CRIMINOLOGY

Third Edition

Frank Schmalleger

Distinguished Professor Emeritus

The University of North Carolina at Pembroke

PEARSON

Boston Columbus Indianapolis New York San Francisco Hoboken
Amsterdam Cape Town Dubai London Madrid Milan Munich Paris Montréal Toronto
Delhi Mexico City São Paulo Sydney Hong Kong Seoul Singapore Taipei Tokyo

Editorial Director: Andrew Gilfillan
Product Manager: Gary Bauer
Program Manager: Tara Horton
Editorial Assistant: Lynda Cramer
Director of Marketing: David Gessell
Marketing Manager: Mary Salzman
Senior Marketing Coordinator: Alicia Wozniak
Marketing Assistant: Les Roberts
Project Management Team Lead: JoEllen Gohr
Project Manager: Jessica H. Sykes
Procurement Specialist: Deidra Skahill
Art Director: Diane Y. Ernsberger
Cover Designer: Diane Y. Ernsberger
Media Project Manager: Leslie Brado
Full-Service Project Management: Christian Holdener, S4Carlisle Publishing Services
Composition: S4Carlisle Publishing Services
Printer/Binder: Courier/Kendallville
Cover Printer: Courier/Kendallville
Text Font: Minion Pro-Regular 10/12

Library of Congress Cataloging-in-Publication Data

Schmalleger, Frank.
Criminology / Frank Schmalleger.—Third edition.
pages cm
Includes bibliographical references and index.
ISBN 978-0-13-380562-8 (alk. paper)—ISBN 0-13-380562-X (alk. paper)
1. Criminology. I. Title.
HV6025.S344 2015
364—dc23
2014035185

Dedication

For Ava and Malia

V011
10 9 8 7 6 5 4 3 2 1

ISBN 10: 0-13-380562-X
ISBN 13: 978-0-13-380562-8

Brief Contents

Contents

PART 3 The Crime Picture—*It's Not Pretty*

Preface

Introducing the Justice Series

When
best-selling
authors

and instructional designers come together focused on one goal—to improve student performance across the criminal justice (CJ) curriculum—they come away with a groundbreaking new series of print and digital content: the *Justice Series*.

Several years ago, we embarked on a journey to create affordable texts that engage students without sacrificing academic rigor. We tested this new format with Fagin's *CJ 2010* and Schmalleger's *Criminology* and received overwhelming support from students and instructors.

The Justice Series expands this format and philosophy to more core CJ and criminology courses, providing affordable, engaging instructor and student resources across the curriculum. As you flip through the pages, you'll notice that this book doesn't rely on distracting, overly used photos to add visual appeal. Every piece of art serves a purpose—to help students learn. Our authors and instructional designers worked tirelessly to build engaging infographics, flowcharts, pull-out statistics, and other visuals that flow with the body of the text, provide context and engagement, and promote recall and understanding.

We organized our content around key learning objectives for each chapter and tied everything together in a new objective-driven end-of-chapter layout. The content not only is engaging to students, but also is easy to follow and focuses students on the key learning objectives.

Although brief, affordable, and visually engaging, the Justice Series is no quick, cheap way to appeal to the lowest common denominator. It's a series of texts and support tools that are instructionally sound and student-approved.

Additional Highlights to the Author's Approach

- The lavish use of figures, charts, and line art visually attracts readers to the subject matter of criminology, making for ease of learning.
- This book moves beyond the confusing terminology found in other criminology texts to provide students with straightforward explanations of criminology's important concepts and most fascinating schools of thought. Content is readily accessible through the use of plain language and commonsense definitions of key terms.
- Cases in every chapter illustrate the principles discussed and provide true-to-life stories of criminal offenders. Thought-provoking questions within the cases provide students with the opportunity to apply what they've learned.

When best-selling authors and instructional designers come together focused on one goal—to improve student performance across the CJ curriculum—they come away with a groundbreaking new series of print and digital content: the *Justice Series*.

New to this Edition

- An entirely new chapter on biosocial theories has been added.
- "Who's to Blame?" boxes, which question the degree to which an offender is responsible for law violations, have been added to the book. The boxes point out that offenders might be influenced by a wide variety of factors in their decision to commit crime, and ask whether some of the responsibility for criminality rests with society.
- All statistics on crime, criminal victimization, probation and parole, jail populations, and imprisonment have been updated.
- New pull quotes can be found throughout the text.

Chapter 1

- A new section, "How Much Crime Is There?" has been added.
- Two "Who's to Blame" boxes have been added; one is about polygamy, while the other asks if "criminology is just a form of academic excuse making."
- A new section on crime facts, to include discussion of the National Crime Victimization Survey, the Uniform Crime Reporting Program, and the National Incident-Based Reporting System, has been added.
- A discussion of crime rates in the United States, along with clearance rates for major crimes, is now included.
- Changing crime rates are now described, and significant shifts in crime rates have been identified.
- A discussion of the dark figure of crime and self-report surveys has been added.
- Questions are now raised about the changing nature of crime, and the need for an evolving understanding of how crime should be measured.
- Evidence-based criminology is now a focus, and the link between evidence-based criminology and effective social policy has been clarified.
- A new case focusing on Colton Harris-Moore (the Barefoot Bandit) has been added to the end of the chapter.
- The decision by the San Francisco Board of Supervisors to ban total public nudity is discussed.
- The recent state legalization of the possession and use of small amounts of marijuana in Colorado and Washington State is mentioned.

- The criminal prosecution of geologists in Italy over a faulty earthquake prediction is used as an example asking "what should be criminal?"
- The section titled "Crime Facts" has been retitled "How Much Crime Is There?"
- Web Extra links have been provided to YouTube videos from the Center for Evidence-based Crime Policy.
- A new case-study box on Adam Lanza, the Sandy Hook Elementary School shooter, concludes the chapter.

Chapter 2

- A new opening story begins the chapter.
- Updated information on capital punishment is provided.
- The 2012 change in California's law relative to three-strikers is discussed.
- The discussion of policy implications of the Classical School has been enhanced to include determinate sentencing, selective incapacitation, and truth in sentencing.
- New studies on the efficacy of capital punishment have been added.
- The impact of the growth of the American prison population is discussed, along with the recent turnaround in growth rates.

Chapter 3

This is a new chapter, having been spun off from the last edition's chapter on biological theories. It summarizes "traditional" biological theories, allowing for a distinction to be made (in Chapter 4) between those perspectives and newer biosocial theories.

Chapter 4

- This is an entirely new chapter focusing on contemporary biological approaches to explaining criminality, especially biosocial theories.
- The chapter also includes new and enhanced materials on the Human Genome Project, the role of genetics and heritability explanations for crime, brain dysfunction as it relates to criminality, and body chemistry theories of criminality.
- A discussion of neurocriminology—a perspective that examines the neurological links between the organism, social factors, and criminal behavior—has been added.
- Similarly, an entirely new discussion of psychobiotics, or the influence of gut bacteria on the human nervous system and behavior, is now included.

Chapter 5

- This chapter has been completely revised to recognize important psychological and psychiatric concepts that had been missing from the previous edition, including:
  - Personality theory, including personality traits and the "Big Five" personality dimensions
  - Moral development theory
  - Cognitive information processing theory
  - Script theory
  - The criminal mindset
  - Criminogenic needs
  - Psychological theories of self-control have been removed from this chapter.

Chapter 6

- The chapter's opening story has been changed.
- A new heading, "Types of Social Structure Theories," helps to distinguish between the three major types of social structure theories.
- The discussion of human ecology has been expanded, and "human ecology" has been added as a new key term, and a definition provided.
- The discussion of the "criminology of place" has been enhanced, and a new key term, "defensible space" has been added to the chapter.
- Some tables have been turned into line art for ease of understanding.
- Older information from Project GangFact has been removed.
- A new Who's to Blame? box now appears in this chapter.

Chapter 7

- Added discussion of Per-Olof H. Wikström's situational action theory.
- The discussion of the general theory of crime (GTC) has been expanded and simplified.
- The discussion of labeling theory has been slightly expanded.
- A new Who's to Blame? box has been added to this chapter.

Chapter 8

- A new chapter-opening story about the 2012 Wall Street protests begins the chapter.
- The chapter now contains a new Who's to Blame? box.
- The distinction between radical and critical criminology is better explained than in the previous edition.

Chapter 9

- A new chapter-opening story sets the tone for the chapter.
- National crime-data-gathering programs are explained in greater detail, and their discussion has been moved to the front of the chapter.
- All crime statistics have been thoroughly updated using the latest *Uniform Crime Reports* of the Federal Bureau of Investigation, and the Bureau of Justice Statistics' National Crime Victimization Survey.
- A new top-level heading, "National Crime-Data-Gathering Programs" has been added to the chapter.

- Added discussion (and definitions) of primary homicide, expressive homicide, and nonprimary homicide.
- The story of James E. Holmes, who opened fire in a crowded Aurora, Colorado, movie theater in 2012, is now described; and Adam Lanza's assault on the Sandy Hook Elementary school in Newtown, Connecticut, is included.
- Results from the 2013 Prison Rape Elimination Act survey are described in some detail.
- Primary and nonprimary homicides are distinguished, and the term "instrumental crimes" is introduced.
- Mass shooters James E. Holmes, Andres Behring Beivik, and Adam Lanza are now discussed, along with the Boston Marathon bombings.
- A new Who's to Blame? box has been added.

Chapter 10

- A new chapter-opening story sets the tone for the chapter.
- All crime statistics in the chapter have been updated.
- A new piece of line art describing various types of burglaries has been added.
- New information on burglary has been added.
- The role of "flash mobs" in larceny is discussed.
- The "Barefoot Bandit" case study has been moved to this chapter.

Chapter 11

- The chapter now begins with a discussion of financial fraud investigations.
- A table showing how white-collar criminal activities are associated with terrorism has been added.
- A discussion of the 2010 Gulf of Mexico oil spill has been added to the environmental crimes section.
- The discussion of Russian organized crime has been expanded, and the term "criminal enterprise" is explained relative to such groups.
- The Sarbanes-Oxley Act has been added to the list of key terms and a definition provided.

Chapter 12

- The chapter has been retitled to better reflect its focus on drug and sex crimes.
- It now begins with a description of the Silk Road website, closed by the federal government in late 2013.
- The discussion of the extent of drug abuse in the United States today has been expanded and now includes data from the National Survey on Drug Use and Health.
- The Obama administration's hands-off approach to state-sanctioned marijuana businesses is now discussed.
- A discussion of the legalization of prostitution in Switzerland has been added to the chapter.
- A new graphic on federal drug control spending has been added.
- A new Who's to Blame? box has been added to this chapter.
- The section on legalizing drugs has been moved to a spot earlier in the chapter.

Chapter 13

- A discussion of the Chinese military as a source of unauthorized cyberintrusions involving U.S.-based computers is discussed within the context of cybercrime.
- A new Who's to Blame? box on computer gaming has been added.
- A discussion of how a hacker in the Netherlands disrupted the computers of a gaming company in New Hampshire has been added to describe the characteristics of computer hackers.
- The 2013 U.S. Supreme Court case of *Maryland* v. *King*—which held that when officers make an arrest supported by probable cause and bring the suspect to the station to be detained, taking a cheek swab of the arrestee's DNA is permissible—is now discussed.

Chapter 14

- The introductory section has been retitled "Transnational Criminal Enterprise."
- A new chapter-opening case begins the chapter.
- A case study on Dzhokhar and Tamerlan Tsarnaev, the Boston Marathon bombers, has been added.
- The term "globalization of knowledge" has been added to describe the increase in understanding that results from a sharing of information between cultures.
- New links to updated antiterrorism documents have been included.
- A new Who's to Blame? box on the making of a suicide bomber is included.
- The description of the Department of Homeland Security has been revised, and a new organizational chart added.
- The most recent Obama administration *National Strategy for Counterterrorism* is now included.

▶ Instructor Supplements

Instructor's Manual with Test Bank

Includes content outlines for classroom discussion, teaching suggestions, and answers to selected end-of-chapter questions from the text. This also contains a Word document version of the test bank.

- *TestGen.* This computerized test generation system gives you maximum flexibility in creating and administering tests on paper, electronically, or online. It provides state-of-the-art features for viewing and editing test bank questions, dragging a selected question into a test you are creating, and printing sleek, formatted tests in a variety of layouts. Select test items from test banks included with TestGen for quick test creation, or write your own questions from scratch. TestGen's random generator provides the option to display different text or calculated number values each time questions are used.
- *PowerPoint Presentations.* Our presentations offer clear, straightforward outlines and notes to use for class lectures or study materials. Photos, illustrations, charts, and tables from the book are included in the presentations when applicable.

To access supplementary materials online, instructors need to request an instructor access code. Go to **www.pearsonhighered.com/irc,** where you can register for an instructor access code. Within 48 hours after registering, you will receive a confirming email, including an instructor access code. Once you have received your code, go to the site and log on for full instructions on downloading the materials you wish to use.

Pearson Online Course Solutions

Criminology is supported by a variety of online course and media solutions. Go to www.pearsonhighered.com or contact your local representative for the latest information.

Alternate Versions

eBooks

This text is also available in multiple eBook formats, including Adobe Reader and *CourseSmart. CourseSmart* is an exciting new choice for students looking to save money. As an alternative to purchasing the printed textbook, students can purchase an electronic version of the same content. With a *CourseSmart* eTextbook, students can search the text, make notes online, print out reading assignments that incorporate lecture notes, and bookmark important passages for later review. For more information, or to purchase access to the *CourseSmart* eTextbook, visit **www.coursesmart.com.**

▶ Acknowledgments

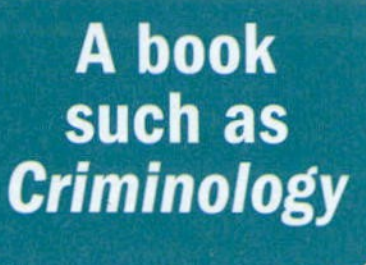
A book
such as
Criminology

draws on the talents and resources of many people and is the end result of much previous effort. This text could not have been written without the groundwork laid by previous criminologists, academics, and researchers; hence, a hearty thank-you is due to everyone who has contributed to the development of the field of criminology throughout the years—and especially to those theorists, authors, and social commentators who are cited in this book. Without their work, the field would be much poorer. I would like to thank, as well, all the adopters—professors and students alike—of my previous textbooks, for they have given me the encouragement and fostered the steadfastness required to write *Criminology*.

The Pearson team members, whom I have come to know so well and who have worked so professionally with me on this and other projects, deserve a special thanks. The team includes Gary Bauer, Lynda Cramer, David Gesell, JoEllen Gohr, Thomas Hayward, Megan Moffo, Santos Shih, Deidra Skahill, Jessica Sykes, Pat Tonneman, and Alicia Wozniak. My thanks also to cover designer Diane Ernsberger and text designer Mary Siener, whose efforts have helped make *Criminology* both attractive and visually appealing.

My friends and professional colleagues Ellen Cohn, Florida International University; Cassandra Renzi, Keiser University; and Karel Kurst-Swanger, Oswego State University helped in many ways. I am especially thankful to Ellen Cohn for the quality products she has created and for her exceptional ability to build intuitively on concepts in the text.

Thanks, too, to Christian Holdener and the folks at S4Carlisle Publishing Services for their insight and vision in keeping the development of this text on track.

This book has benefited greatly from the quick availability of information and other resources through online services and in various locations on the World Wide Web. I am grateful to the many information providers who, although they are too numerous to list, have helped establish such useful resources.

Manuscript reviewers who have contributed to the development of *Criminology* include:

Brittnie Aiello, Merrimack College
Wendi Albert, Keiser University
Desiré J.M. Anastasia, Metropolitan State College of Denver
Joanne Anzenberger, Housatonic Community College
Tiffiney Y. Barfield-Cottledge, University of North Texas–Dallas
Kevin M. Beaver, Florida State University
Kathryn A. Branch, University of Tampa
Thomas Chuda, Bunker Hill Community College
Harold A. Frossard, Moraine Valley Community College
Krista S. Gehring, University of Houston–Downtown

Elizabeth L. Grossi, University of Louisville
John R. Hamilton, Jr., Park University
Lisa A. Kort-Butler, University of Nebraska–Lincoln
Michael J. Leiber, Virginia Commonwealth University
Samantha L. Lewis, Miami Dade College
Allyson Maida, St. John's University
Mark A. Noe, Keiser University
Angela Overton, Old Dominion University
Michael F. Raymond, NHTI, Concord's Community College
Cassandra L. Renzi, Keiser University
Isis N. Walton, Virginia State University
Patricia Y. Warren, Florida State University

Last, but by no means least, I am indebted to a small but very special group of contemporary criminologists who have laid the foundation for our discipline's presence on the Internet. Among them are Cecil Greek at Florida State University, whose online lecture notes are massively informative; Tom O'Connor of Austin Peay State University, whose Megalinks in Criminal Justice provide an amazingly comprehensive resource; Matthew Robinson at Appalachian State University, whose Crime Theory Links allow visitors to vote on what they think are the causes of crime; Bruce Hoffman, whose former Crime Theory site at the University of Washington offers many great insights into the field; and Regina Schekall, volunteer webmaster for the Santa Clara Police Department. All of these excellent resources were used in the development of the first edition of this book—and it is to these modern-day visionaries that *Criminology* owes much of its technological depth.

About the Author

Frank Schmalleger, Ph.D., is professor emeritus at the University of North Carolina at Pembroke, where he is also recognized as Distinguished Professor. Dr. Schmalleger holds degrees from the University of Notre Dame and The Ohio State University, having earned both a master's (1970) and a doctorate in sociology (1974) from The Ohio State University with a special emphasis in criminology. From 1976 to 1994, he taught criminal justice courses at the University of North Carolina at Pembroke. For the last 16 of those years, he chaired the university's Department of Sociology, Social Work, and Criminal Justice. As an adjunct professor with Webster University in St. Louis, Missouri, Schmalleger helped develop the university's graduate program in security administration and loss prevention. He taught courses in that curriculum for more than a decade. Schmalleger also taught in the New School for Social Research's online graduate program, helping build the world's first electronic classrooms in support of distance learning through computer telecommunications. An avid Web user and site builder, Schmalleger is also the creator of award-winning websites.

Frank Schmalleger is the author of numerous articles and many books, including the widely used *Criminal Justice Today: An Introductory Text for the 21st Century* (Pearson, 2015), now in its 13th edition; *Juvenile Delinquency* (with Clemens Bartollas; Pearson, 2016); *Criminal Justice: A Brief Introduction*, 11th edition (Pearson, 2016); *Criminal Law Today*, 5th edition (with Daniel Hall and John Dolatowski; Pearson, 2014); *Crime and the Justice System in America: An Encyclopedia* (Greenwood Publishing Group, 1997); *Trial of the Century: People of the State of California vs. Orenthal James Simpson* (Prentice Hall, 1996); *Career Paths: A Guide to Jobs in Federal Law Enforcement* (Regents/Prentice Hall, 1994); *Computers in Criminal Justice* (Wyndham Hall Press, 1991); *Criminal Justice Ethics* (Greenwood Press, 1991); *Finding Criminal Justice in the Library* (Wyndham Hall Press, 1991); *Ethics in Criminal Justice* (Wyndham Hall Press, 1990); *A History of Corrections* (Foundations Press of Notre Dame, 1983); and *The Social Basis of Criminal Justice* (University Press of America, 1981). Schmalleger is also founding editor of the journal *Criminal Justice Studies* (formerly *The Justice Professional*).

Schmalleger's philosophy of both teaching and writing can be summed up in these words: "In order to communicate knowledge, we must first catch, then hold, a person's interest—whether a student, colleague, or policymaker. Our writing, our speaking, and our teaching must be relevant to the problems facing people today, and they must—in some way—help solve those problems."

If you use this book, the author would like to hear from you. You may contact him at the email address below.

Frank Schmalleger, Ph.D.
Distinguished Professor Emeritus
The University of North Carolina at Pembroke
schmall@justicestudies.com

"Society secretly wants crime, needs crime, and gains definite satisfactions from the present mishandling of it! We condemn crime; we punish offenders for it; but we need it. The crime and punishment ritual is part of our lives!"

—*Karl Menninger*[1]

1 What Is Criminology?

Understanding Crime and Criminals

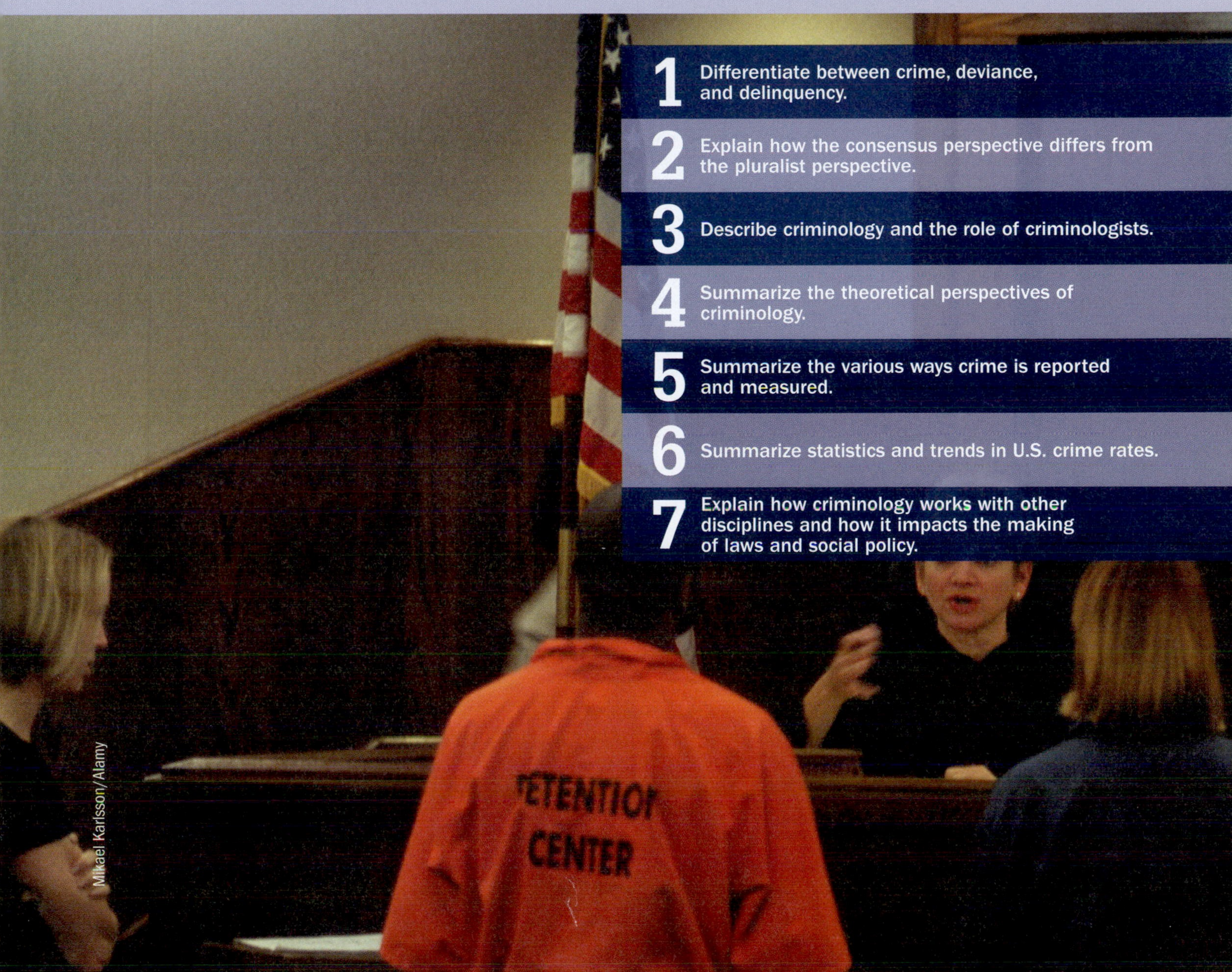

Mikael Karlsson/Alamy

1. Differentiate between crime, deviance, and delinquency.
2. Explain how the consensus perspective differs from the pluralist perspective.
3. Describe criminology and the role of criminologists.
4. Summarize the theoretical perspectives of criminology.
5. Summarize the various ways crime is reported and measured.
6. Summarize statistics and trends in U.S. crime rates.
7. Explain how criminology works with other disciplines and how it impacts the making of laws and social policy.

INTRO A FASCINATION WITH CRIME AND CRIMINALS

According to social commentators, people are simultaneously attracted to and repulsed by crime—especially gruesome crimes involving extreme personal violence. The popularity of today's TV crime shows, Hollywood-produced crime movies, true-crime books and magazines, and websites devoted exclusively to the coverage of crime supports that observation. The CBS TV megahit *NCIS*, for example, was named the number one TV drama in 2014, and received an impressive three nominations for TV's 2014 People's Choice Award.[2] The show was also nominated as "Favorite TV Crime Drama," with individual episodes drawing more than 24 million viewers.[3] Earlier, *CSI: Miami*, which ran for ten seasons, until going off the air in 2012, garnered 50 million regular viewers in more than 55 countries. By its eighth season it had become the most popular television show in the world.[4] In 2012, the CSI series was named the most watched TV show in the world for the fifth time.[5] Other widely followed TV crime series, both past and present, include shows such as *Awake* (NBC), *Criminal Minds* (CBS), *Blue Bloods* (CBS), *Without a Trace* (CBS), *Magic City* (HBO), *Numb3rs* (CBS), *The Unit* (CBS), *The Unusuals* (ABC), *The Sopranos* (in reruns on HBO), *The Killing* (AMC), *White Collar* (USA), *The District* (CBS), *Boardwalk Empire* (HBO), *The Shield* (FX), *The Wire* (HBO), *Cold Case* (CBS), *Prison Break* (Fox), and *Law and Order* (NBC)—along with the *Law and Order* spin-offs, *Law and Order: Criminal Intent* and *Law and Order: Special Victims Unit.* American TV viewers are hungry for crime-related entertainment and have a fascination with criminal motivation and detective work. Visit the home page of the CBS hit show *NCIS* at **Web Extra 1–1**.

Some crimes cry out for explanation. Yet one of the things that fascinates people about crime—especially violent crime—is that it seems to be inexplicable. Some crimes are especially difficult to understand, but our natural tendency is to seek out some reason for the unreasonable. We search for explanations for the seemingly unexplainable. How, for example, can the behavior of child killers be understood, anticipated, and even prevented? What motivates mass shooters? Why don't terrorists acknowledge the emotional and personal suffering they inflict?

AF Archive/Alamy

A photo of the cast from the highly popular CBS TV show *NCIS*. Shown from left to right are Rocky Carroll, Michael Weatherly, David McCallum, Pauley Perrette, Cote de Pablo, Sean Murray, and Mark Harmon. Why do many people like to watch TV crime shows like *NCIS*?

Why do some robbers or rapists kill and even torture, utterly disregarding human life and feelings?

People also wonder about "everyday" crimes such as burglary, drug use, assault, vandalism, and computer intrusion. Why, for example, do people fight? Does it matter to a robber that he may face prison time? How can people sacrifice love, money, careers, and even their lives for access to illegal drugs? What motivates terrorists to give up their own lives to take the lives of others? Why do gifted techno-savvy teens and preteens hack sites on the Internet thought to be secure? While this text may not answer each of these questions, it examines the causative factors in effect when a crime is committed and encourages an appreciation of the challenges of crafting effective crime-control policy.

DISCUSS Why are people fascinated by crime and criminal behavior? How does the popularity of TV crime shows reflect the American mind-set

What Is Crime?

As the word implies, *criminology* is clearly concerned with crime. As we begin our discussion of criminology, let's consider just what the term *crime* means. Like anything else, crime can be defined in several ways. For our purposes, **crime** is *human conduct that violates the criminal laws of a state, the federal government, or a local jurisdiction that has the power to make and enforce the laws.* We prefer this definition because without a law defining a particular form of behavior, there is no crime, no matter how deviant or socially repugnant the behavior in question may be.[6]

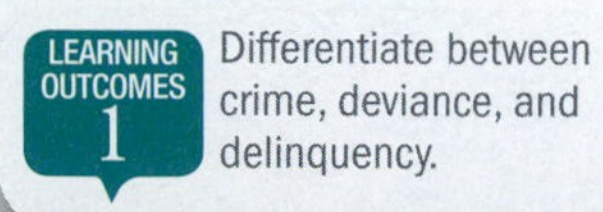
LEARNING OUTCOMES 1 Differentiate between crime, deviance, and delinquency.

Edwin Sutherland, regarded by many as a founding figure in American criminology, said that crime's "essential characteristic . . . is that it is behavior which is prohibited by the State as an injury to the State and against which the State may react . . . by punishment."[7] This is a legalistic perspective, and it recognizes that laws are social products. The legalistic approach to crime assumes that powerful individuals who are in a position to politically influence lawmaking strategies can impose their

WHO'S TO BLAME—The Individual or Society

Should Polygamy Be a Protected Religious Practice?

Taeler Leon, a member of the Fundamentalist Church of Jesus Christ of Latter Day Saints, an ultraconservative offshoot of the Mormon Church, was arrested in a rural area outside of Salt Lake City, Utah, and charged with polygamy and the rape of a child. The charges came after the parents of a 13-year-old girl, whom Leon had "married" in a ceremony performed by a church elder, complained to the Utah State Bureau of Investigation (SBI) that Leon was holding their daughter against her will. SBI agents visited Leon's compound and learned that six of Leon's wives and 16 of his children were living at the compound. The compound, which consisted of four houses and a communal building containing a small school, chapel, and dining and meeting areas, was set in a secluded location well off the main road.

A follow-up investigation revealed that the children's births had been officially registered at the county courthouse and that the needed homeschooling papers had been filed with the State Board of Education for each of the school-aged children living at the compound—meaning that they were exempt from required attendance at public schools.

Polygamy is a criminal offense in Utah and is banned under the state's constitution. It has been officially repudiated by the mainstream Mormon Church since 1890. After determining that Leon was married concurrently to multiple women, SBI agents took him into custody and interviewed each of his wives. Each told much the same story of how she had been promised by her parents to Leon at an early age, how she had been married in a small ceremony, and how she had borne Leon's children. What surprised investigators, though, was the women's agreement that their way of life, while it might not be common in the wider society, was a matter of choice—and that they should be left alone to practice their faith. "Taeler's committed no crime in the eyes of God," said Adaleen, Leon's first wife, speaking for the others. "We should be free to practice our religion just like others are," she said.

Hendy, another of the wives, pointed out that members of the American Indian Church have been allowed to use peyote in their religious ceremonies, even though it is a banned drug, unavailable to non-Native Americans. "If they can smoke peyote, then why can't we get married and live the way we want to?" she asked. "It's our religion, and it's supposed to be a free country."

George Frey/AFP/Newscom

A polygamist family in Utah. Why is the practice of polygamy a violation of the criminal law? Should it be?

Think About It

1. Not all women involved in polygamous unions would agree with Adaleen and Hendy, and those who oppose polygamy argue not only that it is illegal but that it degrades women, devalues the family, and victimizes young women who are forced into arranged unions. Nonetheless, there are those who would agree with Adaleen and Hendy that the practice should be allowed based on constitutional guarantees of freedom of religion. Which perspective makes more sense to you? Why?
2. Do a bit of historical research and see if you can learn the legal history of the practice of polygamy in the United States. When did it become illegal? Why?
3. What rights, if any, should members of minority faiths have when they advocate or engage in behavior that goes beyond social norms or violates the law? Give some examples.
4. Would the rights you identified above extend to the practice of polygamy? Why or why not?

Note: Who's to Blame boxes provide fictionalized critical thinking opportunities, and are not actual cases.

preferred definitions of criminal behavior on lawbreakers. By making their own laws, powerful but immoral individuals might therefore escape the label "criminal" and may escape punishment for wrongdoings they have committed. Although democratic societies such as that of the United States seem immune from legislative process abuse, history demonstrates otherwise. Consequently, crime is socially relative in the sense that it is created by legislative activity. Without a law defining it, there can be no crime. Hence, as social scientists are fond of saying, "Crime is whatever a society says it is." Later in this book, we will focus on the process of *criminalization*, which is used to **criminalize** some forms of behavior—or make them illegal.

Crime is human conduct that violates the criminal law.

Crime, Deviance, and Delinquency

In line with sociological thought, many crimes are seen as deviant or abnormal forms of behavior. The definition of **deviant behavior** that we will use in this text is as follows: Deviant behavior is human activity that violates social norms. Some activities that are not condemned by **statute** are nonetheless regarded as "bad behavior." Sufficiently "bad behavior" calls out

FIGURE 1–1 **The Overlap Between Deviance and Crime.**

for a societal response, echoing, "That ought to be a crime!" or "There should be a law against that!"

Abnormality, deviance, and crime are concepts that do not always easily mesh. Some forms of deviance are not violations of the criminal law, and the reverse is equally true. (See Figure 1–1.) Deviant styles of dress, for example, are not restricted by criminal law unless they violate decency statutes by virtue of lack of clothing. Laws are generally subject to interpretation, and they may be modified as social norms evolve. A few years ago, for example, a Palm Beach County (Florida) judge struck down a law banning baggy pants, calling the measure unconstitutional. The judge agreed with a public defender representing a teenager arrested for exposing his underwear by wearing pants that sagged. The attorney argued that the law was unacceptable because it restricted styles of dress and empowered "the fashion police."[8]

More recently, San Francisco's Board of Supervisors voted to ban total public nudity in their city.[9] The vote came in late 2012 after a series of complaints had been received about men and women strolling through the city's Castro neighborhood without any clothes, and sipping drinks at the city's coffee shops. The local legislation, however, exempted nudity at private beaches and within permitted special events.

Think About It…

Some people say that wearing hoodies or sagging pants are fashion statements, while others say that wearing such clothing paints the wearer in a negative light. Keeping that example in mind, what kinds of human behavior might be deviant but not criminal? What things might be criminal but not necessarily deviant?

Nando Machado/Fotolia

However, some types of behavior, although neither deviant nor abnormal, are still against the law. Although speeding on interstate highways in some circumstances is considered the *norm* and not deviant, it is still illegal. Complicating matters further, certain behaviors are illegal in some jurisdictions but not in others. Commercialized gambling (slot machines and games of chance) are against the law in many parts of the United States, although they are legitimized in Nevada, on some Native American reservations, on cruise ships operating outside U.S. territorial waters, on some Mississippi riverboats, and in some state-sponsored locales. Even state governments seeking to enhance revenues allow gambling through state lotteries—which now operate in 45 states[10]—although online gambling is forbidden in an effort to protect states' lottery revenues. Similarly, prostitution, almost uniformly illegal in the United States, is legal in parts of Nevada if it occurs within licensed brothels that meet state licensing and health requirements. Finally, the consumption of small amounts of marijuana in private for personal recreational use was recently legalized in Colorado and Washington State, although such use remains illegal in other states and on federal property.

We should also add that **delinquency**, a term often used in conjunction with crime and deviance, refers to violations of the criminal law and other misbehavior committed by young people. The laws of many states proclaim that "youth" ends at a person's 18th birthday, although other states specify the 16th or 17th birthday as meeting that requirement. All states, however, specify certain offenses, such as running away from home, being ungovernable, and drinking alcohol, as illegal for children but not adults.

What Should Be Criminal?

By now, you have probably realized that the question "What is crime?" differs from the question "What should be criminal?" Everyone would agree that murder, rape, burglary, and theft are illegal activities, but there is far less agreement about the legal status of controlled substance abuse, abortion and "abortion pills" (RU-486, or Mifeprex), online gambling, and "deviant" forms of consensual adult sexual behavior. State legislatures, along with the general public, have recently debated the pros and cons of same-sex marriages and certain forms of biomedical research (specifically human cloning and stem cell research). In some parts of the country same-sex marriages are now legally performed, and in others state-approved gambling operations are big moneymakers. And, as noted, Colorado and Washington State have legalized the private recreational use of marijuana.

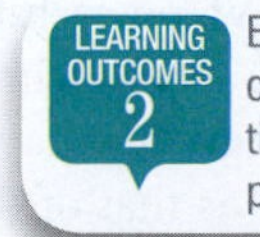

Explain how the consensus perspective differs from the pluralist perspective.

An interesting 2012 story from Italy well illustrates our point. In that year, six Italian scientists and one government official were convicted of criminal manslaughter and sentenced to six years in prison for failing to warn the people of L'Aquila, Italy, of a deadly earthquake that struck in 2009. Before the tragedy, a number of small tremors were felt in L'Aquila. Fearing this activity would lead to a serious earthquake, authorities hired the scientists to study the matter and to instruct townspeople on what to do. The scientists deliberated and a government official relayed their advice. "The scientific community tells me there is no danger, because there is an ongoing discharge of energy," he stated. "The situation looks favorable."

That advice proved to be deadly, however, as a major earthquake devastated the area six days later. Striking at night, it killed more than 300 townspeople, injured at least 1,500, and left thousands homeless. Italian prosecutors indicted the scientists for giving "inexact, incomplete and contradictory information." Prosecutors insisted the case was not about failing to predict the quake, but about being, in effect, misleadingly reassuring.

As many saw it, however, the Italian scientists were accused of failing to predict an inherently unpredictable event. Although Italy has many earthquakes, the last major quake in L'Aquila occurred in 1703. And while half of large earthquakes start with tremors beforehand, only about 5% of tremors presage a large quake. David Rothery, a scientist at the Open University in the United Kingdom, said that before the 2009 earthquake arrived, "the best estimate at the time was that the low-level seismicity was not likely to herald a bigger quake."[11]

As the Italian scientists soon learned, the question "What should be criminal?" can be answered in many different ways. The social and intellectual processes addressing this question can be found in two contrasting points of view: (1) the consensus perspective and (2) the pluralist perspective. The **consensus perspective** holds that laws should be enacted to criminalize given forms of behavior when members of society agree that such laws are necessary. The consensus perspective is most applicable to homogeneous societies with shared values, norms, and belief systems. Multicultural and diverse societies such as the United States find it difficult to achieve shared consensus. Here, even minor matters may spawn complex debates over the issues. For example, a Chicago municipal ordinance banned giving wine to a dog and provided that anyone who did so could be arrested and jailed.[12] While the ordinance seemed reasonable when enacted (after all, dogs sometimes need to be shielded from their owners' indiscretions), others viewed the law as silly and unnecessary. The ordinance pitted wine connoisseurs against collectors, growers, and sellers and animal rights activists against animal protectionists and city council members.[13] Those favoring repeal of the ordinance argued that it was old-fashioned and reflected badly on an acceptable consumer product that is a staple of some ethnic diets. Eventually, the ordinance was repealed, and the hubbub it had inspired ended. The debate, however, shows the inherent difficulties in achieving a consensus over minor matters in our complex society.

The consensus viewpoint holds that laws should be enacted to criminalize given forms of behavior when members of society generally agree that such laws are necessary.

Think About It…

Not everyone agrees about what is moral or immoral; nor do they agree about what should be legal or illegal—and laws vary from one place to another. What are some forms of behavior that are illegal in some jurisdictions (or states) but not in others?

Michael Ireland/Fotolia

In line with the pluralist view of crime, the **pluralist perspective** recognizes the importance of diversity in our society. It states that behaviors are typically criminalized through a political process only after debate over the appropriate course of action. The political process creates legislation and may involve additional appellate court action to interpret the laws passed by the legislature. Following the 2012 random mass shootings at Sandy Hook Elementary School and an Aurora, Colorado, movie theater shooting, for example, state and federal legislatures reexamined gun laws to determine whether new laws would keep guns out of the hands of potential mass killers. With our society's diversity of perspectives, agreement was not easy to reach—and gun-control proponents continue the fight to limit gun ownership.

What Do Criminologists Do?

A typical dictionary definition of a **criminologist** is "one who studies crime, criminals, and criminal behavior."[14] Occasionally, the term *criminologist* describes almost anyone working in the criminal justice field, regardless of formal training. Today, the growing tendency is to reserve applying the term *criminologist* to academics,

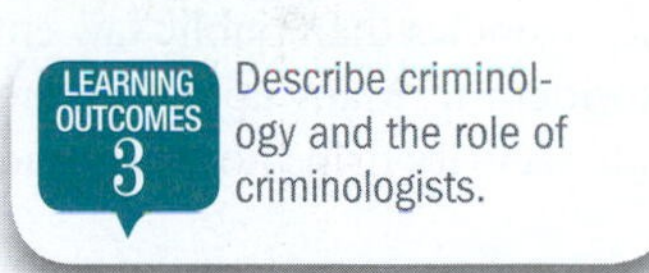

LEARNING OUTCOMES
3
Describe criminology and the role of criminologists.

Think About It…

Some people believe that "there ought to be a law" about some forms of behavior that are currently legal. Others think that people should have more freedom. What forms of behavior that are currently crimes would you like to see legalized? What forms of behavior that are currently legal would you like to criminalize?

Ronald Sumners/Shutterstock

researchers, and policy analysts with advanced degrees who study crime, study trends, and analyze societal reactions to crime. In respect to this designation, we describe highly skilled investigators, crime laboratory technicians, fingerprint experts, crime-scene photographers, ballistics experts, and others who work to solve particular crimes as criminalists. A **criminalist** is "a specialist in the collection and examination of the physical evidence of crime."[15] By contrast, police officers, corrections professionals, probation and parole officers, judges, district attorneys, criminal defense attorneys, and others who do the day-to-day work of the criminal justice system are best referred to as criminal justice professionals.

Academic criminologists and research criminologists generally hold doctoral degrees (Ph.D.) in criminology or criminal justice from accredited universities. Some criminologists hold degrees in related fields such as sociology and political science, specializing in the study and control of crime and deviance. Most Ph.D. criminologists teach criminology or criminology-related subjects in institutions of higher learning, including universities and two- and four-year colleges. Nearly all criminology professors are involved in research or writing projects, thereby advancing criminological knowledge and expertise. Some Ph.D. criminologists are strictly researchers and work for federal agencies such as the National Institute of Justice (NIJ), the Bureau of Justice Statistics (BJS), and the National Criminal Justice Reference Service (NCJRS) or for private (albeit often government-funded) organizations such as RAND Corporation and SEARCH.

With a master's or bachelor's degree in the field of criminology, criminologists often find easy entrance into police investigative or support work, probation and parole agencies, court support activities, and correctional (prison) venues. Criminologists also work for government agencies developing effective social policies intended to deter or combat crime.

In addition, private security offers individuals interested in criminology and criminal justice other career options. Twice as many law enforcement personnel are employed by private security agencies than public law enforcement agencies, and the gap is widening. Many upper- and mid-level private managers at private security firms hold criminology or criminal justice degrees.

Training in criminology offers many career alternatives. (See Table 1–1.) Some people trained in criminology or criminal justice decide to attend law school, while others become teachers or even private investigators. Many criminologists provide civic organizations (such as victims' assistance and justice advocacy groups) with their expertise, work for politicians and legislative bodies, or appear on talk shows debating social policies designed to "fight" crime. Some criminologists even write texts like this one.

What Is Criminology?

This text describes various criminological theories and explains the most popular ones in detail. Let's start by defining the term *criminology*.

Theorists believe that the word *criminology* was coined in 1889[16] by a Frenchman, Paul Topinard, to describe the study of criminal body types within the field of anthropology.[17]

With varying interpretations, numerous definitions of *criminology* are found in literature today. One straightforward definition comes from a linguistic analysis of the word *criminology*, which literally means "the study of criminal accusations"—or simply, "the study of crime."

Edwin H. Sutherland, referred to as the "dean of American criminology," offered definitions of the field, emphasizing its importance as a discipline of study.[18] Sutherland's textbook, first published in 1924, set the stage for much of American criminology. By 1974, in the final printing of that text, Sutherland's original definition of *criminology* was restated as follows: "Criminology . . . includes the processes of making laws, of breaking laws, and of reacting toward the breaking of laws."[19]

For our purposes, we will use a definition that brings together the works of previous writers and recognizes the increasingly

There is some evidence that the term *criminology* was coined by a Frenchman, Paul Topinard, in 1889.

TABLE 1–1 WHAT DO CRIMINOLOGISTS DO?

The term criminologist *refers to credentialed individuals holding advanced degrees in the field and studying crime, criminal behavior, and crime trends. The word* criminalist *describes people who collect and examine the physical evidence associated with specific crimes. Others working in the criminal justice system are called* criminal justice professionals. This table and Figures 1–2 and 1–3 illustrate these differences.

The activities of criminologists include but are not limited to the following:

Data Gathering and Analysis	Public Service
Crime-pattern analysis and trend identification	Study of normal and abnormal social behaviors
Theory construction	Scholarly presentations and publications
Hypothesis testing	Education and training
Social policy creation	Threat assessment and risk analysis
Public advocacy	Service as an expert witness at trial or in other court proceedings

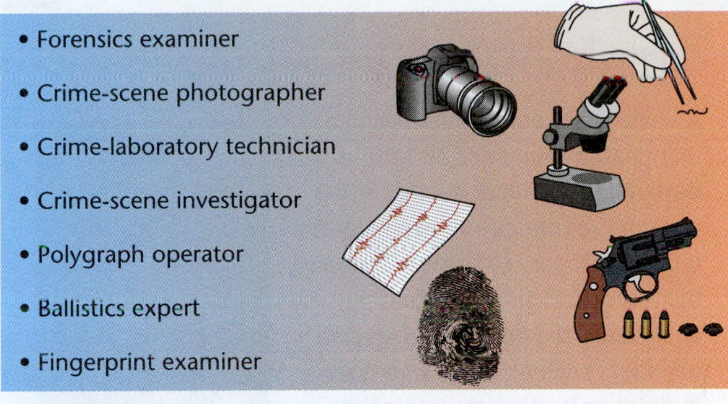

• Forensics examiner
• Crime-scene photographer
• Crime-laboratory technician
• Crime-scene investigator
• Polygraph operator
• Ballistics expert
• Fingerprint examiner

FIGURE 1–2 **Jobs in the Field of Criminalistics.**

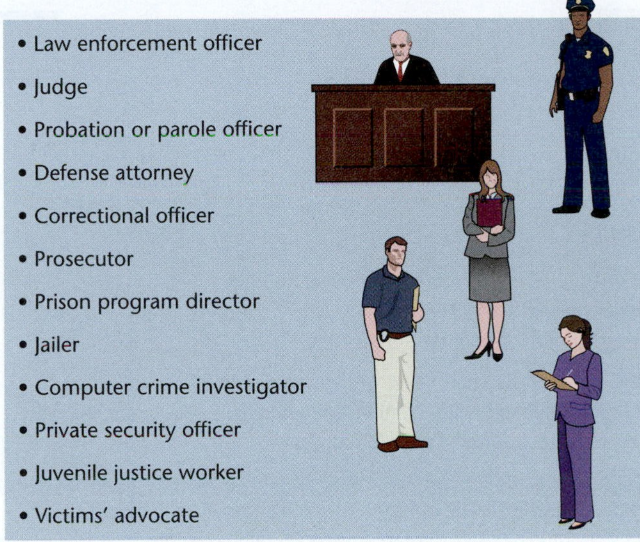

• Law enforcement officer
• Judge
• Probation or parole officer
• Defense attorney
• Correctional officer
• Prosecutor
• Prison program director
• Jailer
• Computer crime investigator
• Private security officer
• Juvenile justice worker
• Victims' advocate

FIGURE 1–3 **Jobs in the Field of Criminal Justice.**

professional status of the criminological enterprise. Throughout this text, then, we view **criminology** as *an interdisciplinary profession built on the scientific study of crime and criminal behavior, including their manifestations, causes, legal aspects, and control.* As this definition indicates, criminology includes consideration of possible solutions to the problem of crime. This text (in later chapters) describes treatment strategies and social policy initiatives that grew out of existing theoretical explanations for crime.

Our definition of *criminology* shows that it is more than a field of study or a collection of theories; it is also a profession.[20] More than a decade ago, experts recognized the importance of controlling crime through the prevention, rehabilitation, and deterrence of repeat offenses. In this way, our society ensures that the criminal justice system reflects the high aspiration we have as a society of "justice for all," which is characterized by the principal goals that motivate the work of the field of criminology.[21]

Notably, criminology also contributes to the discipline of **criminal justice**, which emphasizes application of criminal law and the study of the components of the justice system, especially the police, courts, and correctional systems. As one author stated, "Criminology gives prominence to questions about the *causes of criminality*, while the *control of lawbreaking* is at the heart of criminal justice."[22]

Think About It...

This chapter identifies significant differences between a criminologist and those who work in the field of criminal justice. What are those differences? Given a choice, which type of work would you like to do?

Theoretical Criminology

Theoretical criminology, considered a subfield of general criminology, is the type of criminology that is usually studied in colleges and universities. Theoretical criminology, instead of simply describing crime and its occurrence, offers explanations for criminal behavior. As Edwin Sutherland said, "The problem in criminology is to explain the criminality of behavior. . . . However, an explanation of criminal behavior should be a specific part of [a] general theory of behavior and its task should be to differentiate criminal from noncriminal behavior."[23]

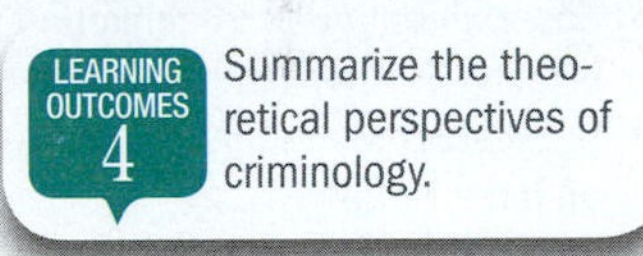

LEARNING OUTCOMES 4
Summarize the theoretical perspectives of criminology.

Criminologists have developed many theories to explain and understand crime. A *theory*, ideally, is made of clearly stated propositions suggesting relationships, often causal, between events and occurrences being studied. An old Roman theory, for example, maintained that insanity was caused by lunar influences and followed its cycles—hence the term *lunacy*.

Theories provide us with explanatory power, aiding our understanding of the phenomenon under study. A **general theory** of crime attempts to explain most forms of criminal conduct through a single, overarching approach. Unfortunately, as prominent scholars observe, "Theories in criminology tend to be unclear and lacking in justifiable generality."[24] When we consider all criminal behaviors—from murder to drug use to white-collar and computer crime—who would imagine that one theory could explain them all? Still, many past theoretical approaches to crime causation were **unicausal**, posing a single identifiable source for all serious deviant and criminal behavior.

An **integrated theory** does not necessarily explain all criminality, but is distinguished because it merges concepts drawn from different sources. As noted criminologist Gregg Barak states, "An integrative criminology . . . seeks to bring together the diverse bodies of knowledge that represent the full array of disciplines that study crime."[25] This is why integrated theories provide potentially wider explanatory power than narrower formulations.

Both theoretical integration and the ability to apply criminological theories to a wide variety of law-violating behavior are appealing concepts. Even far more limited attempts at criminological theorizing, however, often face daunting challenges. As criminologist Don C. Gibbons notes, "Criminologists have not managed to articulate a large collection of relatively formalized arguments in a general or integrated form."[26] Many social scientists insist that to be considered theories, explanations must consist of sets of clearly stated, logically interrelated, and measurable propositions. The fact that only a few of the theories described in this text rise above the level of organized conjecture—and those offer only limited applicability to other settings and have rarely been integrated—is one of the greatest challenges facing criminology today. So although we will use the word *theory* to describe the many explanations for crime covered in this text, the word will only loosely apply to many of the perspectives on crime causation discussed.

Think About It...

A unicausal theory posits a single identifiable source for all serious deviant and criminal behavior. Can you offer (or create) an example of a unicausal theory of crime? Can you think of one explanation that encompasses the behavior of diverse offenders such as those who deal in drugs or participate in prostitution? Why is this exercise especially challenging?

Monkey Business Images/Shutterstock

WHO'S TO BLAME—The Individual or Society?

Is Criminology Really Just a Form of Academic Excuse Making?

Three teenage boys were arrested in the small town of Hillsboro, Maine, and charged with beating a homeless man to death with a baseball bat in an underground parking garage on a cold January evening. A surveillance camera captured the beating, and the youngsters were identified by residents who watched the video clip on local TV news.

Because the boys were juveniles, a storm of controversy swarmed around a local judge's decision to charge them as adults and to bind them over for trial in criminal court–something that state law allows for serious crimes if the suspected offenders were over 14 years of age at the time of the alleged offense.

Soon opinions were being heard from many quarters, and the news media arranged to interview a criminology professor, Dr. Roy Humbolt, at a local college to see if he might be able to shed some light on the boys' behavior.

Cultura Creative/Alamy

A news conference held to provide insight into a seemingly senseless killing. What value do criminological explanations hold for the understanding of criminal activity? How can we benefit from such explanations?

The first question came from a reporter holding a digital voice recorder toward Professor Humbolt. "What happened here? How do you explain this kind of senseless killing?"

"Well," Humbolt began, "it's not senseless. Crime is a social event, not just an isolated instance of individual activity. And in much youth crime we see patterns of co-offending."

Humbolt felt as though he was hitting his stride and started lecturing as though he was in the classroom with his undergraduates. "Criminal behavior is often attributable to social failings rather than to individual choice. Consider, for a moment, the backgrounds of these young men. Were they subjected to physical abuse while they were growing up? Was violence what they learned at the hands of older siblings or parents? Were they, in this instance, involved in some adolescent rite of passage, maybe even an initiation into a gang? Did they feel forced to behave this way because of peer pressure? Was it something they saw on television or in video games that they might have played and then decided to reenact?"

"Dr. Humbolt," the reporter asked, bringing the professor back from his reverie, "even if you find that some of those things are true, isn't criminology just an exercise in excuse making for criminals?"

Think About It

1. What do you think of the explanations offered by Professor Humbolt for the boys' behavior? Which of his explanations, if any, makes the most sense? How can we know for sure if those explanations are accurate?
2. What do you think of the reporter's stinging criticism of the professor? Is the reporter right, that criminology is "just an exercise in excuse making for criminals"? Explain your answer.
3. Generally speaking, does understanding absolve responsibility? In other words, if we can understand why someone does something, then should we hold him or her less responsible for doing it? Why or why not?

Note: Who's to Blame boxes provide fictionalized critical thinking opportunities, and are not actual cases.

The Social Context of Crime

Crime does not occur in a vacuum. For this reason, we say that criminal activity is diversely created and variously interpreted—meaning that different people will have various interpretations regarding the who, what, when, where, and why of crime. We recognize in this text that crime is not an isolated individual activity, but a social event.

Every crime has a unique set of causes, consequences, and participants. Crime affects some people more than others, even impacting those who are not direct participants in the act itself—offenders, victims, police officers, witnesses, and so on. In general, crime provokes reactions from the individuals it victimizes. These reactions flow from concerned groups of citizens to the criminal justice system and sometimes to society as a whole. This can manifest itself in the creation of new social policy, or laws. Reactions to crime, from the everyday to the precedent-setting, may color the course of punishment for future criminal events.[27]

Like other social events, crime is fundamentally a social construction.[28] However, agreeing that crime is a social construction doesn't lessen the impact of victimization experienced by people affected by crime. Nor does this statement trivialize the significance of crime-prevention efforts or the activities of members of the criminal justice system. Crime has a measurable cost to individual victims and to society as a whole. Although a given instance of criminal behavior may have many causes, it may also carry with it many different meanings. There may be one meaning for offenders, another (generally quite different) for victims, and still another for agents of the criminal justice system. In view of this fact, social interest groups (victims' advocates, prisoner "rights" advocates, and gun-control organizations) all interpret lawbreaking behavior from their unique point of view. Then each arrives at different conclusions regarding resolving the so-called problems inherent in crime.

For these reasons, criminologists apply the concept of **social relativity** to the study of criminality.[29] Social relativity means that social events are interpreted differently according to the cultural experiences and personal interests of the initiator, observer, or recipient of that behavior. This is why crime has a different meaning to the offender, the criminologist studying it, the police officer investigating it, and the victim experiencing it firsthand. (See Figure 1–4.)

Think About It…

This text says that "criminal activity is diversely created and variously interpreted." What does that mean? Similarly, what does it mean to say that "crime is fundamentally a social construction"? How does the concept of social relativity come into play in the field of criminology?

Ilya Andriyanov/ Shutterstock

Criminology's Interdisciplinary Nature

Academically, criminology is presently considered primarily a social scientific discipline. Nonetheless, contemporary criminologists recognize that their field is interdisciplinary—drawing on other disciplines to provide an integrated approach to crime in contemporary society and advancing solutions to the social problems that crime creates. Here, anthropology (cultural anthropology, or ethnology), biology, sociology, political science, psychology, psychiatry, economics, ethology (the study of character), medicine, law, philosophy, ethics, and numerous other fields all have something to offer the student of criminology. Other disciplines providing the tools to measure results are found in statistics, computer science, and other forms of scientific and data analysis. (See Figure 1–5.)

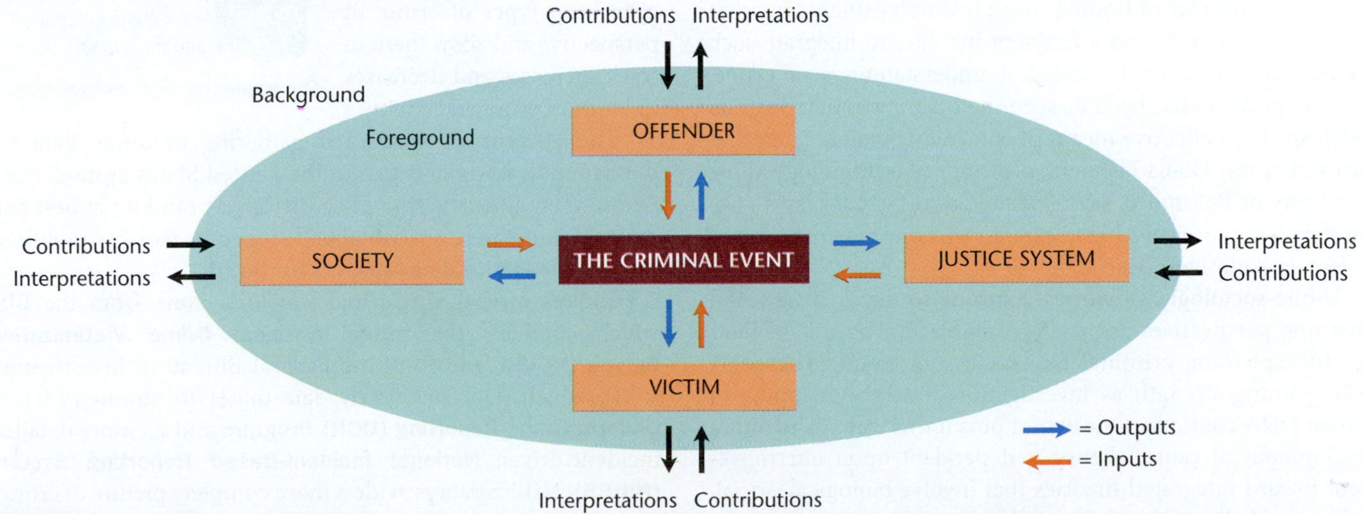

FIGURE 1–4 **Interpreting the Criminal Event.**
Source: From *Criminology Today: An Integrative Introduction*, 7e by Frank A. Schmalleger. Copyright © 2014 by Pearson Education. Used by permission of Pearson Education.

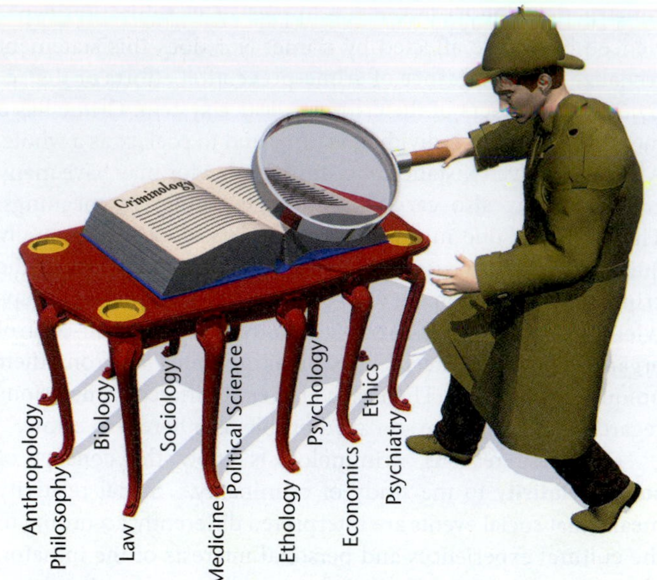

FIGURE 1–5 **Criminology's Many Roots.**

Many contemporary criminologists operate primarily from a sociological perspective. Many of today's theoretical explanations of criminal behavior are routinely presented in the language of social science and emerge within the framework of sociological theory.

Some disagree with people who claim that the sociological perspective should be elevated in importance in today's criminological enterprise. Those who agree with the primacy of sociology emphasize the fact that the study of crime is a social phenomenon. Central to any study of crime, they say, is the social context of the criminal event because it brings victims and criminals together.[30] Moreover, much of contemporary criminology rests on a tradition of social scientific investigation into the nature of crime and criminal behavior, as rooted in European and American sociological thought and traditions that are well over 200 years old.[31]

One of sociology's problems is its apparent reluctance to accept the significance of findings from research gathered in other fields. It traditionally has a frequent inability to integrate such findings into existing sociological understandings of crime. Another problem has been its seeming inability to demonstrate conclusively an effective means of controlling violent and other forms of crime. Diana Fishbein, professor of criminology at the University of Baltimore, says, "Sociological factors play a role. But they have not been able to explain why one person becomes violent and another doesn't."[32]

While sociological theories continue to develop, new and emerging perspectives ask to be recognized. The role of biology in explaining criminal tendencies, for example, appears to be gaining strength as investigations into the mapping of human DNA continue. One expert puts it this way: "The future development of causal theory is dependent upon our movement toward integrated theories that involve biological, social, and cultural dimensions. Our failure to achieve much in the way of understanding the causal sequences of crime is in part a reflection of our slowness in moving toward multidisciplinary, integrated theoretical structures. . . . Fortunately in the last 20 years, this has begun to change. Today we see under way substantial research efforts that are based upon models of explanation that far exceed the traditional sociological approaches."[33]

Think About It…

This chapter says that sociological perspectives continue to dominate the field of criminology, but it also says that criminology is an interdisciplinary discipline. What does the word *interdisciplinary* mean in this context? How can both claims be true?

ad sa/Fotolia

In line with current thought, it is highly likely that sociological perspectives will continue to dominate the field of criminology for some time to come. This dominance is likely to continue because crime—regardless of the causative nuances identified in its development—occurs within the context of a social world. For this reason, the primary significance of crime and criminal behavior is fundamentally social in nature and only workable social policy will effectively curb criminal activity. Read more about the interdisciplinary nature of criminology at **Web Extra 1–2**.

How Much Crime Is There?

To fully understand the nature of crime, it is necessary to gain an appreciation for crime statistics—including how they are gathered, how they affect our understanding of crime, and how they are accessed. Such an appreciation helps criminologists keep types of crime in perspective and allow them to track increases and decreases in kinds of criminal activity.

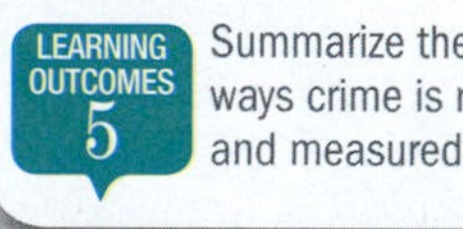

Summarize the various ways crime is reported and measured.

The government-sponsored gathering of crime data for the nation as a whole began in the United States around 1930. Before then, the gathering of statistics was random at best and most accounts were anecdotal and spread by word of mouth or were printed in local newspapers (or both).

Today's official U.S. crime statistics come from the BJS, which conducts the annual **National Crime Victimization Survey (NCVS)**, and from the Federal Bureau of Investigation (FBI), which publishes yearly data under its summary-based **Uniform Crime Reporting (UCR) Program** and its more detailed incident-driven **National Incident-Based Reporting System (NIBRS)**. NIBRS data provide a more complete picture of crimes reported and committed.

NCVS data appear in a number of annual reports, the most important of which is *Criminal Victimization in the United*

States. FBI data take the form of the annual publication *Crime in the United States.* Numerous other surveys and reports are made available through the BJS. Such surveys not only cover the incidence of crime and criminal activity in the United States, but also extend to many other aspects of the criminal justice profession, including justice system expenditures, prisons and correctional data, probation and parole populations, jail inmate information, data on law enforcement agencies and personnel, and information on the activities of state and federal courts. These and other reports are generally made available free of charge to interested parties through the NCJRS.[34] The largest single collection of facts about all aspects of U.S. crime and criminal justice is the *Sourcebook of Criminal Justice Statistics*, which is compiled yearly by the BJS and made available in electronic format.

The UCR/NIBRS and the NCVS each uses its own specialized definitions in deciding which events should be scored as crimes. Sometimes the definitions vary considerably between programs, and none of the definitions used by the reporting agencies are strictly based on federal or state statutory crime classifications.

The National Crime Victimization Survey (NCVS)

The NCVS began collecting data in 1972. It differs from FBI-sponsored programs in one significant way: Rather than depending on reports of crimes to the police (as does UCR/NIBRS), the data contained in the NCVS consist of information from interviews with members of randomly selected households throughout the nation. Hence, the NCVS uncovers a large number of crimes that may not have been reported; therefore, compared to the UCR/NIBRS, the NCVS is regarded by many researchers as being a more accurate measure of the actual incidence of crime in the United States.

NCVS interviewers ask questions about the incidence of rape, personal robbery, aggravated and simple assault, household burglary, personal and household theft, and motor vehicle theft as they have affected household members during the past six months. Information is gathered on victims (including sex, age, race, ethnicity, marital status, income, and educational level), offenders (sex, age, race, and relationship to the victim), and crimes (time and place of occurrence, use of weapons, nature of injury, and economic consequences of the criminal activity for the victim). Questions also cover protective measures used by victims, the possibility of substance abuse by offenders, and the level of previous experience victims may have had with the criminal justice system.

The number of victimizations counted by the NCVS for any single reported criminal occurrence is based on the number of people victimized by the event. Hence, a robbery may have more than one victim and will be so reported in NCVS data. Although this distinction is applied to personal crimes, households are treated as individual units; thus, all household crimes are counted only once, no matter how many members the household contains.

According to the NCVS, on average, only 44% of violent victimizations and 38% of property crimes are reported to the police.[35] While violent crimes are most likely to be reported to the police, personal thefts are the least likely crimes to be reported. NCVS data show that around 77% of motor vehicle thefts are reported to the police, making this the most highly reported crime. Larcenies, at 31%, are least likely to be reported. An interest in recovering property or in receiving insurance payments motivates many victims of property crimes to report their victimization to the police. The two most common reasons for not reporting violent victimizations are that the crime is a personal or private matter and that the offender was unsuccessful and the crime was only attempted.

Larcenies are the least likely crime to be reported.

Critique of the NCVS

Just as the UCR/NIBRS has been criticized for underestimating the actual incidence of criminal activity in the United States, the NCVS can be criticized for possible overreporting. It is difficult to verify the actual occurrence of crimes reported to NCVS interviewers. Hence, no reliable measure exists as to the number of crimes that might be falsely reported or of the number of crimes that might be underreported in NCVS data. Although the proportion is not known, some individuals, when approached by NCVS interviewers, may be unable to resist embellishing crime reports pertaining to their households and may even concoct criminal incidence data for purposes of self-aggrandizement or in an attempt to please the interviewer by providing copious amounts of data.

The NCVS program is much newer than the FBI's UCR Program, and comparisons between the programs are not available before 1973. As with the UCR/NIBRS, definitions of crimes measured by the NCVS do not necessarily correspond to any federal or state statutes or to definitions used for other purposes, making comparisons with other state and federal crime records difficult. Complicating matters still further, changes in NCVS categories have resulted in the inability to easily compare NCVS findings of even a decade ago with current NCVS data.[36]

The Uniform Crime Reporting (UCR) Program

The UCR Program was created by the FBI in 1929 as an official crime-data-gathering program covering the entire United States. The UCR Program developed out of a national initiative by the International Association of Chiefs of Police (IACP), whose goal was to develop a set of uniform crime statistics for use by police agencies and policymakers. The FBI was designated to serve as a national clearinghouse on crime facts, and police agencies around the country began submitting data under the UCR Program. In its initial year of operation, 400 police departments representing cities and towns in 43 states participated in the program.

Early UCR data were structured in terms of seven major offense categories: murder, rape, robbery, aggravated assault, burglary, larceny, and motor vehicle theft. These crimes, called **Part I offenses**, formed the FBI's Crime Index. The Crime Index provided a crime rate that could be compared over time from one geographic location to another. (See Figure 1–6.) Rates of crime under the UCR/NIBRS Program are generally expressed as "*x* number of offenses per 100,000 people." The 2012 rate of criminal homicide, for example, was 4.7 murders for every 100,000 people in the United States.[37]

Rates of crime are generally expressed as the number of offenses per 100,000 people.

In 1979, Congress mandated that arson be added to the list of major crimes offenses. Unfortunately, the inclusion of arson as an eighth index offense made it difficult to compare pre- and post-1979 Crime Indexes. For this and other reasons, the FBI officially discontinued use of the term *crime index* beginning with its report of crime data for 2005.[38]

In today's UCR/NIBRS reports, Part I offenses are subdivided into two categories: violent personal crimes consisting of murder, rape, robbery, and aggravated assault (which will be discussed in Chapter 8) and property crimes consisting of burglary, larceny, motor vehicle theft, and arson (which will be discussed in Chapter 9). Table 1–2 shows the ten most dangerous cities in America ranked according to violent crime data derived from the FBI's 2012 UCR.

Each year, when the FBI issues its annual report, *Crime in the United States*, it includes information within each Part I offense category on the percentage of crimes that have been "cleared." *Cleared crimes* are those crimes for which an arrest has been made or for which the perpetrator is known but an arrest is not possible (as when the offender is deceased or is out

TABLE 1–2 THE TEN MOST DANGEROUS AMERICAN CITIES

Rank	City	Violent Crimes per 100,000	Murders in 2012	Poverty Rate
1	Flint, MI	2,729	63	41%
2	Detroit, MI	2,123	386	41%
3	Oakland, CA	1,993	126	21%
4	St. Louis, MO	1,776	113	27%
5	Memphis, TN	1,750	133	27%
6	Stockton, CA	1,548	71	26%
7	Birmingham, AL	1,518	67	32%
8	New Haven, CT	1,439	17	30%
9	Baltimore, MD	1,406	219	25%
10	Cleveland, OH	1,384	84	34%

Source: FBI, *Uniform Crime Reports*, 2012.

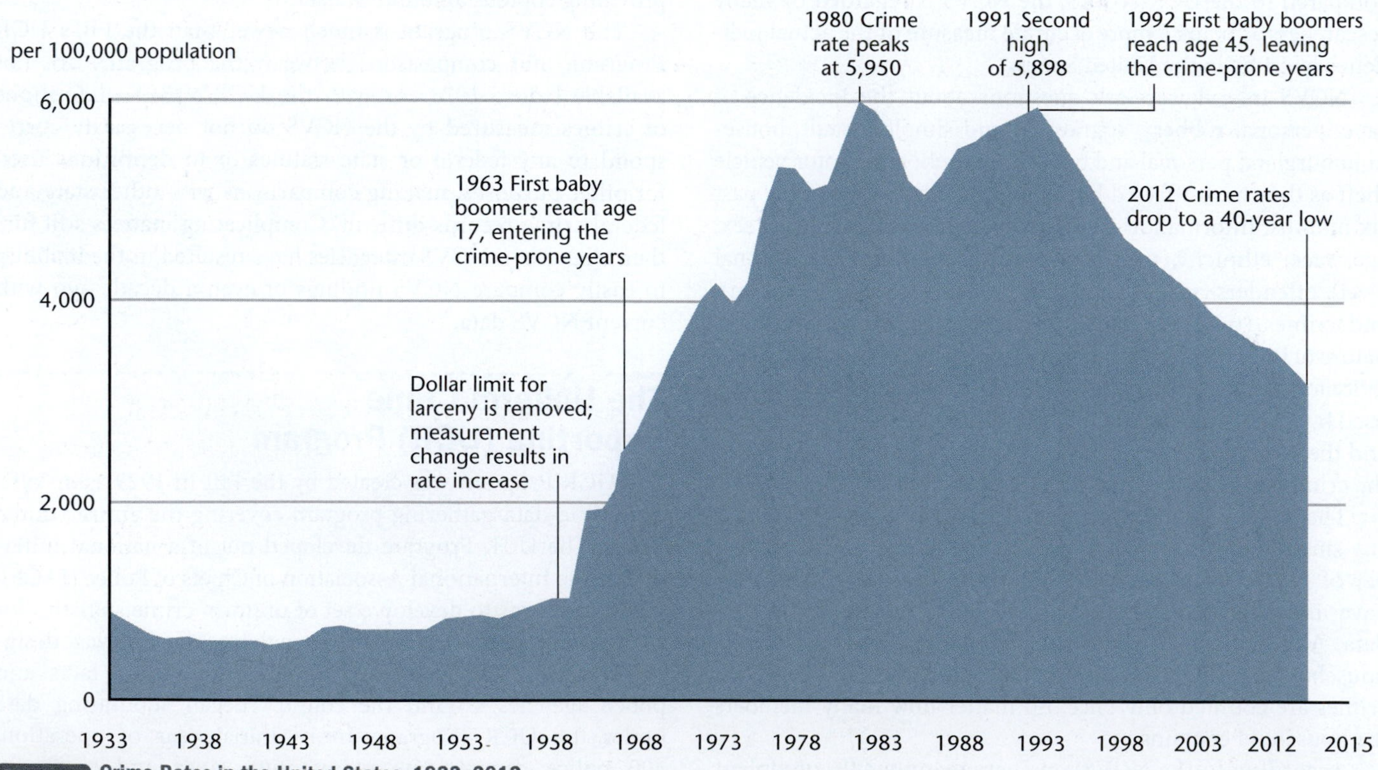

FIGURE 1–6 **Crime Rates in the United States, 1933–2012.**
Source: FBI, *Uniform Crime Reports*, various years.

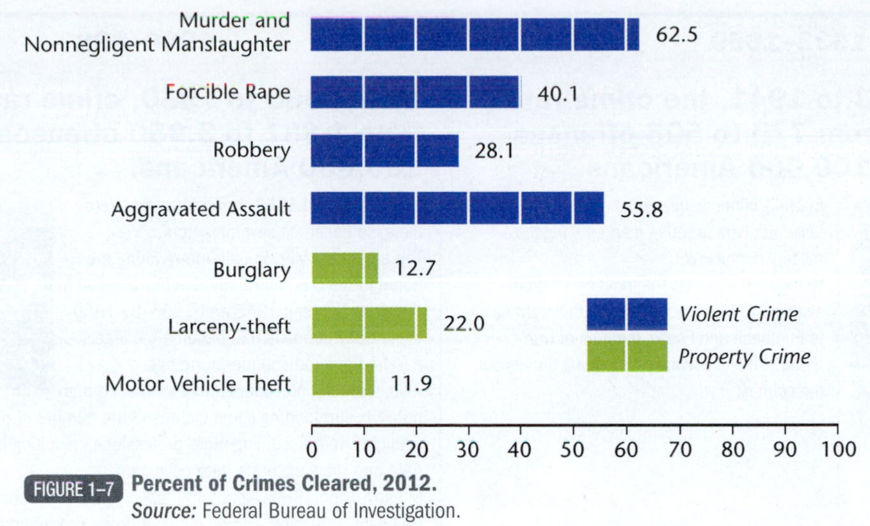

FIGURE 1–7 **Percent of Crimes Cleared, 2012.**
Source: Federal Bureau of Investigation.

of the country). Cleared crimes are also referred to as "solved." Those charged with a crime that is scored as cleared by the FBI may not yet have been adjudicated. In official UCR/NIBRS terminology, a Part I offense is regarded as cleared or solved when (1) "a law enforcement agency has charged at least one person with the offense" or (2) "a suspect has been identified and located and an arrest is justified, but action is prevented by circumstances outside law enforcement control."[39] Clearance rates are reported for each Part I crime category. A **clearance rate** is the proportion of reported or discovered crimes within a given offense category that are solved. Figure 1–7 shows 2012 clearance rates for major crimes.

The most significant feature of the UCR Program is indicated by its name. It is a *reporting* program. In other words, only crimes that are reported to the police (or that are discovered by the police or by others who then report them to the police) are included in the statistics compiled by the program. Most complaints are made by victims.

Because UCR/NIBRS data are based on *reported* crime, the program has been criticized for seriously underestimating the true incidence of criminal activity in the United States—a measurement that would also include unreported crimes. Some experts say, for example, that rape is the most underreported crime in the FBI data, with four to five times as many rapes occurring each year as are reported. Reasons for not reporting a crime such as rape are numerous and include fear of the perpetrator, shame, fears the victim may have of not being believed, and fear of participation in the justice system.

Although rape is indeed seriously underreported (a conclusion drawn from comparison of NCVS and UCR/NIBRS rape statistics), many other crimes are underreported as well. The most seriously underreported crime may be larceny because the theft of small items never makes it into official police reports.

NIBRS: The New UCR Data Format

Recently, the UCR Program has undergone a number of significant changes, and more are scheduled to be implemented shortly as a new, enhanced, incident-driven crime-reporting system is phased in. The new system, the NIBRS, revises the definitions of a number of offenses for reporting purposes, but its "incident-driven" nature is its most important feature. Incident-driven means that the FBI will use the NIBRS system to collect detailed data on the circumstances surrounding each serious criminal incident. NIBRS reports are more detailed than those previously provided under the UCR Program. The NIBRS data-collection format focuses on each single incident and arrest within 22 crime categories, with incident, victim, property, offender, and arrestee information being gathered when available. The 22 NIBRS crime categories are, in turn, made up of 46 specific crimes called "Group A offenses" (as compared with only 8 major offenses on which the old UCR Program gathered data). In addition to Group A offenses, there are 11 Group B offense categories for which only arrest data are reported. The goal of NIBRS is to make data on reported crime more useful by relating them more completely than the old system did to other available information, such as victim and offender characteristics.[40] Because the UCR Program is currently undergoing a transition in format that involves more complete use of NIBRS data, we refer to UCR information that is cited in this text as UCR/NIBRS data.

Changing Crime Patterns

Since official crime statistics were first gathered around 1930, there have been three major shifts in crime rates (Figure 1–8). The first occurred during the early 1940s at the outbreak of the Second World War, when crime decreased sharply due to the large number of young men who entered military service. Young males make up the most "crime-prone" segment of the population, and their participation in the war efforts abroad did much to lower crime rates at home. From 1933–1941, the Crime Index declined from 770 to 508 offenses per every 100,000 members of the U.S. population.[41]

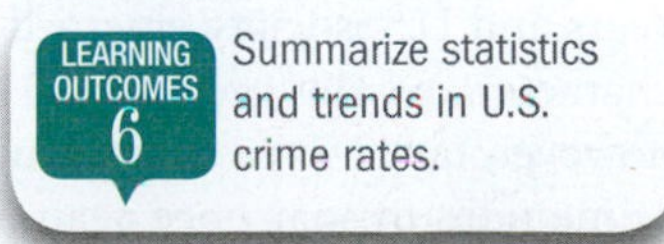

LEARNING OUTCOMES 6
Summarize statistics and trends in U.S. crime rates.

1933–1959

From 1933 to 1941, the crime rate declined from 770 to 508 offenses per every 100,000 Americans.

In 1941 crime decreased sharply based on the large numbers of young men entering the military during WWII.

Young men make up the most crime-prone segment of the population, and their removal to European and Pacific theaters of war reduced the incidence of offending throughout the country.

1960–1989

From 1960 to 1980, crime rates rose from 1,887 to 5,950 offenses per every 100,000 Americans.

Starting around 1960, crime rates began to increase based on several factors.

The end of the war brought many young men home to the U.S., and birthrates skyrocketed in the years between 1945 and 1955. By 1960 these baby boomers had become teenagers and had entered a crime-prone age.

Also, reporting procedures were simplified and publicity surrounding crime increased the number of reports. Police agencies were becoming more professional, resulting in increased data and more accurate data collection.

Moreover, the 1960s were tumultuous years. The Vietnam War, civil rights struggles, and an influx of drugs combined to create an imbalance in society that led to an increase in crime.

1933 1937 1941 1945 1949 1963 1967 1960 1963 1967 1975 1979 1983 1987

FIGURE 1–8 **American Crime Rates: Historical Trends.**
Source: From *Criminal Justice Today: An Introductory Text for the 21st Century*, 13e by Frank A. Schmalleger. Copyright by Pearson Education. Used by permission of Pearson Education.

The second significant shift in offense statistics was a dramatic increase in most forms of crime that began in the 1960s and ended in the 1990s. Many criminologists believe that this shift also had a link to World War II. With the end of the war and the return of millions of young men to civilian life, birth rates skyrocketed between 1945 and 1955, creating a postwar baby boom. By 1960, baby boomers were entering their teenage years. A disproportionate number of young people in the U.S. population produced a dramatic increase in most major crimes.

Other factors contributed to the increase in reported crime during the same period. Crimes that may have gone undetected in the past began to figure more prominently in official statistics. Similarly, the growing professionalization of some police departments resulted in more accurate and increased data collection, making some of the most progressive departments appear to be associated with the largest crime increases.[42] Finally, the 1960s were tumultuous years, punctuated by the Vietnam War, a vibrant civil rights struggle, the heady growth of secularism, dramatic increases in the divorce rate, diverse forms of "liberation," and the influx of psychedelic and other drugs. As a consequence, social norms were blurred and group control over individual behavior declined substantially. According to the FBI, from 1960–1980, crime rates rose from 1,887 to 5,950 offenses per every 100,000 members of the U.S. population.

Crime rates recorded by the FBI continued to remain high, with the exception of a brief decline in the early 1980s, when postwar boomers began to "age out" of the crime-prone years and U.S. society emerged from the cultural drift that had characterized the previous 20 years. At about the same time, however, an increase in drug-related criminal activity led crime rates to soar once again, especially in the area of violent crime. Crime rates peaked around 1991 and have since shown a third major shift, with decreases in the rates of most major crimes being reported since that time. Between 1991 and 2012, the crime rate decreased from 5,898 to 3,246 offenses per every 100,000 citizens, sending it down to levels not seen since 1968.

Decreases in crime since the mid-1990s may have been largely due to an "aging out" of the post–World War II baby-boomer generation (members of which are now mostly too old to continue active criminal lifestyles), new strict laws, expanded justice system and police funding, changes in crime-fighting technologies, economic factors, and the increase in forms of crime not readily counted by official reporting programs.

Moreover, while the two-decade-long decline in crime that took place beginning in 1991 is noteworthy, it did not even begin to bring the overall rate of crime in this country anywhere close to the low crime rates characteristic of the early 1940s and the 1950s. From a long-term perspective, even with recent declines, crime rates in this country remain more than seven times what they were in 1940.

Recent evidence seems to indicate that the decline in crime is ending and that we may be on the cusp of a new cycle of increased criminal activity. Some criminologists think that recent economic uncertainty, an increased jobless rate among unskilled workers, growing state budget deficits resulting in prison closures and an ever-larger number of ex-convicts who are back on the streets, the recent growth in the teenage population in this country, the increasing influence of violent gangs, copycat crimes, and the overall reduction in justice systems resources brought about by the recent recession may soon lead to sustained increases in crime.[43]

1990–2012

From 1991 to 2012, crime rates dropped from 5,897 to 3,246 offenses per every 100,000 Americans.

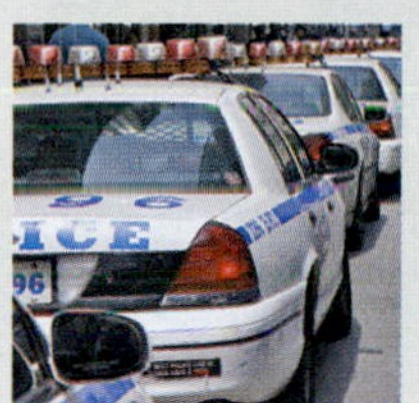

Strict laws, an expanded justice system, and increased police funding for personnel and for crime-fighting technologies are cited as reasons for the drop in crime. Other changes beyond the control of the police may have played a role as well and include economic expansion and an aging population. During the 1990s, unemployment decreased by 36% and likely contributed to the decline in crime rates.

2013–present

In recent years some cities have experienced increases in homicides and other violent crimes.

A fourth shift in crime trends may be about to begin. Economic uncertainty, high jobless rates, a growing number of ex-convicts back on the streets as well as an increase in teen populations and gang activity may soon lead to sustained increases in crime.

1990 1994 1997 2001 2005 2009 2010 2011 2012 2014

Additionally, the specter of random mass shootings, a high number of inner-city murders, and novel forms of criminal activity complicate today's crime picture. Many types of crimes today are Internet-based or involve advanced technology. Neither the UCR nor the NCVS count computer crimes among the major crime categories that they report, although these types of offenses are sometimes subsumed under the category of "larceny" because they frequently involve the theft of money or other things of value. In contrast to earlier periods, today's criminal perpetrators who illegally gain access to digital information (and money) through social media or Internet-based transactions are responsible for a significant level of criminal activity in the virtual world. Such crimes can have very significant impacts on people's lives, although they frequently remain undiscovered, or are found out only with the passage of time.

Unreported Crime

As a comparison of NCVS and UCR/NIBRS data shows, many crimes are not reported, leading criminologists to talk about the "dark figure of crime."[44] The **dark figure of crime** refers to the large number of unreported crimes that never make it into official crime statistics (Figure 1–9). Not only are many crimes not reported, some are not even discovered. If we were to examine all forms of criminal activity, and if we were to become fully aware of all of today's hidden offenses, we would probably find that crimes today have undergone a significant shift away from historical forms of offending to more innovative schemes involving computers and other digital devices.

Many types of crimes today are Internet-based or involve other forms of advanced technology.

Crime's dark figure is sometimes glimpsed through offender self-reports, also known as offender **self-report surveys**, in which anonymous respondents without fear of disclosure or arrest are asked to report confidentially any violations of the criminal law they have committed. A 2010 survey by the Centers for Disease Control and Prevention, for example, found that 1.3 million women said they had been raped during the past 12 months—a number that dwarfs the 83,425 rapes reported to police in 2011.[45] Similarly, a recent Canadian sexual assault survey showed a rate more than 100 times higher than official reports of rape.[46] Self-report surveys, of course, are not free of problems; some respondents may not be fully truthful or may exaggerate when reporting their own victimization. Limitations aside, some criminologists believe that "the development and widespread use of the self-report method of collecting data on delinquent and criminal behavior was one of the most important innovations in criminological research in the twentieth century."[47]

Some of the more recent and best-known self-report surveys include the National Youth Survey (NYS) and the Monitoring the Future study. Begun in 1976, the NYS surveyed a national sample of 1,725 youths between the ages of 11 and 17.[48] Members of the group (or "panel") were interviewed each year for five years between 1977 and 1981 and later at three-year intervals. The survey, which was last conducted in 1993, followed the original respondents into their 30s. Self-report data were compared with official data over time, and data were gathered

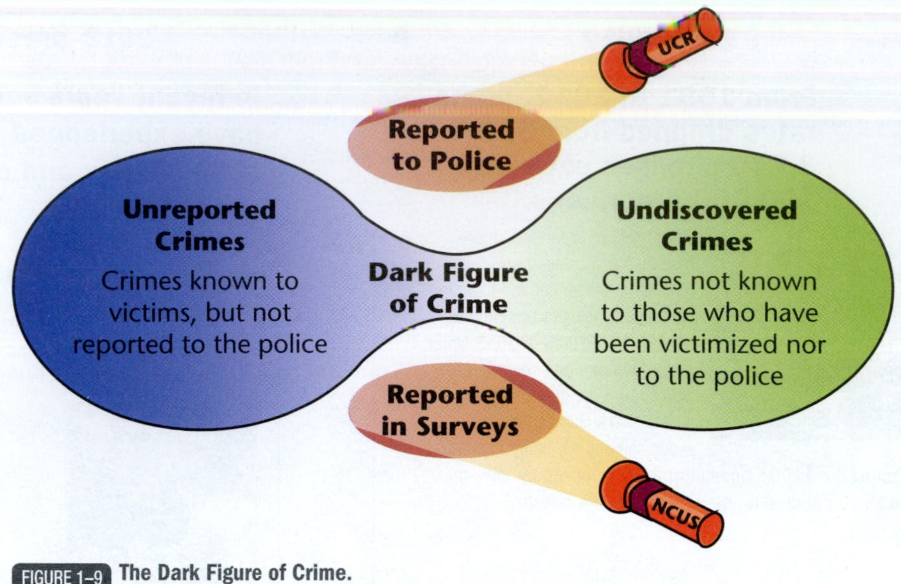

FIGURE 1-9 **The Dark Figure of Crime.**

on a wide variety of variables. Among other things, researchers found that (1) females are involved in a much higher proportion of crime than previously thought, (2) race differentials in crime are smaller than traditional data sources (that is, the UCR/NIBRS) indicated, and (3) violent offenders begin lives of crime much earlier than previous estimates provided by official statistics indicated. The NYS also found a consistent progression from less serious to more serious acts of delinquency over time.

Monitoring the Future[49] is an ongoing national self-report study of the behaviors, attitudes, and values of U.S. secondary school students, college students, and young adults. The study began in 1975, and each year, a total of almost 50,000 8th-, 10th-, and 12th-grade students are surveyed. (Twelfth graders have been surveyed since 1975; 8th and 10th graders, since 1991.) In addition, annual follow-up questionnaires are mailed to a sample of each graduating class for a number of years after students' initial participation.

Criminology and Social Policy

Criminologists make use of contemporary social scientific research methods in the development of criminological theories.

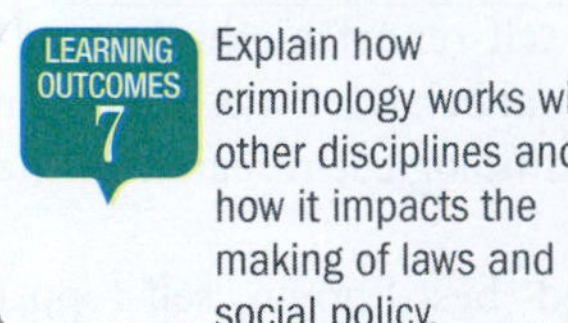

Explain how criminology works with other disciplines and how it impacts the making of laws and social policy.

The use of rigorous social scientific techniques to develop knowledge in the field of criminology is referred to as **evidence-based criminology** (also called knowledge-based criminology). The research conducted by today's criminologists results in a body of scientific evidence applicable to the problems and realities of today's world. Because contemporary criminology is built on a social scientific approach to the subject matter of crime, the discipline has much to offer as we attempt to grapple with the problems of crime and crime control.

Evidence-based criminology is an increasingly popular form of contemporary criminology that is founded on the experimental method.

In 2009, in recognition of the growing significance of evidence-based criminology, the executive board of the American Society of Criminology (ASC) established a new division of experimental criminology; the division's purpose is "the promotion and improvement of experimental evidence and methods in the advancement of criminological theory and evidence-based crime policy."[50] Visit the American Society of Criminology on the Web at **Web Extra 1-3**.

Today, evidence-based criminology is given added voice by the Academy of Experimental Criminology, which is based at the University of Pennsylvania, and by a number of important new journals including the *Journal of Experimental Criminology*, which is the first journal in the field of criminology to focus directly on experimental methods.[51]

The ultimate outcome of criminological research is a set of effective social policies based on scientific evidence. Translating the results of research in the field of criminology into workable social policy is sometimes referred to as **translational criminology**. The NIJ, an arm of the U.S. Department of Justice, explains it this way: "The idea of translational criminology is simple, yet powerful: If we want to prevent, reduce and manage crime, we must be able to translate scientific discoveries into policy and practice."[52]

It is not always easy to translate research into practice, however, even when solid evidence points to needed changes in policy. Some policy implications, such as those relating to the physical environment, are relatively easy to implement. Most criminologists agree that such changes, such as installing brighter lighting in crime-prone areas, can be effective at preventing crime and must be easy to implement.

Other policy innovations, especially those calling for cultural or social changes, can be difficult to implement, even when there is strong evidence for their likely success. In a recent example, an editorial in the highly regarded British magazine *New Scientist* asked this question: "Why are we so reluctant to accept that on-screen violence is bad for us?"[53] The article, entitled "In Denial," noted that "by the time the average U.S. schoolchild leaves elementary school, he or she will have witnessed more than 8,000 murders and 100,000 other acts of violence on television." For children who play computer games and watch cable TV, the numbers will be far higher. Scientific studies show the obvious detrimental effects of media violence, according to the article, "yet every time a study claims to have found a link between aggression, violence, educational, or behavioral problems and TV programs or computer games, there are cries of incredulity. . . ."[54]

Numerous professional groups—including the American Medical Association, the American Academy of Pediatrics, the American Psychological Association, and the American Academy of Child and Adolescent Psychiatry—agree that violence in television, music, video games, and movies leads to increased levels of violent behavior among children.[55] A joint statement issued by those organizations says that the effects of violence in the media "are measurable and long-lasting." The groups reached the conclusion "based on over 30 years of research . . . that viewing entertainment violence can lead to increases in aggressive attitudes, values and behaviors, particularly in children." Moreover, "prolonged viewing of media violence can lead to emotional desensitization toward violence in real life." Similarly, some years ago, the Federal Trade Commission (FTC) issued a report[56] on teenage violence that concluded that "Hollywood aggressively markets violent movies, music and electronic games to children even when they have been labeled as appropriate only for adults."[57] Read the full report at **Web Extra 1–4**.

Numerous professional groups agree that violence in television, music, video games, and movies leads to increased levels of violent behavior among children.

Even with knowledge of these results, however, policymakers are reluctant to slow the production of violent media. For this reason, violence on TV and in video games is still prominent in the United States. *New Scientist* says media vendors dissuade "any criticism of a multibillion-dollar business" where they would lose profits resulting from any policies aimed at crime reduction.[58]

Professional criminologists understand the necessity of linking sound **social policy** to the objective findings of well-conducted criminological research. In the words of the NIJ, "Successful dissemination of the results of criminological research" requires that the evidence be implemented correctly. In other words, "it is not just about finding evidence that something works; it is figuring out why it works and how to implement the evidence in real-world settings."[59] Watch dozens of YouTube videos from the Center for Evidence-Based Crime Policy at **Web Extra 1–5**, and learn more about contemporary crime and public policy at **Web Extra 1–6**.

Think About It…

This chapter says that in an ideal world, evidence-based criminological research should be translated into effective social policy. What is evidence-based criminology? Why doesn't the evidence of "what works" always lead to effective social policy?

jpainting/Fotolia

THE CASE

Adam Lanza and the Sandy Hook School Shootings

On December 14, 2012, 20-year-old Adam Lanza, a socially awkward young man, went on a shooting rampage at Sandy Hook Elementary School in Newtown, Connecticut. In a matter of minutes, Lanza fired 155 bullets and shot to death 20 kindergarten students, 4 teachers, a principal, and the school's psychologist.[i] The shooting spree ended when Lanza turned one of his three guns on himself. Before the massacre, Lanza killed his mother at the house they shared only minutes from the school. The horrific shooting was covered by media services for days and reignited an intense national debate about gun control.

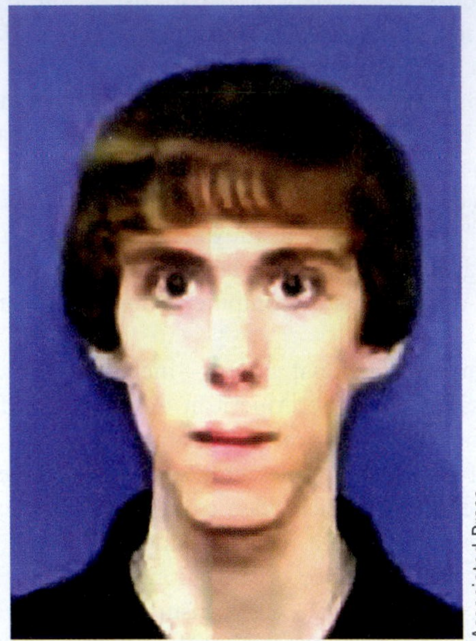

Adam Lanza, the Sandy Hook Elementary School shooter. Why do random mass shootings seem to be so commonplace in the United States today?

Although the Newton shooting stood out as especially horrific because it ended so many innocent young lives, it is but one of a number of random mass shootings in the United States in recent years. In 2012 alone, there were 12 other random mass killings—including a July attack by a lone gunman in an Aurora, Colorado, movie theater where 12 people were killed and another 58 injured during a midnight showing of the movie *The Dark Knight Rises*.[ii] In that crime, the alleged shooter, 24-year-old James Eagan Holmes, who dressed as the Joker (a nefarious character from the film) during the shooting spree, was arrested outside the theater. He remains jailed as this text goes to press, having entered a plea of not guilty by reason of insanity on June 4, 2013.

Experts tell us that the number of random mass shootings is on the increase. According to the *Wall Street Journal*, there "were 18 random mass shootings in the 1980s, 54 in the 1990s, and 87 in the 2000s."[iii] The *Journal*'s emphasis was on *random* shootings, and it noted that other mass killings—in which victims were in some way known to the shooter—had not significantly increased or decreased in number.

A fair question to ask would be "Why are the number of such random incidents increasing?" Some answers might be found in the personal characteristics of the shooters. Lanza and Holmes shared a number of things in common. Both were middle-class white males in their early 20s who were regarded by their peers as unnervingly intelligent. Holmes had been a former neuroscience graduate student at the University of Colorado's Anschutz Campus, whose academic career unraveled shortly before the movie theater shooting. Lanza, once a prominent member of his high school's technology club and an honors student, was said to have been extraordinarily bright by former teachers. Neither shooter had a previous criminal record.[iv]

What may have contributed to both incidents, however, was one additional feature the two men shared—a disordered personality.[v] According to the American Psychiatric Association, most mentally ill people do not turn to violence, although some forms of mental illness have been associated with aggression and criminal activity, especially when combined with illegal drug use.[vi]

Questions about Lanza's mental health were quickly raised following the Sandy Hook shootings by former friends and family members who knew him to be painfully shy, reclusive, and psychologically troubled. Described by personal acquaintances as "very bright" but emotionally disturbed, Lanza may have suffered from a form of Asperger's syndrome and was said to be impervious to physical pain. He had been on numerous medications intended to lower the anxiety that he experienced in everyday social situations, and prior to the Newtown shootings, his mother had repeatedly sought help in controlling her increasingly unresponsive and emotionally withdrawn son. Months after the Sandy Hook shooting, investigators revealed that Lanza had compiled a detailed record to include a timeline of mass shootings across the nation and may have wanted to achieve a "record" of some kind—by killing more than any other attacker ever had.[vii] Holmes, the Colorado shooter, met with at least three mental health professionals prior to the movie theater shooting, and CBS news reports that the fact "adds to the picture of Holmes being clearly on [psychiatrists'] radar in the time period leading up to the shooting."[viii]

Once we understand that guns and certain forms of mental illness can prove to be a dangerous combination, it is important to ask whether something can be done to predict and prevent episodes of random mass violence. Two days after the Newtown shooting, President Obama, for example, told those gathered at a memorial service at the town's high school, "We can't tolerate this anymore,"[ix] and promised to examine federal gun-control options.[x]

Yet the answer may not be as simple as gun control. Lanza and Holmes were known to have serious mental health problems, yet they were able to live freely in society, to arm themselves, and to attack unprotected and innocent people in what should have been safe public places. U.S. society is built on a delicate balance between the demand for *personal freedoms* and the need for *public safety*. The tears that appear in the social and legal fabric woven from the attempt to achieve balance between these two contrasting goals is where crimes like random mass shootings can occur.

Notes

[i]Michael Isikoff, Tom Winter, and Erin McClam, "Investigators: Adam Lanza Surrounded by Weapons at Home; Attack Took Less Than 5 Minutes," NBC News, March 28, 2013, http://openchannel.nbcnews.com/_news/2013/03/28/17501282-investigators-adam-lanza-surrounded-by-weapons-at-home-attack-took-less-than-5-minutes?lite (accessed March 29, 2013).

[ii]"U.S. Mass Shootings in 2012," *The Washington Post*, December 14, 2012, http://www.washingtonpost.com/wp-srv/special/nation/us-mass-shootings-2012 (accessed March 20, 2013). The article, however, notes that there has been no long-term increase in mass shootings, only in *random* mass shootings.

[iii]David Kopel, "Guns, Mental Illness and Newtown," *Wall Street Journal*, December 17, 2012 (accessed March 21, 2013).

[iv]Holly Yan, "Gunman's Family at a Loss to Explain Connecticut Shooting," CNN, December 17, 2012, http://www.cnn.com/2012/12/16/justice/connecticut-shooting-suspect-profile/index.html (accessed March 20, 2013).

[v]The Autism Research Institute's Autistic Global Initiative Project notes that autism and Asperger's syndrome are neurodevelopmental issues and does not consider them to be mental health disorders.

[vi]American Psychiatric Association, Council on Law and Psychiatry, *Access to Firearms by People with Mental Illness: Resource Document* (Arlington, VA: American Psychiatric Association, 2009).

[vii]Howard Koplowitz, "Adam Lanza Spreadsheet: Sandy Hook Shooter Compiled Extensive List of Mass Murderers," *International Business Times*, March 18, 2013, http://www.ibtimes.com/adam-lanza-spreadsheet-sandy-hook-shooter-compiled-extensive-list-mass-murderers-1133557# (accessed March 28, 2013).

[viii]Rick Sallinger, "James Holmes Saw Three Mental Health Professionals before Shooting," CBS News, August 21, 2012, http://www.cbsnews.com/8301-201_162-57497820/james-holmes-saw-three-mental-health-professionals-before-shooting/ (accessed March 21, 2013).

[ix]"Transcript: 'We Have Wept with You'; Obama Says in Newtown Speech," CNN, December 16, 2012, http://politicalticker.blogs.cnn.com/2012/12/16/breaking-we-have-wept-with-you-obama-says-in-newtown-speech (accessed March 20, 1013).

[x]Jared A. Favole, "Obama Says All Gun Buyers Should Face Checks," *Wall Street Journal*, December 19, 2012, http://professional.wsj.com/article/SB10001424127887324461604578188680585236550.html?mod=WSJPRO_hps_MIDDLEThirdNews (accessed March 22, 2013).

The case of Adam Lanza raises a number of interesting questions. Among them are the following:

1. **What led Lanza to attack an elementary school and take so many lives?**
2. **What role did biology, society, and his mental state play in contributing to Lanza's crime?**
3. **Can future random mass shootings be prevented? If so, how?**

CHAPTER 1 What Is Criminology?

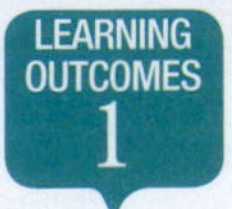

Differentiate between crime, deviance, and delinquency.

Crime is human conduct that violates the criminal law. Without a law defining a particular form of behavior, there is no crime, no matter how deviant or socially repugnant the behavior in question may be. Many crimes are deviant or abnormal forms of behavior. Not all deviance, however, is criminal, and some crimes are not seen as deviant by those who commit them—or by significant segments of the population.

1. What is crime? Who determines what is and is not criminal? How are such determinations made?
2. What is deviance? How do we know what is and is not deviant?
3. How does delinquency differ from crime?

crime Human conduct that violates the criminal laws of a state, the federal government, or a local jurisdiction that has the power to make and enforce the laws.

criminalize To make an act illegal.

deviant behavior Human activity that violates social norms.

statute A formal written enactment of a legislative body.

delinquency Violations of the criminal law and other misbehavior committed by young people.

Explain how the consensus perspective differs from the pluralist perspective.

While it is easy to agree that certain behaviors, such as murder, should be criminal, it is not so easy to agree on other forms of behaviors—especially those that seem to involve willing participants.

1. What is the consensus perspective?
2. What is the pluralistic perspective?
3. How does the consensus perspective differ from the pluralist perspective?

consensus perspective A viewpoint that holds that laws should be enacted to criminalize given forms of behavior when members of society agree that such laws are necessary.

pluralist perspective A viewpoint that recognizes the importance of diversity in our society and says that behaviors are typically criminalized through a political process.

Describe criminology and the role of criminologists.

Criminology is the scientific study of crime and criminal behavior. Criminologists are credentialed individuals holding advanced degrees in the field and studying crime, criminal behavior, and crime trends.

1. What does a criminologist do?
2. How do the duties of a criminologist differ from those of criminalists?
3. How is a criminologist different from a police officer?
4. What is criminology?
5. What do criminologists study?
6. How does criminology cooperate with other disciplines to prevent and solve crimes?

criminologist A person trained in the field of criminology who studies crime, criminals, and criminal behavior.

criminalist A specialist in the collection and examination of the physical evidence of crime.

criminology The scientific study of crime and criminal behavior, including their manifestations, causes, legal aspects, and control.

criminal justice The scientific study of crime, criminal law, the criminal justice system, police, courts, and correctional systems.

Summarize the theoretical perspectives of criminology.

While some crimes are especially difficult to understand, our natural tendency is to seek out explanations for such behavior, and we look to criminology for answers about how to prevent crime. Crime, however, is not an isolated individual activity, but a social event. Consequently, every crime has a unique set of causes, consequences, and participants.

1. What is theoretical criminology?
2. What is a general theory?
3. What does theory integration mean within the context of the study of criminology?
4. Explain how the concept of social relativity applies to crime and to particular types of crimes such as hate crimes.

theoretical criminology The type of criminology that is usually studied in colleges and universities, describes crime and its occurrence, and offers explanations for criminal behavior.

general theory A theory that attempts to explain most forms of criminal conduct through a single, overarching approach.

unicausal Of or having one cause. Theories posing one source for all that they attempt to explain.

integrated theory An explanatory perspective that merges concepts drawn from different sources.

social relativity The notion that social events are interpreted differently according to the cultural experiences and personal interests of the initiator, observer, or recipient of that behavior.

LEARNING OUTCOMES 5

Summarize the various ways crime is reported and measured.

To fully understand the nature of crime, it is necessary to gain an appreciation for crime statistics—including how they are gathered, how they affect our understanding of crime, and how they are accessed. Such an appreciation helps criminologists keep types of crime in perspective and allows criminologists to track increases and decreases in kinds of criminal activity.

1. What federal agency runs the Uniform Crime Reporting Program?
2. What are the eight major crimes about which the Uniform Crime Reporting Program gathers data?
3. What is NIBRS? How does it work to improve the Uniform Crime Reporting Program?
4. What is the National Crime Victimization Survey? How does it differ from the Uniform Crime Reporting Program?

National Crime Victimization Survey (NCVS) An annual survey of selected American households conducted by the Bureau of Justice Statistics to determine the extent of criminal victimization—especially unreported victimization—in the United States.

Uniform Crime Reporting (UCR) Program An FBI statistical reporting program that provides an annual summation of the incidence and rate of reported crimes throughout the United States.

National Incident-Based Reporting System (NIBRS) A new and enhanced statistical reporting system that collects data on each single incident and arrest within 22 crime categories. NIBRS expands the data collected under the Uniform Crime Reporting Program.

Part I offenses The crimes of murder, rape, robbery, aggravated assault, burglary, larceny, and motor vehicle theft, as defined under the FBI's Uniform Crime Reporting Program. Also called major crimes.

clearance rate The proportion of reported or discovered crimes within a given offense category that are solved.

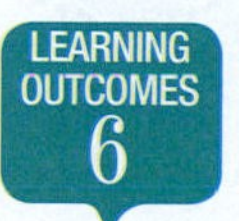

Summarize statistics and trends in U.S. crime rates.

Since official crime statistics were first gathered around 1930, there have been three major shifts in crime rates. The first occurred during the early 1940s at the outbreak of the Second World War, when crime decreased sharply. The second was a dramatic increase in most forms of crime that began in the 1960s and ended in the 1990s. Crime rates peaked around 1991 and have since shown a third major shift, with decreases in the rates of most major crimes being reported since that time.

1. What are the three major shifts in crime rates that have occurred in the United States since the 1930s?
2. Explain what is meant by the term *dark figure of crime*. Why are many crimes not reported?
3. Why are self-report surveys useful in uncovering the true extent of crime in American society?

dark figure of crime The large number of unreported crimes that never make it into official crime statistics.

self-report surveys A survey in which anonymous respondents, without fear of disclosure or arrest, are asked to report confidentially any violations of the criminal law they have committed.

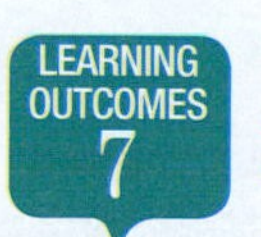

Explain how criminology works with other disciplines and how it impacts the making of laws and social policy.

More important than criminological theorizing are social policies based on research findings. Nonetheless, policy innovations, especially those calling for cultural or social changes, can be difficult to implement, even when there is strong support for their likely success.

1. What is evidence-based criminology? How does the meaning of the word *evidence* in *evidence-based criminology* differ from criminal evidence?
2. How might theoretical understandings of crime causation lead to policies intended to prevent criminal activity?
3. How can evidence-based criminology contribute to the creation of effective social policy?

evidence-based criminology A form of contemporary criminology that makes use of rigorous social scientific techniques, especially randomized controlled experiments, and the systematic review of research results; also called knowledge-based criminology.

translational criminology A form of contemporary criminology that seeks to translate research findings in the field into practical and workable policy initiatives.

social policy A government initiative, person, or plan intended to address problems in society.

"Nature has placed mankind under the governance of two sovereign masters, pain and pleasure."

—Jeremy Bentham

Classical and Neoclassical Criminology

Choice and Consequences

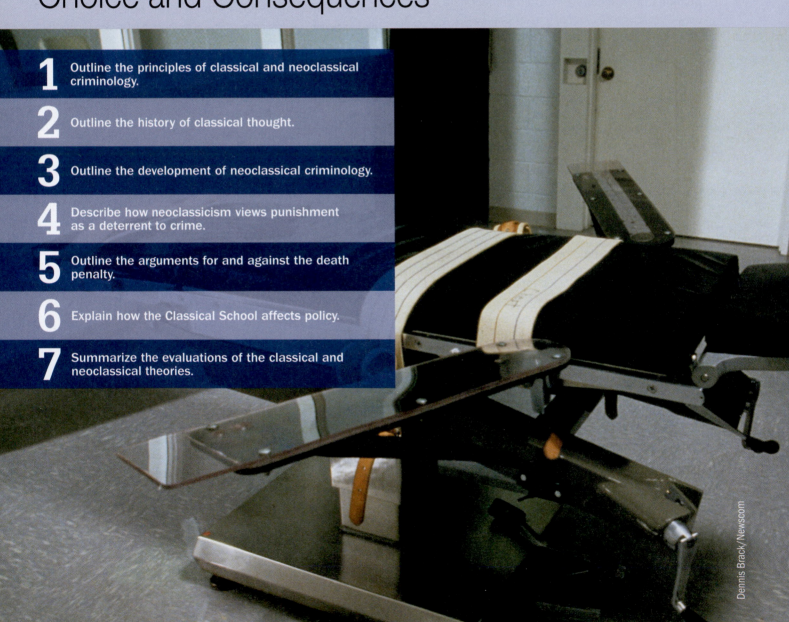

1. Outline the principles of classical and neoclassical criminology.
2. Outline the history of classical thought.
3. Outline the development of neoclassical criminology.
4. Describe how neoclassicism views punishment as a deterrent to crime.
5. Outline the arguments for and against the death penalty.
6. Explain how the Classical School affects policy.
7. Summarize the evaluations of the classical and neoclassical theories.

Dennis Brack/Newscom

INTRO HOW TO COMMIT THE PERFECT CRIME

Some crimes are relatively spontaneous unplanned events that occur in the heat of passion or when an unanticipated opportunity presents itself. A wallet left on the seat of an unlocked car whose window is rolled down, for example, is a clear invitation for anyone walking by to steal the wallet, and some people will be unable to resist the temptation to reach out and grab it. The majority of crimes, however, are likely planned—at least to some degree. Crime planning, which involves rational decision making on the part of the offender, means not only that criminals assess the pros and cons of perpetrating offenses (that is, the benefits versus the likelihood of being caught and punished), but also the means of crime commission. An example of clear thinking in support of criminal activity was recently available on listverse.com, a site that touts itself as "focused on lists that intrigue and educate."[1] One list featured among the site's crime and mystery series is "Top 10 Tips to Commit the Perfect Crime."[2] Among the tips offered are ensuring that anyone contemplating an offense not leave any discoverable DNA at the scene of the crime. Because DNA is ubiquitous, the list author explains that "The best solution . . . is to commit your crime in a place that is likely to have a lot of DNA from strangers." A park, a shopping mall, or "anywhere that a lot of people tend to gather" is recommended as an offense location. The list author opines that "Finding your DNA will be like finding a needle in a haystack."[3]

Dmitrijs Dmitrijevs/Fotolia

DISCUSS Do you think that most crimes are planned, or are they relatively spontaneous events? What kinds of crimes are most likely to be planned?

Principles of Classical and Neoclassical Criminology

Rational thinking is, of course, not confined to criminals; it is a widespread human trait. Even so, Western culture has sometimes emphasized faith and belief, or emotions and fancy, over the need to think rationally. In the eighteenth century, however, a social and intellectual movement known as the Enlightenment swept through Europe. The Enlightenment was based on the idea that rational thought, and the application of reasoned scientific principles, would liberate humankind from superstitious and unfounded beliefs. This emphasis on rational thinking would change the way members of Western society understood their world.

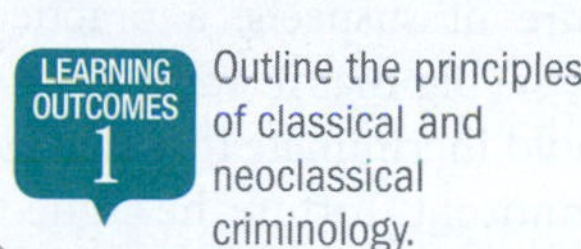
LEARNING OUTCOMES 1 Outline the principles of classical and neoclassical criminology.

Think About It…

Classical thinkers said that most crime is the result of rational decision making. Some criminals, however, appear to act without much thought. What distinguishes between crimes that involve thought and crimes that don't? Is it the type of offender who commits them, or is it the type of crime being committed?

Patleem/Fotolia

The Enlightenment was a powerful intellectual initiative that fueled the fires of social change. It eventually led to the French and American Revolutions and provided many of the intellectual foundations of the U.S. Constitution and the French Declaration of the Rights of Man and of the Citizen. The Enlightenment also inspired other social movements and freed innovative thinkers from old conventional thoughts. Because of this, superstitions—such as the belief that evil spirits caused people to violate the law—were widely discarded. For the first time, men and women began to think for themselves and started exercising freedom of choice in their beliefs. Following the Enlightenment, supernatural explanations for human behavior were largely abandoned. This is important because, at least in Europe, free will and rational thought became the link binding all significant human activity. In summary, the Enlightenment inspired the reexamination of existing doctrines of human behavior from the viewpoint of rational thought.

Within criminology, the Enlightenment led to the development of the **Classical School** of criminological thought. Crime and deviance, which had previously been explained by referencing mythological influences and spiritual shortcomings, came to be understood as products of the exercise of free will. People controlled their own lives, and crime was explained as moral wrongdoing fueled by personal choice. For this reason, the Classical School of criminology became the first modern approach to making sense of crime and criminal behavior. The eight key principles of classical and current-day neoclassical criminology are shown in Figure 2–1.

Key Principles of Classical and Neoclassical Criminology

- Human beings are fundamentally rational, and most human behavior results from free will coupled with rational choice.
- Pain and pleasure are the two central determining factors of human behavior.
- Punishment serves to deter law violators and serves as an example to others who might contemplate violating the law.
- The principles of right and wrong are inherent in our nature and cannot be denied.
- Society exists to provide benefits to individuals that they would not receive living in isolation.
- When people band together for the protection offered by society, they forfeit some of their personal freedoms in order to enjoy the benefits of living among others cooperatively.
- Certain key rights of the individual are necessary for the enjoyment of life, and governments that restrict and prohibit the exercise of those rights should be disbanded.
- Crime lessens the quality of the contractual bond that exists between individuals and their society. Therefore, criminal acts cannot be tolerated by any members if everyone wants to receive the most benefit from living in a cooperative society.

FIGURE 2–1 Key Principles of Classical and Neoclassical Criminology.

▶ *The Roots of Classical Criminology*

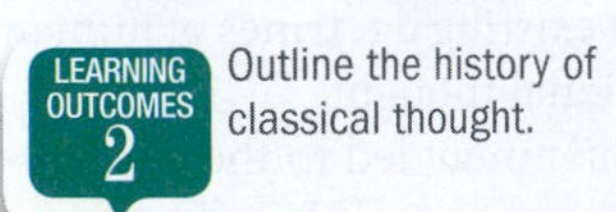

Outline the history of classical thought.

Classical criminology developed out of the writings of a number of influential thinkers. Especially important were the ideas developed by Cesare Beccaria and Jeremy Bentham.

Cesare Beccaria (1738–1794): Punishment as Deterrence

Cesare Beccaria (Cesare Bonesana, who held the title "Marchese di Beccaria") was born in Milan, Italy. He was the eldest of four children, was trained at Catholic schools, and earned a doctor of laws degree at the age of 20.

In 1764, Beccaria published his *Essay on Crimes and Punishments*. Beccaria's purpose in penning the book was not to set forth a theory of crime, but to communicate his observations on the laws and justice system of his time. In his *Essay*, Beccaria distilled the notion of the social contract into the idea that "laws are the conditions under which independent and isolated men united to form a society."[4] More important, his writings contained a philosophy of punishment. Beccaria claimed that although most criminals are punished based on an assessment of their criminal intent, they should be punished instead based on the degree of injury they cause. The purpose of punishment, Beccaria said, should be deterrence rather than retribution, and punishment should be imposed to prevent offenders from committing additional crimes. Beccaria saw punishment as a tool to an end, not an end in itself, and crime prevention was more important to him than revenge.

To help prevent crimes, Beccaria argued, trial and punishment should be swift and, once punishment is decreed, it should be certain. In his words, "The more promptly and the more closely punishment follows upon the commission of a crime, the more just and useful it will be." Punishment that is imposed immediately following crime commission, claimed Beccaria, is connected with the wrongfulness of the offense, both in the mind of the offender and in the minds of others who might see the punishment imposed. Others would thereby learn of the consequences of being involved in criminal activity, and it would act as a deterrent for would-be offenders.

Beccaria concluded that punishment should be only severe enough to outweigh the personal benefits derived from committing crimes. Any additional punishment, he argued, would be superfluous. Beccaria's concluding words on punishment are telling. "In order," he said, "for punishment not to be, in every instance, an act of violence of one or of many against a private citizen, it must be essentially public, prompt, necessary, the least possible in the given circumstances, proportionate to the crimes, [and] dictated by the laws."

Beccaria condemned the torture of suspects, a practice still used in the eighteenth century, saying that it was a device that ensured that weak suspects would incriminate themselves, while strong ones would be found innocent. Torture, he argued, was also unjust by punishing individuals before determining their guilt in a court of law. In Beccaria's words, "No man can be called guilty before a judge has sentenced him, nor can society deprive him of public protection before it has been decided that he has in fact violated the conditions under which such protection was accorded him. What right is it then, if not simply that of might, which empowers a judge to inflict punishment on a citizen while doubt still remains as to his guilt or innocence?"

Beccaria's ideas were widely recognized as progressive by his contemporaries. His principles were incorporated into the French penal code of 1791 and significantly influenced the justice-related activities of European leaders such as Catherine the Great of Russia, Frederick the Great of Prussia, and Emperor Joseph II of Austria. Evidence suggests that Beccaria's *Essay* influenced framers of the U.S. Constitution, and some scholars

Think About It…

Classical thinkers in the field of criminology claimed that rational decision making plays a big role in crime causation. But rationality is different from motivation. What did classical thinkers likely see as motivating factors behind criminal behavior?

Yuri Arcurs/Fotolia

claim that the first ten amendments to the Constitution, known as the Bill of Rights, might not have existed were it not for Beccaria's emphasis on the rights of individuals in the face of state power. Perhaps more than anyone else, Beccaria is responsible for the contemporary belief that criminals have control over their behavior, that they choose to commit crimes, and that they can be deterred by the threat of certain punishment. Learn more about Cesare Beccaria at **Web Extra 2-1**.

Jeremy Bentham (1748–1832): The Pain versus Pleasure Balance

Jeremy Bentham, another founding personality of the Classical School, wrote in his *Introduction to the Principles of Morals and Legislation* (1789) that "nature has placed mankind under the governance of two sovereign masters, pain and pleasure."[5] To reduce crime or, as Bentham put it, "to prevent the happening of mischief," the pain associated with crime commission must outweigh the pleasure to be derived from criminal activity. Bentham's claim rested upon his belief, spawned by Enlightenment thought, that human beings are fundamentally rational and that criminals will weigh the resulting pain of punishment against any pleasures derived from crime commission.

Bentham advocated neither extreme nor cruel punishment—only punishment sufficiently distasteful to the offender so that the discomfort experienced would outweigh the benefits gained from committing crimes. Generally, Bentham argued, the more serious the offense, the more reward it holds for its perpetrator, and therefore the more weighty the resulting punishment. "Pain and pleasure," said Bentham, "are the instruments the legislator has to work with" in controlling antisocial and criminal behavior.

Bentham's approach has been termed **hedonistic calculus** or *utilitarianism* because of its emphasis on the worth any action holds for an individual undertaking it. As Bentham stated, "By the principle of utility is meant that principle which approves or disapproves of every action whatsoever, according to the tendency which it appears to have to augment or diminish the happiness of the party whose interest is in question; or, what is the same thing . . . to promote or to oppose that happiness." In other words, Bentham believed that individuals could weigh, at least intuitively, the consequences of their behavior before acting, thus maximizing pleasure and minimizing pain. The value of any pleasure (or the tendency to avoid pain), according to Bentham, could be calculated by its intensity, duration, certainty, and immediacy (or remoteness in time).

Bentham claimed that the principles surrounding his pleasure–pain perspective were not new. "Nor is this a novel and unwarranted, any more than it is a useless theory," he wrote. "In all this there is nothing but what the practice of mankind, wheresoever they have a clear view of their own interest, is perfectly comfortable to. An article of property, an estate in land, for instance, is valuable, on what account? On account of the pleasures of all kinds which it enables a man to produce, and what comes to the same thing the pains of all kinds which it enables him to avert." Although Bentham's ideas were not new, their application to criminology was innovative at the time. In 1739, David Hume distilled the notion of utilitarianism into a philosophical perspective in his book *A Treatise of Human Nature*. Although Hume's central concern was not to explain crime, scholars who followed Hume observed that human behavior is typically motivated by self-interest more than by anything else.

Utilitarianism is a practical philosophy, and Bentham was quite practical in his suggestions about crime prevention. All citizens, he said, should have their first and last names tattooed on their wrists for the purpose of facilitating police identification. He also recommended the creation of a centralized police force focused on crime prevention and control—a recommendation that found life in the English Metropolitan Police Act of 1829, which established London's New Police under the direction of Sir Robert Peel.

Bentham's other major contribution to criminology was his suggestion that prisons be designed along the lines of what he called a "Panopticon House." The **Panopticon**, as Bentham envisioned it, was to be a circular building with cells along the circumference, each clearly visible from a central location staffed by guards. Bentham recommended that Panopticons be constructed near or within cities, serving as examples to others of what would happen to them should they commit crimes. He also wrote that prisons should be managed by contractors, who could profit from the labor of prisoners. He further suggested that each contractor should "be bound to insure the lives and safe custody of those entrusted to him." Although a Panopticon was never built in Bentham's England, French officials funded a modified version of such a prison, eventually built at Lyons. Subsequently, three prisons modeled after the Panopticon concept were later constructed in the United States.

Bentham advocated neither extreme nor cruel punishment—only punishment sufficiently distasteful to the offender so that the discomfort experienced would outweigh the benefits gained from committing crimes.

Bentham's critics have been quick to point out that punishments often don't work as planned. Even death sentences appear not to affect the incidence of murder and homicidal crimes. Such critics forget Bentham's second tenet: that for punishment to be effective, "it must be swift and certain." For any punishment to have teeth, Bentham said, it not only must mandate a certain degree of displeasure, but also must follow immediately after judgment—and must have no avenue available for avoidance. More information about Jeremy Bentham and the Bentham Project can be found at **Web Extra 2–2** and **Web Extra 2–3**.

Neoclassical Criminology

By the end of the 1800s, classical criminology, with its emphasis on free will and individual choice as the root causes of crime, was replaced by another theory of the Enlightenment era known as "positivism." Positivism, which made use of the scientific method in studying criminality, is discussed in more detail in Chapter 3. For the purposes of this chapter, however, it is important to realize that positivism, in its original formulation, was based upon an acceptance of hard determinism, or the belief that much of human behavior—and therefore crime—results from forces that are beyond the control of the individual. For this reason, the original positivists completely rejected the notion of free will. They turned their attention instead to the impact of socialization, genetics, economic conditions, peer-group influences, and other factors that might determine criminality. Hard determinism implied that offenders were not responsible for their crimes and suggested that crime could be prevented by changing the conditions that produced criminality. (See Figure 2–2.)

LEARNING OUTCOMES 3 Outline the development of neoclassical criminology.

Although positivism remains an important component of contemporary criminology, some of its assumptions were challenged in the 1970s. At that time, several studies showed that offenders could not be rehabilitated, no matter what method was tried to change their attitudes. This precipitated a growing and widespread public fear of crime that led to "get-tough-on-crime" policies and a cultural reaffirmation of belief in the rational nature of human beings. The result was a resurgence of classical ideals that came to be referred to as **neoclassical criminology**. Neoclassical criminology focused on the importance of character (a kind of middle ground between total free will and hard determinism), the dynamics of character development, and the rational choices that people make as they are faced with opportunities for crime.

Free Will	Soft Determinism	Hard Determinism
Classical Criminology		Nineteenth-Century Positivist Criminology

FIGURE 2–2 **Classical Criminology versus Positivism—The Role of Free Will.**

The neoclassical movement appears to have had its start with a number of publications produced in the 1970s. One of these was **Robert Martinson's** national survey of rehabilitation programs.[6] Martinson found that when it came to the rehabilitation of offenders, nothing seemed to work, as most of them resume their criminal careers after being released from prison. The phrase "Nothing works!" became a rallying cry of conservative policymakers everywhere, and the **nothing-works doctrine** received much public attention. Many conservative politicians (and some criminologists) began calling existing notions of crime prevention and rehabilitation into question. This was amidst claims that enhanced job skills, increased opportunities for employment, and lessened punishment did nothing to stem what was then a rising tide of crime.

In 1975, Harvard political scientist James Q. Wilson wrote *Thinking about Crime*, in which he suggested that crime is not a result of poverty or social conditions and cannot be affected by social programs.[7] Wilson argued instead for the lengthy incarceration of offenders and for the elimination of criminal opportunity. Writings by Wilson and others led to the development of the **justice model**, which was predicated on the growing belief that prisons do not rehabilitate or cure offenders, and that criminals *deserve* punishment because of the choices they make.[8]

For the next 20 to 30 years, many states initiated "get tough on crime" campaigns, adapting the justice model to crime-control legislation. In the spring of 1994, for example, California legislators passed the state's now-famous "three-strikes-and-you're-out" law. Amid much fanfare, then-Governor Pete Wilson signed the three-strikes measure into law, calling it "the toughest and most sweeping crime bill in California history." California's law, which is retroactive (counting offenses committed before the date the legislation was signed), requires a mandatory sentence of 25 years to life for three-time felons, with convictions for two or more serious or violent prior offenses. Criminal offenders facing a "second strike" can receive up to double the normal sentence for their most recent offense. Under the law, prisoners are eligible for parole only after serving 80% of their sentence.

Think About It…

Classical and neoclassical criminology assume that human actors have free will. That is, they can make choices and impose those choices through their behavior on the world around them. What role does free will play in crime commission? Might some crimes result from something other than the exercise of free will?

haveseen/Fotolia

In 2003, in two separate cases, the U.S. Supreme Court upheld the three-strikes California convictions of Gary Ewing and Leandro Andrade.[9] In a California courtroom following his conviction for felony grand theft of three golf clubs, Ewing, who had four prior felony convictions, had received a sentence of 25 years to life. Andrade, who also had a long record, had been sentenced to 50 years in prison for two petty-theft convictions.[10] In her opinion, noting the *Ewing* case, Justice Sandra Day O'Connor admitted that states should be able to decide when repeat offenders "must be isolated from society . . . to protect the public safety," even when nonserious crimes trigger the lengthy sentence. In deciding these two Eighth Amendment–based cases, the Court determined that imposing a possible life term for nonviolent felonies with a defendant who had a history of serious or violent criminal convictions was *not* cruel and unusual punishment.

In November 2012, California voters overwhelmingly approved a change to their state's three-strikes law. The changes mean that now only two categories of offenders can be sentenced as three-strikers: (1) those who commit new "serious or violent" felonies as their third offense, and (2) previously released murderers, rapists, or child molesters who are convicted of a new third strike, even if it is not a "serious or violent" felony. Under the new legislation, inmates sentenced under earlier versions of the law are allowed to petition for early release. Estimates are that around 3,000 such inmates may soon be released.

A recent review of three-strikes legislation found that 16 states have modified such laws in response to difficult economic conditions. This means that the high cost of imprisonment is leading legislatures to rethink long prison terms. Modifications have included giving judges more discretion in sentencing and narrowing the types of crimes that count as a "strike." Learn more about crime-control policy at the Center for Law and Social Policy via **Web Extra 2–4**.

Rational Choice Theory

Rational choice theory (RCT), a product of the late 1970s and early 1980s, mirrors many principles found in classical criminology. Rational choice theory holds that criminals make a conscious, rational, and at least partially informed choice to commit crime. (See Figure 2–3.) It employs cost–benefit analysis, resembling similar theories found in economics that view human behavior as resulting from personal choices made after weighing the costs and benefits of available alternatives. Rational choice theory is noteworthy for its emphasis on the rational and adaptive aspects of criminal offending. It "predicts that individuals choose to commit crime when the benefits outweigh the costs of disobeying the law. Crime will decrease," according to such theories, "when opportunities are limited, benefits are reduced, and costs are increased."[11]

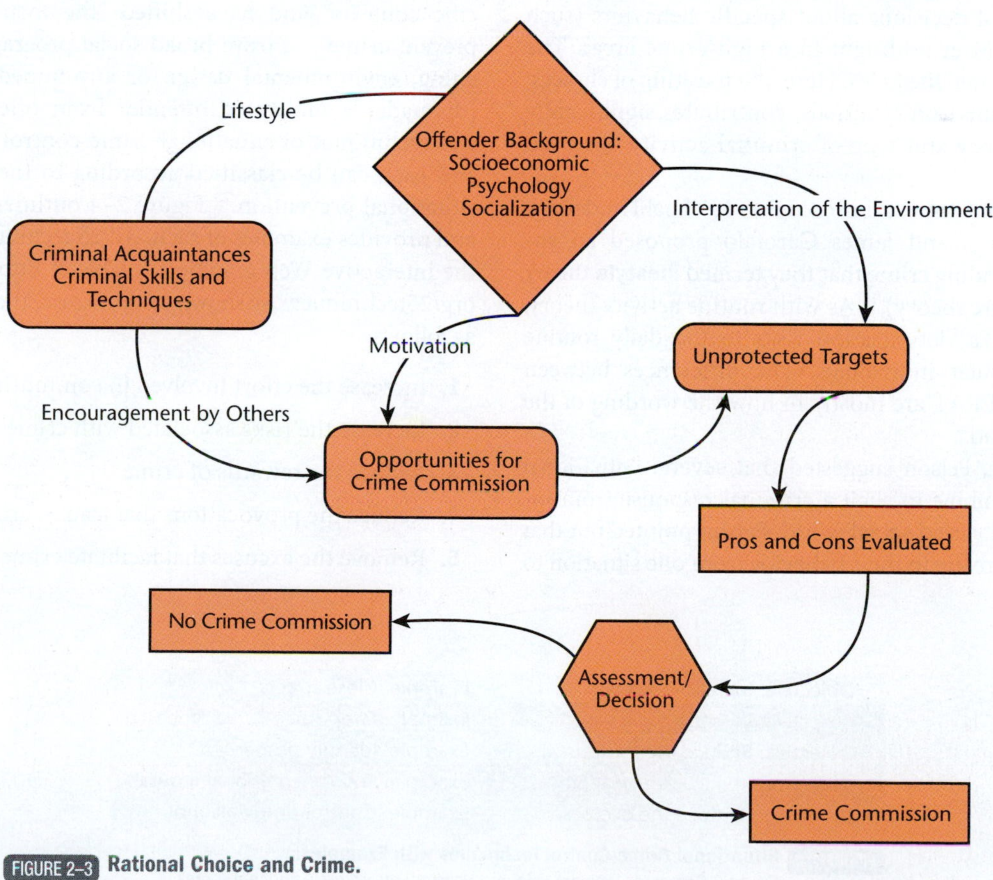

FIGURE 2–3 **Rational Choice and Crime.**

Two varieties of rational choice theory can be identified here. One, which builds on an emerging emphasis on victimization, is called **routine activities theory (RAT)**. A second, which is largely an extension of the rational choice perspective, is called **situational choice theory**.

Routine activities theory was proposed by **Lawrence Cohen** and **Marcus Felson** in 1979.[12] Cohen and Felson suggested that regular, recurrent, and patterned activities contribute significantly to both the volume and type of crime found in any society. The two believed that increased personal affluence and the development of social activities outside the home changed the nature of American society during the 1960s and 1970s. They thought this brought about increased rates of household theft and personal victimization by strangers. Central to the routine activities approach is the claim that crime is likely to occur when a motivated offender and a suitable target come together in the absence of a capable guardian. A **capable guardian**, simply put, is one who effectively discourages crime. So a person who has taken steps toward crime prevention is less likely to be victimized. As Cohen and Felson observe, "The risk of criminal victimization varies dramatically among the circumstances and locations in which people place themselves and their property."[13] For example, a person routinely using an automated teller machine in isolated locations late at night is more likely to be preyed upon by robbers than a person who stays home after dark. Lifestyles that contribute to criminal opportunities are likely to result in crime because they increase the risk of potential victimization.[14] Although noncriminal lifestyles are partly the result of unavoidable social roles assigned to those participating in a given lifestyle, people generally make rational decisions about specific behaviors (such as going to an ATM at midnight in a high-crime area). The same is true of criminal lifestyles. Here, the meshing of choices, made by both victims and criminals, contributes significantly to both the frequency and type of criminal activity observed in society.

At about the same time, criminologists Michael Hindelang, Michael Gottfredson, and James Garofalo proposed an approach to understanding crime that they termed **lifestyle theory** (or lifestyle/exposure theory).[15] As with routine activity theory, lifestyle theory links victimization risks to the daily routine activities of particular individuals. The differences between lifestyle theory and RAT are mostly in how the wording of the concepts is presented.

In a later work, Felson suggested that several "situational insights" might combine to elicit a criminal response from individual actors in a varied social world. Felson pointed out that "individuals vary greatly in their behavior from one situation to another" and said that criminality might flow from temptation, bad company, idleness, or provocation.[16] Convenience stores, for example, create temptations toward theft by displaying merchandise within easy reach of customers. Other authors have defined the term *situation* to mean "the perceptive field of the individual at a given point in time" and have suggested that it can be described "in terms of who is there, what is going on, and where it is taking place."[17]

Situational choice theory is a kind of soft determinism. It views criminal behavior "as a function of choices and decisions made within a context of situational constraints and opportunities."[18] The theory holds that "crime is not simply a matter of motivation; it is also a matter of opportunity."[19] Situational choice theory suggests that the probability of criminal activity can be reduced by changing the features of the environment. **Ronald V. Clarke** and **Derek B. Cornish**, developers of the situational choice perspective, review the choices available in criminal situations. They define *choice-structuring properties* as "the constellation of opportunities, costs, and benefits attaching to particular kinds of crime."[20] Clarke and Cornish suggest using situational strategies such as "cheque guarantee cards, the control of alcohol sales at football matches, supervision of children's play on public housing estates, vandal resistant materials and designs, 'defensible space' architecture, improved lighting, closed-circuit television surveillance"[21] as effective crime-prevention additions to specific situations—all designed to lower criminal victimization in given instances.

In brief, rational choice theorists concentrate on "the decision-making process of offenders confronted with specific contexts" and have shifted "the focus of the effort to prevent crime . . . from broad social programs to target hardening, environmental design or any impediment that would [dissuade] a motivated offender from offending."[22] Twenty-five techniques of situational crime control can be identified, and each can be classified according to the five objectives of situational prevention.[23] Figure 2–4 outlines those techniques and provides examples of each. All 25 techniques can be seen in the interactive Web graphic available at http://www.popcenter.org/25techniques. As shown in the figure, the five objectives are as follows:

1. Increase the effort involved in committing a crime.
2. Increase the risks associated with crime commission.
3. Reduce the rewards of crime.
4. Reduce the provocations that lead to criminal activity.
5. Remove the excuses that facilitate crime commission.

Objective: Increase the effort	Example: Close streets
Objective: Increase the risks	Example: Strengthen surveillance
Objective: Reduce the rewards	Example: Identify property
Objective: Reduce provocations	Example: Reduce emotional arousal
Objective: Remove the excuses	Example: Control drugs/alcohol

FIGURE 2–4 **Situational Crime-Control Techniques with Examples.**
Source: Center for Problem-Oriented Policing, *http://www.popcenter.org*

Think About It...

This chapter refers to 25 situational crime-control techniques. How might situational crime-control techniques be applied to reduce crimes such as shoplifting?

Steve Lovegrove/Fotolia

Although RCT is similar to classical deterrence theory, earlier approaches focused largely on the balance between pleasure and pain to prevent criminal behavior. Rational choice theory places less emphasis on pleasure and emotionality and more on rationality and cognition. Some rational choice theorists distinguish among the types of choices offenders make when moving toward criminal involvement. One type of choice, known as "involvement decisions," is considered "multistaged" and "includes the initial decision to engage in criminal activity as well as subsequent decisions to continue one's involvement or to desist."[24] Another type of choice, called "event decisions," relates to particular instances of criminal opportunity, such as robbing a particular person or letting him or her pass. Event decisions are usually made quickly, in contrast to involvement decisions, which are decided after months or years of thought.

The Seductions of Crime

One criminologist focusing on the relationship between decisions to commit crime and the rewards of those decisions is **Jack Katz**.[25] In his book *Seductions of Crime*, Katz explains that crime is the result of "often wonderful attractions within the lived experience of criminality."[26] Crime, Katz says, is often pleasurable for those committing it, and this pleasure of one sort or another is the major motivation behind crime. As the title of his book indicates, Katz termed these pleasurable experiences **the seductions of crime**. Sometimes, however, the pleasures derived from crime are not immediately obvious. Moreover, as Katz points out, criminologists have often depicted crime as something to be avoided, but have failed to understand just how good some crimes feel to those who commit them.[27]

For many criminal offenders, crime is indeed rewarding, Katz says. It is exciting; it feels good, he tells his readers. "The particular seductions and compulsions [which criminals] experience may be unique to crime," he says, "but the sense of being seduced and compelled is not. To grasp the magic in the criminal's sensuality, we must acknowledge our own."[28] Katz describes the almost sexual attraction shoplifting held for one young offender. As one thief said, "The experience was almost orgasmic for me. There was a buildup of tension as I contemplated the danger of a forbidden act, then a rush of excitement at the moment of committing the crime, and finally a delicious sense of release."[29] Katz's approach, which stresses the sensual dynamics of criminality, says that for many people, crime is sensually compelling. As one writer notes, "Jack Katz argues for a redirection of the criminological gaze—from the traditional focus on background factors such as age, gender, and material conditions to foreground or situational factors that directly precipitate criminal acts and reflect crimes' sensuality."[30] Learn more about Jack Katz's seductions of crime at **Web Extra 2–5**.

Situational Crime-Control Policy

Building on the work of rational and situational choice theorists, Israeli American criminologist David Weisburd describes the advantages of a situational approach to crime prevention. Weisburd points out that crime-prevention efforts have traditionally been concerned with offenders or potential offenders. "Researchers have looked to define strategies that would deter individuals from involvement in crime or rehabilitate them," Weisburd says, "so they would no longer want to commit criminal acts. In recent years, crime-prevention efforts have often focused on the incapacitation of high-rate or dangerous offenders so [that] they are not free to victimize law-abiding citizens. In the public debate over crime-prevention policies, these strategies are usually defined as competing approaches."[31] However, Weisburd says, "They [agree] about crime-prevention research and policy: that efforts to understand and control crime must begin with [understanding] the offender. In all of these approaches, the focus of crime prevention is on people and their involvement in criminality."

"Although this assumption continues to dominate crime prevention research and policy," says Weisburd, "it has begun to be challenged by a very different approach that seeks to shift the focus of crime prevention efforts." The new approach developed in large part as a response to the failures of traditional theories and programs. The 1970s, in particular, saw a shattering of traditional assumptions about the effectiveness of crime-prevention efforts. It led to a reevaluation of research and policy about crime prevention. For many scholars and policymakers, this meant having to rethink their assumptions about criminality and how offenders might be prevented from participating in crime. Others suggested that a more radical reorientation of

Think About It...

Classical thinkers and rational choice theorists seem to say that free will and careful thought play a significant role in crime commission. However, if criminals weigh their choices and the consequences of their behavior before committing a crime, then why do so many crimes seem to happen spontaneously—and apparently without much thought?

Godfer/Fotolia

crime-prevention efforts was needed. They argued to shift the unit of analysis forming the basis of crime-prevention efforts, instead of changing specific strategies or theories already in use at the time. This new crime-prevention effort focuses not on people who commit crime, but on the context in which crime occurs.

This approach, which is called **situational crime prevention**, looks to develop greater understanding of crime and more effective crime-prevention strategies through concern with the physical, organizational, and social environments that make crime possible.[32] The situational approach does not ignore offenders; it merely places them as one part of a broader crime-prevention equation centered on the context of crime. It demands shifting the approach to crime prevention from one concerned primarily with why people commit crime to one that asks why crime occurs in specific settings. It moves the context of crime into central focus and sees the offender as one of several factors that affect it. Situational crime prevention is closely associated with the idea of a "criminology of place," which is discussed in more detail in Chapter 5. Situational crime prevention can be further explored at **Web Extra 2–5** .

Weisburd suggests that a "reorientation of crime prevention research and policy, from the causes of criminality to the context of crime, provides much promise." Says Weisburd, "At the core of situational prevention is the concept of opportunity." In contrast to offender-based approaches to crime prevention that usually focus on the dispositions of criminals, situational crime prevention begins with the opportunity structure of the crime situation. By "opportunity structure," advocates of this perspective refer to the immediate situational and environmental components of the context of crime, not the sociological concepts of anomie (normlessness) or differential opportunity. Their approach to preventing crime is to reduce the opportunities for crime in specifically identified situations. This may involve efforts as simple and straightforward as **target hardening** or access control.[33]

The value of a situational approach lies in the fact that criminologists have found it difficult to identify who is likely to become a serious offender and to predict the timing and types of future offenses that repeat offenders are likely to commit. And, as Weisburd says, "Legal and ethical dilemmas make it difficult to base criminal justice policies on models that still include a substantial degree of statistical error." Moreover, Weisburd adds, "If traditional approaches worked well, of course, there would be little pressure to find new forms of crime prevention. If traditional approaches worked well, few people would possess criminal motivation and fewer still would actually commit crimes."

Situational prevention advocates argue that the context of crime provides a promising alternative to tradit ional offender-based crime-prevention policies.[34] They assume that situations provide a more stable and predictable focus for crime-prevention efforts than do people. In part, this assumption develops from commonsense notions of the relationship between opportunities and crime. Shoplifting, for example, is, by definition, clustered in stores and not residences, and family disputes are unlikely to be a problem outside the home. High-crime places, in contrast to high-crime people, cannot flee to avoid criminal justice intervention, and crime that develops from the specific characteristics of certain places cannot be easily transferred to other contexts.

Another example can be found in street robberies, which are most likely to be found in places where many pedestrians stroll (such as bus stops and business districts), where there are few police or informal guardians (for example, doormen), and where a supply of motivated offenders can be found nearby or at least within easy access to public transportation.[35] Similarly, such places are not likely to be centers for prostitution, which would favor easy access of cars (and little interference by shopkeepers who are likely to object to the obvious nature of street solicitations), or flashing, which is more likely to be found in the more anonymous environments of public parks.

THEORY in PERSPECTIVE

The Classical School and Neoclassical Thinkers

The Classical School is a criminological perspective developed in the late 1700s and early 1800s. It had its roots in the Enlightenment and held that men and women are rational beings and that crime is the result of the exercise of free will and personal choices based on calculations of perceived costs and benefits. Hence, punishment can be effective in reducing the incidence of crime when it negates the rewards to be derived from crime commission.

Classical Criminology

Approach: Application of Classical School principles to problems of crime and justice

Period: 1700s–1880

Theorists: Cesare Beccaria, Jeremy Bentham, others

Concepts: Free will, deterrence through punishment, social contract, natural law, natural rights, due process, Panopticon

Neoclassical Criminology

Approach: Modern-day application of classical principles to problems of crime and crime control in contemporary society, often in the guise of "get-tough" social policies

Period: 1970s–present

Theorists: Lawrence Cohen, Marcus Felson, Ronald V. Clarke, Derek B. Cornish, Jack Katz, many others

Concepts: Rational choice, routine activities theory, capable guardians, situational crime prevention, target hardening, just deserts, determinate sentencing, specific deterrence, general deterrence

Punishment and Neoclassical Thought

Punishment is a central feature of both classical and neoclassical thought. Whereas punishment served as a deterrent to crime in classical thought, in neoclassical thinking, it is expanded to support the ancient concept of retribution. Advocates of retribution see punishment as revenge.

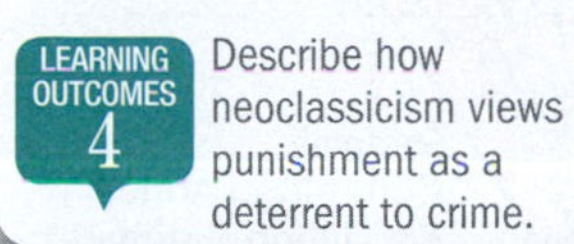

LEARNING OUTCOMES
4
Describe how neoclassicism views punishment as a deterrent to crime.

If a person is attracted to crime and chooses to violate the law, then he or she *deserves* to be punished, according to modern neoclassical thinkers. Because the consequences of crime were known to the offender before the crime was committed, the criminal *must* be punished to curtail future criminal behavior.

Notions of revenge and retribution are morally based. They build on a sense of community indignation at criminal behavior—and on the sense of righteousness inherent in Judeo-Christian notions of morality and propriety. Both philosophies of punishment turn a blind eye to the mundane and practical consequences of any particular form of punishment. Advocates of retributive punishment easily dismiss critics of the death penalty. Those critics are known to frequently challenge the effectiveness of court-ordered capital punishment on the basis that such sentences do little to deter others from committing the same crimes. Wider issues, including general deterrence, are irrelevant when a person focuses narrowly on the emotions that crime and victimization produce in any given instance. Simply put, from the neoclassical perspective, some crimes cry out for vengeance, while others demand little more than a slap on the wrist or an apology from the offender.

Just Deserts

The old adages "He got what was coming to him" and "She got her due" summarize the thinking behind the **just deserts model** of criminal sentencing. Just deserts, a concept inherent in the justice model, means that criminal offenders deserve the punishment they receive at the hands of the law, and that any punishment imposed should be appropriate to the type and severity of crime committed. The idea of just deserts has long been a part of Western thought. The Old Testament dictum of "an eye for an eye, and a tooth for a tooth" has been cited by many as divine justification for strict punishments. Some scholars believe, however, that in reality, the notion of "an eye for an eye" was intended to reduce the barbarism of existing penalties, where a victim might exact the severest of punishments for only minor offenses. In those times, even petty offenses were often punished by whipping, torture, and sometimes death.

According to the neoclassical perspective, doing justice ultimately comes down to an official doling out of what is deserved. Justice is nothing more or less than what that individual deserves after careful consideration of the circumstances.

Deterrence

True to its historical roots, **deterrence** is a hallmark of modern neoclassical thought. In contrast to early thinkers, however, today's neoclassical writers distinguish between **specific deterrence** and **general deterrence**. Specific deterrence is a goal of criminal sentencing that seeks to prevent a particular offender from repeating criminality. General deterrence, in contrast, works by way of example and seeks to prevent others from committing crimes similar to the one for which a particular offender is being sentenced.

Following their classical counterparts, modern-day advocates of general deterrence stress that for punishment to effectively impede crime, it must be swift, certain, and severe enough to outweigh rewards flowing from criminal activity. Unfortunately, those advocating punishment as a deterrent are frustrated by today's complex criminal justice system and the slow handling of cases and punishments. Court-imposed punishments are rarely swift in imposition due to inherent delays in judicial proceedings and stalling tactics used by defense counsel. Similarly, certainty of punishment is practically nonexistent because of ongoing appeals and stumbling blocks built into the system. Often, punishments are ordered and not fully carried out. In contemporary America, offenders sentenced to death, for example, are unlikely to ever have their sentences finalized. For those who do, an average of nearly 16 years passes between the time a sentence of death is imposed and the time it is carried out.[36] Death-row inmates and their lawyers typically solicit appeals at various courts to delay or derail the process of justice. Some win new trials; others receive overturned sentences by blanket U.S. Supreme Court rulings finding fault or trial error. Many others die of natural causes before the notion of fair process is actually served.

An average of nearly 16 years passes between the time a sentence of death is imposed and the time it is carried out.

If the neoclassicists are correct, ideally, criminal punishments should prevent a repetition of crime. Unfortunately, as high rates of contemporary recidivism indicate, punishments in America rarely accomplish that goal. **Recidivism** means repeating criminal behavior by those already involved in crime. Recidivism can also be used to measure the success of a given approach to the problem of crime. When so employed, it is referred to as a recidivism rate, expressed as the percentage of convicted offenders released from prison who are later rearrested for a new crime, generally within five years following release. Some studies show high recidivism rates, reaching 80% to 90%, meaning that eight or nine of every ten criminal offenders released from confinement are rearrested for new crimes within five years of release. Such studies, however, do not measure how many released offenders return to crime but are not caught; nor do they identify those who return to crime more than five years after release from prison. Were such numbers available, recidivism rates would likely be even higher.

Think About It…

Why do we say that "notions of revenge and retribution" are morally based? Is it easier to take revenge on an offender whose crime is believed to be the result of rational thought, instead of an offender whose crimes are undertaken spontaneously?

The Martyrdom of St. Stephen, c.1623 (oil on copper), Stella, Jacques (1596–1657)/Fitzwilliam Museum, University of Cambridge, UK/The Bridgeman Art Library

One reason American criminal justice seems so ineffectual at preventing crime and reducing recidivism may be that the punishments that contemporary criminal law provides are rarely applied to most offenders. Statistics show that few lawbreakers are ever arrested and that of those who are arrested, fewer still are convicted of the crimes with which they have been charged. After lengthy court proceedings, most offenders processed by the justice system are released, fined, or placed on probation. Relatively few are sent to prison, although short of capital punishment, prison is the most severe form of punishment available to authorities today. To represent this situation, criminal justice experts often use a diagram known as a "crime funnel." Figure 2–5 shows the crime funnel for 2014. As the figure shows, fewer than 1% of criminal law violators in America can be expected to spend time in prison as punishment for their crimes.

Complicating the situation is the fact that few inmates ever serve their full sentences. Many serve only a small fraction of their sentences, with early release for good behavior, mandated reentry training, and the practical considerations necessitated by prison overcrowding.

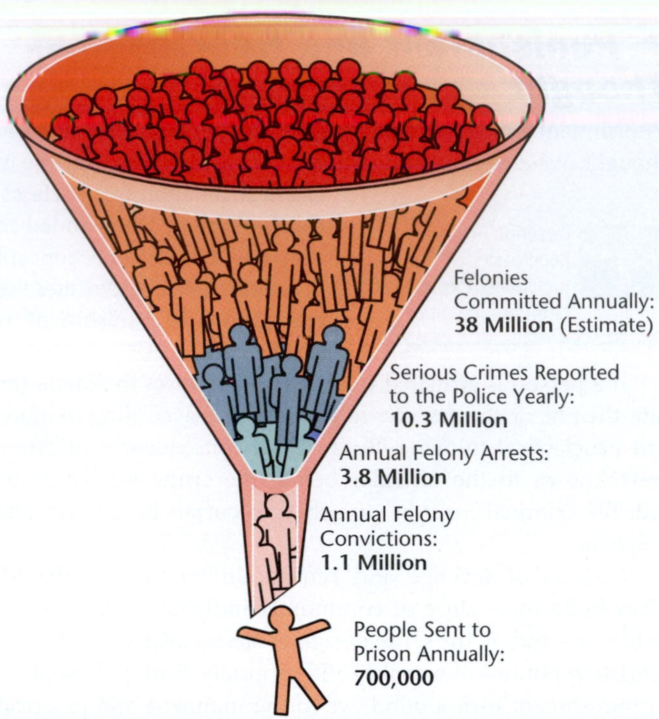

FIGURE 2–5 **The Crime Funnel.**
Note: Includes drug crimes.
Source: Statistics derived from Kathleen Maquire, ed., *Sourcebook of Criminal Justice Statistics,* http://www.albany.edu/sourcebook (accessed May 12, 2014).

The Death Penalty

Notions of deterrence, retribution, and just deserts all come together in **capital punishment**. The many different understandings of crime and crime control, along with arguments over free will and social determinism, combine with varying philosophies of punishment to produce considerable disagreement over death as an appropriate form of criminal sanction.

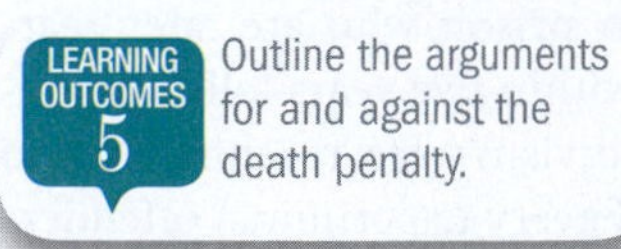

LEARNING OUTCOMES
5
Outline the arguments for and against the death penalty.

Opponents of capital punishment make ten kinds of claims:

1. Capital punishment does not deter crime.
2. The death penalty has, at times, been imposed on innocent people, with no workable system currently in place to prevent the accidental execution of innocents.
3. Human life is sacred, even the life of a murderer.
4. State-imposed death lowers society to the same moral (or amoral) level as the murderer.
5. The death penalty has been haphazardly imposed in seemingly random fashion.
6. The death penalty is imposed disproportionately on minority offenders.
7. Capital punishment goes against most fundamental precepts of organized religion.
8. The death penalty is more expensive than imprisonment.
9. Internationally, capital punishment is widely viewed as inhumane and barbaric.
10. A viable alternative exists in life imprisonment without the possibility of parole.

Advocates of capital punishment discount each of these claims by countering abolitionist arguments of injustice with the proposition that death is *deserved* by those who commit especially heinous acts. Some argue that people deserve to die as retribution for horrible crime and that, in some cases, capital punishment provides the only just response available to society. These arguments have evolved from a natural law perspective, are sometimes supported on religious grounds, and are often based on the notion of just deserts, as discussed earlier.

Strong feelings on both sides of the issue have generated studies of the effectiveness and fairness of capital punishment as a criminal sanction. Although one might expect study results to have produced some agreement, just the opposite seems to have occurred. A relative impasse exists as to the proper interpretation of most death-penalty studies. How the death penalty acts as a general deterrent, for example, has been widely examined. Some researchers[37] have compared murder rates between states eliminating the death penalty with those retaining it, finding little variation in recorded murder rates. Others looked at variations in murder rates over time in jurisdictions eliminating capital punishment, with similar results.[38] A now classic 1988 Texas study provided a comprehensive review of capital punishment by correlating homicide rates with the rate of executions within the state between 1930 and 1986.[39] The study, which was especially important because Texas actively employs capital punishment, failed to find any support for the use of death as a deterrent.

Similarly, in an important study of the deterrent effect of capital punishment published in 2009, Tomislav V. Kovandzic and colleagues found "no empirical support for the argument that the existence or application of the death penalty deters offenders from committing homicide."[40] In 2012, in a succinct summary of studies on the deterrent effect of the death penalty, the Committee on Law and Justice of the National Academies of Sciences released *Deterrence and the Death Penalty*, a publication that included a detailed analysis of previous death-penalty research.[41] The Committee found that "research to date is not informative about whether capital punishment decreases, increases, or has no effect on homicide rates." It concluded that "claims that research demonstrates that capital punishment decreases or increases the homicide rate or has no effect on it should not influence policy judgments about capital punishment." Read the entire National Academy of Sciences report at **Web Extra 2–6**.

Regardless of studies to the contrary, many capital punishment advocates remain unconvinced that the threat of death cannot be an effective deterrent. As with other punishments, a swift and certain death penalty, they point out, is likely to deter others. As noted earlier, however, modern-day capital punishment rarely meets these requirements because offenders sentenced to death are unlikely to ever have their sentences finalized.[42] Even if the threat of death does not effectively deter others, advocates of capital punishment say that it ensures that the people put to death will never commit another crime. Learn about capital punishment issues and statistics at **Web Extra 2–7** .

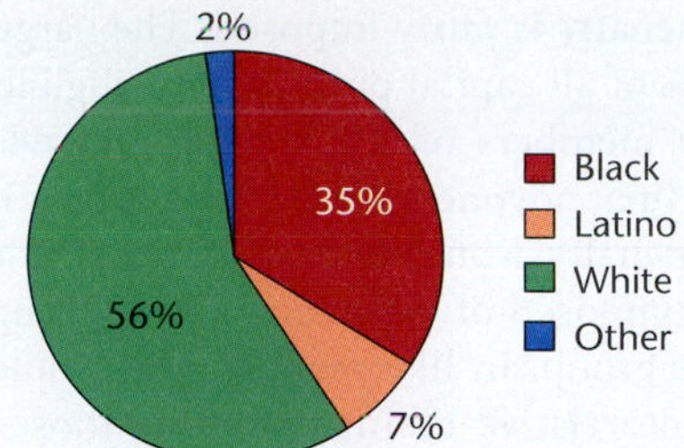

FIGURE 2–6 **Ethnicity of Defendants Executed in the United States, 1976–2013.**
Source: Death Penalty Information Center. Copyright © 2013 by Death Penalty Information Center. Used by permission of Death Penalty Information Center.

Think About It...

People tend to have powerful feelings about capital punishment—they are either strongly in favor of it or strongly opposed to it. Which arguments do you find most convincing about the death penalty—and which side of the death penalty debate are you on? Defend your choice.

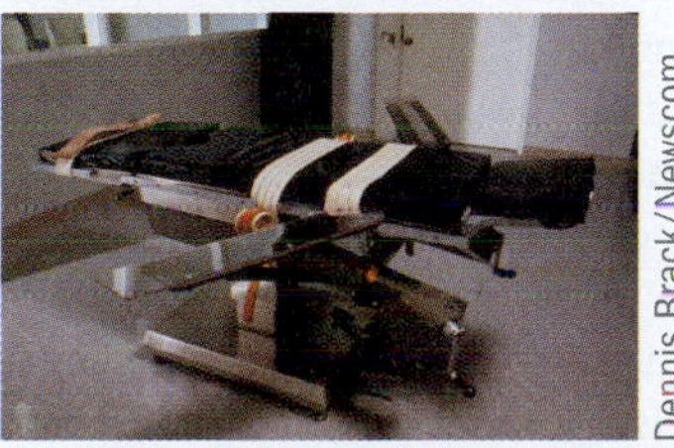

Dennis Brack/Newscom

Capital Punishment and Ethnicity

According to the Washington-based Death Penalty Information Center,[43] the death penalty has been imposed disproportionately on racial minorities throughout most of American history. Statistics maintained by the center show that "since 1930 nearly 90% of those executed for the crime of rape in this country were African Americans. Currently, about 50% of those on the nation's death rows are from minority populations representing 20% of the country's population." The center, a fervent anti–capital punishment organization, claims that "evidence of racial discrimination in the application of capital punishment continues. About 35% of those executed since 1976 have been black [Figure 2–6], even though blacks constitute only 12% of the [nation's total] population. And in almost every death penalty case, the race of the victim is white." The center says that "of the 229 executions that have occurred since the death penalty was reinstated [in 1972], only one has involved a white defendant for the murder of a black person." Figure 2–7 provides this information visually.

On the other hand, capital punishment advocates say that the real question is not whether differences exist in the rate of imposition among ethnic populations of the death penalty, but

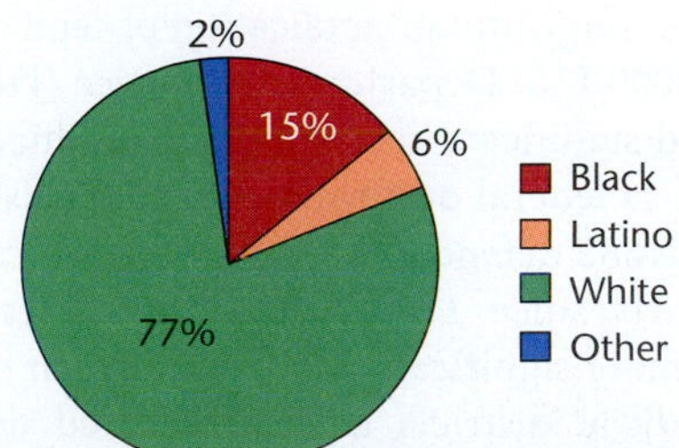

FIGURE 2–7 **Ethnicity of Murder Victims in the United States, 1976–2013.**
Source: Death Penalty Information Center. Copyright © 2013 by Death Penalty Information Center. Used by permission of Death Penalty Information Center.

whether the penalty is *fairly* imposed. They argue, for example, that if 50% of all capital punishment–eligible crimes were committed by members of a particular, but relatively small, ethnic group, then anyone anticipating fairness in imposition of the death penalty would expect to see 50% of death-row populations composed of members of that group—no matter how small the group. In like manner, one would also expect to see the same relative ethnicity among those executed. In short, they say that if fairness is to be any guide, those committing capital crimes should be the ones sentenced to death—regardless of ethnicity, gender, age, or other similar social characteristics.

Although evidence may suggest that African Americans and other minorities in the United States have in the past been unfairly sentenced to die,[44] the present evidence is not so clear. For an accurate appraisal to be made, any claims of disproportionality must go beyond simple comparisons with racial representation in the larger population and must somehow measure both the frequency and the seriousness of capital crimes between and within racial groups. Following that line of reasoning, in the 1987 case of *McCleskey* v. *Kemp*,[45] the Supreme Court held that a simple showing of racial discrepancies in the application of the death penalty does not amount to a constitutional violation.

A Flawed System?

In 1996, researchers at the Institute for Law and Justice in Alexandria, Virginia, published *Convicted by Juries, Exonerated by Science*, a report funded by the National Institute of Justice.[46] The study reviewed 28 cases where postconviction DNA evidence conclusively exonerated defendants sentenced to lengthy prison terms. The 28 cases were selected on the basis of a detailed examination of records indicating that the convicted defendants actually might have been innocent. The men in the study had served an average of seven years in prison, and most were tried and sentenced prior to the widespread availability of reliable DNA testing—although eyewitness testimony and other forensic evidence sealed their convictions. In each case, the DNA results unequivocally demonstrated that the defendants were wrongfully convicted, and each defendant was ultimately set free. Although the study did not specifically involve the death penalty, *Convicted by Juries* showed just how fallible the judicial process can be for those convicted.

More recent studies focus on claimed injustices inherent in the sentencing process, leading to imposition of the death penalty and the seemingly unfair application of capital punishment sentences. A 2000 U.S. Department of Justice (DOJ) study, for example, found significant racial and geographic disparities in the imposition of federal death sentences.[47] The study revealed that 80% of the 682 defendants who have faced capital charges in federal courts since 1995 have been African American. Perhaps even more significant, U.S. attorneys in only 49 of the nation's 94 judicial districts have prosecuted defendants for capital crimes. Critics of the study noted that such numbers are meaningless unless compared with actual proportions of minority defendants qualifying for capital prosecution. The fact that few crimes qualify for prosecution as capital offenses might explain the lack of death-penalty prosecution. This is opposed to the belief that prosecuting attorneys may have exhibited discretion or less-than-eager efforts in seeking those death-penalty convictions.

A potentially more significant study was conducted by Columbia University Law School professors **James Liebman** and **Jeffrey Fagan**. Liebman and Fagan examined 4,578 death penalty appeals during 1973–1995[48] and found that most cases were seriously flawed, necessitating retrials. Death-sentence convictions were thrown out in 68% of the state or federal court cases analyzed. This means that appellate courts found serious, reversible errors in almost seven out of every ten cases involving capital sentences. Eighty-two percent of defendants with death sentences that were overturned by state appellate courts due to serious error were found to deserve a sentence less than death. Of these, 7% were found to be innocent of the capital crime charged. According to the study's authors, "Our 23 years worth of findings reveal a capital punishment system collapsing under the weight of its own mistakes."

According to the Death Penalty Information Center, 143 people in 25 states were released from death rows across the United States between 1973 and mid-2013 after proof of their innocence became available.[49]

Studies such as these have led to an official rethinking of the death penalty in some parts of the country, contributing to what some have called a moratorium movement focused on reform of capital punishment laws.[50] In 2000, for example, Illinois suspended executions after DNA results showed conclusively that 13 death-row prisoners were innocent; and in 2002 Maryland became the second state in modern times to declare a moratorium on executions. The governor decided that "reasonable questions have been raised in Maryland and across the country about the application of the death penalty."[51] Similarly, in 2007, New Jersey governor Jon S. Corzine signed a legislative measure repealing the state's law on capital punishment;[52] and in 2012, Connecticut Governor Dannel Malloy signed legislation making his state the 17th state to abolish capital punishment.

Not all state governors are convinced that the death penalty should be abolished. Instead, some, such as former Massachusetts governor Mitt Romney, believe that capital punishment should be revived. Massachusetts abolished the death penalty in 1984 and has not carried out an execution since 1947.[53] In 2003, however, Governor Romney, having campaigned in favor of the death penalty, established the Governor's Council on Capital Punishment to restore the death penalty in his state. Romney told constituents that he sought to avoid the problems that have cast the death-sentencing systems of other states into doubt. The council's report, issued in 2004, included a recommended requirement that physical or scientific evidence such as DNA be used to corroborate guilt during the sentencing phase of trial. Jurors would also be informed of the demonstrated fallibility of human evidence and eyewitness testimony. Were the state to follow the council's recommendations, jurors would be told that to impose a sentence of death, they must find that there is "no doubt" about the defendant's guilt—a much higher standard of proof than the reasonable doubt standard used elsewhere. In 2014, legislative attempts to abolish the death penalty in New Hampshire and South Dakota were defeated.[54]

In 2004, recognizing that DNA testing exonerates the innocent, President George W. Bush signed the Innocence Protection Act[55] into law. The Innocence Protection Act provides federal funds to eliminate the backlog of unanalyzed DNA samples in the nation's crime laboratories.[56] It sets aside money to improve the capacity of federal, state, and local crime laboratories to conduct DNA analyses.[57] The act also eases access to postconviction DNA testing for those serving time in state[58] or federal prisons or on death row; in addition, the act sets forth conditions under which a federal prisoner asserting innocence may obtain postconviction DNA testing of specific evidence. Similarly, the legislation requires the preservation of biological evidence by federal law enforcement agencies for any defendant under a sentence of imprisonment or death.

Policy Implications of the Classical School

A few years ago, Lawrence Sherman of the University of Pennsylvania described two types of justice, one rational (deterrence-focused) and the other emotional (retribution-focused). These two types, said Sherman, "have competed for primacy" since the dawn of the modern era.

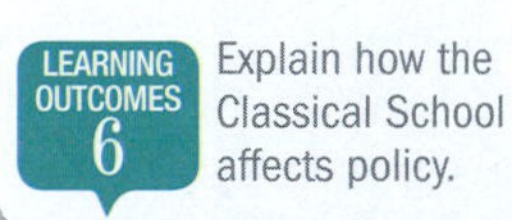

LEARNING OUTCOMES
6
Explain how the Classical School affects policy.

During the past 30 years or so, American justice philosophy has embodied the punishment practices of determinate sentencing and truth in sentencing. Because both determinate sentencing and truth in sentencing are rational forms of justice, most criminologists see them as natural consequences of a classical view of crime and justice.

Determinate sentencing is a strategy that mandates a specified and fixed amount of time to be served for every offense category. Under determinate sentencing schemes, judges may be required to impose seven-year sentences on armed robbers, but only one-year sentences on strong-armed robbers (who use no weapon). Determinate sentencing schemes build upon the twin notions of classical thought that (1) the pleasure of a given crime can be somewhat accurately assessed and (2) a fixed amount of punishment necessary for deterrence can be calculated and specified. **Truth in sentencing** requires judges to assess and publish the actual time an offender will serve once sentenced to prison. Many recently enacted truth-in-sentencing laws require that offenders serve a large portion of their sentence (often 80%) before their release.

Because of the widespread implementation of determinate sentencing strategies and the passage of truth-in-sentencing laws during the last quarter century, prison populations grew tremendously between 1980 and 2012. By early 2013, the nation's state and federal prison population (excluding jails) stood at 1,571,013 inmates, representing an increase of about 700% over 1970.[59] Figure 2–8 shows the U.S. prison population growth rate from 1924 to 2013.

Imprisonment is one component of an incapacitation strategy. **Incapacitation**, simply put, is the use of imprisonment or other means to reduce the likelihood that an offender will be capable of committing future offenses.

Proponents of modern-day incapacitation often distinguish between *selective incapacitation*, where crime is controlled via the imprisonment of specific individuals, and *collective incapacitation*, whereby changes in legislation and/or sentencing patterns lead to removing dangerous individuals from society. Advocates of selective incapacitation as a crime-control strategy point to studies showing that the majority of crimes are perpetrated by a small number of hard-core repeat offenders. The most famous of those studies, conducted by University of Pennsylvania Professor Marvin Wolfgang, focused on 9,000 men born in Philadelphia in 1945.[60] By the time this cohort of men had reached age 18, Wolfgang was able to determine that 627 "chronic recidivists" were responsible for the large majority of all serious violent crimes committed by the group. Other more recent studies show that a small core of criminal perpetrators is probably responsible for most criminal activity in the United States.

Such thinking led to the development of incapacitation as a treatment philosophy, and to the creation of innovative forms of incapacitation without imprisonment, such as home confinement, halfway houses or career training centers for convicted felons, and psychological and/or chemical treatments designed to reduce the likelihood of future crime commission. Similarly, such thinkers argue, the decriminalization of many offenses and the enhancement of social programs designed to combat the root causes of crime, including poverty, low educational levels, a general lack of skills, and inherent or active discrimination, will result in reduced incidence of crime in the future, making high rates of imprisonment unnecessary. Some of these strategies may be about to pay off, as state prison populations began experiencing a slight decline around 2012. Much of the decline,

Think About It...

Prisons in America are full, and prison populations have grown considerably over the past 20 years. At the same time, crime rates are down significantly. Why are America's prisons so full? Could it have anything to do with the influence of neoclassical thinking? Do full prisons equate to lower crime rates? Explain.

Robin Nelson/ZUMA Press/Newscom

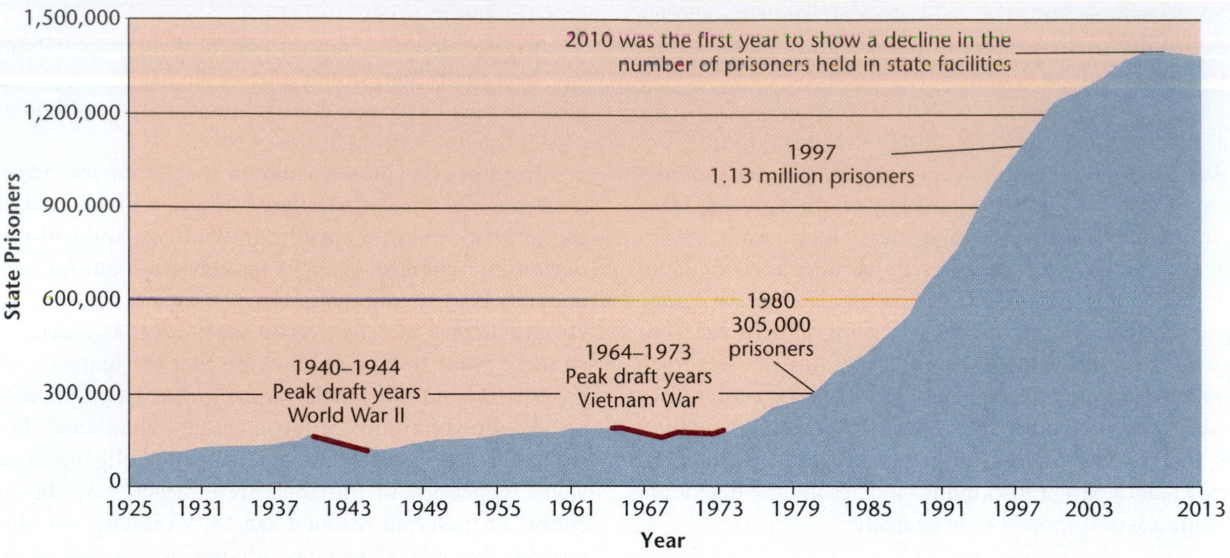

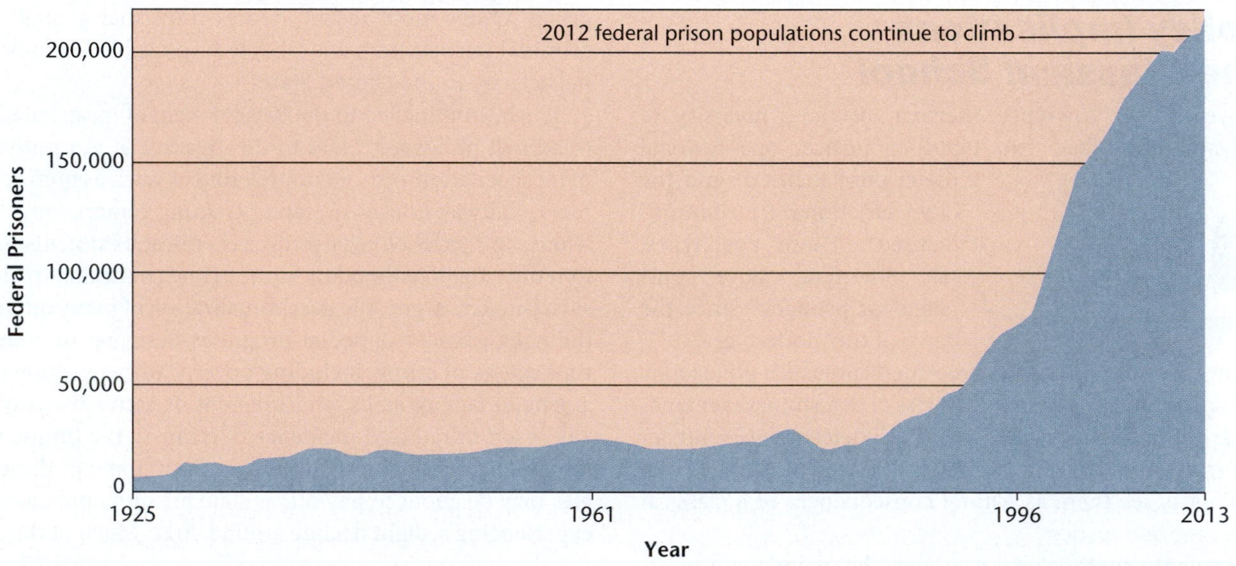

FIGURE 2-8 **U.S. Prison Populations, 1925–2013.**
Source: Bureau of Justice Statistics, *Crime and Justice Atlas 2000* (Washington, DC: Bureau of Justice Statistics, 2001), pp. 42–43; Bureau of Justice Statistics, *Prisoners in 2012* (Washington, DC: Bureau of Justice Statistics, 2013); and other years.

however, may be attributable to fiscal exigencies and underfunded state budgets, which have required cutbacks in state-run programs at many levels—including lengthy incarceration.

A Critique of Classical and Neoclassical Theories

Critics charge that classical thought doesn't fully explain criminal motivation. Other than claims that crime is the result of free will, the personal attractions of crime, and individual choice, the perspective has little to say about crime causation. Why, for example, do some people choose to commit crime, while others in similar situations decide against crime commission? Critics point out that classical theory is largely missing meaningful explanations as to how a choice for or against criminal activity is made. Similarly, classical theory lacks any appreciation for the deeper sources of personal motivation. This includes those motivating factors represented by aspects of human biology, psychology, and the social environment. Moreover, the Classical School, seen first in the writings of Beccaria and Bentham, made claims without any scientific basis behind them. While such musings may make for interesting philosophical debates, their lack of grounding in practical, everyday social research means that any social policies based on them will be fraught with uncertainty.

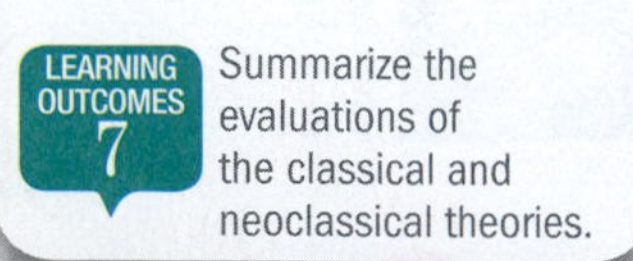

Summarize the evaluations of the classical and neoclassical theories.

Critics charged that the Classical School made many claims without any scientific basis.

WHO'S TO BLAME—The Individual or Society

The Excitement of Crime

Following his arrest for the theft of a police car, Moonbeam Kittaro met with one of his friends in the visiting area of the local jail. Here's what he said:

> I stole a cop car and s***, was it exciting!
>
> I mean, the thing was just sitting there running in the parking lot with the keys in it. Who wouldn't take it?
>
> I've never been so high on pure adrenaline. It was an adrenaline rush being behind the wheel of that f***ing car.
>
> It turned my girlfriend on too.
>
> I drove over to her place with the lights and siren on, and as soon as she saw the car she wanted to go for a ride.
>
> We must have hit 140 on the Interstate!
>
> Then we pulled into a rest stop and made love in the back seat.
>
> It was the whole illegal thing that got her so excited.
>
> But that's when we got arrested.
>
> The cops surrounded the car, guns drawn and all that s***.
>
> We didn't even hear them coming.

Carolina K. Smith MD/Shutterstock

A police car like the one stolen in this story. What kinds of crimes hold the most excitement for offenders?

Think About It

1. Why did Kittaro steal the car? Do you think he knew, before he stole it, that the theft would lead to so much excitement?
2. Can the desire for excitement explain crimes like Kittaro's? Can the same desire explain other kinds of crimes? If so, what might they be?
3. If excitement explains crime commission, then why doesn't everyone commit crime for the excitement it brings?
4. What kinds of crime-prevention programs might be based on the principles illustrated here?

Note: Who's to Blame boxes provide fictionalized critical thinking opportunities and are not actual cases.

A Critique of Neoclassical Thought

Any perspective gains credence if actions taken on the basis of its claims bear fruit. Not surprisingly, advocates of today's neoclassical approaches to crime control take much of the credit for the reduction in crime rates that our nation has been experiencing for the past two decades. After all, following the implementation of "get-tough-on-crime" policies such as the determinate sentencing schemes in the just deserts model, officially reported rates of crime declined substantially. The decrease led mayors, police chiefs, and politicians throughout the country to declare victory in the battle against crime, and many took personal credit for crime's decline. Notable among them were then–New York City mayor Rudy Giuliani, Los Angeles mayor Antonio Villariagosa, and Los Angeles police chief William J. Bratton.

The situation, however, is not so simple. As one journalist recently explained it, taking "responsibility for crime trends depends entirely on whether those trends are good or bad. When . . . crime stats decline, everyone rushes to take credit. The mayor boasts his new initiative is working exactly as he said it would. The police chief proudly declares that the strategy he implemented is a great success. Social service agencies insist their new programs are responsible. And so it goes in city after city. The only thing that varies is the identity of the initiatives, strategies, and programs said to be the cause of the crime drop. . . . Which suggests pretty strongly that all these claims are empty."[61]

The fact that crime has declined significantly in almost every U.S. jurisdiction over the past 20 years means that it has gone down in areas that instituted get-tough policies, as well as in areas that saw little change in their approach to crime prevention. Realistically, those who take credit for actively reducing crime in their cities and towns must also somehow account for crime's decline in other locations over which they had no control. A few years ago, for example, after the mayor and police chief in Los Angeles claimed that their crime-fighting policies had been responsible for an 8% drop in homicides throughout the city, one Los Angeles politician looked at murder rates in the region and found that while murder *inside* the city was down 8%, a decline of 15% had taken place in surrounding cities. "If [the mayor and the police chief] were doing things better than surrounding cities," he asked, "wouldn't the percentage reduction *inside* the city be greater than the reduction *outside* the city?"[62]

Finally, one last criticism of neoclassical perspectives on crime can be offered: Although neoclassical writers are sometimes credited for advancing the scientific approach to crime prevention through studies that appear to have identified

Those who take credit for actively reducing crimes in their cities and towns must also somehow account for crime's decline in other locations.

Think About It…

Classical and neoclassical approaches to criminology are not without their critics. Which of the criticisms of classical and neoclassical thought discussed in this chapter do you find most convincing? Why?

effective forms of deterrence, many such thinkers defend their perspective by referring to purely philosophical ideals such as just deserts. In this respect, they have made little progress beyond the armchair theorizing and philosophical banter of classical perspectives.

A Critique of Rational Choice Theory

Rational and situational choice and routine activities theories are criticized for overemphasizing the importance of individual choice with relative disregard for the role of social factors. Social factors in crime causation are poverty, poor home environment, and inadequate socialization of the would-be offender. One study, for example, found that the routine activities approach explained 28% of property crimes committed in socially disorganized (high-crime) areas of a small Virginia city and explained only 11% of offenses committed in low-crime areas.[63] In the words of the authors, "This research demonstrates more support for routine activities theory in socially disorganized areas than in socially organized areas."[64] So although one could argue that the kinds of routine activities supportive of criminal activity are more likely to occur in socially disorganized areas, it is also true that the presence (or absence) of certain ecological characteristics (that is, the level of social disorganization) may enhance (or reduce) the likelihood of criminal victimization. As the authors state, "Those areas characterized by low socioeconomic status will have higher unemployment rates, thus creating a larger pool of motivated offenders. Family disruption characterized by more divorced or separated families will result in more unguarded living structures, thus making suitable targets more available. Increased residential mobility will result in more non-occupied housing, which creates a lack of guardianship over the property and increases the number of suitable targets."[65]

The most significant contributors to crime's decline in recent years may have been economic and demographic factors that were largely beyond the control of policymakers.

Similarly, according to another study, RCT does not adequately consider the impact of emotional states on cognitive ability and the role of psychopharmacological agents (drugs or alcohol) in decision making.[66] The study examined the effects of alcohol and anger on aggression and found that "alcohol diminishes individuals' perceptions of the costs associated with aggression and, in some instances, actually increases the perceived benefits." Similarly, high arousal levels, such as those associated with anger and other emotions, appear to impair judgment. So when acting under the influence of alcohol or when experiencing strong emotions, "the individual's capacity to anticipate gratification and aversion, success and failure, and cost is diminished."[67] The authors note that other studies show that approximately 40% of offenders are under the influence of alcohol when arrested for committing their crimes. This suggests that future research on the rational choice perspective should include the role of emotions and the potential impact of psychopharmacological agents on the decisions made by people who commit crimes.

Rational choice theory assumes that everyone is equally capable of making rational decisions when, in fact, such is probably not the case. Some individuals are more logical than others by virtue of temperament, personality, or socialization, whereas others are emotional, hotheaded, and unthinking. Empirical studies of RCT have added scant support for the perspective's underlying assumptions, tending to show instead that criminal offenders are often unrealistic in their appraisals of the relative risks and rewards facing them.[68] Similarly, rational and situational choice theories seem to disregard individual psychology and morality, instead emphasizing external situations. Moral individuals, say critics, when faced with easy criminal opportunities, may rein in their desires and turn their backs on temptation.

Finally, the emphasis of rational and situational choice theories upon changing aspects of the immediate situation to reduce crime has been criticized for resulting in the displacement of crime from one area to another.[69] Target hardening,[70] a key crime-prevention strategy among such theorists, has sometimes caused criminals to find new targets of opportunity in other areas.[71]

THE CASE

Gary Stephen Krist

In his youth, Gary Steven Krist was known throughout the tiny Pelican, Washington, community as a troublemaker. Krist's father was a salmon fisherman, and Krist himself described his mother as "a well-intentioned scatterbrain."[i]

The Krists' fishing business kept his parents at sea, and the financial return was not impressive. During his parents' absence, Gary and his brother, Gordon, were left in the care of others. As a preteen in the mid-1950s, Gary showed a propensity for violence when, on one occasion, he fired a shotgun over his babysitter's and brother's heads because the babysitter made him angry by being too bossy. In an article for *Life* magazine, Krist later wrote that this incident illustrated his "absolute hatred for authority." A striking discovery, however, was his parents' attitude toward the reports of theft, vandalism—including blowing up an empty oil drum—and repeated reports of frequent intercourse with an 11-year-old town girl. Krist's parents seemed to view this behavior as simply displays of typical youthful exuberance.

As he entered his teens, Krist's delinquency bloomed into full-fledged criminality. At the age of 14, Krist was arrested with a friend for a series of burglaries, various sexual conquests, and much drinking. He later wrote in a memoir that their "crimes arose, I believe, more from an overpowering hungry curiosity coupled with excess physical energy than from any defined hostility or malice toward others." While on probation for these offenses, Krist stole a car. This offense got him sent to a reform school in Ogden, Utah, where he earned straight-A grades as a student in the local public school. He also unsuccessfully tried to escape on two different occasions, yet later recalled that he was "happy" in this reform school because he was "accepted."

In 1965, after completing a short prison term for vehicle theft, he married and was arrested a year later—again for auto theft. Eight months into a five-year sentence, he engineered an escape during which guards shot his accomplice to death. Since California law permitted capital punishment when a prison escape led to someone's death, Krist worried that he'd get the gas chamber if he were found. So he moved his young family to Boston and created a new identity as George Deacon, an aspiring scientist.

The undeniably intelligent Krist obtained a job as a lab technician at MIT. This led, in September 1968, to his participation in a marine science expedition where the still-married Krist began an affair with a student named Ruth Eisemann Schier. Before the expedition was over a month later, Krist confessed his true identity and criminal past to her, and they formed a plan to run off to Australia.

To finance their planned new life together, Krist and Eisemann Schier plotted to kidnap Emory University student Barbara Jane Mackle, the daughter of a prominent Miami family, and bury her in a homemade box, where she would remain until they received a $500,000 ransom.

Bettmann/Corbis

A bearded Gary Steven Krist is escorted from an elevator by a DeKalb County (Georgia) deputy sheriff en route to jail in 1969. Krist had been found guilty for his part in the kidnapping of Barbara Jane Mackle and was sentenced to life in prison. Paroled after ten years, he entered a new life of crime. Why didn't he reform?

Krist and Eisemann Schier did abduct and bury Mackle, who ultimately survived 83 hours underground before police, informed by Krist of the burial site, were able to find and release her. The kidnappers were subsequently caught and tried in Decatur, Georgia, in May 1969.

Before his trial, Krist's intellect was evaluated by a psychiatrist as "if not at the genius level, then certainly in the near genius category." But the doctor also declared him fit to stand trial, and classified Krist as "having a sociopathic character disorder with no evidence of psychosis." Found guilty, the 23-year-old Krist received a life sentence.

Paroled after ten years, Krist set about lobbying for a complete pardon, which he eventually obtained in 1989. He then enrolled in a medical school in the West Indies and completed his M.D. degree. Several states denied him a medical license before Indiana finally granted him a probationary license in 2001.[ii] That license was revoked two years later when Krist's past criminal record and allegations of sexual assaults on patients surfaced.[iii]

In January 2007, 61-year-old Gary Krist, who once described himself as the "Einstein of crime," went back to prison to serve a five-year, five-month sentence. A federal sting operation busted Krist and his 41-year-old stepson in early 2006 for conspiracy to bring cocaine and illegal aliens into the United States.[iv] In 2011, Krist was released from prison and moved to Mobile, Alabama, where he continues to reside today.

(*continued*)

THE CASE

Gary Stephen Krist (*Continued*)

Notes

[i]MSNBC, "Georgia Man in 1960s Buried Alive Case Gets 5 Years in Drug Case," http://www.msnbc.msn.com/id/16710294/ (accessed May 21, 2010).

[ii]*Cincinnati Enquirer*, The Enquirer Online Edition, "Doctor Found to Have Been Imprisoned for Kidnapping," November 16, 2002, http://www.enquirer.com/editions/2002/11/16/loc_in-felondoc16.html (accessed July 10, 2010).

[iii]Wishtv.com, "Doctor's License Revoked," August 29, 2003, http://www.wishtv.com/Global/story.asp?S=1423007 (accessed May 21, 2010).

[iv]Steve Fennessy, "The Talented Dr. Krist," Atlanta Magazine Online, http://www.atlantamagazine.com/article.php?id=299 (accessed May 21, 2010).

The case of Gary Krist raises a number of interesting questions. Among them are the following:

1. **Seen from a classical perspective, what might Krist have learned in his early years that would have caused him to choose a life of crime later?**
2. **Krist seemed to have a hatred of authority. Can classical criminology explain emotions such as hatred? If so, how would it explain them?**
3. **How might Katz's "seductions of crime" perspective explain the feelings the young Krist reported having?**
4. **Might punishments appropriately applied in Krist's early life have prevented his future criminality?**
5. **Classical criminology says that crime can be rewarding. Might camaraderie with other offenders be one of its rewards?**

CHAPTER 2 Classical and Neoclassical Criminology

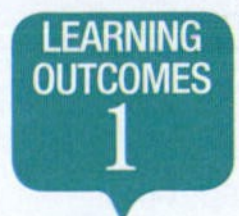

Outline the principles of classical and neoclassical criminology.

Classical and neoclassical criminology see human activity as the product of the exercise of free will and rational thought and explain crime as moral wrongdoing based on personal choice. Both perspectives believe that punishment can be effective in reducing the incidence of crime because it negates the rewards to be derived from violating the law.

1. What is the central distinguishing feature of classical thought in criminology?

Classical School A criminological perspective developed in the late 1700s and early 1800s. It had its roots in the Enlightenment and held that men and women are rational beings and that crime is the result of the exercise of free will and personal choices based on calculations of perceived costs and benefits.

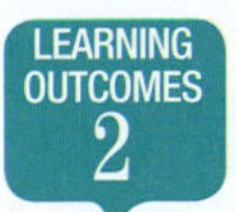

Outline the history of classical thought.

Classical criminology developed out of the writings of a number of influential thinkers. Especially important were the ideas developed by Cesare Beccaria and Jeremy Bentham, who depicted crime as a rational choice. Bentham argued that punishment should be sufficiently distasteful to the offender so that the discomfort experienced would outweigh the benefits gained from committing crimes.

1. Describe hedonistic calculus. What role do pleasure and pain play in the concept?
2. Why did Cesare Beccaria say that the goal of punishment should be deterrence rather than retribution?

hedonistic calculus The belief, first proposed by Jeremy Bentham, that behavior holds value to any individual undertaking it according to the amount of pleasure or pain that it can be expected to produce for that person.

Panopticon A prison designed by Jeremy Bentham that was to be a circular building with cells along the circumference, each clearly visible from a central location staffed by guards.

Key Names

Cesare Beccaria A proponent of judicial reform who believed that the purpose of punishment should be deterrence rather than retribution, and punishment should be imposed to prevent offenders from committing additional crimes. Punishment should be only severe enough to outweigh the personal benefits to be derived from crime commission.

Jeremy Bentham A proponent of social reform who believed that individuals will weigh the consequences of their behavior before acting to maximize their own pleasure and minimize pain.

LEARNING OUTCOMES 3

Outline the development of neoclassical criminology.

In the 1970s, a widespread belief that nothing worked to reform offenders led to the ascent of neoclassical criminology, which focused on the importance of character, the dynamics of character development, and the rational choices that people make as they are faced with opportunities for crime.

1. What are the differences between the Classical School of thought and neoclassical criminology?
2. How does a person's lifestyle contribute to both the volume and type of crime found in a society?
3. Explain the routine activities theory (lifestyle theory) in your own words.
4. Describe situational crime prevention. What kinds of crime-prevention strategies are suggested by situational crime prevention?

neoclassical criminology Focuses on the importance of character, the dynamics of character development, and the rational choices that people make as they are faced with opportunities for crime.

nothing-works doctrine The belief popularized by Robert Martinson in the 1970s that correctional treatment programs have little success in rehabilitating offenders.

justice model A contemporary model of imprisonment in which the principle of just deserts forms the underlying social philosophy.

rational choice theory (RCT) A perspective holding that criminality is the result of conscious choice and predicts that individuals choose to commit crime when the benefits outweigh the costs of disobeying the law.

routine activities theory (RAT) A brand of rational choice theory suggesting that regular, recurrent, and patterned activities contribute significantly to both the volume and type of crime found in any society.

situational choice theory A brand of rational choice theory that views criminal behavior "as a function of choices and decisions made within a context of situational constraints and opportunities."

capable guardian One who effectively discourages crime.

lifestyle theory A perspective holding that lifestyles contribute significantly to both the volume and type of crime found in any society.

the seductions of crime The idea that crime is often pleasurable for those committing it and that pleasure of one sort or another is the major motivation behind crime.

situational crime prevention An approach that looks to develop greater understanding of crime and more effective crime-prevention strategies through concern with the physical, organizational, and social environments that make crime possible.

target hardening The reduction in criminal opportunity for a particular location, generally through the use of physical barriers, architectural design, and enhanced security measures.

Key Names

Robert Martinson A criminologist who believes that nothing works in the area of offender rehabilitation, and most convicted offenders resume their criminal careers after release from prison.

Lawrence Cohen and ***Marcus Felson*** Crime theorists who believe that the risk of criminal victimization varies dramatically among the circumstances and locations in which people place themselves and their property.

Ronald V. Clarke and ***Derek B. Cornish*** Criminologists who suggest the use of situational strategies such as "cheque guarantee cards, the control of alcohol sales at football matches, supervision of children's play on public housing estates, vandal resistant materials and designs, 'defensible space' architecture, improved lighting, closed-circuit television surveillance," and the like as effective crime-prevention additions to specific situations—all of which might lower the likelihood of criminal victimization in given instances.

Jack Katz A criminologist who believes that crime is sensually compelling.

LEARNING OUTCOMES 4

Describe how neoclassicism views punishment as a deterrent to crime.

Punishment is a central feature of both classical and neoclassical thought. Whereas punishment served as a deterrent to crime in classical thought, in neoclassical thinking, it is expanded to support the ancient concept of retribution, in which punishment is deserved.

1. What is the just deserts model? How does it relate to the punishment of criminal offenders?
2. What is the difference between specific and general deterrence? With which form of deterrence is the Classical School most concerned?

just deserts model The notion that criminal offenders deserve the punishment they receive at the hands of the law and that punishments should be appropriate to the type and severity of crime committed.

deterrence A goal of criminal sentencing that seeks to inhibit criminal behavior through the fear of punishment.

specific deterrence A goal of criminal sentencing that seeks to prevent a particular offender from engaging in repeat criminality.

general deterrence A goal of criminal sentencing that seeks to prevent others from committing crimes similar to the one for which a particular offender is being sentenced.

recidivism The repetition of criminal behavior.

LEARNING OUTCOMES 5

Outline the arguments for and against the death penalty.

Opponents of capital punishment claim that it does not deter crime, has been imposed on innocent people, violates the sacredness of life, lowers society to the same amoral level as the offender, is imposed disproportionately on minority offenders, goes against most fundamental precepts of organized religion, is more expensive than imprisonment, and is inhumane and barbaric. Advocates of capital punishment discount each of these claims with the proposition that death is *deserved* by those who commit especially heinous acts.

1. What arguments favor the use of capital punishment?
2. What arguments can be offered to oppose the use of capital punishment?

capital punishment The legal imposition of a sentence of death upon a convicted offender.

Key Names

James Liebman and ***Jeffrey Fagan*** Law school professors who, after examining 4,578 death penalty appeals during 1973–1995, found that most of them were seriously flawed.

LEARNING OUTCOMES 6

Explain how the Classical School affects policy.

During the past 30 years or so, American justice philosophy has embodied punishment practices based on neoclassical principles. These practices include determinate sentencing and truth in sentencing.

1. What is determinate sentencing? How is it consistent with principles underlying the Classical School?
2. What is truth in sentencing? How is it consistent with principles underlying the Classical School?

determinate sentencing A model of criminal punishment in which an offender is given a fixed term of imprisonment that may be reduced by good behavior or other considerations.

truth in sentencing A close correspondence between the sentence imposed upon those sent to prison and the time actually served prior to prison release.

incapacitation The use of imprisonment or other means to reduce the likelihood that an offender will be capable of committing future offenses.

LEARNING OUTCOMES 7

Summarize the evaluations of the classical and neoclassical theories.

Critics charge that classical thought doesn't fully explain criminal motivation. Other than claims that crime is the result of free will, the personal attractions of crime, and individual choice, the perspective has little to say about crime causation. In particular, rational and situational choice and routine activities theories are criticized for overemphasizing the importance of individual choice with relative disregard for the role of social factors such as poverty, poor home environment, and inadequate socialization.

1. What are some of the criticisms of classical and neoclassical thought?

"Today the most compelling modern theories of crime and violence weave social and biological themes together."

—*Terrie E. Moffitt, Duke University*[1]

Early Biological Perspectives on Criminal Behavior

It's What We Are

1. Describe the differences between historical biological and contemporary biosocial theories of crime.
2. Outline the basic principles of biological theories of crime.
3. Describe early biological explanations of criminality.
4. Explain how sociobiology views crime, and demonstrate the importance of altruism, territoriality, and tribalism from that perspective.
5. Identify some criticisms of early biological theories of criminal behavior.

Frank Schmalleger

INTRO DIET AND BEHAVIOR

In 2012, the Dutch Ministry of Justice implemented a program of nutritional supplements in 14 prisons across the Netherlands. Under the program, nearly 500 inmates were provided with healthy diets, devoid of added sugar and supplemented with vitamins and important micronutrients.[2] According to Ap Zaalberg, the project's director, the link between good nutrition and lower levels of antisocial behavior had already been clearly established by studies published in England only a few years earlier, and the Dutch wanted to see if good eating habits could lower levels of violence in their prisons.

Zaalberg's interest came from reading an article published in the *British Journal of Psychiatry* in 2002 by Oxford University professor C. Bernard Gesch.[3] Gesch reported on the results of work he had done in recruiting 231 young British prisoners, assigning half of them to receive carefully selected dietary supplements while the other half received a placebo. Before Gesch's nutritional program was implemented, the placebo and active-treatment groups had been matched according to the number of disciplinary incidents in which each had been involved. Similarly, there were no significant individual or psychological differences between the two groups in terms of IQ, verbal ability, anger, anxiety, or depression. After Gesch's experimental subjects took specially formulated vitamins, minerals, and essential fatty acids for 142 days, he found that prisoners taking the supplements committed an average of 26.3% fewer offenses compared with the placebo group. Moreover, he observed a 35.1% reduction in overall offenses in the group receiving the supplements and a 37% drop in violent incidents. According to Gesch, ". . . evidence is mounting that putting poor fuel into the brain significantly affects social behavior. We need to know more about the composition of the right nutrients. It could be the recipe for peace."[4] Figure 3–1 shows the levels of some of the nutrients in the disadvantaged youths studied by Gesch.

The field of criminology has been slow to give credence to biological theories of deviant behavior.

DISCUSS Do you think that people's diets can significantly influence their behavior? Their state of mind? Have you ever experienced such effects from food or drink (other than alcohol or drugs)?

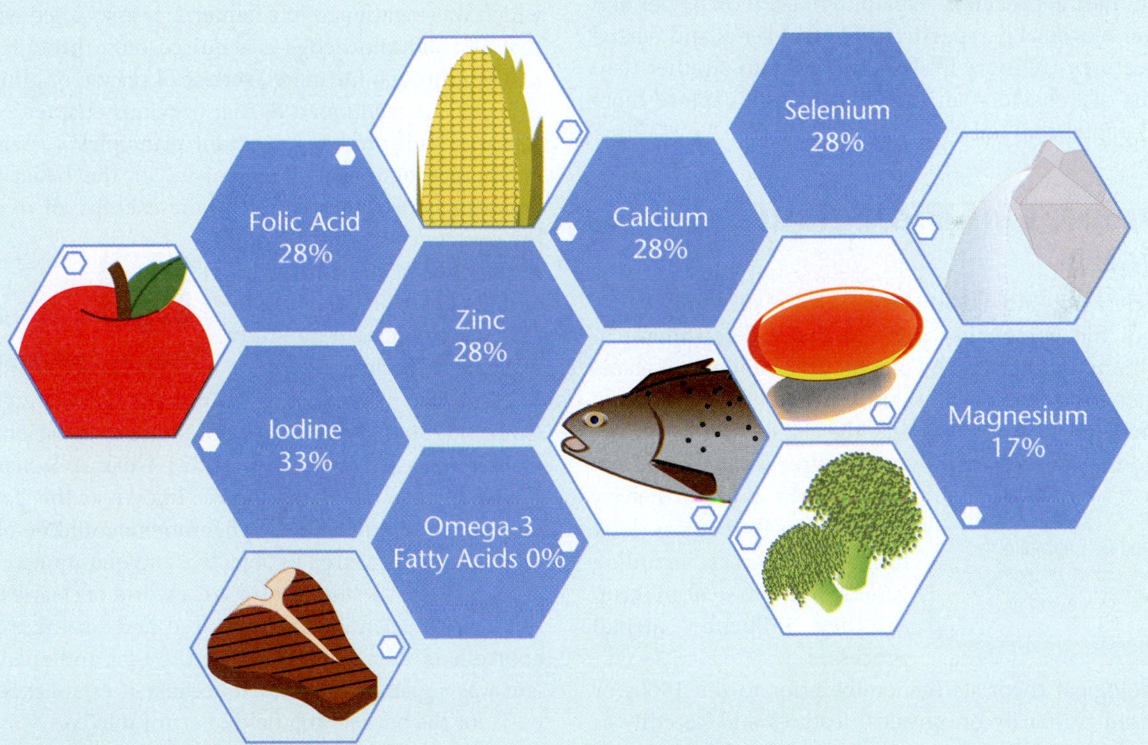

FIGURE 3–1 **Selected Nutrient Levels in Diets of a Sample of Disadvantaged Youth.**
Source: John Bohannon, "The Theory? Diet Causes Violence. The Lab? Prison," *Science*, Vol. 325 (September 25, 2009), p. 1616, http://www.ifbb.org.uk/files/Science-25-9-09.PDF

Traditional Biological versus Modern Biosocial Theories

The field of criminology has been slow to give credence to **biological theories** of deviant behavior. One reason for this, as noted in Chapter 1, is that contemporary criminology's academic roots are grounded in the social sciences. As well-known biocriminologist **C. Ray Jeffery**, commenting on the historical development of the field, observed, "The term *criminology* was given to a social science approach to crime as developed in sociology. Sutherland's [1924] text *Criminology* was pure sociology without any biology or psychology; beginning with publication of that text, criminology was offered in sociology departments as a part of sociology separate from biology, psychology, psychiatry and law. Many of the academicians who call themselves criminologists are sociologists."[5]

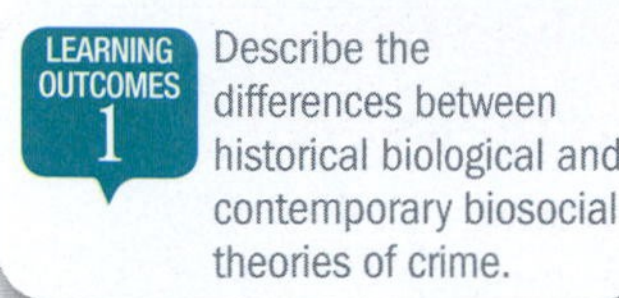

LEARNING OUTCOMES
1
Describe the differences between historical biological and contemporary biosocial theories of crime.

Fortunately for those studying criminology today, the field of criminology is interdisciplinary, recognizing contributions from many different disciplines. This chapter and the next (Chapter 4: Biosocial and Other Contemporary Perspectives) review both historical and contemporary biological perspectives on crime, including modern-day biosocial theories. Many older biological theories, as we will see in this chapter, were relatively simplistic in their approach to explaining human behavior and crime. Newer biosocial perspectives hold that genes and related biological features are more likely to be facilitators rather than determinants of behavior—an idea that we will explore more fully in the chapter that follows.

Principles of Biological Theories

Generally speaking, biological theories focus on the brain as the center of the personality and the major determinant in controlling human behavior. As one biocriminologist explains it, "no matter the source of human behavior, it is necessarily funneled through the brain."[6] Unlike the classical and neoclassical traditions, however, which consider free will and external forces as the cause of behavior, biological theories look to internal sources, including genetic and physical makeup as they influence mental processes.

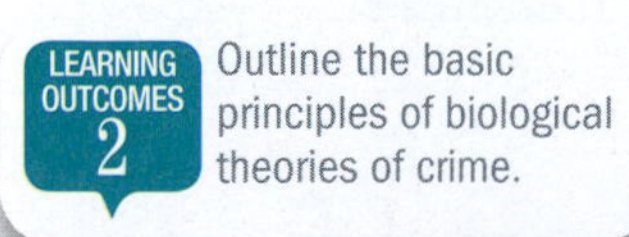

LEARNING OUTCOMES
2
Outline the basic principles of biological theories of crime.

Early biological theorists (generally, prior to the 1960s or 1970s) focused primarily on physical features and heredity as the source of criminal behavior. They considered such physical **traits** as facial features, body type, and shape of the skull as significant causes of criminality. Several early theorists proposed that criminality ran in families and could be inherited, being passed down from one generation to another. Such early approaches, while appropriate for the time in which they were developed, appear relatively simplistic when compared with modern biosocial perspectives.

In contrast, contemporary biological theorists (mostly after 1990) have taken a more in-depth look at human biology, leading them to examine a variety of influences on behavior, including genes and chromosomes, diet, hormonal issues, environmental contaminants, and neurophysical conditions. Nonetheless, both early and contemporary biological perspectives share a number of fundamental assumptions, which are shown in Figure 3–2.

One of the major distinguishing features between historical and contemporary biological theories of criminality is the degree of emphasis that each puts on the last item listed in Figure 3–2 (the interplay between biology and the social and physical environments). While most early biological theories of crime ascribed at least some importance to the role of the social environment in producing behavior, that role was relatively minor. In contrast, contemporary biosocial theorists see the *interaction* between the organism and its environment as the crucial determining factor in almost all behavior.

Early Biological Theories

Early biological theories of crime, while not as sophisticated as their modern counterparts, are especially significant because they built upon the scientific tradition of positivism. **Positivism**, which was mentioned in Chapter 2, is associated with the belief that all valid knowledge is acquired only through observation and not through the mere exercise of reason or blind adherence to belief. As mentioned in that previous chapter, early positivism was built on two important principles: (1) an unflagging acceptance of social determinism, or the belief that human behavior is determined not by the exercise of free choice but by causative factors beyond the control of the individual, and (2) the application of scientific techniques to the study of crime and criminology.

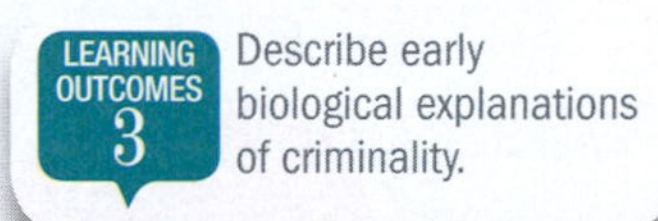

LEARNING OUTCOMES
3
Describe early biological explanations of criminality.

The term *positivism* had its roots in the writings of Auguste Comte (1798–1857), who proposed use of the scientific method in the study of society in his 1851 work *A System of Positive Polity*.[7] Comte, who later became known as the "father of sociology," believed that social phenomena could be observed, explained, and measured in objective and quantitative terms. For a strict positivist, reality consists of a world of clearly defined facts that can be scientifically measured and—some would hope—controlled.[8] As a framework for thought and analysis, positivism was a giant leap forward because it established a scientific basis for the burgeoning field of criminology.

Physical Features and Crime

Some of the earliest studies in the field of criminology used data from the fields of biology and anthropology to identify physical abnormalities that early criminologists thought could be used to distinguish criminal offenders from other people. One of the earliest attempts to use bodily features to identify

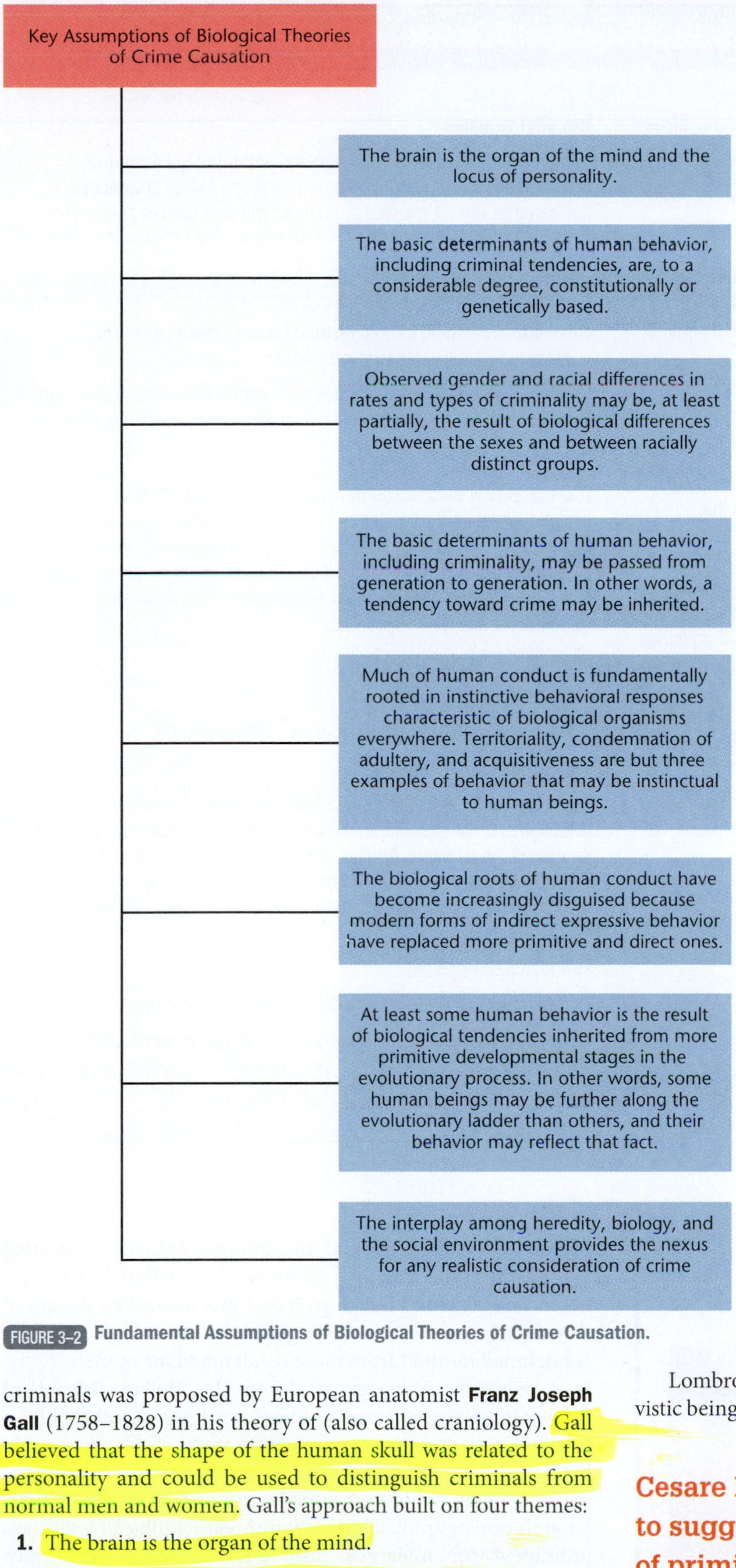

Key Assumptions of Biological Theories of Crime Causation

- The brain is the organ of the mind and the locus of personality.
- The basic determinants of human behavior, including criminal tendencies, are, to a considerable degree, constitutionally or genetically based.
- Observed gender and racial differences in rates and types of criminality may be, at least partially, the result of biological differences between the sexes and between racially distinct groups.
- The basic determinants of human behavior, including criminality, may be passed from generation to generation. In other words, a tendency toward crime may be inherited.
- Much of human conduct is fundamentally rooted in instinctive behavioral responses characteristic of biological organisms everywhere. Territoriality, condemnation of adultery, and acquisitiveness are but three examples of behavior that may be instinctual to human beings.
- The biological roots of human conduct have become increasingly disguised because modern forms of indirect expressive behavior have replaced more primitive and direct ones.
- At least some human behavior is the result of biological tendencies inherited from more primitive developmental stages in the evolutionary process. In other words, some human beings may be further along the evolutionary ladder than others, and their behavior may reflect that fact.
- The interplay among heredity, biology, and the social environment provides the nexus for any realistic consideration of crime causation.

FIGURE 3–2 Fundamental Assumptions of Biological Theories of Crime Causation.

criminals was proposed by European anatomist **Franz Joseph Gall** (1758–1828) in his theory of (also called craniology). Gall believed that the shape of the human skull was related to the personality and could be used to distinguish criminals from normal men and women. Gall's approach built on four themes:

1. The brain is the organ of the mind.
2. Particular aspects of personality are associated with specific locations in the brain.
3. Portions of the brain that are well developed cause personality characteristics associated with them to be more prominent in the individual under study, whereas poorly developed brain areas lead to a lack of associated personality characteristics.
4. The shape of a person's skull corresponds to the shape of the underlying brain and is therefore indicative of the personality.

Gall was one of the first Western writers to firmly locate the roots of personality in the brain. Prior to his time, it was thought that aspects of personality resided in various organs throughout the body—a fact reflected in linguistic anachronisms that survive to the present day (for example, when someone is described as being "hard-hearted" or having "a lot of gall"). Greek philosopher Aristotle was said to believe that the brain served no function other than to radiate excess heat from the body, so Gall's perspective, although relatively primitive by today's standards, did much to advance physiological understandings of the mind–body connection in Western thought.

One of Gall's students, German physician **Johann Gaspar Spurzheim** (1776–1853), brought phrenological theory to America and helped to spread its influence through a series of lectures and publications on the subject. Phrenology's prestige in America extended into the twentieth century, finding a place in classification schemes employed to evaluate newly admitted prisoners. Learn more about **phrenology** at **Web Extra 3–1**.

The Italian School

One of the best-known early scientific biological theorist—nineteenth-century Italian army prison physician **Cesare Lombroso** (1836–1909)—coined the term **atavism** to suggest that criminality was the result of primitive urges that survived the evolutionary process in modern-day human throwbacks. Lombroso, whose work had consisted mostly of postmortem studies of the bodies of executed offenders and deceased criminals, measured the bodies in many different ways.[9] He claimed that, using his system, not only could criminal offenders be separated from the general population, but even specific types of criminals could be identified.

Lombroso described "the nature of the criminal" as "an atavistic being who reproduces in his person the ferocious instincts

Cesare Lombroso coined the term *atavism* to suggest that criminality was the result of primitive urges that survived the evolutionary process.

THEORY in PERSPECTIVE

Early Biological Theories

Biological theories adhere to the principle that many predispositions relating to human behavior, including aggression, risk taking, and criminality, are constitutionally or physiologically influenced and inherited. This chapter discusses early biological approaches to crime.

Early Positivism

Early positivism used data from the fields of biology and anthropology to identify physical abnormalities that early criminologists thought could be used to distinguish criminal offenders from other people.

Period: 1790s–1880s

Theorists: Franz Joseph Gall, Johann Gaspar Spurzheim

Concepts: phrenology

Criminal Anthropology

Criminal anthropology is the scientific study of the relationship between human physical characteristics (in particular, bodily features) and criminality. Today the word is mostly applied to the Italian School of criminology, whose contributors built on scientific, or positivistic, principles like the use of measurement and observation in applying evolutionary concepts to the study of crime and criminals. Criminal anthropology saw criminals as throwbacks to earlier evolutionary epochs.

Period: 1860s–1930

Theorists: Cesare Lombroso, Enrico Ferri, Raffael Garofalo, Charles Buckman Goring, Earnest A. Hooton

Concepts: Italian School, positivism, criminal anthropology, atavism, born criminals, criminaloids

Constitutional Theories

These biological theories, sometimes called constitutional theories, explain criminality by reference to offenders' body types, inheritance, genetics, or external observable physical characteristics.

Period: classical constitutional theories, 1930s–1940s; modern constitutional theories, 1960s–present

Theorists: Ernst Kretschmer, William H. Sheldon, Patricia Jacobs

Concepts: Somatotyping, mesomorph, ectomorph, endomorph, XYY supermale

Criminal Families

In the late 1800s the focus of criminal anthropology turned to the identification of criminal families, or those family groups that appeared to exhibit criminal tendencies through several generations. The study of criminal families built on developing notions of heredity and genetics.

Period: 1870s–1940s

Theorists: Sir Francis Galton, Richard Louis Dugdale, Arthur H. Estabrook, Henry Herbert Goddard

Concepts: heredity, behavioral genetics, criminal families (Jukes and Kallikaks), genetic determinism, eugenics, eugenic criminology

Sociobiology

This theoretical perspective developed by Edward O. Wilson applies evolutionary theory to social behavior and says that most social behaviors are shaped by natural selection. Sociobiology includes the systematic study of the biological basis of all social behavior, which is a branch of evolutionary biology and particularly of modern population biology.

Period: 1975–present

Theorist: Edward O. Wilson

Concepts: altruism, tribalism, survival of the gene pool

Twin Studies and Heredity

Genetics and heredity, combined with processes of natural selection, including sexual selection, can produce biologically based differences in behavior. Studies of twins attempted to identify the role that heredity played in criminal behavior, especially among twins who were separated at birth and raised in vastly different environments.

Period: 1920s–present

Theorists: Karl O. Christiansen, Sarnoff Mednick, and others

Concepts: twin studies (dizygotic and monozygotic twins), genetic determinism

---

Think About It...

Lombroso claimed that criminals could be identified by the atavistic traits they displayed. What would such traits include? Might some primitive traits survive in modern-day humans? If so, would they likely be related to the behavior of those who possessed them? Explain.

Piotr Marcinski/Fotolia

of primitive humanity and the inferior animals."[10] Writing around the same time as Lombroso, Italian Raffael Garofalo noted that "One has but to go into a prison, and by the aid of this description one can distinguish almost at a glance those condemned for theft from those condemned for murder."

Lombroso's ideas gave rise to the **Italian School of Criminology**, also referred to today as criminal anthropology. **Criminal anthropology** is the scientific study of the relationship between human physical characteristics (in particular anthropometric features, or bodily measurements) and criminality. Criminal anthropology probably derives from earlier subjective feelings, prominent for millennia, that unattractiveness, deformity, and disfigurement are somehow associated with evil, spiritual malaise, and general uncleanliness.

Although the earlier works of Gall and others might be subsumed under the umbrella of criminal anthropology, the term is usually reserved in today's criminological literature for the work of Lombroso and other members of the Italian School of Criminology, especially **Enrico Ferri** and **Raffael Garofalo**.

Lombroso has been called "the father of modern criminology" because he was the first criminologist of note to employ the scientific method—particularly measurement, observation, and generalization—in his work. Other writers have preferred to limit his influence, referring to him simply as the father of the Italian School of criminology in recognition of the fact that nineteenth-century positivism began in Italy under his tutelage.

Lombroso's most famous term, *atavism,* implies that criminals are born that way. Lombroso was continuously reassessing his estimates of the proportion, from among all offenders, of **born criminals**. At one point, he asserted that fully 90% of offenders committed crimes because of atavistic influences; he later revised the figure downward to 70%, admitting that normal individuals might be pulled into lives of crime. In addition to the category of born criminal, Lombroso described other categories of offenders, including the insane, **criminaloids** (occasional criminals), and criminals incited by passion. The insane were said to include mental and moral degenerates, alcoholics, drug addicts, and so forth. Learn more about Lombroso and the theory of atavism via **Web Extra 3–2**.

Following in Lombroso's positivistic footsteps around the turn of the twentieth century, English physician **Charles Buckman Goring** (1870–1919) conducted a well-controlled statistical study of Lombroso's thesis of atavism. Using newly developed but advanced mathematical techniques to measure the degree of correlation between physiological features and criminal history, Goring examined nearly 3,000 inmates at Turin prison beginning in 1901. Enlisting the aid of London's Biometric Laboratory, he concluded that "the whole fabric of Lombrosian doctrine, judged by the standards of science, is fundamentally unsound."[11] Goring compared the prisoners with students at Oxford and Cambridge Universities, British soldiers, and non-criminal hospital patients and published his findings in 1913 in his lengthy treatise *The English Convict: A Statistical Study.*[12]

Constitutional Theories

Constitutional theories explain criminality by reference to offenders' body types, genetics, or external observable physical characteristics. A constitutional, or physiological, orientation that found its way into the criminological mainstream during the early and mid-twentieth century was that of **somatotyping** (classifying according to body types), primarily associated with the work of **Ernst Kretschmer** and **William H. Sheldon**. Kretschmer, a professor of psychiatry at the German University of Tubingen, proposed a relationship between body build and personality type and created a rather detailed "biopsychological constitutional typology."

Influenced by Kretschmer, Sheldon utilized measurement techniques to connect body type with personality.[13] Sheldon studied 200 boys between the ages of 15 and 21 at the Hayden Goodwill Institute in Boston and concluded that four basic body types characterized the entire group, as shown in Figure 3–3. Mesomorphs, said Sheldon, were the most likely to be criminal.

Criminal Families

Sir Francis Galton (1822–1911) was the first Western scientist to systematically study **heredity**, or the passing of traits from parent to child, and its possible influence on human behavior.[14] In 1907, Galton wrote that "the perpetuation of the criminal class by heredity is a question difficult to grapple with on many accounts.

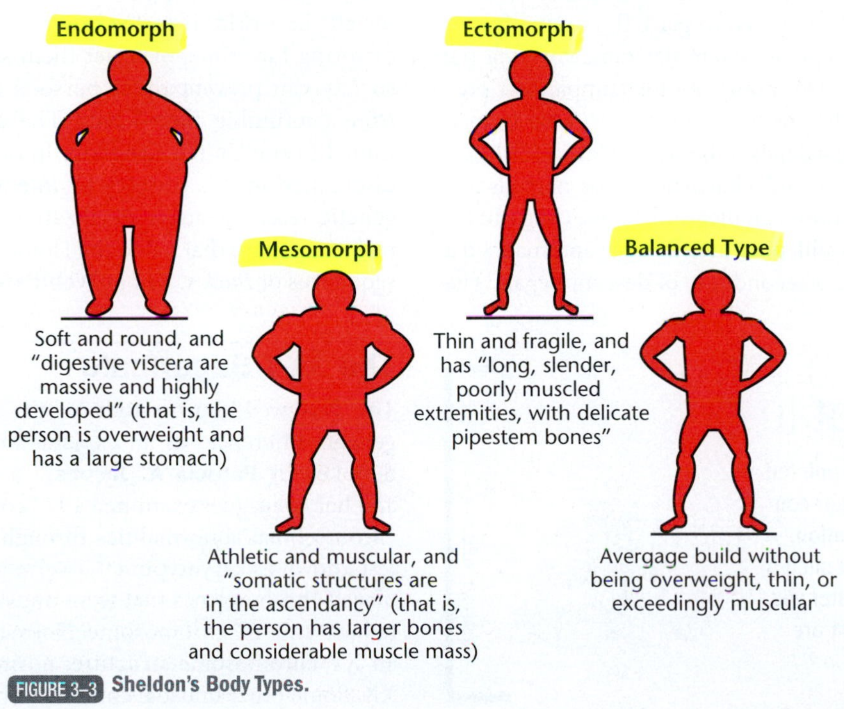

Endomorph
Soft and round, and "digestive viscera are massive and highly developed" (that is, the person is overweight and has a large stomach)
Ectomorph
Thin and fragile, and has "long, slender, poorly muscled extremities, with delicate pipestem bones"
Mesomorph
Athletic and muscular, and "somatic structures are in the ascendancy" (that is, the person has larger bones and considerable muscle mass)
Balanced Type
Avergage build without being overweight, thin, or exceedingly muscular

FIGURE 3–3 **Sheldon's Body Types.**

Think About It...

Some biological theorists claimed to have identified a relationship between body type and criminal behavior. Might there be any truth to such claims? If so, how can we be sure?

Andreas Gradin/Fotolia

It is, however, easy to show that the criminal nature tends to be inherited. . . . The criminal population receives steady accessions from those who, without having strongly marked criminal natures, do nevertheless belong to a type of humanity that is exceedingly ill suited to play a respectable part in our modern civilization, though it is well suited to flourish under half-savage conditions, being naturally both healthy and prolific."[15] Galton's work contributed to the development of the field of **behavioral genetics**, the study of genetic and environmental contributions to individual variations in human behavior. See **Web Extra 3–3** for more about behavioral genetics and crime.

Beginning in the late 1800s, and supported by burgeoning notions of heredity, researchers in the field of criminal anthropology focused on criminal families, or families that appeared to exhibit criminal tendencies across decades. In 1877, American sociologist **Richard Louis Dugdale** (1841–1883) published a study of the **Juke family**, which he described as criminogenic by nature.[16] In 1916, **Arthur H. Estabrook** published a follow-up to Dugdale's work in which he identified additional descendants, including prostitutes, paupers, and various types of criminal offenders.[17]

Following in the tradition of family-tree researchers, **Henry Herbert Goddard** (1866–1957) published a study of the **Kallikak family** in 1912.[18] Goddard attempted to place the study of deviant families within an acceptable scientific framework via the provision of a kind of control group, so for comparison purposes he used two branches of the same family. One branch began as the result of a sexual liaison between Martin Kallikak, a Revolutionary War soldier, and a barmaid whose name is unknown; as a result of this union, an illegitimate son (Martin, Jr.) was born. After the war, Kallikak returned home and married a righteous Quaker girl, and a second line of descent began. The legitimate branch produced only a few minor deviants, but the illegitimate line resulted in 262 feebleminded births and various other epileptic, alcoholic, and criminal descendants. (The term *feebleminded*, which was much in vogue at the time of Goddard's study, was later recast as "mentally retarded," and people exhibiting similar characteristics today might be referred to as "mentally handicapped" or "mentally challenged.") Because feeblemindedness appeared to occur with some predictability in Goddard's study, but criminal activity seemed to be only randomly represented among the descendants of both Kallikak lines, Goddard concluded that a tendency toward feeblemindedness was inherited but that criminality was not.

Like the ideas of the Italian School, constitutional theories and studies of criminal families have largely been discarded today as biosocial researchers develop more sophisticated perspectives on criminology. Early biological theories, however, because they tended to encourage the **eugenics** movement of the late 1880s and early 1900s, were vigorously opposed by many in the criminological community throughout the latter part of the twentieth century. The eugenics movement proposed selective human breeding as a course to improvement of the human species, and **eugenic criminology**, an offshoot of the movement,[19] held that the root causes of criminality were largely passed from generation to generation in the form of "bad genes."

Eugenic criminology, which accepted the idea of **genetic determinism**, or the belief that genes are the major determining factor in human behavior, replaced the idea of the "feebleminded criminal" with the "defective delinquent," and social policies developed during the eugenics movement called for the sterilization of mentally handicapped women to prevent their bearing additional offspring.[20] Those policies were supported by the federal Eugenics Record Office, which funded studies of "cacogenic," or "bad-gened," families and were endorsed by the 1927 U.S. Supreme Court case of ***Buck* v. *Bell***.[21] In *Buck*, Justice Oliver Wendell Holmes, Jr., writing in support of a Virginia statute permitting sterilization, said, "It is better for all the world, if instead of waiting to execute degenerate offspring for crime, or to let them starve for their imbecility, society can prevent those persons who are manifestly unfit from continuing their kind." The eugenics movement continued in the United Kingdom into the 1960s but was largely discredited in this country by intense condemnation of Nazi genetic research, mass sterilization, and eugenics programs, including those that led to the Holocaust. Learn about the consequences of *Buck* v. *Bell* at **Web Extra 3–4**.

Think About It...

Some researchers have pointed to the role of excess sugar consumption in crime causation. What is the evidence for such a link? How do *you* feel after you consume food items that are high in sugar?

Picsfive/Fotolia

The XYY Supermale

The first well-known study of the modern era to focus on genetic differences as an explanation for criminality was undertaken by **Patricia A. Jacobs**,[22] a British researcher. Jacobs and her colleagues examined 197 Scottish prisoners in 1965 for chromosomal abnormalities through a relatively simple blood test known as karyotyping.[23] Twelve members of the group displayed chromosomes that were unusual, and seven were found to have an XYY chromosome. Normal male individuals possess an XY chromosome structure; normal female individuals are XX. Some other unusual combinations might be XXX, wherein

Think About It...

Studies of families such as the Jukes and Kallikaks supported the idea of eugenics. What is eugenics? What dangers did some see in eugenic criminology?

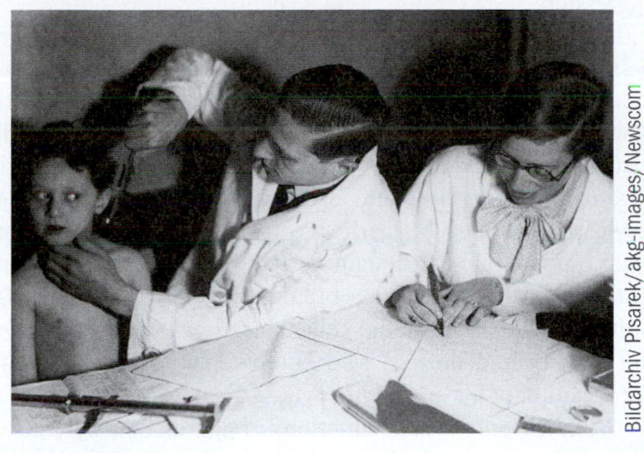

Bildarchiv Pisarek/akg-images/Newscom

a woman's genetic makeup contains an extra X chromosome, and XXY (also called Klinefelter's syndrome), in which a man might carry an extra X, or female, chromosome. Klinefelter's men often have male genitalia but are frequently sterile and have evidence of breast enlargement and intellectual retardation.[24] The XYY man, however, whose incidence in the prison population was placed at around 3.5% by Jacobs, was quickly identified as potentially violent and was termed a **supermale**.

Following the introduction of the supermale notion into popular consciousness, a number of offenders attempted to offer a chromosome-based defense. In 1969, for example, Lawrence E. Hannell, who was adjudged a supermale, was acquitted of murder in Australia on the grounds of insanity.[25] Such a defense, however, did not work for Richard Speck, who also claimed to be an XYY man but was convicted of killing eight Chicago nursing students in 1966; it was later learned that Speck did not carry the extra Y chromosome. See the Criminal Profiles box for more on Richard Speck.

The supermale phenomenon (also called the XYY syndrome) appears to have been based more on sensationalism than on fact. Today, little evidence exists to suggest that XYY men actually commit crimes of greater violence than do other men, although they may commit somewhat more crimes overall.[26]

Twin Studies and Heredity

More recently, studies of the criminal tendencies of fraternal and identical twins have provided a methodologically sophisticated technique for ferreting out the role of heredity in crime causation. Fraternal twins, or **dizygotic (DZ) twins**, develop from different fertilized eggs and share only the genetic material common among siblings; identical twins, or **monozygotic (MZ) twins**, develop from the same egg and carry virtually the same genetic material. Hence, if human behavior has a substantial heritable component, twins would display similar behavioral characteristics despite variations in their social environment, with any observed relationship being stronger among MZ twins than among DZ twins.

Christiansen and Mednick found significant statistical support for the notion that criminal tendencies are inherited.

A large twin study was begun in 1968 by European researchers **Karl O. Christiansen** and **Sarnoff Mednick**, who analyzed all twins (3,586 pairs) born on a selected group of Danish islands between 1881 and 1910.[27] Christiansen and Mednick found significant statistical support for the notion that criminal tendencies are inherited: 52% of identical twins and 22% of fraternal siblings displayed the same degree of criminality within the twin pair. Such similarities remained apparent even among twins separated at birth and raised in substantially different environments.

The Minnesota Twin Family Study began in 1983.[28] The Minnesota registry conducted personality and interests tests with more than 8,000 twin pairs and family members (by mail), and its findings seemed to show that MZ twins reared apart are about as similar as MZ twins reared together in personality and temperament, occupational and leisure-time interests, and social attitudes. Study authors warned, however, that "this evidence for the strong heritability of most psychological traits, sensibly construed, does not detract from the value or importance of parenting, education, and other . . . interventions."[29]

The study of twins is still common practice in criminology today, and the area of twin studies provides something of an overlap between this chapter and the next; that is, between early and contemporary biological theories. In 1996, for example, British researchers studying 43 MZ and 38 DZ same-sex twins through the use of self-report questionnaires stated that "common bad behaviors of the sort admitted to by the majority of adolescents have a substantially heritable component. Additive genetic effects account for most of the variation, with no evidence of a contribution from shared environment."[30]

In 2003, researchers examined the behavior of 1,116 pairs of five-year-old twins participating in a longitudinal study and asked mothers, teachers, study examiners, and the children themselves to evaluate the degree of the children's level of antisocial behavior.[31] Findings showed that antisocial children can be identified early in life, that their behavior can be nearly impossible to control by the time they reach kindergarten, and that heredity plays a far greater role in determining such behavior than does home life or parenting. Because of similar behavior among twin pairs, the researchers concluded that genetic influences were extremely powerful determinants of antisocial behavior across diverse social settings, writing that "research and theory on the etiology of childhood antisocial behavior must look beyond the current focus on socioeconomic contexts and parenting processes, to incorporate genetic explanations and develop new theories of nature-nurture interplay."[32]

Sociobiology

In the introduction to his insightful article summarizing **sociobiology**, Arthur Fisher wrote, "Every so often, in the long course of scientific progress, a new set of ideas appears, illuminating and redefining what has gone before like a flare bursting over a darkened landscape."

To some, sociobiology—which burst upon the social science scene in 1975—held the promise of just such a new **paradigm**, or model. The development of this novel paradigm, however, was preceded by the work of ethnologists, including Englishman John H. Cook, Sir Julian Huxley, and Austrian zoologist **Konrad Lorenz**, who studied the social behavior of both people and animals and laid the groundwork for later sociobiological perspectives.

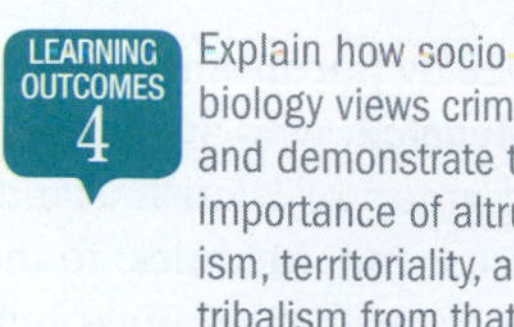

Explain how socio biology views crime, and demonstrate the importance of altruism, territoriality, and tribalism from that perspective.

The Biological Roots of Human Aggression

In 1966, Konrad Lorenz published his now-famous work *On Aggression*. In it, Lorenz described how aggression permeates the animal kingdom and asked, "What is the value of all this fighting?" He wrote, "In nature, fighting is such an ever-present process, its behavior mechanisms and weapons are so highly developed and have so obviously arisen under the pressure of a species-preserving function, that it is our duty to ask this question."

Lorenz focused on instinctive behavior in animals, and accepted the evolutionary thesis of nineteenth-century biologist **Charles Darwin** that intraspecies aggression favored the strongest and best animals in the reproductive process, but he concluded that aggression serves a variety of other purposes as well. Aggression, said Lorenz, ensures an "even distribution of animals of a particular species over an inhabitable area" and provides for a defense of the species from predators. Human aggression, he claimed, meets many of the same purposes but can take on covert forms, and the drive to acquire wealth and power, which was so characteristic of Western men at the time of his writing, is part of the human mating ritual whereby a man might "win" a prized woman through displays of more civilized forms of what could otherwise be understood as intraspecies aggression.

Lorenz's greatest contribution to the study of human behavior may have been his claim that all human behavior is, at least to some degree, "adapted instinctive behavior"; in other words, much of human conduct is fundamentally rooted in instinctive behavioral responses characteristic of biological organisms everywhere and present within each of us in the form of a biological inheritance from more primitive times. Even rational human thought derives its motivation and direction from instinctual aspects of human biology, and the highest human virtues, such as the value placed on human life, "could not have been achieved," said Lorenz, "without an instinctive appreciation of life and death."

Building on the root functions of aggression, Lorenz concluded that much of what we today call "crime" is the result of overcrowded living conditions combined with a lack of legitimate opportunity for the effective expression of aggression. Crowding increases the likelihood of aggression, whereas contemporary socialization works to inhibit it. In the words of Lorenz, "In one sense we are all psychopaths, for each of us suffers from the necessity of self-imposed control for the good of the community." When people break down, said Lorenz, they become neurotic or delinquent, and crime may be the result of stresses that have been found to typically produce aggression throughout the animal kingdom.

Lorenz's explanations, like many early biologically based theories, appear to be more applicable to certain forms of crime than to others, but it is important to recognize that modern frustrations and accompanying manifestations of aggression may be symbolically—rather than directly—expressed. Hence, a stockbroker who embezzles a client's money, spurred on by the need to provide material goods for an overly acquisitive family, may be just as criminal as a robber who beats his victim and steals her purse to have money to buy liquor.

The New Synthesis

Evolutionist **Edward O. Wilson** is credited with coining the term *sociobiology*. In his ground-breaking book *Sociobiology: The New Synthesis*, Edwards defined *sociobiology* as "the systematic study of the biological basis of all social behavior [that is] a branch of evolutionary biology and particularly of modern population biology." Wilson applied evolutionary theory to social behavior and claimed that most social behaviors are shaped by natural selection. Because of the important role of biology in social evolution that Wilson was able to demonstrate, his work brought renewed attention to biological theories throughout the social sciences.

Through studies of primates, Wilson was able to demonstrate that the human brain and mind are the products of natural selection that occurred early in human evolution as developing hominids overcame the limits to sociality posed by the

Think About It...

Some people think that there is a gene for crime—or at least a gene that might predispose those who carry it to behaviors that could result in law violation. If you were a parent, would you want your children tested to see if they might be biologically predisposed to crime? What would you do if the test results came back positive?

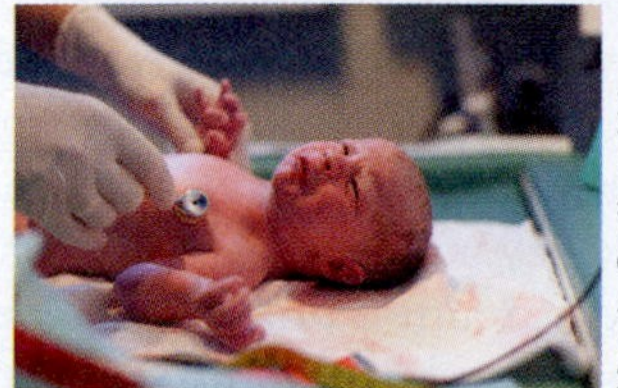

Marcin Sadlowski/ Fotolia

Wilson was able to demonstrate that the human brain and mind are the products of natural selection.

weak social ties that are characteristic of most primates. In so doing, they were able to develop close-knit social groups based upon strong social ties. Wilson then showed how the ability to form large-scale societies contributed to the long-term survival of the social group.

Through his entomological study of social insects (especially ants), Wilson provided examples of **altruism** (selfless, helping behavior) in multiple species and, contrary to the beliefs of some evolutionary biologists, he found that helping behavior facilitated the continuity of the **gene pool** among altruistic individuals. The primary determinant of behavior, including human behavior, said Wilson, was the need to ensure the survival and continuity of genetic material from one generation to the next—and altruism played a role in survival.

Territoriality, according to Wilson's writings, explained many of the conflicts, including homicide, warfare, and other forms of aggression, between and among species—especially human beings. In Wilson's words, "Part of man's problem is that his intergroup responses are still crude and primitive, and inadequate for the extended extraterritorial relationships that civilization has thrust upon him." The "unhappy result," as Wilson terms it, may be **tribalism**, expressed through the contemporary proliferation of street gangs, racial tension, and hardened encampments of survivalist and separatist groups, as well as the resilience of ethnic divides in the Middle East and throughout Europe and Asia.

Sociobiological theory not only tells us that the violence and aggressiveness associated with territoriality are often reserved for strangers but also explains intragroup aggression (violence occurring within groups). Wilson's theory suggested that within the group, "a particularly severe form of aggressiveness should be reserved for actual or suspected adultery. In many human societies, where sexual bonding is close and personal knowledge of the behavior of others detailed, adulterers are harshly treated. The sin is regarded to be even worse when offspring are produced."

Hence, territoriality and acquisitiveness extend to location, possessions, and even other people. Human laws, explained Wilson, are designed to protect genetically based relationships that people have with one another, as well as their material possessions and their claimed locations in space, so violations of these intuitive relationships result in crime and in official reactions by the legal system.

The importance of Wilson's work was its recognition that human nature is not so much an inherent quality of our species, but rather the "result of culture workings its ways on a biology that somewhat channeled (but did not fix) the subsequent nature of our species."

Today, many open-minded scholars are beginning to sense the growing need for a new synthesis, a way to integrate the promise of biological theories like sociobiology and insights drawn from studies of twins with other long-accepted perspectives like sociology and psychology in explaining human behavior. As a result, the field of criminology appears ripe for a new integrative approach, with some saying that this approach can be found in contemporary biosocial explanations of criminal behavior—to which we turn our attention in the next chapter. Learn more about sociobiology at **Web Extra 3–5**.

Critique of Early Biological Theories of Criminal Behavior

Identify some criticisms of early biological theories of criminal behavior.

A central concern with all early biological theories of criminal behavior has to do with the fact that they seemed to relegate the role of free will in human behavior to a kind of philosophical dustbin. If a person's behavior is largely determined, for example, by inherent and unchangeable atavistic features, then he or she may be condemned to a life of crime, and efforts at reformation can be expected to have little positive effect on future behavior. Consequently, some people continue to shy away from biological explanations for criminality and disordered behavior because phrases like "genetic determinism," which are often voiced by the popular media, have come to be synonymous with inevitability. People unschooled in criminology or modern biology tend to believe that "biological" equals "hopeless,"[33] as the physical makeup of a person is hard to change.

Other concerns stem from aligning the concept of crime with biological variables because crime is itself a social construction and its meaning varies from place to place and from time to time. Years ago, for example, it was illegal to own physical gold for investment purposes in the United States, but today such ownership is permitted. Similarly, Islamic law in Saudi Arabia makes it a crime for a woman to drive a car while unaccompanied by a male relative, while in the United States (and much of the rest of the world) such activity is far from criminal. Although it is possible to hypothesize, for example, that a particular biological trait leads to a desire for gold ownership (or for ownership of shiny things of value), or produces the urge to drive a motor vehicle, the fact that such ownership (or driving) may or may not be criminal makes it hard to link specific biological features with potential criminality. Similarly, it would seem unlikely that any biological feature (or a combination of

Think About It…

Do you think that biological approaches to the study of crime tell the whole story? Or do you believe that they provide only one piece of the crime-causation puzzle? If so, what might the other "pieces" be?

seralex/Fotolia

features) could explain the wide variety of criminal offending today—from insider stock trading and while-collar crime to violent attacks, rape and murder.

A more sensible approach might be to work to identify biological influences on characteristics that most criminals share. Such characteristics could include the level of aggression, risk taking, and danger seeking that individuals demonstrate. Possession of these characteristics may be found to increase the likelihood that some people will gravitate toward criminal activity, or to related behaviors. Even if that is true, however, such characteristics might be shared by people who routinely violate the law as well as by those who enforce it. Many on both sides of the law, for example, may be risk takers, danger seekers, and aggressive personalities. Consequently, in some ways criminals and enforcement agents may share any number of characteristics, and even some genes related to behavior propensities, but differ significantly in their orientation toward social life. What separates one from the other might be the nature of the social environment to which people are exposed when growing up.

Given the difficulty in sorting out this kind of complex relationship, it may be impossible to identify any biological features shared solely by criminals. Moreover, as today's theorists understand, the influence of biology on behavior of any kind is more often the result of an interaction among genetic, hormonal, and other biological features of an individual and his or her social and physical environments. In other words, as the following chapter will show, biological influences are not likely to be the direct cause of crime or conformity, but are mediated through a person's surroundings to produce behavior of one sort or another.

THE CASE

Richard Benjamin Speck—"Born to Raise Hell"

In an appalling crime ranked number ten on *Time*'s list of the top 25 crimes of the twentieth century,[i] Richard Speck committed the mass murder of eight nurses from a community hospital in Chicago on the night of July 14, 1966.

Born the seventh of eight children on December 6, 1941, Speck had an early upbringing in Kirkwood, Illinois, that included strict adherence to Baptist religious teachings. When he was just six years old, his father died, and his mother subsequently married a hard-fisted drinker with an arrest record. After the family relocated to Dallas, Texas, Speck performed poorly in school and began sinking into increasingly serious delinquent behavior. His drunken stepfather's response was typically the administration of severe physical punishment for each of Speck's continuing transgressions.[ii] Speck himself became a heavy drinker, an affliction that would haunt him for the remainder of his life.

Interspersed with a series of incarcerations for various burglaries, thefts, check forgeries, and other low-level crimes, 18-year-old Speck married 15-year-old Shirley Malone in November 1962. Their brief marriage was marked by his repeated absence while imprisoned, punctuated by his physical abuse of both his wife and his mother-in-law whenever he was not in jail. The abuse of his wife included frequent instances of rape at knifepoint.[iii]

In January 1966, the couple divorced, and Speck left Texas to return by bus to Illinois, ending up in Monmouth, a small town near the Iowa border. Following the rape of a 65-year-old woman in early April and the murder of a barmaid 11 days later, Speck was interrogated. He was let go when he became physically ill, but he promised to return for further questioning. When he failed to show up, investigators who went looking for him found he had fled on a bus headed east, presumably to the Chicago area. Before leaving, he had the phrase *Born to Raise Hell* tattooed on his forearm.

Late on the evening of July 13, 1966, a drunken Speck invaded a townhouse where nursing students from nearby South Chicago Community Hospital resided. Within the first hour, he was able to capture and tie up nine women. After securing all the victims, Speck spent the next three hours systematically taking each student to another room within the townhouse and killing her. Each was violently murdered by strangulation, multiple stab wounds, and/or a cut throat; one was also raped.

Speck lost count of the number of women he had captured, and as a result, one of the women survived by rolling under a bed and hiding there. Speck left the townhouse at approximately 3:30 A.M. The survivor, Corazon Amurao, huddled in terror under the bed until almost 6 A.M. before she finally crawled out a window and began calling for help.[iv]

Bettmann/Corbis

Mass murderer Richard Speck. Speck killed eight young nurses in 1966, and he admitted during an interview that they would be alive today if one of the women had not spit in his face as he raped her. Speck's case helped popularize the notion of supermales—predators with a distinctive genetic makeup. Do contemporary understandings of biology support the idea of a supermale?

Speck was soon arrested and tried in Peoria, Illinois. The jury returned a guilty verdict in just 49 minutes, and Speck was sentenced to death.[v]

Speck achieved notoriety in the national press when his lawyers offered the claim that he was an XYY supermale, apparently hoping that the claim could provide a defense to the charges against him. At the time the claim was made, the XYY theory was being debated in academic circles and had become popular with the public. Later tests showed, however, that Speck did not carry the extra Y chromosome.

Speck's death sentence was commuted to 50 to 100 years in prison when the U.S. Supreme Court voided the death penalty in 1972. He died of a heart attack on December 5, 1991.

Notes

[i] Howard Chua-Eoan, "The Top 25," *Crimes of the Century, Time*, http://www.time.com/time/2007/crimes/9.html (accessed May 22, 2007).

[ii] David Lohr, "Richard Speck," *Crime Magazine: An Encyclopedia of Crime*, August 2003, http://crimemagazine.com/03/richardspeck,0820.htm (accessed May 22, 2007).

[iii] Connie Fillippelli, "Richard Speck: Born to Raise Hell," Chapter 11, CourtTV Crime Library, 2007, http://www.crimelibrary.com/serial_killers/predators/speck/hell_11.html (accessed May 22, 2007).

[iv] Ibid., Chapter 16, http://www.crimelibrary.com/serial_killers/predators/speck/hell_16.html (accessed May 22, 2007).

[v] Ibid., Chapter 16.

The case of Richard Speck raises a number of interesting questions. Among them are the following:

1. **What caused Richard Speck to go on a murderous crime spree? Do you think it was his background or his biology, or a combination of both?**
2. **How is the Speck case illustrative of the current debate between advocates of biological theories of crime causation and those who advocate sociological theories?**
3. **How might a psychologist explain Speck's crimes? A sociologist?**

CHAPTER 3 Early Biological Perspectives on Criminal Behavior

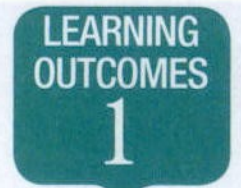

Describe the differences between historical biological and contemporary biosocial theories of crime.

Early proponents of biological theories argued that at least some human behavior is the result of biological propensities inherited from more primitive developmental stages in the evolutionary process. Contemporary biosocial theories suggest that human behavior is the result of complex interactions between biology and features of the physical and social environments.

1. How do historical and contemporary biological perspectives differ?
2. Do you believe that people today can be influenced by "primitive urges" or "primitive features" that are somehow carried over from earlier evolutionary periods of human development?
3. What does C. Ray Jeffery mean when he writes, "Open inquiry requires objective consideration of all points of view and an unbiased examination of each for its ability to shed light on the subject under study"? Do you agree or disagree with this assertion? Why?

biological theories Perspectives maintaining that the basic determinants of human behavior, including criminality, are constitutionally or physiologically based and often inherited.

Key Names

C. Ray Jeffery A criminologist who believes that a biologically based program of crime control and crime prevention includes biological monitoring and research.

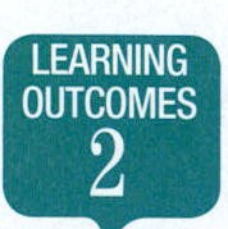

Outline the basic principles of biological theories of crime.

Biological theories advance the principle that the basic determinants of human behavior, including criminality, are constitutionally or physiologically based and are largely inherited. This chapter lists eight fundamental assumptions of biological theories of crime causation, including that the brain is the organ of the mind and the locus of personality.

1. What are the central assumptions of biological theories of crime?
2. What does it mean to say that "the brain is the organ of the mind"?

trait A notable feature or quality of a biological entity. Traits may be classified as physical, behavioral, or psychological. Traits are passed on from generation to generation.

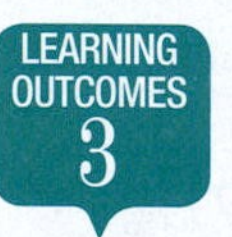

Describe early biological explanations of criminality.

Early biological explanations of criminality built upon positivism, an early scientific approach to the study of crime and its causation. Positivism was founded upon evolutionary principles and saw criminals as throwbacks to earlier evolutionary epochs. Like positivism, other early biological theories contended that there was a relationship between criminal behavior and physical characteristics and suggested that deviant behavior could be explained by correlating it to aspects of human evolution.

1. What is positivism? How can positivism inform criminological theorizing?
2. What is atavism? What evidence did early criminologists offer for the existence of atavistic traits?
3. What body types did William H. Sheldon identify? Which of these did he think was most likely to be criminal?

positivism A scientific approach to the study of crime and its causation. Early positivism was built upon evolutionary principles and saw criminals as throwbacks to earlier evolutionary epochs.

phrenology The study of the shape of the head to determine anatomical correlates of human behavior.

atavism A term used by Cesare Lombroso to suggest that criminals are physiological throwbacks to early stages of human evolution.

Italian School of Criminology A perspective on criminology developed in the late 1800s holding that criminals can be identified by physical features and are throwbacks to earlier stages of human evolution. The Italian School was largely based on studies of criminal anthropology.

criminal anthropology The scientific study of the relationship between human physical characteristics and criminality.

born criminal An individual who is born with a genetic predilection toward criminality.

criminaloids A term used by Cesare Lombroso to describe occasional criminals who were pulled into criminality by environmental influences.

constitutional theories Biological theories that explain criminality by reference to offenders' body types, inheritance, genetics, or external observable physical characteristics.

somatotyping Classifying according to body types.

heredity The passing of traits from parent to child.

behavioral genetics The study of genetics and environmental contributions to individual variations in human behavior.

Juke family A well-known "criminal family" studied by Richard Dugdale.

Kallikak family A well-known "criminal family" studied by Henry H. Goddard.

eugenics The study and implementation of hereditary improvement by genetic control (i.e., selective breeding to "improve" the human race).

eugenic criminology A perspective holding that the root causes of criminality are passed from generation to generation in the form of "bad genes."

genetic determinism The belief that genes are the major determining factor in human behavior.

Buck* v. *Bell A Supreme Court case that upheld the practice of sterilization as a way to rid society of those people with criminal tendencies.

supermale A male individual displaying the XYY chromosome structure.

dizygotic (DZ) twins A twin who develops from a separate ovum and who carries the genetic material shared by siblings.

monozygotic (MZ) twins Twins who develop from the same egg and have virtually the same genetic material.

Key Names

Franz Joseph Gall An early criminological anthropologist who believed that the shape of the human skull is indicative of the personality and can be used to predict criminal behavior.

Johann Gaspar Spurzheim A student of Franz Joseph Gall who introduced phrenology, the correlation between the shape of the human skull and human behavior, to America, where it became part of the classification method used to evaluate newly admitted prisoners.

Cesare Lombroso A well-known early scientific biological theorist who said that criminality is the result of primitive urges that survived the evolutionary process in modern-day human throwbacks.

Enrico Ferri and ***Raffael Garofalo*** Members of the Italian School of Criminology, which was founded by Cesare Lombroso.

Charles Buckman Goring An English physician around the beginning of the twentieth century who believed that the theory of atavism, the correlation of physical features with criminal behavior, is unfounded when assessed by scientific methods.

Ernst Kretschmer A professor of psychiatry who claimed that body build could be related to personality type.

William H. Sheldon A psychologist who, like Ernst Kretschmer, believed that body build could be related to personality type; he popularized the concept of somatotyping.

Sir Francis Galton The first Western scientist to systematically study heredity.

Richard Louis Dugdale An American sociologist who published a study of the Juke family in the late 1800s, which he described as criminogenic by nature.

Arthur H. Estabrook A sociological researcher who published a follow-up to Richard Dugdale's work in 1916.

Henry Herbert Goddard A researcher who conducted a study of the Kallikak family in 1912 using an acceptable scientific framework. The study indicated that criminal tendencies existed among the offspring of the union of Kallikak and a barmaid, whereas a subsequent liaison with a virtuous Quaker woman resulted in offspring that did not demonstrate criminal tendencies.

Patricia A. Jacobs A British researcher who examined Scottish prisoners for chromosomal abnormalities through a relatively simple blood test known as karyotyping.

Karl O. Christiansen A European researcher who worked with Sarnoff Mednick to analyze thousands of pairs of twins in an effort to determine whether criminal tendencies might be inherited.

Sarnoff Mednick A European researcher who worked with Karl O. Christiansen to analyze thousands of pairs of twins in an effort to determine whether criminal tendencies might be inherited.

Explain how sociobiology views crime, and demonstrate the importance of altruism, territoriality, and tribalism from that perspective.

Sociobiology is a theoretical perspective developed by Edward O. Wilson that applies evolutionary theory to social behavior and says that most social behaviors are shaped by natural selection. Sociobiology includes "the systematic study of the biological basis of all social behavior." It is a branch of evolutionary biology and particularly of modern population biology.

1. What is sociobiology? What contributions has sociobiology made to the study of criminality?
2. What role does altruism play in the continuity of the gene pool?

sociobiology A theoretical perspective developed by Edward O. Wilson that includes "the systematic study of the biological basis of all social behavior." It is a branch of evolutionary biology and particularly of modern population biology.

paradigm An example, a model, or a theory.

altruism Selfless, helping behavior.

gene pool The total genetic information of all the individuals in a breeding population.

tribalism The attitudes and behavior that result from strong feelings of identification with one's own social group.

Key Names

Konrad Lorenz An Austrian zoologist who studied instinctive behavior in animals with a focus on intraspecies aggression.

Charles Darwin A nineteenth-century English biologist known for his contributions to evolutionary theory.

Edward O. Wilson A researcher and author who believes that behavior can be explained through a synthesis of biological and evolutionary ecology.

Identify some criticisms of early biological theories of criminal behavior.

Some criminologists fear that acceptance of biological theories of crime causation might spark another eugenics movement in which people are judged more on their biology than their behavior. Other critics say that biological theories of crime fail to adequately conceptualize criminality or that difficulty in accurately estimating the degree of criminality among sample populations clouds the link between theory and reality.

1. What is eugenics?
2. What warnings does eugenics offer anyone interested in studying biological theories of crime?
3. Why have biological approaches to crime causation encountered stiff criticism?

"Biological explanations shaped criminology at its inception, and today they are reemerging with fresh vigor and increased potential."

—Nicole Rafter[1]

Biosocial and Other Contemporary Perspectives—Interaction Is Key

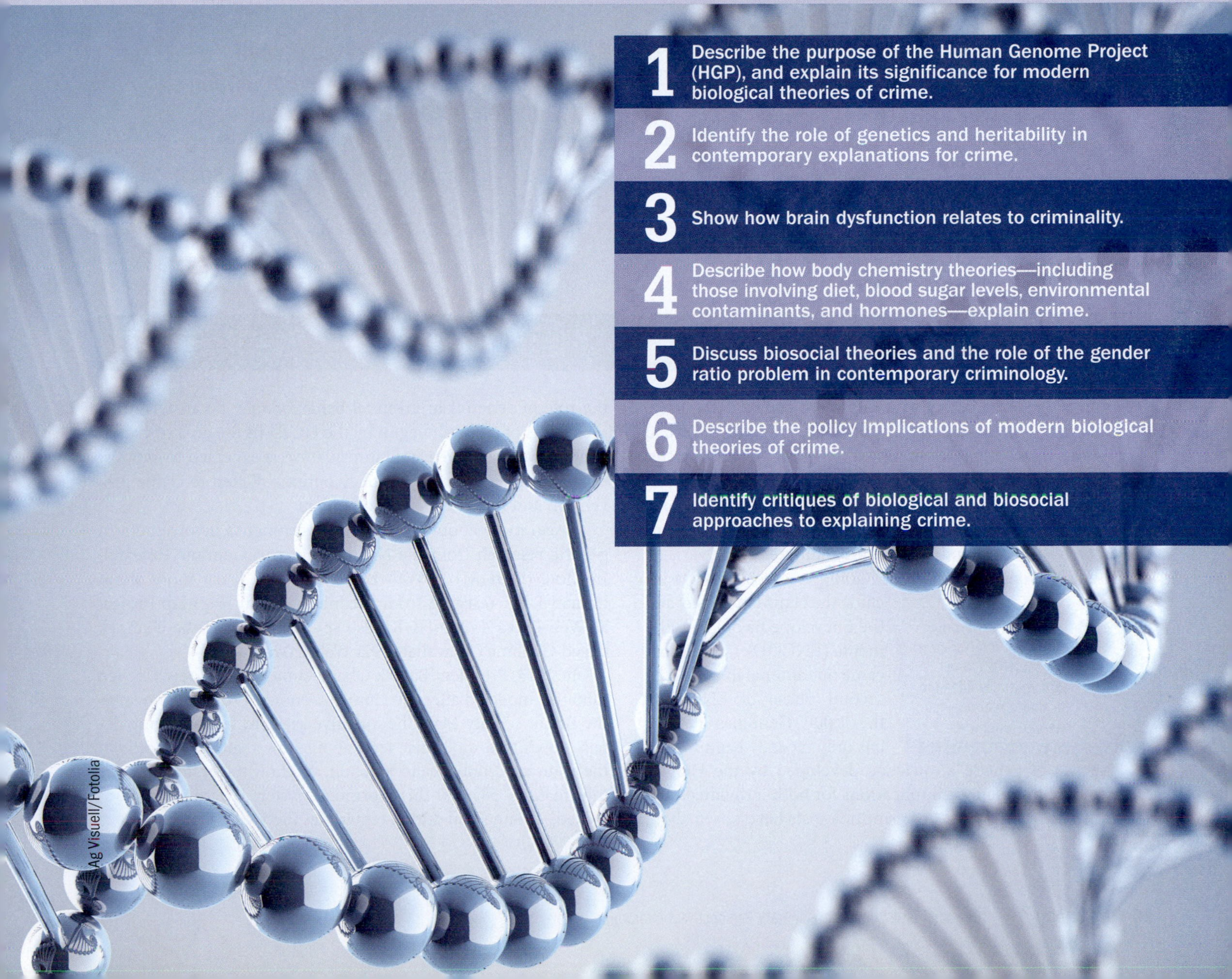

1. Describe the purpose of the Human Genome Project (HGP), and explain its significance for modern biological theories of crime.
2. Identify the role of genetics and heritability in contemporary explanations for crime.
3. Show how brain dysfunction relates to criminality.
4. Describe how body chemistry theories—including those involving diet, blood sugar levels, environmental contaminants, and hormones—explain crime.
5. Discuss biosocial theories and the role of the gender ratio problem in contemporary criminology.
6. Describe the policy implications of modern biological theories of crime.
7. Identify critiques of biological and biosocial approaches to explaining crime.

THE DNA REVOLUTION

In 2013, Connecticut Chief Medical Examiner H. Wayne Carver ordered the testing of Newton, Connecticut, school shooter Adam Lanza's DNA in an effort to determine "if he possessed any genetic abnormalities that could have led to his violent behavior."[2] In issuing that order, Carver was relying on new technologies that have recently been developed to map and explore the biological mechanisms that underlie human behavior.

One of the most important recent efforts in understanding human nature is the Human Genome Project (HGP), an international research program designed to construct detailed maps of the human genome. The HGP began in the United States in 1990 through a joint effort of the Department of Energy and the National Institutes of Health. It had as its goal the determination of the complete chemical sequence of human DNA. Researchers participating in the project worked together to localize the nearly 100,000 genes within the human genome, and to determine the sequences of the 3 billion chemical base pairs that make up human DNA. The HGP was officially declared completed on April 14, 2003—almost exactly 50 years after James Watson and Francis Crick published their historic findings on the double-helix three-dimensional structure of DNA.[3]

The HGP marked the beginning of a new era of research into human biology, and recast understandings of human nature, disease, cognition, and behavior. Because the HGP offered radical new insights into fundamental human qualities, we use it as the point of demarcation between earlier biological theories of criminality and those that have been recently developed.

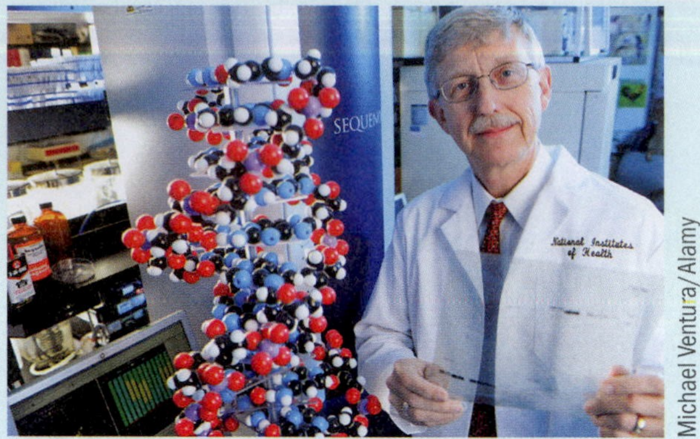
Michael Ventura/Alamy

Dr. Francis Collins, former director of the Human Genome Project and current director of the National Institutes of Health. The National Center for Human Genome Research at the National Institutes of Health supported the international Human Genome Project, a research program that determined the complete nucleotide sequence of human DNA. What ethical, legal, and social implications are inherent in such a project?

DISCUSS **Do you believe that biological theories have something of significance to contribute to the discussion of causes of crime and deviance? Will such theories ever be able to fully explain such behavior?**

The Human Genome Project

The human genome refers to a complete copy of the entire set of human gene instructions.[4] **Genes** are made of DNA and carry coded instructions for making everything the body needs. **Chromosomes** are bundles of genes.[5] After completion of the HGP, which resulted in the sequencing of the entire genome sequence of a "reference human genome," the focus of genomics research turned to finding individual differences or variants from that reference sequence.[6] Ongoing research projects include the HapMap Project and the Encyclopedia of DNA Elements (ENCODE), which became operational in 2007. The second phase of ENCODE, the 1,000 Genomes Project, has only recently begun.

LEARNING OUTCOMES 1 Describe the purpose of the Human Genome Project (HGP), and explain its significance for modern biological theories of crime.

The use of genetic knowledge developed by the HGP is likely to have momentous implications for both individuals and society. Many of the questions criminologists have raised about the role of genetics in criminal behavior may be answered by the results of research begun by the HGP.[7] In the area of crime-control policy, HGP-related information is expected to support the development of public policy options related to crime prevention and the treatment of offenders.

Learn more about the federal government's involvement in genetic research from the National Human Genome Research Institute (NHGRI) at **Web Extra 4–1**, and learn more about human DNA research from the international HapMap Project at **Web Extra 4–2**. NHGRI also sponsors a YouTube channel, called GenomeTV, available via **Web Extra 4–3**.

In 2013, President Barack Obama announced a new U.S.-led initiative modeled after the Human Genome Project.[8] Known as the Brain Activity Map, the initiative seeks to learn specific details down to a molecular level about how regions and cells in the brain interconnect and function, and how the brain processes information.[9] "There's this enormous mystery, awaiting to be unlocked," Obama said during remarks at the White House.[10]

Some criminologists claim that the evidence is very clear that there is a genetic factor involved in crime.

Genetics and Heritability

In 1993, only three years after the launch of the HGP, Dutch criminologists caught worldwide attention with their claim that they had uncovered a specific gene with links to criminal behavior. Researcher **H. Hilger Ropers**, geneticist **Han Brunner**, and collaborators studied what media sources called "the Netherlands' most dysfunctional family."[11] Although members of the unnamed family displayed IQs in the near-normal range, they seemed unable to control their impulses and often ended up being arrested for violations of the criminal law. The arrests, however, were always of men. Tracing the family back five generations, Brunner found 14 men whom he classified as genetically driven to criminality, but none of the women in the family displayed criminal tendencies, although they were said to have often been victimized by their crime-prone male siblings.

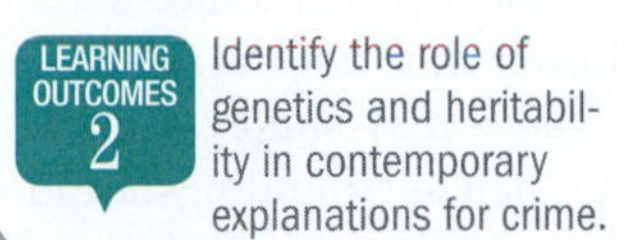

LEARNING OUTCOMES
2
Identify the role of genetics and heritability in contemporary explanations for crime.

According to Ropers and Brunner, because men have only one X chromosome, they are especially vulnerable to any defective gene, whereas women (with two X chromosomes) have a kind of backup system in which one defective gene may be compensated for by another correctly functioning gene carried in the second X chromosome. After a decade of study, Ropers and Brunner announced that they had isolated the specific mutation that caused the family's criminality.[12] This gene, they said, is responsible for the production of an enzyme called monoamine oxidase A (MAOA), which is crucially involved in the process by which signals are transmitted within the brain. MAOA breaks down the chemicals serotonin (a hormone that plays the role of a neurotransmitter, and that we discuss in more detail later in this chapter) and noradrenaline (another neurotransmitter). **Neurotransmitters** are the chemicals that facilitate the flow of electrical impulses from one neuron to the next across nerve synapses; and the presence or absence of both serotonin and noradrenaline have been linked to aggressive behavior in human beings. Because men with the mutated gene do not produce enough of the enzyme necessary to break down a lot of chemical transmitters, the researchers surmised, their brains are overwhelmed with stimuli, resulting in uncontrollable urges and, ultimately, criminal behavior. Research that examines the relationship between neurotransmitters and behavior falls into the field of **neurophysiology**.

Also in the 1990s, researchers at the University of Texas Health Science Center in San Antonio announced the discovery of a pleasure-seeking gene that, they suspected, plays a role in deviant behavior, addictions, and maybe even murder and violence. The gene, which is a variation (also called an **allele**) of a gene known as "DRD2 A1" is normally involved in controlling the flow of dopamine (a powerful brain chemical that gives people a sense of well-being). When defective, however, the DRD2 A1 allele diminishes dopamine function, which may drive a person to take drugs, drink, or engage in activity that provides a dopamine-like experience. "We think they're seeking out ways of fixing the lack of pleasure," said researcher Kenneth Blum. "You might be a pleasure seeker for alcohol, drugs, sex or maybe you get it from violence or murder."[13]

Think About It…

Some neurophysiologists claim that all of human consciousness and behavior can be explained by an examination of the chemical and neural structure of the brain. Would you agree?

Yellowj/Fotolia

In 2002, **Avshalom Caspi** and **Terrie E. Moffitt** and their colleagues offered a model of *gene-environment interaction* which recognized that childhood maltreatment appears to be a "universal risk factor for antisocial behavior" in adulthood. Previous research had demonstrated that children who experience abuse—especially those exposed to erratic, coercive, and punitive parenting—frequently develop conduct disorders and display antisocial personality symptoms, and they are known to be at greater risk of becoming violent adult offenders than children who do not experience such maltreatment.[14] Earlier research had also shown that the younger children are when they experience maltreatment, the more likely they are to display such problems in later life.

Using data from the Dunedin Multidisciplinary Health and Development Study—a longitudinal study of 1,037 children born in the maternity hospital in Dunedin, New Zealand, between April 1, 1972, and March 31, 1973—Caspi and Moffit noted that not all maltreated children grow up to become criminal,[15] but hypothesized that the development of antisocial behavior is mediated by an interaction between a gene

Childhood maltreatment appears to be a "universal risk factor for antisocial behavior" in adulthood.

responsible for the production of the enzyme MAOA and an environment variable (maltreatment). Researchers demonstrated a significant biosocial interaction between MAOA and early child abuse, leading to violence later in life.[16] Their findings showed that maltreatment "has lasting neurochemical correlates in human children" and that deficient MAOA activity may cause "neural hyperreactivity" in children in response to threats. The researchers concluded that "childhood maltreatment predisposes most strongly to adult violence among children whose MAOA is insufficient to constrain maltreatment-induced changes to neurotransmitter systems."[17] Maltreated children with high MAOA activity did not develop antisocial behavior. The finding was supported by two separate Swedish studies published in 2007.[18]

A 2008 analysis of data from the National Longitudinal Study of Adolescent Health (also known as Add Health) by Kevin M. Beaver of Florida State University and associates found that low MAOA activity can interact with neuropsychological deficits (defined in this study as poor scores on verbal skills tests) to produce low self-control and delinquency. Hence, according to Beaver, data analysis findings "are supportive of an interdisciplinary scientific approach to the study of crime and delinquency, which views antisocial behavior as a multifactorial phenotype that is the result of genetic factors, neural substrates, and environmental factors working independently and synergistically."[19] In other words, in at least some cases, genetic predispositions plus interaction with the surrounding social and physical environments combine to produce delinquency.

Continued focus on the gene related to MAOA production led to the announced finding of a "warrior gene," and in 2010 National Geographic Television produced a show entitled "Inside the Warrior Gene" featuring men who felt that their lives were controlled by a deep-seated and constant anger that might be ascribed to such a biological condition.[20] Variants of the gene were found in boys more likely to engage in violence, to use weapons, and to join gangs.

In 2007, researchers at the University of Texas Southwestern Medical Center discovered that mice carrying certain mutations in what is called the clock gene exhibited manic behaviors, such as recklessness and hyperactivity, and also displayed a preference for addictive substances, such as cocaine, but that treatment with the antipsychotic medicine lithium caused them to behave normally. Somewhat later, Francis McMahon of the National Institute of Mental Health in Bethesda, Maryland, reported finding a number of specific genes that act by influencing how the brain responds to neurotransmitters such as dopamine and that might be associated with bipolar disorder.[21]

In 2008, researchers with the National Institute on Drug Abuse announced that "as much as half of an individual's risk of becoming addicted to nicotine, alcohol, or other drugs depends on his or her genes."[22] The researchers stated, "Pinning down the biological basis for this risk is an important avenue of research for scientists trying to solve the problem of drug abuse."

In 2011, making a genetic argument for at least some forms of callous, unemotional behavior, **Nathalie Fontaine** of Indiana University and colleagues, reported that **heritability** (which is a statistical construct that estimates the amount of variation in the traits of a population that is attributable to genetic factors) leads to persistently high levels of such behavior among twin boys.[23] The data on which Fontaine reported were derived from the United Kingdom's ongoing Twin Early Development Study (TEDS), which uses information gathered from over 15,000 families to explore how people change through childhood and adolescence.[24] A 2014 study by Eric Lacourse and colleagues at the University of Montreal found that aggression in toddlers is strongly associated with genetic factors.[25] Lacourse studied 667 monozygotic and dizygotic twin pairs born in the greater Montreal area between April 1995 and December 1998, asking their mothers to report their children's behavior at 20, 32, and 50 months. Lacourse noted that his "gene-environment analyses revealed that early genetic factors were pervasive in accounting for developmental trends, explaining most of the stability and change in physical aggression. . . ." He also warned that "early childhood propensities may evoke negative responses from parents and peers," and that "early physical aggression needs to be dealt with, with care."

Some of the studies discussed here may appear to point to criminal genes that, once inherited, inevitably produce antisocial behavior. Such a conclusion, however, is not warranted. As we shall see later in this chapter, genes may simply influence the way in which people respond to their surroundings. As one researcher puts it, "genes and environments operating in tandem [are] required to produce significant antisocial behavior."[26] Hence, so-called criminal genes may be nothing more than genetic predispositions to respond in certain ways to a criminogenic environment.

The study of the chemical reactions that occur within a genome, and that switch parts of the genome on or off at strategic times and locations, is referred to as **epigenetics**. Epigenetics is informed by the principle that "the genome dynamically responds to the environment. Stress, diet, behavior, toxins and other factors activate chemical switches that regulate **gene expression**."[27] A video explaining epigenetics can be found at **Web Extra 4-4**.

Future Directions in the Study of Genes and Crime

The HGP, the Brain Activity Mapping project, and studies like those cited here notwithstanding, behavioral geneticists examining the crime problem face some daunting issues: coming up with a generally acceptable definition of criminality, determining how best to measure criminality once it has been defined, separating the influences of the social and physical environments from genetic influences on behavior, and distinguishing among the multiple and potentially interrelated influences of many genes. In the final analysis, the explanatory power of heritability appears to be limited by the fact that it may apply only to specific environments that existed at the time of a given study. For example, red roses grown under optimal conditions will likely all be similar in size, shape, and color, but grow the same roses in a desert or put food coloring in their water, and their appearance is likely to change substantially. As one noted geneticist says, "If the population or the environment changes, the heritability most likely will change as well. Most important, heritability statements provide no basis for predictions about

The interaction of genes and the behavioral possibilities that they represent, with features of the social and physical environments, produce meaningful human activity.

the expression of the trait in question in any given individual."[28] In other words, even red roses watered with blue food coloring are unlikely to end up being red.

New understandings about how genes operate also seem to call into question previous notions that genes are strong determinants of human behavior. Researchers in the field of neurobiology, for example, have found 17 genes, known as CREB genes, that are switched on and off in response to environmental influences. The CREB genes lay down neural pathways in the brain and form the basis of memory; the act of learning turns the CREB genes on and is made possible by them.[29] Hence, the CREB genes respond to human experience rather than determine it. One writer explains it this way: "These genes are at the mercy of our behavior, not the other way around."[30] The FOXP2 gene on chromosome 7 allows the development of language skills in human beings. The CREB and FOXP2 genes have taught researchers that genes are not just carriers of heredity; they are active during life and respond to the environment.

In sum, it is important to recognize that genes are both the cause and the consequence of our actions—and that they do not so much *determine* human action as *enable* it. Nonetheless, evidence seems to show that disadvantaged environments can suppress prosocial gene expression and enhance antisocial gene action. As one researcher puts it, "Single genes can have quite large effects, though, when they are paired with criminogenic environments."[31]

Learn more about the HGP by visiting the National Human Genome Research Institute via **Web Extra 4–5**; you might also want to visit the Human Genome Project Information Archive site at **Web Extra 4–6**.

The Dysfunctional Brain

Numerous contemporary researchers have explored brain dysfunction as it relates to criminality. For example, studies using positron emission tomography (PET) of the prefrontal cortex of subjects' brains have shown interesting results. Among other things, PET technology can measure the uptake of glucose by the brain. In a 1994 study conducted by University of Pennsylvania psychologist **Adrian Raine** and his colleagues, PET scans of the brains of 22 murderers (including some who had only attempted murder) revealed that the study subjects showed much lower levels of glucose uptake in the prefrontal cortex than did members of a control group.[32] "The differences that Raine observed were not related to age, gender, handedness, ethnicity, motivation, history of head injury, or presence of schizophrenia. In addition, no subjects were taking psychoactive drugs at the time of the test."[33] Raine observed that their data strongly suggested that "deficits localized to the prefrontal cortex may be related to violence" in some offenders (Figure 4–1). He also noted that "frontal damage is associated with impulsivity, loss of self-control, immaturity, lack of tact, inability to modify and inhibit behavior appropriately, and poor social judgment."[34]

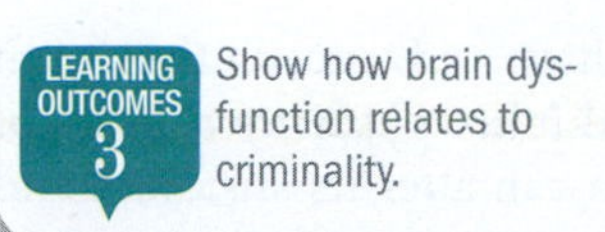

LEARNING OUTCOMES 3
Show how brain dysfunction relates to criminality.

PET scans of the brains of murderers showed much lower levels of glucose uptake in the prefrontal cortex than did those of the controls.

Raine and other researchers who were involved in the study explained that prefrontal cortex dysfunction must be evaluated in terms of how individuals who exhibit the condition interact with features of the environment, including social and psychological influences. Because prefrontal cortex dysfunction may result in failure in school, inability to hold a job, problems in relationships, and so forth, it may not be a direct cause of crime but might predispose someone afflicted with the condition to "a criminal and violent way of life."[35] Raine later replicated the study using 41 murderers who had claimed to be not guilty by reason of insanity (NGRI), and who were matched with 41 "normal" controls. Similar results were obtained, leading Raine to conclude "that murderers pleading NGRI are characterized by . . . reduced glucose metabolism in (the) bilateral prefrontal cortex."[36] Still later, Raine and his colleagues used PET studies to show that differences exist between the brains of people prone to impulsive violence and those who preplan violent crimes.[37]

Seventeen years later, in a 2011 presentation made to the American Association for the Advancement of Science, Raine identified an 18% reduction of the volume of the portion of the brain called the amygdala in psychopaths when compared to nonpsychopaths, along with reductions in the size of prefrontal cortex.[38] Raine claimed that by examining the brains of children as young as three years of age, criminologists could already see signs indicating the potential for troubled behavior in the future.[39] Today, Raine's approach has become known as **neurocriminology**, a perspective that examines the neurological links between the organism, social factors, and criminal behavior.

Other researchers, using less sophisticated techniques, have been able to show that "violent psychopathology in youth is associated with structural and functional damage" to the brain's orbital cortex.[40] The orbital cortex is that part of the brain that is directly over the orbits of the eyes. Some researchers have termed the neuroanatomical findings from studies like these the **frontal brain hypothesis**.[41]

Other brain mechanisms may also be involved in aggression. In the 1990s, for example, an Italian research team identified what they termed "mirror cells" in the brain which become active as we watch other people move.[42] Mirror cells seem to be associated with movement pathways in the brains of the observer, but merely fire in sympathy with those whose movements are being observed. They do not produce movement in the observer, but seem to reflect a kind of interpretation of

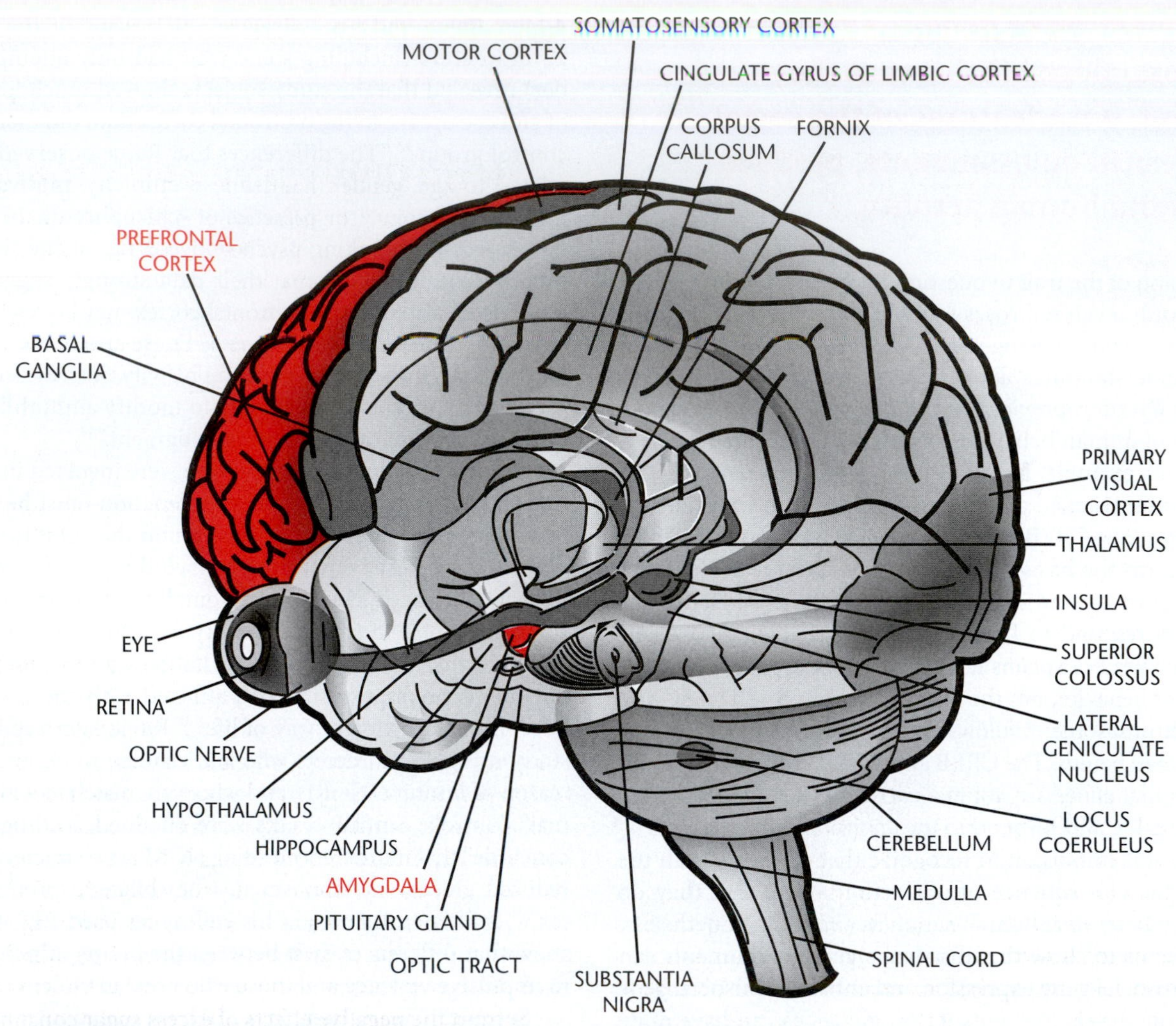

FIGURE 4–1 **The Human Brain Showing the Prefrontal Cortex and the Amygdala.**

what others are doing. Some researchers have suggested that people who are deficient in mirror cells, or whose mirror cells do not work the way they do in others, can produce a lack of empathy, psychopathy and even autism.[43]

Similarly, allergic reactions to common foods have been reported as the cause of violence and homicide by a number of investigators.[44] Some foods—including milk, citrus fruit, chocolate, corn, wheat, and eggs—are thought to produce allergic reactions in sensitive individuals, leading to a swelling of the brain and the brain stem. Such swelling is thought to impede the higher faculties, reducing people's sense of morality and creating conditions that support impulsive behavior. Involvement of the central nervous system in such allergies may reduce the amount of learning that occurs during childhood and may contribute to delinquency as well as to adult criminal behavior.

Additionally, physical injuries, emotional trauma, disease, and even long-term exposure to stress can lead to changes in the brain. One 2010 study found that the brains of monkeys whose mothers had the flu while they were pregnant exhibited physical changes similar to those in people with schizophrenia.[45] Researchers noted that their findings supported the suggestion that flu in human mothers-to-be can impact brain development.

Similarly, in 2010, Princeton University's Douglas S. Massey discovered a link between stressors in the social environment and brain structure. Massey, who studied the impact of social stratification on thought processes among residentially segregated minorities, found that "people who are exposed to high levels of stress over a prolonged period of time are at risk of having their brains re-wired in a way that leaves them with fewer cognitive resources."[46] Consequently, Massey concluded that residential segregation based on race produces life-long stressors, including exposure to violence, social disorder, and poverty, that result in high-risk behavior, including criminality, among deprived minorities.

Recently, some scientists have advanced the term **neuroplasticity** (sometimes called *brain plasticity* or *cortical plasticity*), to mean that the brain can alter its structure and function in response to experience or injury, and to explain why some people experience significant changes in personality when undergoing powerful new experiences. It is well known, for example, that when portions of the brain are physically damaged through trauma, stroke, or other types of injury, adjacent parts of the brain can assume some of the psychological or motor functions that would have otherwise been lost.

Think About It...

The concept of neuroplasticity seems to explain the profound personality changes that some people undergo as a result of powerful experiences. How might such experiences lead to changes in the brain?

Blend Images/Alamy

In 2011, researchers at University College London scanned the brains of dozens of children and found that those who had experienced physical violence at the hands of caregivers showed extra activity in the amygdala and the anterior insula—regions of the brain involved in threat perception and the anticipation of pain. The changes were the same, the researchers said, as those found in soldiers exposed to combat. Eamon McCrory, one of the researchers, explained that "Maltreated kids and active soldiers are adapting to survive in a threatening or dangerous environment."[47]

Finally, in 2013, researchers in New Mexico reported on having scanned the brains of 96 male prisoners just prior to their release to assess impulsivity and inhibitory control.[48] They found that prisoners who showed less activity in the anterior cingulate cortex (ACC)—which is located in the front of the brain—were about twice as likely to reoffend over the next four years, compared with those who showed more activity in that specific region of the brain.

In a symposium that concluded not long before this text went to press, researchers with the U.S. National Academy of Sciences and the Canadian Institute for Advanced Research reported advances in research on biological *embedding*, or the process by which social experiences change neural circuitry in the brain.[49] Changes in brain structure brought about by embedded stressful and traumatic childhood experiences were found to influence a child's development and to persist throughout life. In the words of the researchers, "experiences of childhood adversity affect cellular pathways and translate into the molecular and genetic changes that result in biological effects on development and health."[50] Some suggest that the interplay between heredity, biology, and the social and physical environments may be much more complicated than once thought and may provide the key nexus in any consideration of crime causation.

Biological theories are theories of criminality, not crime.

Body Chemistry and Criminality

Today's biological theorists have made significant progress in studies in linking violent or disruptive behavior to body chemistry. Body chemistry is influenced by things such as eating habits, vitamin deficiencies, environmental contaminants, and the endocrine system—and it is to those issues that we now turn.

Describe how body chemistry theories—including those involving diet, blood sugar levels, environmental contaminants, and hormones—explain crime.

Ingested Substances and Blood Sugar Levels

One of the first studies to focus on chemical imbalances in the body as a cause of crime was reported in the British medical journal *Lancet* in 1943.[51] The authors of the study linked murder to **hypoglycemia**, or low blood sugar. Low blood sugar, produced by too much insulin in the blood or by near-starvation diets, was said to reduce the mind's capacity to reason effectively or to judge the long-term consequences of behavior. More recent studies have linked excess consumption of refined white sugar to hyperactivity, aggressiveness, excitability, and impairment of the ability to make reasoned decisions, and popular books like *Sugar Blues* provide guides for individuals seeking to free themselves from the negative effects of excess sugar consumption.[52]

Even the courts have accepted the notion that excess sugar consumption resulting in hyperglycemia may be linked to crime. In the early 1980s, for example, Dan White, a former San Francisco police officer, was given a reduced sentence after his lawyers used what came to be known as the "Twinkie Defense."[53] They argued that White's nightlong binge on large numbers of Coca-Colas and Twinkies before he murdered San Francisco Mayor George Moscone and City Councilman Harvey Milk was evidence of White's unbalanced mental state; the consumption of junk food was presented as evidence of depression, as White was normally very health conscious.

Some studies have implicated food additives, such as the flavor enhancer monosodium glutamate, dyes, and artificial flavorings, in producing criminal violence.[54] Other research has found that coffee and sugar may trigger antisocial behavior;[55] researchers were led to these conclusions through finding that inmates consumed considerably greater amounts of coffee, sugar, and processed foods than others.[56] It is unclear, however, whether inmates drink more coffee because of boredom or whether "excitable" personalities feel a need for the kind of stimulation available through coffee consumption. On the other hand, habitual coffee drinkers in nonprison populations have

"You are what you eat" may contain more than a grain of truth.

THEORY in PERSPECTIVE

Modern Biological Theories

Modern biological theories of criminality stress the interaction between biological influences and the surrounding social and physical environments. Unlike earlier biological theories, modern biosocial perspectives recognize the role of the environment in shaping both biological processes and behavioral propensities that are related to those processes.

Genetics and Heritability

Genetic characteristics and variations in human chromosomes are thought to play a role in aggression and crime causation. Although contemporary criminologists do not believe that there is one single and identifiable "criminal gene," they do believe that individuals who are genetically predisposed to certain types of behavior may become aggressive or criminal through interaction with the surrounding physical and social environments. Sex-linked chromosomes have special explanatory power by virtue of the fact that the majority of violent offenders are male.

Period: 1965–present

Theorists: Patricia A. Jacobs, Nathalie Fontaine, H. Hilger Ropers, Han Brunner, Adrian Raine, Darrell J. Steffensmeier, Thomas Bernard

Concepts: genes, genome, chromosomes, heritability

Brain Dysfunction

Organic problems with the brain may lead to behavioral anomalies, including crime and deviance.

Period: 1990s–present

Theorists: Adrian Raine, and others

Concepts: neurocriminology, frontal brain hypothesis, neuroplasticity, embedding

Body Chemistry Theories

Violent or disruptive behavior can sometimes be linked to nutrition, vitamin deficiencies, and other conditions that affect the body. Studies of eating habits, endocrinology, and environmental contaminants have all contributed to advances in understanding such behavior.

Period: 1940s–present

Theorists: Adrian Raine, Stephen Schoenthaler, Alexander G. Schauss, David Fergusson

Concepts: hypoglycemia, frontal brain hypothesis, environmental pollution, psychobiotics, toxic metals, vitamins, food allergies, and environmental pollution, prenatal exposure to toxins

Hormones and Criminality

These biological theories explain violent or disruptive and criminal behavior by identifying hormonal influences on human cognition and action.

Period: 1940s–present

Theorists: Alan Booth, D. Wayne Osgood, Paul C. Bernhardt, Kevin Beaver, Anthony Walsh, Lee Ellis

Concepts: testosterone, evolutionary perspective, serotonin, premenstrual syndrome (PMS), hormones (testosterone, cortisol, norepinephrine) neurotransmitters (dopamine), monoamine oxidase inhibitors (MAOIs), neurophysiology

Biosocial Criminology

This theoretical perspective sees the interaction between biology and the physical and social environments as key to understanding human behavior, including criminality.

Period: 1987–present

Theorists: James Q. Wilson, Richard J. Herrnstein, Hans J. Eysenck, Anthony Walsh, Avshalom Caspi, Terrie E. Moffitt, Kevin M. Beaver

Concepts: Biosocial perspectives incorporate many of the concepts previously listed in this box, including genetics, heritability, hormones, brain dysfunction, body chemistry, the gender ratio problem, and natural and sexual selection. Neuroplasticity and epigenetics are additional associated concepts. The most important contribution from this perspective, however, comes in recognizing the influence of biological factors as they are mediated through the physical and social environments in producing criminal behavior

---

not been linked to crime, and other studies, like the one conducted by Mortimer Gross of the University of Illinois, showed no link between the amount of sugar consumed by inmates and hyperactivity.[57] Nonetheless, some prison programs have been designed to limit intake of dietary stimulants through nutritional management and substitution of artificial sweeteners for refined sugar.

Other studies appear to show that diets deficient in various vitamins and other nutrients can increase aggressiveness and agitation, and can open the door to crime. In recent years, for example, **Stephen Schoenthaler**, a researcher at the California State University in Stanislaus, has demonstrated significant declines in bad behavior in incarcerated adults and in school children receiving specifically designed vitamin and mineral supplementation.[58] In one of Schoenthaler's studies, for example, school children receiving vitamin supplements showed a 47% lower rate of antisocial behavior than children who received placebos.[59] More important, the drop in disciplinary infractions among children taking the supplements was due mostly to a decrease in infractions by those who had been identified as habitual offenders before entering the study.

Recently, a study of the relationship between omega-3 intake levels and chronic hostility among 3,600 urban young adults concluded that higher consumption of omega-3 fatty acids was related to significantly lower levels of hostility, with researchers stating that "high dietary intake of DHA and consumption of fish rich in omega-3 fatty acids may be related to lower likelihood of high hostility in young adulthood."[60] Similarly, a 2007 study conducted in the United Kingdom found that antisocial behavior could be reduced in children through dietary supplementation with polyunsaturated fatty acids.[61] Read more about diet and its possible contribution to criminal behavior at **Web Extra 4–7**.

High dietary intake of DHA and consumption of fish rich in omega-3 fatty acids may be related to lower likelihood of high hostility in young adulthood.

Environmental Pollution

Various substances found in our environment have been shown to be linked to criminal behavior. In 1997, British researchers Roger D. Masters, Brian Hone, and Anil Doshi published a study purporting to show that industrial and other forms of environmental pollution cause people to commit violent crimes.[62] The study used statistics from the Uniform Crime Reporting Program of the Federal Bureau of Investigation (FBI) and data from the U.S. Environmental Protection Agency's Toxic Release Inventory. A comparison between the two data sets showed a significant correlation between juvenile crime and high environmental levels of both lead and manganese. Masters and his colleagues suggested an explanation based on a *neurotoxicity hypothesis*. Another author stated, "According to this approach, toxic pollutants—specifically the toxic metals lead and manganese—cause learning disabilities, an increase in aggressive behavior, and—most importantly—loss of control over impulsive behavior. These traits combine with poverty, social stress, alcohol and drug abuse, individual character, and other social and psychological factors to produce individuals who commit violent crimes."[63]

It has long been established that lead is a potent neurotoxin, and that lead poisoning causes increased aggression, especially among young children, whose small, growing bodies are sensitive to even tiny amounts of lead. Lead interferes with normal brain development in children by destroying the myelin sheaths that surround brain cells, interfering with neurotransmission.

In 2012, a study published in *Environment Research* measured the impact of lead poisoning on crime rates over more than two decades, as affected children grew up and became criminals.[64] In the study, researchers examined the amounts of lead released in six cities from 1950 to 1985. They correlated these rates with levels of aggravated assaults 22 years later, after the exposed children had grown up. The study found that for each 1% increase in the amount of environmental lead, aggravated assaults rose 0.46%. "Up to 90 percent of the variation in aggravated assault across the cities is explained by the amount of lead dust released 22 years earlier," researchers wrote.[65]

The largest study of lead contamination and its effects on behavior was an examination of 1,000 black children in Philadelphia that showed that the level of exposure to lead was a reliable predictor of the number of juvenile offenses among the exposed male population, the seriousness of juvenile offenses, and the number of adult offenses. More recent studies, including many that Masters was unaware of, seem to support his thesis.[66]

The researchers reasoned that toxic metals affect individuals in complex ways. Because lead diminishes a person's normal ability to detoxify poisons, it may heighten the effects of alcohol and drugs; industrial pollution, automobile traffic, lead-based paints, and aging water-delivery systems are all possible sources of lead contamination. In a recent interview, Roger D. Masters, Research Professor at Dartmouth College, noted that "The presence of pollution is as big a factor [in crime causation] as poverty. It's the breakdown of the inhibition mechanism that's the key to violent behavior."[67] When brain chemistry is altered by exposure to heavy metals and other toxins, people lose the natural restraint that holds their violent tendencies in check.

More recent studies have focused on **prenatal substance exposure** to things like marijuana, tobacco smoke, and alcohol. In 2000, for example, L. Goldschmidt and colleagues reported the results of a ten-year study that monitored the development of children of more than 600 low-income women. The study, which began during the women's pregnancies, found that prenatal marijuana use was significantly related to increased hyperactivity, impulsivity, inattention, increased delinquency, and externalizing problems;[68] the findings remained significant even when researchers controlled for other lifestyle features.

In 1998, **David Fergusson** and colleagues, in a study of 1,022 New Zealand children who had been followed for 18 years, found that "children whose mothers smoked one pack of cigarettes or more per day during their pregnancy had mean rates of conduct disorder symptoms that were twice as high as those found among children born to mothers who did not smoke during their pregnancy."[69] The observed relationship was twice as strong among male teens as among females. Similar relationships between prenatal smoking and both aggression and hyperactivity in later life have been reported by Dutch researchers.[70] A similar 2006 meta-analysis by researchers at Washington State University found that smoking by pregnant mothers contributed slightly to their children's subsequent antisocial behavior.[71]

Prenatal alcohol exposure also seems to be linked to delinquency and psychiatric problems later in life.[72] Learn more about the role of environmental contaminants, fetal alcohol exposure, and other factors and their contributions to criminality at **Web Extra 4–8**. Read about pollution's possible link to crime and toxic threats to child development at **Web Extras 4–9** and **4–10**.

Psychobiotics

Within the last few years, a new field of study called **psychobiotics** has begun to emerge that focuses on the psychological and behavioral effects that bacteria can have on the mind, feelings, emotions, and behavior.[73] The central focus of study is what are referred to as *gut bacteria*—or those bacteria that live in the digestive system. Although bacteria are single-celled organisms, they are generally far smaller than human tissue cells; and there are far more bacteria living in a symbiotic relationship in any mammal than that animal has body cells. In human beings, gut bacteria, taken in total, weigh more than the human brain.

Recent research has demonstrated that gut bacteria carry a vast array of genes that can produce thousands of chemicals. Many of these chemicals, once produced, are absorbed through the digestive system into the blood. Some of them are linked to brain signaling, and include bacteria-produced dopamine, serotonin, and gamma-aminobarytic acid (GABA).[74] In other words, gut bacteria appear to produce chemical messengers that interact with the brain and nervous system. Some studies have even led to the notion that chemicals from gut bacteria help to build and shape the physical structure of the developing brain.

Studies of mice raised in the absence of gut bacteria showed that memory, emotional state, and behavior were far different among the subject mice than those exposed to normal environmental bacteria. These studies give support to earlier reports that the absence of the bacterium *Bifidobacterium infantis* in the intestines of human beings can lead to depression. Further, neuroimaging studies show that an identifiable mixture of specific digestive bacteria are associated with "the reduced response of a brain network involved in the processing of emotion and sensation."[75]

Scientists now speculate that a chemical gut–brain axis exists within the body, with the two body regions involved in a constant form of chemical communication. They suggest that introducing the proper bacteria into the digestive system could produce positive results in mood and behavior by reducing blood levels of the stress hormone cortisol and by fighting inflammatory molecules produced by the immune system. The study of the interaction between gut bacteria and behavior is still in its infancy, and more studies will be required before any definitive statements can be made about the relationship between such bacteria and neurobiological conditions.

Heart Rate and Crime

One of the clearest biological relationships established to date is that between resting heart rate and criminality. In 2014, a group of researchers declared that "a low resting heart rate is considered the best-replicated biological correlate of antisocial behavior."[76] Heart rate is determined by the activity of the autonomic nervous system (ANS), and numerous early studies implicated ANS involvement in psychopathy, aggression, and antisocial behavior.[77] Studies of children as young as three, that measured heart rates have been able to predict with considerable accuracy which children will become antisocial in their early- to mid-teens.[78] The relationship between low resting heart rate and crime, while well established, has not been fully explained. Some researchers suggest that low resting heart rate is a marker of low autonomic arousal, and that low arousal is an unpleasant physiological state akin to boredom—causing people who routinely experience it to seek added stimulation and excitement. Others say that a low heart rate reflects a relative lack of fear, and that fearlessness can lead to poor choices and be reflected in increased aggression.[79] It should be noted that low resting heart rate appears to be associated only with antisocial behavior among males and not females; and that low heart rates are frequently found in well-conditioned athletes—and that no one has suggested that athletic conditioning plays a role in crime causation.

Hormones and Criminality

A **hormone** is a chemical substance produced by the body that regulates and controls the activity of certain cells or organs. Hormones have come under scrutiny as potential behavioral determinants. The male sex hormone **testosterone**, for example, has been linked to aggression, and appears to play an important role in increasing the propensity toward violence and aggression among men. Testosterone is a steroid hormone from the androgen group that is primarily secreted by the testes. Although females produce some testosterone, it is normally present in far higher quantities in the blood and tissues of males.

A few authors have suggested that testosterone is the agent *primarily* responsible for male criminality and that its relative lack in women leads them to commit fewer crimes. A growing body of evidence supports just such a hypothesis. Studies have shown, for example, that female fetuses exposed to elevated testosterone levels during gestation develop masculine characteristics, including a muscular build and a demonstrably greater tendency toward aggression later in life.[80] Other studies show that testosterone continues to strongly influence behavior, and that it creates what some have called "sexually dismorphic brains."[81]

Most studies on the subject have consistently shown a relationship between high blood testosterone levels and increased aggressiveness in men, and focused studies have unveiled a direct relationship between the amount of the chemical present and the degree of violence used by sex offenders.[82] Other researchers have linked anabolic steroid abuse among bodybuilders to destructive urges and psychosis.[83] Anabolic steroids are man-made drugs that have similar effects to testosterone in the body.

Some contemporary investigations have demonstrated a link between testosterone levels and aggression in teenagers,[84] and others have shown that adolescent problem behavior and teenage violence rise in proportion to the amount of testosterone in the blood of young men.[85]

In what may be the definitive work to date on the subject, **Alan Booth** and **D. Wayne Osgood** concluded that there is a "moderately strong relationship between testosterone and adult deviance" but suggested that the relationship "is largely mediated by the influence of testosterone on social integration and on prior involvement in juvenile delinquency."[86] In other words, measurably high levels of testosterone in the blood of young men may have some effect on behavior, but that effect is likely to be moderated by the social environment.

A few limited studies have attempted to measure the effects of testosterone on women. Although women's bodies manufacture roughly one-tenth the amount of the hormone secreted by men, subtle changes in testosterone levels in women have been linked to changes in personality and sexual behavior.[87] One such study showed that relatively high blood levels of testosterone in female inmates were associated with "aggressively dominant behavior" in prison.[88]

Fluctuations in the level of female hormones may also bear some relationship to law violation. In 1980, a British court exonerated Christine English of charges that she murdered her live-in lover after English admittedly ran him over with her car after an argument; English's defense rested on the fact that she was suffering from premenstrual syndrome (PMS) at the time of the homicide. An expert witness, Dr. Katharina Dalton, testified at

Aggressive behavior in men may be influenced by high testosterone levels combined with low brain levels of the neurotransmitter serotonin.

WHO'S TO BLAME—The Individual or Society?

Hormones and Criminal Behavior

Lamont Ridgeway, 22, was arrested and charged with rape after 21-year-old Nicole Bachman called police to her Minneapolis home at 2:00 A.M. Ridgeway and Bachman had met in an evening art class at the local community college, and Bachman invited Ridgeway to her apartment for a glass of wine after the class was over. Officers couldn't help but notice that Bachman was an unusually attractive young woman whose clothes were in disarray and that she was visibly intoxicated and slurred her words as she spoke; Ridgeway was passed out on her couch, apparently after having had far too much to drink.

"He raped me!" Bachman told the two officers who responded to her call for help. "I told him to stop, and he wouldn't," she said.

Ridgeway was roused from sleep, arrested, searched, handcuffed, and taken to jail, where he was booked and charged with rape. After being advised of his rights not to speak and to have a lawyer represent him, he decided to tell the officers who were questioning him that it wasn't really rape. "She came on to me," he said. "She took her blouse off, then her pants. And she gave me a lot to drink. Yeah, she said 'No,' but by then we were already there. I couldn't stop. Why would she want to, anyway?"

When Ridgeway's lawyer arrived, he advised Ridgeway not to say anything more. The lawyer, hired by Ridgeway's wealthy parents, read the statement that he had given to the police and then hired a psychiatrist to help in building a defense that might stand up in court.

When the case went to trial two months later, the psychiatrist testified as an expert witness for the defense. He told the jury that blood tests showed that Ridgeway had abnormally large amounts of testosterone naturally occurring in his blood, that testosterone was the chemical messenger responsible for the male sex drive (which, he said, differed substantially from that of women), and that Ridgeway had consequently been unable to control his behavior on the night of the alleged rape. "The young man was simply doing what his hormones made him do," the psychiatrist testified. "It's my professional opinion," he concluded, "that with that amount of testosterone affecting his judgment, he really didn't have much choice in his behavioral responses once he was offered alcohol and was then visually stimulated by the young woman's removal of her clothes. If this was my patient," the psychiatrist added, "I'd treat him with the testosterone antagonist Depo-Provera, and we would see the strength of his sex drive substantially diminished. You could be sure that this kind of thing wouldn't happen again."

Kanzefar/Fotolia

In response, the prosecution called their own expert, a noted biochemist who, citing various studies, said that there was no clearly established link between blood levels of testosterone and aggressive sexual behavior in human beings. "Even if there were," he said, "people are not mindless animals. We have free choice. We are not so driven by our blood chemistry that we cannot decide what we are going to do in any given situation."

Think About It

1. With which expert witness do you agree more—the psychiatrist or the biochemist? Why?
2. Do you believe that blood chemistry can ever be an explanation for behavior? For crime?
3. If you answered "Yes" to the previous question, then do you think that blood chemistry can ever be an effective excuse for criminality? If you answered "No," then why not?
4. How do our understandings of criminal motivation and crime causality influence our policies on the treatment, punishment, and reformation of those who violate the law?

Note: Who's to Blame boxes provide fictionalized critical thinking opportunities, and are not actual cases.

the trial that PMS had caused English to be "irritable, aggressive, and confused, with loss of self-control."[89]

Serotonin

A 1997 study by **Paul C. Bernhardt** found that testosterone might not act alone in promoting aggression.[90] Bernhardt discovered that aggressive behavior in men may be influenced by high testosterone levels combined with low brain levels of the neurotransmitter **serotonin**. Serotonin, a neurotransmitter, is a hormone that is commonly found in the pineal gland, the digestive tract, the central nervous system, and in blood platelets. Serotonin plays an important role in the regulation of learning, mood, and sleep, as well as in the constriction of blood vessels. Most of the body's serotonin is in the intestines, where it regulates intestinal movements. The rest is found in the neurons of the central nervous system.

Bernhardt postulated that testosterone's true role is to produce dominance-seeking behavior, but not necessarily overt aggression. According to Bernhardt, when individuals are frustrated by their inability to achieve dominance, serotonin acts to reduce the negative psychological impact of frustration, producing calmer responses. Men whose brains are lacking in serotonin, however, feel the effects of frustration more acutely and therefore tend to respond to frustrating circumstances more aggressively, especially when testosterone levels are high.

Serotonin has been called a "behavior-regulating chemical," and animal studies have demonstrated a link between low levels of serotonin in the brain and aggressive behavior. For example, monkeys with low serotonin levels in their brains have been found to be more likely to bite, slap, and chase others of their kind. Studies at the National Institute on Alcohol Abuse and Alcoholism have linked low serotonin levels in humans

Low cortisol levels were associated with early onset of aggression.

to impulsive crimes. Men convicted of premeditated murder, for example, have been found to have normal serotonin levels, whereas those convicted of crimes of passion had lower levels.[91]

One study of 781 men and women age 21 found a clear relationship between elevated *blood* levels of serotonin (which correspond to lower *brain* levels of the chemical) and violence in men.[92] According to the study's authors, "This is the first study to demonstrate that a possible index of serotonergic function is related to violence in the general population. The epidemiological serotonin effect was not small [but rather] indicated a moderate effect size in the population."[93]

Similar research by Swedish neuropsychiatrists in 2003 found that a "dysregulation of serotonin" in the brain and central nervous system could lead to increased impulsivity, irresponsibility, aggression, and need for stimulation.[94] The researchers examined the cerebrospinal fluid (CSF) of 28 violent and sexual offenders and noted that an imbalance between levels of serotonin and dopamine was highly associated with psychopathic traits.

In other studies, hormones, such as testosterone and the thyroid hormone T_3, along with the neurotransmitter dopamine and the stress hormones cortisol and norepinephrine, have all been implicated in delinquency and poor impulse control.[95]

A few years ago, two separate Swedish studies found evidence suggesting that elevated levels of the thyroid hormone T_3 were related to alcoholism, psychopathy, and criminality.[96] Blood serum levels of the thyroid hormone T_4 (thyroxine), on the other hand, were negatively related to antisocial behavior. The researchers concluded that the results of their studies indicate an intimate relationship between T_3 and T_4 and abuse and antisocial behavior. They emphasize the importance of further studies on T_3 as a biological marker for abuse, social deviance, and repeated violent behavior.

Not all hormones produce aggression or are linked to violence, of course. A 2012 study of what has been billed as the "trust molecule" showed that increased levels of a chemical messenger known as oxytocin helps to explain why some people are routinely giving and altruistic, while others are seen as coldhearted and stingy.[97] In the brain oxytocin appears to be the chemical that creates bonds of trust in all types of human relationships. Although oxytocin is primarily a female reproductive hormone that controls contractions during labor, it is also responsible for the bond that forms between mothers and their babies. It is even thought to be responsible for the warm feelings that people feel during lovemaking, or when giving and sharing hugs. The 2012 study found that when oxytocin levels rise in the blood, people respond generously and caringly even to strangers.

As Georgia State University criminologist Leah E. Daigle points out, however, "changes in hormone levels alone do not account for aggressive behavior. Instead, these hormonal changes may affect a third, unspecified variable (such as self-control or social bonds) that lead to aggressive responses."[98] In other words, says Daigle, "rather than directly affecting behavior, hormones may instead interact with social factors to produce criminal behavior."

▶ Biosocial Criminology

In the mid-1980s, criminologist **James Q. Wilson** and psychologist **Richard J. Herrnstein** teamed up to write *Crime and Human Nature*, a book-length treatise that restated and refined many of the arguments proposed by biological criminologists over the preceding century.[99] Part of their purpose was to reopen discussion of biological causes of crime. "We want to show," Herrnstein said, "that the pendulum is beginning to swing away from a totally sociological explanation of crime."[100] Their avowed goal was "not to state a case just for genetic factors, but to state a comprehensive theory of crime that draws together all the different factors that cause criminal behavior."[101]

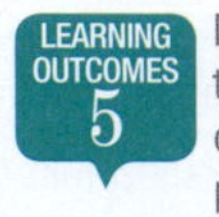

Discuss biosocial theories and the role of the gender ratio problem in contemporary criminology.

Wilson and Herrnstein cited several constitutional factors that they believed made important and undeniable contributions to criminal behavior:[102] (1) gender (male), (2) age (young adulthood), (3) body type (mesomorphic), (4) intelligence (low), and (5) personality (impulsive, aggressive, and cruel).

Although personality, behavioral problems, and intelligence may be related to and at least partially determined by environment, the authors said that "each involves some genetic inheritance." Wilson and Herrnstein recognized social factors in the development of personality but suggested that constitutional factors predispose a person to specific types of behavior and that societal *reactions* to such predispositions may determine, to a large degree, the form of continued behavior.

In the 1990s, **Anthony Walsh** of Boise State University, who is one of today's best known proponents of **biosocial criminology**, continued the movement toward recognizing biology's contributions to understanding criminal behavior. Walsh emphasized the importance of the *interaction* between biology and the environment in the formation of behavioral responses to given situations. "Biological factors do not operate in an environmental vacuum," said Walsh, "nor do environmental factors operate in a biological vacuum, and we must cease formulating our theories as if they do."[103]

Walsh became one of the first proponents of contemporary biosocial criminology—a scientific endeavor that attempts to take all that is known about the biological underpinnings of human behavior, and to use that knowledge to assess how human biology interacts with the surrounding physical, cultural, and social environments in producing a criminal event. Biosocial criminology is not so much a theory about crime as it is a perspective on criminality that recognizes the importance of the interaction between biology and the surrounding physical and social environments.

Walsh observes that biosocial perspectives are theories of criminality, not crime.[104] He goes on to explain that crime is

Biological factors do not operate in an environmental vacuum, nor do environmental factors operate in a biological vacuum.

a "legal label" that is placed on specific behaviors that violate the criminal law. Criminality, on the other hand, says Walsh, "is a property of individuals, a continuous trait that is itself an amalgam of other continuous traits, and thus belongs to a more inclusive kind of criminology."[105] According to Walsh, criminality can be seen as the willingness to violate individual rights and social norms, whether or not such behavior is against the law. Criminality, says Walsh, consists of "a relative lack of empathy, conscience, self-control, and fear, as well as self-centeredness, and a penchant for risky behavior."[106] Seen this way, biosocial explanations of criminality are more likely to be couched in terms of a propensity for violence, aggression, deceit, recklessness, fearlessness, and so on—and features of the surrounding environment determine how such propensities will be expressed.

Behavioral science expert Diana Fishbein of the Research Triangle Institute (RTI) puts it this way: "numerous behavioral science subdisciplines, including molecular and behavioral genetics, neurobiology, physiology, psychology, cognitive neuroscience, endocrinology, and forensic psychiatry, provide substantial evidence" that certain traits possessed by individuals lead to increased risk for antisocial behavior.[107]

Fishbein notes that "the vast range of studies from these disciplines on vulnerability to antisocial personality disorder, violence, and drug abuse . . . reveal a pattern that may characterize vulnerable individuals." These patterns, which include individual biological differences in resting heart rate, hormone levels, and electroencephalogram (EEG) recordings, demonstrate that "vulnerability to antisocial behavior is partially a function of genetic and biological makeup," which is expressed, says Fishbein, "during childhood as particular behavioral, cognitive, and psychological traits, such as impulsivity, attention deficits, aggressiveness, and conduct disorder."

Echoing Walsh, Fishbein notes that "biological differences do not function in a vacuum to increase risk." Instead, she writes, that biological factors interact dynamically with many social and environmental conditions "to contribute to or protect from social dysfunction." It is this emphasis on *interaction* between biology and the environment—especially culture and the social environment—that differentiates biosocial criminology from other biological perspectives on crime.

Researchers are beginning to understand just how complex the relationship between biology, behavior, and the social environment can be. Biosocial criminology attempts to recognize this complexity by embracing the role of a multitude of factors leading to criminality (Figure 4–2), to include the interaction of those factors with the surrounding environment.

Gender Differences in Criminality

Numerous contemporary writers propose that criminologists must recognize that "the male is much more criminalistic than the female."[108] With the exception of crimes such as

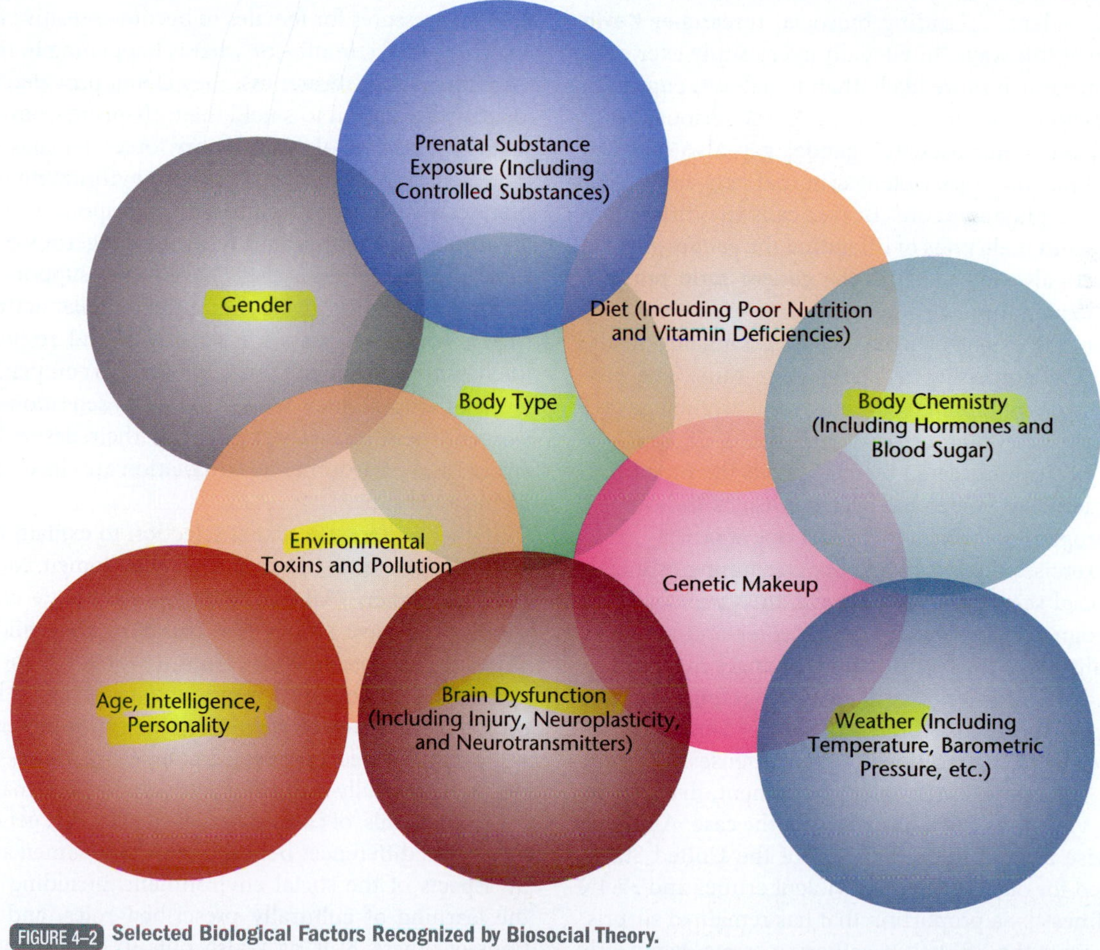

FIGURE 4–2 **Selected Biological Factors Recognized by Biosocial Theory.**
Source: From *Criminology Today: An Integrative Introduction,* 7e by Frank A. Schmalleger. Copyright © 2014 by Pearson Education. Used by permission of Pearson Education.

Think About It…

Biosocial perspectives recognize the complexity of the interaction between biology and the surrounding physical and social environments. Do they have more explanatory power than theories that are purely sociological? If so, why?

Photocreo Bednarek/Fotolia

prostitution and shoplifting, the number of crimes committed by men routinely far exceeds the number of crimes committed by women in almost all categories, and when women commit crimes, they are far more likely to assume the role of followers than leaders.[109] Leading biosocial researcher **Kevin Beaver** explains it this way: "In virtually every study ever conducted, males are much more likely than females to engage in violence, aggression, and serious crimes. As the seriousness of the offense/behavior increases, the gender gap also tends to increase, such that the most violent criminal acts are almost exclusively a male phenomenon." Beaver calls the differences between female and male rates of offending the *gender gap*. He and other writers also refer to it as the **gender ratio problem** and call for its explanation.[110]

The data on the extent of male–female criminality in the United States show surprising regularity over time: The proportion of homicides committed by men versus women has remained more or less constant for decades (Figure 4–3). Similarly, the proportion of men murdered by men versus the proportion of women murdered by women has been consistent, indicating a much greater propensity for men to murder one another.

If culture exercises the major role in determining criminality, as many social scientists today believe, then we would expect to see recognizable increases in the degree and nature of female criminality over time, especially as changes in socialization practices, cultural roles, and other ethnographic patterns increase the opportunity for women to commit what had previously been regarded as traditionally male offenses. With the exception of a few crimes, such as embezzlement, drug abuse, and liquor-law violations, such has not been the case. Although women comprise 51% of the population of the United States, they are arrested for only 19.9% of all violent crimes and 37.4% of property crimes[111]—a proportion that has remained surprisingly constant since the FBI began gathering crime data nearly a century ago—in spite of all the cultural changes creating new possibilities for women to commit crimes. These gender differences also can be seen in cross-cultural studies.

Penn State criminologist **Thomas Bernard**, and colleagues Jeffrey Snipes and Alexander Gerould, have advanced the proposition that "the issue of why always and everywhere males commit more criminal acts than females is the 'single most important fact that criminology theories must be able to explain.'"[112]

Biosocial criminologists suggest that the organic correlates of gender provide the needed explanation. Walsh, for example, says that the gender ratio problem is only a problem "if we are constrained to operate under sociology's strict environmentalist paradigm, which is suspicious of psychological or biological factors that differentiate among individuals and categories of individuals. . . ."[113] If we admit, Walsh writes, that "there is something about gender per se" that is responsible for the observed differences, the problem is resolved.[114]

One of the primary contemporary paradigms useful in understanding gender differences in criminality is the concept of **sexual selection**. Sexual selection, which is a form of natural selection that influences an individual's ability to attain or choose a mate, derives from Charles Darwin's theory of evolution.[115] Although Darwin was most concerned with explaining how the process of natural selection (survival of the fittest) determines trait differences between species, the concept of sexual selection seeks to explain male/female differences within species. Contemporary writers, for example, claim that the important roles of child bearing, child protection, and child rearing created evolutional pressures for females to become sensitive to immediate environmental stimuli—or what is happening in their immediate vicinity. Such awareness, they claim, provided the ability to identify threats and to shield their offspring from danger. Consequently, because of evolutionary forces, females today may be more sensitive than men to many environmental stimuli, are more easily aroused, are quicker to respond to what is going on around them, and tend to avoid dangerous or threatening situations. Some researchers have found support for just such an argument in discoveries that the reticular activating system (RAS), which accounts for sensitivity and response, is more finely tuned in women than in men.[116] To compensate for lower levels of arousal, men tend to be more sensation-seeking than women, these researchers say, and their desire for increased arousal and environmental stimulation are closely linked to risk taking and crime.[117]

Other writers use sexual selection to explain differences in levels of aggression between men and women. Men, they note, can father many children with relatively little effort, whereas women can have only a few children; and child bearing requires much greater effort from a woman than it does from a man.[118] Consequently, reproductive success, a key theme in evolutionary theories, drives males toward greater levels of aggression—especially toward competing males—and may result in successfully acquiring access to fertile females.

None of this, of course, denies the fact that genetically based behavioral differences between men and women are moderated by aspects of the social environment, including socialization, the learning of culturally prescribed roles, and the expectations of others. Still, as Walsh puts it, criminological theories that continue to deny the important role of biology and gender

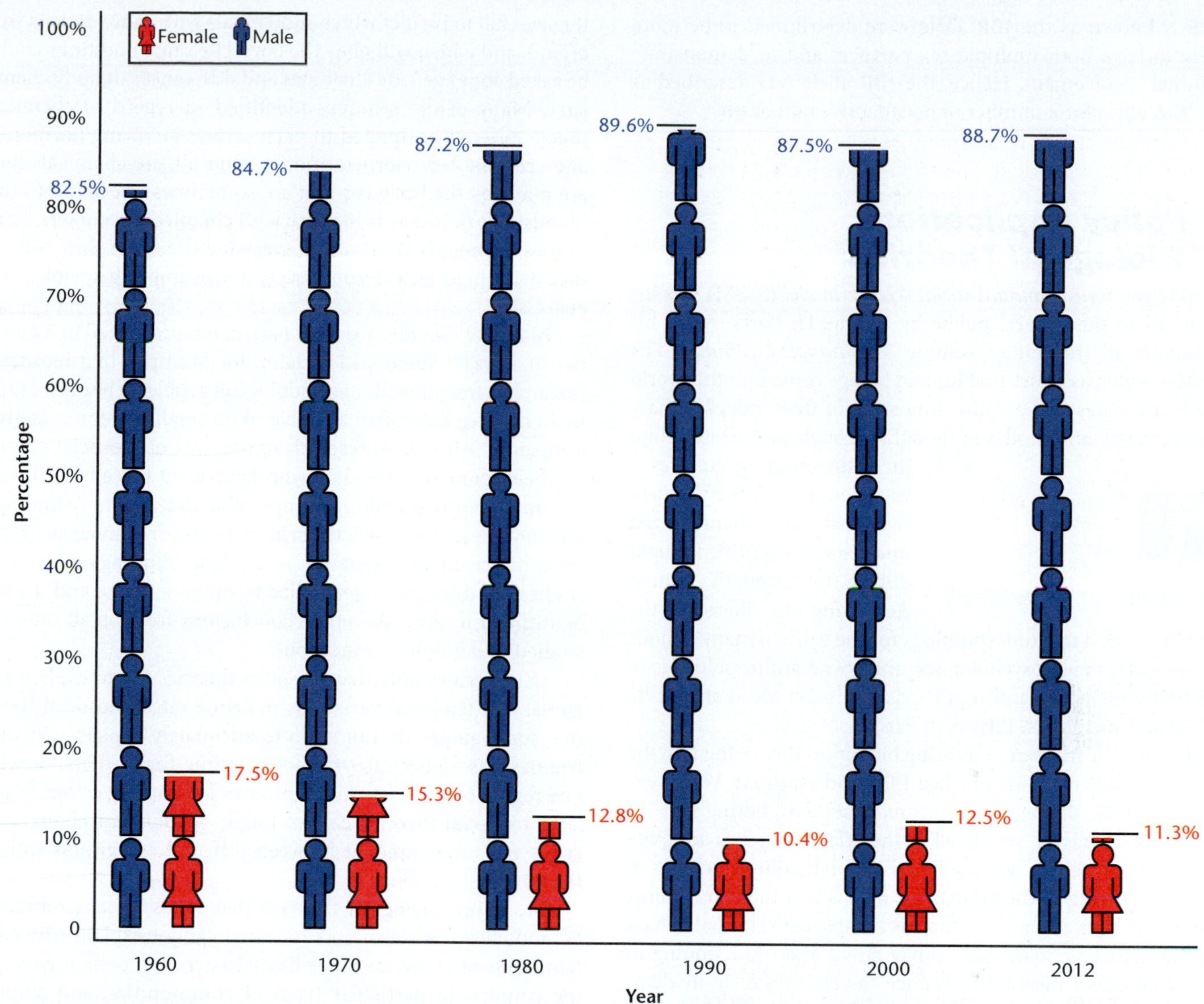

FIGURE 4–3 **Male and Female Murder Perpetrators as a Percentage of All Arrests for Homicide, 1960–2012.**
Source: Federal Bureau of Investigation.

differences in criminality are akin to the "drunk who knew he hadn't lost his keys under the lamppost, but perversely continued looking there anyway because that's where the light is." In sum, Walsh concludes, "we must realize that gender socialization rests on the solid bedrock of sex-differentiated biology forged by countless thousands of years of contrasting sexual selection pressures."[119]

Evolutionary Theory

In 2010, Kevin M. Beaver, John P. Wright, and Anthony Walsh discovered that the number of sexual partners that men have is associated with criminal involvement.[120] In other words, the greater the number of partners, the higher the likelihood of criminal involvement. The researchers noted, however, that "the question . . . is why there is a high degree of covariation between criminal involvement and the number of sexual partners."

Genetically based behavioral differences between men and women are moderated by aspects of the social environment.

Utilizing an **evolutionary perspective**—or one that (1) seeks to explain behavior with reference to human evolutionary history[121] and (2) recognizes the influence that genes have over human traits—they came to the conclusion that behavioral traits are "manifestations of multiple genes working independently and synergistically" in response to the environment. They proposed that some of the same genes must be involved in both reproductive activity and criminality. Through an analysis of data from the National Longitudinal Study of Adolescent Health (also known as Add Health), they concluded that differing versions of the dopamine transporter gene known as DAT1 were "related to both a greater number of sexual partners and to increased involvement in antisocial behavior for adult males."

Different versions of the same gene are referred to as *polymorphism*, and the word *allele* (used earlier in this chapter) is used to describe an alternative form of a gene that is located at a given position on a specific chromosome. Men who possessed what is known as the 10R allele were determined to be more likely to have both multiple sex partners and to demonstrate criminal involvement. Hence, the 10R allele was described as the "risk allele for a number of maladaptive outcomes."

Policy Implications of Biological Theories

In 1992 the term *standard social science model* (SSSM) was introduced to the general public by Jerome H. Barkow and his colleagues in the edited volume *The Adapted Mind*.[122] The SSSM—which assumes that human beings come into this world like blank slates and acquire almost all of their values, behavioral patterns, and modes of thought through socialization into their surrounding cultures—was identified as the perspective that had characterized much social scientific thought during the twentieth century. According to Barkow, the SSSM provided the underpinnings for the work of many famous sociologists, social psychologists, and social anthropologists of the 1900s, including anthropologists Margaret Mead and Leslie White and sociologist Ellsworth Faris.

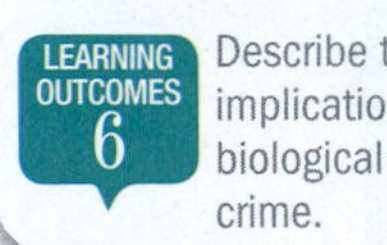

Describe the policy implications of modern biological theories of crime.

In 1997, in an attempt to bring biological theorizing into the criminological mainstream, Lee Ellis and Anthony Walsh expanded on the theme of *genetic predispositions*, noting that "in the case of behavior, nearly all of the effects of genes are quite indirect because they are mediated through complex chains of events occurring in the brain. This means that there are almost certainly no genes for something as complex as criminal behavior. Nevertheless, many genes may affect brain functioning in ways that either increase or reduce the chances of individuals learning various complex behavior patterns, including behavior patterns that happen to be so offensive to others that criminal sanctions have been instituted to minimize their recurrence."[123] More than a decade later, Terrie Moffitt, through a meta-analysis of more than 100 studies of genetic influences on antisocial behavior, was able to conclude that "genes influence 40% to 50% of population variation in antisocial behavior."[124]

Critiques of Biological and Biosocial Theories

This chapter discusses a variety of biological and biosocial approaches to explaining crime, including those related to genetics, brain dysfunction, body chemistry, and contemporary understandings of evolutionary theory. Many such perspectives have been criticized because they fail to accurately predict criminality while purporting to understand its causes. If, for example, a particular defect in the brain is associated with a greater tendency toward law violation, then why would such theories fail to predict which individuals with those deficits will offend, and which will obey the law? The same questions could be asked about genetic attributes and differences in body chemistry. Many of the critiques identified in regard to chemical precursors can be applied to perspectives involving hormones and criminal behavior. Hormones, after all, are chemicals that are made by the body (or that are sometimes injected into the bloodstream). Just as is the case with chemical precursors, hormones apparently don't affect everyone the same way. Not all men with high testosterone levels, for example, are violent or aggressive.

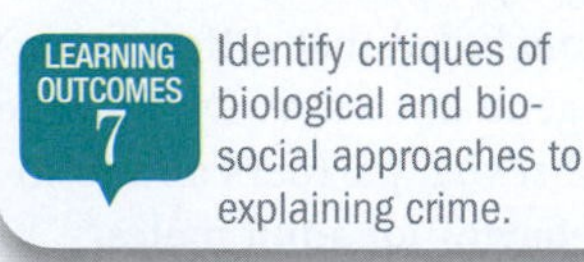

Identify critiques of biological and biosocial approaches to explaining crime.

Biosocial theories, for their part, can be criticized in a number of ways.[125] Some critics claim, for example, that biosocial research is fraught with methodological problems because studies in the area have often been based on small, unrepresentative samples.[126] Also, most research in the area of biosocial theory has been done on offenders who have been placed in clinical treatment settings, making it impossible to tell if study findings are only relevant to convicted criminals in correctional facilities, or to the criminal population as a whole. Findings from such studies are difficult to generalize to other settings, and it may be difficult to draw definitive conclusions from small samples studied under unique conditions.

Other critics note that biosocial theories fail to explain regional and temporal variations in crime rates. Biosocial theories, for example, do not seem to adequately explain why one country has higher rates of violent crime than others, or why one region of a city has different rates of property crime. Similarly, biosocial theories cannot totally account for changes in crime rates over time, or between different age groups within the same population.

Moreover, biological theories that focus on environmental and chemical precursors to crime cannot explain why certain kinds of crime are more likely to occur in certain parts of the country, in particular types of communities, and among members of specific subcultures rather than in others. Such differences imply that much more is at work than chemicals themselves and suggest that cultural differences play a significant role in criminality.

Critics also claim that theories involving chemical precursors cannot account for changes in crime rates over time. Crime rates have trended substantially downward over the past two or three decades, during the same time period that exposure to chemical substances of all types throughout the general population has expanded.

Finally, some biosocial criminologists have been accused of racial and class bias for failing to explain why disproportionate numbers of certain kinds of crime are committed by poor people and by racial and ethnic minorities.[127] Critics say that it would be more useful to focus on social settings rather than on biological variables to explain such differences, and that elements of the social environment—including things such as racism, oppression, discrimination, and economic strain—are more effective at explaining differences in criminality between racial and ethnic groups and social classes. These critics also note that some people may try to use biosocial perspectives to support their own biases, and to justify continued social inequality.

THE CASE

Jodi Arias

How could a petite, soft-spoken woman who had no record of past violence shoot her former lover in the face, slit his throat from ear to ear, and stab him 27 times?

Jodi Arias first denied any role in the 2008 killing, then confessed, claiming she did it in self-defense. At the end of a four-month trial, however, a jury found her guilty of first-degree murder, deciding it was so brutal that it could merit the death penalty.

The victim, Travis Alexander, was a leader of the Mormon Church in the Phoenix, Arizona, area who hid his steamy sexual relationship with Arias even from friends. Her highly attended trial was punctuated with photos of the couple having kinky sex, a 30-minute tape of phone sex between them and photos of them both naked, apparently just moments before the murder was committed.[i]

The prosecution portrayed the pretty Northern Californian as an obsessed stalker who went ballistic when Alexander wanted to date other women. Before the murder, witnesses said she slashed his tires, looked into his windows, and hacked into his Facebook account.[ii]

However, an examination of Arias's past revealed little evidence of the sex-crazed stalker that seemed to emerge after she met Alexander. She claimed her parents had beaten her, but she had no problems with previous boyfriends, at work, or with friends. She had no arrests, convictions, or other legal issues.

Arias grew up in the small town of Yreka, California. "She was a sweet girl, you know, the kind of girl that you just always wanted to be around," her best friend told the HLN network. She "definitely wasn't" promiscuous, she added.[iii]

The obsessive, on-again, off-again relationship between Arias and Alexander ended up in murder. They met in Las Vegas in September 2006, at a conference for Prepaid Legal Services, a nationwide company where they both worked. They were both single and about the same age. In addition to being a company salesman, he worked as a motivational speaker. She had recently discovered the Mormon faith. Two months later, he baptized her into the faith and they had sex afterward.[iv]

Alexander's image as a devout Mormon virgin, which he projected to friends, clashed with the erotic adventures he had with Arias. A friend who lived with Alexander testified that he did not admit he was having sex, saying it could have led to excommunication from the church. Arias's defense attorney said she was "his dirty little secret."[v] The prosecution speculated that Arias took pictures of Alexander in sex acts to blackmail him if he tried to leave her.

The couple carried on a long-distance romance between her home in California and his in Mesa, Arizona. They broke up in June 2007 but continued to see each other for sex. Arias moved to Mesa that summer, waiting tables and cleaning Alexander's home for income, then moved back to California in the spring of 2008.

AP Photo/The Arizona Republic/Rob Schumacher, Pool/Thomson Reuters (Markets) LLC

Jodi Arias, convicted in 2013 of the brutal murder of her boyfriend, Travis Alexander. Why did the televised trial draw such large media audiences?

"I want you to understand how evil I think you are," Alexander wrote her in an email a week before he died.[vi] He had invited another woman to go to Cancun, Mexico, with him. In early June, Arias drove to Mesa, arriving at his home at 4 A.M., and killed him later that day.

Friends found Alexander's mangled body slouched in his shower. Arias's palm print was found in blood at the scene, along with nude photos of them from the day of the killing. When she was later arrested, she denied any involvement and blamed it on masked intruders. It was two years later that she first admitted to killing Alexander, saying he became violent after she dropped his new camera, which she was using to take pictures of their sex play.

At the trial, she showed little emotion when asked about the killing. The jurors didn't accept Arias's plea of self-defense and wrote to her: "After all the lies you have told, why should we believe you now?"

Notes

[i]Tamara Holder, "Four Reasons Why Jodi Arias Should be Found Guilty of Murder," FoxNews, April 2, 2013, http://www.foxnews.com/opinion/2013/04/02/four-reasons-why-jodi-arias-should-be-found-guilty-murder (accessed May 8, 2014).

[ii]Dale Archer, "Is Jodi Arias a Sociopath?" *Psychology Today*, March 11, 2013, http://www.psychologytoday.com/blog/reading-between-the-headlines/201303/is-jodi-arias-sociopath (accessed May 8, 2014).

[iii]Kat McCullough and Beth Carey, "Arias' Childhood Best Friend: 'She Was a Sweet Girl,'" HLN, April 17, 2013, http://www.hlntv.com/article/2013/04/17/jodi-arias-childhood-best-friend-she-was-sweet-girl (accessed May 8, 2014).

(*continued*)

THE CASE

Jodi Arias (*Continued*)

[iv]"Timeline of Events in Jodi Arias Murder Case," ABC News, May 15, 2013, http://abcnews.go.com/US/wireStory/timeline-events-jodi-arias-murder-case-19185819#.UZPcUXCCMUU (accessed May 8, 2014).

[v]Ryan Owens, "Jodi Arias: Who Is the Admitted Arizona Killer?" ABC News, January 8, 2013, http://abcnews.go.com/US/jodi-arias-admitted-arizona-killer/story?Id=18159181#.UZPvN3CCMUU (accessed May 8, 2014).

[vi]Brian Skoloff, "Prosecutor Calls Jodi Arias a Manipulative Liar," Associated Press, May 2, 2013, http://news.yahoo.com/prosecutor-calls-jodi-arias-manipulative-liar-195750776.html (accessed May 8, 2014).

The case of Jodi Arias raises some interesting questions. Among them are the following:

1. **How could a woman who had no record of past violence perform such a gruesome murder?**
2. **What was it about Arias's and Alexander's relationship that led to the killing?**

CHAPTER 4 Biosocial and Other Contemporary Perspectives

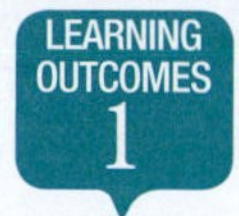

Describe the purpose of the Human Genome Project (HGP), and explain its significance for modern biological theories of crime.

The Human Genome Project (HGP), which had as its goal identifying and mapping the total genes of the human genome, was completed in 2003, and corresponds to the start of a new era of biosocial theories in criminology.

1. What was the purpose of the Human Genome Project? Did it meet its goals?
2. Why does the author of this text use the HGP as a point of demarcation between historical and contemporary biological theories of crime?

gene A molecular unit of DNA that carries coded instructions for making everything the body needs.

chromosomes Bundles of genes.

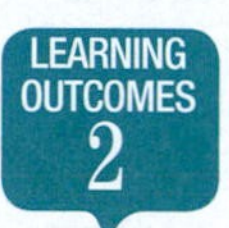

Identify the role of genetics and heritability in contemporary explanations for crime.

Genetic characteristics and variations in human chromosomes are thought to play an important role in aggression and crime causation. The contemporary study of human genetics builds upon a model of gene–environment interaction and employs the concept of heritability to help explain law-violating behavior. Although contemporary criminologists do not believe that there is one single and identifiable "criminal gene," they do believe that individuals who are genetically predisposed to certain types of behavior may become aggressive or criminal through interaction with the surrounding physical and social environments.

1. How convincing are research findings linking genetics and crime?
2. What have research studies in the field of genetics had to say about possible causes of crime?

neurotransmitters Chemical substances that facilitate the flow of electrical impulses from one neuron to the next across nerve synapses.

neurophysiology A field of research that examines the relationship between neurotransmitters and behavior.

allele Variation of a gene.

heritability The proportion of variation in traits within a group of people that can be attributed to variations in their genes rather than to their environment.

epigenetics The study of the chemical reactions that occur within a genome, and that switch parts of the genome on or off at strategic times and locations.

gene expression The process by which the coded information that is stored within a gene is used to create a biological product, usually a protein. Also, the manifestation of a trait in an individual carrying the gene or genes that determine that trait.

Key Names

H. Hilger Ropers and ***Han Brunner*** Geneticists who studied what they called "the Netherlands' most dysfunctional family." They concluded that genetics played a significant role in the production of antisocial behavior.

Avshalom Caspi and ***Terrie E. Moffitt*** Offered a model of gene–environment interaction which recognized that childhood maltreatment appears to be a universal risk factor for antisocial behavior in adulthood.

Nathalie Fontaine An Indiana University researcher who found that heritability leads to persistently high levels of callous and unemotional behavior among twin boys.

Show how brain dysfunction relates to criminality.

Some criminologists have explored brain dysfunction, resulting in the development of the frontal brain hypothesis, which references physical changes in certain parts of the brain to explain criminality. Neuroplasticity, or the ability of the brain to alter its structure and function in response to experience or injury, may be useful in explaining changes in personality and behavior.

1. What is brain dysfunction? How might it lead to crime?
2. What is the frontal brain hypothesis? Why might people with damage to the prefrontal cortex be more crime-prone?

neurocriminology A perspective that examines the neurological links between the organism, social factors, and criminal behavior.

frontal brain hypothesis A perspective that references physical changes in certain parts of the brain to explain criminality. The belief, supported by studies, that people who suffer damage to the prefrontal cortex of the brain tend to be more aggressive than others and that patients who suffer from frontal brain lesions tend to be more uninhibited and impulsive.

neuroplasticity The ability of the brain to alter its structure and function in response to experience.

Key Names

Adrian Raine A University of Pennsylvania psychologist known for his research into the neurobiological and biosocial causes of antisocial and criminal behavior.

LEARNING OUTCOMES 4

Describe how body chemistry theories—including those involving diet, blood sugar levels, environmental contaminants, bacteria, and hormones—explain crime.

Body chemistry theories say that violent or disruptive behavior can sometimes be linked to nutrition, vitamin deficiencies, and other conditions that affect the body. Studies of eating habits, endocrinology, and environmental contaminants have all contributed to advances in understanding such behavior.

1. Are high blood levels of testosterone likely linked to criminality? If so, how?
2. What environmental contaminants appear to be significantly related to deviant behavior and law violation?

hypoglycemia A medical condition characterized by low blood sugar.

prenatal substance exposure Fetal exposure to maternal drug and alcohol use. Prenatal substance exposure can significantly increase a child's risk for developmental and neurological disorders.

psychobiotics The study of the psychological and behavioral effects that bacteria (primarily those found in the human gut) can have on the mind, feelings, emotions, and behavior.

hormone A chemical substance produced by the body that regulates and controls the activity of certain cells or organs.

testosterone The primary male sex hormone. It is produced in the testes, and its function is to control secondary sex characteristics and sexual drive.

serotonin A neurotransmitter that is commonly found in the pineal gland, the digestive tract, the central nervous system, and in blood platelets.

Key Names

Stephen Schoenthaler A researcher at the California State University in Stanislaus who demonstrated significant declines in bad behavior in incarcerated adults and in school children receiving specifically designed vitamin and mineral supplementation.

David Fergusson A researcher who studied the effects of mothers' smoking during pregnancy, and found that children whose mothers smoked evidenced conduct disorders twice as frequently as those whose mothers did not smoke during pregnancy.

Alan Booth and ***D. Wayne Osgood*** Researchers who established a relationship between measurably high levels of testosterone in the blood of young men and aggressive behavior, noting that the effect is likely to be moderated by the social environment.

Paul C. Bernhardt A researcher who discovered that aggressive behavior in men may be influenced by high testosterone levels combined with low brain levels of the neurotransmitter serotonin.

LEARNING OUTCOMES 5

Discuss biosocial theories and the role of the gender ratio problem in contemporary criminology.

Biosocial criminology sees the interaction between biology and the physical and social environments as key to understanding human behavior, including criminality. It holds that genetic predispositions and their interaction with the surrounding social and physical environments may combine to produce criminality. Neuroplasticity, a concept that is central to some biosocial perspectives, may influence and facilitate much of human behavior.

1. What is biosocial criminology? How is criminality explained from a biosocial perspective?
2. What is the gender ratio problem in criminology? What traditional explanations have been offered for the "problem"? Why is the gender ratio problem not a "problem" from the point of view of biosocial criminology?

biosocial criminology A theoretical perspective that sees the interaction between biology and the physical and social environments as key to understanding human behavior, including criminality.

gender ratio problem The need for an explanation of the fact that the number of crimes committed by men routinely far exceeds the number of crimes committed by women in almost all categories.

sexual selection A form of natural selection that influences an individual's ability to attain or choose a mate.

evolutionary perspective A theoretical approach that (1) seeks to explain behavior with reference to human evolutionary history, and (2) recognizes the influence that genes have over human traits.

Key Names

James Q. Wilson and ***Richard J. Herrnstein*** Authors of the book *Crime and Human Nature,* which, in the mid-1980s, sought to reopen discussion of biological theories of crime. They cited a number of constitutional factors that they believed contributed to criminality.

Anthony Walsh A leading contemporary proponent of biosocial theories of criminology and a co-author with Kevin Beaver.

Kevin Beaver A leading contemporary proponent of biosocial theories of criminology and a co-author with Anthony Walsh.

Thomas Bernard A professor of sociology and criminal justice at the Pennsylvania State University who helped to bring attention to the gender gap in crime commission. Bernard identified the issue of why, always and everywhere, males commit more criminal acts than females as the single most important fact that theories of criminology need to explain.

LEARNING OUTCOMES 6

Describe the policy implications of modern biological theories of crime.

In the past, biology was often seen as deterministic. The eugenics movement, Nazi extermination programs, and enforced sterilization all resulted from an inaccurate assessment of the power of genes or other physical factors to determine behavior. At the same time, the once widely held belief that the human organism was a blank slate at birth appears now to be a fallacy. A contemporary crime-prevention program needs to be based on modern understandings of the link between biology and crime. Some say that environmental contaminants, diet, and exposure to chemical substances that control the expression of genes could be vital to crime control. A medical perspective could replace the current legalistic interpretation of criminality, leading to the right to treatment for criminal offenders.

1. What are the social policy implications of biological and biosocial theories of crime?
2. What modern-day social policies reflect the biological and biosocial approaches to crime causation?

LEARNING OUTCOMES 7

Identify critiques of biological and biosocial approaches to explaining crime.

As is the case with many other perspectives, biological criminology has suffered from the lack of a workable definition of criminality. Few biological studies adequately conceptualize criminality, methodological problems have been found in many studies attempting to evaluate the role of genetics in crime, and results obtained outside the United States may not be applicable within this country. Many criminologists continue to believe that although biology provides a context for human behavior, biological predispositions are overshadowed by the role of volition, mechanisms of human thought, and the undeniable influences of socialization and acculturation.

1. What are the shortcomings of biological theories of criminal behavior?
2. Why have biological approaches to crime causation encountered stiff criticism?

Follow the author's tweets about the latest crime and justice news **@schmalleger**.

5

“Thank you for the free kill. She died in front of me.”

—*Jared Loughner’s ramblings at his first court appearance*

Psychological and Psychiatric Foundations of Criminal Behavior—

It’s How We Think

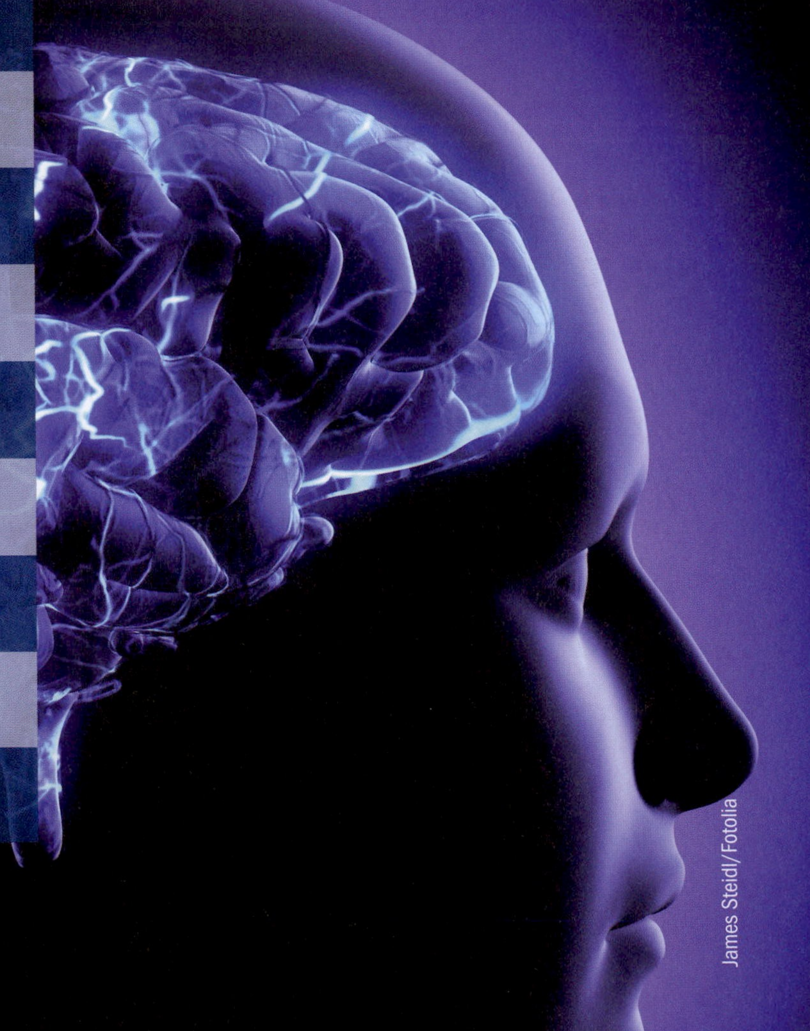

James Steidl/Fotolia

1. Describe the main features of the psychological perspective on criminal behavior.
2. Describe the two major ideas that characterized early psychological theories and explain the difference between them.
3. Explain how personality impacts criminality, and define *psychopath*.
4. Describe cognitive theories and identify the two types of cognitive theories that this chapter discusses.
5. Describe the insights that the psychoanalytic perspective offers into criminal behavior.
6. Demonstrate how behavior theory explains the role of rewards and punishments in shaping behavior.
7. Describe some of the policy and treatment implications of psychological understandings of criminality.
8. Provide a critique of psychological and psychiatric theories of crime.
9. Explain the fundamental assumption underlying the practice of criminal psychological profiling.

GUNS AND MENTAL DISORDER

On January 8, 2012, survivors of a Tucson, Arizona, shooting that seriously injured U.S. Democratic Representative Gabrielle Giffords and killed six other people, including a nine-year-old girl and an Arizona District Court chief judge, gathered to support one another.[1] One year earlier, a total of 19 people were shot in the parking lot of a Safeway store when 22-year-old Tucson resident Jared Lee Loughner shot Giffords in the head and then fired indiscriminately into the crowd that had gathered to hear her speak. After emptying the first clip in his 9mm semiautomatic pistol, Loughner stopped to reload, but fumbled and dropped a second clip to the ground, providing an opportunity for members of the crowd to overpower him and hold him until police arrived. Dozens of people witnessed the shooting, and it was captured by video surveillance cameras.

On May 25, 2011, while being held at the Federal Correctional Institution at Phoenix, Loughner appeared before a federal judge, who found Loughner incompetent to stand trial on the basis of two medical evaluations that had been performed while he was in custody. On August 7, 2012, however, after being forcibly medicated with antipsychotic drugs for more than a year in a Missouri prison medical facility, Loughner was ruled legally competent. He entered a plea of guilty to killing 6 people and wounding 13 others. Loughner's plea spared him the death penalty, but he was sentenced to seven life sentences in federal prison without the possibility of parole.[2]

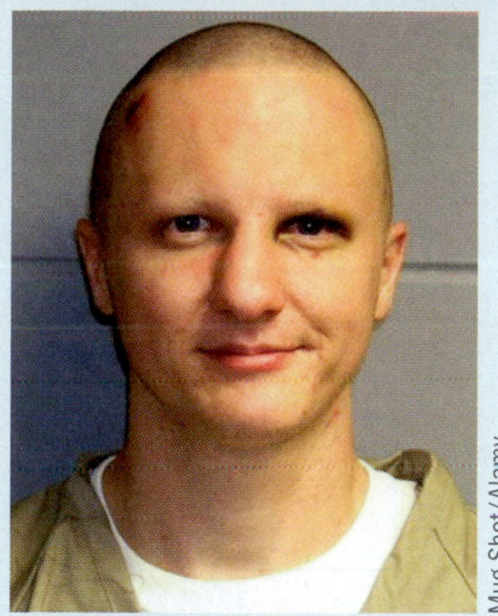

Mug Shot/Alamy

Jared Loughner, sentenced to life in prison without parole after pleading guilty to 19 charges of murder and attempted murder in an attack on people gathered to hear U.S. Representative Gabrielle Giffords speak in Tucson, Arizona, in 2011. What role did Loughner's personality play in the shootings?

DISCUSS **How does the ready availability of guns combine with the incidence of mental disorders in the United States to produce random violence perpetrated upon strangers?**

Principles of Psychological and Psychiatric Theories

Anyone who saw early courtroom recordings of Jared Loughner knew that he was psychologically damaged. Courtroom images showed Loughner, with his hair dyed bright orange, sitting in front of a judge who read the charges against him and asked if he understood those charges. Loughner grimaced and squirmed, and seemed to want to fall asleep repeatedly, but then jerked his eyes wide open. An even earlier photo taken by the Pima County Sheriff's Office following Loughner's arrest showed an intense-looking young man with a vacant expression—whom some likened to a person without a soul. The *Washington Post* described the picture as "smirking and creepy, with hollow eyes ablaze."[3] Was Loughner insane at the time of the shootings? Even if his behavior and state of mind did not meet the judicial standards for insanity, can we identify features of his personality that led to crime commission? If so, might he have been stopped? Questions like these concern all criminologists, but they are especially relevant from a psychological perspective.

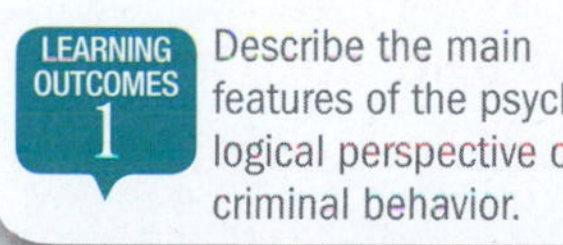

LEARNING OUTCOMES 1 Describe the main features of the psychological perspective on criminal behavior.

Psychological determinants of deviant or criminal behavior are couched in various terms, such as *exploitative personality characteristics*, *poor impulse control*, *emotional arousal*, *an immature personality*, and so forth. Before beginning a discussion of psychological theories, however, it is necessary to provide a brief overview of the terminology used to describe the psychological study of crime and criminality. **Forensic psychology**, one of the fastest growing subfields of psychology, is the application of the science and profession of psychology to questions and issues relating to law and the legal system.[4] Forensic psychology is sometimes referred to as **criminal psychology**, and forensic psychologists are also called "criminal psychologists," "correctional psychologists," and "police psychologists." Unlike forensic psychologists (who generally hold Ph.D.s), forensic psychiatrists are medical doctors, and **forensic psychiatry** is a medical subspecialty that applies psychiatry to the needs of crime prevention and solution, criminal rehabilitation, and issues of criminal law.[5] The assumptions that characterize psychological and psychiatric theories of crime causation are shown in Figure 5–1.

Assumptions of Psychological and Psychiatric Theories of Crime Causation

- The individual is the primary unit of analysis.
- Personality is the major motivational element within individuals because it is the seat of drives and the source of motives.
- Crimes result from abnormal, dysfunctional, or inappropriate mental processes within the personality.
- Criminal behavior, although condemned by the social group, may be purposeful for the individual insofar as it addresses certain felt needs. Behavior can be judged "inappropriate" only when measured against external criteria purporting to establish normality.
- Normality is generally defined by social consensus—that is, what the majority of people in any social group agree is "real," appropriate, or typical.
- Defective, or abnormal, mental processes may have a variety of causes, including a diseased mind, inappropriate learning or improper conditioning, the emulation of inappropriate role models, and adjustment to inner conflicts.

FIGURE 5–1 Assumptions of Psychological and Psychiatric Theories of Crime Causation.

History of Psychological Theories

Two major ideas characterized early psychological theories: **personality** and **behaviorism**. Personality theory built on the burgeoning area of cognitive science, including personality disturbances, the process of moral development, and diseases of the mind; behaviorism (also known as *behavior theory*) examined social learning with an emphasis on behavioral **conditioning**. Together, these two areas formed the early foundation of psychological criminology. This chapter discusses theories of cognitive science and behaviorism as they relate to criminality. A separate discussion of **psychoanalytic theory**, an outgrowth of personality theory, rounds out this chapter.

LEARNING OUTCOMES 2 Describe the two major ideas that characterized early psychological theories and explain the difference between them.

Personality Disturbances

Psychologists working in the first half of the twentieth century adapted the disease model—a paradigm that had worked so well in the field of medicine—in an effort to cure mental and emotional problems. Consequently, early cognitive perspectives in psychology were couched in terms of mental disease, personality disorder, and **psychopathy**.

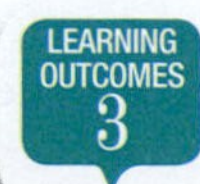
LEARNING OUTCOMES 3 Explain how personality impacts criminality, and define *psychopath*.

Psychologists and psychiatrists today distinguish between the terms *psychopathy* and *psychopathology*. In the psychological literature, psychopathology "refers to any sort of psychological disorder that causes distress either for the individual or for those in the individual's life."[6] Today, depression, **schizophrenia**, attention deficit hyperactivity disorder, alcoholism, and bulimia are all considered forms of psychopathology, or mental disease. One of the most serious of mental diseases is psychopathy, "a very specific and distinctive type of psychopathology"[7]

The Psychopath

Psychopathy is a personality disorder characterized by antisocial behavior and by a lack of sympathy, empathy, and embarrassment. Psychopaths, many of whom are known as effective manipulators, and who clearly understand the motivations of others, are said to especially lack empathy or sensitivity toward others.

The concept of psychopathy, called "one of the most durable, resilient and influential of all criminological ideas,"[8] may have evolved from the work of French physician Philippe Pinel (1745–1826), who described a form of "insanity without delirium." The term *psychopathy* comes from the Greek words *psyche* (meaning soul or mind) and *pathos* (meaning "suffering" or "illness"). The word, which appears to have been coined by German neurologist Richard von Krafft-Ebing (1840–1902),[9] made its way into English psychiatric literature through the writings of Polish-born American psychiatrist Bernard H. Glueck (1884–1972)[10] and British psychiatrist William Healy (1869–1963).[11]

The **psychopath** has been historically viewed as perversely cruel, often without thought or feeling for his or her victims.[12] By the Second World War, the role of the psychopathic personality in crime causation had become central to psychological theorizing. The concept of a psychopathic personality, which by its very definition is antisocial, was fully developed by neuropsychiatrist **Hervey M. Cleckley** in his 1941 book *The Mask of Sanity*[13]—a work that had considerable impact on the field of psychology. Cleckley described the psychopath as a "moral idiot," or as one who does not feel empathy for others, even though that person may be fully aware of what is happening around him or her. The central defining characteristic of a

Forensic psychiatry is a medical subspecialty that applies psychiatry to the needs of crime prevention and solution, criminal rehabilitation, and issues of criminal law.

psychopath was described as a "poverty of affect," or the inability to fully appreciate how others think and feel. Therefore, it becomes possible for a psychopath to inflict pain and engage in cruelty without appreciation for the victim's suffering. Charles Manson, for example, whom some regard as a psychopath, once told a television reporter, "I could take this book and beat you to death with it, and I wouldn't feel a thing. It'd be just like walking to the drugstore."[14]

In *The Mask of Sanity*, Cleckley describes numerous characteristics of the psychopathic personality, some of which are shown in Figure 5–2. For Cleckley, "psychopathy was defined by a constellation of dysfunctional psychological processes as opposed to specific behavioral manifestations."[15] Cleckley noted that in cases he had observed, the behavioral manifestations of psychopathy varied with the person's age, gender, and socioeconomic status.

Even though psychopaths have a seriously flawed personality, they can easily fool others into trusting them—hence the title of Cleckley's book. According to Cleckley, indicators of psychopathy appear early in life, often in the teenage years. They include lying, fighting, stealing, and vandalizing. Even earlier signs may be found, according to some authors, in bed-wetting, cruelty to animals, sleepwalking, and fire setting.[16] Others have described psychopaths as "individuals who display impulsiveness, callousness, insincerity, pathological lying and deception, egocentricity, poor judgment, an impersonal sex life, and an unstable life plan."[17]

Cleckley believed that there were two kinds of psychopaths: primary and secondary. In later work, psychologist David Lykken refined those terms, saying that *primary psychopaths* are somehow neurologically different from other people, and that makes them behave the way they do.[18] Hence, primary psychopaths are born with psychopathic personalities, whereas *secondary psychopaths* (sometimes called **sociopaths**) are born with a "normal" personality, but personal experience (frequently physical and emotional abuse) when they are young cause them to develop psychopathic characteristics.

Superficial charm and "good intelligence"
Absence of delusions, hallucinations, or other signs of psychosis
Absence of nervousness or psychoneurotic manifestations
Inability to feel guilt or shame
Unreliability
Chronic lying
Ongoing antisocial behavior
Poor judgment and inability to learn from experience
An impersonal, trivial, and poorly integrated sex life
Unresponsiveness in general interpersonal relations
Failure to follow any life plan
Self-centeredness and incapacity to love

FIGURE 5–2 Selected Characteristics of the Psychopathic Personality.

Other types of psychopaths have also been identified, including the *charismatic psychopath* and the *distempered psychopath*. The charismatic type of psychopath is charming and attractive, but also a habitual liar. Charismatic psychopaths manipulate others to achieve their personal goals, without considering others' feelings. Distempered psychopaths are easily offended and fly into rages even at slight provocations. They have been characterized as having strong urges, including sexual drives, that often lead to addiction.

A definitive modern measure of psychopathy can be found in the Psychopathy Checklist (PCL), developed by Robert Hare (sometimes called the Hare Psychopathy Checklist).[19] The checklist, when used by qualified experts employing information from subject interviews and official records, produces a series of ratings assessing degree of psychopathy. The checklist uses two kinds of indicators: affective and interpersonal traits (glibness, emotional detachment, egocentricity, superficial charm, shallow affect) and traits associated with a chronic unstable and antisocial lifestyle (irresponsibility, impulsivity, criminality, proneness to boredom).[20] Hence, psychopathy has both emotional and behavioral components.

Some have questioned whether psychopaths merely lack empathy or really don't know the difference between right and wrong. Recent research seems to show that the ability to tell right from wrong is something that human beings are born with, that the human brain is hard-wired to make moral distinctions, and that the same distinctions tend to be made across cultures.[21] You can test your own sense of right and wrong by taking the Moral Sense Test (MST) online. The MST, which researchers are using to detail the nature of moral psychology, is accessible through Harvard University's Cognitive Evolution Laboratory online at **Web Extra 5-1**.

Traditionally, psychopathology has been regarded as difficult or impossible to treat. But a recent study of adolescent psychopaths found that "youth with psychopathic features who received intensive treatment" in sanction-based programs that held them accountable for their actions, "had significantly lower rates of violent recidivism and a longer time to rearrest for violent behavior" than those who received treatment in a typical juvenile correctional facility.[22] Learn more about the concept

Think About It...

Ivan Pavlov demonstrated the importance of conditioned reflexes in animals. Might some human behavior also be explained through the concept of a conditioned response? If so, how much behavior might be amenable to change?

Aliaksei Hintau/Fotolia

Individuals exhibiting an antisocial personality are said to be suffering from antisocial personality disorder.

of the psychopath as a clinical construct by visiting the Society for Research in Psychopathology via **Web Extra 5–2**. Read about the issues involved in identifying criminal psychopaths via **Web Extra 5–3**.

Antisocial Personality Disorder

In recent years, the terms *sociopath* and *psychopath* have fallen into disfavor. In an attempt to identify sociopathic individuals, some psychologists have come to place greater emphasis on the type of behavior exhibited rather than on identifiable personality traits. By 1968, the American Psychiatric Association's (APA's) *Diagnostic and Statistical Manual of Mental Disorders* had completely discontinued using the words *sociopath* and *psychopath*, replacing them with the terms *antisocial personality* and *asocial personality*.[23] In that year, the APA manual changed to a description of **antisocial personality** types as "individuals who are basically unsocialized and whose behavior pattern brings them repeatedly into conflicts with society. They are incapable of significant loyalty to individuals, groups, or social values. They are grossly selfish, callous, irresponsible, impulsive, and unable to feel guilt or to learn from experience and punishment. Frustration tolerance is low. They tend to blame others or offer plausible rationalization for their behavior."[24] In most cases, individuals exhibiting an antisocial personality through their behavioral patterns are said to be suffering from **antisocial personality disorder** (sometimes referred to in clinical circles as "APD," "ASPD," or "ANPD").

The causes of ASPD are unclear. Somatogenic causes (those based on physiological features) are said to include a malfunctioning of the central nervous system, which is characterized by a low state of arousal driving the sufferer to seek excitement, and brain abnormalities, which may have been present since birth. Some studies show that an **electroencephalogram (EEG)** taken of an individual diagnosed as having ASPD is frequently abnormal, reflecting "a malfunction of some inhibitory mechanisms" that makes it unlikely that someone characterized by ASPD will "learn to inhibit behavior that is likely to lead to punishment."[25] It is difficult, however, to diagnose ASPD through physiological measurements because similar EEG patterns show up in patients with other types of disorders. Psychogenic causes (those rooted in early interpersonal experiences) include inability to form attachments to parents or other caregivers early in life, sudden separation from the mother during the first six months of life, and other forms of insecurity during the first few years of life. In short, a lack of love or the sensed inability to unconditionally depend upon one central loving figure (typically the mother in most psychological literature) immediately following birth is often posited as a major psychogenic factor contributing to the development of ASPD.

Most studies of ASPD have involved male subjects. Only rarely have researchers focused on women with antisocial personalities, and it is believed that only a small proportion of those afflicted with ASPD are women.[26] What little research there is suggests that females with ASPD possess many of the same definitive characteristics as their male counterparts and that they assume their antisocial roles at similarly early ages.[27] The lifestyles of antisocial females, however, appear to include sexual misconduct and abnormally high levels of sexual activity, but such research can be misleading because the cultural expectations of female sexual behavior inherent in early studies may not always have been in keeping with reality; that is, early researchers may have had so little accurate information about female sexual activity that the behavior of women judged to possess antisocial personalities may have actually been far closer to the norm than originally believed.

Trait Theory

In 1964, **Hans J. Eysenck**, a British psychologist, published *Crime and Personality*, a book in which he explained crime as the result of fundamental personality characteristics, or **traits**, which he believed are largely inherited.[28] Psychological traits are stable personality patterns that tend to endure throughout the life course and across social and cultural contexts. They include behavioral, cognitive, and affective predispositions to respond to a given situation in a particular way. According to trait theory, as an individual grows older or moves from one place to another, his or her personality remains largely intact—defined by the traits that comprise it. Trait theory links personality (and associated traits) to behavior, and holds that it is an individual's personality, combined with his or her intelligence and natural abilities,[29] that determines his or her behavior in a given situation.[30]

Eysenck believed that the degree to which just three universal *supertraits* are present in an individual accounts for his or her unique personality. He termed these supertraits (1) introversion/extraversion, (2) neuroticism/emotional stability, and (3) psychoticism. Eysenck, like many other psychologists, accepted the fact that personality holds steady throughout much of life, but stressed that it is largely determined by genetics. He argued that what we call *personality* is a reflection of variations in the component operating systems of major brain–behavioral pathways.

In support of his idea of the genetic basis of personality, Eysenck pointed to twin studies showing that identical twins display strikingly similar behavioral tendencies, whereas fraternal twins demonstrate far less likelihood of similar behaviors. Eysenck also argued that psychological conditioning occurs more rapidly in some people than in others because of biological differences, and that antisocial individuals are difficult to condition (or to socialize) because of underlying genetic characteristics. He believed that up to two-thirds of all "behavioral variance" could be strongly attributed to genetics.[31]

Of Eysenck's three personality dimensions, one in particular—psychoticism—was thought to be closely correlated with criminality at all stages.[32] According to Eysenck, psychoticism is defined by such characteristics as lack of empathy, creativeness, tough-mindedness, and antisociability. Extroverts, Eysenck's second personality group that was associated with criminality, are described as carefree, dominant, and venturesome, operating with high levels of energy. "The typical extrovert," Eysenck wrote, "is sociable, likes parties, has many friends, needs to have people to talk to, and does not like reading or studying by himself."[33] Neuroticism, the third of the personality characteristics Eysenck described, is said to be typical of people who are irrational, shy, moody, and emotional.

According to Eysenck, psychotics are the most likely to be criminal because they combine high degrees of emotionalism with similarly high levels of extroversion; individuals with such characteristics are especially difficult to socialize and to train and do not respond well to the external environment. Eysenck cited many studies in which children and others who harbored characteristics of psychoticism performed poorly on conditioning tests designed to measure how quickly they would respond appropriately to external stimuli. Because conscience is fundamentally a conditioned reflex, Eysenck said, an individual who does not take well to conditioning will not fully develop a conscience and will continue to exhibit the asocial behavioral traits of a very young child. In essence, criminality can be seen as a personality type characterized by self-centeredness, indifference to the suffering and needs of others, impulsiveness, and low self-control—which, taken together, lead to law-violating behavior.

Today, trait theories of personality have expanded beyond Eysneck's basic three-trait model to encompass five basic traits: (1) openness to experience, (2) extraversion, (3) conscientiousness, (4) neuroticism and (5) agreeableness. People are said to possess more or less of any one trait, and the combination of traits and the degree to which they are characteristic of an individual define that person's personality. Psychologists call these traits the *Big Five*, and they form the basis of the **Five Factor Model** of psychology (see Figure 5–3). According to many psychologists, "the Big Five are strongly genetically influenced, and the genetic factor structure of the Big Five appears to be invariant across European, North American, and East Asian samples,"[34] which suggests that personality traits, to a greater or lesser degree, are universally shared by all peoples. Conscientiousness, for example, is related to self-control, and is unlikely to be associated with criminality.

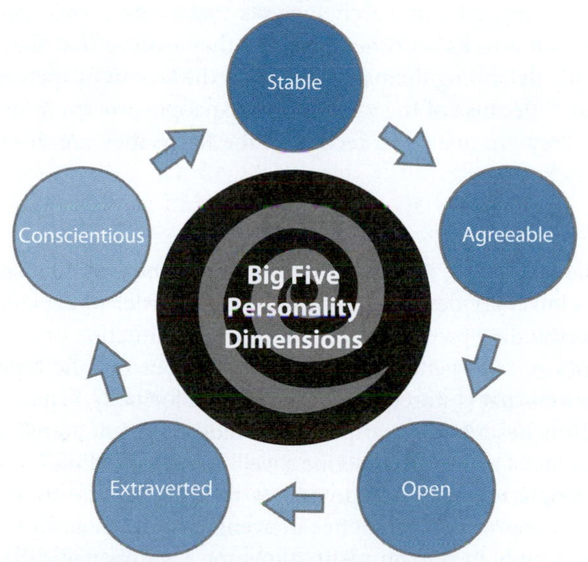

FIGURE 5–3 **The Big Five Personality Dimensions.**
Source: From *Criminology Today: An Integrative Introduction*, 7e by Frank A. Schmalleger. Copyright © 2014 by Pearson Education. Used by permission of Pearson Education.

Cognitive Theories

Theories of cognition form a third area of personality theory. Cognitive approaches are learning theories that examine thought processes, and seek to explain how people: (1) learn to solve problems, including those that involve questions of value and morality, and (2) perceive and interpret the social environment. Cognitive theory has a number of branches, including one that focuses on moral and intellectual development, and another that examines how people process information.

Describe cognitive theories and identify the two types of cognitive theories that this chapter discusses.

Moral Development Theory

The first branch of cognitive theory, **moral development theory**, holds that individuals become criminal when they have not successfully completed their intellectual development from child- to adulthood. One of the first comprehensive maps of human psychological development was created by Swiss developmental psychologist **Jean Piaget**. Piaget believed that human thinking and intellectual processes go through a number of biopsychological stages of development—something that Piaget saw as a natural extension of evolutionary adaptation. Just as a species adapts to its environment, Piaget believed, individual human beings respond to their environment by developing intellectually. He posited four stages of human intellectual development:[35]

1. The *sensory-motor stage*, which lasts from birth to age two. During this stage children are extremely egocentric (or focused on themselves and their personal experiences), and learn about the world through physical senses and the movement of their bodies.
2. The *preoperational stage*, which lasts from ages two to seven. During this stage children are not able to reason well or to use logical thinking; but egocentrism begins to weaken, and motor skills are acquired. Piaget said that this stage was dominated by magical thinking, explaining why beliefs in Santa Claus, the Easter Bunny, and similar mythical characters are typical among younger children.
3. The *concrete operational stage*, which runs from age 7 to 11. In this stage children start to develop the ability to reason and to think logically, although they are very concrete in their thinking, and often require objects like buttons or coins to aid in counting and arithmetic. By the time children reach the end of this stage they are no longer egocentric, but are able to appreciate the needs and feelings of others.
4. The *formal operational stage*, which lasts from age 11 to 16, and which continues into adulthood. During this stage, the developing adolescent acquires abstract reasoning skills, and learns how to think and reason without the need for external aids.

Central to Piaget's perspective on moral development is the idea that as children grow and learn, they become able to reflect on their own actions—acquiring a sense of the unspoken rules

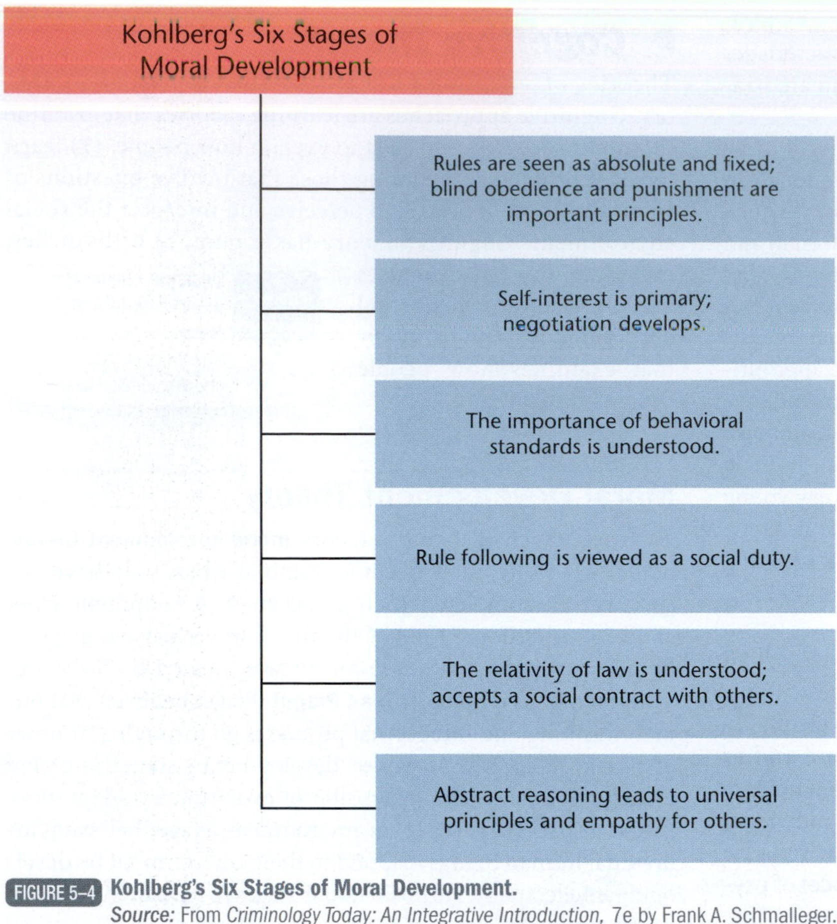

Kohlberg's Six Stages of Moral Development
Rules are seen as absolute and fixed; blind obedience and punishment are important principles.
Self-interest is primary; negotiation develops.
The importance of behavioral standards is understood.
Rule following is viewed as a social duty.
The relativity of law is understood; accepts a social contract with others.
Abstract reasoning leads to universal principles and empathy for others.

FIGURE 5–4 **Kohlberg's Six Stages of Moral Development.**
Source: From *Criminology Today: An Integrative Introduction,* 7e by Frank A. Schmalleger. Copyright © 2014 by Pearson Education. Used by permission of Pearson Education.

that govern human interaction. According to Piaget, children apply their burgeoning ability to reflect and use it to examine themselves; and in the process they learn right from wrong. In his words, "the child is someone who constructs his own moral world view, who forms ideas about right and wrong, and fair and unfair, that are not the direct product of adult teaching and that are often maintained in the face of adult wishes to the contrary."[36]

Once a child has moved through the four developmental stages, said Piaget, he would have moved from moral absolutism (in which he unquestioningly accepts the dictates of his parents or caregivers), to moral relativism (where actions are seen as right or wrong depending on the circumstances in which they are undertaken).

Following Piaget, American psychologist **Lawrence Kohlberg** offered an expanded cognitive structural theory of morality in a six-stage typology (Figure 5–4).[37] In Kohlberg's first stage, people only obey the law because they are afraid of being punished if they don't. By the final, or sixth stage, however, obedience to the law becomes an obligation that is willingly assumed, and people chose not to violate the law because they value the principle of fairness and believe in interpersonal justice. Those who have evolved to higher stages of moral reasoning are unlikely to commit crimes because they appreciate not only their own needs, but the needs and interests of others as well.

Kohlberg argued that a preference for higher levels of moral thinking must be universal in human beings, although not necessarily inborn. He believed that people who have successfully moved through all stages of moral development have developed the ability to objectively evaluate opinions and either accept them or reject them without irrationally clinging to their own beliefs. Kohlberg posited that people may turn to crime if they are unsuccessful at making the normal transitions between developmental stages of moral reasoning.

Research based on Kohlberg's work has demonstrated that offenders have less ability at making moral judgments than do noncriminals, even when they have similar backgrounds and experiences.[38]

Cognitive Information-Processing Theory

A second major area of cognitive theory applicable to criminology is **cognitive information-processing theory (CIP)**. CIP involves the study of human perceptions, information processing, and decision making. Psychological research suggests that people make decisions by engaging in a series of complex thought processes, or steps. In the first step, they encode and interpret the information they are presented with or the experiences they have. In the next stage they search for an appropriate response; in the third stage they act on their decision.[39]

Some information-processing theorists believe that violent individuals may be using information incorrectly when making decisions. Violence-prone individuals, for example, may see people as more aggressive or threatening than they actually are. Such a view may result in violence even at the slightest provocation. Supportive research suggests that some people engage in violent attacks on others because they believe that they are actually defending themselves, even in the face of misperceived threat.[40] Because of the way that some people process information, they are unable to recognize the harm they are doing to others.[41]

Script Theory

In the late 1970s, **Roger C. Schank** and **Robert P. Abelson** of Yale University developed script theory in order to explain the understanding process that occurs during a situation or event.[42] **Scripts** refer to generalized knowledge about specific types of situations that is stored in the mind. More formally, Schank and Abelson described a script as "a predetermined, stereotyped sequence of actions that define a well-known situation."

People use ready-made scripts in everyday life to anticipate an appropriate sequence of events in a given context. We build scripts in our minds to allow for a number of different roles for those actors (others than ourselves) whose presence is anticipated to play out in the script, and we allow for possible variations in the physical scene and in the progression of events. In this sense, scripts are like stories that we use to structure our expectations of and reactions to circumstances that we expect to typically encounter. Take, for example, the internal script that we might use for restaurant dining. We know that when we arrive at a restaurant we should check with the host or hostess to see if a table is available. We expect that he or she will take us to our table and that a server will arrive soon after we are seated to present us with a menu and to take our drink order. We have similar expectations as to what will occur as our dinner progresses, including the eventual arrival of the bill, and the amount or percentage of a tip to be left at the completion of the evening. Because most events play out according to the scripts that we have in mind, things typically go smoothly. Sometimes, however, we can be surprised and find ourselves forced to innovate. In our restaurant example, we might unexpectedly be served the wrong meal, or (worse) the server might trip and spill food onto us. Unless we are surprised, however, things generally go according to plan and events fit with previous experiences we have had involving the same kind of activity.

According to Helen Gavin and David Hockey, two British criminologists writing in 2010, "scripts are used to guide behavior because the script provides the holder with a set of expectations about what will happen during the unfolding of an event, thus offering a way of predicting the outcome and aid[ing] the individual to act accordingly."[43] Gavin and Hockey recognize that people develop scripts based on the learning opportunities and experiences that are presented to them within their social environment. The idea is similar to that involved in role-playing, whereby children engage in role play as a kind of practice for the adult roles they will assume later in life.

The applicability of scripts to criminal behavior can be seen in the fact that career offenders routinely follow developed scripts to guide them through criminal activity. Gavin and Hockey say that these particular kinds of scripts "consist of a goal aim, a criminal belief system, a criminally motivated perception, and a self-serving set of distorted cognitions that protect the individual's low self-esteem." Criminals use scripts in their approach to crime commission, much of which becomes routine over time. Consequently, criminal motivations and drives underpin criminal scripts.

In their 2010 study of criminal scripts, Gavin and Hockey detailed the scripts of career offenders and found that they could "be acquired through. . . . various relevant psychological processes,"[44] along with other more conservative scripts that most people use in their daily lives. Moreover, they concluded that criminal scripts help to form a criminal identity once they have been internalized.

The Criminal Mindset

In 1970 **Stanton E. Samenow**, a young clinical psychologist, began working with psychiatrist **Samuel Yochelson** in the Program for the Investigation of Criminal Behavior at St. Elizabeths Hospital—a large federal psychiatric facility in Washington, D.C. Yochelson had abandoned a lucrative psychiatric practice in New York and moved to Washington to direct the criminal behavior research project, which studied and treated serious criminal offenders. After Samenow joined the program, he and Yochelson began to realize that many of the patients they were seeing "were in conflict with society [and] not suffering from internal psychological conflicts."[45] The two came to believe that criminals make entirely different assumptions about living and behaving than noncriminals do because of ingrained and pervasive errors of thinking.

After more than six years of working together, Yochelson and Samenow published a three-volume series, *The Criminal Personality*, in which they wrote that many offenders share an identifiable mindset that is largely immune to environmental influences and that, for the most part, develops independently of social experience.[46]

In 1984 Samenow published the book *Inside the Criminal Mind*, which was republished 20 years later in a revised edition. The criminal personality, Samenow claims, develops early in childhood and consists of ways of thinking that are characteristic of many types of criminals, but that are not shared by noncriminals. In the theoretical model that Samenow developed, he focuses largely on the criminal mindset, and notes that criminals think differently than do noncriminals. Characteristics of the criminal mindset include anger as a way of life, a focus on excitement without any real consideration of the cost to others, a lack of any feelings of obligation to others, lack of empathy, and prejudgment with which offenders approach most situations. The mindset of a criminal is not "caused" by poverty, mental illness, or social conditions, Samenow argued, but rather by the need for excitement. It manifests, Samenow said, through personal choices made by offenders.

Although offenders come from a diversity of backgrounds, and although they engage in many different patterns of criminal behavior, Samenow argued that almost all criminal offenders are alike in the way they think. "A gun-toting, uneducated criminal off the streets of Southeast Washington, D.C., and a crooked Georgetown business executive are extremely similar in their view of themselves and the world," he wrote. The difference between a person with a criminal worldview and one with a conformist worldview is so different, said Samenow, that "it's as though the criminal were a different breed."

Samenow wrote that "the criminal chooses crime; he chooses to reject society long before society rejects him." Seen this way, crime resides within the person, Samenow said, and is "caused" by the way he thinks, not by his environment.[47] Criminal offenders are driven by excitement and self-interest, Samenow believed, and he suggested that if certain forms of criminal behavior were legalized they would lose their excitement—causing people committed to a life of law violations to engage in some other form of forbidden behavior. "No matter how many victims he has and how much damage he does," Samenow argues, "the criminal has little, if any, remorse and continues to regard himself as a good person."

Samenow believed that "behavior follows in the wake of thought,"[48] so the only way to rehabilitate an offender, he said, is to force him to see himself realistically and help him to develop responsible patterns of thought. Changed thoughts will lead to a reassessment of the criminal worldview and, hopefully, to positive behavioral change.

Psychiatric criminology envisions a complex set of drives and motives operating from hidden recesses deep within the personality to determine behavior.

Sublimation is the psychological process whereby one item of consciousness is symbolically substituted for another.

The Psychoanalytic Perspective—Criminal Behavior as Maladaptation

Psychiatric criminology (also called *forensic psychiatry*) envisions a complex set of drives and motives operating from hidden recesses deep within the personality to determine behavior. Perhaps the best-known psychiatrist of all time is **Sigmund Freud** (1856–1939). Freud coined the term **psychoanalysis** in 1896 and based an entire theory of human behavior on it.

Describe the insights that the psychoanalytic perspective offers into criminal behavior.

Freud said nothing about criminal behavior, and it wasn't until later that other psychoanalysts began to apply concepts that Freud had developed to criminal behavior. From the point of view of psychoanalysis, criminal behavior is maladaptive, or the product of inadequacies in the offender's personality. Significant inadequacies may result in full-blown mental illness, which can be a direct cause of crime. The psychoanalytic perspective encompasses diverse notions such as personality, **neurosis**, and **psychosis** and more specific concepts such as transference, **sublimation**, and repression. **Psychotherapy**, referred to in its early days as the "talking cure" because it relied on patient–therapist communication, is the attempt to relieve patients of their mental disorders through the application of psychoanalytic principles and techniques.

According to Freud, the personality is made up of three components—the id, the ego, and the superego—as shown in Figure 5–5. The **id** is the fundamental aspect of the personality from which drives, wishes, urges, and desires emanate. Freud focused primarily on love, aggression, and sex as fundamental drives in any personality. The id operates according to the pleasure principle, seeking full and immediate gratification of its needs. Individuals, however, according to Freud, are rarely fully aware of the urges that manifest (occasionally into awareness) from the id because it is a largely unconscious region of the mind. Nonetheless, from the Freudian perspective, each of us carries within our id the prerequisite motivation for criminal behavior. We are, each one of us, potential murderers, sexual aggressors, and thieves—our drives and urges kept in check only by other controlling aspects of our personalities.

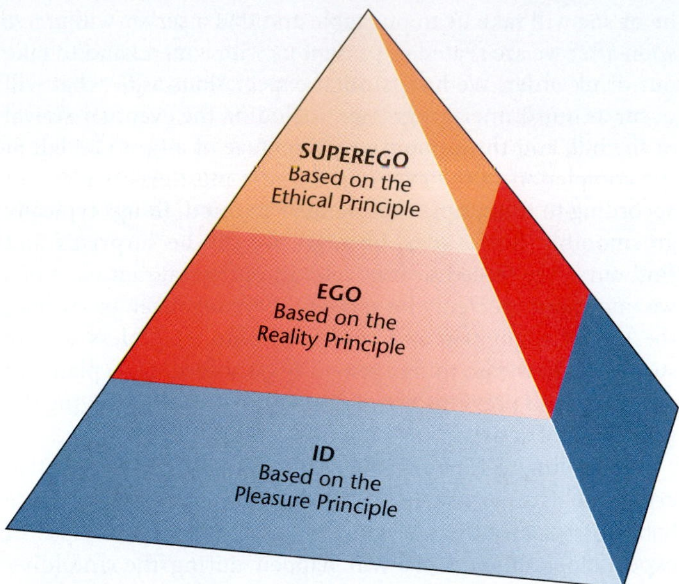

FIGURE 5–5 **The Psychoanalytic Structure of Personality.**

The **ego** is primarily charged with reality testing. Freud's use of the word *ego* should not be confused with popular usage, whereby a person might talk about an "inflated ego" or an "egotistical person." For Freud, the ego was primarily concerned with how objectives might be best accomplished. The ego tends to effect strategies for the individual that maximize pleasure and minimize pain. It lays out the various paths of action that can lead to wish fulfillment. The ego inherently recognizes that it may be necessary to delay gratification to achieve a more fulfilling long-term goal.

The **superego** is much like a moral guide to right and wrong. If properly developed, it evaluates the ego's plans, dismissing some as morally inappropriate while accepting others as ethically viable. The id of a potential rapist, for example, might be filled with lustful drives, and his ego may develop a variety of alternative plans whereby those drives might be fulfilled, some legal and some illegal. His superego will, if the individual's personality is relatively well integrated and the superego is properly developed, turn the individual away from law-violating behavior based on his sensual desires and guide the ego to select a path of action that is in keeping with social convention. When the dictates of the superego are not followed, feelings of guilt may result. The superego is one of the most misunderstood of Freudian concepts. In addition to elements of conscience, the superego also contains what Freud called the "ego-ideal," which

Think About It…

Sigmund Freud developed the psychoanalytic perspective and gave meaning to the terms *id*, *ego*, and *superego*. Which of the three aspects of the personality posited by psychoanalysis can be expected to contribute the most to criminal or abnormal behavior?

MARKA/Alamy

is a symbolic representation of what society values. The ego-ideal differs from the conscience in that it is less forceful in controlling behavior in the absence of the likelihood of discovery.

Although, as previously mentioned, Freud did not directly address crime, he did spend much of his time examining abnormal behaviors, many of which might lead to violations of the criminal law. One way in which a person might be led into crime, according to the perspective of psychoanalysis, is as the result of a poorly developed superego. In the individual without a fully functional superego, the mind is left to fall back on the ego's reality-testing ability. To put it simply, the ego, operating without a moral guide, may select a path of action that, although expedient at the time, violates the law. Consequently, without a fully functioning superego, offenders come to be characterized by id-dominated personalities, and the id's need for instant gratification determines their behavior. Individuals suffering from poor superego development are unlikely to give thought to the long-term consequences of the choices they make.

Although Freud actually wrote very little about criminality, **August Aichorn**, another psychoanalyst, did. Aichorn saw the behavior of violent criminals as dominated by the id, leaving them unable to control their impulsive and pleasure-seeking drives that stemmed from the id.[49] Aichorn believed that, as a result of negative life experiences, especially at an early age, violence-prone individuals suffer from damaged egos that are too weak to be able to deal with stressful circumstances and urges that well up from the id.

Another path to criminality from a psychiatric viewpoint is through repressed needs. The psychoanalytical concept of **repression** holds that individuals may seek to reject their own desires and impulses towards pleasurable instincts by excluding them from their own consciousness, thereby removing them from awareness and rendering them unconscious.

One secret need of many criminals, according to some psychologists, is the need to be punished, which arises, according to psychiatric theory, from a sense of guilt. Psychiatrists who suggest that the need to be punished is a motivating factor in criminal behavior are quick to point out that this need may be a closely guarded secret, unknown even to the offender. Hence, from the psychiatric point of view, many drives, motives, and wishes are unconscious or even repressed by people who harbor them. The concept of repression holds that the human mind may choose to keep certain aspects of itself out of consciousness, possibly because of shame, self-loathing, or a simple lack of adequate introspection.

Freudian theory was very popular during the middle part of the twentieth century, but by the 1980s, the notions of ego and id were considered antiquated by most psychiatrists. Attention shifted to the study of chemical imbalances in the brain, and psychopharmacology supplemented—if not replaced—the earlier ideas of Freud and his followers. Marti Olsen Laney, a neuroscience researcher in Portland, Oregon, found that the brains of introverted children functioned somewhat differently from those of extroverts. Brain scans of introverted kids found much more overall activity—especially in the brain's frontal lobes, which are areas associated with problem solving, introspection, complex thinking, and planning.[50]

The need to be punished is a motivating factor in some criminal behavior.

The field of psychiatry has seen a rekindling of interest in Freudian psychology, however, because psychopharmacology (the use of drugs to treat psychiatric symptoms and disorders) has been unable to provide an alternative grand theory of personality, emotion, and motivation.[51] Moreover, today's neuroscientists are busily creating a chemical map of the mind that seems to validate the general sketch that Freud provided decades ago, and soon a new unified perspective that reconciles the work of neurologists and psychiatrists may emerge. The recognition of just such a possibility prompted Eric R. Kandel of Columbia University, the 2000 Nobel laureate in physiology and medicine, to say that psychoanalysis is "still the most coherent and intellectually satisfying view of the mind."[52]

The Psychotic Offender

Some seemingly inexplicable forms of criminality may be the result of psychosis. People with psychotic disorders are out of touch with reality in some fundamental way, possibly suffering from hallucinations, delusions, or other breaks with reality. Psychoses may be either organic (resulting from physical damage to or abnormalities in the brain) or functional (having no known physical cause). Canadian criminologist Gwynn Nettler said, "Thought disorder is the hallmark of psychosis. People are called crazy when, at some extremity, they cannot 'think straight.'"[53] She identified three characteristics of psychotic individuals: "(1) a grossly distorted conception of reality, (2) moods, and swings of mood, that seem inappropriate to circumstance, and (3) marked inefficiency in getting along with others and caring for oneself."[54]

Psychiatrists today recognize at least nine different types of psychotic disorders, and one important category is schizophrenia. Schizophrenics (mentioned earlier) are characterized by disordered or disjointed thinking, in which the types of logical associations they make are atypical of other people. **Paranoid schizophrenics**, one of the four major subgroup of schizophrenics, also suffer from delusions and hallucinations. Schizophrenia is a disorganization of the personality, and in its most extreme form, it may manifest itself in seemingly irrational behavior as well as hallucinations and delusions.

A recent study of male schizophrenics found that 37% started a criminal career, and 13% had committed their first violent crime before any contact with the psychiatric hospital system. Study authors concluded that "the criminality committed [by schizophrenics] before first contact to the psychiatric hospital system is substantial, especially among males with schizophrenia."[55] Many studies confirm the association between violence and schizophrenia, but recent evidence from a study conducted in the U.K. suggests that the proportion of violent crime directly attributable to schizophrenia is below 10%.[56] When substance abuse is added to the mix, however, the amount of violence associated with schizophrenia increases considerably. Consequently, a 2009 article in the *Journal of the American Medical Association* (JAMA) found that schizophrenics are four to six times as likely as members of the general population to commit a violent crime, and noted that current medical guidelines "recommend that violence **risk assessment** should be conducted for all patients with schizophrenia."[57]

Not all people who are psychotic commit crime, and many remain law abiding throughout their entire lives. Psychoses, however, may lead to crime in a number of ways. Following the Vietnam War, for example, several American soldiers suffering from a kind of battlefield psychosis killed friends and family members, thinking they were Vietcong soldiers (the enemy). These men, who had been traumatized by battlefield experiences in Southeast Asia, relived their past on American streets. In other crimes committed by psychotics, thought disorders may be less obvious or may exist only temporarily.

Recognizing the potential link between full-blown psychosis and violent aggressive acts, in 2013 the state of Maryland approved special funding for a new Center for Excellence on Early Intervention for Serious Mental Illness.[58] Its creation was spurred in part by random mass shootings that had occurred throughout the United States a year or two earlier.

Frustration–Aggression Theory

In his early writings, Freud suggested that aggressive behavior is a natural response to the frustration and limitations imposed upon a person. This *frustration–aggression thesis* was later developed more fully in the writings of J. Dollard, Albert Bandura, Richard H. Walters, and others. Dollard's frustration–aggression theory held that although frustration can lead to various forms of behavior—including regression, sublimation, and aggressive fantasy—direct aggression toward others is its most likely consequence.[59] Because everyone suffers frustration at times in life (beginning with weaning and toilet training), aggression is a natural consequence of living, but that aggression can be manifested in socially acceptable ways (contact sports, military or law enforcement careers, simple verbal attacks) and/or engaged in vicariously by observing others who are acting violently (in movies, on television, in fiction).

Dollard applied the psychoanalytical term *displacement* to the type of violence that is vented on something or someone who is not the source of the original frustration and suggested that satisfying one's aggressive urges via observation was a form of "catharsis."

Some psychologists have tried to identify what it is that causes some individuals to displace aggression or to experience it vicariously, while others respond violently and directly toward the immediate source of their frustrations. Andrew F. Henry and James F. Short, Jr., for example, suggested that child-rearing practices are a major determining factor in such a causal nexus.[60] Restrictive parents who both punish and love their children, said Henry and Short, will engender in their children the ability to suppress outward expressions of aggression, but when one parent punishes and the other loves, or when both punish but neither shows love, children can be expected to show anger directly and perhaps even immediately because they will not be threatened with the loss of love. Physical punishment rarely threatens the loss of love, and children so punished cannot be expected to refrain from direct displays of anger.

In 1960, Stewart Palmer studied murderers and their siblings to determine the degree of frustration to which they had been exposed as children.[61] He found that male murderers had experienced much more frustration than their brothers and that more than twice as many frustrating experiences—ranging from difficult births to serious illnesses, childhood beatings, severe toilet training, and negative school experiences—were reported by the murderers than by their law-abiding siblings.

Crime as Adaptation

Some psychiatrists see crime as an adaptation to life's stresses. According to **Seymour L. Halleck**, a psychiatrist and adjunct professor of law at the University of North Carolina at Chapel Hill, turning to crime can provide otherwise disenfranchised individuals with a sense of power and purpose.[62] Halleck says that crime can also provide "excellent rationalizations" for perceived inadequacies—especially for those whose lives have been failures when judged against the benchmarks of the wider society. "The criminal is able to say. . ., 'I could have been successful if I had not turned to crime. All my troubles have come to me because I have been bad.' " Thus, crime, according to Halleck, provides "a convenient resource for denying, forgetting or ignoring . . . other inadequacies."[63]

Insofar as the choice of crime reduces stresses the individual faces by producing changes in the environment (empowerment), it is referred to as **alloplastic adaptation**. When crime leads to stress reduction as a result of internal changes in beliefs, value systems, and so forth, it is called **autoplastic adaptation**. The offender who is able to deny responsibility for other failures by turning to crime is said to be seeking autoplastic adaptation. Because other forms of behavior also may meet many of the same needs as crime, Halleck points out, an individual may select crime over various other behavioral alternatives only when no reasonable alternatives are available or when criminal behavior has inherent advantages—as might be the case under instances of economic or social oppression. That is, individuals who are actively discriminated against may find personal and political significance in violating the laws of the oppressing society.

From Halleck's point of view, crime "has many advantages even when considered independently of the criminal's conscious or unconscious needs for gratification."[64] Even though crime

Think About It…

Alloplastic adaptation reduces stresses that individuals face by producing external changes in the environment and by creating a sense of empowerment. Autoplastic adaptation reduces stresses by producing internal changes, or changes in the mind. Can one type of crime produce both forms of adaptation? If so, what sort of crime might it be?

RioPatuca/Fotolia

can be immediately rewarding or intensely pleasureful, such a reward is more like a "fringe benefit"; its central significance is that it "is an action which helps one survive with dignity."[65] Halleck explained that "we cannot understand the criminal unless we appreciate that his actions are much more than an effort to find a specific gratification."[66]

In another approach to stress as a causative agent in crime commission, Arnold S. Linsky, Ronet Bachman, and Murray A. Straus suggested that stress may lead to aggression toward others and toward oneself (self-destructive behavior such as suicide, smoking, and abuse of alcohol).[67] Linsky and his colleagues measured stress at the societal level, arguing that although the relationship between stress and aggression has been studied at the individual level, "the neglect of social stress as an explanation for society-to-society differences in aggression may be partially due to a lack of an objective means of comparing the stressfulness of life in different societies."[68] Concluding that societal stress levels heighten levels of aggression, the authors suggested that social policies should be created to reduce the impact of such stressful events as having to stop work, foreclosing on a mortgage, and dropping out of school.

Finally, we should recognize that perceptions vary and that although criminal behavior may appear to be a valid choice for some individuals who are seeking viable responses to perceived stresses and oppression, their perceptions may not be wholly accurate.

Criminogenic Needs

In 1998 **Donald A. Andrews** and **James Bonta** identified major risk factors associated with criminal conduct that they termed **criminogenic needs**.[69] Criminogenic needs, which Andrews and Bonta referred to in later writings as "criminogenic domains,"[70] can be described as dynamic attributes of offenders and their circumstances that are associated with rates of recidivism.[71] Among the "needs" or risk factors that Andrews and Bonta listed are (1) antisocial attitudes, values, and beliefs; (2) antisocial personality, including low self-control; (3) antisocial associates and friends; (4) low levels of social achievement, to include a lack of educational, vocational, or financial achievement; (5) family factors, to include marital instability, a criminal family, and poor parenting skills; (6) substance abuse; and (7) a lack of prosocial pursuits. Criminogenic needs, because they are dynamic or amenable to change, can be targeted by treatment strategies intended to reduce criminality and recidivism.

In other writings, Andrews and Bonta used the term "criminogenic domain" to refer to major risk factors for continuing criminality. They identified criminal history as a major "criminogenic domain," and said that it in combination with antisocial attitudes, criminal associates, and antisocial personality represent the "big four" risk factors. Andrews and Bonta were careful, however, not to include criminal history as a criminogenic need because it is a static element unamenable to change.[72]

Attachment Theory

Another psychological approach to explaining crime and delinquency is **attachment theory**, first proposed by English child psychiatrist **John Bowlby** (1907–1990) who observed children during his tenure at the London Child Guidance Clinic after World War II.[73] Bowlby was especially interested in the maladjusted behavior of children who lacked a solid relationship with a mother figure, and he concluded that for healthy personality development to occur, "the infant and young child should experience a warm, intimate, and continuous relationship with his mother (or permanent mother substitute) in which both find satisfaction and enjoyment."[74]

The successful development of secure attachment provides the basic foundation for future psychological development.

Bowlby identified three forms of attachment: secure attachment, anxious-avoidant attachment, and anxious-resistant attachment.[75] Only the first is healthy, and it develops early in life when a child is confident that the mother figure will be responsible and available when needed. The successful development of secure attachment between children and their primary caregivers, Bowlby said, provides the basic foundation for all their future psychological development, with children developing a secure psychological base when they are "nourished physically and emotionally, comforted if distressed [and] reassured if frightened."[76]

According to attachment theory, delinquent behavior arises when nonsecure attachments are created. Anxious-avoidant attachment develops when children feel rejection and lack confidence concerning parental support and care. Anxious-resistant attachment develops from similar experiences and results in feelings of uncertainty, causing the child (and later, the adult) to feel anxious, to be fearful of his or her environment, and to cling to potential caregivers or partners. Bowlby called delinquents "affectionless," meaning they did not form intimate attachments as children and cannot form such attachments later in life. Attachment theory predicts that the most problematic individuals will be those who were abandoned at an early age, who experienced multiple placements (in foster homes and so on), who had to deal with the early absence of one or both parents, and who faced traumatic conditions (physical, sexual, or other abuse) in early childhood.

Tests of attachment theory seem to confirm that difficulties in childhood (especially before the age of eight) produce criminality later in life.[77] Studies have shown that children who were raised in insecure environments are likely to engage in violent behavior as adults and that childhood insecurity leads to a relative lack of empathy.[78] Some attachment theorists believe that the development of empathy is the single most important factor leading to conformity. When children do not receive empathy from those around them, they appear to also be unable to see others as deserving of empathy and become more likely to inflict injury on others. Learn more about attachment theory by visiting the Attachment Research Center via **Web Extra 5–4**, and read about the development of attachment theory at **Web Extra 5–5**.

THEORY in PERSPECTIVE

Types of Psychological and Psychiatric Theories

Psychological and psychiatric theories of criminology are derived from the behavioral sciences and focus on the individual as the unit of analysis. This chapter breaks their discussion down into a number of areas, as shown in this box.

Personality Theory

This approach envisions a complex set of drives and motives operating from recesses deep within the personality to determine behavior.

Period: 1930s–present

Theorists: Hervey M. Cleckley, Hans J. Eysenck, many others

Concepts: personality, psychopath, sociopath, antisocial personality, traits, Five Factor Model

Frustration–Aggression Theory

Frustration is a natural consequence of living and a root cause of crime in this theory, where criminal behavior can be a form of adaptation when it results in stress reduction.

Period: 1940s–present

Theorists: J. Dollard, Albert Bandura, Richard H. Walters

Concepts: Frustration, aggression, displacement

Crime as Adaptation

Criminal activity facilitates individual adaptation to the environment by reducing life stresses, and by producing environmental changes.

Period: 1970s–present

Theorists: Seymour L. Halleck, Donald A. Andrews, James Bonta, John Bowlby

Concepts: alloplastic and autoplastic adaptation, criminogenic needs, criminogenic domains, attachment theory

Behavior Theory

A psychological perspective, behavior theory posits that individual behavior that is rewarded will increase in frequency and behavior that is punished will decrease in frequency.

Period: 1940s–present

Theorists: B. F. Skinner, others

Concepts: Operant behavior, operant conditioning, classical conditioning, stimulus-response, reward, punishment

Modeling Theory

This theory states that people learn how to behave by modeling themselves after others whom they have the opportunity to observe.

Period: 1950s–present

Theorists: Gabriel Tarde, Albert Bandura, others

Concepts: Imitation, interpersonal aggression, social cognition theory, modeling, disengagement

Cognitive Theory

Cognitive theory, also known as moral development theory, holds that individuals become criminal when they have not successfully completed their intellectual development from child- to adulthood.

Period: 1930s–present

Theorists: Jean Piaget, Lawrence Kohlberg, Roger C. Schank, Robert P. Abelson, Stanton E. Samenow, Samuel Yochelson

Concepts: moral development, cognitive-information processing, scripts, criminal mindset

Psychoanalytic Criminology

This psychiatric approach, developed by Austrian psychiatrist Sigmund Freud, emphasizes the role of personality in human behavior and sees deviant behavior as the result of dysfunctional personalities or maladaptation to the social environment.

Period: 1920s–present

Theorists: Sigmund Freud, August Aichorn, others

Concepts: psychiatric criminology, id, ego, superego, psychoanalysis, psychotherapy, neurosis, psychosis, sublimation, paranoid schizophrenics

Behavior Theory

Behavior theory, the second main thrust of early psychological theorizing, built upon the concept of conditioned behavior. The idea that behavior could be "conditioned" or *shaped*, was popularized through the work of Russian physiologist Ivan Pavlov (1849–1936), whose work with dogs won the Nobel Prize in Physiology or Medicine in 1904. The dogs, which salivated when food was presented to them, were always fed in the presence of a ringing bell. Soon, Pavlov found, the dogs would salivate as if in preparation for eating when the bell alone was rung, even when no food was present. Hence, salivation, an automatic response to the presence of food, could be conditioned to occur in response to some other stimulus, demonstrating that animal behavior could be predictably altered via association with external changes arising from the environment surrounding the organism. The kind of conditioning that Pavlov demonstrated, which is the association of a particular response to a conditioned stimulus, is referred to today as *classical conditioning*.

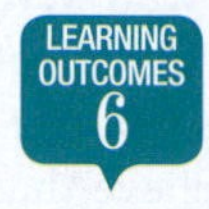

Demonstrate how behavior theory explains the role of rewards and punishments in shaping behavior.

Behavioral Conditioning

Behavior theory has sometimes been called the "stimulus-response theory of human behavior." When an individual's

The concept of conditioned behavior was popularized through the work of Russian physiologist Ivan Pavlov.

Think About It...

Behavior theory has sometimes been called the "stimulus-response approach to human behavior." Describe the stimulus-response approach in your own words. How is it applicable to criminal behavior?

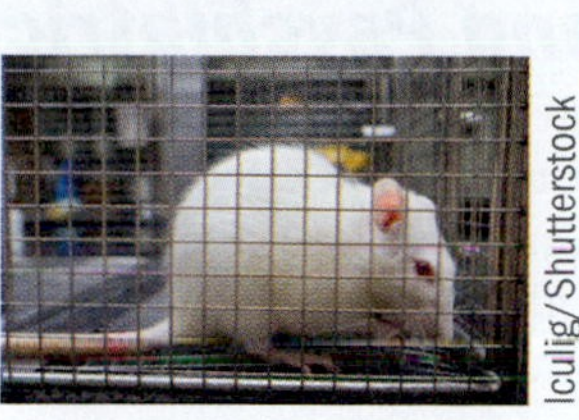
Iculig/Shutterstock

behavior results in rewards or feedback that the individual regards as pleasurable and desirable, then that the behavior will likely become more frequent. Under such circumstances, the behavior in question is reinforced, and the rewards themselves are referred to as *reinforcements*. Conversely, when punishment follows behavior, chances are that the frequency of that type of behavior will decrease. The individual's responses are termed **operant behavior** because a person's behavioral choices effectively operate on the surrounding environment to produce consequences for the individual.

Behavior theory is often used by parents seeking to control children through a series of **rewards** and **punishments**. Young children may be punished, for example, by being spanked, by having a favored toy taken away, and by the television being turned off. Older children are often told what rules they are expected to obey and what rewards they can anticipate if they adhere to those rules. They also know that punishments will follow if they do not obey the rules.

Rewards and punishments have been further divided into four conceptual categories: (1) positive reinforcements, which increase the frequency of approved behavior by adding something desirable to the situation—as when a "good" child is given a toy; (2) negative reinforcements, which increase the frequency of approved behavior by removing something distressful from the situation—as when a "good" child is permitted to skip the morning's chores; (3) positive punishments, which decrease the frequency of unwanted behavior by adding something undesirable to the situation—as when a "bad" child is spanked; and (4) negative punishments, which decrease the frequency of unwanted behavior by removing something desirable from the situation—as when a "bad" child's candy is taken away. According to behavior theory, it is through the application of rewards and punishments that behavior is shaped.

Behavior theory differs from other psychological theories in that the major determinants of behavior are envisioned as existing in the environment surrounding the individual rather than actually in the individual. Perhaps the best-known proponent of behavior theory is **B. F. Skinner** (1904–1990), who created the term *operant conditioning*. Skinner, a former Harvard professor, rejected unobservable psychological constructs, focusing instead on patterns of responses to external rewards and stimuli. Skinner did extensive animal research involving behavioral concepts and created the notion of programmed instruction, which allows students to work at their own pace and provides immediate rewards for learning accomplishments.

Behavior theory is important in the study of criminology because much human behavior is the result of conditioning, and people can be conditioned to respond to situations with either prosocial or antisocial conduct. It's important, too, because it is the foundation on which social cognition theory (which is discussed in the following section) is built. In fact, teachers and parents often use punishments and rewards in an effort to condition their students and children, respectively, to engage in appropriate or desired behavior. Consequently, from the perspective of behavior theory, crime can be explained as the result of inappropriate behavioral conditioning.

Social Cognition and the Role of Modeling

One of the earliest attempts to explain crime and deviance as learned behavior can be found in the work of **Gabriel Tarde** (1843–1904), a French social theorist of the late 1800s. Tarde discounted the biological theories of Lombroso and others. The basis of any society, Tarde believed, was imitation, the tendency of people to pattern their behavior after the behavior of others. Tarde developed a theory of human behavior that built upon three laws of imitation and suggestion.[79] Tarde's first law held that individuals in close intimate contact with one another tend to imitate each other's behavior. His second law stated that imitation moves from the top down. This means that poor people tend to imitate wealthy people, youngsters tend to emulate those who are older, lower-class people tend to imitate members of the upper class, and so forth. The third law of imitation is the law of insertion, which says that new acts and behaviors tend to either reinforce or replace old ones. Hence, the music of each generation replaces the music of the one that preceded it, the politics of young people eventually become the politics of the nation, faddish drugs are substituted for traditional ones, and new forms of crime tend to take the place of older ones (for example, when computer criminals become a more serious threat to financial institutions than bank robbers).

More recently, **Albert Bandura** developed a comprehensive **social cognition theory** of aggression that depends for its explanatory power on cognitive processes. Bandura believed that reinforcement theory could not account for all types of learning. Although everyone is capable of aggression, Bandura said, "people are not born with . . . repertories of aggressive behavior. They must learn them."[80] Bandura, a psychology professor at Stanford University and past president of the American Psychological Society, is often referred to as the creator of *social learning theory* in the field of psychology (a parallel tradition of social learning theories in sociology will be discussed in later chapters). Because of the central role of cognition in Bandura's learning theory, however, he preferred to call his approach *social cognition theory*. Central to Bandura's theory are the ideas of observation, imitation, and modeling.

The concept of **modeling** acknowledges the fact that people learn how to act through their life experiences, and especially by observing others. Bandura wrote that "Most human behavior is learned observationally through modeling: from observing others, one forms an idea of how new behaviors are performed, and on later occasions this coded information serves as a guide for action."[81] In some of his early work, Bandura experimented with children who observed adult role models striking inflatable cartoon characters. When the children were observed after their encounter with adult behavior, they, too, exhibited similarly aggressive behavior. Bandura also studied violence on television and concluded that "television is an effective tutor. Both laboratory and controlled field studies in which young children and adolescents are repeatedly shown either violent or nonviolent fare, disclose that exposure to film violence shapes the form of aggression and typically increases interpersonal aggressiveness in everyday life."[82] A later study by other researchers showed that even after ten years, the level of violence that young adults engaged in was directly related to the degree of violent television they had been exposed to as children.[83]

Aggression can be provoked, Bandura suggests, through physical assaults and verbal threats and insults, as well as by thwarting a person's hopes or obstructing his or her goal-seeking behavior. Deprivation and "adverse reductions in the conditions of life" (a lowered standard of living, the onset of disease, a spouse leaving or caught cheating, for example) are other potential triggers of aggression. Bandura adds, however, that a human being's ability to foresee the future consequences of present behavior adds another dimension to the activation of learned patterns of aggression. That is, aggressive behavior can be perceived as holding future benefits for individuals exhibiting it. In short, it can be seen as a means to a desired end.

Bandura also says that individuals sometimes become aggressive because they are rewarded for doing so. The early-twentieth-century American concept of a "macho"—virile and masculine—male figure, for example, was often associated with the expectation of substantial reward. Whether this perception was accurate, a significant proportion of American men subscribed to it nonetheless, and for many decades, it served as a guide to daily behavior.

Another form of reward can flow from aggression. Bandura called it the "reduction of aversive treatment." By this, he meant that simply standing up for oneself can improve the way one is treated by others. For example, standing up to a bully may be the most effective way of dealing with the harassment one might otherwise face. Bandura recognized that everyone has self-regulatory mechanisms that can inhibit the tendency toward aggression. People reward or punish themselves, Bandura said, according to internal standards they have for judging their own behavior. Thus, aggression may be inhibited in people who, for example, value religious, ethical, or moral standards of conduct such as compassion, thoughtfulness, and courtesy. Bandura concluded that people who devalue aggression may still engage in it via a process he called *disengagement*. Disengagement may result from (1) "attributing blame to one's victims"; (2) dehumanization through bureaucratization, automation, urbanization, and high social mobility; (3) vindication of aggressive practices by legitimate authorities; and (4) desensitization resulting from repeated exposure to aggression in any of a variety of forms.

Policy and Treatment Implications of Psychological and Psychiatric Approaches

No discussion of social policy as it relates to the insights of criminal psychology would be complete without mention of correctional psychology. **Correctional psychology** is concerned with the diagnosis and classification of offenders, the treatment of correctional populations, and the rehabilitation of inmates and other law violators.

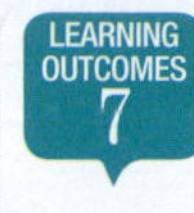

Describe some of the policy and treatment implications of psychological understandings of criminality.

Various forms of psychological and psychiatric treatments for criminal offenders have been developed based on the theories discussed in this chapter. In 2006, John C. Norcross and colleagues used a panel of 101 experts to generally assess the effectiveness of differing psychological assessments and treatments.[84] Fifty-nine treatments and 30 assessment techniques were evaluated, with the experts scoring each on a scale of 1 (not at all discredited) to 5 (totally discredited). Discredited assessment measures included the Luscher Color Test, the Szondi Test, and the Lowenfeld Mosaic Test for personality assessment, along with handwriting analysis (graphology). Similarly, voice stress analysis for lie detection received a failing grade from the experts. Although it is beyond the scope of this chapter to discuss these and most other techniques in detail, the panel of experts found that the Myers-Briggs Type Indicator and the Rorschach Technique, along with some others, were useful assessment techniques.

The most successful techniques for psychological treatment were identified as behavior therapy for sex offenders, cognitive behavioral interventions (discussed below), psychodrama, and laughter or humor therapy (for treatment of depression). The least successful treatment techniques included "fringe" methods, such as the use of pyramids for energy restoration, Orgone therapy (use of an orgone energy accumulator), crystal healing, rebirthing, and past lives therapy.

Although there are many different psychological and psychiatric treatments available today, including psychotherapy, guide group interaction, behavioral modification, parent training, peer programs, and individual counseling, some of the most successful have aimed to change impulsivity and other offender personality characteristics. One of the most effective correctional techniques, as the Norcross study (just mentioned) showed, is *cognitive behavioral intervention (CBI).* CBI is based on the belief that offenders need to acquire better social skills in order to become more prosocial. Cognitive skill-building enables offenders to modify their cognitive processes to control themselves and interact positively with others. According to one source, "the goal of cognitive skills is to teach offenders to manage their own behavior by engaging in processes that develop self-control, making them responsible for and in charge of their actions no matter how stressful the situation. These specific skills include problem solving, social skills training (learned behaviors that enable one to interact with others in ways that elicit

WHO'S TO BLAME—The Individual or Society?

The Video Game Killer

In early 2013, 17-year-old Jason Sutter was pulled over in a small midwestern town for various traffic offenses, including going 70 mph in a 35-mph zone, running a red light, failing to yield for a blue light and siren, and driving recklessly. When officers discovered that he didn't have a driver's license, Sutter was handcuffed, briefly searched, placed in the back of a patrol car, and driven to the local police station for booking.

Auremar/Fotolia

After he was photographed and fingerprinted, detective Joe Lockman sat down with him in a small interrogation room. Lockman, a 25-year veteran of the force, was working late and was in the station at 2:00 A.M. when Sutter arrived. The building was nearly empty, so Lockman decided to remove Sutter's handcuffs for what he hoped would be an informal chat. Sutter, who stood only 5 feet 4 inches tall and weighed 135 pounds, reminded Lockman of his son, and the detective hoped that he could teach the boy something about right and wrong.

As Lockman leaned forward to unshackle Sutter, a number of unfortunate events came together with deadly results. Sutter was a high school dropout and video game fanatic who spent most of his waking hours playing violence-themed games—including three in which the "heroes" killed pursuing police officers. Sutter had been improperly handcuffed with his hands in front, giving him easy access to Lockman's service revolver. Lockman carried an older model .38-caliber revolver (instead of a 9mm semiautomatic pistol), which was loaded with deadly hollow-point ammunition and did not have a safety. When Sutter grabbed the weapon, he was able to immediately pull the trigger and fire two shots into Lockman's chest, killing him instantly.

Sutter fled out the front door of the police station past the surprised desk sergeant. The sergeant, realizing what had happened, pursued Sutter through the front door, and the two exchanged shots. Sutter was wounded in the exchange and captured; he was taken to an area hospital where he underwent surgery and recovered. He was charged with the murder of Detective Lockman, and the district attorney said that he would seek to have Sutter put away for the rest of his life.

Sutter's parents hired an attorney to defend their son. The lawyer held a press conference during which he announced his defense strategy—that Sutter had been brainwashed by video games and that at the time of the shooting he had been unable to distinguish reality from fantasy. "Jason was confused by all that happened. He thought that he was playing a game," the attorney said. "He didn't realize that someone might really get hurt." He also announced that he was filing a lawsuit against the two media companies that had made the games Sutter played.

Think About It

1. Who is primarily responsible for the murder of Detective Lockman, Sutter or the video game manufacturers? Do both bear at least some responsibility?
2. What role, if any, did society play in Detective Lockman's death? Should government regulations control the content of video games?
3. What role did free will and individual choice play in Sutter's quick decision to take Lockman's gun and shoot him? How much control did Sutter have over his own behavior, and how much of his behavior was merely a response to experiences he had in the past?

Note: Who's to Blame boxes provide fictionalized critical thinking opportunities, and are not actual cases.

positive responses), anger management, and empathy training."[85] CBI programs not only target the offender's environment, behavioral responses, and skill development, they also seek to increase the offender's reasoning skills and problem-solving abilities, and expand the offender's empathy toward others.

CBI is based, in part, on the work of Stanton Samenow (discussed earlier in this chapter) and was first outlined in a six-part video series entitled *Commitment to Change* that Samenow created. The first three parts of the series emphasize the value of looking at one's own thinking and help to define and identify thinking errors. The next video addresses specific thinking errors that are crucial in problem solving, and the last two parts outline various methods useful in overcoming thinking errors.

Finally, it should be noted that psychopathology has been regarded as notoriously resistant to treatment of any kind. One of the first comprehensive studies of treatments intended for psychopaths, conducted by the NATO Advanced Study Institute, concluded that "no demonstrably effective treatment has been found." However, a more recent survey by Frederich Losel, a psychology professor at the University of Nurnberg (Germany) found that only a small proportion of 500 English psychiatrists shared that viewpoint.[86] Losel concluded that effective treatment with psychopaths should involve behavior modification techniques, educational measures, involvement in therapeutic communities, and pharmacological agents.

Critique of Psychological and Psychiatric Theories of Crime

Critics say that by focusing on the individual, psychological and psychiatric theories of criminality do not sufficiently take into account social or environmental conditions that produce crime. In fact, if social conditions are the primary cause of crime, as some claim, then individual change brought about by psychological or psychiatric interventions will not necessarily reduce levels of criminal offenses or lower rates of crime.

Provide a critique of psychological and psychiatric theories of crime.

Similarly, psychological and psychiatric theories place the locus of control within the individual by positing a sense of moral reasoning. However, effective social control may actually stem from within the social and physical arrangements that comprise the environment in which the individual functions. In other words, physical and social barriers to crime (such as the presence of a police officer) may be more effective at preventing crime than the sense of right or wrong that psychological theories find so important.

Freudian theory, discussed earlier, has been criticized on several levels. The first and most fundamental criticism of this perspective is its lack of scientific support. Critics point out that Freud's theories are not research-based and that there is no substantial support for his concepts. As such, Freudian theory has been seen as less of a scientific explanation for human behavior based on sound methodology and more of a belief system, valuable as a tool for literary and philosophical interpretation.[87]

Moreover, some claim that psychiatric theories, as distinguished from psychological ones, are appropriate only for explanations of abnormal cognition and do not apply well to otherwise normal people who turn to crime. In fact, some criminologists point to the fact that criminological predicators such as offense history are more accurate in forecasting future offenses than are psychological assessments and diagnosis even among individuals characterized as mentally disordered.[88]

Think About It...

Psychological and psychiatric theories of crime control stress a well-developed internal moral sense. Do you believe that an internal sense of moral reasoning is more important in preventing crime than crime control that results from social and physical arrangements in the external environment? How can we know?

Federico Rostagno/Shutterstock

Think About It...

Psychiatric theories focus more on the individual and on what goes on in a person's mind than on the social group or external factors. Might it be possible to develop psychological or psychiatric theories of crime that also consider social or environmental conditions? Explain.

olly/Fotolia

Freudian theory was very popular during the middle part of the twentieth century. By the 1980s, however, the notions of ego and id were considered antiquated by most psychiatrists. Attention shifted to the study of chemical imbalances in the brain, and psychopharmacology, or the use of drugs to treat psychiatric symptoms and disorders, has supplemented—if not replaced—the earlier ideas of Freud and his followers. Recently, however, the field of psychiatry has seen a rekindling of interest in Freudian psychology. The reason, according to some contemporary thinkers, is that psychopharmacology has been unable to provide an alternative grand theory of personality, emotion, and motivation.[89] Moreover, today's neuroscientists are busily creating a chemical map of the mind that seems to validate the general sketch that Freud provided decades ago. Soon a new and unified perspective that reconciles the work of neurologists and psychiatrists may emerge.

Behavior theory has been criticized for ignoring the role that cognition plays in human behavior. Martyrs, for example, persist in what may be defined by the wider society as undesirable behavior, even in the face of severe punishment—including the loss of their own lives. Rewards and punishments as controls over human behavior seem to lose any explanatory power because even the most severe punishment is unlikely to deter a martyr who answers to some higher call. Similarly, criminals who are punished for official law violations may find that their immediate social group interprets criminal punishment as status-enhancing—meaning that punishment actually becomes a reward.

Modeling theory, a more sophisticated form of cognitive theory, has been criticized for lacking comprehensive explanatory power. How, for example, can striking differences in sibling behavior, when early childhood experiences were likely much the same, be explained? Similarly, why do apparent differences exist between the sexes with regard to degree and

Modeling theory, a form of social learning theory, asserts that people learn how to act by observing others.

type of criminality, irrespective of social background and early learning experiences? More recent versions of modeling theory, sometimes called "cognitive social learning theory,"[90] attempt to account for such differences by hypothesizing that reflection and cognition play a significant role in interpreting what one observes and in determining responses. Hence, few people are likely to behave precisely as others do because they will have their own ideas about what observed behavior means and about the consequences of imitation.

Criminal Psychological Profiling

During World War II, the U.S. War Department recruited psychologists and psychiatrists in an attempt to predict the future moves that enemy forces might make. In addition, psychological and psychoanalytic techniques were applied to the study of German leader Adolf Hitler, Italian leader Benito Mussolini, Japanese general and prime minister Hideki Tojo, and other Axis leaders. Such psychological profiling of enemy leaders may have given the Allies the edge in battlefield strategy.

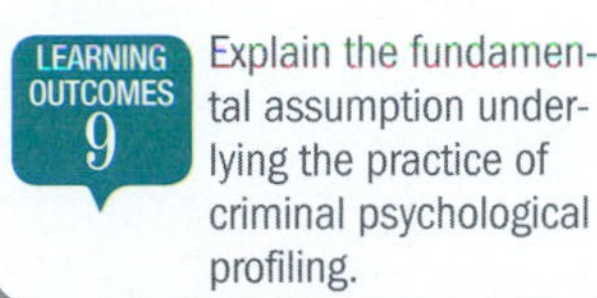

Explain the fundamental assumption underlying the practice of criminal psychological profiling.

After the war ended, little work was done in the field, until the 1970s when Federal Bureau of Investigation (FBI) special agent Howard Teten and others began to apply psychological profiling techniques to violent criminal behavior. In July 1984, the Bureau opened the National Center for the Analysis of Violent crime (NCAVC) on the grounds of the FBI National Academy in Quantico, Virginia. One division within NCAVC, the Behavioral Sciences Unit (later renamed the Behavioral Analysis Unit), began to look for unique psychological patterns in the behavior of serial rapists and killers and launched the practice of routinely profiling high-interest criminal offenders.

Today, **psychological profiling** (also called *criminal profiling* and *behavioral profiling*) is used to assist police investigators seeking to better understand individuals wanted for serious offenses. Psychological profiling is built on the idea that behavioral clues left behind at a crime scene may reflect the personality of the offender.

During an interview, famed profiler John Douglas, the retired FBI special agent who became the model for the Scott Glenn character in Thomas Harris's *Silence of the Lambs*, described criminal profiling: "It is a behavioral composite put together of the unknown subject after analyzing the crime scene materials, to include the autopsy protocol, autopsy and crime scene photographs, as well as the preliminary police reports. It is also a detailed analysis of the victim and putting that information together. To me, it's very much like an internist in medicine who now attempts to put a diagnosis, say, on an illness; I'm trying to put a diagnosis on this particular case that's relative to motive, as well as the type of person(s) who would perpetrate that type of crime."[91]

Profilers develop a list of typical offender characteristics and other useful principles by analyzing crime-scene and autopsy data, in conjunction with interviews and studies of past offenders, in the belief that almost any form of conscious behavior (including behavior the offender engaged in during a criminal episode) is symptomatic of the individual's personality. The way a kidnapper approaches victims, the type of attack used by a killer, and the specific sexual activities of a rapist—all of these might help paint a picture of the offender's motivations, personal characteristics, and likely future behavior. Sometimes psychological profiles can provide clues as to what an offender might do following an attack: Some offenders have been arrested after returning to the crime scene, a behavior typically predicted by specific behavioral clues left behind, and a remorseful type can be expected to visit the victim's grave, permitting fruitful stakeouts of a cemetery.

Although criminal profiling may not be useful in every case, it can help narrow the search for an offender in repetitive crimes involving one offender, such as serial rape or murder. Knowledge gleaned from profiling can also help in the interrogation of suspects and can be used to identify and protect possible victims before the offender has a chance to strike again.

Criminal profiling techniques have also been used in hostage negotiation, where law enforcement officers need to know as much as possible about the hostage taker; and in the analysis of anonymous communications—especially when those communications contain threats of violence. To analyze such communications, profilers have developed a "threat dictionary," in which words contained in the message are weighted and compared to standard speech patterns.[92] An analysis of the communications may indicate the educational level, gender, financial standing, and social group of the writer. Similarly, "signature" words or phrases that appear unique to the writer may help to identify him or her.

Profilers have also contributed to the criminological literature. In a well-known study of lust murderers (men who kill and often mutilate victims during or following a forced sexual episode), FBI Special Agents Robert R. Hazelwood and John E. Douglas distinguished between the organized nonsocial and the disorganized asocial types.[93] The organized nonsocial lust murderer exhibits complete indifference to the interests of society and is completely self-centered, methodical, cunning, and "fully cognizant of the criminality of his act and its impact on society."[94] The disorganized asocial lust murderer was described this way: "[He] exhibits primary characteristics of societal aversion. This individual prefers his own company to that of others and would be typified as a loner. He experiences difficulty in negotiating interpersonal relationships and consequently feels rejected and lonely. He lacks the cunning of the nonsocial type and commits the crime in a more frenzied and less methodical manner. The crime is likely to be committed in close proximity to his residence or place of employment, where he feels secure and more at ease."[95]

Critics of psychological profiling say that it is still more art than science. In a recent article published on the American Psychological Association's website, for example, psychologist Lea Winerman says that psychological profiling "is still a relatively new field with few set boundaries or definitions. Its practitioners don't always agree on methodology or even terminology."[96] Moreover, many early FBI profilers were not psychologists, and the techniques they developed were not necessarily based on accepted psychological perspectives or accepted methodology.

Terms like *offender profiling* and *crime action profiling* are used today to describe the work of profilers. Today's profilers tend to analyze crime-scene data and offender interviews, searching for commonalities that can be used to distinguish between types of offenders. Another term commonly used today is *investigative psychology*, which can be defined as "the scientific discipline of applying, analyzing, or developing psychological principles, theories or empirical findings to aid investigations and the legal process."[97]

Some contemporary psychologists discount the value of profiling. In 2007 a meta-analysis of profiling studies found that "trained profilers did only slightly better than non-profilers at estimating the overall characteristics of offenders from information about their crimes."[98] The studies compared the ability of profilers with non-profilers to gauge an offenders physical characteristics, thinking processes (including motives), and personal habits.[99] Nonetheless, profiling remains highly visible in today's media and continues to be popular with the public. Visit the Center for Investigative Psychology at the University of Liverpool at **Web Extra 5–6**, and learn more about the FBI's Behavioral Science Unit via **Web Extra 5–7**.

THE CASE

Andrea Yates

Few crimes have shocked American society as deeply as the drowning of five young children by their mother, Andrea Pia (Kennedy) Yates, in a bathtub in their suburban Houston, Texas, home on June 20, 2001. Her subsequent trial, conviction, life sentence, successful appeal, and second trial brought under intense scrutiny the insanity defense based on a claim of postpartum psychosis.

Yates's early life showed promise for future success. High school valedictorian and swim team captain, she went on to earn an undergraduate degree in nursing from the University of Texas. After obtaining a job as a registered nurse, she met Rusty Yates. Their shared deep Christian faith was a significant factor in their attraction to each other.

When Andrea and Rusty finally married, they planned on having as many children as God intended. The birth of their first child, Noah, a year after their marriage, however, brought unexpected difficulties.

Unaware of the extent of mental illness that had plagued her own family, the new mother was tormented when she began to have violent visions of stabbings and came to believe that Satan was speaking directly to her. Yates hid these frightening experiences from everyone, including her husband. The Yates had two more children, after which Andrea miscarried. She then had their fourth child, but the birth was followed by pronounced depressive manifestations—including chewed fingers, uncontrollable shaking, hallucinations, voices in her head, suicidal and homicidal thoughts, and two suicide attempts. Soon she entered into a series of psychiatric counseling sessions with various doctors. A wide variety of drug therapies were tried, many of which Andrea rejected by flushing the prescriptions down the toilet.

Despite extensive hospitalizations and medication for her ongoing depression and emerging psychosis—and against the advice of her psychiatrist—Yates became pregnant again, delivering her fifth child, Mary, in November 2000. The pregnancy had resulted from the urging of her husband, who also ignored the strong medical opposition to the birth of another child.[i]

When Yates's father died just four and a half months after her fifth child was born, her mental health declined dramatically.[ii] Both a hospitalization at the end of March and her medication, however, were terminated by her psychiatrist, Dr. Mohammed Saeed, because, he claimed, she did not seem psychotic. Yates returned to the hospital again for ten days in May. Upon her release, she was advised to think positive thoughts and to see a psychologist.

ASSOCIATED PRESS

Two days later, she systematically drowned each of her five children.

Following a sensational trial, Yates was convicted and sentenced to life in prison. That conviction was subsequently overturned. In July 2006, Yates was retried, but this time she was acquitted of capital murder charges and found not guilty by reason of insanity. She was immediately ordered to be committed to a mental hospital, where she will remain until she is no longer considered a threat to herself or others.[iii] Today, Yates is held at the Kerrville State Hospital, located 70 miles south of San Antonio. She has been diagnosed with bipolar disorder, and is medicated by daily injection.[iv]

Notes

[i]Charles Montaldo, "Profile of Andrea Yates," About.com: Crime/Punishment, 2007, http://crime.about.com/od/current/p/andreayates.htm (accessed June 16, 2010).

[ii]Ibid.

[iii]"Jury: Yates Not Guilty by Reason of Insanity," July 26, 2006, MSNBC/Associated Press, http://www.msnbc.msn.com/id/14024728 (accessed June 16, 2007).

[iv]Andrew Cohen, "How Andrea Yates Lives, and Lives with Herself, A Decade Later," *The Atlantic*, March 12, 2012, http://www.theatlantic.com/national/archive/2012/03/how-andrea-yates-lives-and-lives-with-herself-a-decade-later/254302 (accessed July 3, 2013).

The case of Andrea Yates raises several interesting questions. Among them are the following:

1. **Could Yates have been considered a psychopath? Why or why not?**
2. **How could Yates's mental issues be seen in light of the theories presented in this chapter?**

CHAPTER 5 Psychological and Psychiatric Foundations of Criminal Behavior

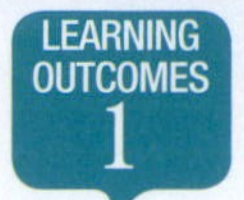

LEARNING OUTCOMES 1

Describe the main features of the psychological perspective on criminal behavior.

Psychological and psychiatric theories of criminal behavior emphasize individual propensities and characteristics in explaining criminality. Whether the emphasis is on conditioned behavior, human cognition, or the psychoanalytic structure of the human personality, these approaches see the wellsprings of human motivation, desire, and behavioral choice as being firmly rooted in the individual.

1. What are the major principles of psychological perspectives on criminal behavior?
2. How do psychological theories of criminal behavior differ from other types of theories presented in this book?

forensic psychology The application of the science and profession of psychology to questions and issues relating to law and the legal system; also called *criminal psychology*.

criminal psychology The application of the science and profession of psychology to questions and issues relating to law and the legal system; also called *forensic psychology*.

forensic psychiatry A branch of psychiatry having to do with the study of crime and criminality.

LEARNING OUTCOMES 2

Describe the two major ideas that characterized early psychological theories and explain the difference between them.

Two major ideas characterized early psychological theories: personality and behaviorism. Personality theory built on the burgeoning area of cognitive science, including personality disturbances and diseases of the mind; behaviorism examined social learning with an emphasis on behavioral conditioning.

1. What two ideas characterized early psychological theories? Explain them.
2. What is behaviorism?

personality The characteristic patterns of thoughts, feelings, and behaviors that make a person unique, and that tend to remain stable over time. Personality influences an individual's thoughts, behavior, and emotions.

behaviorism A psychological perspective that stresses observable behavior and disregards unobservable events that occur in the mind.

conditioning A psychological principle that holds that the frequency of any behavior can be increased or decreased through reward, punishment, or association with other stimuli.

psychoanalytic theory A perspective developed by psychiatrist Sigmund Freud in the early 1900s that explains the structure of personality and behavior in terms of both conscious and unconscious components and the conflicts between them.

LEARNING OUTCOMES 3

Explain how personality impacts criminality, and define *psychopath*.

Some early psychologists adapted the disease model, which had worked so well in the field of medicine, in an effort to cure mental and emotional problems. Hence, early psychological perspectives were couched in terms of mental disease, antisocial personality disorder, and psychopathy. The psychopathic personality, one that is cunning and self-serving but without empathy, offers an explanation for personality found in the unrestrained desires of offenders. The antisocial personality, in contrast, is essentially unsocialized and generally in conflict with society. Other important personality components are traits, or stable personality patterns that tend to endure throughout the life course and across social and cultural contexts.

1. How would you define *personality*? How might personality relate to criminality?
2. What are some of the characteristics of a psychopath?
3. How do the terms *psychopath* and *antisocial personality* differ?
4. What are *traits*, and how might they contribute to criminal behavior?

psychopathy A personality disorder characterized by antisocial behavior and lack of affect.

schizophrenia A serious mental illness that distorts the way a person thinks, feels, and behaves. A primary feature of schizophrenia is the inability to distinguish between real and imagined experiences and the inability to think logically.

psychopath An individual who has a personality disorder, especially one manifested in aggressively antisocial behavior, and who is lacking in empathy; also called *sociopath*.

sociopath An individual who has a personality disorder, especially one manifested in aggressively antisocial behavior, and who is lacking in empathy; also called *psychopath*.

antisocial personality An individual who is unsocialized and whose behavior pattern brings him or her into repeated conflict with society.

antisocial personality disorder (ASPD) A psychological condition exhibited by individuals who are basically unsocialized and whose behavior pattern brings them repeatedly into conflict with society.

electroencephalogram (EEG) The electrical measurement of brain-wave activity.

traits (psychological) Stable personality patterns that tend to endure throughout the life course and across social and cultural contexts.

Five Factor Model A psychological perspective that builds on the Big Five core traits of personality.

Key Names

Hervey M. Cleckley A neuropsychiatrist who described a psychopath as a "moral idiot," or one who does not feel empathy for others, even though that person may be fully aware of what is happening around him or her.

Hans J. Eysenck A British psychologist who explained crime as the result of fundamental personality characteristics, or traits, which he believed are largely inherited.

LEARNING OUTCOMES 4

Describe cognitive theories and identify the two types of cognitive theories that this chapter discusses.

Cognitive theories are learning theories that examine thought processes, and seek to explain how people learn to solve problems and how they perceive and interpret their social environment. Cognitive theory has a number of branches, including one that focuses on moral and intellectual development, and another that examines how people process information.

1. What is moral development theory, and what are some of its ideas?
2. How does moral development theory explain crime?

moral development theory A perspective on crime causation holding that individuals become criminal when they have not successfully completed their intellectual development from child- to adulthood.

cognitive information-processing theory (CIP) A psychological perspective that involves the study of human perceptions, information processing, and decision making.

scripts Generalized knowledge about specific types of situations that is stored in the mind.

Key Names

Jean Piaget A Swiss developmental psychologist who believed that human thinking and intellectual processes go through a number of biopsychological stages of development.

Lawrence Kohlberg An American psychologist who offered an expanded cognitive structural theory of morality in a six-stage typology.

Roger C. Schank and ***Robert P. Abelson*** Yale University co-researchers who developed script theory to explain the understanding process that occurs during a situation or event.

Stanton E. Samenow and ***Samuel Yochelson*** Mental health coworkers who suggested that criminals think in fundamentally different ways than nonoffenders.

LEARNING OUTCOMES 5

Describe the insights that the psychoanalytic perspective offers into criminal behavior.

Psychiatric criminology, or forensic psychiatry, sees crime as caused by biological and subconscious psychological urges mediated through consciousness. From the point of view of psychoanalysis, criminal behavior is maladaptive, the product of inadequacies in the offender's personality. The psychoanalytic perspective, advanced by Sigmund Freud in the early 1900s, encompasses diverse notions such as personality, neurosis, and psychosis as well as transference, sublimation, and repression. Some psychiatric perspectives see criminality as a form of adaptive behavior to stresses, holding that law violation represents an individual's most satisfactory method of adjustment to inner conflicts that he or she cannot otherwise express.

1. What insights into criminal behavior does the psychoanalytic perspective offer?
2. How can crime be a form of adaptation to one's environment? Why would an individual choose such a form of adaptation over others that might be available?
3. How does attachment theory explain behavior, and what are the three forms of attachment?
4. What are criminogenic needs? How might the concept of criminogenic needs be useful in the reformation of offenders?

psychiatric criminology A theory that is derived from the medical sciences (including neurology) and that, like other psychological theories, focuses on the individual as the unit of analysis. Psychiatric theories form the basis of psychiatric criminology.

psychoanalysis The theory of human psychology founded by Sigmund Freud on the concepts of the unconscious, resistance, repression, sexuality, and the Oedipus complex.

neurosis A functional disorder of the mind or of the emotions involving anxiety, phobia, or other abnormal behavior.

psychosis A form of mental illness in which sufferers are said to be out of touch with reality.

sublimation The psychological process whereby one aspect of consciousness comes to be symbolically substituted for another.

psychotherapy A form of psychiatric treatment based on psychoanalytical principles and techniques.

id The aspect of the personality from which drives, wishes, urges, and desires emanate. More formally, this division of the psyche is associated with instinctual impulses and demands for immediate satisfaction of primitive needs.

ego The reality-testing part of the personality; also called the *reality principle.* More formally, this personality component is conscious, most immediately controls behavior, and is most in touch with external reality.

superego The moral aspect of the personality, much like the conscience. More formally, this division of the psyche develops by the incorporation of the perceived moral standards of the community, is mainly unconscious, and includes the conscience.

repression The psychological process through which a person rejects his or her own desires and impulses toward pleasurable instincts by excluding them from consciousness, thereby removing them from awareness and rendering them unconscious.

paranoid schizophrenic A schizophrenic individual who suffers from delusions and hallucinations.

risk assessment The practice of using a structured instrument that combines information about individuals in order to classify them as being at low, moderate, or high risk for violent behavior, reoffending, or continued criminal activity.

alloplastic adaptation A form of adjustment that results from changes in the environment surrounding an individual.

autoplastic adaptation A form of adjustment that results from changes within an individual.

criminogenic needs Dynamic attributes (also known as *dynamic risk factors*) of offenders and their circumstances that are associated with rates of recidivism.

attachment theory A social-psychological perspective on delinquent and criminal behavior holding that the successful development of secure attachment between a child and his or her primary caregiver provides the basic foundation for all future psychological development.

Key Names

Sigmund Freud A psychiatrist who maintained that the personality is made up of three components—the id, the ego, and the superego.

August Aichorn A psychoanalyst who adapted Freud's work to explanations of violent criminal behavior, suggesting that violent offenders are dominated by the id and act impulsively.

Seymour L. Halleck A psychiatrist who says that crime provides otherwise disenfranchised individuals with a sense of power and purpose.

Donald A. Andrews and ***James Bonta*** Co-researchers responsible for developing the concept of criminogenic needs.

John Bowlby An English child psychiatrist who developed attachment theory.

LEARNING OUTCOMES 6

Demonstrate how behavior theory explains the role of rewards and punishments in shaping behavior.

Behavior theory (or the stimulus–response approach to human behavior) holds that behavior is directly determined by the environmental consequences it produces for the individual exhibiting the behavior. When an individual's behavior results in rewards or positive feedback, that behavior will increase in frequency; when punishment follows behavior, that behavior will decrease. Behavior theory differs from other psychological theories in that the major determinants of behavior are envisioned as existing in the environment surrounding the individual rather than within the individual.

1. How does behavior theory explain the role of rewards and punishments in shaping behavior?
2. Which do you feel would be more effective in shaping behavior: punishments or rewards?
3. How does behavior theory differ from other psychological theories?

behavior theory A psychological perspective positing that behavior that is rewarded will increase in frequency and behavior that is punished will decrease in frequency.

operant behavior Behavior that affects the environment so as to produce responses or further behavioral cues.

reward A desirable behavioral consequence likely to increase the frequency of occurrence of that behavior.

punishment An undesirable behavioral consequence likely to decrease the frequency of occurrence of that behavior.

social cognition theory A perspective stating that people learn how to act by observing others.

modeling A form of learning in which individuals imitate actions or performances by observing other people in order to add those actions to their own behavioral repertoire.

Key Names

B. F. Skinner A proponent of behavior theory who rejected unobservable psychological constructs, focusing instead on patterns of responses to external rewards and stimuli.

Gabriel Tarde A mid-nineteenth century French social theorist who developed a theory of human behavior that built upon laws of imitation and suggestion.

Albert Bandura A psychologist who developed a comprehensive modeling theory of aggression stating that everyone is capable of aggression, but people must learn aggressive behaviors.

LEARNING OUTCOMES 7

Describe some of the policy and treatment implications of psychological understandings of criminality.

Although there are many different psychological and psychiatric treatments available today, including psychotherapy, guide group interaction, behavioral modification, parent training, peer programs, and individual counseling, some of the most successful have aimed to change impulsivity and other offender personality characteristics. One of the most effective correctional techniques is cognitive behavioral intervention (CBI). CBI is based on the belief that offenders need to acquire better social skills in order to become more prosocial.

1. What types of crime-control policies might be based on psychological understandings of criminality?
2. How would the perspectives discussed in this chapter suggest that offenders might be prevented from committing additional offenses? How might they be rehabilitated?

correctional psychology The branch of forensic psychology concerned with the diagnosis and classification of offenders, the treatment of correctional populations, and the rehabilitation of inmates and other law violators.

LEARNING OUTCOMES 8

Provide a critique of psychological and psychiatric theories of crime

By focusing on the individual, psychological and psychiatric theories of criminality may not sufficiently take into account social or environmental conditions that produce crime. Moreover, psychological and psychiatric theories place the locus of control within the individual by positing a sense of moral reasoning. However, effective social control may actually stem from within social and physical arrangements that comprise the environment in which the individual functions. A specific aspect of the psychological perspective, behavior theory, has been criticized for ignoring the role that cognition plays in human behavior.

1. What are some of the critiques of psychological and psychiatric theories that this chapter identifies?
2. How might behavior theory be criticized?

LEARNING OUTCOMES 9

Explain the fundamental assumption underlying the practice of criminal psychological profiling.

Psychological profiling of criminal offenders is based on the belief that almost any form of conscious behavior is symptomatic of the individual's personality.

1. What is the fundamental assumption behind criminal psychological profiling?

psychological profiling The attempt to categorize, understand, and predict the behavior of certain types of offenders based on behavioral clues they provide; also called *criminal profiling* and *behavioral profiling*.

"Society prepares the crime; the criminal commits it."

—*Chinese proverb*

Social Structure—

It's How We Live

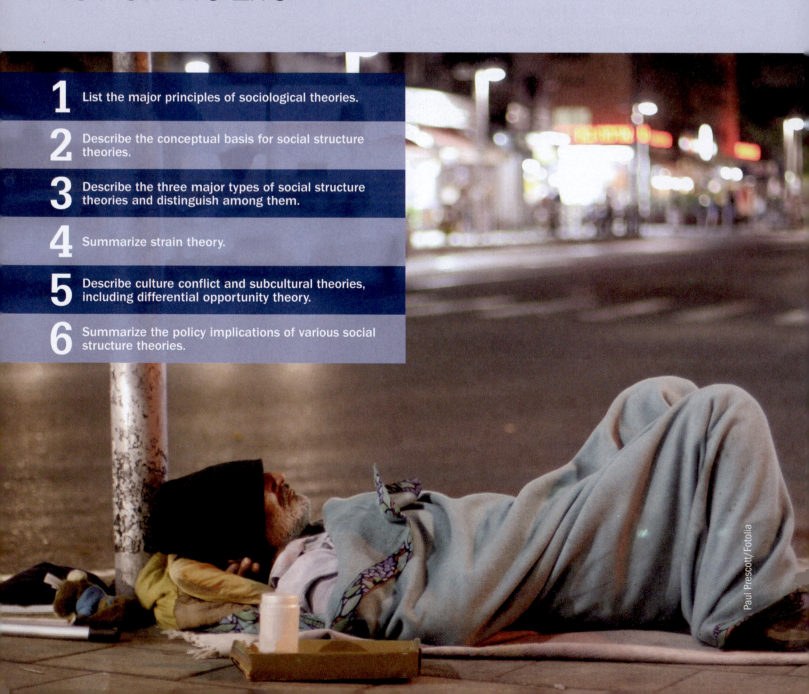

1. List the major principles of sociological theories.
2. Describe the conceptual basis for social structure theories.
3. Describe the three major types of social structure theories and distinguish among them.
4. Summarize strain theory.
5. Describe culture conflict and subcultural theories, including differential opportunity theory.
6. Summarize the policy implications of various social structure theories.

Paul Prescott/Fotolia

POVERTY AND CRIME

There's an old saying, something to the effect that you can take the criminal out of a bad environment, but you can't take the bad environment out of the criminal. Although we don't necessarily believe this to be true, some suggest that negative influences of the social environment—especially things like poverty, lack of education, broken families, disorganized neighborhoods, episodes of discrimination, and socialization into unproductive values—predispose certain people to lives of crime and that such negative influences may remain active even when people's circumstances change. Central to this perspective is the idea that crime is a social phenomenon, and central to any understanding of crime is the role that society, social institutions, and social processes play in its development and control.

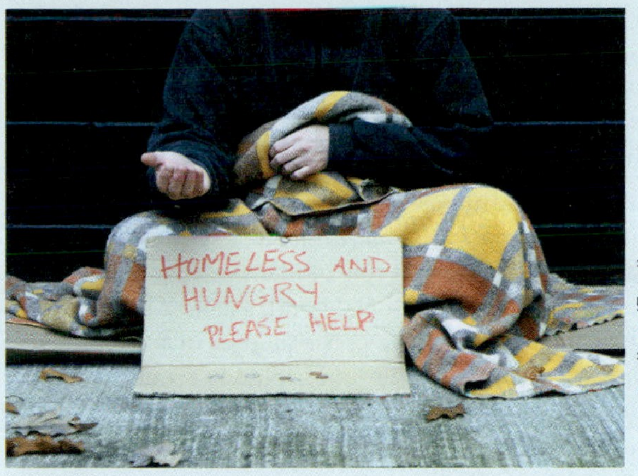
HOMELESS AND
HUNGRY
PLEASE HELP

margaretwallace/Fotolia

DISCUSS **Can a person's social environment lead that person into crime? If so, how? Can changes in the social environment end criminal involvement?**

Major Principles of Sociological Theories

Theories that explain crime by examining the structure of society are only one of three major sociological approaches to crime causation. The other two are social process theories and social conflict approaches. Although sociological perspectives on crime causation are diverse, most build upon the principles shown in Figure 6–1.

LEARNING OUTCOMES 1
List the major principles of sociological theories.

Sociological theories analyze institutional arrangements within society (that is, **social structure**) and the interaction among social institutions, individuals, and groups (that is, **social processes**) as they affect socialization and have an impact on social behavior (that is, **social life**). Sociological theories also examine the nature of existing power relationships between social groups and focus on the influences that various social phenomena bring to bear on the types of behaviors that tend to characterize *groups* of people. In contrast to more individualized psychological theories, which have what is called a "micro" focus, sociological approaches utilize a "macro" perspective, stressing the type of behavior likely to be exhibited by group members rather than attempting to predict the behavior of specific individuals.

Although all sociological perspectives on crime share the characteristics identified in this section, particular theories give more or less weight to the various components of social life. Hence, we can identify three key sociological explanations for crime:

- *Crime is the result of an individual's location within the structure of society.* This approach focuses on the social

Major Principles of Sociological Theories of Crime

- Social groups, social institutions, the arrangements of society, and social roles all provide the proper focus for criminological study.
- Group dynamics, group organization, and subgroup relationships form the causal nexus out of which crimes develop.
- The structure of society and its relative degree of organization or disorganization are important factors contributing to criminal behavior.
- Although it may be impossible to predict the specific behavior of a given individual, statistical estimates of group characteristics are possible. Hence, the probability that members of a certain group will engage in a specific type of crime can be estimated.

FIGURE 6–1 **Major Principles of Sociological Theories of Crime.**

and economic conditions of life, including poverty, alienation, social disorganization, weak social control, personal frustration, relative deprivation, differential opportunity, alternative means to success, and deviant subcultures and subcultural values, that conflict with conventional values. (These are the primary features of *social structure theories*, which are discussed in this chapter.)

- *Crime is the end product of various social processes, especially inappropriate socialization and social learning.* This approach stresses the role of interpersonal relationships, the strength of the social bond, a lack of self-control, and the personal and group consequences of societal reactions to deviance as they contribute to crime. (These are the primary characteristics of social *process theories* and *social development theories*, which are discussed in Chapter 6.)
- *Crime is the product of class struggle.* This perspective emphasizes the nature of existing power relationships between social groups, the distribution of wealth within society, the ownership of the means of production, and the economic and social structure of society as it relates to social class and social control. (These are the primary features of *conflict theories*, which are discussed in Chapter 7.)

> **Social structure theories explain crime by reference to the economic and social arrangements of society.**

Social Structure Theories

Social structure theories explain crime by reference to the economic and social arrangements of society. They see the various formal and informal arrangements between social groups (that is, the structures of society) as the root causes of crime and deviance. Structural theories predict that negative aspects of societal structures, such as disorganization within the family, poverty or income inequality within the economic arrangements of society, and disadvantages brought about by a lack of success for some in the educational process, produce criminal behavior.

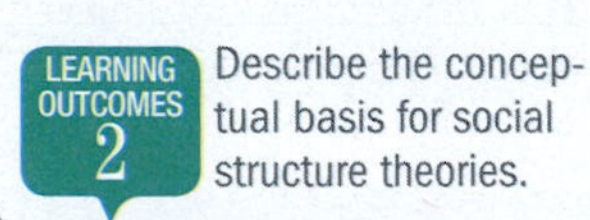

LEARNING OUTCOMES
2
Describe the conceptual basis for social structure theories.

Although different kinds of social structure theories have been advanced to explain crime, they all have one thing in common: They highlight those arrangements within society that contribute to the low socioeconomic status of identifiable groups as significant causes of crime. Social structure theorists view members of socially and economically disadvantaged groups as being more likely to commit crime, and they see economic and social disenfranchisement as fundamental causes of crime. Poverty, lack of education, an absence of salable skills, and subcultural values conducive to crime are all thought to be predicated on the social conditions surrounding early life experiences, and they provide the foundations of social structure theories. Environmental influences, socialization, and traditional and accepted patterns of behavior are all used by social structuralists to portray the criminal as a product of his or her social environment—and the immediate social environment is itself viewed as a consequence of the structure of the society to which the offender belongs. Although criminality is recognized as a form of acquired behavior, it is depicted as the end result of social injustice, racism, and feelings of disenfranchisement to which existing societal arrangements give rise. Similarly, social structure, insofar as it is unfair and relatively unchangeable, is believed to perpetuate the fundamental conditions that cause crime. Consequently, viewed from a social structure perspective, crime is seen largely as a lower-class phenomenon, and the criminality of the middle and upper classes is generally discounted as less serious, less frequent, and less dangerous.

Types of Social Structure Theories

This chapter describes three major types of social structure theories: (1) social disorganization theory (also called the "ecological approach"), (2) strain theory, and (3) culture conflict theory (also called "cultural deviance" theory). All have a number of elements in common, and the classification of a theory into one subcategory or another is often a matter of which aspects a writer chooses to emphasize rather than the result of any clear-cut definitional elements inherent in the perspectives themselves.

Describe the three major types of social structure theories and distinguish among them.

Think About It…

Theories of social structure seem to imply that economic conditions and the location of a person within society can create the conditions that propel people into crime. How might economic deprivation lead to crime? Is it inevitable that someone living an economically disadvantaged life will turn to crime? How do physical environments such as city life and urban environment contribute to crime?

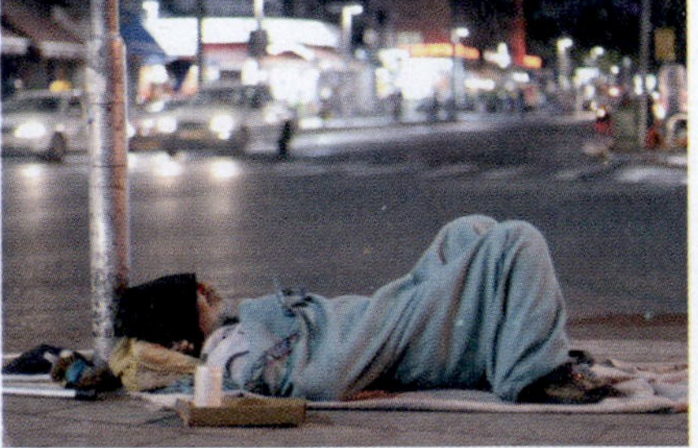
paul prescott/Fotolia

Social Structure Theories—From Past to Present

Social disorganization theory, which depicts social change, social conflict, and lack of social consensus as the root causes of crime and deviance, is closely associated with the ecological school of criminology. Much early criminology in the United States is rooted in the human ecology movement of the early twentieth century. *Ecology* is a term borrowed from biology that describes the interrelationships between living organisms and their environment, and social scientists use the term **human ecology** to describe the interrelationship between human beings and the physical and cultural environments in which they live.[1] Pioneers in the human ecology movement saw cities as superorganisms that incorporated areas adapted to specific groups, including ethnic groups ("Little Italy," "Chinatown"), which were functional enclaves within a larger organized whole that possessed its own dynamics.

The idea of the community as a functional whole that directly determines the quality of life for its members was developed and explored around the beginning of the twentieth century by sociologists **Emile Durkheim** (1858–1917),[2] Ferdinand Toennies (1855–1936),[3] and Georg Simmel (1858–1918).[4] Durkheim believed that crime was a normal part of all societies and that law was a symbol of social solidarity. Hence, for Durkheim, an act was "criminal when it offends strong and defined states of the collective conscience."[5]

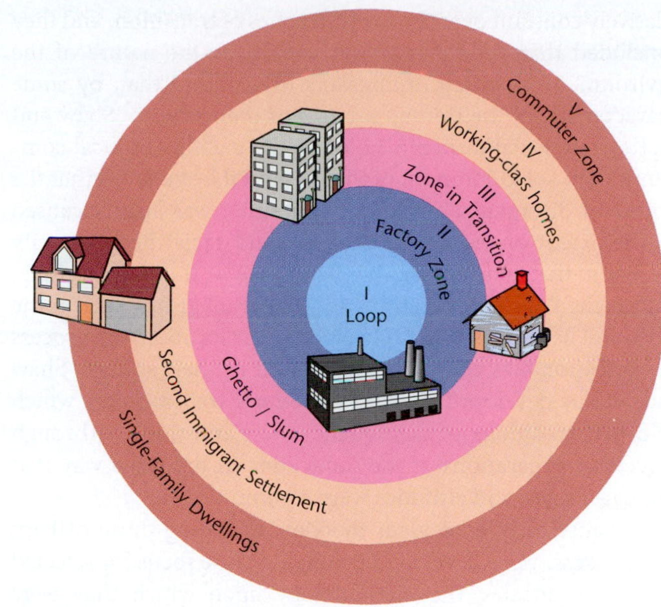

FIGURE 6–2 **Chicago's Concentric Zones.**
Source: Robert E. Park, Ernest W. Burgess, and R. D. McKenzie, *The City* (Chicago: University of Chicago Press, 1925), p. 55. Copyright © 1925 University of Chicago Press. Used by permission of University of Chicago Press.

The Chicago School

Some of the earliest sociological theories to receive widespread recognition can be found in the writings of **Robert Park** and **Ernest Burgess**.[6] In the 1920s and 1930s, Park and Burgess, through their work at the University of Chicago, developed what became known as **social ecology**, or the ecological school of criminology. The social ecology movement, which was influenced by the work of biologists on the interaction of organisms with their environments, concerned itself with how the structure of society adapts to the quality of natural resources and to the existence of other human groups.[7] Because ecological models build upon an organic analogy, it is easy to portray **social disorganization** as a disease or pathology.[8] Hence, social ecologists who studied crime developed a disease model built around the concept of **social pathology**. In its initial statement, social pathology was defined as "those human actions which run contrary to the ideals of residential stability, property ownership, sobriety, thrift, habituation to work, small business enterprise, sexual discretion, family solidarity, neighborliness, and discipline of will."[9] The term referred simply to behavior not in keeping with the prevalent norms and values of the social group. Over time, however, the concept of social pathology changed, and it came to represent the idea that aspects of society may be somehow pathological, or "sick," and may produce deviant behavior among individuals and groups living under or exposed to such social conditions.

Social disorganization—and therefore social pathology—may arise when a group is faced with "social change, uneven development of culture, maladaptation, disharmony, conflict, and lack of consensus."[10] Due to the rapid influx of immigrant populations at the beginning of the twentieth century, American cities were caught up in swift social change, and Park and Burgess saw in them an ideal focus for the study of social disorganization. Park and Burgess viewed cities in terms of concentric zones, which were envisioned much like the circles on a target (Figure 6–2). Each zone had its unique characteristics wherein unique populations and typical forms of behavior could be found. Park and Burgess referred to the central business zone as Zone I, or the "Loop," in which retail businesses and light manufacturing were typically located. Zone II, surrounding the city center, was home to recent immigrant groups and was characterized by deteriorated housing, factories, and abandoned buildings. Zone II was an area that was in transition from residential to business uses. Zone III contained mostly working-class tenements, while Zone IV was occupied by middle-class citizens with single-family homes, each with its own yard and garage. Zone V, consisting largely of suburbs, was called the "commuter zone." Significantly, Park and Burgess noticed that residents of inner-city zones tended to migrate to outer zones as their economic positions improved.

Clifford Shaw and **Henry McKay**, other early advocates of the ecological approach, applied the concentric zone model to the study of juvenile delinquency. They conducted empirical studies of arrest rates for juveniles in Chicago during the years 1900–1906, 1917–1923, and 1927–1933. These years were associated with high rates of neighborhood transition, during which one immigrant group after another moved in rapid succession from the inner city toward the suburbs—a process that was repeated with the arrival of each new wave of immigrants. Shaw and McKay found that rates of offending remained relatively constant over time within zones of transition, and they concluded that delinquency was caused by the nature of the environment in which immigrants lived rather than by some characteristic of the immigrant groups themselves.[11] Shaw and McKay saw social disorganization as the inability of local communities to solve common problems, and they believed that the degree of disorganization in a community was largely caused by the extent of residential mobility and racial heterogeneity present in that community. In effect, as a new immigrant group, such as the Polish, replaced an old immigrant group, such as the Irish, and became dominant in a particular location, the process of succession was complete. As a result of their studies, Shaw and McKay developed the idea of **cultural transmission**, which held that traditions of delinquency were transmitted through successive generations of the same zone in the same way that language, roles, and attitudes were communicated.

Because early **ecological theories**, including those of Park and Burgess, were developed through a close focus on selected geographic locales, the methodology upon which they were predicated came to be known as "area studies," and because Chicago in the 1920s served as the model for most such studies, they became collectively referred to as the **Chicago School of criminology**. Although the applicability of these early studies to other cities or to other time periods was questionable, it was generally accepted that the Chicago School had demonstrated the tendency for criminal activity to be associated with urban transition zones, which, because of the turmoil or social disorganization that characterized them, were typified by lower property values, impoverished lifestyles, and a general lack of privacy.

The greatest contribution the ecological school made to criminological literature can be found in its claim that society, in the form of the community, wields a major influence on human behavior.[12] Similarly, ecological theorists of the Chicago School formalized the use of two sources of information: (1) official crime and population statistics and (2) ethnographic data. Population statistics, or demographic data, when combined with crime information, provided empirical material that gave scientific weight to ecological investigations. Ethnographic information, gathered in the form of life stories, or ethnographies, described the lives of city inhabitants. By comparing demographic data with ethnographic data, ecological investigators were able to show that life experience varied from one location to another and that personal involvement in crime had a strong tendency to be associated with place of residence. Learn more about social disorganization theories of crime at **Web Extra 6–1**.

The Criminology of Place

Ecological approaches to crime causation have found a modern rebirth in the **criminology of place**. The *criminology of place*, also called **environmental criminology**, is a perspective that emphasizes the importance of geographic location and architectural features as they are associated with the prevalence of victimization. Such "hot spots" of crime, including neighborhoods, specific streets, and even individual houses and businesses, have been identified by recent writers. Lawrence W. Sherman, for example, tells of a study that revealed that 3% of places (addresses and intersections) in Minneapolis produce 50% of all calls to the police.[13] Crime, noted Sherman, although relatively rare in Minneapolis and similar urban areas, is geographically concentrated.

Policing hot spots, also known variously as *place-based policing* and *place-based crime prevention*, is a concept that was popularized by George Mason University's David Weisburd, University of Maryland's John Eck, Harvard University professor Anthony Braga, and others.[14] Place-based crime prevention has been shown to be a potentially effective crime-reduction technique. In a 2004 report, the National Research Council Committee to Review Research on Police Policy and Practices concluded that "[t]here has been increasing interest over the past two decades in police practices that target very specific types of crimes, criminals, and crime places. In particular, policing crime hot spots has become a common police strategy for reducing crime and disorder problems. . . . [A] strong body of evidence suggests that taking a focused geographic approach to crime problems can increase the effectiveness of policing."[15]

Reflecting the questions first addressed by Shaw and McKay, another contemporary researcher, Rodney Stark, asks, "How is it that neighborhoods can remain the site of high crime and deviance rates despite a complete turnover in their populations? . . . There must be something about places as such that sustains crime."[16] Stark has developed a theory of deviant neighborhoods. It consists of 30 propositions, including the following:[17]

- To the extent that neighborhoods are dense and poor, homes will be crowded.
- Where homes are more crowded, there will be a greater tendency to congregate outside the home in places and circumstances that raise levels of temptation and offer opportunity to deviate.
- Where homes are more crowded, there will be lower levels of supervision of children.
- Reduced levels of child supervision will result in poor school achievement, with a consequent reduction in stakes in conformity and an increase in deviant behavior.
- Poor, dense neighborhoods tend to be mixed-use neighborhoods.
- Mixed use increases familiarity with and easy access to places offering the opportunity for deviance.

Central to the criminology of place is the **broken windows theory**, which holds that physical deterioration and an increase in unrepaired buildings lead to increased concerns for personal safety among area residents.[18] Heightened concerns, in turn, lead to further decreases in maintenance and repair and to increased delinquency, vandalism, and crime among local residents, which cause even further deterioration in both a sense of safety and the physical environment. Offenders from other neighborhoods are then increasingly attracted by the area's perceived vulnerability. In short, physical evidence of disorder, left unchecked, leads to crime by driving residents indoors and sending a message to would-be offenders that a neighborhood is out of control.[19] A YouTube video about broken windows theory can be found at **Web Extra 6–2**.

Think About It…

The broken windows theory says that physical deterioration and an increase in unrepaired buildings lead to increased concerns for personal safety among residents living in such areas and may contribute to heightened crime rates. If this is true, how do run-down conditions in a neighborhood translate into criminal activity? Are such conditions the *cause* of crime? Explain.

elxeneize/Fotolia

The criminology of place employs the concept of **defensible space**,[20] meaning "the range of mechanisms—real and symbolic barriers, strongly defined areas of influence, and improved opportunities for surveillance—that combine to bring an environment under the control of its residents."[21] The criminology of place holds that location can be as predictive of criminal activity as lifestyles of victimized individuals or social features of victimized households. (*Place* has been defined by researchers as "a fixed physical environment that can be seen completely and simultaneously, at least on its surface, by one's naked eyes."[22]) Places can be criminogenic because they have certain routine activities associated with them or because they provide the characteristics that facilitate crime commission.

One problem with place-based crime prevention is the spatial displacement of criminal activity from areas targeted for crime reduction to other areas. Increased police patrols in one part of a city, for example, may cause criminals to simply pick up and move—resulting in a decrease in crime in one part of the city but an increase in another part.[23] A YouTube video on situational crime prevention is online at **Web Extra 6–3**.

Critique of Ecological Theory

Some authors have suggested that ecological theories give too much credence to the notion that spatial location determines crime and delinquency. The nature of any given location changes over time, they say, and evolutions in land-use patterns, such as a movement away from homeownership and toward rental or low-income housing, may seriously affect the nature of a neighborhood and the character of the social organization found there. Similarly, rates of neighborhood crime and delinquency may be "an artifact of police decision-making practices"[24] and may bear little objective relationship to the actual degree of law violation in an area. Such police bias (that is, enforcement efforts focused on low-income inner-city areas) may seriously mislead researchers into categorizing certain areas as high in crime when enforcement decisions made by police administrators merely make them appear that way.

Environmental criminology says that physical disorder in a community leads to crime.

Another critique of the ecological school can be found in its seeming inability to differentiate between the condition of social disorganization and the things such a condition is said to cause. What, for example, is the difference between social disorganization and high rates of delinquency? Isn't delinquency a form of the very thing said to cause it? As Stephen J. Pfohl has observed, early ecological writers sometimes used the incidence of delinquency as "both an example of disorganization and something caused by disorganization,"[25] making it difficult to gauge how accurate their explanatory approach is.

Similarly, those who criticize the ecological approach note that many crimes occur outside geographic areas said to be characterized by social disorganization. Murder, rape, burglary, incidents of drug use, assault, and so forth all occur in affluent, "well-established" neighborhoods as well as in other parts of a community. Likewise, white-collar, computer, environmental, and other types of crime may actually occur with greater frequency in socially well-established neighborhoods than elsewhere. Hence, the ecological approach is clearly not an adequate explanation for all crime, nor for all types of crime.

Strain Theory

Strain theory depicts delinquency as a form of adaptive, problem-solving behavior, usually committed in response to problems involving frustrating and undesirable social environments. Strain can be thought of as the pressure that individuals feel to reach socially determined goals (Figure 6–3).[26] The classic statement of **strain theory** was offered in 1938 by **Robert K. Merton**, who developed the concept of *anomie*. *Anomie*, a French word meaning "normlessness," was popularized by Emile Durkheim in his 1897 book *Suicide*.[27] Durkheim used the term to explain how a breakdown of predictable social conditions can lead to

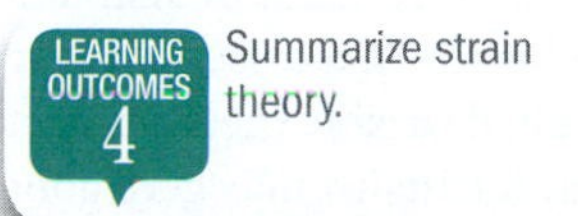
LEARNING OUTCOMES
4
Summarize strain theory.

	GOALS	MEANS
Conformity	+	+
Innovation	+	–
Ritualism	–	+
Retreatism	–	–
Rebellion	±	±

FIGURE 6–3 **Goals and Means Disjuncture.**
Source: Adapted from Robert K. Merton, "Social Structure and Anomie," *American Sociological Review*, Vol. 3, No. 5 (October 1938), pp. 672–682. Used by permission of *American Sociological Review*.

feelings of personal loss and dissolution. In Durkheim's writings, *anomie* was a feeling of strain that resulted from not being embedded personally in society. It marked the loss of a sense of belonging.

Merton's use of the term *anomie* was somewhat different. In Merton's writings, **anomie** came to mean a disjunction between socially approved means to success and legitimate goals.[28] Merton maintained that legitimate goals, involving such things as wealth, status, and personal happiness, are generally portrayed as desirable for everyone. The widely acceptable means to these goals, however, including education, hard work, and financial savings, are not equally available to all members of society. As a consequence, crime and deviance tend to arise as alternative means to success when individuals feel the strain of being pressed to succeed in socially approved ways but find that the tools necessary for such success are not available to them. Strain increases as the gulf between goals and the availability of the means necessary to achieve them widens. Complicating the picture further, Merton maintained, is the fact that not everyone accepts the legitimacy of socially approved goals. Merton diagrammed possible combinations of goals and means as shown in Figure 6–3, referring to each combination as a mode of adaptation.

The upper-left box in Figure 6–3 (*Conformity*) signifies acceptance of the goals that society holds as legitimate for everyone, with ready availability of the means approved for achieving those goals. The mode of adaptation associated with this combination of goals and means, conformity, typifies most middle- and upper-class individuals.

Innovation, the second form of adaptation, arises when an emphasis on approved goal achievement combines with a lack of opportunity to participate fully in socially acceptable means to success. This form of adaptation is experienced by many lower-class individuals who have been socialized to want traditional success symbols, such as expensive cars, large homes, and big bank accounts, but who do not have ready access to approved means of acquiring them, such as educational opportunity. Innovative behavioral responses, including crime, can be expected to develop when individuals find themselves so deprived.

The third form of adaptation, *ritualism*, describes the form of behavior that arises when members of society participate in socially desirable means but show little interest in goal achievement. A ritualist may get a good education, work every day in an acceptable occupation, and appear outwardly to be leading a solid middle-class lifestyle, yet that person may care little for the symbols of success, choosing to live an otherwise independent lifestyle.

Retreatism describes the behavior of those who reject both the socially approved goals and means. They may become dropouts, drug abusers, or homeless people or participate in alternative lifestyles such as communal living. These individuals are often socially and psychologically separate from the larger society around them.

Merton's last category, *rebellion*, signifies a person, or rebel, who wants to replace socially approved goals and means with some other system. Political radicals, revolutionaries, and antiestablishment agitators may fit into this category. Merton believed that conformity was the most common mode of adaptation prevalent in society, whereas retreatism was least common.

Messner and Rosenfeld suggest that inconsistencies in the ability to achieve the American Dream are to be blamed for most criminal activity.

Relative Deprivation

Relative deprivation refers to the economic and social gap that exists between rich and poor people who live in close proximity to one another. This contemporary version of Merton's anomie theory has been proposed by Steven F. Messner and Richard Rosenfeld, who suggest that inconsistencies in the ability to achieve the American Dream are to be blamed for most criminal activity.

According to sociologists **Judith Blau** and **Peter Blau**, two proponents of the relative deprivation concept, people assess their position in life by comparing themselves with things and people they already know.[29] Inner-city inhabitants, for example, develop an increasing sense of relative deprivation when they grow up in impoverished communities and witness well-to-do lifestyles in nearby neighborhoods. According to the Blaus, relative deprivation creates feelings of anger, frustration, hostility, and social injustice on the part of those who experience it. Relative deprivation is also related to the notion of **distributive justice**, which refers to an individual's perception of his or her rightful place in the reward structure of society. Thus, according to the principle of distributive justice, even wealthy and socially privileged individuals may feel slighted or shortchanged if they believe they have been inadequately rewarded for their behavior or accomplishments.

General Strain Theory (GST)

In 1992, strain theory was reformulated by **Robert Agnew** and others who molded it into a comprehensive perspective called **general strain theory (GST)** (Figure 6–4).[30] GST sees lawbreaking behavior as a coping mechanism that enables those who engage in it to deal with the socioemotional problems generated by negative social relations. According to GST, strain occurs when others do the following: (1) prevent or threaten to prevent an individual from achieving positively valued goals, such as autonomy or financial success; (2) remove or threaten to remove positively valued stimuli that a person possesses, such as the loss of a romantic partner or the death of a loved one; or (3) present or threaten to present someone with noxious or negatively

General strain theory sees law-breaking behavior as a coping mechanism that enables those who engage in it to deal with the socioemotional problems generated by negative social relations.

FIGURE 6–4 A Visual Representation of Strain Theory.

valued stimuli, such as verbal insults or physical abuse. In 2006, Agnew restated the six central propositions of general strain theory as shown in Figure 6–5.

Factors that increase the likelihood of criminal (as opposed to conformist) coping include poor conventional coping skills and resources; the availability of criminal skills and resources; low levels of conventional social support; routine association with criminal others; personal beliefs and values that are favorable to crime; frequent exposure to situations where the costs of crime are low; low levels of social control, including weak bonds to conventional others; and a lack of investment in conventional institutions.

Strategies for reducing exposure to strains include eliminating strains conducive to crime, altering strains to make them less conducive to crime, removing individuals from exposure to strain, and equipping individuals with the traits and skills needed to avoid strains that are conducive to crime.

GST expands on traditional strain theory in several ways. First, it significantly widens the focus of strain theory to include all types of negative relations between an individual and others.

The Six Central Propositions of General Strain Theory

- Strains refer to events and conditions that are disliked by individuals. There are three major sources of strain: Individuals may (a) lose something they value, (b) be treated in an aversive or negative manner by others, and (c) be unable to achieve their goals.
- Strains increase the likelihood of *particular* crimes primarily through their impact on a range of negative emotional states. Certain kinds of strains, for example, might lead to revenge seeking, while others cause those who experience them to steal things of value.
- Those strains most likely to cause crime are perceived (a) as high in magnitude or, (b) as unjust, (c) are associated with low self-control, and (d) create some pressure or incentive to engage in criminal coping.
- The likelihood that individuals will react to strains with criminal behavior depends on a range of factors that influence the individual's (a) ability to engage in legal coping, (b) costs of crime, and (c) disposition of crime.
- Patterns of offending over the life course, group differences in crime, and community and societal differences in crime can be partly explained in terms of differences in the exposure to strains conducive to crime.
- Crime can be reduced by reducing individuals' exposure to strains that are conducive to crime and by reducing their likelihood of responding to strains with crime.

FIGURE 6–5 **The Six Central Propositions of General Strain Theory.**
Source: Adapted from: Robert Agnew, "Pressured into Crime: An Overview of General Strain Theory," in Francis T. Cullen and Robert Agnew, eds., *Criminological Theory: Past to Present* (Los Angeles: Roxbury, 2003), pp. 201–209.

Second, GST maintains that strain is likely to have a cumulative effect on delinquency after reaching a certain threshold. Third, GST provides a more comprehensive account of the cognitive, behavioral, and emotional adaptations to strain than do traditional strain approaches. Finally, GST more fully describes the wide variety of factors affecting the choice of delinquent adaptations to strain.

Agnew sees the crime-producing effects of strain as cumulative and concludes that whatever form it takes, "strain creates a predisposition for delinquency in those cases in which it is chronic or repetitive."[31] Predispositions may be manifested in the form of **negative affective states**, or emotions such as anger, fear, depression, and disappointment.

Think About It…

GST suggests that positive relationships with other people reduce the likelihood of crime and delinquency. What is the nature of relationships that GST considers positive? Are close relationships necessarily the same as positive ones? Explain.

BestPhotoStudio/Fotolia

An analysis by Agnew of other strain theories found that all such theories share at least two central explanatory features.[32] Strain theories, Agnew said, (1) focus "explicitly on negative relationships with others, relationships in which the individual is not treated as he or she wants to be treated," and (2) argue that "adolescents are pressured into delinquency by the negative affective states—most notably anger and related emotions—that often result from negative relationships."[33] Watch a YouTube presentation by Robert Agnew on the topic of strain theory at **Web Extra 6–4**.

Critique of Strain Theory

From a social responsibility perspective, those who criticize strain theory note that Merton's original formulation of strain theory is probably less applicable to American society today than it was in the 1930s. That's because in recent times, considerable effort has been made toward improving opportunities for success for all Americans, regardless of ethnic heritage, race, or gender. Hence, it is less likely that individuals today will find themselves without the opportunity for choice, as was the case decades ago. Travis Hirschi criticizes contemporary strain theory for its inability "to locate people suffering from discrepancy" and notes that human beings are naturally optimistic—a fact, he says, that "overrides . . . aspiration-expectation disjunction." Hirschi concludes that "expectations appear to affect delinquency, but they do so regardless of aspirations, and strain notions are neither consistent with nor required by the data."[34] Similarly, recent studies have found that, contrary to what might be expected on the basis of strain theory, "delinquents do not report being more distressed than other youth."[35] Delinquent youths who are not afforded the opportunities for success that are available to others appear to be well shielded from sources of stress and despair through their participation in delinquency. Hence, "although strain theorists often have portrayed the lives of delinquents in grim terms . . . this depiction does not square well with the lived world of delinquency."[36]

THEORY in PERSPECTIVE

Types of Social Structure Theories

Social structure theories emphasize poverty, lack of education, absence of marketable skills, and deviant subcultural values as fundamental causes of crime. These theories, which portray crime as the result of an individual's location within the structure of society and focus on the social and economic conditions of life, are divided into three types.

Social Disorganization

Social disorganization depicts social change, social conflict, and the lack of social consensus as the root causes of crime and deviance; an offshoot, social ecology, sees society as a kind of organism and crime and deviance as a disease or social pathology.

Period: 1920s–1930s

Theorists: Robert Park, Ernest Burgess, Clifford Shaw, Henry McKay

Concepts: social ecology, ecological theories, social pathology, social disorganization, Chicago School, Chicago Area Project, demographics, concentric zones, delinquency areas, cultural transmission (criminology of place, environmental criminology, and the broken windows theory represent, at least in part, a contemporary reinterpretation of early ecological notions)

Strain Theory

Strain theory points to a lack of fit between socially approved success goals and the availability of socially approved means to achieve those goals. As a consequence, according to the perspective of strain theory, individuals who are unable to succeed through legitimate means turn to other avenues (crime) that promise economic and social recognition.

Period: 1930s–present

Theorists: Robert K. Merton, Steven F. Messner, Richard Rosenfeld, Peter Blau and Judith Blau, Robert Agnew

Concepts: anomie, goals, means, innovation, retreatism, ritualism, rebellion, differential opportunity, relative deprivation, distributive justice, general strain theory (GST)

Culture Conflict

The theory of culture conflict sees the root cause of crime in a clash of values between variously socialized groups over what is acceptable or proper behavior.

Period: 1920s–present

Theorists: Thorsten Sellin, Walter Miller, Gresham Sykes, David Matza, Franco Ferracuti, Marvin Wolfgang, Richard A. Cloward, Lloyd E. Ohlin, Albert Cohen, many others

Concepts: subculture, violent subcultures, socialization, focal concerns, delinquency and drift, techniques of neutralization, illegitimate opportunity structures, reaction formation, conduct norms

Culture Conflict Theory

Culture conflict theory (also called "cultural deviance theory") suggests that the root cause of criminality can be found in a clash of values between differently socialized groups over what is acceptable or proper behavior. The culture conflict concept is inherent in ecological criminology and its belief that zones of transition, because they tend to be in flux, harbor groups of people whose values are often at odds with those of the larger surrounding society.

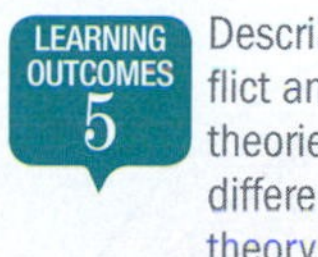

Describe culture conflict and subcultural theories, including differential opportunity theory.

In his 1938 book *Culture Conflict and Crime*,[37] **Thorsten Sellin** maintained that the root cause of crime could be found in different values about what is acceptable or proper behavior. According to Sellin, **conduct norms**, or expectations for human behavior within a social group, are acquired early in life through childhood socialization. The clash of norms between variously socialized groups results in crime. Because crime is a violation of laws established by legislative decree, the criminal event itself, from this point of view, is nothing more than a disagreement over what should be acceptable behavior. For some social groups, what we tend to call "crime" is simply part of the landscape—something that can be expected to happen to you unless you take steps to protect yourself. From this point of view, those to whom crime happens are not so much victimized as they are ill-prepared.

Sellin described two types of culture conflict. The first type, *primary conflict*, arises when a fundamental clash of cultures occurs. Sellin's classic example was that of an immigrant father who killed his daughter's lover following an old-world tradition that demanded a family's honor be kept intact. The other type of conflict, *secondary conflict*, arose, according to Sellin, when smaller cultures within the primary one clashed. Because criminal laws are based on middle-class values, the social phenomenon called crime occurs when middle-class values are at odds with inner-city or lower-class norms.

In Sellin's day, prostitution and gambling provided plentiful examples of secondary conflict. Many lower-class inner-city groups accepted gambling and prostitution as a way of life. Today, drug use and drug abuse provide more readily understandable examples. In some parts of America, drug dealing is an acceptable form of business. To those who make the laws, however, it is not. It is from the clash of these two opposing viewpoints that conflict and crime emerge.

Subcultural Theory

Subcultural theory is a sociological perspective that emphasizes the contribution made by variously socialized cultural groups to the phenomenon of crime. **Culture** is a collection of values, ideas, beliefs, and traits that characterize a human group—usually one defined by geographic boundaries, such as a nation. Like the larger culture, or the dominant culture, of which it is a part, a **subculture** is a collection of values and preferences that is communicated to subcultural participants through a process of socialization. Subcultures differ from the larger culture in that they claim the allegiance of smaller groups of people. Whereas the wider American culture, for example, may proclaim that hard work and individuality are valuable, a particular subculture may espouse the virtues of deer hunting, male bonding, and recreational alcohol consumption. Although it is fair to say that most subcultures are not at odds with the surrounding culture, some subcultures do not readily conform to the parameters of national culture. Countercultures, which tend to reject and invert the values of the surrounding culture, and criminal subcultures, which may actively espouse deviant activity, represent the other extreme.

In 1958, **Walter Miller** attempted to detail the values that drive members of lower-class subcultures into delinquent pursuits. Miller described *lower-class culture* as "a long established, distinctively patterned tradition with integrity of its own."[38]

Miller also outlined what he termed the **focal concerns**, or key values, of delinquent subcultures. Such concerns included trouble, toughness, smartness, excitement, fate, and autonomy. Miller concluded that subcultural crime and deviance are not the direct consequences of poverty and lack of opportunity, but emanate from specific values characteristic of such subcultures. Just as middle-class concerns with achievement, hard work, and delayed gratification lead to socially acceptable forms of success, said Miller, lower-class concerns provide a path to subculturally recognized success for lower-class youth.

Miller found that trouble is a dominant feature of lower-class culture. Getting into trouble, staying out of trouble, and dealing with trouble when it arises become focal points in the lives of many members of lower-class culture. Miller recognized that getting into trouble is not necessarily valued in and of itself, but is seen as an oftentimes necessary means to valued ends. In Miller's words, "[For] men, 'trouble' frequently involves fighting or sexual adventures while drinking; for women, sexual involvement with disadvantageous consequences."

Like many theorists of the time, Miller was primarily concerned with the criminality of men. The lower-class masculine concern with toughness that he identified, Miller admitted, may have been a product of the fact that many men in the groups he examined were raised in female-headed families. Miller's "toughness," then, may reflect an almost obsessive concern with masculinity as a reaction to the perceived threat of overidentification with female role models. Miller described "smartness" as the "capacity to outsmart, outfox, outwit, dupe, take, [or] con another or others and the concomitant capacity to avoid being outwitted, taken or duped oneself. . . . In its essence," said Miller, "smartness involves the capacity to achieve a valued entity—material goods, personal status—through a maximum use of mental agility and a minimum of physical effort."

Excitement was seen as a search for thrills—often necessary to overcome the boredom inherent in lower-class lifestyles. Miller claimed that fighting, gambling, picking up women, and making the rounds were all derived from the lower-class concern with excitement. Fate is related to the quest for excitement and to the concept of luck or of being lucky. As Miller stated, "Many lower-class persons feel that their lives are subject to a set of forces over which they have relatively little control. These . . . relate to a concept of 'destiny' or man as a pawn. . . . This often implicit world view is associated with a conception of the ultimate futility of directed effort toward a goal."

Focal concerns include key values of delinquent subcultures, such as trouble, toughness, smartness, excitement, fate, and autonomy.

Autonomy, as a focal concern, manifests itself in statements such as "I can take care of myself" and "No one's going to push me around." Autonomy produces behavioral problems from the perspective of middle-class expectations when it occurs in work environments, public schools, or other social institutions built on expectations of conformity.

Miller's work is derived almost entirely from his study of black inner-city delinquents in the Boston area in the 1950s. As such, it may have less relevance to members of lower-class subcultures in other places or at other times.

Delinquency and Drift

Members of delinquent subcultures are, to at least some degree, participants in the larger culture that surrounds them. How is it, then, that subcultural participants may choose behavioral alternatives that seemingly negate the norms and values of the larger society?

Gresham Sykes and **David Matza** suggested that offenders and delinquents are aware of conventional values, understand that their offending is wrong, but overcome feelings of responsibility through **techniques of neutralization**.[39] When involved in crime commission, offenders may use one or more of these five types of justification (Figure 6–6):

- *Denying responsibility*, by pointing to one's background of poverty, abuse, lack of opportunity, and so forth. Example: "The trouble I get into is not my fault."

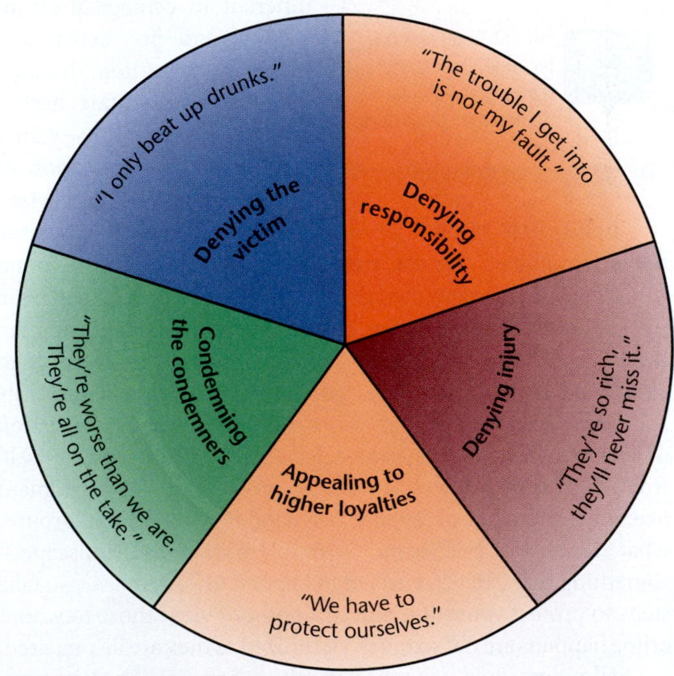

FIGURE 6–6 Techniques of Neutralization.

- *Denying injury*, by explaining how insurance companies, for example, cover losses. Claims that "everyone does it" or that the specific victim could "afford it" fall into this category. Example: "They're so rich, they'll never miss it."
- *Denying the victim*, or justifying the harm done by claiming that the victim, for whatever reason, deserved the victimization. Example: "I only beat up drunks."
- *Condemning the condemners*, by asserting that authorities are corrupt or responsible for their own victimization. Offenders may also claim that society has made them into what they are and must now suffer the consequences. Example: "They're worse than we are. They're all on the take."
- *Appealing to higher loyalties*, as in defense of one's family honor, gang, significant other, or neighborhood. Example: "We have to protect ourselves."

A few years later, Matza went on to suggest that delinquents tend to drift into crime when available techniques of neutralization combine with weak or ineffective values espoused by the controlling elements in society. In effect, said Matza, the delinquent "drifts between criminal and conventional action," choosing whichever is more expedient at the time. By employing techniques of neutralization, delinquents need not be fully alienated from the larger society. When opportunities for crime present themselves, such techniques provide an effective way of overcoming feelings of guilt and of allowing for ease of action. Matza used the term *soft determinism* to describe drift, saying that delinquents are neither forced to make choices because of fateful experiences early in life nor entirely free to make choices unencumbered by the realities of their situation.

Think About It...

Gresham Sykes and David Matza believed that offenders and delinquents are aware of conventional values and understand that crime is wrong, but that they overcome feelings of responsibility through what Sykes and Matza called "techniques of neutralization." They identified five such techniques. Of the five, which do you think are most important? The most widely used? Might there be other such techniques that they did not list? If so, what might they be?

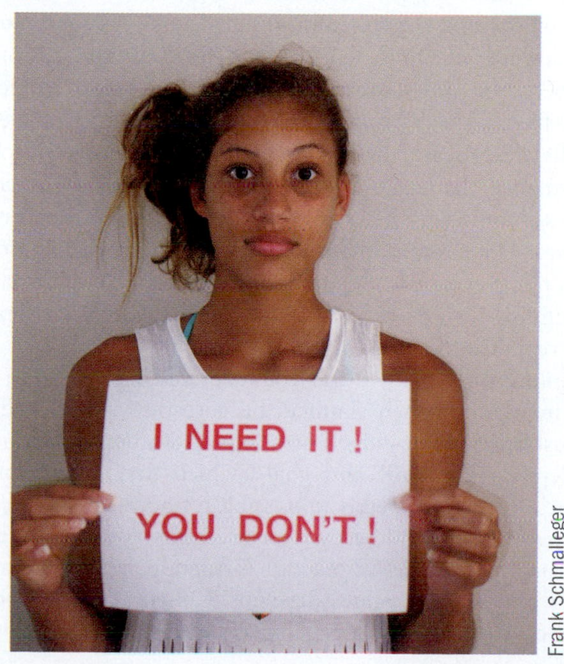

Frank Schmalleger

Some subcultures are decidedly violent and are built around violent themes and around values supporting violent activities. **Franco Ferracuti** and **Marvin Wolfgang** drew together many of the sociological perspectives previously advanced to explain delinquency and crime and claimed that violence is a learned form of adaptation to certain problematic life circumstances.[40] Learning to be violent, then, takes place within the context of a subculture that emphasizes the advantages of violence over other forms of adaptation. Such subcultures are characterized by songs and stories that glorify violence, by gun ownership, and by rituals that tend to stress macho models. They are likely to teach that a quick and decisive response to insults is necessary to preserve one's prestige within the group. Subcultural group members have a proclivity for fighting as a means of settling disputes. Subcultures of violence both expect violence from their members and legitimize it when it occurs.

Differential Opportunity Theory

In 1960, **Richard A. Cloward** and **Lloyd E. Ohlin** published *Delinquency and Opportunity*,[41] a report on the nature and activities of juvenile gangs that blended the subcultural thesis with ideas derived from strain theory. Cloward and Ohlin identified two types of socially structured opportunities for success: illegitimate and legitimate. They observed that whereas **legitimate opportunities** are generally available to individuals born into a middle-class culture, participants in lower-class subcultures are often denied access to them. As a consequence, illegitimate opportunities for success are often seen as quite acceptable by participants in so-called illegitimate subcultures.

Cloward and Ohlin used the term **illegitimate opportunity structure** to describe preexisting subcultural paths to success that are not approved of by the wider culture. Where illegitimate paths to success are not already in place, alienated individuals may undertake a process of ideational evolution through which "a collective delinquent solution" or a "delinquent means of achieving success" may be decided upon by members of a gang. Because the two paths to success, legitimate and illegitimate, differ in their availability to members of society, Cloward and Ohlin's perspective has been called "differential opportunity."

According to Cloward and Ohlin, delinquent behavior may result from the ready availability of illegitimate opportunities and the effective replacement of the norms of the wider culture with subcultural rules. Hence, delinquency and criminality may be seen as legitimate in the eyes of gang members and may even form the criteria used by other subcultural participants to judge successful accomplishments.

WHO'S TO BLAME—The Individual or Society?

Like Father, Like Son

Reginald Barfield, age 22, was arrested for driving under the influence (DUI) of alcohol and taken to jail. A judge set bail at $500, and his mother came to the jail to post bond for her son. She didn't have much money, so she used the services of a bondsman, who charged her a $70 fee and arranged for Reginald's release. As she drove her son home, she began yelling at him, telling him that he had turned out just like his father, who had had a long-standing problem with alcohol.

"You're just like your father, and if you don't change, you'll end up just like him—dead."

Reginald became angry and blurted out that he drank because that was all he had known as a child. "What do you mean?" his mother asked.

"Whenever Dad had a problem or when you two fought," Reginald said, "Dad broke open a bottle and killed the pain. It worked for him. It works for me. So you're right. I'm just like him. But it's not my fault. I learned it from him. You didn't stop him. And you didn't stop me."

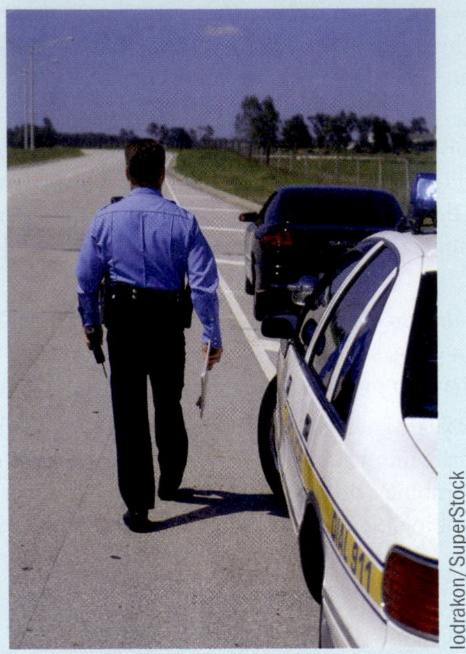

Iodrakon/SuperStock

Think About It

1. Is Reginald right? Did he learn his problem behavior from his father? What other factors might have contributed to his excessive use of alcohol?
2. Might the concept of reaction formation help explain Reginald's behavior? If so, how?
3. If you were Reginald's mother, to what degree would you hold your son responsible for his problem drinking? To what degree would you hold him responsible if you were a judge hearing his case in court?
4. Are questions about responsibility merely exercises in blame shifting? Is blame shifting ever appropriate when assessing criminal responsibility?

Note: Who's to Blame boxes provide fictionalized critical thinking opportunities, and are not actual cases.

Cloward and Ohlin noted that a delinquent act can be "defined by two essential elements: it is behavior that violates basic norms of the society, and, when officially known, it evokes a judgment by agents of criminal justice that such norms have been violated."[42] For Cloward and Ohlin, however, deviance is as much an effort to conform, albeit to subcultural norms and expectations, as is conformity to the norms of the wider society. Cloward and Ohlin described three types of delinquent subcultures: (1) criminal subcultures, in which criminal role models are readily available for adoption by those being socialized into the subculture; (2) conflict subcultures, in which participants seek status through violence; and (3) retreatist subcultures, where drug use and withdrawal from the wider society predominate. Each subculture is thought to emerge from a larger, all-encompassing "parent" subculture of delinquent values. According to Cloward and Ohlin, delinquent subcultures have at least three identifiable features: (1) "acts of delinquency that reflect subcultural support are likely to recur with great frequency," (2) "access to a successful adult criminal career sometimes results from participation in a delinquent subculture," and (3) "the delinquent subculture imparts to the conduct of its members a high degree of stability and resistance to control or change."[43] A video describing strain theory is available at **Web Extra 6–5**.

Reaction Formation

Another criminologist whose work is often associated with both strain theory and the subcultural perspective is **Albert Cohen**. Like Cloward and Ohlin, Cohen's work focused primarily on the gang behavior of delinquent youth. Cohen argued that young people from all backgrounds are generally held accountable to a "middle-class measuring rod" of expectations related to school performance, language proficiency, cleanliness, punctuality, neatness, nonviolent behavior, and allegiance to other similar standards. Like strain theorists, Cohen noted that, unfortunately, not everyone is prepared, by virtue of the circumstances surrounding his or her birth and subsequent socialization, for effectively meeting such expectations.[44]

Children, especially those from deprived backgrounds, turn to delinquency, Cohen claimed, because they experience status frustration when judged by adults and others according to middle-class standards and goals, which they are unable to achieve. Because it is nearly impossible for nonmainstream children to succeed in middle-class terms, they may overcome anxiety through the process of reaction formation, in which hostility toward middle-class values develops. Cohen adapted **reaction formation** from psychiatric perspectives and used it to mean

Albert Cohen adapted the concept of reaction formation from psychiatric perspectives and used it to mean "the process in which a person openly rejects that which he wants, or aspires to, but cannot obtain or achieve."

"the process in which a person openly rejects that which he wants, or aspires to, but cannot obtain or achieve."[45]

Cohen discovered the roots of delinquent subcultures in what he termed the "collective solution to the problem of status."[46] When youths who experience the same kind of alienation from middle-class ideals band together, they achieve a collective and independent solution and create a delinquent subculture.

The Code of the Street

Elijah Anderson, a University of Pennsylvania sociology professor, studied African American neighborhoods along Philadelphia's Germantown Avenue and published the results of his findings in a 1990 book entitled *The Code of the Street*.[47] In *Code*, Anderson details aspects of contemporary street code that stress a hyperinflated notion of manhood that rests squarely on the idea of respect. "At the heart of the code is the issue of respect," says Anderson, "loosely defined as being treated 'right' or being granted one's 'props' (or proper due) or the deference one deserves." In street culture, a man's sense of worth is determined by the respect he commands when in public. The violent nature of street subculture, however, means that a man cannot back down from threats—no matter how serious they may be. Working-class African American families place high value on the man as head of the household, and he is expected to be a provider and strict disciplinarian. Economic and social circumstances, however, conspire to limit opportunities for legitimate success—driving many families to alternative means of making money. Men who are not able to live up to the role of provider tend to abandon their mates and their children and may then move through a series of unsuccessful relationships.

A crucial distinction between both families and individuals in inner-city neighborhoods such as Germantown can be expressed as what Anderson calls the "decent family" and the "street family." "Decent" and "street" are labels that residents themselves use, says Anderson, and they mark people as either trying to uphold positive values or being oriented toward the street. Street life, he says, involves displays of physical strength and intellectual prowess meant to demonstrate that "I can take care of myself" and "I can take care of my own." Those who wholeheartedly embrace the street code are proud to live the "thug life" and identify with role models such as rap-legends Tupac Shakur and Snoop Dogg. A street orientation, says Anderson, means that people and situations become obstacles to be overcome or subdued. Hence, individuals who are street-wise learn to outsmart, or "hustle," others while avoiding being hustled themselves.

Gangs Today

Gangs have become a major source of concern in contemporary American society. Although the writings of investigators such as Cohen, Cloward, and Ohlin focused on the illicit activities of juvenile gangs in the nation's inner cities, most gang-related crimes of the period involved vandalism, petty theft, and battles over turf. The ethnic distinctions that gave rise to gang culture in the 1920s through the 1950s are today largely forgotten. Italian, Hungarian, Polish, and Jewish immigrants, whose children made up many of the early gangs, have been, for the most part, successfully integrated into the society that is modern America.

Today's gangs are quite different from the gangs of the first half of the twentieth century. More than one-third of jurisdictions covered by the 2011 National Youth Gang Survey (NYGS) reported experiencing gang problems in 2011, which is up considerably from 2001 when only 25% of jurisdictions reported gang problems.[48] Overall, an estimated 3,500 jurisdictions served by city and county law enforcement agencies reported gang problems. Survey results also indicated that an estimated 782,500, gang members and nearly 30,000 gangs were active in the United States during 2011.

The 2011 NYGC Survey confirmed previous findings that gang members are often involved in a variety of serious and violent crimes. Almost half of the law enforcement agencies reporting gang problems are involved in collaborative efforts with other law enforcement and criminal justice agencies to combat youth gangs and the serious and violent crimes they commit.

In addition to conducting the National Youth Gang surveys, the NYGC provides a compilation of gang-related legislation, maintains a repository of gang-related literature, analyzes gang-related data and statistics, and coordinates the activities of the Youth Gang Consortium.

Members of modern youth gangs generally identify with a name (such as the "Crips" and "Bloods," which are well-known Los Angeles–area gangs), a particular style of clothing, symbols, tattoos, jewelry, haircuts, and hand symbols.

Gangs can be big business. In addition to traditional criminal activities such as burglary, extortion, vandalism, and protection rackets, drug dealing has become a mainstay of many inner-city gangs. Los Angeles police estimate that at least four city gangs earn over $1 million each per week through cocaine sales.[49] The potential for huge drug-based profits appears to have changed the nature of gangs, making them more prone to violence and cutthroat tactics. Gang killings, including the now infamous drive-by shootings, have become commonplace in our nation's cities.

Rodney Dailey, a self-avowed former Boston-area drug dealer and gun-wielding gang member, says that in today's gang world, "shoot before you get shot is the rule." According to Dailey, "Things that normally people would have had fist-fights about can get you shot or stabbed" today.[50] Dailey is the founder of Gang Peace, an outreach group that tries to reduce gang-related violence.

Guns have become a way of life for many young gang members. As a young man named Jamaal, hanging around with friends outside Boston's Orchard Park housing project, recently put it, "We don't fight, we shoot." Police in the area describe how values among youth have changed over the past decade or two. Today they "think it's fun to pop someone," the police say.[51]

Critique of Culture Conflict Theories

Subcultural approaches, which constitute the last of the three types of social structure explanations for crime discussed in this chapter, have been questioned by some criminologists who see them as lacking in explanatory power. Canadian criminologist Gwynn Nettler, for example, criticizes the notion of violent subcultures by insisting that it is tautological, or circular. Nettler argues that saying that people fight because they are violent or that "they are murderous because they live violently" does little to explain their behavior. Attributing fighting to "other spheres of violence," he says, may be true, but it is fundamentally "uninformative."[52]

The subcultural approach has also been criticized for being racist because many so-called violent subcultures are said to be populated primarily by minorities. Margaret Anderson says that "the problem with this explanation is that it turns attention away from the relationship of black communities to the larger society and it recreates dominant stereotypes about blacks as violent, aggressive, and fearful. Although it may be true that rates of violence are higher in black communities, this observation does not explain the fact."[53] In sociological jargon, one might say that an observed correlation between race and violence does not necessarily provide a workable explanation for the relationship.

Policy Implications of Social Structure Theories

Theoretical approaches that fault social structure as the root cause of crime point in the direction of social action as a solution. In the 1930s, for example, Clifford Shaw, in an effort to put his theories into practice, established the **Chicago Area Project**. Through the Chicago Area Project, Shaw sought to reduce delinquency in transitional neighborhoods. Shaw analyzed oral histories gathered from neighborhood citizens to determine that delinquents were essentially normal youngsters who entered into illegal activities at early ages, often through street play. Hence, he worked to increase opportunities for young people to embark on successful work careers.

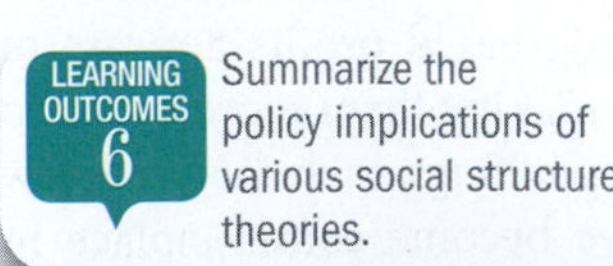

LEARNING OUTCOMES 6
Summarize the policy implications of various social structure theories.

The Chicago Area Project attempted to reduce social disorganization in slum neighborhoods through the creation of community committees. Shaw staffed these committees with local residents rather than professional social workers. The project had three broad objectives: (1) improving the physical appearance of poor neighborhoods, (2) providing recreational opportunities for youths, and (3) involving project members directly in the lives of troubled youths through school and courtroom mediation. The program also made use of "curbside counselors," street-wise workers who could serve as positive role models for inner-city youth. Although no effective assessment programs were established to evaluate the Chicago Area Project during the program's tenure, in 1984, Rand Corporation reviewers published a 50-year review of the program, declaring it "effective in reducing rates of juvenile delinquency."[54]

Similarly, Mobilization for Youth, which operated in New York City during the 1960s, provides a bold example of the treatment implications of social structure theories. Mobilization for Youth sought not only to provide new opportunities, but also to change the fundamental arrangements of society and thereby address the root causes of crime and deviance through direct social action. Leaders of Mobilization for Youth decided that "what was needed to overcome . . . formidable barriers to opportunity . . . was not community organization but community action" that attacked entrenched political interests. Accordingly, the program promoted "boycotts against schools, protests against welfare policies, rent strikes against 'slum landlords,' lawsuits to ensure poor people's rights, and voter registration."[55] A truly unusual government-sponsored program for its time, Mobilization for Youth was eventually disbanded amid protests that "the mandate of the President's Committee was to reduce delinquency, not to reform urban society or to try out sociological theories on American youths."[56]

The War on Poverty declared by the Kennedy and Johnson administrations during the 1960s and subsequent federal and state-run welfare programs that provide supplemental income assistance have been cited[57] as examples of programs that at least held the potential to reduce crime rates by redistributing wealth in American society.[58] Such programs, however, have come under increasing fire recently, and the federal Welfare Reform Reconciliation Act of 1996[59] reduced or eliminated long-term benefits that had previously been available through avenues such as the federal Aid to Families with Dependent Children (AFDC) program. The 1996 legislation also established stricter work requirements for welfare recipients through a new Welfare-to-Work program under the Personal Responsibility and Work Opportunity Reconciliation Act of 1996.[60]

Think About It...

This chapter says that theoretical approaches that fault social structure as the root cause of crime point in the direction of social action as a solution. What contemporary social action measures can you think of that might be effective at fighting crime or preventing it from increasing?

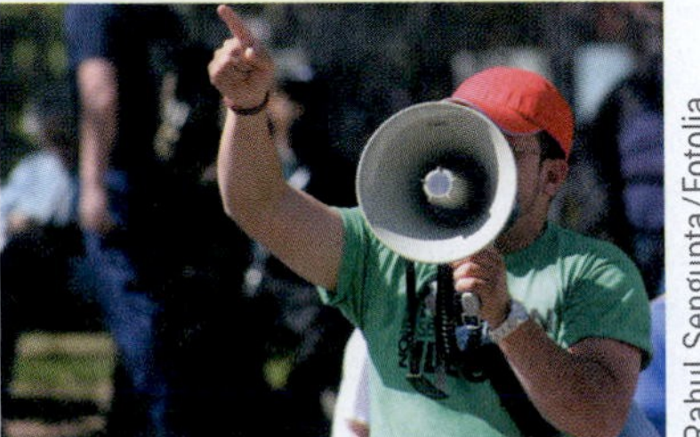

Rahul Sengupta/Fotolia

THE CASE

Sanyika Shakur, aka Monster Kody Scott

Born in the tumultuous 1960s (1963), 11-year-old Kody Scott (he adopted the name Sanyika Shakur in prison some years later) earned initiation into the infamous Crips street gang–and into a life of persistently violent criminal conduct–with eight blasts from a shotgun at a group of the notorious Bloods, a rival gang. His teen years were an odyssey of violent crime interspersed with repeated stays in various juvenile detention centers and, ultimately, the California State Penitentiary.

His "Monster" moniker came from one such crime. After robbing and beating a man, the victim had the audacity to strike Shakur in the face. In retaliation, Shakur further "beat him, and stomped him and disfigured him," leaving the young man in a coma.[i] The severity of the damage caused one investigating police officer to observe that whoever had done the beating was a monster. Shakur decided to adopt the name later that night when he saw the looks on the faces of the people in his neighborhood. "[I]t was just power," he says proudly. "And I felt it. And I just took that name."[ii]

Feared even by his fellow Crips, Shakur rose through the gang's leadership ranks until he eventually became one of its top leaders and achieved status as an Original Gangster (O.G.), the highest "honor" a gang member can receive. Throughout his autobiography, *Monster: The Autobiography of an L.A. Gang Member*, Shakur speaks with pride of committing his crimes out of an honor-bound "duty" to stand with his fellow Crips. To his way of thinking, adherence to the code of the gang justifiably trumps social prohibitions against killing and maiming–as long as one does so for the purpose of supporting the criminal activities of one's fellow lawbreakers.

In *Monster*, Shakur shrouds his behavior in a cloak of inevitability, asserting that there are no other options available to him and those like him by which they can achieve success within the legitimate American social system. He "portrays himself as the inevitable product of a hellish environment."[iii] Shakur speaks out against what he perceives as a contrived systematic mechanism for preventing minorities from advancement and gives one the sense that he is attempting to create a Robin Hood–esque mystique about his criminality.

Shakur has been dubbed an "iconic figure" of the hip-hop culture by independent filmmaker Billy Wright, who further asserts that Shakur's "real life encapsulates what hip hop imagery is all about."[iv] Wright's recent project, entitled *Can't Stop, Won't Stop*, tells the story of Shakur's life. Wright describes the film as a "tribute" to close friend Shakur.

Susan Ragan/Associated Press

Sanyika Shakur (born Kody Scott), aka Monster Kody Scott, photographed at Pelican Bay Prison in June 1993 through Plexiglas. The gangster thug of the literary set was sent back to prison in 2008 for beating a man and stealing his car while out on parole. Is Shakur a villain or a hero?

In December 2006, already a fugitive for numerous parole violations (he was, at the time, out on parole from yet another term in the California State Penitentiary), Shakur allegedly broke into a man's home and beat him in order to steal the victim's car. In 2008, he pleaded no contest to carjacking and robbery charges and is now serving a sentence of six years in state prison.

Notes

[i]Mandalit Del Barco, "Gang Member Turned Author Arrested in L.A.," *Morning Edition*, National Public Radio, March 9, 2007, http://www.npr.org/templates/story/story.php?storyId=7793148 (accessed July 14, 2007).

[ii]Ibid.

[iii]Mark Horowitz, "In Search of Monster," *The Atlantic*, December 1993, http://www.theatlantic.com/doc/199312/monster (accessed July 2, 2009).

[iv]"America's O.G. Gangster–Monster Kody (aka Sanyika Shakur)," RapIndustry.com, 2007.

The case of Sanyika Shakur raises several interesting questions. Among them are the following:

1. **How does Shakur's life demonstrate the principles of reaction formation?**
2. **Sykes and Matza suggest that offenders use five techniques of neutralization to justify their actions, even when they know offending is wrong. Which of these techniques might Shakur be expressing?**
3. **How is filmmaker Billy Wright demonstrating Cloward and Ohlin's notion of illegitimate opportunity structure to explain his admiration of Shakur?**
4. **How might strain theory be used to explain Shakur's actions?**

CHAPTER 6 Social Structure—*It's How We Live*

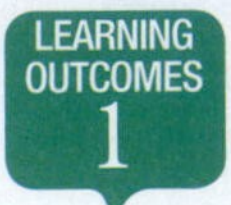

List the major principles of sociological theories.

Sociological perspectives on crime causation are diverse and include three major approaches to crime causation: social structure theories, social process theories, and social conflict approaches. Still, all make certain assumptions, one of which is that social groups, social institutions, the arrangements of society, and social roles all provide the proper focus for criminological study.

1. What are the principle assumptions upon which sociological perspectives on crime causation rest?
2. What is the difference between social structure and social process?

sociological theories A group of perspectives that focus on the nature of the power relationships that exist between social groups and on the influences that various social phenomena bring to bear on the types of behaviors that tend to characterize groups of people.

social structure The stable pattern of social relationships that exists within a society.

social process The interaction between and among social institutions, individuals, and groups.

social life The ongoing and (typically) structured interaction that occurs between people in a society, including socialization and social behavior in general.

LEARNING OUTCOMES 2

Describe the conceptual basis for social structure theories.

Social structure approaches emphasize the role of poverty, lack of education, absence of marketable skills, and subcultural values as fundamental causes of crime. Social structure approaches portray crime as the result of an individual's location within the structure of society and focus on the social and economic conditions of life.

1. How do social structure theories explain crime?
2. What do all social structure theories have in common?

social structure theories Theories that explain crime by reference to some aspect of the social fabric. These theories emphasize relationships among social institutions and describe the types of behavior that tend to characterize groups of people rather than individuals.

LEARNING OUTCOMES 3

Describe the three major types of social structure theories and distinguish among them.

This chapter describes three major types of social structure theories: (1) social disorganization theory (also called the "ecological approach"), (2) strain theory, and (3) culture conflict theory (also called "cultural deviance" theory). All have a number of elements in common, and the classification of a theory into one subcategory or another is often a matter of which aspects a writer chooses to emphasize rather than the result of any clear-cut definitional elements inherent in the perspectives themselves.

1. What are the three major types of social structure theories that this chapter discusses?
2. What is meant by the term *social disorganization*?
3. How does social disorganization lead to crime?

social disorganization theory A perspective on crime and deviance that highlights the role that the breakdown of social institutions, such as the family, the economy, education, and religion, plays in crime causation.

human ecology The interrelationship between human beings and the physical and cultural environments in which they live.

social ecology (also called *ecological school of criminology*) An approach to criminological theorizing that attempts to link the structure and organization of a human community to interactions with its localized environment.

social disorganization A condition said to exist when a group is faced with social change, uneven development of culture, maladaptiveness, disharmony, conflict, and lack of consensus.

social pathology A concept that compares society to a physical organism and sees criminality as an illness or a disease.

cultural transmission Through a process of social communication, the transmission of delinquency through successive generations of people living in the same area.

ecological theory A type of sociological approach that emphasizes demographics (the characteristics of population groups) and geographics (the mapped location of such groups relative to one another) and that sees the social disorganization that characterizes delinquency areas as a major cause of criminality and victimization.

Chicago School of criminology An ecological approach to explaining crime that examined how social disorganization contributes to social pathology.

criminology of place A perspective that emphasizes the importance of geographic location and architectural features as they are associated with the prevalence of criminal victimization.

environmental criminology An emerging perspective that emphasizes the importance of geographic location and architectural features as they are associated with the prevalence of criminal victimization.

broken windows theory A perspective on crime causation that holds that physical deterioration in an area leads to increased concerns for personal safety among area residents and to higher crime rates in that area.

defensible space The range of mechanisms that combine to bring an environment under the control of its residents.

Key Names

Emile Durkheim A sociologist who believed that crime is a normal part of all societies and law is a symbol of social solidarity. He introduced the concept of *anomie*.

Robert Park and ***Ernest Burgess*** Sociologists who developed the theory purporting that the structure and organization of a human community can be linked to interactions with its localized environment.

Clifford Shaw and ***Henry McKay*** Theorists who found that juvenile delinquency can be explained by concentric zone theory, a theory that considers the effects of neighborhoods in transition.

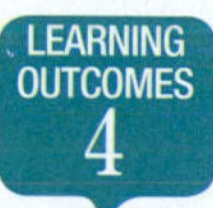

LEARNING OUTCOMES 4

Summarize strain theory.

Strain theory depicts delinquency as a form of adaptive, problem-solving behavior, usually committed in response to problems involving frustrating and undesirable social environments.

1. Briefly explain strain theory. From where does strain come?
2. How does the organization and structure of society contribute to strain?
3. What is anomie?
4. How can anomie lead to crime?

strain theory A sociological approach that posits a disjuncture between socially and subculturally sanctioned means and goals as the cause of criminal behavior.

anomie A social condition in which norms are uncertain or lacking.

relative deprivation A sense of social or economic inequality experienced by those who are unable, for whatever reason, to achieve legitimate success within the surrounding society

distributive justice The rightful, equitable, and just distribution of rewards within a society.

general strain theory (GST) A perspective that suggests that lawbreaking behavior is a coping mechanism that enables those who engage in it to deal with the socioemotional problems generated by negative social relations.

negative affective states Adverse emotions that derive from the experience of strain, such as anger, fear, depression, and disappointment.

Key Names

Robert K. Merton A sociologist who developed the classic statement of strain theory as a disjunction between socially approved means to success and legitimate goals.

Judith Blau and ***Peter Blau*** Sociologists who maintained that people assess their position in life by comparing themselves with things and people they already know.

Robert Agnew A criminologist who believed that lawbreaking behavior is a coping mechanism that enables those who engage in it to deal with the socioemotional problems generated by negative social relations.

LEARNING OUTCOMES 5

Describe culture conflict and subcultural theories, including differential opportunity theory.

Culture conflict perspectives rely on the proposition that the root cause of crime is a clash of values between variously socialized groups over what is acceptable or proper behavior. Subcultural theory emphasizes the contribution made by variously socialized cultural groups to the phenomenon of crime. Differential opportunity approaches say that delinquent behavior may result from the ready availability of illegitimate opportunities and the effective replacement of the norms of the wider culture with subcultural rules.

1. What is culture? What is subculture?
2. How do culture conflict theories explain crime?
3. What is reaction formation? Why does it occur?

culture conflict theory A sociological perspective on crime that suggests that the root cause of criminality can be found in a clash of values between variously socialized groups over what is acceptable or proper behavior.

conduct norms Shared expectations of a social group relative to personal conduct.

subcultural theory A sociological perspective that emphasizes the contribution made by variously socialized cultural groups to the phenomenon of crime.

culture A collection of values, ideas, beliefs, and traits that characterize a human group—usually one defined by geographic boundaries, such as a nation.

subculture A collection of values and preferences that is communicated to subcultural participants through a process called socialization.

focal concerns The key values of any culture, especially the key values of a delinquent subculture.

techniques of neutralization Culturally available justifications that can provide criminal offenders with the means to disavow responsibility for their behavior.

legitimate opportunities Opportunities generally available to individuals born into a middle-class culture; participants in lower-class subcultures are often denied access to them.

illegitimate opportunity structure Subcultural pathways to success of which the wider society disapproves.

reaction formation The process by which a person openly rejects that which he or she wants or aspires to but cannot obtain or achieve.

Key Names

Thorsten Sellin A sociologist who maintained that the root cause of crime could be found in different values about what is acceptable or proper behavior.

Walter Miller A theorist who described a lower-class culture as "a long established distinctively patterned tradition with integrity of its own."

Gresham Sykes and ***David Matza*** Theorists who claimed that offenders understand that their offending is wrong, but engage in neutralizing self-talk before offending to mitigate the anticipated shame and guilt associated with violating societal norms.

Franco Ferracuti and ***Marvin Wolfgang*** Theorists who said that violence is a learned form of adaptation to certain problematic life circumstances and that learning to be violent takes place within the context of a subculture that emphasizes the advantages of violence.

Richard A. Cloward and ***Lloyd E. Ohlin*** Criminologist who identified two types of socially structured opportunities for success: illegitimate and legitimate.

Albert Cohen A criminologist who claimed that young people from all backgrounds are generally held accountable to the norms of the wider society through a "middle-class measuring rod" of expectations related to school performance, language proficiency, cleanliness, punctuality, neatness, nonviolent behavior, and allegiance to other similar standards.

LEARNING OUTCOMES 6

Summarize the policy implications of various social structure theories.

Theoretical approaches that fault social structure as the root cause of crime point in the direction of social action as a solution. The War on Poverty, waged during the Kennedy and Johnson administrations, is an example of a large-scale social action project that would be in keeping with solutions offered by social structure theories.

1. What are the policy implications of social structure theories in the area of crime prevention?

Chicago Area Project A program originating at the University of Chicago during the 1930s that focused on urban ecology and attempted to reduce delinquency, crime, and social disorganization in transitional neighborhoods.

"I am truly regretful for what I have done. I feel very bad."

—*Convicted murderer Joran van der Sloot*

Social Process and Social Development— It's What We Learn

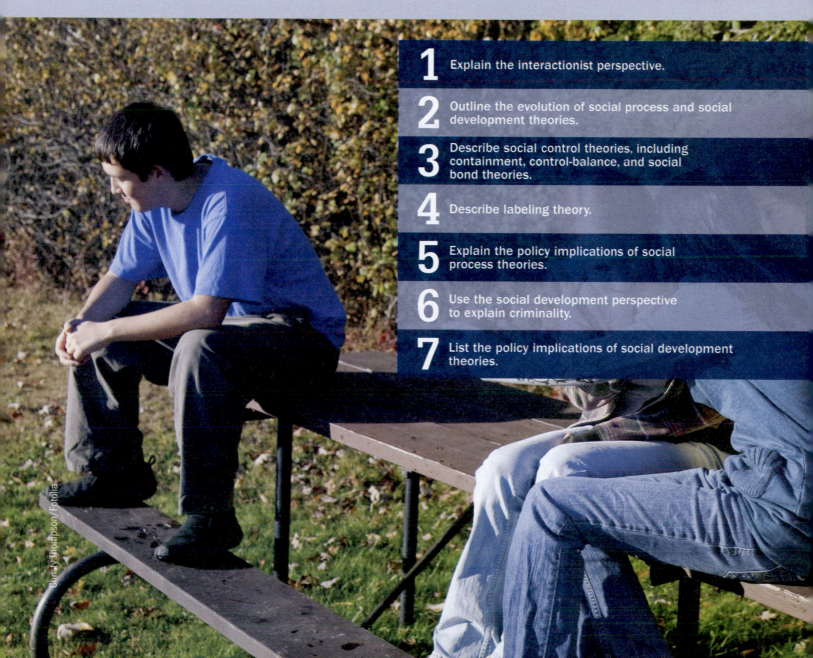

1. Explain the interactionist perspective.
2. Outline the evolution of social process and social development theories.
3. Describe social control theories, including containment, control-balance, and social bond theories.
4. Describe labeling theory.
5. Explain the policy implications of social process theories.
6. Use the social development perspective to explain criminality.
7. List the policy implications of social development theories.

Christy Thompson/Fotolia

INTRO

LABELING A KILLER

In 2012, 24-year-old Joran van der Sloot stood before a Peruvian judge and pled guilty to the 2010 murder of 21-year-old Stephany Flores in a Lima, Peru, hotel room. "Yes, I want to plead guilty. I wanted from the first moment to confess sincerely," he told the judge. "I truly am sorry for this act. I feel very bad."[1] Van der Sloot, who gained notoriety as the prime suspect in the 2005 disappearance of 18-year-old Alabama cheerleader Natalee Holloway while she was vacationing on the island of Aruba, fled to Chile after the murder, but was extradited to face prosecution in Peru. Prior to sentencing, attorneys for van der Sloot asked the judge for leniency, saying that their client killed Flores as a result of "extreme psychological trauma" that he had suffered as a result of the intense negative publicity he had received in the international news media following Holloway's disappearance. Rejecting his pleas, the judge imposed a sentence of 28 years in prison and ordered him to pay the Flores family $75,000 in reparations. He will be eligible for parole in 2026.[2]

Paolo Aguilar/EPA/Newscom

DISCUSS **Prior to sentencing, van der Sloot's attorneys asked the judge to consider the extreme psychological trauma resulting from intense negative publicity that followed from charges he had killed American Natalee Holloway years earlier. Why do people tend to accept labels applied to them? Can labeling a killer such as van der Sloot cause him or her to kill again? Explain.**

The Perspective of Social Interaction

The theories discussed in the first part of this chapter are called **social process theories**, or *interactionist perspectives*, because they depend on the process of interaction between individuals and society for their explanatory power. The various types of social process theories include social learning theory, social control theory, and labeling theory. The second part of this chapter focuses on **social development theories**, which tend to offer an integrated perspective and place a greater emphasis on changes in offending over time. Figure 7–1 details the principles of social process and social development theories. Learn more about social development from the Early Growth & Development Study (EGDS) at **Web Extra 7–1**.

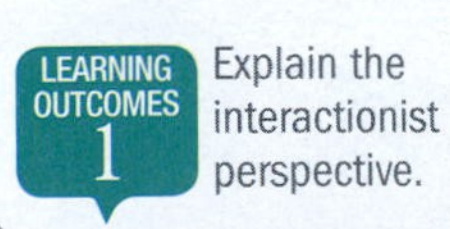

LEARNING OUTCOMES 1 Explain the interactionist perspective.

History of Social Process and Social Development Theories

Social **learning theory** says that all behavior is learned in much the same way and that crime, like other forms of behavior, is also learned. People learn to commit crime from others by learning the norms, values, and patterns of behaviors conducive to crime. Hence, according to learning theory, criminal behavior is a product of the social environment and not an innate characteristic.

LEARNING OUTCOMES 2 Outline the evolution of social process and social development theories.

Differential Association

One of the earliest and most influential forms of learning theory was advanced by **Edwin Sutherland** in 1939. Sutherland's thesis was that criminality is learned through a process of **differential association** with others who communicate criminal values and who advocate the commission of crimes.[3] Sutherland emphasized the role of social learning as an explanation for crime because he believed that many of the concepts popular in the field of criminology at the time—including social pathology, genetic inheritance, biological characteristics, and personality flaws—could not fully explain why an otherwise normal individual turns to crime. Sutherland was the first well-known criminologist to suggest that all significant human behavior is learned and that crime, therefore, is not substantively different from any other form of behavior.

Sutherland's nine principles of differential association were presented in complete form three years before his death in the fourth edition of his famous book *Principles of Criminology*:

1. Criminal behavior is learned.
2. Criminal behavior is learned in interaction with others in a process of communication.

Major Principles of Social Process and Social Development Theories

- Social process theories of crime causation assume that everyone has the potential to violate the law and that criminality is not an innate human characteristic.
- Criminal behavior is learned through interaction with others, and the socialization process that occurs as the result of group membership is seen as the primary route through which learning occurs.
- Among the most important groups contributing to the process of socialization are family, peers, work groups, and reference groups with which one identifies.
- This is the process through which criminality is acquired; deviant self-concepts are established; and criminal behavior results are active, open-minded, and ongoing throughout a person's life.
- Individuals who have low stakes in conformity are more likely to be influenced by the social processes and contingent experiences that lead to crime. Criminal choices, once made, tend to persist because they are reinforced by the reaction of society to those whom it has identified as deviant.
- The social development perspective understands that development begins at birth (and perhaps even earlier) and occurs primarily within a social context.
- Human development occurs on many levels simultaneously, including psychological, biological, familial, interpersonal, cultural, societal, and ecological. Hence, social development theories tend to be integrated theories, or theories that combine various points of view on the process of development.
- Social development theories focus more on individual rates of offending and seek to understand both increases and decreases in rates of offending over the individual's lifetime. Social development theories generally use longitudinal (over time) measurements of delinquency and offending, and they pay special attention to the transitions that people face as they move through the life cycle.
- Most theories of social development recognize that a critical transitional period occurs as a person moves from childhood to adulthood.

FIGURE 7–1 Principles of Social Process and Social Development Theories.

3. The principal part of the learning of criminal behavior occurs within intimate personal groups.
4. When criminal behavior is learned, the learning includes (a) techniques of committing the crime, which are sometimes very complicated and sometimes very simple, and (b) the specific direction of motives, drives, rationalizations, and attitudes.
5. The specific direction of motives and drives is learned from definitions of the legal codes as favorable or unfavorable.
6. A person becomes delinquent because of an excess of definitions favorable to law violation over definitions unfavorable to law violation.
7. Differential associations may vary in frequency, duration, priority, and intensity.
8. The process of learning criminal behavior by association with criminal and anticriminal patterns involves all of the mechanisms that are involved in any other learning.
9. Although criminal behavior is an expression of general needs and values, it is not explained by those general needs and values because noncriminal behavior is an expression of the same needs and values.

Differential association found considerable acceptance among mid-twentieth-century theorists because it combined then-prevalent psychological and sociological principles into a coherent perspective on criminality. Crime as a form of learned behavior quickly became the catchword of mid-twentieth-century criminology, and biological and other perspectives were largely abandoned. A brief YouTube video on differential association theory is available at **Web Extra 7–2**.

Critique of Differential Association

Perhaps the most potent criticism of differential association is the claim that Sutherland's initial formulation of the approach is not applicable at the individual level because even people who experience an excess of definitions favorable to law violation may still not become criminal. Likewise, those who rarely associate with recognized deviants may still turn to crime. In addition, the theory is untestable because most people experience a multitude of definitions—both favorable and unfavorable to law violation—and it is up to them to interpret just what those experiences mean. Hence, classifying experiences as either favorable or unfavorable to crime commission is difficult at best.

Other critics suggest that differential association alone is not a sufficient explanation for crime. If it were, then we might expect correctional officers, for example, to become criminals by virtue of their constant and continued association with prison inmates. Similarly, wrongly imprisoned people might be expected to turn to crime upon release from confinement. Little evidence suggests that either of those scenarios actually occurs. In effect, differential association theory does not seem to provide for free choice in individual circumstances, nor does it explain why some individuals, even when surrounded by associates who are committed to lives of crime, are still able to hold onto other noncriminal values. Finally, differential association theory fails to account for the emergence of criminal values, addressing only the communication of those values.

Social Process: Social Control Theories

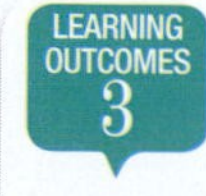

Describe social control theories, including containment, control-balance, and social bond theories.

According to Charles R. Tittle, a sociologist specializing in crime and deviance, **social control theories**, which fall under the general category of the social process perspective, emphasize "the inhibiting effect of social and psychological integration with others whose potential negative responses, surveillance, and expectations regulate or constrain criminal impulses."[4] In other words, social control theorists seek to identify those features of the personality and the environment that keep people from committing crimes. Social control theorists, however, take a step beyond static aspects of the personality and physical features of the environment in order to focus on the *process* through which social integration develops. It is the extent of a person's integration with positive social institutions and significant others that determines his or her resistance to criminal temptations; social control theorists focus on the process through which such integration develops. Rather than stressing causative factors in criminal behavior, however, social control theories tend to ask *why* people obey rules instead of breaking them.[5]

Containment Theory

In the 1950s, **Walter C. Reckless** tackled head-on the realization that most sociological theories lacked the ability to predict precisely which individuals, even those exposed to various causes of crime, would become criminal. Crime, Reckless wrote, was the consequence of social pressures to involve oneself in violations of the law, as well as of failure to resist such pressures. Reckless called his approach **containment theory**, and he compared it with a biological immune response, saying that only some people exposed to a disease actually come down with it. Thus sickness, like crime, results from the failure of control mechanisms—some internal to the person and others external.

In the case of crime, Reckless wrote, *external containment* consists of "the holding power of the group."[6] Under most circumstances, Reckless said, "the society, the state, the tribe, the village, the family, and other nuclear groups are able to hold the individual within the bounds of the accepted norms and expectations."[7] *Inner containment*, said Reckless, "represents the ability of the person to follow the expected norms, to direct himself."[8] Such ability is said to be enhanced by a positive self-image, a focus on socially approved goals, personal aspirations that are in line with reality, a good tolerance for frustration, and a general adherence to the norms and values of society. A person with a positive self-image can avoid the temptations of crime simply by thinking, "I'm not that kind of person." A focus on socially approved goals helps keep people on the straight and narrow path. Reckless's containment theory is diagrammed in Figure 7–2. "Pushes toward Crime" represents those factors in an individual's background that might propel him or her into criminal behavior. They include a criminogenic background or upbringing that involves participation in a delinquent subculture, deprivation, biological propensities toward deviant behavior, and psychological maladjustment. "Pulls toward Crime" signifies all the perceived rewards crime may offer, including financial gain, sexual satisfaction, and higher status. **Containment** is a stabilizing force and, if effective, blocks such pushes and pulls from leading the individual toward crime.

Critique of Reckless's Containment Theory

Reckless's pushes and pulls against crime have been cited as purely personal interpretation. They are not part of a fixed formation of psychological impulses and drives, many critics claim, but simply the feelings of the moment that may have been conditioned through individual thought processes.

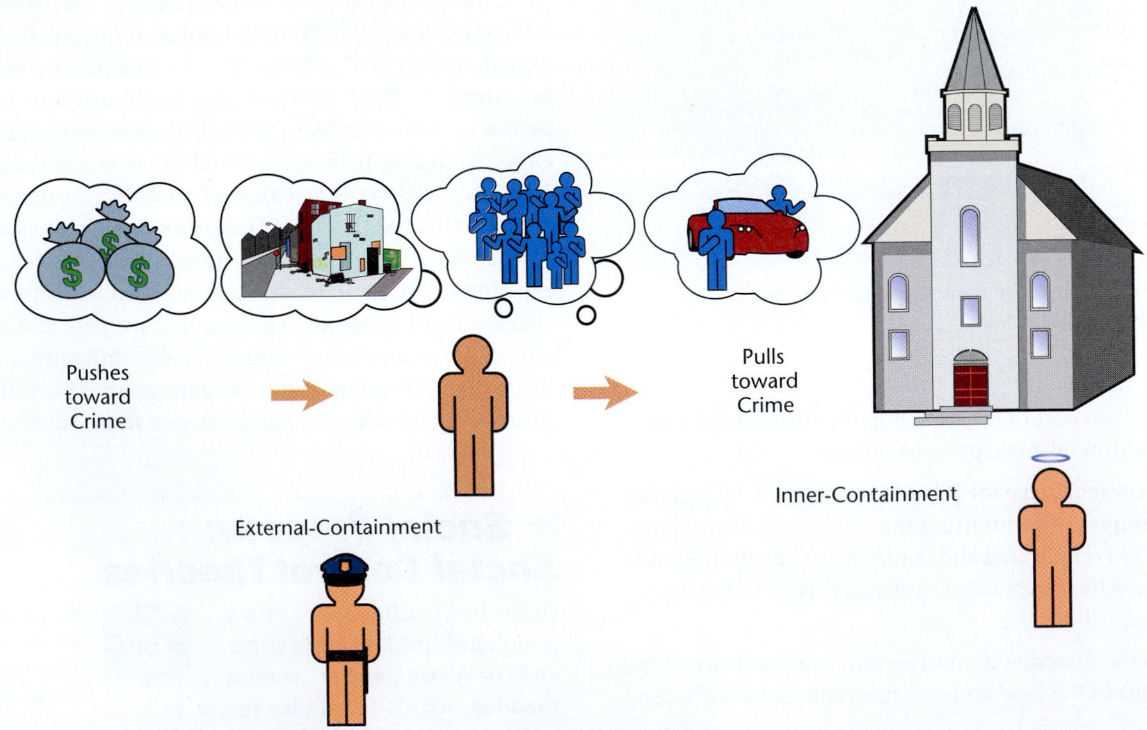

FIGURE 7–2 **A Diagrammatic Representation of Containment Theory.**
Source: From *Criminology Today: An Integrative Introduction*, 7e by Frank A. Schmalleger. Copyright © 2014 by Pearson Education. Used by permission of Pearson Education.

Think About It…

Numerous studies link low self-esteem and delinquent behavior. How does peer group acceptance build self-esteem?

Christy Thompson/ Fotolia

Delinquency and Self-Esteem

An innovative perspective on social control was offered by **Howard B. Kaplan** in the mid-1970s.[9] Kaplan proposed that people who are ridiculed by their peers suffer a loss of self-esteem; assess themselves poorly; and, as a result, abandon the motivation to conform.

Numerous studies appear to support the idea that **low self-esteem** fosters delinquent behavior.[10] At the same time, however, delinquency also seems to enhance self-esteem, at least for some delinquents.[11] One study has found that delinquent behavior enhances self-esteem in adolescents whose self-esteem is already very low.[12]

Social Bond Theory

An important form of control theory called *social bond theory* was popularized by **Travis Hirschi** in his 1969 book *Causes of Delinquency*.[13] Hirschi argued that through successful socialization, a bond forms between individuals and the social group. When that bond is weakened or broken, deviance and crime may result. As shown in Figure 7–3, there are four components of the **social bond**.

The first component, attachment, refers to a person's shared interests with others. In his writings, Hirschi cites the psychopath as an example of the kind of person whose attachment to society is nearly nonexistent.[14] Other relatively normal individuals may find their attachment to society loosened through "the process of becoming alienated from others [which] often involves or is based on active interpersonal conflict," says Hirschi. "Such conflict could easily supply a reservoir of socially derived hostility sufficient to account for the aggressiveness of those whose attachments to others have been weakened."[15]

FIGURE 7–3 **The Four Components of the Social Bond.**

The second component of the social bond—commitment—reflects a person's investment of time and energies into conforming behavior versus the potential loss of the rewards that would otherwise accrue from that behavior. In Hirschi's words, "The idea, then, is that the person invests time, energy, himself, in a certain line of activity—say, getting an education, building up a business, acquiring a reputation for virtue. Whenever he considers deviant behavior, he must consider the costs of this deviant behavior, the risk he runs of losing the investment he has made in conventional behavior."[16] For such a traditionally successful person, says Hirschi, "a ten-dollar-holdup is stupidity" because the potential for losing what has already been acquired through commitment to social norms far exceeds what stands to be gained. Recognizing that his approach applies primarily to individuals who have been successfully socialized into conventional society, Hirschi adds, "The concept of commitment assumes that the organization of society is such that the interests of most persons would be endangered if they were to engage in criminal acts."[17]

Involvement, for Hirschi, means "engrossment in conventional activities."[18] It can also be described as the amount of time spent with others in shared activities. In explaining the importance of involvement in determining conformity, Hirschi cites the old saying that "idle hands are the devil's workshop." Time and energy, he says, are limited, and if a person is busy at legitimate pursuits, he or she will have little opportunity for crime and deviance.

Belief, the last of Hirschi's four aspects of the social bond, describes a shared value and moral system. It is his emphasis upon belief that sets Hirschi's control theory apart from subcultural approaches. Hirschi says that unlike subcultural theory, "control theory assumes the existence of a common value system within the society or group whose norms are being violated. We not only assume the deviant has believed the rules, we assume he believes the rules even as he violates them."[19] How can a person simultaneously believe it is wrong to commit a crime and still commit it? Hirschi's answer is that "many persons do not have an attitude of respect toward the rules of society."[20] That is, although they know the rules exist, they basically do not care. They invest little of their sense of self in moral standards.

The General Theory of Crime

In 1990, Hirschi, in collaboration with **Michael Gottfredson**, proposed a **general theory of crime** (GTC) based on the concepts advanced earlier in control theory.[21] The general theory of crime claims to be *general*, in part, due to its assertion that the operation of a single mechanism, low self-control, accounts for "'all crime, at all times'; acts ranging from vandalism to homicide, from rape to white-collar-crime." Gottfredson and Hirschi defined *self-control* as the degree to which a person is vulnerable to temptations of the moment. They proposed that self-control is acquired early in life and that low self-control is the premier individual-level cause of crime. It develops by the end of childhood and is fostered through parental emotional investment in the child, monitoring the child's behavior, recognizing deviance when it occurs, and punishing the child.

Nearly all crimes, claim Gottfredson and Hirschi, are mundane, simple, trivial, easy acts aimed at satisfying desires of the moment. Hence, their general theory is built on a classical or rational choice perspective—that is, the belief that crime is a natural consequence of unrestrained human tendencies to seek pleasure and avoid pain. Crime, say Gottfredson and Hirschi, is little more than a subset of general deviant behavior. Hence, they conclude, crime bears little resemblance to the explanations offered in the media, by law enforcement officials, or by most academic thinkers on the subject.

According to Gottfredson and Hirschi, the offender is neither the diabolical genius of fiction nor the ambitious seeker of the American Dream often portrayed by other social scientists. On the contrary, offenders appear to have little control over their own desires. When personal desires conflict with long-term interests, those who lack self-control often opt for the desires of the moment, thus contravening legal restrictions and becoming involved in crime.[22] Gottfredson and Hirschi define *self-control* as the degree to which a person is vulnerable to temptations of the moment.[23]

Central to Gottfredson and Hirschi's thesis is the belief that a well-developed social bond will result in the creation of effective mechanisms of self-control. They propose that self-control is acquired early in life and that low self-control is the premier individual-level cause of crime. Self-control, say Gottfredson and Hirschi, develops by the end of childhood and is fostered through parental emotional investment in the child, which includes monitoring the child's behavior, recognizing deviance when it occurs, and punishing the child. They also argue that self-control is a lasting feature of the individual. Some researchers have called the argument that self-control develops early in childhood and persists over time the *stability thesis*.

Gottfredson and Hirschi recognize that the link between self-control and crime depends substantially upon criminal opportunity, which in itself is a function of the structural or situational circumstances that an individual encounters. Thus, these theorists suggest that "the link between self-control and crime is not deterministic, but probabilistic, affected by opportunities and other constraints."[24]

More recently, **Per-Olof H. Wikström** at the University of Cambridge proposed that self-control could best be analyzed as a situational concept (i.e., a factor in the process of choice), rather than as an individual trait. Wikstrom's **situational action theory (SAT)** suggests that an individual's ability to exercise self-control is an outcome of the interaction between his or her personal traits and the situation in which he or she takes part. SAT adopts the situation as the core unit of analysis, and places emphasis on a person's sense of morality, which expresses itself when an individual is faced with a particular set of circumstances.

Think About It...

Social bond theory highlights the importance of the bond between individuals and the group. What are the four major components of the social bond? How would you rank them in terms of importance? Also, do you agree with the general theory of crime that low self-control accounts for most crime? What other factors are likely to be involved?

Auremar/Fotolia

Critique of the General Theory of Crime and Social Bond Theory

Hirschi's social bond theory has been criticized for its basic premise that those who commit deviant behavior know that it is against social norms and the law but commit it anyway. Social bonds, it would appear, are not strong enough to negate the propensity toward criminal behavior even in those where the bond is strong. In addition, Hirschi and Gottfredson's general theory of crime has been criticized for providing merely a general view of crime that is overly simplistic and ignores the complexity of the criminal process. Human behavior is more complex, especially in terms of criminal behavior, than Gottfredson and Hirschi take into account, critics contend. Some well-adjusted teenagers, for example, participate in crime during their teen years and become law-abiding citizens once they reach adulthood.[25] For other critiques of the concept of self-control as it relates to criminality, refer to Chapter 4.

Control-Balance Theory

A novel form of control theory can be found in **Charles R. Tittle**'s control-balance perspective.[26] Tittle's control-balance approach results from a blending of the social bond and containment perspectives. Too much control can be just as dangerous as too little. The crucial concept in the approach is what is called the **control ratio**. The control ratio is the amount of control to which a person is subject versus the amount of control that person exerts over others. The control ratio is said to predict not only the probability that one will engage in deviance but also the specific form that deviance will take (Figure 7–4).

High levels of control, or overcontrol, are termed "control surplus," whereas low levels are called "control deficit." Individuals with *control surpluses* are able to exercise a great deal of control over others and will work to extend their degree of control even further. Their efforts lead to deviant actions involving exploitation, plunder, and decadence—frequently seen in cases of white-collar crime and political corruption.[27] Control surpluses are built upon "the fundamental drive toward autonomy." Such a drive involves "a desire to extend control as far as possible" and results in forms of deviance that Tittle terms "autonomous."[28]

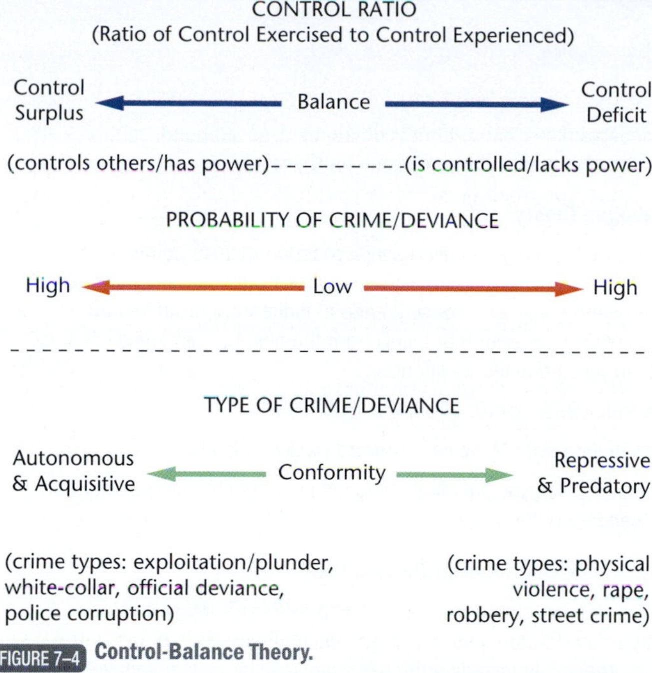

FIGURE 7–4 **Control-Balance Theory.**

A *control deficit* exists for people unable to exercise much control over others (and who are hence overly controlled). Control deficits result in deviance as an attempt to escape repressive controls. Deviance caused by control deficit takes the form of predation (for example, physical violence, theft, sexual assault, and robbery), defiance (challenges to conventional norms, including vandalism, curfew violations, and sullenness), or submission (which Tittle describes as "passive, unthinking, slavish obedience to the expectations, commands, or anticipated desires of others"[29]). Thus, control imbalance only sets the stage for deviance. Deviance ultimately occurs once a person realizes, at some level, that acts of deviance can reset the control ratio in a favorable way. Finally, opportunity also plays a significant role. "No matter how favorable the motivational and constraint configuration," says Tittle, "the actual likelihood of deviance occurring depends on there being an opportunity for it to happen."[30]

Critique of Social Control Theories

Social control theories have been criticized because they make the assumption that all people are automatically noncomformist unless they are socialized through control mechanisms. Human choice, then, is minimized in favor of creating the right kind and level of social self-controls to help individuals avoid deviance and achieve conformity. Consequently, the individual is seen as somehow naturally "evil" and it is society's job to institute moral order to bring about conformity.

Just as troubling to critics of social control theories is the fact that these theories do not recognize the role of human motivation or the conditions that propel people to associate with and learn from others. Instead, the assumption is simply made that most of us would commit crime if we had the chance. Although associations and relationships can mitigate or escalate deviant behavior, it is unclear how those relationships are formed.

Labeling Theory

Society's response to known or suspected offenders determines the individual futures of those labeled as criminals and contributes to the incidence of criminality by reducing the behavioral options available to labeled offenders. In 2012, Margaret Colgate Love, reporting on a conference of journalists at John Jay College in New York City, pointed out that the word "felon" carries with it a great deal of social significance—especially for those who have been labeled with it. Love wrote, "the word 'felon' . . . arouses fear and loathing in most of us. I confess that it arouses those visceral feelings in me. I do not want to live or work around felons. I do not want to socialize with them."[31]

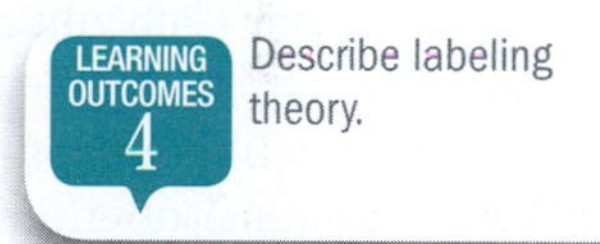

Tagging is a term that explains what happens to offenders following arrest, conviction, and sentencing. From the community's point of view "the individual who used to do bad and mischievous things becomes a bad and unredeemable human being."[32]

Once a person has been defined as bad, few legitimate opportunities remain open to him or her. As a consequence, the offender finds that only other people who have been similarly defined by society as bad are available to associate with him or her. This continued association with negatively defined others leads to continued crime.

One of the best-known views of labeling comes from **Edwin M. Lemert**. Lemert called an offender's initial acts of deviance **primary deviance** and the offender's continued acts of deviance, especially those resulting from forced association with other offenders, **secondary deviance**. Primary deviance may be undertaken to solve some immediate problem or to meet the

Think About It…

Control-balance theory says that conformity results from just the right balance between control surpluses and control deficits. How would you explain control-balance in your own words?

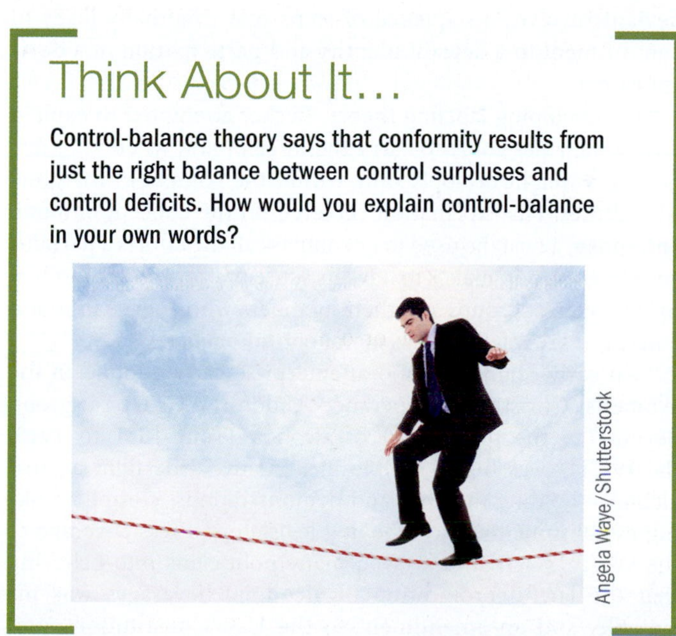

Angela Waye/Shutterstock

THEORY in PERSPECTIVE

Types of Social Process Theories

Social process theories (also called *interactionist theories*) depend on the process of interaction between individuals and society for their explanatory power. They assume that everyone has the potential to violate the law and that criminality is not an innate human characteristic; instead, criminal behavior is learned in interaction with others, and the socialization process that occurs as the result of group membership is seen as the primary route through which learning occurs.

Social Learning Theory

Social learning theory (also called *learning theory*) says that all behavior is learned in much the same way and that crime is also learned. The theory places primary emphasis on the roles of communication and socialization in the acquisition of learned patterns of criminal behavior and the values supporting that behavior.

Period: 1930s–present

Theorists: Edwin Sutherland, others

Concepts: Differential association

Social Control Theory

Social control theory focuses on the strength of the bond people share with the individuals and institutions around them, especially as those relationships shape people's behavior, and seeks to identify those features of the personality and of the environment that keep people from committing crimes.

Period: 1950s–present

Theorists: Walter C. Reckless, Howard B. Kaplan, Travis Hirschi, Michael Gottfredson, Charles R. Tittle, Per-Olof H. Wikström, others

Concepts: Inner and external containment, social bond, control-balance, general theory of crime (GTC), situational action theory (SAT)

Labeling Theory

Labeling theory (also called *social reaction theory*) points to the special significance of society's response to the criminal and sees continued crime as a consequence of limited opportunities for acceptable behavior that follow from the negative responses of society to those defined as offenders.

Period: 1938–1940, 1960s–1980s, 1990s

Theorists: Edwin M. Lemert, Howard Becker, others

Concepts: Tagging, labeling, outsider, moral enterprise, primary and secondary deviance

The Social Development Perspective

The social development perspective provides an integrated view of human development that examines multiple levels of maturity simultaneously, including the psychological, biological, familial, interpersonal, cultural, societal, and ecological levels.

Period: 1980s–present

Theorists: Sheldon and Eleanor Glueck, Terrie E. Moffitt, Robert J. Sampson, John H. Laub, Glen H. Elder, Jr., David P. Farrington and Donald J. West, Marvin Wolfgang, Lawrence E. Cohen and Richard Machalek, Terrence Thornberry, and others

Concepts: human development, social development perspective, life-course criminology, career criminal, life-course, human agency, turning points, social capital, life-course-persistent offenders, adolescence-limited offenders, persistence, desistance, evolutionary ecology

---

expectations of one's subcultural group. Hence, the robbery of a convenience store by a college student temporarily desperate for tuition money, although not a wise undertaking, may be the first serious criminal offense ever committed by the student. The student may well intend for it to be the last, but if arrest ensues and the student is tagged with the status of a criminal, then secondary deviance may occur as a means of adjustment to the negative status. Secondary deviance becomes especially important because of the forceful role it plays in causing tagged individuals to internalize the negative labels that have been applied to them. Through such a process, labeled individuals assume the role of the deviant.

The name most often associated with labeling theory is that of **Howard Becker**, who described the deviant subculture of jazz musicians and the process by which an individual becomes a marijuana user, among other things. His primary focus, however, was to explain how a person becomes labeled as an *outsider*, as "a special kind of person, one who cannot be trusted to live by the rules agreed on by the group."[33] The central fact about deviance, says Becker, is that society creates both deviance and the deviant person by its response to circumscribed behaviors. The person who engages in sanctioned behavior is, as part of the process, labeled a deviant.[34] For Becker, as for other labeling theorists, no act is intrinsically deviant or criminal, but is defined as such by others. Becoming deviant involves a sequence of steps that eventually leads to commitment to a deviant identity and participation in a deviant career.

In developing labeling theory, Becker attempted to explain how some rules come to carry the force of law, whereas others have less weight or apply only within the context of marginal subcultures. His explanation centered on the concept of **moral enterprise**, a term he used to encompass all the efforts a particular interest group makes to have its sense of propriety embodied in law. Interest groups and their members who engage in moral enterprise are referred to as **moral entrepreneurs**.

An early example of moral enterprise can be found in the Women's Christian Temperance Union (WCTU), a group devoted to the prohibition of alcohol. From 1881 to 1919, the WCTU was highly visible in its nationwide fight against alcohol—holding marches and demonstrations, closing drinking establishments, and lobbying legislators. Press coverage of the WCTU's activities swayed many politicians into believing that the lawful prohibition of alcoholic beverages was inevitable, and an amendment to the U.S. Constitution soon followed, ushering in the age of prohibition.

A more contemporary example of moral enterprise is NORML—the National Organization for the Reform of Marijuana Laws. NORML says that its mission is "to move public opinion sufficiently to achieve the repeal of marijuana prohibition so that the responsible use of cannabis by adults is no longer subject to penalty."[35] Within the past couple of years, NORML's efforts seem to have paid off, with Washington state and Colorado legalizing the possession and nonpublic use of marijuana for recreational purposes. Other recent examples of moral entrepreneurs can be found in those individuals and organizations that lobbied for the creation of Amber Alert systems and the passage of Megan's Laws (which authorize local law enforcement agencies to notify the public about convicted sex offenders living or working nearby) following the abduction and murder of young girls.

Moral enterprise is used, Becker claimed, by groups seeking to support their own interests with the weight of law. Often the group that is successful at moral enterprise does not represent a popular point of view. The group is simply more effective than others at maneuvering through the formal bureaucracy that accompanies legislation.

Becker was especially interested in describing deviant careers—the processes by which individuals become members of deviant subcultures and take on the attributes associated with the deviant role. Becker argued that most deviance, when it first occurs, is unlikely to occur again. However, deviance can become part of a person's behavioral repertoire through the labeling process. Once a person is labeled "deviant," most opportunities that remain open are deviant ones. Hence, throughout the person's career, the budding deviant increasingly exhibits deviant behavior because his or her choices are restricted by society. In addition, successful deviants must acquire the techniques and resources necessary to undertake the deviant act (be it drug use or bank robbery) and must develop the mindset characteristic of others like them. Near the completion of a deviant career, the person who has been labeled a deviant internalizes society's negative label, assumes a deviant self-concept, and is likely to become a member of a deviant subgroup. In this way, says Becker, deviance finally becomes a "self-fulfilling prophecy." Labeling, then, is a cause of crime insofar as society's calling the rule-breaker "deviant" pushes the person further in the direction of continued deviance.

Think About It...

This chapter provides some early examples of moral enterprise, such as the WCTU, a group devoted to the prohibition of alcohol that was active from 1881 to 1919, and NORML, a marijuana legalization group that is still active. Can you think of any other examples of contemporary moral entrepreneurs? If so, what are they?

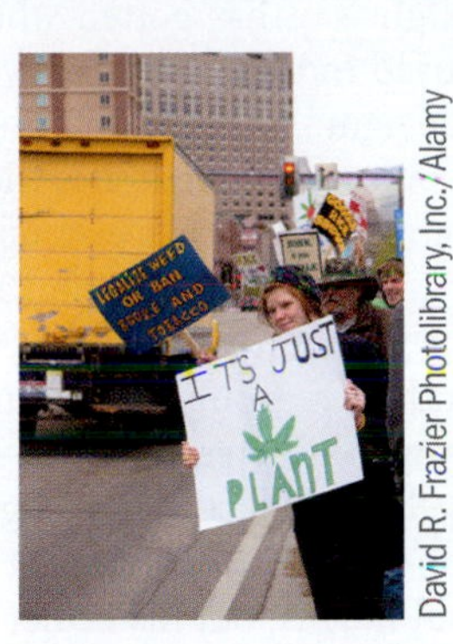

David R. Frazier Photolibrary, Inc./Alamy

Labeling theory contributed a number of unique ideas to the criminological literature, including the following:

- Deviance is the result of social processes involving the imposition of definitions rather than the consequence of any quality inherent in human activity itself.
- Deviant individuals achieve their status by virtue of social definition rather than because of inborn traits.
- The reaction of society to deviant behavior and to those who engage in such behavior is the major element in determining the criminality of the person and of the behavior in question.
- Negative self-images do not precede delinquency; instead, they result from processing by the criminal justice system.
- Labeling by society and handling by the justice system tend to perpetuate crime and delinquency rather than reduce it.

Becker's typology of delinquents demonstrates the labeling approach (Figure 7–5). It consists of (1) the pure deviant, (2) the falsely accused deviant, and (3) the secret deviant. The pure deviant is one who commits norm-breaking behavior and whose behavior is accurately appraised as such by society.

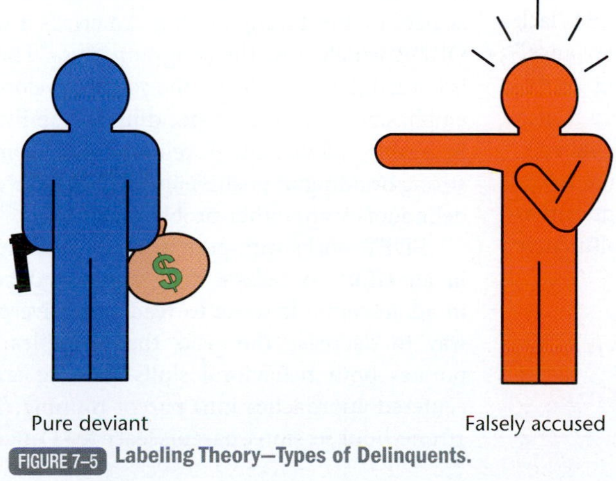

FIGURE 7–5 Labeling Theory—Types of Delinquents.

An example might be the burglar who is caught in the act of burglary and then is tried and convicted. Such a person, we might say, has gotten what he or she deserves. The falsely accused individual is one who, in fact, is not guilty but is labeled "deviant" nonetheless. The falsely accused category in Becker's typology demonstrates the power of social definition. Innocent people sometimes end up in prison, and one can imagine that the impact of conviction and the experiences that attend prison life can leave the falsely accused with a negative self-concept and with group associations practically indistinguishable from those of the true deviant. In effect, the life of the falsely accused is changed just as thoroughly as is the life of the pure deviant by the process of labeling. Finally, the secret deviant violates social norms, but his or her behavior is not noticed, and negative societal reactions do not follow. The secret deviant again demonstrates the power of societal reaction—in this case, by the very lack of consequences.

Although labeling theory fell into disregard during the late 1970s and early 1980s due to accusations that it was vague and ambiguous, criminologists have recently recast the theory as one that points out the cumulative effects over time of official intervention on future life chances and opportunities for approved success. Contemporary proponents of the labeling perspective, however, generally see labeling as only one factor contributing to cumulative disadvantages in life chances. In 2003, Jon Gunnar Bernburg and Marvin D. Krohn studied the impact of negative official intervention on young men in Rochester, New York. Data on the men were available from the time they were (on average) 13.5 years old until they reached the age of 22. In keeping with what labeling theory would predict, Bernburg and Krohn found that official intervention during adolescence led to increased criminality in early adulthood because it reduced life chances for educational achievement and successful employment. For additional insight into labeling theory, visit Professor Tom O'Connor's web page via **Web Extra 7-3**.

Critique of Labeling Theory

The labeling approach, although it successfully points to the labeling process as a reason for continued deviance and as a cause of stabilization in deviant identities, has been criticized because it does little to explain the origin of crime and deviance. In addition, few, if any, studies seem to support the basic tenets of the theory. Critics of labeling have pointed to its "lack of firm empirical support for the notion of secondary deviance," and "many studies have not found that delinquents or criminals have a delinquent or criminal self-image."[36] There is also a lack of unequivocal empirical support for the claim that contact with the justice system is fundamentally detrimental to the personal lives of criminal perpetrators. Even if that supposition were true, however, one must ask whether it would ultimately be better if offenders were not caught and forced to undergo the rigors of processing by the justice system. Although labeling theory hints that official processing makes a significant contribution to continued criminality, it seems unreasonable to expect that offenders untouched by the system would forgo the rewards of future criminality. Finally, labeling theory has little to say about *secret deviants*, or people who engage in criminality but are never caught. An important question about secret deviants, for example, is whether they can be expected to continue in lives of deviance if they are never caught.

Labeling theory has been criticized for doing little to explain the origin of crime and deviance.

Policy Implications of Social Process Theories

Social process theories suggest that crime prevention programs should work to enhance self-control and to build **prosocial bonds**. One program that seeks to build strong prosocial bonds while attempting to teach positive values to young people is the **Juvenile Mentoring Program (JUMP)** of the Office of Juvenile Justice and Delinquency Prevention (OJJDP). Fundamentally a social control initiative, JUMP was funded by Congress in 1992 under an amendment to the Juvenile Justice and Delinquency Prevention Act of 1974.[37] OJJDP-sponsored JUMP programs commenced operation in 1996. JUMP places at-risk youth in a one-on-one relationship with favorable adult role models. At-risk youths are defined as those who are at risk of delinquency, gang involvement, educational failure, or dropping out of school. General demographic information is used in conjunction with scores on a standardized risk-assessment instrument known as the Problem Oriented Screening Instrument for Teenagers in order to identify potential JUMP participants.

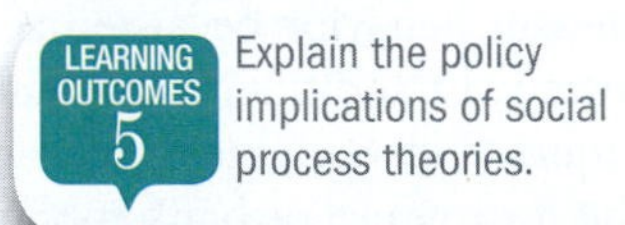

LEARNING OUTCOMES
5
Explain the policy implications of social process theories.

Most recent data show that 9,200 youths were enrolled in more than 200 JUMP programs nationwide. The average age at the time of enrollment was just under 12 years. Although complete evaluation data are only beginning to come in on the project, both youth and mentors were very positive when rating various aspects of their mentoring experiences. Another social control–based program is **Preparing for the Drug Free Years (PDFY)**.[38] PDFY is designed to increase effective parenting and is part of the Strengthening America's Families Project. The OJJDP, which runs the program, says, "The PDFY curriculum is guided theoretically by the social development model, which emphasizes the role of bonding to family, school, and peers in healthy adolescent development. The model specifies that strong bonding to positive influences reduces the probability of delinquency and other problem behaviors."[39]

PDFY works with parents of children in grades 4 through 8 in an effort to reduce drug abuse and behavioral problems in adolescents. It seeks to teach effective parenting skills as a way to decrease the risks that juveniles face. PDFY incorporates both behavioral skills training and communication-centered approaches into parent training. Through a series of 10 one-hour sessions, parents learn to (1) increase their children's

WHO'S TO BLAME—The Individual or Society

Sexual Abuser Claims Victim Status

Mortimer Rataway was arrested after authorities received a report of a man struggling with a boy in a Short Stop food and beverage store. A police officer on nearby patrol arrived at the scene within minutes and observed Rataway forcing the boy, nine-year-old Justin, into an old sedan outside the convenience store. When the officer asked Rataway what was going on, the boy blurted out that he had been kidnapped.

The officer had heard reports on his radio describing the kidnapping of a nine-year-old boy from a school bus stop in an adjacent city two days earlier, and he quickly took Rataway into custody on suspicion of kidnapping.

Justin was taken to a special area reserved for juveniles in the local police station where he told detectives that he was the boy who had been kidnapped. Although he was physically okay, he told police that Rataway had forced him to engage in repeated masturbation and that Rataway had taken many photographs of him naked.

A search of Rataway's apartment uncovered a number of digital cameras and a computer Web server hosting a child pornography site. The camera and computer contained photos of many other young boys; some of the photos had probably been purchased over the Internet, but Rataway later admitted taking others.

"I never hurt anybody," Rataway told investigators. "Most of the boys agreed to serve as models after I paid them. But I got carried away and grabbed Justin because I thought he'd make one of my best models.

"Yeah, I'm gay," Rataway told the police in a recorded statement. "And, sure, I like boys. But it isn't my fault. When I was growing up as a young Catholic I was taught to enjoy my body and to like other men by the parish priest. Now I know that most priests are good men and that the crisis in the church has been way overblown by the media. But if that hadn't happened to me, I know I would have been straight, and I'm sure I would have gotten married and had kids of my own. Because of what happened to me when I was a kid, I'm as much a victim as anybody. It doesn't matter how much you punish me, I'm never going to change my sexual orientation."

Angela Waye/Shutterstock

Think About It

1. Do you see Rataway as a criminal or a victim (as he claims)? Might he be both?
2. Some people describe child molesters as "sick." Is Rataway "sick"? If so, how can he be cured?
3. Will sending Rataway to prison rehabilitate him? Why or why not? How can you ensure that he won't pose a future threat if he is released back into society someday?
4. How does this case illustrate the way our understandings of criminal motivation and crime causality influence our notions of fairness and justice in the treatment of offenders?

Note: Who's to Blame boxes provide fictionalized critical thinking opportunities, and are not actual cases.

opportunities for family involvement, (2) teach needed family-participation and social skills, and (3) provide reinforcement for positive behavior and appropriate consequences for misbehavior. Early studies show that program participation (session attendance) tends to be high and that the program is effective at improving general child-management skills among parents.[40]

A program that emphasizes the development of self-control is the **Montreal Preventive Treatment Program**.[41] It addresses early childhood risk factors for gang involvement by targeting boys from poor socioeconomic backgrounds who display disruptive behavior while in kindergarten. The program offers training sessions for parents that are designed to teach family crisis management, disciplining techniques, and other parenting skills. The boys participate in training sessions that emphasize the development of prosocial skills and self-control. At least one evaluation of the program showed that it was effective at keeping boys from joining gangs.[42]

The Social Development Perspective

Over the past 25 years, an emerging appreciation for the process of **human development** has played an increasingly important role in understanding criminality.[43] Human development refers to the relationship between the maturing individual and his or her changing environment and to the social processes that relationship entails. The **social development perspective** acknowledges that human development begins at birth and takes place within a social context. Students of human development recognize that the process of development occurs through reciprocal and dynamic interactions that take place between individuals and various aspects of their environment.

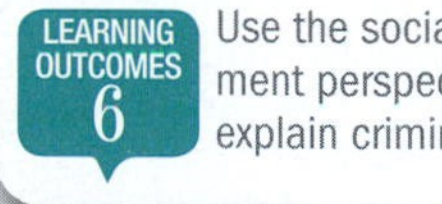

Use the social development perspective to explain criminality.

The Life-Course Perspective

Developmental theories of crime and delinquency demonstrate that criminal behavior tends to follow a distinct pattern across the life cycle. Criminality is relatively uncommon during childhood; it tends to begin as sporadic instances of delinquency during late adolescence and early adulthood and then diminishes and sometimes completely disappears by age 30 or 40. Of course, some people never commit crimes or do so only rarely, whereas others become career criminals and persist in lives of crime.

The life-course perspective, which is quite popular among criminologists today, shifted the traditional focus away from asking why people begin offending to questions about the dimensions of criminal offending over the entire life-course.[44] Also known as **life-course criminology**, the contemporary life-course perspective has its roots in a 1986 National Academy of Sciences (NAS) panel report.[45] The NAS report emphasized the importance of the study of criminal careers and of crime over the life-course. The NAS panel defined a **criminal career** as "the longitudinal sequence of crimes committed by an individual offender."[46] The report was especially important for its analysis of "offending development," a concept that underlies the life-course perspective (Figure 7–6).

Think About It...

Life-course criminology emphasizes the importance of the study of criminal careers and of crime over the life-course. What do life-course researchers mean when they talk about "trajectories" and "transitions" through the "age-differentiated life span"?

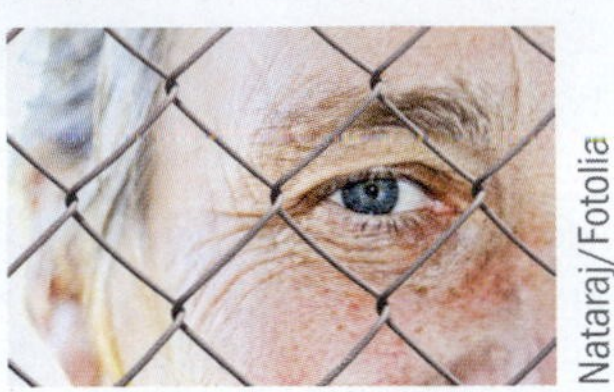

Nataraj/Fotolia

The panel noted (Figure 7–7) that criminal careers can be described in terms of four dimensions: participation, frequency, duration, and seriousness. *Participation*, which refers to the fraction of a population that is criminally active, depends on the scope of criminal acts considered and the length of the observation period.[47] *Frequency* refers to the number of crimes committed by an individual offender per unit of time. Hence, a

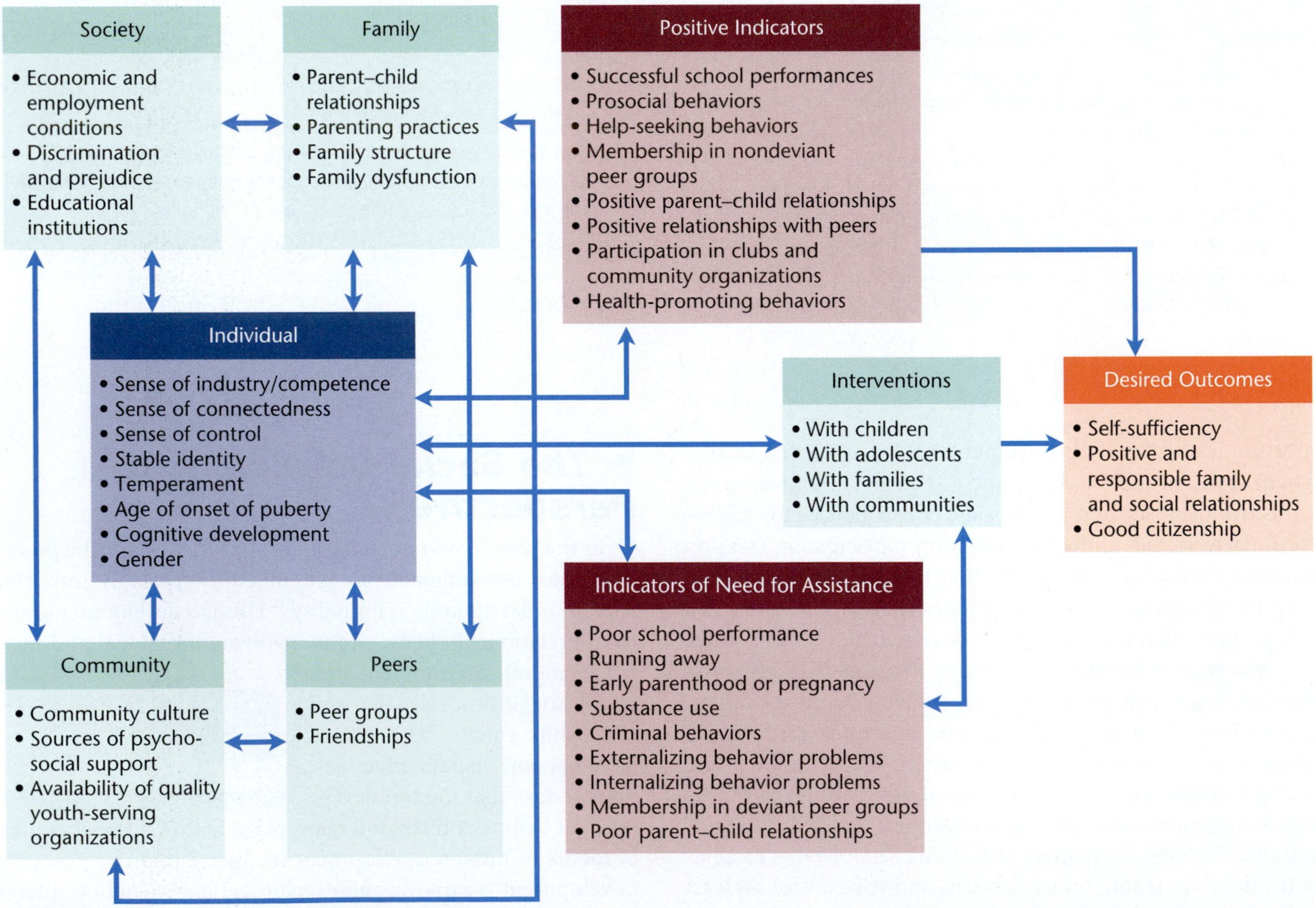

Society
- Economic and employment conditions
- Discrimination and prejudice
- Educational institutions

Family
- Parent–child relationships
- Parenting practices
- Family structure
- Family dysfunction

Positive Indicators
- Successful school performances
- Prosocial behaviors
- Help-seeking behaviors
- Membership in nondeviant peer groups
- Positive parent–child relationships
- Positive relationships with peers
- Participation in clubs and community organizations
- Health-promoting behaviors

Individual
- Sense of industry/competence
- Sense of connectedness
- Sense of control
- Stable identity
- Temperament
- Age of onset of puberty
- Cognitive development
- Gender

Interventions
- With children
- With adolescents
- With families
- With communities

Desired Outcomes
- Self-sufficiency
- Positive and responsible family and social relationships
- Good citizenship

Indicators of Need for Assistance
- Poor school performance
- Running away
- Early parenthood or pregnancy
- Substance use
- Criminal behaviors
- Externalizing behavior problems
- Internalizing behavior problems
- Membership in deviant peer groups
- Poor parent–child relationships

Community
- Community culture
- Sources of psychosocial support
- Availability of quality youth-serving organizations

Peers
- Peer groups
- Friendships

FIGURE 7–6 **A Conceptual Model of Adolescent Development.**
Source: Family and Youth Services Bureau, *Understanding Youth Development: Promoting Positive Pathways of Growth* (Washington, DC: U.S. Department of Health and Human Services, 2000).

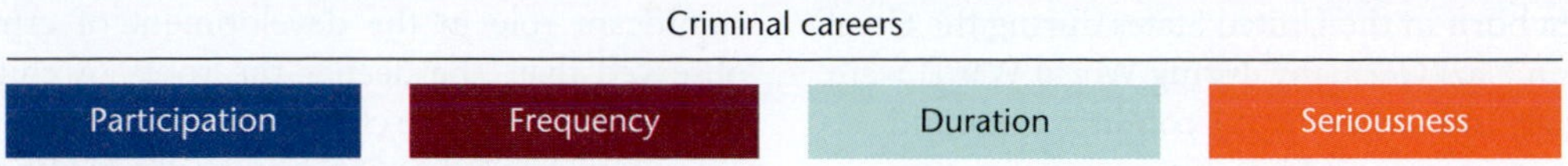

Criminal careers

Participation | Frequency | Duration | Seriousness

FIGURE 7–7 **Aspects of Criminal Careers.**

burglar who commits one burglary a year has a much lower frequency than one who is active monthly or weekly. Frequency is generally not constant and varies over the life-course—even for habitual offenders. *Duration* refers to the length of the criminal career. A criminal career can be very short, consisting of only one offense, or it can be quite long, as in the case of habitual or chronic criminals. *Seriousness* is relatively self-explanatory, although it is worthwhile to note that some offenders with long criminal careers commit only petty crimes, whereas others are serious habitual offenders, and still others commit offenses with a mixed degree of seriousness.

Life-course criminology was given its name in a book written by **Robert J. Sampson** and **John H. Laub** in 1993.[48] Earlier, the **life-course** concept had already been defined as "pathways through the life span involving a sequence of culturally defined, age-graded roles and social transitions enacted over time."[49] Life-course theories, which build on social learning and social control principles, recognize that criminal careers may develop as the result of various criminogenic influences, which affect individuals over the course of their lives.

Researchers who focus on the life-course as it leads to delinquency, crime, and criminal identities are interested in evaluating the prevalence, frequency, and onset of offending, as well as identifying different developmental pathways to delinquency. Life-course researchers ask a variety of questions: How do early childhood characteristics (for example, antisocial behavior) lead to adult behavioral processes and outcomes? How do life transitions (for example, shifts in relationships from parents to peers, transitions from same-sex peers to opposite-sex peers, transitions from attending school to beginning work, marriage, and divorce) influence behavior and behavioral choices? How do offending and victimization interact over the life cycle?[50]

Life-course researchers examine "trajectories and transitions through the age-differentiated life span."[51] A trajectory is a pathway or line of development through life that is marked by a sequence of transitions in such areas as work, marriage, parenthood, and criminal behavior. "Trajectories refer to longer-term patterns and sequences of behavior, whereas transitions are marked by specific life events (for example, first job or the onset of crime) that are embedded in trajectories and evolve over shorter time spans."[52] The concept of age differentiation (or age grading) recognizes the fact that certain forms of behavior and some experiences are more appropriate (in terms of their social consequences) in certain parts of the life cycle than in others.

Life-course theories recognize that criminal careers may develop as the result of criminogenic influences, which affect individuals over the course of their lives.

Having a baby, for example, is more manageable when a woman is married, has a spouse with a dependable job and income, and is covered by health insurance than when she is an adolescent. Life-course theorists search for evidence of continuity between childhood or adolescent experiences and adult outcomes or lifestyles.

Three sets of dynamic concepts are important to the life-course perspective: (1) activation, (2) aggravation, and (3) desistance.[53] *Activation* refers to the factors that stimulate delinquent behaviors, once initiated, and the processes that shape the continuity, frequency, and diversity of delinquency. Three types of activation are possible: (1) acceleration, or increased frequency of offending over time; (2) stabilization, or increased continuity over time; and (3) diversification, or the tendency of individuals to become involved in more diverse delinquent activities. *Aggravation*, the second dynamic process, refers to the existence of a developmental sequence of activities that escalate, or increase in seriousness, over time. *Desistance*, the third process, describes a slowing down in the frequency of offending (deceleration), a reduction in its variety (specialization), or a reduction in its seriousness (deescalation).[54] Desistance is discussed in greater detail later in this chapter.

Another central organizing principle of life-course theories is linked lives. The concept of linked lives refers to the fact that human lives "are typically embedded in social relationships with kin and friends across the life span."[55] Family, friends, and coworkers exercise considerable influence on the life-course of most people.

Glen H. Elder, Jr., has identified five important life-course principles that, taken together, provide a concise summary of life-course theory (Figure 7–8).[56] They are:

1. *The principle of historical time and place.* The life-course of individuals is embedded in and shaped by the historical times and places they experience over their lifetime.

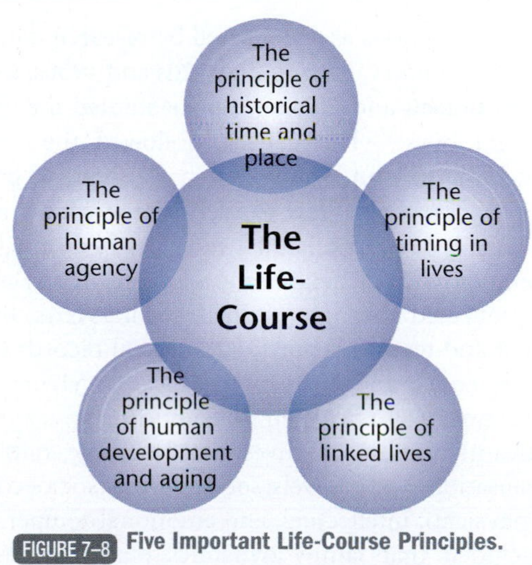

FIGURE 7–8 **Five Important Life-Course Principles.**

Hence, children born in the United States during the Great Depression or in Nazi Germany during World War II were no doubt strongly influenced by the conditions around them. Similarly, surviving children whose parents were lost in the Holocaust experienced trajectories in their life-course that probably would have been far different had they been born in a different place or at a different time.

2. *The principle of timing in lives.* The developmental impact of a succession of life transitions or events is contingent on when they occur in a person's life. Early marriage, for example, or childbearing at an early age can significantly influence the course of people's lives through the long-term consequences of such events. People who start families early may find themselves excluded from further schooling by the demands of parenthood, and those who leave home and marry at an early age may find that parental financial support is not as readily available to them as it might have been if they had continued to live at home.
3. *The principle of linked lives.* Lives are lived interdependently, and social and historical influences are expressed through this network of shared relationships. If a child or a spouse develops a serious illness, for example, the lives of other family members are likely to be affected. Caring for an ill family member is emotionally and financially costly, and it takes time. Because of such costs, opportunities that might have been otherwise available are likely to be lost.
4. *The principle of human agency.* **Human agency**, which is closely related to the concept of free will, refers to the fact that individuals construct their own life-course through the choices they make and the actions they take within the opportunities and constraints of history and social circumstances. The example that Elder gives is of hard-pressed Depression-era parents who "moved their residence to cheaper quarters and sought alternative forms of income." In making such choices, they were involved in the process of building a new life-course.
5. *Principle of human development and aging as lifelong processes.* Human behavior cannot be fully explained by restricting analysis to one life stage, whether it be adolescence, midlife, or old age.

Life-course theories are supported by research dating back well over half a century. During the 1920s and 1930s, for example, **Sheldon Glueck** and **Eleanor Glueck** studied the life cycles of delinquent boys.[57] The Gluecks followed the careers of 500 nondelinquents and 500 known delinquent boys and another 500 girls in an effort to identify the causes of delinquency. Study group participants were matched on age, intelligence, ethnicity, and neighborhood residence. Data were originally collected through psychiatric interviews with subjects; parent and teacher reports; and official records obtained from police, court, and correctional files. Surviving subjects were interviewed again between 1949 and 1965.

Significantly, the Gluecks investigated possible contributions to crime causation on four levels: sociocultural (socioeconomic), somatic (physical), intellectual, and emotional-temperamental. They concluded that family dynamics played an especially significant role in the development of criminality, and they observed that "the deeper the roots of childhood maladjustment, the smaller the chance of adult adjustment."[58] Delinquent careers, then, tend to carry over into adulthood and frequently lead to criminal careers.

In 2012, in an interesting test of life-course theory and turning points, David S. Kirk at the University of Texas at Austin showed that former prisoners returning home to New Orleans were far less likely to continue lives of crimes if they moved to new neighborhoods. Kirk found that the displacement produced by Hurricane Katrina generally led to lower rates of recidivism among those former prisoners because it resulted in a reduction of criminal opportunities and a loss of association with former criminal peers.[59]

Critique of Life-Course Theory

Like the social structure approaches discussed in Chapter 5, life-course theories are intimately associated with the social problems approach. For policymakers, an important question is what role individual choice plays, if any, in human development. Do people actively select components of the life-course? Do they influence their own trajectories? Because so many important life-course determinants are set in motion in early childhood and during adolescence, should those who make wrong choices be held accountable?

Laub and Sampson's Age-Graded Theory

Almost 20 ago, John H. Laub and Robert J. Sampson analyzed 60 cartons of nearly forgotten data that had been collected by the Gluecks and were stored in the basement of the Harvard Law School.[60] Laub and Sampson found that children who turned to delinquency were frequently those who had trouble at school and at home and who had friends who were already involved in delinquency. They also found that two events in the life-course—marriage and job stability—seemed to be especially important in reducing the frequency of offending in later life.

Using a sophisticated computerized analysis of the Gluecks' original data, Laub and Sampson developed an "age-graded theory of informal social control."[61] Laub and Sampson suggest that delinquency is more likely to occur when an individual's bond to society is weak or broken. Their theory, however, also recognizes "that social ties embedded in adult transitions (for example, marital attachment and job stability) explain variations in crime unaccounted for by childhood deviance."[62] Hence, although it incorporates elements of social bond theory, Laub and Sampson's perspective also emphasizes the significance of continuity and change over the life-course.

Central to Laub and Sampson's approach is the idea of **turning points**, or crucial life experiences that can change behavior, in a criminal career. According to the age-graded theory, "the interlocking nature of trajectories and transitions may generate turning points or a change in the life-course."[63] One highly significant turning point, for example, may occur when a person becomes a first-time parent and decides to settle down and abandon a carefree or even "fringe" lifestyle. Given the importance of turning points—which may turn a person either toward or away from criminality and delinquency—a clear-cut relationship between early delinquency and criminality later in life cannot be assumed.

Although turning points can occur at any time in the life-course, Sampson and Laub identified two especially significant turning points: employment and marriage. Employers who are willing to give "troublemakers" a chance and marriage partners who insist on conventional lifestyles seem to be able to successfully redirect the course of a budding offender's life. Other important turning points can occur in association with leaving home, having children, getting divorced, graduating from school, and receiving a financial windfall, for example. Even chronic offenders can be reformed when they experience the requisite turning points, whereas individuals with histories of conventionality can begin offending in response to events and circumstances that undermine previously restraining social bonds.[64]

Because transitions in the life-course are typically associated with age and because events (such as marriage) either enhance or weaken the social bond, Sampson and Laub contend that "age-graded changes in social bonds explain changes in crime." Because these events are not the result of "purposeful efforts to control," they are dubbed "informal social controls."[65]

Another important concept in Laub and Sampson's theory is **social capital**. Laub and Sampson use the concept of social capital to refer to the degree of positive relationships with other people and with social institutions that individuals build up over the course of their lives.[66] Social capital can be enhanced by education, a consistent employment background, enriching personal connections, a "clean" record, and a good marriage and family life. Social capital impacts directly on life-course trajectories: The greater a person's social capital, the less the chance of criminal activity.[67]

Critique of Age-Graded Theory

Age-graded theory, although supported by research, still leaves a number of research questions unanswered. For instance, why does social capital prevent some individuals from participating in criminal activity and not others? A second key question is this: Does social capital actually change a criminal's behavior or simply limit his or her access to crime? Of course, just what constitutes a "positive" relationship is open to interpretation. And some otherwise positive relationships might actually increase the opportunity for crime, as when an individual who has been successful in the world of business finds himself or herself introduced to corrupt politicians or is offered bribes to bend the rules and regulations that should be followed in the normal course of business activities.

Moffitt's Dual Taxonomic Theory

Criminologists have long noted that although adult criminality is usually preceded by antisocial behavior during adolescence, most antisocial children do not become adult criminals. Psychologist **Terrie E. Moffitt** developed a two-path (dual taxonomic) theory of criminality that helps to explain this observation.[68] Moffit's theory contends that as a result of neuropsychological deficits (specifically, early brain damage or chemical imbalances) combined with poverty and family dysfunction, some people come to display more or less constant patterns of misbehavior throughout life.[69] These people are called **life-course–persistent offenders** or "life-course persisters." Life-course persisters tend to fail in school and become involved in delinquency at an early age. As a consequence, their opportunities for legitimate success become increasingly limited with the passage of time.

Other teenagers, says Moffitt, go through limited periods where they exhibit high probabilities of offending. Probabilities of offending are generally highest for these people, says Moffitt, during the mid-teen years. This second group, called **adolescence-limited offenders**, is led to offending primarily by structural disadvantages, according to two-path theory. The most significant of these disadvantages is the status anxiety of teenagers that stems from modern society's inadequacy at easing the transition from adolescence to adulthood for significant numbers of young people. Moffitt hypothesizes that a significant source of adolescent strain arises from the fact that biological maturity occurs at a relatively early age (perhaps as early as 12) and brings with it the desire for sexual and emotional relationships as well as personal autonomy.[70] Society, however, does not permit the assumption of autonomous adult roles until far later (around age 18). As adolescents begin to want autonomy, they are prevented from achieving it because of preexisting societal expectations and societally limited opportunities, resulting in what Moffitt calls a "maturity gap." They might be told, "You're too young for that," or "Wait until you grow up." Lacking the resources to achieve autonomy on their own, they are drawn into delinquent roles by lifelong deviants who have already achieved autonomy and serve as role models for others seeking early independence. At least an appearance of autonomy is achievable for adolescence-limited offenders by engaging in actions that mimic those routinely undertaken by life-course–persistent offenders. Once adolescence-limited offenders realize the substantial costs of continuing misbehavior, however, they abandon such social mimicry and the participation in delinquent acts that characterizes it. As they mature, they begin to aspire toward achieving legitimate autonomy. Those who fail to make the transition successfully add to the ranks of the life-course–persistent population.

Moffitt notes that adolescence-limited offenders display inconsistencies in antisocial behavior from one place to another. They might, for example, participate in illicit drug use with friends or shoplift in stores. They might also experiment sexually. Still, their school behavior is likely to remain within socially acceptable bounds, and they will probably act with respect toward teachers, employers, and adults. Life-course–persistent offenders, on the other hand, consistently engage in antisocial behavior across a wide spectrum of social situations.

Research findings indicate that positive developmental pathways are fostered when adolescents are able to develop (1) a sense of industry and competency, (2) a feeling of connectedness to others and to society, (3) a belief in their ability to control their future, and (4) a stable identity.[71] Adolescents who develop these characteristics appear more likely than others to engage in prosocial behaviors, exhibit positive school performances, and be members of nondeviant peer groups.

Competency, connectedness, control, and identity are outcomes of the developmental process. They develop through a person's interactions with his or her community, family, school, and peers. The following kinds of interactions appear to promote development of these characteristics:

- Interactions in which children engage in productive activities and win recognition for their productivity
- Interactions in which parents and other adults control and monitor adolescents' behaviors in a consistent and caring manner while allowing them a substantial degree of psychological and emotional independence
- Interactions in which parents and other adults provide emotional support, encouragement, and practical advice to adolescents
- Interactions in which adolescents are accepted as individuals with unique experiences based on their temperament; gender; biosocial development; and family, cultural, and societal factors

Critique of Moffitt's Dual Taxonomic Theory

Moffit has been criticized because her research could not definitely show that family and psychological dysfunction was directly related to parent control or individual trajectories. Generally, however, her ideas are well supported and have achieved broad acceptance within the field of criminology.

Farrington's Delinquent Development Theory

Life-course theorists use the term **persistence** to describe continuity in crime, or continual involvement in offending. **Desistance**, on the other hand, refers to the cessation of criminal activity or to the termination of a period of involvement in offending behavior (that is, abandoning a criminal career). In **Farrington's Delinquent Development Theory**, desistance (which was mentioned earlier in this chapter) can be unaided or aided. *Unaided desistance* refers to desistance that occurs without the formal intervention or assistance of criminal justice agencies such as probation or parole agencies, the courts, or prison or jail. *Aided desistance*, which does involve agencies of the justice system, is generally referred to as "rehabilitation." As noted earlier in our discussion of adolescence-limited offenders, delinquents often mature successfully and grow out of offending. Even older persistent offenders, however, may tire of justice system interventions or lose the personal energy required for continued offending. Such offenders are said to have "burned out."

A number of early criminologists noted the desistance phenomenon where offenders appear to undergo relatively intense periods of criminal involvement during the teenage years, with continued involvement into their 20s and even 30s. By age 35 or so, however, spontaneous desistance seems to occur. Marvin Wolfgang described the process as one of "spontaneous remission." The Gluecks later developed the concept of maturational reform to explain the phenomenon and suggested that the "sheer passage of time" caused delinquents to "grow out" of this transitory phase and to "burn out" physiologically. "Ageing is the only factor," they concluded, "which emerges as significant in the reformative process."[72]

In 1985, Walter R. Grove proposed a maturational theory of biopsychosocial desistance that sees the desistance phenomenon as a natural or normal consequence of the aging process.[73] Grove wrote, "As persons move through the life cycle, (1) they will shift from self-absorption to concern for others; (2) they will increasingly accept societal values and behave in socially appropriate ways; (3) they will become more comfortable with social relations; (4) their activities will increasingly reflect a concern for others in their community; and (5) they will become increasingly concerned with the issue of the meaning of life."[74]

Longitudinal studies of crime in the life-course conducted by **David P. Farrington** and **Donald J. West** have shown far greater diversity in the ages of desistance than in the ages of onset of criminal behavior.[75] In 1982, in an effort to explain the considerable heterogeneity of developmental pathways, Farrington and West began tracking a cohort of 411 boys born in London in 1953. The study, known as the **Cambridge Study in Delinquent Development**, is ongoing. It uses self-reports of delinquency as well as psychological tests and in-depth interviews. To date, participants have been interviewed nine times. Although respondents are now 60 years old, the earliest interviews were conducted at age 8.

The Cambridge study reveals that life-course patterns found in the United States are also characteristic of English delinquents. Farrington found that the study's persistent offenders suffered from "hyperactivity, poor concentration, low achievement, an antisocial father, large family size, low family income, a broken family, poor parental supervision, and parental disharmony."[76] Other risk factors for delinquency included harsh discipline, negative peer influences, and parents with offense histories of their own. Chronic offenders were found to have friends and peers who were also offenders, and offending was found to begin with early antisocial behavior, including aggressiveness, dishonesty, problems in school, truancy, hyperactivity, impulsiveness, and restlessness. Consistent with other desistance studies, Farrington found that offending tends to peak around the age of 17 or 18 and then declines. By age 35, many subjects were found to have assumed conforming lifestyles, although they were often separated or divorced with poor employment records and patterns of residential instability. Many former offenders were also substance abusers and consequently served as very poor role models for their children.

In 1990, Rolf Loeber and Marc LeBlanc identified four components of desistance.[77] Desistance, they said, can be conceptualized in terms of (1) *deceleration*, or a slowing down in the frequency of offending; (2) *specialization*, or a reduction in the variety of offenses; (3) *deescalation*, or a reduction in the seriousness of offending; and (4) *reaching a ceiling*, or remaining at a certain level of offending and not committing more serious offenses. Until desistance is better defined and conceptualized, it will remain difficult for researchers to investigate the topic.

Critique of Farrington's Delinquent Development Theory

Delinquent Development Theory has been criticized for its methodology. Although studies of desistance are becoming increasingly common, one of the main methodological problems for researchers is determining when desistance has occurred. Some theorists conceptualize desistance as the complete or absolute stopping of criminal behavior of any kind, whereas others see it as the gradual cessation of criminal involvement.[78]

Some criminologists argue, however, that the claim that aging causes desistance is meaningless because it doesn't explain the actual mechanisms involved in the desistance phenomenon. In other words, the claim that an offender "ages out" of crime offers no more explanatory power than the claim that turning 16 causes delinquency.

Evolutionary Ecology

Because life-course theory uses a developmental perspective in the study of criminal careers, life-course researchers typically use longitudinal research designs involving cohort analysis. **Cohort analysis** usually begins at birth and, until participants reach a certain age, traces the development of a population whose members share common characteristics. One well-known analysis of a birth cohort, undertaken by **Marvin Wolfgang** during the 1960s, found that a small nucleus of chronic juvenile offenders accounted for a disproportionately large share of all juvenile arrests.[79]

Wolfgang studied male individuals born in Philadelphia in 1945 until they reached age 18. He concluded that a few violent offenders were responsible for most of the crimes committed by the cohort. Six percent of cohort members accounted for 52% of all arrests (Figure 7–9). A follow-up study found that the seriousness of the offenses among the cohort increased in adulthood, but that the actual number of offenses decreased as the cohort aged.[80] More recently, Wolfgang published a cohort analysis of 5,000 individuals born in the Wuchang district of the city of Wuhan in China. The study, from which preliminary results were published in 1996, used Chinese-supplied data to compare delinquents with nondelinquents. It found "striking differences in school deportment, achieved level of education, school dropout rate, type of employment, and unemployment rate" between the two groups.[81]

The ecological perspective on crime control, pioneered by **Lawrence E. Cohen** and **Richard Machalek**, provides a contemporary example of a life-course approach.[82] Like other life-course theories, **evolutionary ecology** blends elements of previous perspectives—in this case, building upon the approach of social ecology—while emphasizing developmental pathways encountered early in life. According to University of Wyoming criminologist Bryan Vila, "The evolutionary ecological approach draws attention to the ways people develop over the course of their lives. Experiences and environment early in life, especially those that affect child development and the transmission of biological traits and family management practices across generations, seem particularly important."[83] According to Vila, evolutionary ecology "attempts to explain how people acquire criminality—a predisposition that disproportionately favors criminal behavior—when and why they express it as crime, how individuals and groups respond to those crimes, and how all these phenomena interact as a dynamic self-reinforcing system that evolves over time."[84]

Critique of Evolutionary Ecology

Wolfgang's analysis has since been criticized for its lack of a second cohort, or control group, against which the experiences of the cohort under study could be compared.[85] Similarly, the dropping out of cohort members can bias the results of any cohort analysis. Such dropping out can occur when contact is lost with members, when cohort members move away, or when they die. It can be expected, for example, that the most crime-prone individuals in any cohort are those most likely to be difficult to keep in touch with and may themselves suffer death or incapacitation—making it impossible to determine what their future behavior might have entailed.

Thornberry's Interactional Theory

Terence Thornberry has proposed what he calls an **interactional theory** of crime, which integrates social control and social learning explanations of delinquency.[86] In constructing his approach, Thornberry was attentive to the impact of social structure on behavior and noted how delinquency and crime seem to develop within the context of reciprocal social arrangements. Reciprocity was especially important to Thornberry because he believed that too many other theories were simplistic in their dependence on simple unidirectional causal relationships.

According to interactional theory, the fundamental cause of delinquency is a weakening of a person's bond to conventional society.[87] Thornberry points out that adolescents who

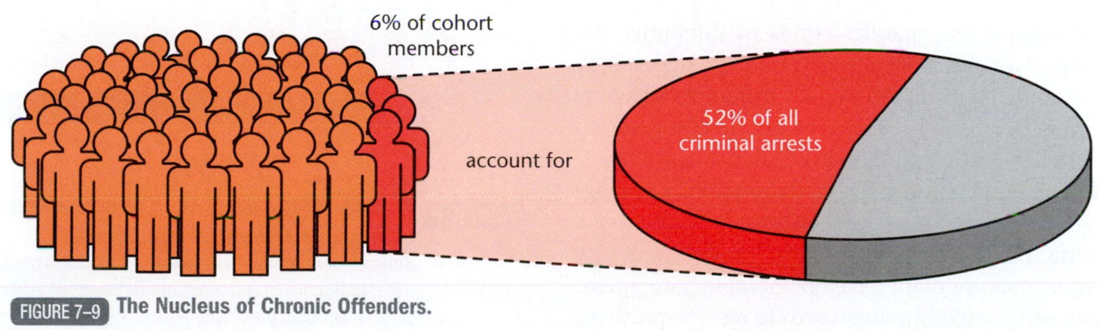
6% of cohort members
account for
52% of all criminal arrests

FIGURE 7–9 **The Nucleus of Chronic Offenders.**

are strongly attached to their parents and family and who strive to achieve within the context of approved social arrangements, such as education, rarely turn to serious delinquency. It takes more than weak conventional bonds, however, for delinquency to develop. A further requirement is the presence of an environment in which delinquency can be learned and in which rule-violating behavior can be positively rewarded. Delinquent peers are especially important in providing the kind of environment necessary for criminal behavior to develop, and gang membership can play a highly significant role in the development and continuation of such behavior. Associating with delinquent peers, says Thornberry, leads to delinquent acts, but also creates a causal loop because those who commit delinquent acts continue associating with others like themselves, reinforcing the behavior and creating escalating levels of criminal activity. Thornberry also predicts that delinquents will seek out association with ever-more delinquent groups if their delinquency continues to be rewarded. Hence, delinquency, from the perspective of interactional theory, is seen as a process that unfolds over the life-course.

In a test of interactional theory,[88] Thornberry used data drawn from the Rochester Youth Development Study, a multiwave panel study designed to examine drug use and delinquent behavior among adolescents in the Rochester, New York, area. Study findings, discussed in more detail to come, supported the loop-back aspects of interactional theory and showed that delinquency is part of a dynamic social process, and not merely the end result of static conditions. The study also found that the development of beliefs supportive of delinquent behavior tends to follow that behavior in time. In other words, commitment to delinquent values may be more a product of delinquent behavior that is rewarded than an initial cause of such behavior.

Critique of Thornberry's Interactional Theory

Those who criticize Thornberry say that his theory does not fully appreciate the notion of childhood maltreatment (as measured by official records) as an important element of the developmental process leading to delinquency.[89] Researchers have also found that the degree of maltreatment experienced in childhood bears at least some relationship to the extent of delinquent involvement later in life. While maltreatment appears to weaken the bond to conventionality, it also weakens the family bond.

Developmental Pathways

Researchers have found that manifestations of disruptive behaviors in childhood and adolescence are often age-dependent, reflecting a developing capability to display different behaviors with age.[90] Budding behavioral problems can often be detected at an early age. In 1994, for example, Rolf Loeber and Dale F. Hay described the emergence of opposition to parents and aggression toward siblings and peers as a natural developmental occurrence during the first two years of life.[91] Loeber and Hay found, however, that as toddlers develop the ability to speak, they become increasingly likely to use words to resolve conflicts.

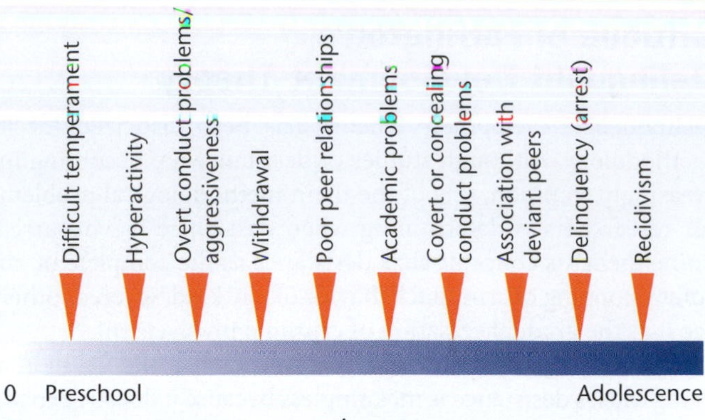

FIGURE 7–10 **Manifestations of Disruptive and Antisocial Behaviors in Childhood and Adolescence.**
Source: Barbara Tatem Kelley et al., *Developmental Pathways in Boys' Disruptive and Delinquent Behavior* (Washington, DC: Office of Juvenile Justice and Delinquency Prevention, December 1997).

As a consequence, oppositional behaviors decline between ages three and six. Children who are unable, for whatever reason, to develop adequate verbal coping skills, however, distinguish themselves from the norm by committing acts of intense aggression, initiating hostile conflict, and being characterized by parents as having a difficult temperament.[92] Figure 7–10 shows the order in which disruptive and antisocial childhood behaviors tend to manifest between birth and late adolescence. Figure 7–11, in contrast, shows the order of development of skills and attitudes deemed necessary for successful prosocial development during childhood and adolescence.

One of the most comprehensive studies to date that has attempted to detail life pathways leading to criminality began in 1986. The study, called the Program of Research on the Causes and Correlates of Delinquency, is sponsored by the U.S. Department of Justice's OJJDP. The program, a longitudinal study that is producing ongoing results, intends to improve the understanding of serious delinquency, violence, and drug use by examining how youths develop within the context of family, school, peers, and community.[93] It has compiled data on 4,500 youths from three distinct but coordinated projects: the Denver Youth

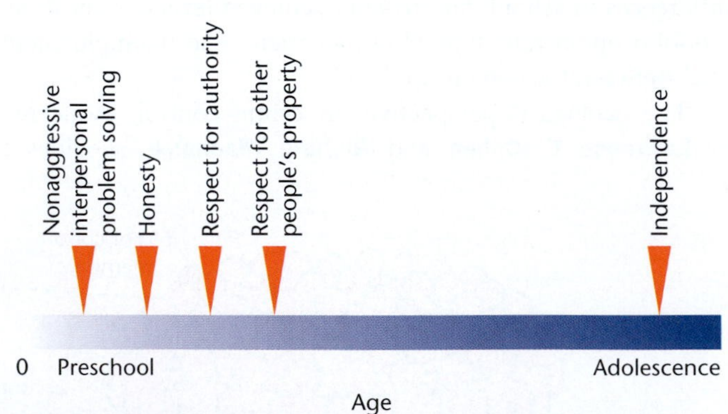

FIGURE 7–11 **The Order of Development of Skills and Attitudes Necessary for Successful Prosocial Development.**
Source: Barbara Tatem Kelley et al., *Developmental Pathways in Boys' Disruptive and Delinquent Behavior* (Washington, DC: Office of Juvenile Justice and Delinquency Prevention, December 1997).

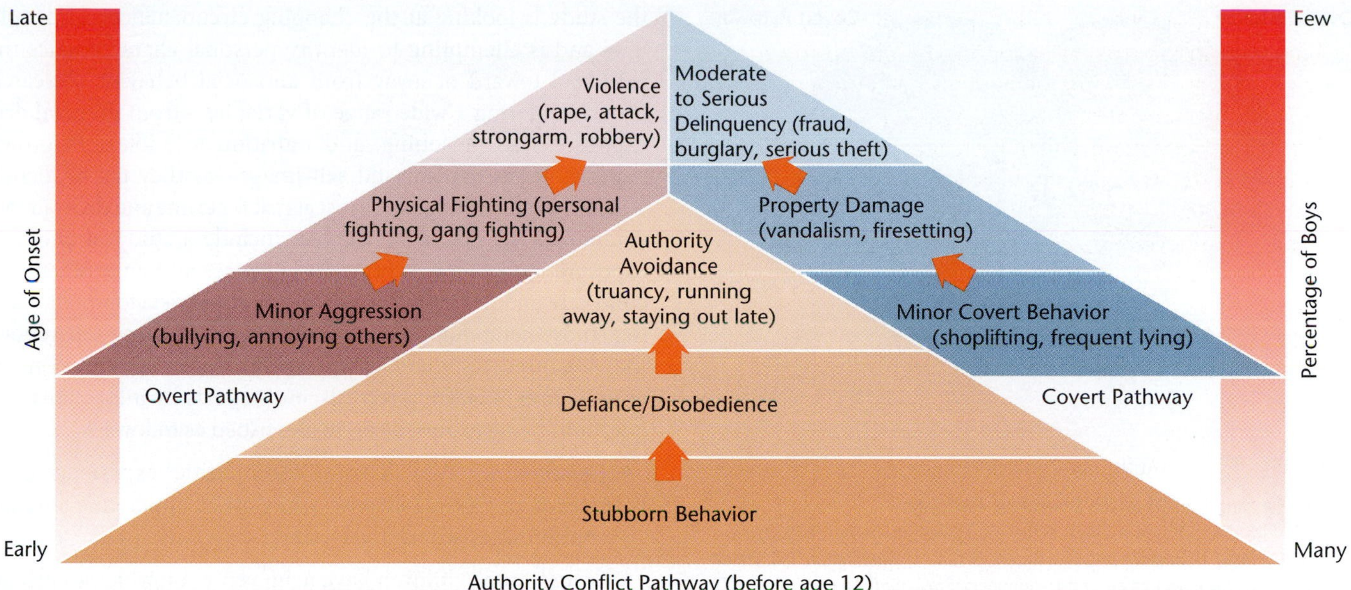

FIGURE 7–12 **Three Pathways to Disruptive Behavior and Delinquency.**
Source: Barbara Tatem Kelley et al., *Developmental Pathways in Boys' Disruptive and Delinquent Behavior* (Washington, DC: Office of Juvenile Justice and Delinquency Prevention, December 1997).

Survey, conducted by the University of Colorado; the Pittsburgh Youth Study, undertaken by University of Pittsburgh researchers; and the Rochester Youth Development Study, fielded by professors at the State University of New York at Albany.

The Causes and Correlates projects all use a similar research design. All of the projects are longitudinal investigations involving repeated contacts with youths during a substantial portion of their developmental years. In each project, researchers conduct individual, face-to-face interviews with inner-city youths considered to be at high risk for involvement in delinquency and drug abuse. Multiple perspectives on each child's development and behavior are obtained through interviews with the child's primary caretakers and in interviews with teachers. In addition to interview data, the studies collect extensive information from official agencies, including police, courts, schools, and social services.[94]

Program results show that (1) delinquency is related to individual risk factors such as impulsivity; (2) the more seriously involved in drugs a youth is, the more seriously that juvenile will be involved in delinquency; (3) children who are more attached to and involved with their parents are less involved in delinquency; (4) greater risks exist for violent offending when a child is physically abused or neglected early in life; (5) students who are not highly committed to school have higher rates of delinquency, and delinquency involvement reduces commitment to school; (6) poor family life, and especially poor parental supervision, exacerbates delinquency and drug use; (7) affiliation with street gangs and illegal gun ownership are both predictive of delinquency; (8) living in a "bad" neighborhood doubles the risk for delinquency; and (9) family receipt of public assistance (welfare) is associated with the highest risk of delinquency (followed by low socioeconomic status).[95] Results also showed that peers who were delinquent or used drugs had a great impact on other youth. In terms of desistance, program results show that "the best predictors of success were having conventional friends, having a stable family and good parental monitoring, having positive expectations for the future, and not having delinquent peers."[96]

Perhaps the most significant result of the Causes and Correlates study is the finding that three separate developmental pathways to delinquency exist. The pathways identified by the study are shown in Figure 7–12. They are the following:[97]

- The *authority conflict pathway*, on which subjects appear to begin quite young (as early as three or four years of age). "The first step," say the study authors, "was stubborn behavior, followed by defiance around age 11, and authority avoidance—truancy, staying out late at night, or running away."
- The *covert pathway*, which begins with "minor covert acts such as frequent lying and shoplifting, usually around age 10." Delinquents following this path quickly progress "to acts of property damage, such as firestarting or vandalism, around age 11 or 12, followed by moderate and serious forms of delinquency."
- The *overt pathway*, in which the first step is marked by minor aggression such as "annoying others and bullying—around age 11 or 12." Bullying was found to escalate into "physical fighting and violence as the juvenile progressed along this pathway." The overt pathway eventually leads to violent crimes such as rape, robbery, and assault.

Researchers have found that these three pathways are not necessarily mutually exclusive and can at times converge (Figure 7–13). Self-report data show that simultaneous progression along two or more pathways leads to higher rates of delinquency than would otherwise occur.[98] Visit the Network on Transitions to Adulthood to explore further issues in social development. Findings from an earlier program, the Causes and Correlates of Delinquency Program, are summarized at **Web Extra 7–4**.

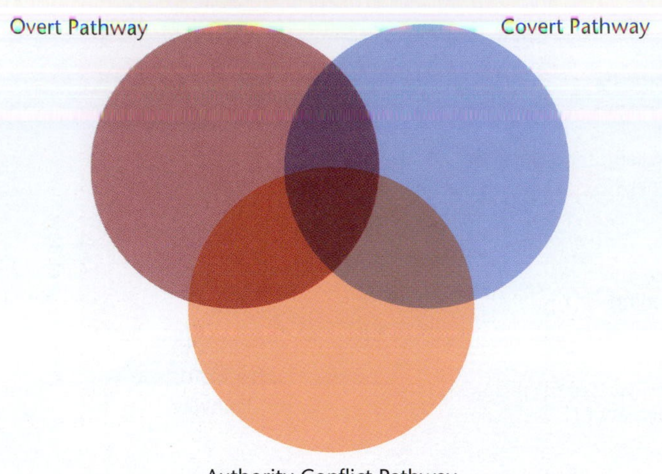

FIGURE 7–13 **Single or Multiple Disruptive Pathways.**
Source: Barbara Tatem Kelley et al., *Developmental Pathways in Boys' Disruptive and Delinquent Behavior* (Washington, DC: Office of Juvenile Justice and Delinquency Prevention, December 1997).

Critique of Developmental Pathways

As with other social development theories, the idea of developmental pathways suffers from definitional issues. What, for example, do life-course concepts such as turning points and pathways really mean? A related fundamental question, especially for policymakers, is the role that individual choice plays, if any, in human development.

The Chicago Human Development Project

Another study that could produce substantially significant results began in 1990. Known as the **Project on Human Development in Chicago Neighborhoods (PHDCN)**,[99] it is directed by physician Felton J. Earls, professor of human behavior and development at Harvard University's School of Public Health. Also involved in the project are Robert Sampson, professor of sociology at the University of Chicago, and Stephen Raudenbush, professor of education at Michigan State University. Earls and Albert J. Reiss describe the ongoing research as "the major criminological investigation of this century."[100]

The PHDCN, which consists of a longitudinal analysis of how individuals, families, institutions, and communities evolve together, is now "tracing how criminal behavior develops from birth to age 32."[101] It involves experts from a wide range of disciplines, including psychiatry, developmental and clinical psychology, sociology, criminology, public health and medicine, education, human behavior, and statistics.

The project is actually two studies combined into a single, comprehensive design. The first is an intensive study of Chicago's neighborhoods. This aspect of the project is evaluating the social, economic, organizational, political, and cultural components of each neighborhood. It seeks to identify changes that took place in the neighborhoods over the study's eight-year data-gathering period. The second project component consists of a series of coordinated longitudinal evaluations of 7,000 randomly selected children, adolescents, and young adults. This aspect of the study is looking at the changing circumstances of people's lives and is attempting to identify personal characteristics that may lead toward or away from antisocial behavior. Researchers are exploring a wide range of variables—from prenatal drug exposure, lead poisoning, and nutrition to adolescent growth patterns, temperament, and self-image—as they try to identify which individuals might be most at risk for crime and delinquency. Additional features of the project include a study of children's exposure to violence and its consequences and an evaluation of child care and its impact on early childhood development. Varying study methodologies are being used, including self-reports, individualized tests and examinations, direct observation, the examination of existing records, and reports by informants. The questions being explored can be described as follows:[102]

- *Communities.* Why do some communities experience high rates of antisocial behavior while other, apparently similar communities are relatively safe?
- *School.* Some children have achievement problems early in school. Others have behavioral or truancy problems. Some exhibit both kinds of problems, and others neither. Why do these differences exist? What are the causes and effects?
- *Peers.* Delinquent youths tend to associate with delinquent peers and usually act in groups. Does the association lead to delinquency, or is it simply a case of "like finding like"? Are the influences of peers equally important for girls and for boys, or are their development pathways entirely different?
- *Families.* Poor parenting practices are strongly associated with substance abuse and delinquency, but are they the cause of such behavior? If so, then social programs in parenting skills could make a difference. But what if there are underlying factors, such as temperamental characteristics or social isolation, that cause problems in both parents and children?
- *Individual differences.* What health-related, cognitive, intellectual, and emotional factors in children promote positive social development? What factors put children at risk of developing antisocial behaviors?

The PHDCN is producing results and has led to targeted interventions intended to lower rates of offending. According to Sampson, "Instead of external actions (for example, a police crackdown), we stress in this study the effectiveness of 'informal' mechanisms by which residents themselves achieve public order. In particular, we believe that collective expectations for intervening on behalf of neighborhood children is a crucial dimension of the public life of neighborhoods."[103] Life-course perspectives, like the perspective that informs the PHDCN, often point to the need for early intervention with nurturing strategies that build self-control through positive socialization. As Bryan Vila points out, "There are two main types of nurturing strategies: those that improve early life experiences to forestall the development of strategic styles based on criminality, and those that channel child and adolescent development in an effort to improve the match between individuals and their environment."[104] The Project on Human Development in Chicago Neighborhoods can be found at **Web Extra 7–5**.

Life-course perspectives point to the need for early intervention using nurturing strategies that build self-control.

Policy Implications of Social Development Theories

Social development strategies have been widely applied to juvenile justice and human services settings. The OJJDP has adopted the social development model as the foundation for its **Comprehensive Strategy for Serious, Violent,** and **Chronic Juvenile Offenders program**. The Comprehensive Strategy program provides participating communities with a framework for preventing delinquency; intervening in early delinquent behavior; and responding to serious, violent, and chronic offending. It assists communities in establishing or modifying a juvenile justice "continuum of care" through risk-focused prevention, risk and needs assessment, structured decision making, and graduated sanctions training and technical assistance. The OJJDP's Comprehensive Strategy program centers around the following six components:

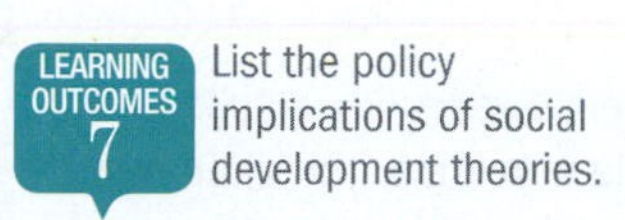
LEARNING OUTCOMES
7
List the policy implications of social development theories.

- Strengthening families in their role of providing guidance and discipline and instilling sound values as the first and primary teacher of children
- Supporting core social institutions, including schools, churches, and other community organizations, so that they can reduce risk factors and help children develop their full potential
- Promoting prevention strategies that enhance protective factors and reduce the impact of negative risk factors affecting the lives of young people at risk for high delinquency
- Intervening immediately and constructively when delinquent behavior first occurs
- Identifying and controlling a small segment of violent and chronic juvenile offenders
- Establishing a broad spectrum of *sanctions* that ensures accountability and a continuum of services

Another contemporary example of social intervention efforts tied to a developmental model is Targeted Outreach, a program operated by Boys and Girls Clubs of America.[105] The program has its origins in the 1972 implementation of a youth development strategy based on studies undertaken at the University of Colorado, which showed that at-risk youths could be effectively diverted from the juvenile justice system through the provision of positive alternatives. Using a wide referral network made up of local schools, police departments, and various youth service agencies, club officials work to end what they call the "inappropriate detention of juveniles."[106]

The program's primary goal is to provide a positive, productive alternative to gangs for the youths who are most vulnerable to their influences or are already entrenched in gang activity. Currently, the program recruits at-risk youngsters—many as young as seven years old—and diverts them into activities that are intended to promote a sense of belonging, competence, usefulness, and self-control. A sense of belonging is fostered through clubs that provide familiar settings where each child is accepted. Competence and usefulness are developed through opportunities for meaningful activities, which young people in the club program can successfully undertake. Finally, Targeted Outreach provides its youthful participants with a chance to be heard and, consequently, with the opportunity to influence decisions affecting their future. Organizers hope that Targeted Outreach will eventually involve more than 1.5 million youngsters between the ages of 7 and 17. Targeted Outreach stands as an example of the kind of program that theorists who focus on the social structure typically seek to implement.

THE CASE

Seung-Hui Cho

Shortly after 7 A.M. on April 16, 2007, Seung-Hui Cho shot and killed two people near the Virginia Polytechnic Institute and State University (Virginia Tech) campus in Blacksburg, Virginia. Cho, an English major at the university who was in his senior year, had previously been accused of stalking two female students. When police mistakenly believed the shootings to have been the result of a lovers' quarrel between one of the victims and her off-campus boyfriend, Cho found the time he needed to make his final preparations for another attack.[i]

Entering the campus's Norris Hall around 9:30 A.M., Cho secured the interior door handles with chains, then systematically set about slaughtering everyone he encountered. During the next 15 minutes, he fired more than 175 rounds of ammunition from two weapons, leaving 30 people dead within Norris Hall. When Cho heard police blast through the entrance doors to gain access to the building, he turned the gun on himself. His rampage is the worst event of its kind in U.S. history,[ii] leaving a total of 32 victims dead. Seventeen others were wounded by gunshots, and still more were hurt when they jumped out of the building's second-story windows to escape.

The attacks on the Virginia Tech campus were planned and executed with near-military precision. In the weeks before the shootings, Cho acquired two handguns, extra magazines, ammunition, and lengths of chain with which to secure the doors of classroom buildings so that potential victims would be unable to escape. Just days before the killings, he videotaped a raging manifesto-like diatribe/suicide note in which he blamed society for making him into what he'd become.[iii] In the video, Cho praised the Columbine High School shooters as martyrs, pronounced himself a Christ figure, and ranted against the hedonistic behavior, trust funds, and high-class living of the financially elite.[iv]

On April 18, 2007, a package from Cho was delivered to NBC News. The date and time post marked on the mailing showed a time between the first and second shooting episodes, showing that Cho had made a trip to the post office before continuing his shooting spree. Inside the package were an 1,800-word manifesto, photos, and 27 digitally recorded videos in which Cho likened himself to Jesus Christ and expressed his hatred of the wealthy. In the video, he proclaimed, "You forced me into a corner and gave me only one option. . . . You just loved to crucify me. You loved inducing cancer in my head, terror in my heart and ripping my soul all this time."

Cho's background was not especially remarkable. He was born on January 18, 1984. Cho came to the United States from the Republic of Korea when he was just eight years old, a sullen, withdrawn, and brooding child. People who knew him when he was young said that he rarely talked and possessed a disassociated manner with an "empty face." He seemed to display little reaction to what was occurring around him. Some people think that he may have had symptoms of autism, although he was never diagnosed as autistic.

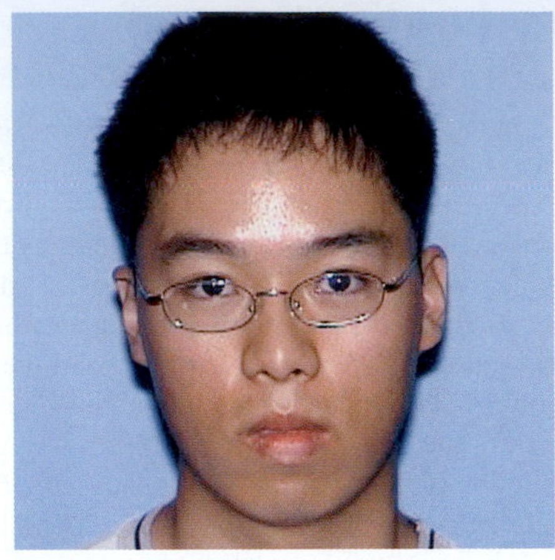
Virginia State Police/Associated Press

After coming to the United States and moving to the tight-knit Korean community in Centreville, Virginia, the family maintained an "uncommonly private"[v] existence. Cho's progression through elementary school was unremarkable. At nearby Chantilly, Virginia's Westfield High School, the slight, slender boy appeared to be too young to be there. The taciturn Cho was teased and bullied more than most of the boys, especially about his poor English and deep-throated voice, which didn't seem to fit his small body.[vi]

Cho's freshman, sophomore, and junior years as an English major at Virginia Tech were noteworthy for the anger in his writings. Although he never threatened to kill people or mentioned guns, the disturbingly violent nature of his papers caused the chairperson of the English Department to remove him from a creative writing class. She attempted to teach him one-on-one, then sought assistance from the university's counseling department and other university officials.

Author's Note: Not long after the events described here, the then-governor of Virginia, Timothy M. Kaine, established a panel of nationally recognized experts from a variety of fields to perform an independent review of the shootings. The group, known as the Virginia Tech Review Panel, studied the shooting incident in detail and released a comprehensive report that can be viewed at http://www.governor.virginia.gov/tempcontent/techpanelreport.cfm.

Notes

[i]Ned Potter, David Schoetz, Richard Esposito, Pierre Thomas, and the staff of ABC News, "Killer's Note: You Caused Me to Do This," ABC News, April 28, 2007, http://abcnews.go.com/US/Story?id=3048108&page=1 (accessed July 1, 2010).

[ii]Aamer Madhani, E. A. Torriero, and Rex W. Huppke, "Danger Signs Festered below Aloof Surface," *Chicago Tribune*, April 17, 2007.

[iii]Ibid.

[iv]"High School Classmates Say Gunman Was Bullied," MSNBC, April 19, 2007.

[v]Benedict Carey, "When the Group Is Wise," *New York Times*, April 22, 2007, http://www.nytimes.com/2007/04/22/weekinreview/22carey.html?_r=1&ref=weekinreview&oref=slogin (accessed July 1, 2010).

[vi]Ned Potter et al., "Killer's Note: You Caused Me to Do This."

The case of Seung-Hui Cho raises some interesting questions. Among them are the following:

1. **Which social process or social development perspective might apply to Cho?**
2. **Might the life-course approach help explain Cho's later behavior? If so, how?**
3. **What turning points can you identify in Cho's life?**
4. **Might there be value in a control-balance perspective when examining Cho's behavior? If so, how would it be of value?**
5. **Which of the three pathways to delinquent behavior described in this chapter seem most applicable to Cho?**

CHAPTER 7 Social Process and Social Development—*It's What We Learn*

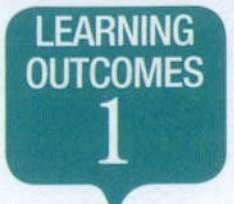

Explain the interactionist perspective.

The theories discussed in the first part of this chapter are called social process theories, or *interactionist perspectives*, because they depend on the process of interaction between individuals and society for their explanatory power. The various types of social process theories include social learning theory, social control theory, and labeling theory. Social process theories see criminal behavior as a product of the social environment and not as an innate characteristic.

1. How does the process of social interaction contribute to criminal behavior?
2. What are the differences between theories of social process and social development?
3. What are the similarities between theories of social process and social development?

social process theories Theories that suggest that criminal behavior is learned in interaction with others and that socialization and learning processes occur as the result of group membership and relationships.

social development theories An integrated view of human development that examines multiple levels of maturation simultaneously, including the psychological, biological, familial, interpersonal, cultural, societal, and ecological levels.

LEARNING OUTCOMES 2

Outline the evolution of social process and social development theories.

One of the earliest and most influential forms of learning theory was advanced by Edwin Sutherland in 1939. Sutherland emphasized the role of social learning as an explanation for crime and held that virtually all criminality is learned through association with others who communicate criminal values and who advocate the commission of crimes.

1. What is the role of communication and socialization in the acquisition of learned patterns of behavior? How do they contribute to criminal behavior?
2. What is meant by the concept of differential association?

learning theory A perspective that places primary emphasis upon the role of communication and socialization in the acquisition of learned patterns of criminal behavior and the values that support that behavior.

differential association An explanation for crime and deviance that holds that people pursue criminal or deviant behavior to the extent that they identify themselves with real or imaginary people from whose perspective their criminal or deviant behavior seems acceptable.

Key Name

Edwin Sutherland A criminologist who suggested that all significant behavior is learned and crime, therefore, is not substantively different from any other form of behavior.

LEARNING OUTCOMES 3

Describe social control theories, including containment, control-balance, and social bond theories.

Social control theories, which fall under the general category of the social process perspective, seek to identify those features of the personality and the environment that keep people from committing crimes. Like social process theories, they see criminal behavior as a product of the social environment and not as an innate characteristic. Social control theorists focus on the process through which social integration develops and say that it is the extent of a person's integration with positive social institutions and significant others that determines his or her resistance to criminal temptations.

1. What are some of the factors of inner containment? Of external containment? How do the two sets of factors work together to prevent crime?
2. What is the general theory of crime? What is its central feature?

social control theories A perspective that predicts that when social constraints on antisocial behavior are weakened or absent, delinquent behavior emerges.

containment theory A form of control theory that suggests that a series of both internal and external factors contributes to law-abiding behavior.

containment The stabilizing force that, if effective, blocks pushes and pulls from leading an individual toward crime.

low self-esteem A reduced sense of self-worth, to include lowered self-assurance and lowered self-respect. Low self-esteem is linked to delinquency.

social bond The link created through individuals and the society of which they are a part.

general theory of crime A theory that attempts to explain all (or at least most) forms of criminal conduct through a single, overarching approach and holds that low self-control accounts for all crime at all times.

situational action theory (SAT) A perspective that suggests that an individual's ability to exercise self-control is an outcome of the interaction between his or her personal traits and the situation in which he or she takes part.

control ratio The amount of control to which a person is subject versus the amount of control that person exerts over others.

Key Names

Walter C. Reckless A theorist who contended that crime is like sickness because it results from the failure of control mechanisms, some internal to the person and others external.

Howard B. Kaplan A theorist who proposed that people who are ridiculed by their peers suffer a loss of self-esteem; assess themselves poorly; and, as a result, abandon the motivation to conform.

Travis Hirschi A theorist who believed that through successful socialization, a bond forms between individuals and the social group. When that bond is weakened or broken, deviance and crime may result.

Michael Gottfredson Criminologist who believed that nearly all crimes are mundane, simple, trivial, easy acts aimed at satisfying the desires of the moment.

Per-Olof H. Wikström a University of Cambridge social scientist who proposed that self-control could best be analyzed as a situational concept (i.e., a factor in the process of choice), rather than as an individual trait.

Charles R. Tittle A sociologist who contended that the control-balance approach results from a blending of social bond and containment perspectives.

LEARNING OUTCOMES 4

Describe labeling theory.

Labeling theory (also called *social reaction theory*) points to the special significance of society's response to the criminal and sees continued crime as a consequence of limited opportunities for acceptable behavior that follow from the negative responses of society to those defined as offenders.

1. What's the difference between primary and secondary deviance? Which of the two is caused by labeling?
2. What is meant by the idea of moral enterprise? What is the result of successful moral enterprise?

tagging A term that explains what happens to offenders following arrest, conviction, and sentencing.

primary deviance Initial deviance often undertaken to deal with transient problems in living.

secondary deviance Deviant behavior that results from official labeling and from association with others who have been so labeled.

moral enterprise The efforts made by an interest group to have its sense of moral or ethical propriety enacted into law.

moral entrepreneurs Individuals or groups engaged in the process of moral enterprise.

Key Names

Edwin M. Lemert A theorist who believed that primary deviance is undertaken to solve an immediate problem. Secondary deviance is important after an arrest has taken place and an individual is "tagged" as a deviant. The deviance then becomes more forceful and serious.

Howard Becker A theorist who described society as creating both deviance and the deviant person by its response to circumscribed behaviors.

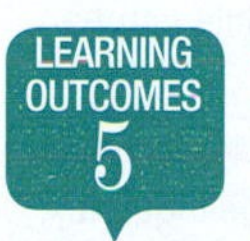

Explain the policy implications of social process theories.

Social process theories suggest that crime-prevention programs should work to enhance self-control and to build prosocial bonds.

1. What kinds of social policy initiatives might be based on social process theories of crime causation?
2. What is meant by the term *prosocial bonds*? How are such bonds formed?

prosocial bonds Bonds between the individual and the social group that strengthen the likelihood of conformity. Prosocial bonds are characterized by attachment to conventional social institutions, values, and beliefs.

Juvenile Mentoring Program (JUMP) A program that places at-risk youth in a one-on-one relationship with favorable adult role models.

Preparing for the Drug Free Years (PDFY) A program designed to increase effective parenting for children in grades 4 through 8 in an effort to reduce drug abuse and behavioral problems.

Montreal Prevention Treatment Program A program designed to address early childhood risk factors for gang involvement by targeting boys in kindergarten who exhibit disruptive behavior.

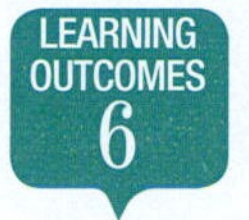

Use the social development perspective to explain criminality.

The social development perspective acknowledges that human development begins at birth and takes place within a social context. Students of human development recognize that the process of development occurs through reciprocal and dynamic interactions that take place between individuals and various aspects of their environment.

1. What are the central concepts of social development theories?
2. What do criminologists mean when they talk about "life-course criminology"?
3. What is "social capital"? How is it accumulated?

human development The relationship between the maturing individual and his or her changing environment, as well as the social processes that the relationship entails.

social development perspective An integrated view of human development that examines multiple levels of maturity simultaneously, including the psychological, biological, familial, interpersonal, cultural, societal, and ecological levels.

life-course criminology A developmental perspective that draws attention to the fact that criminal behavior tends to follow a distinct pattern across the life cycle.

criminal career The longitudinal sequence of events committed by an individual offender.

life-course Pathways through the life span involving a sequence of culturally defined, age-graded roles and social transitions enacted over time.

human agency The idea that individuals construct their own life-course through the choices they make and the actions they take within the opportunities and constraints of history and social circumstances.

turning points Crucial life experiences that can change behavior.

social capital The degree of positive relationships with others and with social institutions that individuals build up over the course of their lives.

life-course–persistent offenders Offenders who, as a result of neuropsychological deficits combined with poverty and family dysfunction, display patterns of misbehavior throughout life.

adolescence-limited offenders Juvenile offenders who abandon delinquency upon reaching maturity.

persistence Continuity in crime, or continual involvement in offending.

desistance The cessation of criminal activity or the termination of a period of involvement in offending behavior (that is, abandoning a criminal career).

Farrington's Delinquent Development Theory A theory in which persistence describes continuity in crime and desistance refers to cessation of criminal activity or to a termination in a period of involvement in offending behavior.

Cambridge Study in Delinquent Development A longitudinal (life-course) study of crime and delinquency tracking a cohort of 411 boys in London.

cohort analysis A social scientific technique that, over time, studies a population with common characteristics. Cohort analysis usually begins at birth and traces the development of cohort members until they reach a certain age.

evolutionary ecology A theory that blends elements of previous perspectives—building upon social ecology while emphasizing developmental pathways.

interactional theory A theoretical approach to exploring crime and delinquency that blends social control and social learning perspectives.

Project on Human Development in Chicago Neighborhoods (PHDCN) A longitudinal analysis of how individuals, families, institutions, and communities evolve together.

Key Names

Robert J. Sampson and ***John H. Laub*** Researchers who, after reexamining the Gluecks' data, found that two events in the life-course—marriage and job stability—were especially important in reducing the frequency of offending in later life.

Glen Elder, Jr. A sociologist who identified four important life-course principles: historical time and place, timing in lives, linked lives, and human agency.

Sheldon Glueck and ***Eleanor Glueck*** Criminologists who studied the life cycles of delinquent boys during the 1930s in the United States and concluded that family dynamics play an especially significant role in the development of criminality. The deeper the maladjustment is, the Gluecks noted, the smaller the chance that these children will become nondeviant adults.

David P. Farrington and ***Donald J. West*** Criminologists who showed that there is a far greater diversity in the ages of distance than in the ages of onset behavior.

Terrie E. Moffitt A theorist who distinguished between two types of criminals—life-course-persistent offenders and adolescence-limited offenders.

Marvin Wolfgang A criminologist who found through cohort analysis that a small nucleus of chronic juvenile offenders accounted for a disproportionately large share of all delinquents.

Lawrence E. Cohen and ***Richard Machalek*** Criminologists who defined evolutionary ecology, which blends social ecology theories while emphasizing the pathways encountered early in life.

Terence Thornberry A criminologist whose interactional theory of crime integrates social control and social learning explanations of delinquency.

LEARNING OUTCOMES 7

List the policy implications of social development theories.

Advocates of the social development perspective believe that at-risk youth can be effectively diverted from the juvenile justice system through the provision of positive alternatives. Strengthening families; assisting core social institutions such as schools, churches, and other community organizations; and promoting active prevention strategies are thus all important policy initiatives from the point of view of social development theorists.

1. What kinds of social policy initiatives might be suggested by social development perspectives?

Comprehensive Strategy for Serious, Violent, and Chronic Juvenile Offenders program A program that works to strengthen families and core institutions in their efforts to reduce risk factors for juvenile offenders and develop their full potential.

"Conflict is a fundamental aspect of social life that can never be fully resolved."

Social Conflict—
It's How We Relate

1. Explain social conflict theories, including radical theories.
2. Describe the history of conflict theory in contemporary criminology.
3. Review how radical-critical and Marxist criminology reflect the principles inherent in the social conflict perspective.
4. Explain how social problems might be solved from the perspective of peacemaking criminology.
5. Discuss the relationship between feminist criminology and feminist thought generally.
6. Describe convict criminology and explain how it differs from the other theories discussed in this chapter.
7. Show what all postmodern criminologies have in common.
8. Explain the implications of conflict theory for crime-control policy.

Jim West/Alamy

INTRO IS IT A CRIME TO MAKE MONEY?

In 2012, a series of protests swept through New York City's financial district. Known as the Occupy Wall Street movement, the movement's organizers wanted protestors to fight "back against the corrosive power" that they said major banks and multinational corporations held over the democratic process. They said that they were also protesting the "role of Wall Street in creating an economic collapse that has caused the greatest recession in generations."[1] One of the slogans adopted by the movement was "We are the 99 percent," referring to the widespread belief that the wealthiest 1% of Americans control the economic and political system of the United States. A website, whose URL was *wearethe99percent.com* welcomed visitors with these words:

> America has been in the grip of accelerating inequality for decades. Politicians have been supporting policies that benefit the few at the expense of everyone else. No matter what you call it—trickle down economics, free market fundamentalism, crony capitalism—it is all rooted in the idea that if you take care of the people at the very top, everyone benefits. That is a lie and we reject it.[2]

B Christopher/Alamy

Occupy Wall Street Protests in 2012. How did American economic conditions influence these protestors?

DISCUSS **The Constitution says that all men and women are created equal; many people understand that to mean that all Americans should have the same opportunity to achieve success. Yet, others think that economic success achieved by a few people later in life is somehow unfair. Do you think that the "99 percenters," if they had their way, would make it a crime to be rich? Explain.**

Principles of the Social Conflict Perspective

The social conflict perspective, which is shared among social sciences generally and is not unique to criminology, says that conflict is a fundamental aspect of social life that can never be fully resolved. At best, the conflict perspective says, formal agencies of social control, including the police, the courts, and the correctional establishment, merely coerce the unempowered or the disenfranchised to comply with the rules established by those in power.

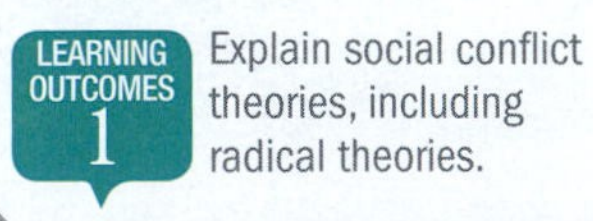

LEARNING OUTCOMES 1 Explain social conflict theories, including radical theories.

Social order, rather than being the result of any consensus, is seen as resting upon the *exercise of power through law*. From the conflict point of view, laws are a tool of the powerful, useful in keeping the unempowered from wresting control over important social institutions. Those in power must work ceaselessly to remain there, although the structure they impose on society—including patterns of wealth building that they define as acceptable and circumstances under which they authorize the exercise of legal power and military might—gives them all the advantages they are likely to need. Hence, according to the conflict perspective, the body of laws that characterize any society is a political statement and crime is a political definition imposed largely upon those whose interests lie outside those that the powerful, through the law, define as acceptable. In short, from a conflict perspective, crime is defined in terms of the concept of oppression.[3]

Central to the social conflict perspective is the notion of **social class**. The concept of social class entails distinctions made among individuals on the basis of significant defining characteristics, such as race, religion, education, profession, income, wealth, family background, housing, artistic tastes, aspirations, cultural pursuits, child-rearing habits, speech, and accent. Individuals are assigned to classes by others and by themselves on the basis of characteristics that are both ascribed and achieved. *Ascribed characteristics* are those with which a person is born, such as race or gender, whereas *achieved characteristics* are acquired through personal effort or chance over the course of one's life and include such things as level of education, income, place of residence, and profession. Figure 8–1 shows the six major principles of the social conflict perspective.

Major Principles of the Social Conflict Perspective

- Society is made up of many social groups each with their own values, traditions and accepted forms of behavior. Diversity is also based on important distinctions, such as gender, sexual orientation, and social class.
- Each group holds different understandings of right and wrong. Both moral and behavioral standards vary from group to group.
- Conflict between groups is inevitable, and is based on differences held to be socially significant. It is unavoidable because groups compete for power, wealth, and other forms of recognition. One of the most significant forms of conflict is class conflict.
- The basic nature of group conflict centers on the exercise of political power. Political power is the key to the accumulation of wealth and to other forms of influence.
- Law is a tool of power and furthers the interest of those powerful enough to make the law. Laws allow those in control to gain what they define through legitimate access to scarce resources and to deny lawful access to the politically disenfranchised.
- Those in power are always interested in maintaining their power against those who would usurp it.

FIGURE 8–1 **Major Principles of the Social Conflict Perspective.**
Source: From *Criminology Today: An Integrative Introduction,* 7e by Frank A. Schmalleger. Copyright © 2014 by Pearson Education. Used by permission of Pearson Education.

A History of Social Conflict Theory in Criminology

Marx: Social Conflict as Class Struggle

The conflict perspective in the social sciences has a long history. One of the best-known early writers on social conflict is **Karl Marx**. Born in Germany in 1818, Marx became well known as a revolutionary economist and sociologist following the publication of *The Communist Manifesto* in 1848. His writings, including another famous book, *Das Kapital,* focused on conflicts inherent in capitalism and led to the formulation of communist ideals, becoming part of the intellectual foundation of twentieth-century communist societies.

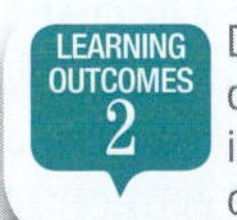

LEARNING OUTCOMES 2 Describe the history of conflict theory in contemporary criminology.

According to Marx, two fundamental social classes exist within any capitalist society: the haves and the have-nots. Marx called these two groups the **bourgeoisie** and the **proletariat**, respectively. He defined the bourgeoisie, also called capitalists, as the wealthy owners of the means of production (for example, factories, businesses, land, and natural resources). Marx's proletariat encompasses the large mass of people, those who are relatively uneducated and who are without power. In short, the proletariat comprises the workers.

According to Marx, the proletariat, possessing neither capital nor the means of production, must earn their living by selling their labor. The bourgeoisie, from their very position within society, stand opposed to the proletariat in an ongoing class struggle. Marx saw the struggle between classes as inevitable in the evolution of any capitalist society and believed that its natural outcome would be the overthrow of the capitalist social order and the birth of a truly classless, or communist, society.

Although Marx concerned himself with only two social classes, most social scientists today refer to at least three groups—the upper, middle, and lower classes—with some, such as sociologist Vance Packard, distinguishing up to five while further subdividing classes "horizontally" according to ascribed characteristics such as race and religion.[4] Societies, including our own, vary as to the relative proportion of each class, although a number of commentators have noted what they call a shrinking of the middle class in a number of today's post-industrial countries.

In 1905, Dutch sociologist Willem Bonger echoed Marx, describing the ongoing struggle between the haves and the have-nots as a natural consequence of capitalist society.[5] Bonger advanced the notion that in such societies, only those who lack power are routinely subject to the criminal law. In 1908, German sociologist Georg Simmel highlighted the role of social conflict in two- and three-person groups, which Simmel called diads and triads, respectively.[6] The notion of culture conflict,

Think About It…

Marx defined the *bourgeoisie* as wealthy capitalists who owned the factories of his day. The *proletariat* were the workers. It was the struggle between these two classes of people that led to social change and, others would later say, to crime. Is the concept of social class still relevant to criminology today? Does the Marxist perspective hold any significance for contemporary American society? Why or why not?

Nickolae/Fotolia

proposed in 1938 by University of Pennsylvania criminologist Thorsten Sellin, incorporates the idea of social conflict.

Vold: Crime as Political Conflict

In his 1958 book *Theoretical Criminology*, **George B. Vold** describes crime as the product of political conflict between groups, a natural expression of the ongoing struggle for power, control, and material well-being.[7] According to Vold, conflict is "a universal form of interaction" and groups are naturally in conflict because their interests and purposes "overlap, encroach on one another and [tend to] be competitive."[8] Vold also addresses the issue of social cohesion, noting, "It has long been realized that conflict between groups tends to develop and intensify the loyalty of group members to their respective groups."[9] Vold, whose writings led to the development of **conflict theory** in criminology, succinctly observes conflict's contribution to crime: "The whole political process of law making, law breaking, and law enforcement becomes a direct reflection of deep-seated and fundamental conflicts between interest groups. Those who produce legislative majorities win control over the power and dominate the policies that decide who is likely to be involved in violation of the law."[10]

According to Vold, powerful groups make laws, and those laws express and protect the groups' interests. He compares the criminal with a soldier, fighting through crime commission for the very survival of the group whose values he or she represents: "The individual criminal is then viewed as essentially a soldier under conditions of warfare: his behavior may not be 'normal' or 'happy' or 'adjusted'—it is the behavior of the soldier doing what is to be done in wartime."[11] Vold's analogy, probably influenced by World War II, expresses the idea that crime is a manifestation of denied needs and values—that is, the cultural heritage of members of disenfranchised groups who are powerless to enact their interests in legitimate fashion. Hence, theft becomes necessary for many poor people, especially those left unemployed or unemployable by the socially acceptable forms of wealth distribution defined by law.

Crime, Social Class, Power, and Conflict

Writers on social conflict in the early and mid-1900s saw in social class the rudimentary ingredients of other important concepts such as authority, power, and conflict. German sociologist **Ralf Dahrendorf**, for example, wrote in the 1950s that "classes are social conflict groups the determinant of which can be found in the participation in or exclusion from the exercise of authority."[12] For Dahrendorf, conflict is ubiquitous, a fundamental part of and coextensive with any society. "Not the presence but the absence of conflict is surprising and abnormal," he writes, "and we have good reason to be suspicious if we find a society or social organization that displays no evidence of conflict."[13]

From Dahrendorf's perspective, it is power and authority that are most at issue between groups and over which class conflicts arise. Dahrendorf also recognized that situations characterized by conflict are rarely static and that conflict is a source of change, whether destructive or constructive. Destructive change brings about a lessening of social order; constructive change increases cohesiveness within society. Dahrendorf's 1959 *Class and Class Conflict in Industrial Society* set the stage for the radical writers of the 1960s and 1970s.

Another theorist, University of California sociologist **Austin Turk**, states that when searching to explain criminality, "one is led to investigate the tendency of laws to penalize persons whose behavior is more characteristic of the less powerful than of the more powerful and the extent to which some persons and groups can and do use legal processes and agencies to maintain and enhance their power position vis-à-vis other persons and groups."[14] In 1969's *Criminality and Legal Order*, Turk writes that in any attempt to explain criminality, "it is more useful to view the social order as mainly a pattern of conflict" rather than to offer explanations for crime based on behavioral or psychological approaches.[15] Like most other conflict criminologists, Turk saw the law as a powerful tool in the service of prominent social groups seeking continued control over others. Crime is the natural consequence of such intergroup struggle because it results from the definitions imposed by the laws of the powerful upon the disapproved strivings of the unempowered.

Modern Radical-Critical and Marxist Criminology

During the late 1960s and early 1970s, the term *Marxist criminology* came into vogue. **Marxist criminology** was the intellectual child of three important historical circumstances: (1) the ruminations of nineteenth-century social utopian thinkers, including Karl Marx, Friedrich Engels, Georg W. F. Hegel, and others; (2) the rise of the conflict perspective in the social sciences around 1900; and (3) the dramatic radicalization of American academia in the 1960s and 1970s. Learn more about Karl Marx and his writings at **Web Extra 8–3.**

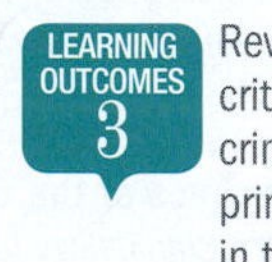

Review how radical-critical and Marxist criminology reflect the principles inherent in the social conflict perspective.

Radical-critical criminology is an outgrowth of Marxist criminology, although both forms of thought coexisted and influenced each other throughout much of the 1970s. Consistent with its roots, contemporary radical-critical criminology holds that the causes of crime can be found in social conditions that empower the wealthy and the politically well organized but disenfranchise those who are less fortunate. Some writers distinguish between radical and critical criminology, saying that the latter simply critiques social relationships that lead to crime, whereas the former constitutes a proactive call for change in the underlying social conditions. That is, critical criminology, when viewed separately, provides a focused critique of current social and economic arrangements as they are related to crime; whereas radical criminology issues a call to action and asks for changes in political and economic systems that are responsible for fostering enhanced levels of criminality.

WHO'S TO BLAME—The Individual or Society?

Human Trafficking, Illegal Aliens, and the American Dream

Jose Gonzales, a naturalized U.S. citizen who worked for a Houston-based trucking company, was driving a tractor trailer through a U.S. Customs checkpoint on the Mexican border near San Diego when his truck was searched and found to contain 45 illegal immigrants concealed in Brazilian-made caskets that were being shipped to Los Angeles. Each of the immigrants had been supplied with plastic bottles containing water, and a few even had portable radios to keep them entertained on what had been planned as an hours-long trip.

AP Photo/Alexandre Meneghini

The illegal immigrants were interrogated and fingerprinted and then taken back across the border to the Mexican border town of Tijuana in a U.S. Customs and Border Protection van. They were released into the custody of a Mexican Federal Investigative Agency official at a local police station, with instructions not to attempt an illegal return into the United States.

Gonzales's fate was quite different. Arrested and charged under the federal Immigration and Nationality Act with attempting to bring unauthorized aliens into the United States, he was held in a federal jail in southern California, where he met with his court-appointed lawyer. The lawyer, Felix Alverez, told Gonzales that agents had him cold, and that he might as well confess in return for a plea bargain that might get him only a brief stint in a federal correctional facility. "Why confess?" Gonzales replied. "I was only trying to help those people have better lives. Many of them were my friends. I didn't even take money for what I was doing."

"Why you were doing what you were doing doesn't matter," Alverez said. "You broke the law, and they are going to punish you."

"No," Gonzales replied. "I am a citizen. I want a trial. You can show them that I was only trying to help unfortunate people live the American Dream. Most of the people who live here and are going to be on a jury have immigrant ancestors. A lot of them were illegal. They won't dare find me guilty." **Web Extras 8-1** and **8-2** relate to this box.

Think About It

1. Why did Gonzales attempt to smuggle illegal immigrants into the United States? Do you think it was primarily for money or for altruistic motives?
2. How likely would Gonzales have been to commit this offense if he had a different ancestry—say, African American or European?
3. What do you think of Gonzales's claim that a jury won't find him guilty? Should he be held responsible for violating the law? Why or why not?

Note: Who's to Blame boxes provide fictionalized critical thinking opportunities, and are not actual cases.

Radical-critical criminology holds that the causes of crime can be found in social conditions that empower the wealthy and the politically well organized but disenfranchise those who are less fortunate.

Chambliss: Crime and Economic Stratification

William J. Chambliss gained prominence during this period, giving voice to the theories of contemporary and earlier Marxist and radical-critical criminologists. He succinctly summarizes the theoretical perspective: "What makes the behavior of some criminal is the coercive power of the state to enforce the will of the ruling class."[16] In 1971, Chambliss and **Robert T. Seidman** coauthored the critically acclaimed *Law, Order, and Power,* which represented something of a bridge between earlier writers on social conflict and Marxist and radical-critical criminologists. Emphasizing social class, class interests, and class conflict, *Law, Order, and Power* presents a Marxist perspective stripped of overt references to capitalism as the root cause of crime. "The more economically stratified a society becomes," Chambliss and Seidman write, "the more it becomes necessary for the dominant groups in the society to enforce through coercion the norms of conduct which guarantee their supremacy."[17] They outline their position in four propositions:[18]

- The conditions of one's life affect one's values and norms. Complex societies are composed of groups with widely different life conditions.
- Complex societies are therefore composed of highly disparate and conflicting sets of norms.
- The probability of a given group having its particular normative system embodied in law is not distributed equally, but is closely related to the political and economic position of that group.
- The higher a group's political or economic position, the greater the probability that its views will be reflected in laws.

Socialist societies, Chambliss claims, should reflect much lower crime rates than capitalist societies because a "less intense class struggle should reduce the forces leading to and the functions of crime."

Inherent in this perspective is the notion that no act is intrinsically criminal or immoral, but is made so by the successful application of negative labels to individuals and activities through the exercise of legislative power by those who are in control of government.

Chambliss also believes that middle- and upper-class criminals are more apt to escape apprehension and punishment by the criminal justice system, not because they are any smarter or more capable of hiding their crimes than are lower-class offenders, but because of a "very rational choice on the part of the legal system to pursue those violators that the community will reward them for pursuing and to ignore those violators who have the capability for causing trouble for the agencies."[19]

Through the 1970s, Chambliss's radical-critical writings assumed a more directly Marxist flavor. In 1975, he once again recognized the huge power gap separating the haves from the have-nots.[20] Crime, he said, is created by actions of the ruling class that define as criminal such undertakings and activities that contravene the interests of the rulers. At the same time, members of the ruling class will inevitably be able to continue to violate the criminal law with impunity because it is their own creation: "As capitalist societies industrialize and the gap between the bourgeoisie and the proletariat widens, penal law will expand in an effort to coerce the proletariat into submission."[21]

For Chambliss, the economic consequences of crime within a capitalist society are partially what perpetuate it: "Crime reduces surplus labor by creating employment not only for the criminals but for law enforcers, welfare workers, professors of criminology, and a horde of people who live off the fact that crime exists."[22] Socialist societies, Chambliss claims, should reflect much lower crime rates than capitalist societies because a "less intense class struggle should reduce the forces leading to and the functions of crime."[23]

Quinney: Capitalism and Crime

Although Chambliss provides much of the intellectual bedrock of contemporary radical-critical criminology, it finds its most eloquent expression in the writings of social philosopher **Richard Quinney**. In 1974, Quinney, in an attempt to challenge and change American social life for the better, set forth his six Marxist propositions for an understanding of crime:

- American society is based on an advanced capitalist economy.
- The state is organized to serve the interests of the dominant economic class—that is, the capitalist ruling class.
- Criminal law is an instrument of the state and ruling class used to maintain and perpetuate the existing social and economic order.
- Crime control in a capitalist society is accomplished through a variety of institutions and agencies established and administered by a governmental elite, representing ruling class interests, for the purpose of establishing domestic order.
- The contradictions of advanced capitalism—the disjunction between existence and essence—require that the subordinate classes remain oppressed by whatever means necessary, especially through the coercion and violence of the legal system.
- Only with the collapse of the capitalist society and the creation of a new society, based on socialist principles, will there be a solution to the crime problem.[24]

Quinney's portrayal of criminology as being closely associated with capitalist modes of production in contemporary society underlies conflict criminology to this day. "Criminological theory and practice," he writes, "are materially based. Moreover, criminology is a cultural production under the late stages of capitalism. It is a form of production: the production of knowledge and consciousness."[25]

A few years later, Quinney further contributed to the development of radical-critical criminology with *Class, State, and Crime*, in which he argues that almost all crimes committed by members of the lower classes are necessary for the survival of individual members of those classes. Crimes, writes Quinney—reminiscent of Vold's criminal as soldier—are actually an attempt by the socially disenfranchised "to exist in a society where survival is not assured by other, collective means."[26] Quinney concludes that "crime is inevitable under capitalist conditions" because crime is "a response to the material conditions of life. Permanent unemployment—and the acceptance of that condition—can result in a form of life where criminality is an appropriate and consistent response."[27] His solution to the problem of crime is the development of a socialist society. "The ultimate meaning of crime in the development of capitalism," he writes, "is the need for a socialist society."[28] A wealth of critical criminology information and resources, including web links and archived papers, is available at **Web Extra 8–4**.

Critique of Radical-Critical and Marxist Criminology

Radical-critical criminology has been criticized for its nearly exclusive emphasis on mechanisms of social change at the expense of developed, testable theory. As William V. Pelfrey explains, "It is in the Radical School of Criminology that theory is almost totally disregarded, except as something to criticize, and radical methods are seen as optimum."[29]

Radical-critical criminologists may also be criticized for failing to recognize what appears to be a fair degree of public consensus about the nature of crime—that crime is undesirable and that criminal activity is to be controlled. Were criminal activity a true expression of the sentiments of the politically and economically disenfranchised, then public opinion might be expected to offer support for at least certain forms of crime. However, even the sale of illicit drugs—a type of crime that may provide an alternative path to riches for the otherwise disenfranchised—is frequently condemned by residents of working-class communities.[30]

An effective criticism of Marxist criminology, in particular, is that by allowing personal values and political leanings to enter the criminological arena, Marxist criminologists have frequently appeared to sacrifice their objectivity. Jackson Toby, for example, claims that Marxist and radical thinkers are simply building upon an "old tradition of sentimentality toward those who break social rules," which can be easily discounted when we realize that "color television sets and automobiles are stolen more often than food and blankets."[31] In a now-classic critique of radical criminology,[32] Carl Klockars in 1979 charged that Marxists are unable to explain low crime rates in some capitalist countries, such as Japan, and seem equally unwilling to acknowledge or address the problems of communist countries, which often have terrible human rights records. Klockars claimed that Marxist criminologists behaved more like "true believers" in a "new religion" who were unwilling to objectively evaluate their beliefs.[33]

Marxist criminology has also been criticized for failing to appreciate the multiplicity of issues that contribute to the problem of crime. For example, criminologist Hermann Mannheim showed how "subsequent developments" have revealed that Marx was wrong in thinking that there could be only two classes in a capitalist society.[34] Mannheim pointed out that the development of a semiskilled workforce along with the advent of highly skilled and well-educated workers has resulted in a multiplicity of classes within contemporary capitalist societies, effectively spreading the available wealth in those societies where such workers are employed and reducing the likelihood of revolution.

The Evolution of Radical-Critical Criminology

Radical-critical criminology attributes much of the existing propensity toward criminality to differences in social class—in particular, to those arrangements within society that maintain class differences. As Quinney puts it, "Classes are an expression of the underlying forces of the capitalist mode of production."[35] "Thus," he writes, "all social life, including everything associated with crime, must be understood in terms of the objective economic conditions of production and the subjective struggle between classes that is related to those conditions."[36]

Elliott Currie amplifies Quinney, stating that "'market societies'—those in which the pursuit of private gain becomes the dominant organizing principle of social and economic life—are especially likely to breed high levels of violent crime."[37] The conditions endemic to market societies—free enterprise, free market economies, the pursuit of personal wealth—lead to high crime rates because they undercut and overwhelm more traditional principles that "have historically sustained individuals, families, and communities." The United States is the world's premier market society, says Currie, and its culture provides "a particularly fertile breeding ground for serious violent crime." Similarly, the recent and dramatic rise in crime rates in former communist countries throughout Europe can be explained by the burgeoning development of new market societies in those nations.

Marxist criminology has suffered a considerable loss of prestige among many would-be followers in the wake of the collapse of the former Soviet Union and its client states in Eastern Europe and other parts of the world. With the death of Marxist political organizations and their agendas, Marxist criminology seems to have lost much of its impetus. Consequently, today's radical-critical criminologists have largely rescinded calls for revolutionary change and no longer employ traditional Marxist rhetoric. They continue nonetheless to escalate their demands for the eradication of gender, racial, and other inequalities in the criminal justice system; for the elimination of prisons; for the abolition of capital punishment; and for an end to police misconduct.

The ideas associated with mid- to late-twentieth-century Marxist criminology, and the more recent radical-critical criminology, contributed to the formation of a number of new and innovative social conflict theory–based approaches to crime and criminology. Four of the most interesting of those theories are (1) peacemaking, (2) feminist, (3) convict, and (4) postmodern criminology. For additional insight into conflict theory in criminology, see **Web Extra 8–5**.

Think About It…

Some say that communism's rise and later fall in Eastern Europe means that only capitalism can provide a stable economic basis for society. Do you agree? Why or why not? At the same time, others argue that market societies, or those based on free enterprise, are especially likely to have high levels of violent crime. Do you agree? Why or why not?

JLImages/Alamy

Peacemaking Criminology

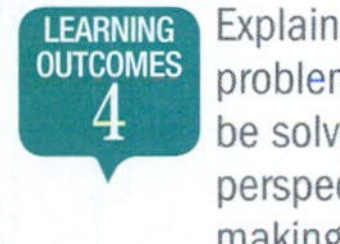

Explain how social problems might be solved from the perspective of peacemaking criminology.

Throughout the development of Western culture, formal agencies of social control, especially the police, officials of the courts, and correctional personnel, have been seen

Four of the most interesting new theories are peacemaking, feminist, convict, and postmodern criminology.

as pitted against criminal perpetrators and would-be wrongdoers in a kind of epic struggle in which only one side can emerge victorious. Since the late 1980s, however, **peacemaking criminology**, a form of postmodern criminology with its roots in Christian and Eastern philosophies, has advanced the notion that social control agencies and the citizens they serve should work together to alleviate social problems and human suffering and thus reduce crime.[38] Also called "compassionate criminology," it includes the notion of service to others and suggests that "compassion, wisdom, and love are essential for understanding the suffering of which we are all a part and for practicing a criminology of nonviolence."[39]

Peacemaking criminology has been popularized by the works of **Harold (Hal) E. Pepinsky**[40] and Richard Quinney,[41] who restate the problem of crime control from one of "how to stop crime" to one of "how to make peace" within society and between citizens and criminal justice agencies (Figure 8–2). Pepinsky puts it this way: "Peacemaking, as I see it, is different from conventional criminology [because it] postulates that violence, even violence committed to stop other violence—as in policing, criminal justice, and wars on crime—breeds more violence."[42]

Peacemaking criminology draws attention to such issues as (1) perpetuating violence through social policies based on current criminological theory, (2) the role of education in peacemaking, (3) "commonsense theories of crime," (4) crime control as human rights enforcement, and (5) conflict resolution within community settings.[43]

Quinney and John Wildeman summarize well the theoretical underpinnings: "A criminology of peacemaking—a nonviolent criminology of compassion and service—seeks to end suffering and thereby eliminate crime."[44] Elsewhere, Quinney writes, "A society of meanness, competition, greed, and injustice is created by minds that are greedy, selfish, fearful, hateful, and crave power over others. Suffering on the social level can be ended only with the ending of suffering on the personal level. . . . We must become one with all who suffer from lives of crime and from the sources that produce crime. Public policy must then flow from this wisdom."[45]

Contributors to peacemaking criminology include **Bo Lozoff**, **Michael Braswell**, and **Clemens Bartollas**. In *Inner Corrections*, Lozoff and Braswell claim that "we are fully aware by now that the criminal justice system in this country is founded on violence. It is a system which assumes that violence can be overcome by violence, evil by evil. Criminal justice at home and warfare abroad are of the same principle of violence. This principle sadly dominates much of our criminology."[46]

Bartollas and Braswell apply New Age principles to correctional treatment. "Most offenders suffered abusive and deprived childhoods," they write. "Some New Age teachings tempered by the ancient spiritual traditions may offer offenders the hope they can create a future that . . . may include growing out of the fear of victimization, becoming more positive and open to possibilities, . . . understanding the futility of violence, and attaining emotional and financial sufficiency."[47]

In a fundamental sense, peacemaking criminologists exhort their colleagues to transcend personal dichotomies to end the political and ideological divisiveness that separates people, asking "If we ourselves cannot know peace, how will our acts disarm hatred and violence?"[48] As Lozoff and Braswell write, "Human transformation takes place as we change our social, economic and political structure. And the message is clear: without peace within us and in our actions, there can be no peace in our results. Peace is the way."[49]

Critique of Peacemaking Criminology

Peacemaking criminology has been criticized as being naïve and utopian, as well as for failing to recognize the realities of crime control and law enforcement. Few victims, for example, would expect to gain much from attempting to make peace with their victimizers (although such strategies do sometimes work). Such criticisms, however, may be improperly directed at a level of analysis that peacemaking criminologists have not assumed. In other words, peacemaking criminology, while it involves work with individual offenders, envisions positive change on the societal and institutional levels and does not suggest that victims attempt to effect personal changes in offenders.

TRADITIONAL PUNISHMENT
Once an ex-con always an ex-con

I drew a circle that shut him out.

THE PEACEMAKING PROCESS
Reintegration into society

We drew a circle that drew him in.

FIGURE 8–2 **The Differences between Peacemaking and Traditional Punishment.**

Think About It…

Peacemaking criminology aims to end human suffering as a way of stopping crime. It's an idealistic theory, but can it work? If you were the victim of a crime, would you be more interested in revenge or in peacemaking?

Jeff Greenberg/Alamy

Feminist Criminology

Feminist criminology applies various forms of feminist thought to infuse gender awareness into mainstream criminology. From the point of view of feminism, there are huge differences between *gender* and *sex*. Gender refers to the complex "sociocultural and psychological shaping, patterning, and evaluating of female and male behavior,"[50] whereas sex merely refers to the "biological based categories of 'female' and 'male.'"[51] Such differences imply, of course, that a variety of gender roles can be assumed by individuals independent of their biology.

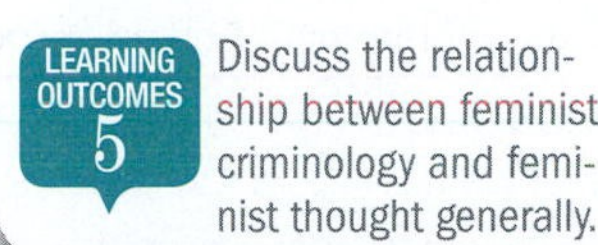

LEARNING OUTCOMES 5 Discuss the relationship between feminist criminology and feminist thought generally.

Feminism, generally speaking, is a way of seeing the world. Two well-known feminist scholars, **Kathleen Daly** and **Meda Chesney-Lind,** say that feminism can be loosely described as "a set of theories about women's oppression and a set of strategies for change."[52] Feminist thought views gender in terms of power relationships, revealing the inequities inherent in patriarchal structures. **Patriarchy** refers to "social relations of power in which the male gender appropriates the labor power of women and controls their sexuality."[53] The patriarchal structure of Western society has long excluded women from much socially significant decision making, affecting both fundamental social roles and personal expectation at all levels.

According to feminist criminologists, evidence of patriarchy can be found throughout criminology. Crime is often seen as an act of aggression, for example, which helps perpetuate the idea that men have a biologically aggressive nature that must be channeled and controlled. This belief has led to the socialization of women as passive actors, excluding them from criminological study and making them more susceptible to continued victimization by men. In other words, traditional criminology, like the larger society, has been male-centered, and women have been largely ignored by criminologists, heightening their sense of powerlessness and dependence upon men.

As one author observes, "Women have been virtually invisible in criminological analysis until recently and much theorizing has proceeded as though criminality is restricted to men."[54]

Feminist criminology applies various forms of feminist thought to infuse gender awareness into mainstream criminology.

Another puts it this way: "Criminological theory assumes a woman is like a man."[55]

Feminist Thought and Criminological Theory

The forms of feminist thought that have most influenced criminology are radical, liberal, socialist, and Marxist feminism, each of which argues that conflict in society derives from gender-based inequalities, although they differ in their focus. **Radical feminism** asserts that because in patriarchal society men control the law, women are defined as subjects. Women who act reasonably to avoid men's exploitation may thus become criminalized. **Liberal feminism** asserts that gender inequalities arise from "separate and distinct spheres of influence and traditional attitudes about the appropriate role of men and women."[56] **Socialist feminism** sees gender oppression as a consequence of the economic structure of society. **Marxist feminism** sees capitalism as perpetuating economic inequality, dependence, and political powerlessness, ultimately leading to unhealthy gender relations. Proponents of each advocate eliminating male domination and restructuring power relationships to reduce crime rates for women and "even [to] precipitate a decrease in male violence against women."[57]

Early feminist criminological works include *Sisters in Crime*[58] by **Freda Adler** and *Women and Crime* by **Rita J. Simon,**[59] both published in 1975. These authors attribute gender divergences in crime rates primarily to socialization rather than to biology. Carol Smart, in *Women, Crime and Criminology* (1977),[60] asserts that men and women experience and perceive the world in different ways, and thus women must have a voice in interpreting the behavior of other women.

Feminist theorizing has heightened awareness of the need to apply feminist thinking to criminological analysis. Feminist criminologists Daly and Chesney-Lind, referred to earlier, suggest that feminist thought is more important for the way it informs and challenges existing criminology than for the new theories it offers, and they state that more research on gender-related issues is badly needed. Traditional understandings of what is "typical" about crime are derived from a study of men only or, more precisely, from that relatively small group of men who commit most crimes. They write, "criminologists should begin to appreciate that their discipline and its questions are a product of white, economically privileged men's experiences"[61] and note that rates of female criminality, lower than those of males (Figure 8-3)—a fact rarely accorded criminological significance—"suggest that crime may not be so normal after all."[62] Hence, feminism's fundamental challenge to criminology: Do existing theories of crime causation apply as well to women as they do to men? Or as Daly and Chesney-Lind ask, "Do theories of men's crime apply to women?"[63]

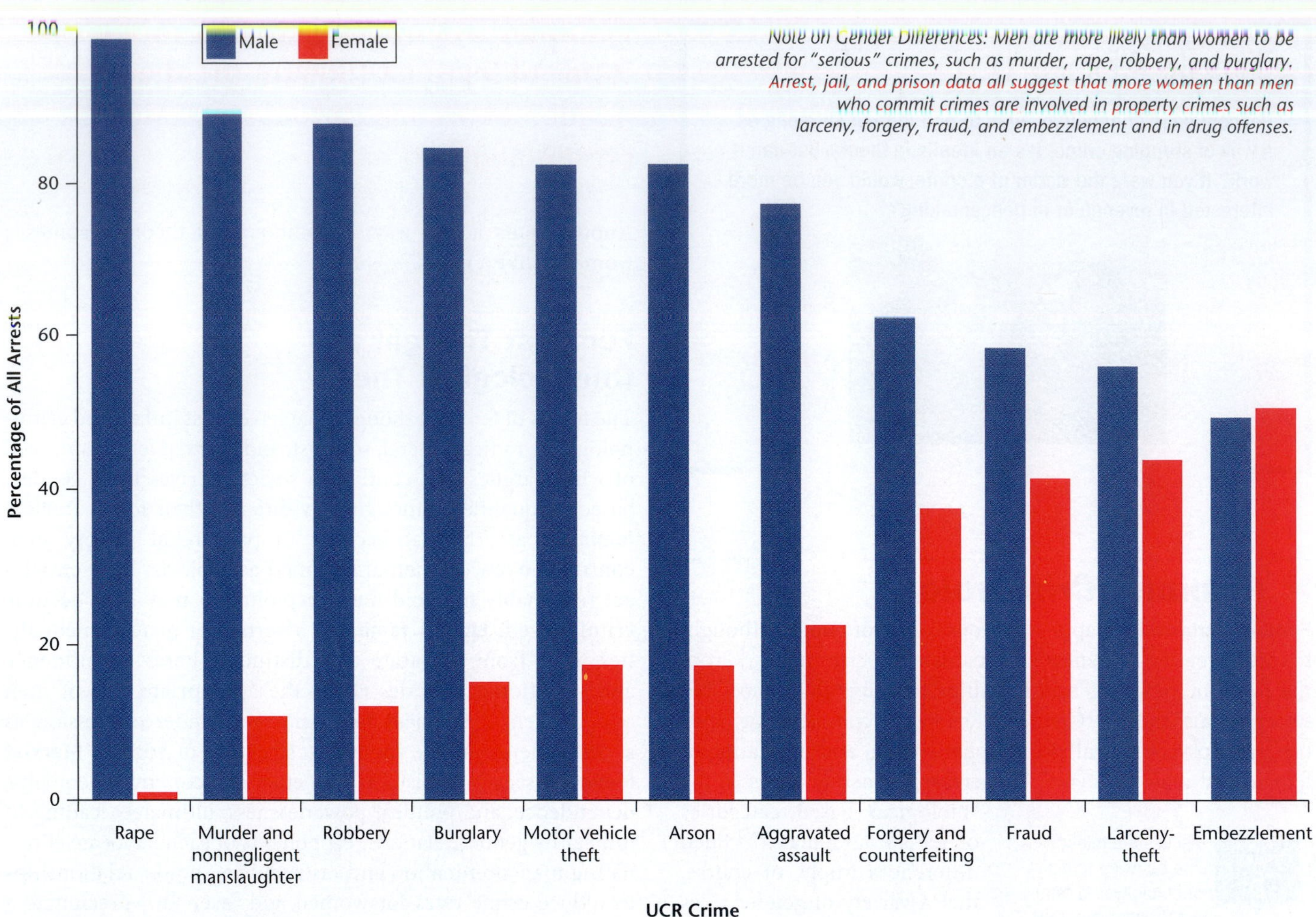
Male
Female
Note on Gender Differences: Men are more likely than women to be arrested for "serious" crimes, such as murder, rape, robbery, and burglary. Arrest, jail, and prison data all suggest that more women than men who commit crimes are involved in property crimes such as larceny, forgery, fraud, and embezzlement and in drug offenses.
Percentage of All Arrests
100
80
60
40
20
0
Rape
Murder and nonnegligent manslaughter
Robbery
Burglary
Motor vehicle theft
Arson
Aggravated assault
Forgery and counterfeiting
Fraud
Larceny-theft
Embezzlement
UCR Crime

FIGURE 8–3 **Male and Female Involvement in Crime: Offense Patterns, 2012.**
Source: Federal Bureau of Investigation, *Crime in the United States, 2012* (Washington, DC: U.S. Department of Justice, 2013).

Other feminists have analyzed the legislative process and have concluded that criminal statutes reflect traditionally male ways of organizing the social world.[64] For example, *assault* (or, more precisely, battery) is defined as an attack by one person upon another. Until the close of the twentieth century, however, in many jurisdictions, domestic violence statutes tended to downplay the seriousness of such attacks, implying that occurrences within the home—whose victims were typically women—weren't as important to the justice system as other forms of assault.[65] Similarly, some argue, legal definitions of prostitution, pornography, and rape derive primarily from men's understanding of the behavior in question and not from women's experiences. Hence, women receive special protection because they are considered vulnerable to crime, but women's experiences do not define the nature of the law or of the justice system's response.

John Hagan, in a perspective known as **power-control theory**, suggests that "family class structure shapes the social reproduction of gender relations, and in turn the social distribution of delinquency."[66] Hagan believes that power relationships existing in the wider society are "brought home" to domestic settings and are reflected in everyday relationships between men, women, and children within the context of family life. Hagan writes, "Work relations structure family relations, particularly relations between fathers and mothers and, in turn, relations between parents and their children, especially mothers and their daughters."[67] In most middle- and upper-middle-class families, says Hagan, a paternalistic model, in which the father works and the mother supervises the children, is the norm. Under the paternalistic model, girls are controlled by both parents—through male domination and by female role modeling. Boys, however, are less closely controlled and are relatively free to deviate from social norms, resulting in higher levels of delinquency among males. In lower-class and lower-middle-class families, however, the paternalistic model is frequently absent. Hence, in such families, there is less "gender socialization and less maternal supervision of girls," resulting in higher levels of female delinquency.[68]

In the area of social policy, feminist thinkers have pointed to the need for increased controls over men's violence toward women, for the creation of alternatives (to supplement the home and traditional family structures) for women facing abuse, and for the protection of children. Most agree that the structure of the justice system itself—gender-biased from years of male domination—must change. Many advocate a balanced approach, believing that individuals of both genders have much to contribute to a workable justice system.[69] Feminist criminology can be further explored at **Web Extra 8–6**.

THEORY in PERSPECTIVE

Social Conflict Theories

Social conflict theories emphasize the role of conflict within society, which is thought to be based largely on inequities between social classes.

Radical Criminology

Radical criminology holds that the causes of crime are rooted in social conditions empowering the wealthy and the politically well organized but disenfranchising those who are less successful.

Period: 1960s–present

Theorists: Karl Marx, Ralf Dahrendorf, George B. Vold, Richard Quinney, William J. Chambliss, Raymond J. Michalowski, Austin Turk

Concepts: Social class, bourgeoisie, proletariat

Feminist Criminology

This radical criminological approach to the explanation of crime sees the conflict and inequality present in society as being based primarily on gender.

Period: 1970s–present

Theorists: Freda Adler, Rita J. Simon, Kathleen Daly, Meda Chesney-Lind, John Hagan

Concepts: Power-control issues, gender socialization

Peacemaking Criminology

Peacemaking criminology holds that crime-control agencies and citizens must work together to alleviate social problems, including crime.

Period: 1980s–present

Theorists: Harold E. Pepinsky, Richard Quinney

Concepts: Compassionate criminology, restorative justice

Convict Criminology

Convict criminology consists of writings and musings on criminology by convicted felons and ex-inmates who have acquired academic credentials or are associated with credentialed others.

Period: 2001–present

Theorists: Jeffrey Ian Ross, Stephen Richards, John Irwin, K. C. Carceral, Thomas J. Bernard

Concepts: Issues-based writings, personal experience as valid information, critical of system

Critique of Feminist Criminology

Critics argue that in the area of theoretical development, feminist criminology has yet to live up to its promise. As one writer puts it, "Feminist theory is a theory in formation."[70] From the late 1970s through the early 1990s, few comprehensive feminist theories of crime were proposed; feminist criminology instead focused on descriptive studies of female involvement in crime[71] and on women's victimization. To date, feminist analysis has hardly advanced beyond a framework for the "deconstruction" and reevaluation of existing theories in light of feminist insights.[72] A fair assessment would probably conclude that the greatest contributions of thought to criminological theory building are yet to come.

Feminist criminology has also faced other criticism. Predicted increases in female crime rates have failed to materialize as social opportunities available to both genders have become more balanced. The **gender gap** in crime—males accounting for much more law violation than females—continues to exist. As criminologist Karen Heimer notes, "The relationship holds, regardless of whether the data analyzed are arrest rates, victimization incidence reports on characteristics of offenders, or self-reports of criminal behavior [and] as far as we can tell, males have always been more criminal than females, and gender differences emerge in every society that has been studied systematically."[73]

Some critics argue that a feminist criminology is impossible. Daly and Chesney-Lind, for example, agree that although feminist thought may inform criminology, "a feminist criminology cannot exist because neither feminism nor criminology is a unified set of principles and practices."[74] Even with such a caveat, however, it should still be possible to construct a gender-aware criminology that incorporates feminist concerns.

Convict Criminology

The newest radical paradigm to emerge within the field of criminology is **convict criminology**. Formalized in 2001 with the publication of "Introducing the New School of Convict Criminology" by **Stephen C. Richards** in the journal *Social Justice*,[75] convict criminology (also called "alternative criminology") is not so much a school of thought as it is a body of writings and musings on criminology by convicted felons and ex-inmates who have acquired academic credentials or who are associated with credentialed others. In 2002, with the publication of *Convict Criminology* by Jeffrey Ian Ross and Stephen Richards, the writings of convict criminologists went mainstream and began receiving attention from within the discipline and from the media.

Describe convict criminology and explain how it differs from the other theories discussed in this chapter.

Convict criminology offers a blend of writings by credentialed ex-inmates and critical criminologists who have joined forces in distrust of mainstream criminology.[76] Convict criminology is largely issues-based and personal. As its adherents admit, convict criminology is not without an agenda and tends to assume a critical perspective with regard to the justice system—especially corrections. Similarly, the language of convict criminologists is different from that of academic criminologists who do not share the convict background. Convict criminologists tend to write about "convicts" instead of "offenders" and "inmates" instead of "prisoners." The distinction is an important one because the terminology used by academic criminologists is "managerial" in the sense that it is consistent with the language of controlling agents in the justice system—police officers, correctional officers, probation and parole officers, court officials, and so forth. By using the language of convict insiders, convict criminologists signify their allegiance to an insider's perspective and refer to traditional criminology as *managerial criminology*.[77]

The primary method used by convict criminologists is ethnographic. *Ethnography* is a branch of anthropology that involves studying other cultures, in this case, inmate society. Ethnographers depend upon lived experiences and oral communications about them (for example, interviews, stories, and long hours spent listening to those whom they are studying). The advantage of convict criminologists is that they are their own subjects, and the long hours needed to gather experiences have already been spent—usually in prison or in personal interaction with the justice system.

The prototype convict criminologist is **John Irwin**, who spent five years in California's Soledad Prison in the 1950s for armed robbery. While imprisoned, Irwin earned college credits and after release went on to attend San Francisco State College and UCLA. Irwin says, "The point is, I made my transition from the life of a thief, drug addict, and convict to one of a 'respectable' professional. . . ." Irwin went on to write *The Felon*,[78] an academic work that shared the career criminal's point of view with interested readers.

Some of the most recent works in the area of convict criminology are the result of collaboration between traditional criminologists and ex-convicts. Among them are *Behind a Convict's Eyes*[79] and *Prison, Inc.*[80]—both by the author team of **K. C. Carceral** (a convict serving life in prison who holds an associate's degree in paralegal studies), **Thomas J. Bernard** (a criminologist at Penn State University)—and others.

Convict criminology is the source of a number of recommendations for improving the justice system, stemming primarily from the lived experiences of the convict criminologists and not from traditional forms of social scientific research. Nonetheless, the claim is sometimes made that experience is itself a kind of research, albeit a very personal one. Convict criminologists say the following:[81]

1. Prisons hold far too many people, do not effectively reduce crime, and hold too many people who have committed minor crimes.
2. Prison expansion has disproportionately and unfairly impacted the nation's poor—especially young men of color—who have made bad decisions in their lives and committed relatively harmless and bothersome crimes.
3. A substantial reduction in the number of federal and state prisoners is needed. Convict criminologists point out that many of today's prisoners are nonviolent drug offenders who committed property crimes in support of drug habits or those who were caught with drugs in their possession either for personal use or resale. Diversion and treatment are recommended as viable alternatives to incarceration. Similarly, the nation's war on drugs—which they see as having a negative impact on all of society— should be terminated.
4. Corrections today can benefit significantly from the use of smaller prisons in place of the large institutions that now characterize many state facilities. Smaller prisons should become a model for U.S. corrections because they are less dangerous than large ones and tend to result in heightened rates of rehabilitation.
5. Treatment should be given precedence over security because most inmates will eventually return to society, and it is treatment that offers the best hope for desistance from crime. Not only should institutional priorities be reversed, but treatment programs need to receive top-level funding.

Think About It...

The text says that convict criminology is not so much a school of thought as it is a body of writings and musings on criminology by convicted felons and ex-inmates who have acquired academic credentials or who are associated with credentialed others. Do you think that convicts (or former convicts) have any special insight into the causes of crime or in how to prevent crime? If so, how would such insight be useful in the study of criminology?

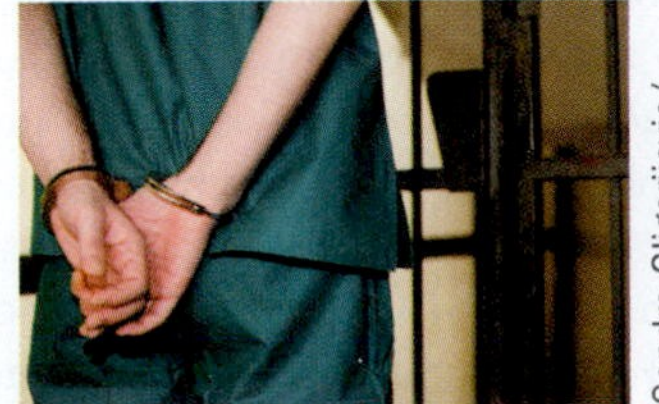
Sandra Gligorijevic/ Fotolia

Critique of Convict Criminology

Convict criminology has been critiqued by those who say that most of the authors working in the field are white males, and not all are ex-convicts.[82] Feminist nonconvict criminologists have also begun contributing to the literature through their prison research, moving the field even further from its roots.

Convict criminologists tend to write about "convicts" instead of "offenders" and "inmates" instead of "prisoners." The distinction is an important one because the terminology used by academic criminologists is "managerial" in the sense that it is consistent with the language of controlling agents in the justice system.

Convict criminologists have been faulted for their activism and partisan approach, and their research has been questioned in light of their thinly veiled agendas. Finally, not everyone agrees that convict criminology offers an edge over traditional criminology. Critics say that having been in prison might actually distort a criminologist's view of his or her field rather than enhance it. Moreover, personal experience rarely gives anyone the entire picture needed to understand a phenomenon. Focusing on the injustices of prison life, for example, might keep one from appreciating the reformative effects of punishment.

Postmodern Criminology

Postmodern criminology applies understandings of social change inherent in postmodern philosophy to criminological theorizing and to issues of crime control. Postmodern philosophy, which developed primarily in Europe after World War II, represents "a rejection of the enlightenment belief in scientific rationality as the main vehicle to knowledge and progress."[83] As a philosophical movement, postmodernism is skeptical of science and the scientific method.[84] One important aspect of postmodern social thought can be found in its efforts to demonstrate the systematic intrusion of sexist, racist, capitalist, colonialist, and professional interests into the very content of science. Feminist scholar Joycelyn M. Pollock puts it this way: "Post-modernism questions whether we can ever 'know' something objectively; so-called neutral science is considered a sham and criminology's search for causes is bankrupt because even the question is framed by **androcentric**, sexist, classist, and racist definitions of crime, criminals, and cause."[85] According to postmodernists, "truth" is a social construction and a form of domination because it represents a way of looking at things that is imposed by those with power.[86]

Show what all postmodern criminologies have in common.

Postmodernist thought began to influence criminology in the late 1980s. Today's postmodernist criminology is not so much a theory as it is a group of new criminological perspectives that have emerged since 1990, all informed by the tone of postmodernism. At the leading edge of postmodern criminology can be found novel paradigms with such intriguing names as "chaos theory," "discourse analysis," "topology theory," "catastrophe theory," "Lacanian thought," "Godel's theorem," "constitutive theory," and "anarchic criminology."[87]

All postmodern criminologies build on the belief that past criminological approaches have failed to realistically assess the true causes of crime and have therefore failed to offer workable solutions for crime control—or if they have, that such theories and solutions may once have been appropriate but do not apply to the postmodern era. Hence, much postmodern criminological theory is deconstructionist. **Deconstructionist theories** are approaches that challenge existing perspectives to debunk them and attempt to replace them with approaches more relevant to the postmodern era. They intend to offer freedom from perceived oppressive forms of thought by deconstructing—pulling apart the foundations of—existing thought, knowledge, and belief in modern Western culture.

Henry and Milovanovic: Constitutive Criminology

Two especially notable authors in the field of postmodern criminology are **Stuart Henry** and **Dragan Milovanovic**,[88] whose **constitutive criminology** claims that crime and crime control are not "object-like entities," but, rather, constructions produced through a social process in which offender, victim, and society are all involved.[89]

A central feature of constitutive criminology is its assertion that individuals shape their world while also being shaped by it. Hence, the behaviors of those who offend and victimize others cannot be understood in isolation from the society of which they are a part. Individuals, however, tend to remain unaware of the role they play in the social construction of their subjective worlds and generally fail to realize that, at least to some degree, they are able to create new meanings while freeing themselves from old biases.

One area that demonstrates such constructionist notions is the sociology of law, which highlights the inherent interrelatedness between law and social structure. Milovanovic, for example, suggests the application of semiotics to the study of law.[90] *Semiotics* is a term akin to semantics; both derive from the Greek *sêma*, meaning "sign." Milovanovic sees semiotics as being especially useful in the study of law and criminology because everything we know, say, do, think, and feel is mediated through signs—a sign being anything that stands for something else. Hence, language, gestures, sensations, objects, and events are all interpreted by the human mind through the use of signs. A semiotic criminology is concerned, therefore, with identifying how language systems (for example, those of medicine, law, education, gangs, sports, prison communities, criminal justice practitioners, and criminologists) communicate uniquely encoded values. Such values are said to "oppress those who do not communicate meaning from within the particular language system in use" because they may prevent effective discourse with those in power.[91]

The application of **semiotics** to the study of law can be illustrated by the term *mental illness*. As a sign, this term is imbued with multiple—perhaps even contradictory—meanings, including a disease in need of treatment and a person needing psychiatric services. Moreover, mental illness means something different in the law (wherein the proper term is *legal insanity*) than it does in medicine or in the lay community. Different interpretations reflect different values, and these values can be traced to divergent interest groups. Moreover, as Milovanovic notes, the meaning of mental illness has changed over time—and continues to change.

Semiotics can also be applied directly to the notion of crime, as crime itself is a "socially constructed category," or sign. In the words of Henry and Milovanovic, crime "is a categorization of the diversity of human conflicts and transgressions into a single category 'crime,' as though these were somehow all the same. It is a melting of differences reflecting the multitude of variously motivated acts of personal injury into a single entity."[92] Such a statement, to the minds of constitutive criminologists, lays bare the true meaning of the word *crime*, effectively "deconstructing" it.

Crime should be understood, say Henry and Milovanovic, as an integral part of society—not as something separate and apart from it. From this perspective, a kind of false consciousness, or lack of awareness, gives rise to criminal activity. According to Werner Einstadter and Stuart Henry, crime is seen to be the culmination of certain processes that allow people to believe that they are somehow not connected to other humans and society. These processes place others into categories or stereotypes and make them different or alien, denying them their humanity. These processes result in the denial of responsibility for other people and to other people. Hence, from a constitutive point of view, crime is simply "the power to deny others" and crime is caused by "the structure, ideology and invocation of discursive practices that divide human relations into categories, that divide responsibility from others and to others into hierarchy and authority relations."[93]

Critique of Postmodern Criminology

Ian Taylor, a British sociologist who lent focus to radical-critical criminology in the 1970s with the publication of two well-received books,[94] criticizes postmodern approaches to crime and deviance for their "increasing incoherence."[95] Not only do postmodern criminologists employ vaguely defined terminology, but, Taylor seems to say, the "battle with orthodox criminology" has led postmodern approaches to increasingly obscure their most basic claims. A second result, says Taylor, "has been the development of a social account of crime that entirely lacks a value or ethical foundation."[96] Deconstructionism, for example, may challenge traditional theories, but unless it offers viable alternatives for crime control and prevention, it does little good. Taylor criticizes what he calls "privileged academic commentators working within the postmodern tradition" for being "nihilistic."[97] Finally, some detractors have said that postmodern criminology is more a collection of ideas about social reality rather than any sort of comprehensive or well-stated theory.[98]

Policy Implications of Conflict Criminology

Three different levels of policy implications emanate from conflict theory in criminology. The first relates to the macro, or wider, societal level, advocating widespread social change intended to redistribute wealth on the premise that crime rates will fall as poverty and social inequalities are eliminated. Raymond J. Michalowski summarizes well the idealistic policy directions envisioned by some radical-critical criminologists when he says, "We cannot be free from the crimes of the poor until there are no more poor; we cannot be free from domination of the powerful until we reduce the inequalities that make domination possible; and we cannot live in harmony with others until we begin to limit the competition for material advantage over others that alienates us from one another."[99]

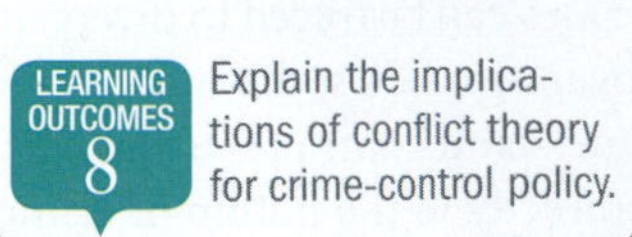

LEARNING OUTCOMES
8
Explain the implications of conflict theory for crime-control policy.

As noted previously, radical-critical criminologists have had to come to terms with the collapse of the Soviet Union, a society that represented utopian Marxism in practice. They have also had to recognize that a sudden and total political reversal within the United States is highly unlikely. As a consequence, many have begun to focus on the second policy level, promoting a gradual transition to a more equitable society and to socialized forms of government activity as a means for crime reduction. These mid-level approaches involve "equal justice in the bail system, the abolition of mandatory sentences, prosecution of corporate crimes, increased employment opportunities, and promoting community alternatives to imprisonment"[100] and include programs to reduce prison overcrowding, efforts to highlight current injustices, the elimination of racism and other forms of inequality in the handling of both victims and offenders, and increased equality in criminal justice system employment (Figure 8–4).

Other critical criminologists promote a raise in the minimum wage, full and quality employment for those who want to work, increased educational opportunities, enhanced social services, programs to help the economically disadvantaged, and the use of social networking websites to achieve social justice.[101] The U.S. Department of Education's *National Assessment of Educational Progress* found, for example, that in 2011, fourth- and eighth-grade students in public schools in our nation's capital were ranked lowest in the country in math and reading proficiency.[102] In 2012, the Alliance for Excellent Education, using numbers from that report, published an estimate showing that a 5% increase in graduation rates for young men in Washington, D.C., could be expected to produce an annual savings of $66.5 million in crime-related expenses for the District of Columbia.[103]

Participatory and Restorative Justice

It is safe to say that few radical-critical criminologists expect to see dramatic social or cultural changes in the near future. Consequently, a third, and some would say more pragmatic, approach to reducing crime lies in applying conflict resolution principles at the micro level—that of the individual and the community.

Think About It…

What would happen if the socially disenfranchised made the laws? What kinds of laws would we have? Would we have a better society? Why or why not?

roman023/Fotolia

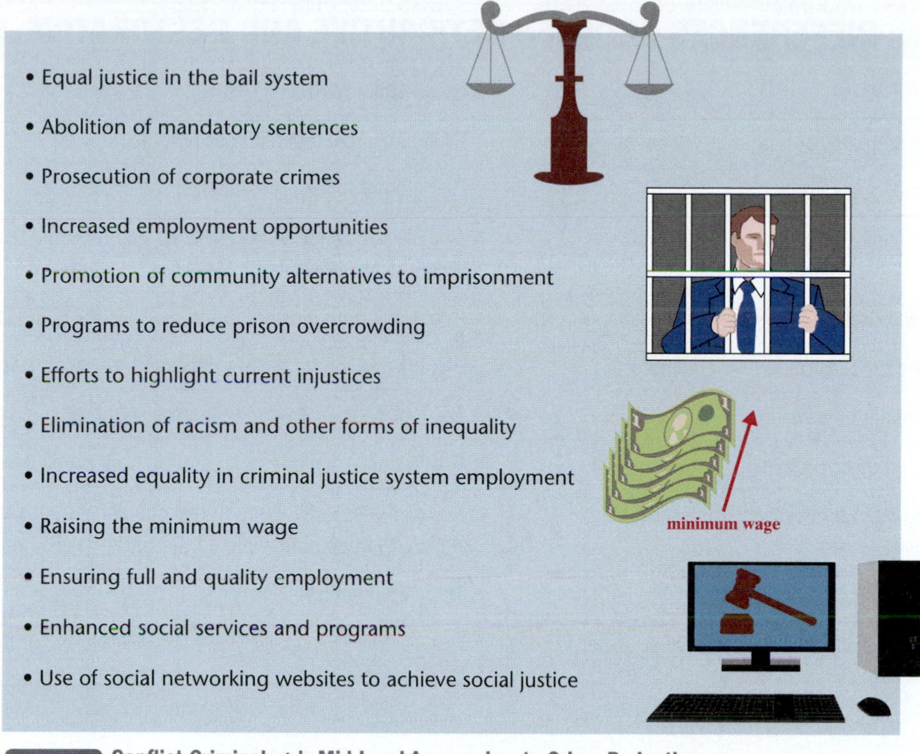
• Equal justice in the bail system
• Abolition of mandatory sentences
• Prosecution of corporate crimes
• Increased employment opportunities
• Promotion of community alternatives to imprisonment
• Programs to reduce prison overcrowding
• Efforts to highlight current injustices
• Elimination of racism and other forms of inequality
• Increased equality in criminal justice system employment
• Raising the minimum wage
• Ensuring full and quality employment
• Enhanced social services and programs
• Use of social networking websites to achieve social justice
minimum wage

FIGURE 8–4 **Conflict Criminology's Mid-Level Approaches to Crime Reduction.**
Source: From *Criminology Today: An Integrative Introduction,* 7e by Frank A. Schmalleger. Copyright © 2014 by Pearson Education. Used by permission of Pearson Education.

Peacemaking criminology suggests that effective crime control at these levels can best be achieved by adopting a model based on cooperation rather than retribution. This **peace model** of crime control focuses on effectively developing a shared consensus on critical issues that may seriously affect the quality of life. These issues may include major crimes such as murder and rape, but also extend to gambling, drug use, sexual preference, nonviolent sexual deviance, noise complaints, simple child custody claims, and minor public offenses—all of which require few resources beyond those immediately available in the community.

Alternative dispute resolution mechanisms play an important role in peacemaking perspectives.[104] Mediation programs such as neighborhood justice centers are characterized by cooperative efforts to resolve disputes rather than by the adversarial-like proceedings characteristic of most U.S. courts. Dispute resolution programs are based on the principle of **participatory justice**, in which all parties to a dispute accept a kind of binding arbitration by neutral parties. Currently operating in over 200 areas throughout the country, dispute resolution centers often utilize administrative hearings and ombudsmen and are staffed by volunteers who work to resolve disputes without assigning blame.

Many alternative dispute resolution strategies are forms of restorative justice. Postmodern writers describe restorative justice as "a new system based on remedies and restoration rather than on prison, punishment and victim neglect"[105] and see it as "a system rooted in the concept of a caring community."[106] It is in fact a modern social movement meant to reform the criminal justice system. Restorative justice stresses healing rather than retribution and is based on three principles. The first is a view of crime "as more than simply law-breaking, an offense against governmental authority; [instead] crime is understood to cause multiple injuries to victims, the community and even the offender. Second, proponents argue that the criminal justice process should help repair those injuries. Third, they protest the government's apparent monopoly over society's response to crime,"[107] insisting that victims, offenders, and their communities must also be involved in a concerted effort to heal the harm caused by crime. Restorative justice programs differ from traditional approaches in that their central features prescribe clear outcomes directed at the three primary stakeholders in the justice system—offenders, victims, and the community. These outcomes, in turn, provide the basis for developing concrete performance measures to gauge the success of justice system programs, agencies, and interventions.

Restoration, or the act of repairing the harm done by crime and rebuilding relationships in the community, is the primary goal of restorative justice. The effectiveness of restorative justice programs is measured by how much relationships are healed rather than by how much punishment is inflicted on the offender. Table 8–1 highlights significant differences between traditional (retributive) justice and **restorative justice**.

Many of those involved in the restorative justice movement have begun to focus on the second policy level, promoting a gradual transition to a more equitable society and to socialized forms of government activity as a means for crime reduction.

TABLE 8–1 DIFFERENCES BETWEEN RETRIBUTIVE AND RESTORATIVE JUSTICE

Retributive Justice	Restorative Justice
Crime is an act against the state, a violation of a law, an abstract idea.	Crime is an act against another person or the community.
The criminal justice system controls crime.	Crime control lies primarily with the community.
Offender accountability is defined as taking punishment.	Offender accountability is defined as assuming responsibility and taking action to repair harm.
Crime is an individual act with individual responsibility.	Crime has both individual and social dimensions of responsibility.
Victims are peripheral to the process of resolving a crime.	Victims are central to the process of resolving a crime.
The emphasis is on adversarial relationships.	The emphasis is on dialogue and negotiation.
Pain is imposed to punish, deter, and prevent.	Restitution is a means of restoring both parties; the goal is reconciliation.
The response is focused on the offender's past behavior.	The response is focused on harmful consequences of the offender's behavior; the emphasis is on the future and on reparation.
There is dependence on proxy professionals.	There is direct involvement by both the offender and the victim.

Source: Adapted from Gordon Bazemore and Mark S. Umbreit, *Balanced and Restorative Justice: Program Summary* (Washington, DC: OJJDP, 1994), p. 7.

The Balanced and Restorative Justice (BARJ) Model

One form of restorative justice is the **Balanced and Restorative Justice Model (BARJ)** (Figure 8–5). Under this model, the community, victim, and offender should all receive balanced attention and all three should gain tangible benefits from their interactions with the justice system. Its three components may be described as follows:[108]

- *Accountability.* When an offense occurs, an obligation to the victim results. Victims and communities should have their losses restored by the actions of offenders making reparation, and victims should be empowered as active participants in the justice process.
- *Community protection.* The public has a right to a safe and secure community and must be protected during the time the offender is under supervision. The justice system must provide a range of intervention alternatives geared to the varying risks presented by the offenders.
- *Competency development.* Offenders who come within the jurisdiction of the court should leave the system capable of being productive and responsible in the community. Rather than simply receiving treatment and services aimed at suppressing problem behavior, offenders should make measurable improvements in their ability to function as productive, responsible citizens.

FIGURE 8–5 **The Balanced and Restorative Justice (BARJ) Model.** *Source:* Office of Juvenile Justice and Delinquency Prevention, *Balanced and Restorative Justice: Program Summary* (Washington, DC: OJJDP, no date), p. 1.

Restorative justice programs make use of a number of techniques, but central to all of them is restorative conferencing, also called "community conferencing," in which victim, offender, and affected community members meet face-to-face in a safe setting with an impartial facilitator to discuss the facts and the impact of a particular offense.[109] The victim can ask questions and express directly to the offender how the crime has affected his or her life. Conferencing provides the victim with greater access to the criminal justice process and a strong voice in the process.[110] Conferencing also humanizes the incident for the offender so that he or she may better understand the real human consequences of his or her wrongdoing. The offender can propose steps that he or she can take to help restore the harm caused to the victim and the community. Participation in conferences is voluntary for victims and offenders. In some cases, a victim unwilling to participate in a face-to-face meeting may make a written statement to be used in the conference, or a surrogate victim may take his or her place. Visit the website for the Center for Restorative Justice & Peacemaking via **Web Extra 8–7**.

THE CASE

Theodore John "Ted" Kaczynski (The Unabomber)

Between 1978 and 1995, Theodore John ("Ted") Kaczynski left or sent a total of 16 homemade pipe bombs, primarily targeting universities and airline-related activities. (The Federal Bureau of Investigation [FBI] designated the investigation the "Unabomb"—or Unabomber—case from these early university targets.) The bombing campaign caused three deaths and numerous serious injuries.

Kaczynski's intermittent attacks were shrouded in anonymity, a trait he inexplicably broke when he sent letters to a newspaper threatening to bomb an airplane. He also stated that he would stop the bombings if his 35,000-word manifesto was published in the *Washington Post*. In this manifesto, Kaczynski railed against contemporary life, claiming that "The Industrial Revolution and its consequences have been a disaster for the human race."[i]

Upon reading the manifesto, David Kaczynski, Ted's younger brother, immediately recognized that its tone and approach "almost had the feeling for me of one of Ted's angry letters over the years. . . . Some of those letters were addressed to the theme of technology just as the manifesto was."[ii] Although not convinced that his brother was the long-sought Unabomber, David Kaczynski contacted the FBI.

That slim investigative thread led the FBI to Kaczynski's cabin in the Montana wilderness, where they found overwhelming evidence that he was, in fact, the Unabomber. A live bomb, meticulous notes of past bombings, bomb-making materials, and the original copy of his infamous manifesto made the ensuing trial almost anticlimactic—and its results an almost foregone conclusion.

On January 22, 1998, Kaczynski pled guilty in the U.S. District Court in Sacramento to four bombings that occurred in 1985, 1993, and 1995. In accordance with his plea agreement, Kaczynski admitted to the three deaths his bombings had caused, all other pending charges were resolved, and he was sentenced to a life term without parole. Kaczynski remains imprisoned at the maximum-security federal prison in Florence, Colorado. Nine years after he entered prison, Kaczynski filed suit against the federal government and a group of his victims, seeking to prevent the sale of more than 40,000 pages of his original writings and correspondence.[iii]

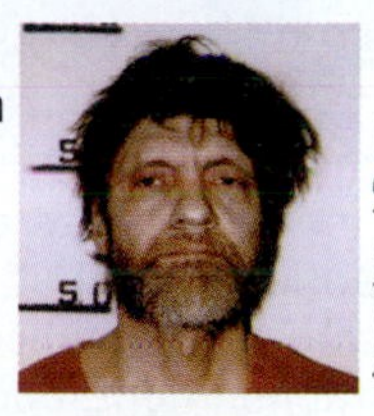
Associated Press

From what can be learned about his background, Kaczynski was a shy, intelligent youth who did not socialize easily or well and who periodically underwent episodes of intense and brooding withdrawal. As he grew older, the episodes were increasingly accompanied by a seething rage. Upon completing his Ph.D., Kaczynski accepted an assistant professorship in mathematics at the University of California at Berkeley in 1967. However, in June 1969, declaring that there was "no relevance" to what he was doing, he quit his teaching post. From 1969 through his arrest in 1996, he worked sporadically, including a brief time at the University of Michigan, and he usually worked only out of financial necessity. He ended up living off the land, assuming a hermit's existence of self-exile in a ramshackle cabin in the remote Montana wilderness that was to last almost 25 years.

Kaczynski also experienced lifelong difficulties with sexual relationships. While at the University of Michigan, he came to believe that he should undergo a sex change operation because fantasies of being a woman intensely excited him. He initiated the process at the school's health care facility, but when finally seen by a doctor, he claimed to be there for a different reason entirely and then left in a rage. He described the experience as shameful and humiliating. Later, he infrequently sought health system support as he attempted to establish meaningful relationships with women, but was never able to do so.

Author's Note: Kaczynski's entire manifesto remains available in the *Washington Post* archives at http://www.washingtonpost.com/wp-srv/national/longterm/unabomber/manifesto.text.htm.

An FBI video showing the inside of Kaczynski's cabin can be viewed at http://www.newseum.org/news/2008/06/video-inside-the-unabomber-s-cabin.html.

Notes

[i] Theodore Kaczynski, *Industrial Society and Its Future* (no date).

[ii] "When Your Brother Is 'the Unabomber,' " Interview with David Kaczynski, MSNBC News, December 29, 2006. Web available at http://www.msnbc.msn.com/id/16304477 (accessed July 4, 2011).

[iii] Serge F. Kovaleski, "Unabomber Wages Legal Battle to Halt Sale of Papers," *New York Times*, January 22, 2007, http://www.nytimes.com/2007/01/22/us/22unabomber.html?ex=1327122000&en=3fda08d949905a96&ei=5088&partner=rssnyt&emc=rss (accessed May 28, 2010).

The case of Ted Kaczynski raises a number of interesting questions. Among them are the following:

1. **Although Kaczynski is not a criminologist, it is likely that he would agree with some of the principles of the social conflict perspective. With which of those principles do you think he would be most comfortable? Why?**
2. **How does Kaczynski's being a loner fit with the crimes he committed? Might it indicate that he was in conflict with the wider society? Explain.**
3. **How might Kaczynski's difficulties with gender relationships provide further evidence of his difficulties with social life in general?**
4. **What similarities do you see between Kaczynski's writings and those of Karl Marx? (Learn more about Marx at http://www.philosophypages.com/ph/marx.htm.)**

CHAPTER 8 Social Conflict—*It's How We Relate*

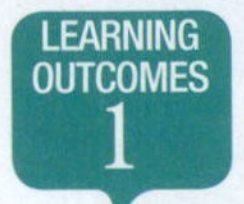

Explain social conflict theories, including radical theories.

Social conflict theories in criminology emphasize the central significance of conflict within society, which is seen as a natural consequence of inequities that exist between social classes. Conflict theories hold that formal agencies of social control, including the police, the courts, and the correctional establishment, coerce the unempowered or the disenfranchised to comply with the rules established by those in power. Consequently, social order, rather than being the result of any consensus, is seen as resting upon the *exercise of power through law*. From the conflict point of view, laws are a tool of the powerful, useful in keeping the unempowered from wresting control over important social institutions.

1. What do conflict theorists see as the natural source of conflict within society?
2. What is social class? What distinguishes one class from another?

social class Distinctions made between individuals on the basis of important defining social characteristics.

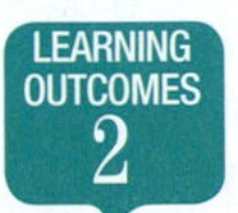

Describe the history of conflict theory in contemporary criminology.

One of the best-known early writers on social conflict was Karl Marx. Later, selected criminologists applied the principles that Marx developed to the study of crime and proposed that the causes of crime are rooted in social conditions that empower the wealthy and the politically well organized but disenfranchise those who are less fortunate. Today, for the most part, Marxist criminology has been superseded by radical-critical criminology.

1. How does the Marxist perspective explain conflict? What does Marxism see as the basic cause of social conflict?
2. What's the difference between the proletariat and the bourgeoisie?

bourgeoisie The class of people who own the means of production.

proletariat The working class.

conflict theory A perspective that applies the principles and concepts developed by Karl Marx to the study of crime and holds that the causes of crime are rooted in social conditions that empower the wealthy and the politically well organized, but disenfranchise those who are less fortunate. Also sometimes referred to as *Marxist criminology*.

Key Names

Karl Marx A writer on social conflict who said that there are two fundamental social classes within any capitalist society—the haves and the have-nots—which creates conflict.

George B. Vold A theorist who wrote that conflict is a natural result of the struggle for power in society.

Ralf Dahrendorf A sociologist who wrote that conflict is a fundamental part of any society.

Austin Turk A sociologist who states that the actions of the less powerful are penalized by those who are more powerful.

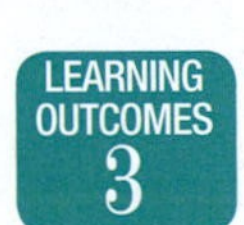

Review how radical-critical and Marxist criminology reflect the principles inherent in the social conflict perspective.

Radical-critical criminology is an outgrowth of Marxist criminology, although both forms of thought coexisted and influenced each other throughout much of the 1970s. Consistent with its roots, contemporary radical-critical criminology holds that crime is engendered by the unequal distribution of wealth, power, and other resources that its adherents believe is especially characteristic of capitalist societies. The causes of crime, according to radical-critical criminologists, can be found in social conditions that empower the wealthy and the politically well organized but disenfranchise those who are less fortunate.

1. What is a "market society"? Why do some radical-critical criminologists think that market societies are especially likely to breed high levels of violent crime?
2. What are the differences, if any, between Marxist criminology and radical-critical criminology?

Marxist criminology A perspective on crime and crime causation based on the writings of Karl Marx.

radical-critical criminology A conflict perspective that sees crime as engendered by the unequal distribution of wealth, power, and other resources that its adherents believe is especially characteristic of capitalist societies.

Key Names

William J. Chambliss and ***Robert T. Seidman*** Theorists who say that the more stratified a society becomes, the more the dominant members will use coercion to enforce their will. No act is intrinsically criminal, but is determined to be so by those in power.

Richard Quinney A social philosopher who believes that advanced capitalistic society requires that the subordinate classes remain oppressed, especially through the coercion and violence of the legal system.

Elliot Currie A theorist who thinks that market societies are especially likely to breed high levels of violent crime. These ideas contribute to the formation of a number of new theories, the most interesting of which are peacemaking, feminist, convict, and postmodern criminology.

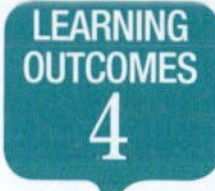

Explain how social problems might be solved from the perspective of peacemaking criminology.

Peacemaking criminology holds that social control agencies and the citizens they serve should work together to alleviate social problems and human suffering and thus reduce crime.

1. What is peacemaking criminology? What are its basic tenants?
2. According to peacemaking criminologists, who should participate in the peacemaking process?

peacemaking criminology A criminological perspective that holds that crime control agencies and the citizens they serve should work together to alleviate social problems and human suffering and thus reduce crime.

Key Names

Harold (Hal) E. Pepinsky A criminologist who says that peacemaking promotes a nonviolent criminology of compassion and service, seeking to end suffering and thereby eliminate crime.

Bo Lozoff A peacemaking criminologist who says that the criminal justice system is founded on violence.

Michael Braswell and ***Clemens Bartollas*** Peacemaking criminologist who believe that human transformation takes place when we change our social, economic, and political structure.

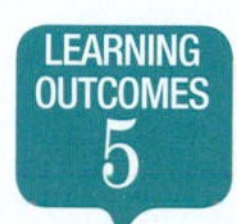

Discuss the relationship between feminist criminology and feminist thought generally.

Feminist criminology applies various forms of feminist thought to infuse gender awareness into mainstream criminology. Feminist thought sees gender in terms of power relationships, revealing the inequities inherent in traditional patriarchal structures. Feminist criminology also points out that traditional criminology has been male-centered and that women have been largely ignored by criminologists, heightening their sense of powerlessness and dependence upon men.

1. What is the relationship between feminist criminology and feminist thought generally?
2. What are the different kinds of feminist thought identified in this chapter? Which is most applicable to the study of crime?
3. How would feminists change the study of crime?

feminist criminology A corrective model of social analysis intended to redirect the thinking of mainstream criminologists to include gender awareness.

patriarchy The tradition of male dominance.

radical feminism A perspective that holds that any significant change in the social status of women can be accomplished only through substantial changes in social institutions such as the family, law, and medicine.

liberal feminism A perspective that holds that the concerns of women can be incorporated within existing social institutions through conventional means and without the need to drastically restructure society.

socialist feminism A perspective that examines social roles and the gender-based division of labor within the family, seeing both as a significant source of women's subordination within society.

Marxist feminism A perspective that sees capitalism as the root cause of women's oppression because it perpetuates economic inequality, dependence, and political powerlessness, ultimately leading to unhealthy social relations between men and women.

power-control theory A perspective that holds that the distribution of crime and delinquency within society is to some degree founded upon the consequences that power relationships within the wider society hold for domestic settings and for the everyday relationships between men, women, and children within the context of family life.

gender gap The observed differences between male and female rates of criminal offending in a given society such as the United States.

Key Names

Kathleen Daly and ***Meda Chesney-Lind*** Feminist scholars who state that traditional understanding of what is "typical" about crime is derived from the study of men.

Freda Adler and ***Rita J. Simon*** Criminologists who assert that differences in crime rates by gender are attributable to socialization rather than biology.

John Hagan A theorist who suggests that family structure and social structure are intertwined.

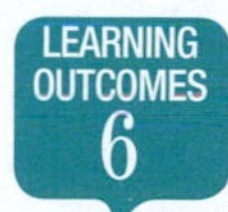

Describe convict criminology and explain how it differs from the other theories discussed in this chapter.

Convict criminology is a new radical paradigm consisting of writings on the subject matter of criminology by convicted felons and ex-inmates who have acquired academic credentials or who are associated with credentialed others. As its adherents admit, convict criminology is not without an agenda and tends to assume a critical perspective with regard to the justice system—especially corrections.

1. What new perspective does convict criminology bring to the study of crime?
2. Does convict criminology have an agenda? If so, what is it?

convict criminology A radical paradigm consisting of writings on criminology by convicted felons and ex-inmates who have acquired academic credentials or who are associated with credentialed others; also called *alternative criminology*.

Key Names

Stephen C. Richards, John Irwin, K. C. Carceral, and ***Thomas J. Bernard***. Those who maintain that much can be learned from the lived experiences of convicts themselves.

LEARNING OUTCOMES 7

Show what all postmodern criminologies have in common.

All postmodern criminologies build on the belief that past criminological approaches have failed to realistically assess the true causes of crime and have therefore failed to offer workable solutions for crime control—or if they have, that such theories and solutions may once have been appropriate but do not apply to the postmodern era.

1. What does it mean to say that traditional theories of crime need to be "deconstructed"? What role does deconstructionist thinking play in postmodern criminology?
2. What is semiotics? How is it applicable to the study of crime?

postmodern criminology A brand of criminology that developed following World War II and builds on the tenets inherent in postmodern social thought.

androcentric A single-sex perspective, as in the case of criminologists who study only the criminality of males.

deconstructionist theories A postmodern perspective that challenges existing criminological theories in order to debunk them and works toward replacing traditional ideas with concepts seen as more appropriate to the postmodern era.

constitutive criminology The assertion that individuals shape their world while also being shaped by it.

semiotics The theory that everything we know, say, do, think, and feel is mediated through signs. Semiotic criminology identifies how language systems communicate uniquely encoded values.

Key Names

Stuart Henry and ***Dragan Milovanovic*** Authors whose writings discuss crime and crime control as constructions produced through a social process in which offender, victim, and society are involved.

Ian Taylor A sociologist who believes that deconstructionism does not offer viable alternatives for crime control and prevention.

LEARNING OUTCOMES 8

Explain the implications of conflict theory for crime-control policy.

Three different levels of policy implications derive from conflict theory in criminology. The first intends to redistribute wealth on the premise that crime rates will fall as poverty and social inequalities are eliminated. The second seeks to promote a gradual transition to a more equitable society and to socialized forms of government activity as a means for crime reduction. A third approach to reducing crime lies in applying conflict resolution principles through the use of peacemaking techniques or by adopting a model based on cooperation rather than retribution.

1. What three different levels of policy implications derive from conflict theory in criminology?

peace model An approach to crime control that focuses on effective ways for developing a shared consensus on critical issues that could seriously affect the quality of life.

participatory justice A relatively informal type of criminal justice case processing that makes use of local community resources rather than requiring traditional forms of official intervention.

restorative justice A postmodern perspective that stresses "remedies and restoration rather than prison, punishment and victim neglect."

Balanced and Restorative Justice Model (BARJ) A model of restorative justice in which the community, victim, and offender should all receive balanced attention.

> PROSECUTOR: "Why did you have these potential 'hits'? Was this to gratify some sexual interest?"
> DENNIS RADER: "Yes sir. I had a lot of them . . . if one didn't work out, I just moved to another one."
>
> —*Testimony from the Trial of Dennis Rader*

Crimes against Persons—What We Fear

1 Describe the major national crime-data-gathering programs and explain the differences between them.

2 Summarize various types and patterns of murder.

3 Provide a closer look at the crime of murder.

4 Define *serial murder* and list the different types of serial killers.

5 Explain how mass murder differs from serial murder and list the different types of mass murderers.

6 Show how definitions of rape differ and describe the various perspectives that have been offered to explain the crime of rape.

7 Summarize the various types and patterns of rape and violence against women.

8 Describe the types and patterns of child physical and sexual abuse.

9 Describe the crime of robbery.

10 Compare the different types of assault.

11 Describe other violent crimes, including hate crimes, workplace violence, and stalking.

Fotolia

INTRO UNSAFE CITIES

In October 2012, as the Detroit Tigers prepared to play the Oakland Athletics in playoff baseball, members of the Detroit Police Officer Association (DPOA) stood outside the Tigers' Comerica Park stadium holding signs warning tourists to "Enter at Your Own Risk."[1] DPOA spokesperson Donato Iorio told onlookers that "Detroit is America's most violent city, its homicide rate is the highest in the country and yet the Detroit Police Department is grossly understaffed." It turns out that Iorio was mistaken. According to the Federal Bureau of Investigation (FBI), Detroit has the *second* highest rate of violent crime in the country—just behind that of Flint, Michigan, only 66 miles away. According to the FBI, Flint's violent crime rate in 2012 was 2,729 per every 100,000 residents, whereas Detroit's was "only" 2,123 per 100,000.[2]

Naokit/Fotolia

The Detroit Tiger's Comerica Park. The stadium recently became the scene of a protest by Detroit police officers against underfunded and understaffed working conditions. Why would any police department be underfunded?

DISCUSS **Crime statistics are significantly influenced by the definitions of crime used by reporting agencies. Similarly, measures purporting to show the total amount of "crime" in American society depend on the types of illegal activities that are counted. If you wanted to create a comprehensive measure of crime in this country, what kinds of illegal activities would you include in the count?**

▶ *National Crime-Data-Gathering Programs*

Before 1930, Detroit officials would not have known how their city ranked in terms of violent crime rates. That's because the government-sponsored gathering of crime data for the nation as a whole began in 1930 in the United States. Before then, the gathering of statistics was random at best, and most accounts were anecdotal and either spread by word of mouth or printed in local newspapers (or both). Today's official U.S. crime statistics come from the Bureau of Justice Statistics (BJS), which conducts the annual **National Crime Victimization Survey (NCVS)**, and from the FBI, which publishes yearly data under its summary-based **Uniform Crime Reporting (UCR) program** and its more detailed **National Incident Based Reporting System (NIBRS)**; the latter provides a more complete picture of crimes reported and committed.

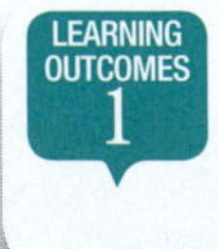

LEARNING OUTCOMES 1 Describe the major national crime-data-gathering programs and explain the differences between them.

NCVS data appear in a number of annual reports, the most important of which is *Criminal Victimization in the United States*, and FBI data take the form of the annual publication *Crime in the United States*. Numerous other surveys and reports are made available through the BJS and cover not only the incidence of crime and criminal activity in the United States but also many other aspects of the criminal justice profession, including justice system expenditures, prisons and correctional data, probation and parole populations, jail inmate information, law enforcement agencies and personnel data, and information on state and federal courts. These and other reports are generally made available free of charge to interested parties through the National Criminal Justice Reference Service (NCJRS).[3]

The largest collection of facts about all aspects of U.S. crime and criminal justice is the *Sourcebook of Criminal Justice Statistics*, using data compiled yearly by the BJS and made available through the auspices of the State University of New York at Albany on the Web at http://www.albany.edu/sourcebook. The UCR/NIBRS and the NCVS both use their own specialized definitions in deciding which events should be scored as crimes. Sometimes the definitions vary considerably between programs, and none of the definitions used by the reporting agencies is strictly based on federal or state statutory crime classifications. For the most part, the definitions and statistics that we will use in this chapter and the next are consistent with those used by the FBI and its annual publication *Crime in the United States*. This chapter discusses violent crimes, including murder, rape, robbery, and aggravated assault (Figure 9–1).

Murder and Nonnegligent Homicide	The willful (nonnegligent) killing of one human being by another. The UCR does not include deaths caused by negligence, suicide, or accident; justifiable homicides; or attempts to murder or assaults to murder, which are classified as aggravated assaults.
Forcible Rape	The carnal knowledge of a person forcibly and against his or her will. Attempts to commit rape by force or threat of force are also included; however, statutory rape (without force) and other sex offenses are excluded.
Robbery	Taking or attempting to take anything of value from the care, custody, or control of a person or persons by force or threat of force, or violence and/or by putting the victim in fear.
Aggravated Assault	An unlawful attack by one person upon another for the purpose of inflicting severe bodily injury. Aggravated assault is usually accompanied by the use of a weapon or by means likely to produce death or great bodily harm.

FIGURE 9–1 **Violent Crimes and Their Definitions.**
Source: Federal Bureau of Investigation, Uniform Crime Reporting Program.

Murder

The terms *homicide* and **murder** are often used interchangeably, although they are not the same. Homicide is the willful killing of one human being by another, whereas murder is an unlawful homicide. Some homicides, such as those committed in defense of oneself or one's family, may be justifiable and therefore legal. The term used by most courts and law enforcement agencies to describe murder is **criminal homicide**. In legal parlance, *criminal homicide* means "the causing of the death of another person without legal justification or excuse."

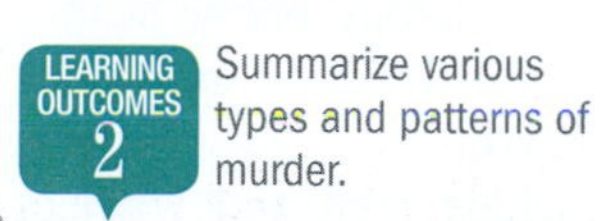

LEARNING OUTCOMES
2
Summarize various types and patterns of murder.

According to the UCR/NIBRS, 14,827 murders were committed throughout the United States in 2012.[4] The 2012 rate of criminal homicide was 4.7 people murdered for every 100,000 individuals in the U.S. population. As is the case with other major crimes, rates of criminal homicide in the United States increased between 1960 and the early 1990s, but then began decreasing until they reached levels not seen since the 1960s (Figure 9–2). General features of criminal homicide in the United States today are shown in Figure 9–3.

Jurisdictions generally distinguish among various types of murder. Among the distinctions made are **first-degree murder**, also called "premeditated murder"; **second-degree murder**; and third-degree murder, or **negligent homicide**. First-degree murder differs from the other two types of murder in that it is planned. It involves what some statutes call "malice aforethought," which may become evident by someone "lying in wait" for the victim, but can also be proved by a murderer's simple action of going into an adjacent room to find a weapon and returning with it to kill. In effect, any activity in preparation to kill that demonstrates the passage of time, however brief, between formation of the intent to kill and the act of killing itself is technically sufficient

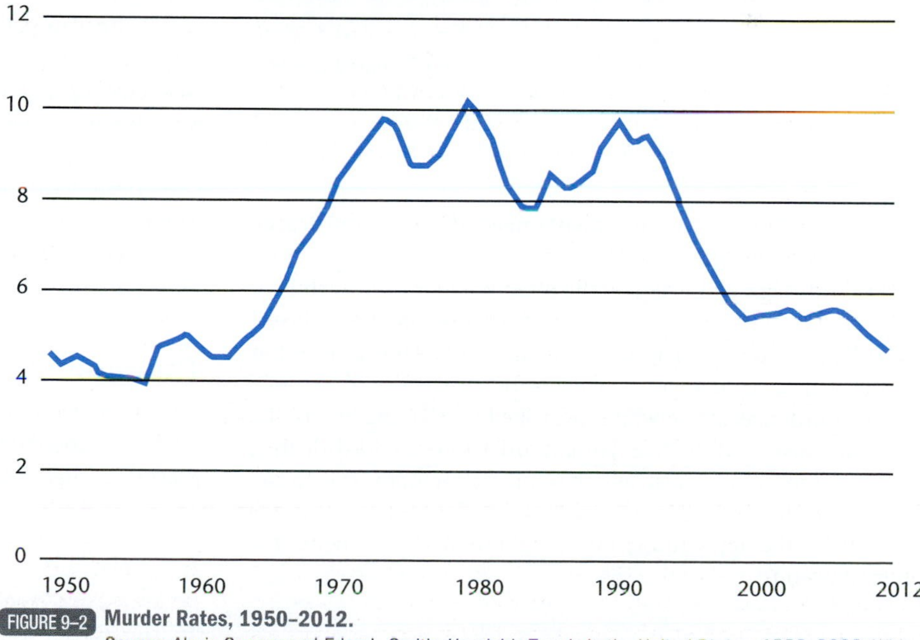

FIGURE 9–2 **Murder Rates, 1950–2012.**
Source: Alexis Cooper and Erica L. Smith, *Homicide Trends in the United States, 1980–2008: With Annual Rates for 2009 and 2010* (Washington, DC: Bureau of Justice Statistics, November 2011), p. 2; and FBI, *Crime in the United States, 2012* (Washington, DC: U.S. Department of Justice, 2013).

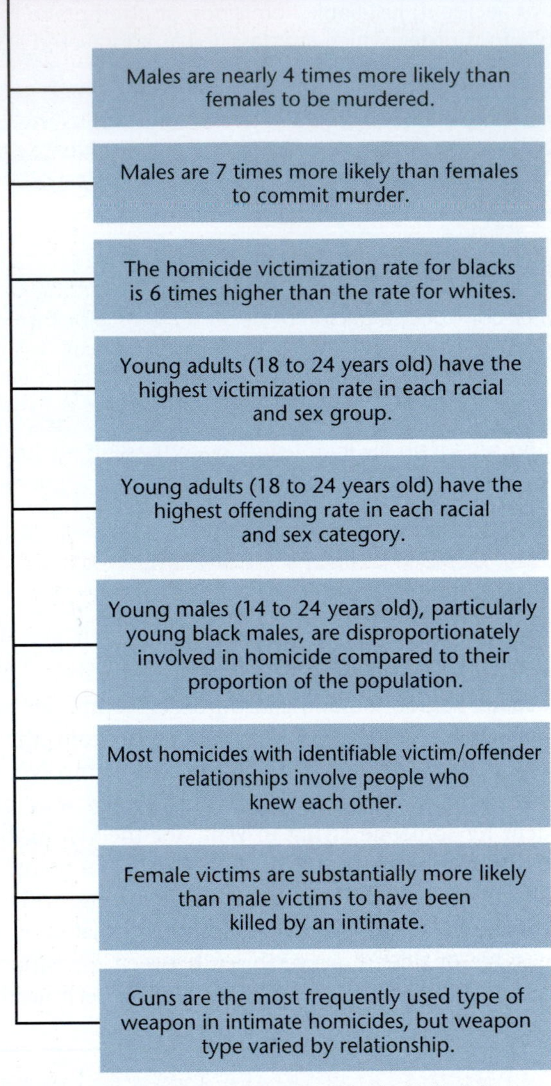

General Features of Criminal Homicide in the United States
Males are nearly 4 times more likely than females to be murdered.
Males are 7 times more likely than females to commit murder.
The homicide victimization rate for blacks is 6 times higher than the rate for whites.
Young adults (18 to 24 years old) have the highest victimization rate in each racial and sex group.
Young adults (18 to 24 years old) have the highest offending rate in each racial and sex category.
Young males (14 to 24 years old), particularly young black males, are disproportionately involved in homicide compared to their proportion of the population.
Most homicides with identifiable victim/offender relationships involve people who knew each other.
Female victims are substantially more likely than male victims to have been killed by an intimate.
Guns are the most frequently used type of weapon in intimate homicides, but weapon type varied by relationship.

FIGURE 9–3 **General Features of Criminal Homicide in the United States.** *Source:* Alexis Cooper and Erica L. Smith, *Homicide Trends in the United States, 1980–2008: With Annual Rates for 2009 and 2010* (Washington, DC: Bureau of Justice Statistics, November 2011).

to establish the legal requirements needed for a first-degree murder prosecution.

Second-degree murder, on the other hand, is a true crime of passion. It is an unlawful killing in which the intent to kill and the killing itself happen almost simultaneously. Hence, a person who kills in a fit of anger is likely to be charged with second-degree murder, as is one who is provoked into killing by insults, physical abuse, and the like. For a murder to be second-degree, however, the killing must follow immediately upon the abuse. Time that elapses between abuse or insults and the murder itself allows the opportunity for thought to occur and hence for premeditation.

Homicide offending is very much patterned in terms of sociodemographics.

Both first- and second-degree murderers intend to kill. Third-degree murder, although it varies in meaning between jurisdictions, most often refers to homicides that are the result of some action that is unlawful or negligent. Hence, it is frequently called "negligent homicide," "negligent manslaughter," "manslaughter," or "involuntary manslaughter." Under negligent homicide statutes, for example, a drunk driver who causes a fatal accident may be charged with third-degree murder even though that person had not the slightest intent to kill.

Some jurisdictions have created a special category of **felony murder**, whereby an offender who commits a crime during which someone dies can be found guilty of first-degree murder even though the person committing the crime had no intention of killing anyone. Bank robberies in which one of the robbers is shot to death by police, for example, or in which a bank patron succumbs to a fear-induced heart attack may leave a surviving robber subject to the death penalty under the felony murder rule. Hence, felony murder is a special class of criminal homicide whereby an offender may be charged with first-degree murder when that person's criminal activity results in another person's death.

Significant contributions to the understanding of the crime of homicide are being made today by the Homicide Research Working Group (HRWG). The HRWG brings together researchers, academicians, and investigators working in the area of interpersonal violence from numerous disciplines. Prior to the creation of the HRWG, work in lethal violence had been scattered among numerous disciplines and was largely uncoordinated. To address this lack of coordination, homicide experts from various disciplines, including criminology, public health, demography, medicine, sociology, criminal justice, and other fields, joined together to create the HRWG.

Although homicide offenders include men and women, young and old, rich and poor, homicide offending is very much patterned in terms of sociodemographics, with members of some groups being disproportionately represented as offenders. Distinctive patterns of homicide can be identified by such factors as individual characteristics, cultural norms, community characteristics, geographic region, availability of weapons and weapons used, gang activity and affiliation, and the victim–offender relationship. All of these sociodemographic features have been used to further our understanding of homicide patterns and to create typologies surrounding homicide. Learn more about the crime of murder by visiting the Homicide Research Working Group on the Web at **Web Extra 9–1**.

The Subculture of Violence Thesis

Within the United States, there has been strong research interest in the subculture of violence thesis originally formulated by Marvin Wolfgang and Franco Ferracuti,[5] which was discussed

The subculture of violence thesis holds that certain groups share norms and values that contribute to lifestyles involving violence.

in Chapter 6. These authors stressed that certain groups share norms and values in lifestyles of violence. Ethnic and racial differences in criminal activity rely on interaction with others, including a shared sense of history, language, values, and beliefs. A subculture requires a sufficient number of people who share not only values and beliefs, but also a social forum that expresses membership. Such a forum may be something as elusive as a street corner. It is primarily the nature of this situation that makes it difficult to test empirically. The subculture of violence thesis has been the primary theoretical perspective used to explain the similarity between homicide victims and offenders. First, homicide statistics reveal that victims and offenders share similar sociodemographic characteristics such as age, gender, and race. African Americans are disproportionately represented in the homicide statistics as both victims and offenders (Figures 9–4 and 9–5).[6] Second, victims and offenders who know each other well are disproportionately represented in homicide statistics. An analysis of supplemental homicide reports shows that approximately 60% of victims and offenders have some prior relationship.[7]

The subculture of violence thesis has also been explored at the community level, where the emphasis is on the importance of "critical masses" as support for the existence of subcultures.[8] Early research argued that the disproportionate rate at which African Americans commit homicide is associated with the presence of a large African American population, the "critical mass" necessary for the "transmission of violence-related models" and subcultural behavior patterns.[9] However, most of the research that found higher homicide rates to be associated with higher percentages of African Americans in the population did not take into consideration socioeconomic status, level of education, and so forth.[10] Research by Robert Sampson, using more sophisticated measures and stronger research designs, revealed that the racial composition of an area alone did not have a significant effect on the homicide rates for either whites or African Americans.[11]

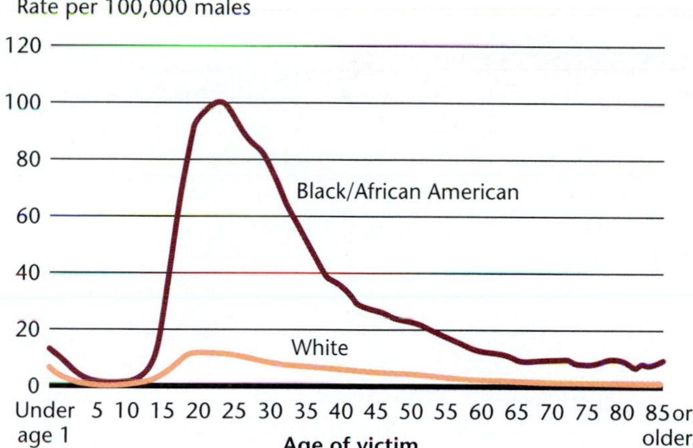

FIGURE 9–4 **Male Homicide Rates, by Victim Age and Race, 2002–2011.** *Source:* Erica L. Smith and Alexia Cooper, *Homicide in the U.S. Known to Law Enforcement*, 2011 (Washington, DC: Bureau of Justice Statistics), p. 5.

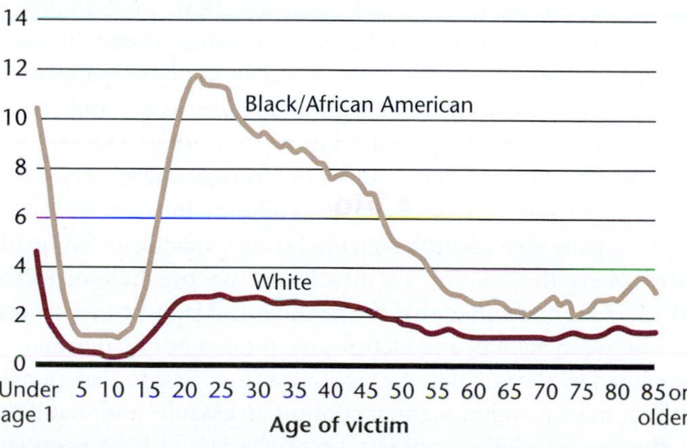

FIGURE 9–5 **Female Homicide Rates, by Victim Age and Race, 2002–2011.** *Source:* Erica L. Smith and Alexia Cooper, *Homicide in the U.S. Known to Law Enforcement*, 2011 (Washington, DC: Bureau of Justice Statistics), p. 5.

Homicide: A Closer Look

Marvin Wolfgang's now-famous 1958 study of homicides in Philadelphia revealed that approximately 25% of all homicides were between family members and that women were far more likely than men to be both offenders and victims within this category than within any other.[12] Males were more likely to be killed by friends and strangers than by their family members. However, when a male was killed by a female, the offender was most likely to be his spouse.[13] Other researchers have emphasized qualitative differences in the pattern of homicide within the victim–offender relationship. Figure 9–6 shows the relationship between killers and their victims.

LEARNING OUTCOMES 3
Provide a closer look at the crime of murder.

Primary and Nonprimary Homicide

The work of **Robert Nash Parker** and Dwayne Smith represented the first systematic research that focused on differentiating homicide according to the victim–offender relationship.[14] Their work used two classifications of homicide: primary and nonprimary. **Primary homicides** are the most frequent and involve family members, friends, and acquaintances, and they are usually characterized as **expressive homicides** because they often result from interpersonal hostility, based on jealousy, revenge, romantic triangles, and minor disagreements.[15]

Nonprimary homicides involve victims and offenders who have no prior relationship and usually occur in the course of another crime such as robbery; these are referred to as **instrumental crimes** because they involve some degree of premeditation by the offender and are less likely to be precipitated by the victim.

Not all homicide offenders intend to kill their victims. This may be the case when the incident begins as a robbery motivated by instrumental ends, such as getting money. An argument may also precede a homicide, but this circumstance is expressive rather than instrumental because "the dominant motivation is the violence itself," even if lethal violence is not planned in

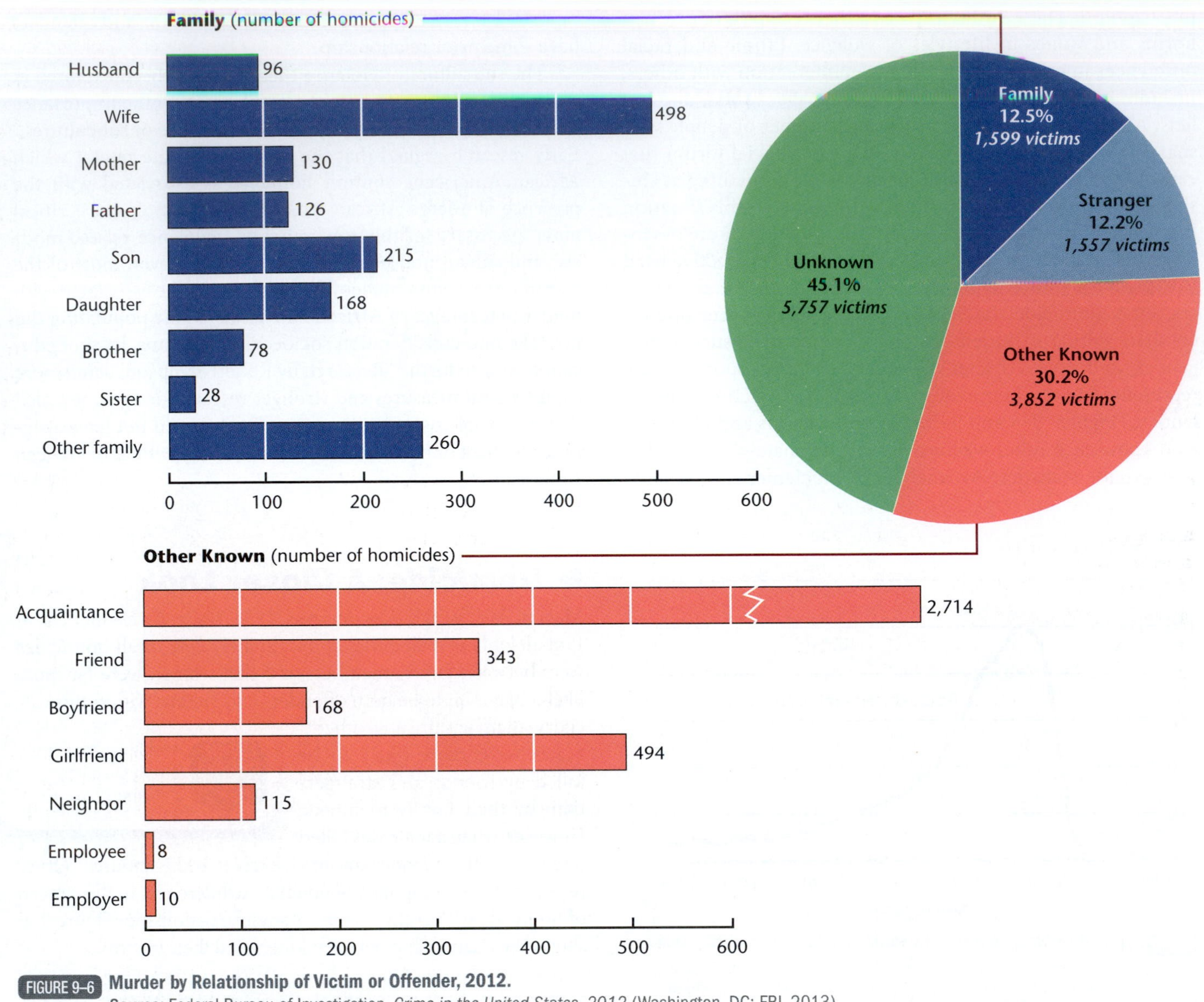

FIGURE 9–6 **Murder by Relationship of Victim or Offender, 2012.**
Source: Federal Bureau of Investigation, *Crime in the United States, 2012* (Washington, DC: FBI, 2013).

advance.[16] The importance of instigating incidents is explored in research by Carolyn Rebecca Block and Richard Block.[17] The Blocks use the term **sibling offense** to refer to the incident that begins the homicide. A sibling offense may be a crime, such as robbery, or another incident, such as a lover's quarrel. It is crucial to take these sibling offenses into account because they help explain why some robberies end in murder while others do not. The Blocks developed an elaborate typology of homicide to illustrate how an understanding of the patterns of nonlethal violence can assist in the prevention of lethal violence. For example, there are a great many incidents of street gang violence, most of which do not end in death, and understanding those nonlethal incidents can assist in preventing homicides.[18]

Victim Precipitation

The concept of **victim precipitation** focuses on the characteristics of victims that may have precipitated their victimization. Victim precipitation seems to blame the victim, which makes it quite controversial. From a scholarly point of view, however, the thrust of the concept of victim precipitation is not to blame the victim for the event, but to examine both individual and situational factors that may have contributed to and initiated the crime. This is especially important in studying patterns of homicide because quite often a homicide begins as a fight or an argument between people who know each other. The circumstances of the particular encounter determine whether the event will end as some type of assault or as a homicide.

Wolfgang also identified alcohol use as a factor in homicide cases where the "victim is a direct, positive precipitator in the crime."[19] He concluded that the positive and significant association between alcohol and victim-precipitated homicides may be explained by the fact that the victim was the "first to slap, punch, stab, or in some other manner commit an assault" and that if the victim had not been drinking, he or she would have been less violent.[20] Wolfgang's research on homicide revealed that most victims of spousal homicide had been drinking at the time of the incident, a situation that did not apply to homicide offenders.[21]

Think About It…

Victim precipitation is an especially important concept when studying homicide. This chapter says that the thrust of the concept is not to blame the victim for the event, but to examine both individual and situational factors that may have contributed to and initiated the crime. What kinds of individual and situational precipitating factors can you identify that might increase the likelihood of homicide victimization?

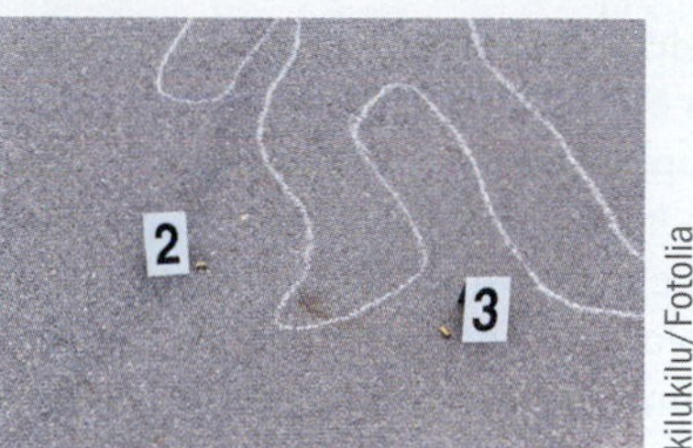

kilukilu/Fotolia

Weapon Use

There are different perspectives on the role that weapons play in crime, with most of the discussion centering on the role of firearms in homicide. In examining the relationship between guns and homicide, it is important to differentiate between instrumentality and availability. *Instrumentality* refers to the fact that the type of weapon used in a particular encounter has an effect on whether the encounter ends in death. For example, the involvement of a gun may mean the difference between a criminal event ending as an assault or a homicide. When guns are used in robberies, the fatality rate is "three times as high as for robberies with knives and 10 times as high as for robberies with other weapons."[22]

Availability refers to issues surrounding how access to guns may increase their presence in all types of interactions, including criminal ones.[23] The ease of availability is important, given the relative spontaneity of some violent encounters. The availability of guns is important at the individual level as well as the community level because the greater the presence of guns in a particular neighborhood, the easier the access for individuals beyond their immediate households. Compared to gun instrumentality then, gun availability may be a much stronger factor in explaining lethal violence.[24]

Serial Murder

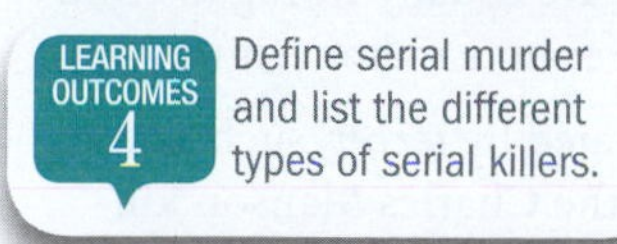
LEARNING OUTCOMES 4 Define serial murder and list the different types of serial killers.

Serial murder is a criminal homicide that "involves the killing of several victims in three or more separate events."[25] Criminologists **James Alan Fox** and **Jack Levin** have written extensively on both serial killing and mass murder.

Contrary to some commonly held beliefs, the vast majority of serial killers are not legally insane or medically psychotic. "They are more cruel than crazy," according to Fox and Levin. "Their crimes may be sickening but their minds are not necessarily sick."[26] Many serial killers are diagnosed as sociopaths, a term for those with antisocial personalities. Because they lack a conscience, sociopaths do not consider the needs or basic humanity of others in their decision making or their view of the world. They do not see themselves as being bound by conventional rules or by the expectations of others. Sociopaths view other people as "tools to be manipulated for the purpose of maximizing their personal pleasure."[27] However, many sociopaths are neither serial killers nor involved in violent crime, even though "they may lie, cheat, or steal."[28]

Although not an exclusive characteristic of serial killers, sexual sadism is a strong pattern. In many of the typologies developed by researchers, this characteristic forms the basis for a type of serial killer. Typologies of serial killers are organized around different, but generally related, themes. Some criminologists identify four different types of serial killers: **Visionary serial killers** hear voices and have visions that are the basis for a compulsion to murder; **comfort serial killers** are motivated by financial or material gain; **hedonistic serial killers** murder because they find it enjoyable and derive psychological pleasure from killing; and **power seekers** operate from some position of authority over others, and their killings usually involve a period where the killer plays a kind of cat-and-mouse game with the victim.[29] Fox and Levin offer a three-part typology. They classify serial murderers as thrill-motivated, mission-oriented, or expedience-directed. *Thrill-motivated killers*, the most common type of serial killer, may be of two types: the sexual sadist and the dominance killer. *Mission-oriented killers* are not as common and generally have either a reformist or visionary orientation. Reformists want to rid the world of evil, and visionaries hear voices commanding them to do certain activities. Visionary killers are quite rare and tend to be genuinely psychotic. *Expedience-directed serial killers* are driven by either profit or protection. Profit-driven killers may kill for financial or material gain, and protection-oriented killers commit murder to mask other crimes, such as robbery.[30]

Female Serial Killers

Although the vast majority of serial killers are male, there have been female serial killers, and the patterns of their activities are sometimes distinct from those of male serialists.[31] Female serial killers typically select their victims from among people they know, unlike male serial killers, who tend to target strangers.[32] A type of serial killer found primarily among women is the *disciple killer*, who murders as the result of the influence of a charismatic personality. The women who killed at the behest of Charles Manson were of this type. The geographic area in which serial killers operate may be either stable or transient, with no clear preference among male serial killers. However, geographic stability characterizes almost all of the known female serial killers.[33]

Michael D. Kelleher and C. L. Kelleher researched female serial killers from a historical perspective and developed a typology based on motivation. Arguing that there are two broad categories of female serial killers—those who act alone and those who work in partnership with others—Kelleher and Kelleher present a typology based on distinct motivation, selection of victim, and method of killing.[34] The categories include the *black widow*, who generally kills spouses and usually for economic profit, and the *angel of death*, who generally kills "those in her care or who rely on her for some form of medical attention or similar support."[35] The typical career of a female serial killer is longer than that of her male counterpart. Other than women who commit their crimes with others, usually men, female serial killers tend to approach their crimes in a systematic fashion—a characteristic that may explain their longer careers.[36]

Apprehending Serial Killers

It is extremely difficult to identify and apprehend serial killers because of the cautiousness and skill with which most of them operate. Ironically, it is these very factors that allow them to operate long enough to be labeled serial killers. Individuals who are less skillful or cautious are generally apprehended because of evidence at the crime scene or the selection of their victim. A detailed multidisciplinary perspective on serial murders and techniques used to apprehend them can be read on the FBI's website via **Web Extra 9–2**.

Mass Murder

Mass murder is the illegal killing of three or more individuals in a single event or during a short period of time.[37] Some mass murders occur on the a large scale, as was the case in the 1995 Oklahoma City bombing, in which 168 individuals, including children, were killed. Other mass murders have been described as "small scale," although no particular number of casualties separates small- from large-scale mass murders. Mass murder can follow the political motivations of the offenders, as was the case with the 2013 Boston Marathon bombings, in which two pressure-cooker bombs exploded at the event's finish line, killing 3 people and injuring 264 others. Other mass murderers kill for more personal reasons. The mass killing of 32 people at the Virginia Polytechnic Institute and State University (Virginia Tech) campus in Blacksburg, Virginia, in 2007 by student gunman Seung-Hui Cho (described in Chapter 6) appears to have been at least partially motivated by a seething anger against those whom Cho perceived as being more successful than he. Similarly, the 2014 slaying of six people in Santa Barbara near the Alpha Phi sorority house by 22-year-old Elliot Rodger (who committed suicide at the scene) appears to have been motivated by psychological problems, including the killer's simmering hatred of women. Before the attack, Rodger placed a 137-page outline of his plans to kill online, a version of which was still recently available at http://www.latimes.com/local/lanow/la-me-ln-isla-vista-document-20140524-story.html. In it, he wrote:

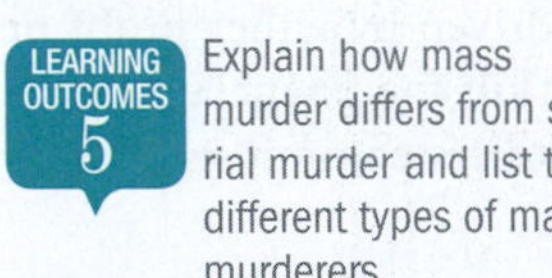

Explain how mass murder differs from serial murder and list the different types of mass murderers.

> I will torture some of the good looking people before I kill them, assuming that the good looking ones had the best sex lives. All of that pleasure they had in life, I will punish by bringing them pain and suffering. I have lived a life of pain and suffering, and it was time to bring that pain to people who actually deserve it. I will cut them, flay them, strip all the skin off their flesh, and pour boiling water all over them while they are still alive, as well as any other form of torture I could possibly think of. . . . The Second Phase will represent my War on Women. I will punish all females for the crime of depriving me of sex. They have starved me of sex for my entire youth, and gave that pleasure to other men. In doing so, they took many years of my life away.[38]

Mass murderers tend to surprise their victims because they often attack in everyday locales that are considered safe and because they erupt spontaneously. In 2012, for example, alleged-shooter James E. Holmes opened fire in a crowded movie theater at a midnight showing of the movie *The Dark Knight Rises* in Aurora, Colorado, killing 12 people and injuring 58.[39] Because mass murders often contain the element of surprise, they are sometimes described as *random*. The term "random mass murder," however, is often used to indicate both (1) the fact that such killings are very difficult to predict before they occur, and (2) the fear that such events inspire in the rest of the population. Such events are not random from the perspective of the perpetrator, however, who often carefully plans his attack.

Although mass murders do not occur with great frequency, they cause great concern because they shatter the sense of safety that usually characterizes everyday life. Given the number of mass shootings that have occurred over the past few years, a number of schools, hospitals, and businesses across the nation are taking steps to deal with such an event, indicating that such events are becoming significantly more frequent than in the past.[40]

Fox and Levin offer a four-part typology of mass murder that differentiates these crimes by motive:[41]

- *Revenge* murderers represent the largest category of such killers. They are motivated by *revenge* against either particular individuals or groups of individuals. Other revenge-motivated murderers may be less specific in the selection of a target, as in the case of George Hennard, who hated "all of the residents of the county in which he lived." In 1991, Hennard drove his truck through the front window of Luby's Cafeteria in Killeen, Texas, and then "indiscriminately opened fire on customers as they ate their lunch, killing 23."[42]
- Mass murderers motivated by *love* have a sense of love that is distorted and obsessive. They often commit suicide after they murder, and in the case of a spouse killing, the may also kill their children.
- Mass murders who kill for *profit* are usually trying to eliminate witnesses in an effort to cover up a major crime.
- Some mass murderers are motivated by *terror*, such as the individuals who participated in the Charles Manson killings. These people want to send a message to society.

Although most mass murders strike the public as senseless acts of a crazy person, Levin and Fox contend that "most massacres are not madmen."[43] Yet why would a person such as 32-year-old right-wing extremist Anders Behring Beivik, who killed

Mass murderers are usually easy to apprehend because they rarely leave the scene of their crime.

77 people at a youth summer camp in Norway in 2011, shoot so many victims at random, many of whom were children?[44] And why would Adam Lanza, who spent much of his time playing video games at him home, suddenly drive to the Sandy Hook Elementary school in Newtown, Connecticut—armed with a hunting rifle, two handguns, and a shotgun—shoot and kill 26 people in 2012, 20 of them schoolchildren between the ages of six and seven?[45]

Levin and Fox argue that factors such as frustration, isolation, blame, loss, failure, and other external and internal motivations and situational elements contribute to the activities of mass murders. They delineate three types of contributing factors: *predisposers*, "long-term and stable preconditions that become incorporated into the personality of the killer," which are nearly always present in his or her biography; *precipitants*, "short-term and acute triggers," that is, catalysts; and *facilitators*, conditions, usually situational, that "increase the likelihood of a violent outburst but are not necessary to produce that response."[46] Using this typology to explain why, for example, most mass murderers are middle-aged, Levin and Fox contend that it takes a long time to accumulate the kind of rage and frustration that sets off some mass murderers. Mass murderers often select targets that have some significance for them, such as workers at a site of former employment. As Fox and Levin state, "A majority of mass killers target victims who are specially chosen, not just in the wrong place at the wrong time. The indiscriminate slaughter of strangers by a 'crazed' killer is the exception to the rule."[47] Unlike serial murderers, mass murderers are usually easy to apprehend because they rarely leave the scene of their crime either because they commit suicide after the killing or because they stay long enough to be detected.

Rape

The FBI began using a new gender-neutral definition of rape for statistical reporting purposes in 2012. The definition of **rape** now used by the FBI reads "The penetration, no matter how slight, of the vagina or anus with any body part or object, or oral penetration by a sex organ of another person, without the consent of the victim."[48] In keeping with the revised terminology, the CJIS Division of the FBI revised its definition of forcible rape, also making it gender-neutral. Under the FBI's UCR program, the term **forcible rape** now means "the carnal knowledge of a person forcibly and against their will."[49]

LEARNING OUTCOMES 6 Show how definitions of rape differ and describe the various perspectives that have been offered to explain the crime of rape.

UCR/NIBRS statistics on rape, as currently reported, include cases of both rape and attempted rape. Statutory rape (sexual relations between an underage female minor and an adult male) and other sex offenses are excluded from the count of rape crimes. In 2012, 84,376 rapes were reported nationwide under the UCR Program, a slight increase over the previous year. The rate of reported forcible rape was officially put at 53.8 rapes per 100,000 women. As Figure 9–7 shows, the risk of sexual assault victimization for both females and males varies greatly by age. Figure 9–8 details the age at time of first rape victimization among females.

Reports to the police of the crime of rape rarely reveal its true incidence. In 2011, the National Center for Injury Prevention and Control (a part of the federal Centers for Disease Control and Prevention) released its *National Intimate Partner and Sexual Violence Survey*. Using data from a 2010 survey, the report showed

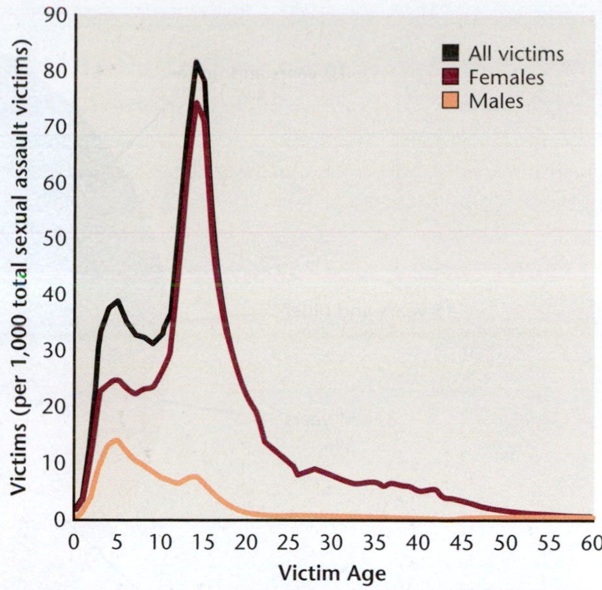

FIGURE 9–7 **Sexual Assault Victimization Rates by Age and Sex.** *Source:* Office of Juvenile Justice and Delinquency Prevention, *Juvenile Offenders and Victims: 2006 National Report* (Washington, DC: OJJDP, 2006), p. 31.

Think About It…

As this chapter shows, the FBI began using a new definition of rape for statistical reporting purposes in 2012. What was the old definition? What is the new one? Why did the FBI change its definition of rape?

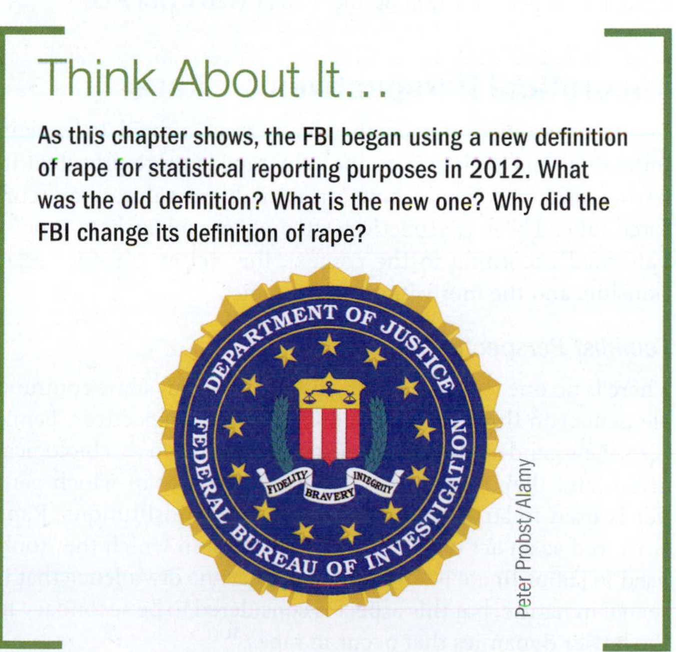

Peter Probst/Alamy

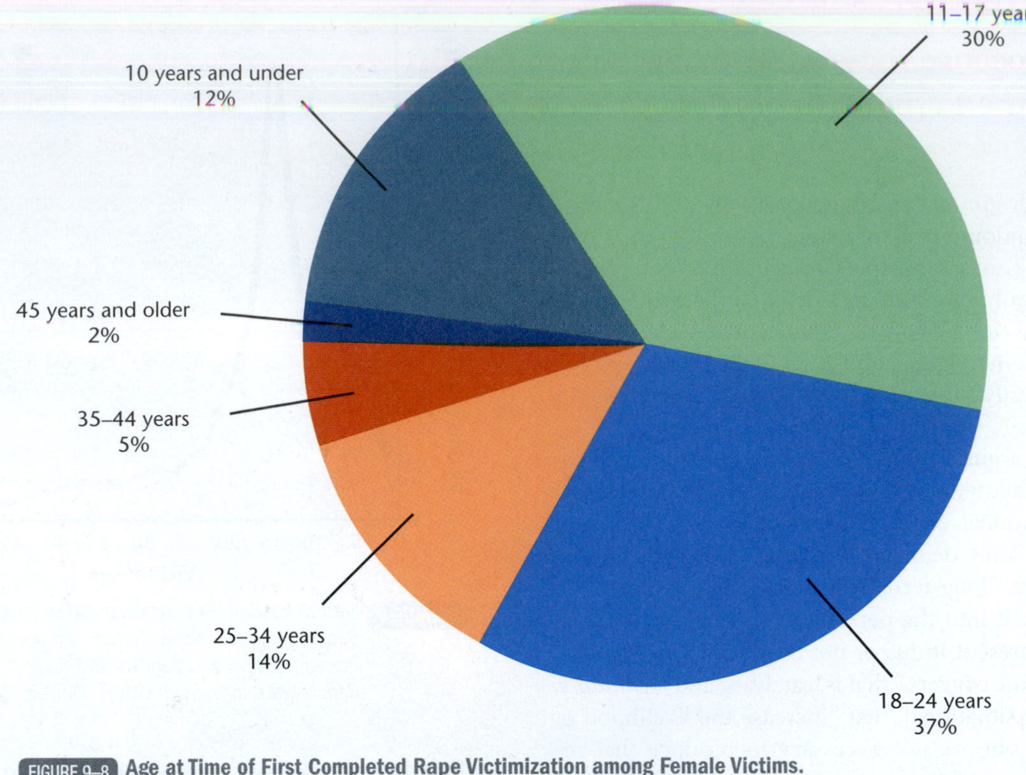

FIGURE 9–8 **Age at Time of First Completed Rape Victimization among Female Victims.**
Source: Centers for Disease Control, National Center for Injury Prevention and Control, *The National Intimate Partner and Sexual Violence Survey Factsheet* (Atlanta, GA: Centers for Disease Control and Prevention, National Center for Injury Prevention and Control, November 2011).

that nearly 1 in 5 women (18.3%) and 1 in 71 men (1.4%) in the United States have been raped at some time in their life, including completed forced penetration, attempted forced penetration, or alcohol- or drug-facilitated completed penetration. The survey also found that 51.1% of female victims of rape reported being raped by an intimate partner and 40.8% by an acquaintance.[50] Read the executive summary of the National Intimate Partner and Sexual Violence Survey at on the Web at **Web Extra 9-3**.

Theoretical Perspectives on Rape

Several theoretical perspectives have been offered to explain individual motivations for rape, why rape is more prevalent in particular contexts, and how certain cultural values may reinforce rape. These perspectives attempt to explain how rape is patterned according to the context, the victim–offender relationship, and the motivations of the rapist.

Feminist Perspectives

There is no one feminist perspective on rape, but some common elements run through the various feminist perspectives. Feminists view gender as a social construct rather than as a biological given, and they regard as problematic the way in which gender is used to structure social relations and institutions. Rape is viewed as an act of power or domination in which the "tool" used to subordinate is sexual. Rape is a crime of violence that is sexual in nature, but this aspect is considered to be secondary to the power dynamics that occur in rapes.[51]

Socialization patterns, cultural practices, structural arrangements, media images, norms surrounding sexuality, and women's status in society all combine to create a rape culture in which both men and women come to view male aggression as normal.[52] Within this culture, which feminist thinkers repudiate, women are blamed for their own rape by virtue of the fact that males are naturally incapable of controlling their sexual desire.

The Psychopathological Perspective

The psychopathological perspective on rape is based on two assumptions: (1) Rape is the "result of idiosyncratic mental disease," and (2) "it often includes an uncontrollable sexual impulse."[53] While acknowledging that rape is connected to issues such as power and anger, **Nicholas Groth**,[54] based on an analysis of 348 imprisoned convicted rapists, found that 55% reported that rape was committed to exert control over the women—a type of crime Groth labeled *power rape*. Power rapists, unlike anger rapists, did not purposefully set out to harm the victim. Power rapes are generally planned, Groth said, "although the actual assault may be opportunistic in origin."[55] In the attacks that Groth labeled *anger rapes*, which totaled about 40% of the sample, the men attacked their victims in anger; usually, the attack was impulsive and involved no prior planning on the part of the offender. These assaults were often quite brutal, and following the rape, the offender felt relief because he was able to relieve his anger. The remaining 5% were considered *sadistic rapes* because they involved a combination of power and anger motives and often involved torture.[56]

Evolutionary/Biological Perspectives

Within the evolutionary perspective, "propagation is the key to survival of a trait, as a genetic predisposition can be passed on only through offspring."[57] Natural selection favors those traits that are most adaptive, and over several generations, it is these traits that survive. An evolutionary perspective does not identify rape per se as an adaptation; rather, it focuses on certain motives and ends that are conducive to rape. According to Randy Thornhill and Craig T. Palmer, "[s]election favored different traits in females and males, especially when the traits were directly related to mating. Although some of these differences could have arisen from what Darwin called natural selection, most of them are now believed to have evolved through sexual selection."[58] *Sexual selection* refers to the fact that some traits appear to survive not because they are related to survival, but because they increase the attraction of mates or the defense against competition over mates. This is said to apply primarily to males because "male fitness is limited by access to the opposite sex much more directly than is female fitness, with the result that females compete for mates much less than do males."[59] The evolutionary perspective has been severely criticized for justifying rape as "natural." Proponents of the usefulness of evolutionary perspectives argue that "biology provides understanding, not justification, of human behavior."[60]

Typologies of Rapists

Several researchers have attempted to develop typologies of rapists. Nicholas Groth's work represented one of the first systematic attempts to do this based on empirical evidence, gathered in his capacity as a prison psychologist. As noted, Groth identified three types of serial rapists: the anger rapist, the power rapist, and the sadistic rapist.[61] Similarly, **Robert R. Hazelwood** and **Ann Burgess** developed a four-part typology of rapists based on the motivation of the offender and revolving around the themes of power, anger, and sadism:[62] power–assertive, power–reassurance, anger–retaliatory, and anger–excitation.

Based on interviews with 61 serial rapists (all incarcerated in a South Carolina maximum-security prison for the crime of rape), Dennis J. Stevens offered a typology of his own based on motivations. Using Groth's "Protocol for the Clinical Assessment of the Offender's Sexual Behaviors" to structure the interview, Stevens explored the areas of premeditation, victim selection, style of attack, degree of violence associated with the rape, accompanying fantasies, and role of aggression. One of his major findings was the role of lust as a primary motive among a large proportion of the rapists (42%). While acknowledging that "lust is not a new idea concerning predatory rape," Stevens believed it to be a primary rather than a secondary motive for

WHO'S TO BLAME—The Individual or Society

Exotic Dancer Claims Rape

Twenty-one-year-old Carla Truluv called 9-1-1 from her cell phone at 3:00 A.M. on a Sunday morning, telling the 9-1-1 operator who answered that she had just been raped.

"Ma'am, are you injured? Are you in need of immediate medical assistance?" the operator asked.

"No, no, I'm okay," Carla told her.

"Are you safe? Is anyone threatening you? Is anyone there with you?" the operator continued.

"I'm okay. I'm back home. Alone," Carla said.

Carla gave her address, and the operator dispatched a patrol car to the location.

The female officer who arrived encouraged Carla to go with her to the hospital for an examination and for evidence collection. Once Carla had been signed in at the emergency room, the officer took a report of the incident.

Carla described herself as an exotic dancer and for-hire personal companion, who spent her evenings entertaining men of all ages. "I show them a good time," she said, "and there's nothing illegal about that. But that don't give them the right to rape me," she told the officer.

Carla then went on to tell the officer how she had been hired by two men who were attending a local convention to come to their hotel room with a friend and put on a show. "Dancing, that's all we were supposed to do," she said. The men, she said, called a number of their friends into their room to watch the show. At some point, Carla told the officer, she had to go to the bathroom. That's when, she said, a man followed her and pushed her into the small room, locking the

Michael Kemp/Alamy

door behind them. "That's when it happened," she said. "He put his hand around my throat, and he raped me."

Think About It

1. Assuming that Carla is telling the truth about what happened, how would you explain this crime? That is, why did it happen, and how might it have been prevented?
2. In your opinion, does Carla bear any responsibility for her own victimization? Why or why not?

Note: Who's to Blame boxes provide fictionalized critical thinking opportunities, and are not actual cases.

rapists.[63] A constant theme emerging throughout Stevens's interviews with the rapists was that for most of them, the amount of force that accompanied the rape was just enough to accomplish the victim's submission, but in cases in which extreme violence accompanied all stages of the rape, the violence would have been present regardless of the level of victim resistance. Therefore, one of the conclusions reached by Stevens is that advocating the idea that women should not resist their attackers is ill-advised.

Another way to approach a typology of men who rape is represented in the work of **Diana Scully**, a professor at Virginia Commonwealth University.[64] Scully's research involved intensive interviews with 114 convicted rapists in seven prisons, all of whom volunteered to be interviewed. Scully rejected the psychopathological perspective on rape and instead employed a feminist sociocultural perspective premised on several assumptions. First, rape is "socially learned behavior," involving "not only behavioral techniques, but also a host of values and beliefs, like rape myths, that are compatible with sexual aggression against women."[65] This premise is based on the assumption that both positive and negative forms of social behavior are learned "socially through direct association with others as well as indirectly through cultural context."[66] Second, Scully viewed rape not as a reflection of pathology but as a reflection of a continuum of normality in which it is important to understand "how sexual violence is made possible in a society [and] what men who rape gain from their sexually violent behavior."[67] Scully thus approached these interviews with convicted rapists from the feminist perspective of wanting to understand the explanations given by the rapists and their sociocultural beliefs about women and sexual violence. Scully identified several patterns to the rationalizations used by men who rape, and she organized these according to two broad types of rapists: admitters and deniers.

In the interviews, Scully explored how these two groups could operate from an understanding of reality that justified their behavior and tended to normalize it as well as what they gained from such behavior. Although some of the rapists in the admitter group relied on rape myth ideology, this was a more prevalent pattern among the deniers. The rape myths' definition of a very narrow group of individuals as legitimate rape victims was a common theme in the interviews given by these rapists. Although variations existed, the majority of rapists in both groups expressed little guilt or empathy for their victims. Read more about the violent criminal victimization of women in America via **Web Extras 9–4** and **9–5**.

Changing Understandings of Rape

The crime of rape has generated much controversy over the years. To understand why, it is important to examine the changing legal definitions of *rape* as well as our societal understanding of rape.

Until the 1970s in the United States and the 1980s in Canada, most jurisdictions followed a **common law definition of rape**, which saw the crime as "carnal knowledge of a woman not one's wife by force or against her will." Rape was construed quite narrowly and specifically and did not recognize men as victims. The law also did not recognize rape within marriage, did not

Rape shield laws, first introduced in the 1970s, were intended to protect rape victims by ensuring that defendants did not introduce irrelevant facts about the victim's sexual past into evidence.

allow for acts of sexual penetration other than vaginal penetration by a penis, and did not allow for various means by which force could occur. Moreover, the rules of evidence required that the victim who claimed rape had to demonstrate physical resistance to the attack and must have some form of corroboration (such as physical injuries) to show that the rape had actually occurred. The victim's previous sexual history could be admitted as relevant information. Furthermore, the understanding of rape relied on gender stereotypes in which only certain kinds of women were deemed to be credible victims and only certain kinds of men were regarded as possible offenders.

Rape Law Reform

Rape law reform attempted to make statutory definitions of rape compatible with those of other violent crimes. Rape investigations, especially at the trial stage, too often forced the victim through further trauma rather than focusing on assessing the offender's guilt or innocence.[68] Feminist groups were joined by law enforcement officials and prosecutors who supported efforts "to remove obstacles to the apprehension and conviction of offenders."[69] In 1975, Michigan became the first state to dramatically redefine *rape* to encompass a broader range of sexually assaultive behaviors, circumstances, and victims. Other states followed Michigan's lead, and by 1992, all states had made significant statutory changes to the common law offense definition of rape.[70]

In one key way, individual rape law reform in states and at the federal level proceeded along a common route: **rape shield laws**. Rape shield laws, first introduced in the 1970s, were intended to protect rape victims by ensuring that defendants did not introduce irrelevant facts about the victim's sexual past into evidence. Previously, no guidelines prevented the defense from bringing into evidence the victim's sexual history as a way to discredit her. Rape shield laws sent the message that the courts would no longer be a party to a "second assault" on the victim.[71]

▶ *Rape: A Closer Look*

Although rape can occur in almost any social context, certain social situations are characterized by a higher prevalence of rape and by a difference in the offender's motivation.

LEARNING OUTCOMES
7
Summarize the various types and patterns of rape and violence against women.

Acquaintance Rape

The vast majority of rapes occur when the victim and the offender have some prior relationship—although not necessarily an intimate or familial one. Some researchers and activists who work with rape victims have stated that **acquaintance rape** is the most common scenario for rapes. Among adults, acquaintance rape usually occurs within the context of a dating relationship and is sometimes referred to as *date rape*.

Researchers have identified college campuses as places that typically have a high incidence of rape. Societal awareness and concern for rape on college campuses did not emerge until the 1980s. Helping to publicize the problem have been a number of high-profile rape cases on college campuses in which the victims not only went public with their experiences, but also grabbed headlines and the covers of major publications such as *Time*, *Newsweek*, and *People*.[72] Media publicity has emphasized the reality of the college setting as a site of rape, and in 1992, the Campus Sexual Assault Victims' Bill of Rights Act became law.[73] It requires campus authorities to "conduct appropriate disciplinary hearings, treat sexual assault victims and defendants with respect, making their rights and legal options clear, and cooperate with them in fully exercising those rights."[74]

A great deal of the research on rape in college settings has focused on identifying the unique factors of campus life that may be conducive to rape. Some researchers contend that college fraternities "create a sociocultural context in which the use of coercion in sexual relations with women is normative and in which the mechanisms to keep this pattern of behavior in check are minimal at best and absent at worst."[75] The increased awareness of campus rape has led to the development of services and programs that assist victims of sexual violence and present information that challenges rape myths. A National Institute of Justice's report, *The Sexual Victimization of College Women*, is posted at **Web Extra 9-6**.

Spousal Rape

As previously mentioned, until the 1970s, under common law, a legally married husband could not be charged with raping his wife. Rape, as research indicates, happens to many women within marriage as part of a practice of *spousal abuse* that may involve beatings and other violence. Until 1976, **spousal rape** could not be prosecuted in any state. Today, it is illegal in every state in the United States.

The first researcher to systematically examine spousal rape was **Diana E. H. Russell**. Based on an analysis of interview data, Russell developed a four-part typology of men who rape their wives:

- Husbands who prefer raping their wives to having consensual sex with them
- Husbands who are able to enjoy both rape and consensual sex with their wives or who are indifferent to which it is
- Husbands who would prefer consensual sex with their wives but are willing to rape them when their sexual advances are refused
- Husbands who might like to rape their wives but do not act out these desires

Thus, rather than being one-dimensional, rape within marriage has several forms that reflect the various nuances of motivation on the part of offenders.

Prison Rape

Prison rape, which is generally considered to involve physical assault, represents a special category of sexual victimization behind bars. In 2003, Congress mandated the collection of statistics on prison rape as part of the Prison Rape Elimination Act (PREA)[76] with the goal of reducing the number of incidents of rape in prison.

The PREA requires the Bureau of Justice Statistics (BJS) to collect data in federal and state prisons, county and city jails, and juvenile institutions, with the U.S. Census Bureau acting as the official repository for collected data.

In 2013, the BJS published the results of its third annual National Inmate Survey (NIS).[77] The survey was conducted in 233 state and federal prisons, 358 local jails, and 15 special confinement facilities operated by Immigration and Customs Enforcement (ICE). A total of 92,449 inmates participated. The survey was also administered to 527 juveniles ages 16 to 17 held in state prisons and 1,211 juveniles of the same age held in local jails. Among the findings:

- An estimated 4.0% of state and federal prison inmates and 3.2% of jail inmates reported experiencing one or more incidents of sexual victimization by another inmate or facility staff in the past 12 months.
- Among state and federal prison inmates, 2.0% (or an estimated 29,300 prisoners) reported an incident involving another inmate, 2.4% (34,100) reported an incident involving facility staff, and 0.4% (5,500) reported both an incident by another inmate and by staff.
- About 1.6% of jail inmates (11,900) reported an incident with another inmate, 1.8% (13,200) reported an incident with staff, and 0.2% (2,400) reported both an incident by another inmate and by staff.
- An estimated 1.8% of juveniles ages 16 to 17 held in adult prisons and jails reported being victimized by another inmate, compared to 2.0% of adults in prisons and 1.6% of adults in jails; an estimated 3.2% of juveniles ages 16 to 17 held in adult prisons and jails reported experiencing staff sexual misconduct.
- Inmates who reported their sexual orientation as gay, lesbian, bisexual, or other were among those with the highest rates of sexual victimization. Among non-heterosexual inmates, 12.2% of prisoners and 8.5% of jail inmates reported being sexually victimized by another inmate; 5.4% of prisoners and 4.3% of jail inmates reported being victimized by staff.

PREA surveys are only a first step in understanding and eliminating prison rape. As the BJS notes, "Due to fear of reprisal from perpetrators, a code of silence among inmates, personal embarrassment, and lack of trust in staff, victims are often reluctant to report incidents to correctional authorities."[78]

Lee H. Bowker, a criminologist who specializes in studying life inside prisons, summarizes studies of sexual violence in prison with the following observations:[79]

- Most sexual aggressors do not consider themselves homosexuals.

- Sexual release is not the primary motivation for sexual attack.
- Many aggressors must continue to participate in gang rapes to avoid becoming victims themselves.
- The aggressors have themselves suffered much damage to their masculinity in the past.

As in cases of heterosexual rape, sexual assaults in prison are likely to leave psychological scars on the victim long after the physical event is over.[80] Victims of prison rape live in fear, may feel constantly threatened, and can turn to self-destructive activities.[81] Many victims question their masculinity and undergo a personal devaluation.

Child Sexual Abuse (CSA)

Child sexual abuse (CSA) is a term encompassing a variety of criminal and civil offenses in which an adult engages in sexual activity with a minor, exploits a minor for purposes of sexual gratification, or exploits a minor sexually for purposes of profit. The term includes a variety of activities and motivations, including child molestation, child sexual exploitation (CSE), and the commercial sexual exploitation of children (CSEC).

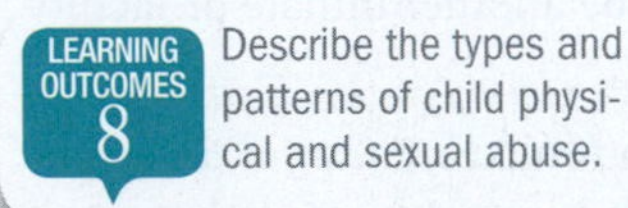

Describe the types and patterns of child physical and sexual abuse.

The National Institute of Justice (NIJ) observes that "few criminal offenses are more despised than the sexual abuse of children, and few are so little understood in terms of incidence (the number of offenses committed), prevalence (the proportion of the population who commit offenses), and reoffense risk."[82]

The NIJ also notes that sexual offenses are more likely than other types of criminal conduct to elude the attention of the criminal justice system. Self-reports from both sex offenders and sexually abused children reveal far more abuse than officially reported.[83] The Child Molestation Research and Prevention Institute, based in Atlanta, Georgia, estimates that at least two out of every ten girls and one out of every ten boys are sexually abused by the time they turn 14.[84]

One of the most informative offender self-report studies on the adult sexual victimization of children comes from research conducted slightly more than two decades ago.[85] In that study, investigators recruited 561 adult subjects who engaged in what the researchers described as "child-focused sexual behavior." The subjects, who were guaranteed anonymity, were recruited through health care workers, through media advertising, through presentations at meetings, and in other ways. All were free from confinement at the time of the interviews. The 561 adults interviewed reported a total of 291,737 "paraphiliac acts" over the course of their adult lives committed against 195,407 victims under the age of 18. The results of this study make it clear that in cases of CSA, a relatively small number of offenders can commit a large number of crimes.

Self-reports from both sex offenders and sexually abused children reveal far more abuse than officially reported.

Types of Child Sex Abusers

Almost all pedophiles are male, with one study of more than 4,400 offenders finding fewer than 0.5% of convicted child sex offenses committed by females.[86] Other than that, little can be said about similarities among child sexual abusers. As individuals, they tend to be highly dissimilar from one another in terms of personal characteristics, life experiences, and criminal histories. No single "molester profile" exists.[87] Child molesters appear to arrive at deviancy via multiple pathways and engage in many different sexual and nonsexual "acting-out" behaviors. Figure 9–9 shows the number of registered predatory child sex offenders by state.

In 1983, Nicholas Groth and his associates proposed a simple two-part distinction among pedophiles whereby offenders were classified as either "regressed" or "fixated."[88] Regressed offenders, said Groth, are attracted sexually primarily to their own age groups but are passively aroused by minors. Generally speaking, the use of alcohol, drugs, or other inhibition-lowering substances, combined with social circumstances providing opportunity, can cause the regressed offender to act out his or her interest in having sexual encounters with children. Fixated offenders, said Groth, are adult pedophiles who engage in planned sexual acts with children and whose behavior is not necessarily influenced by drugs or alcohol.

A U.S. Department of Justice publication representing a compilation of studies produced by the NIJ shows that most victims of childhood sexual abuse do not go on to become child molesters.[89] However, the NIJ points out that sexual victimization as a child, if accompanied by other factors—such as the co-occurrence of physical and verbal abuse—may contribute to the child-victim's development as a perpetrator of CSA later in life. Similarly, says the NIJ, social competence deficits are significant in child molestation, but an individual's inadequate social and interpersonal skills do not, by themselves, make his or her sexual abuse of children inevitable.

Some evidence exists to suggest that child molestation may be related to an offender's restaging of his or her own childhood sexual victimization.[90] Tests of the restaging theory on a sample of 131 rapists and child molesters revealed that child molesters who committed their first assault when they were 14 or younger were sexually victimized at a younger age than offenders who committed their first assault in adulthood; they also experienced more severe sexual abuse than offenders with adult onset of sexual aggression.[91]

Nonetheless, sexual victimization alone is unable to fully explain child molestation. Studies show that most victims of childhood sexual abuse do not go on to become perpetrators.[92] As is true for other kinds of maltreatment, childhood sexual victimization may be one critical element in the presence or absence of a variety of other factors (for example, co-occurrence of other types of abuse, availability of supportive caregivers, ego strength of child-victim at the time of abuse, and availability of treatment), all of which appear to moderate the likelihood of becoming a child molester.

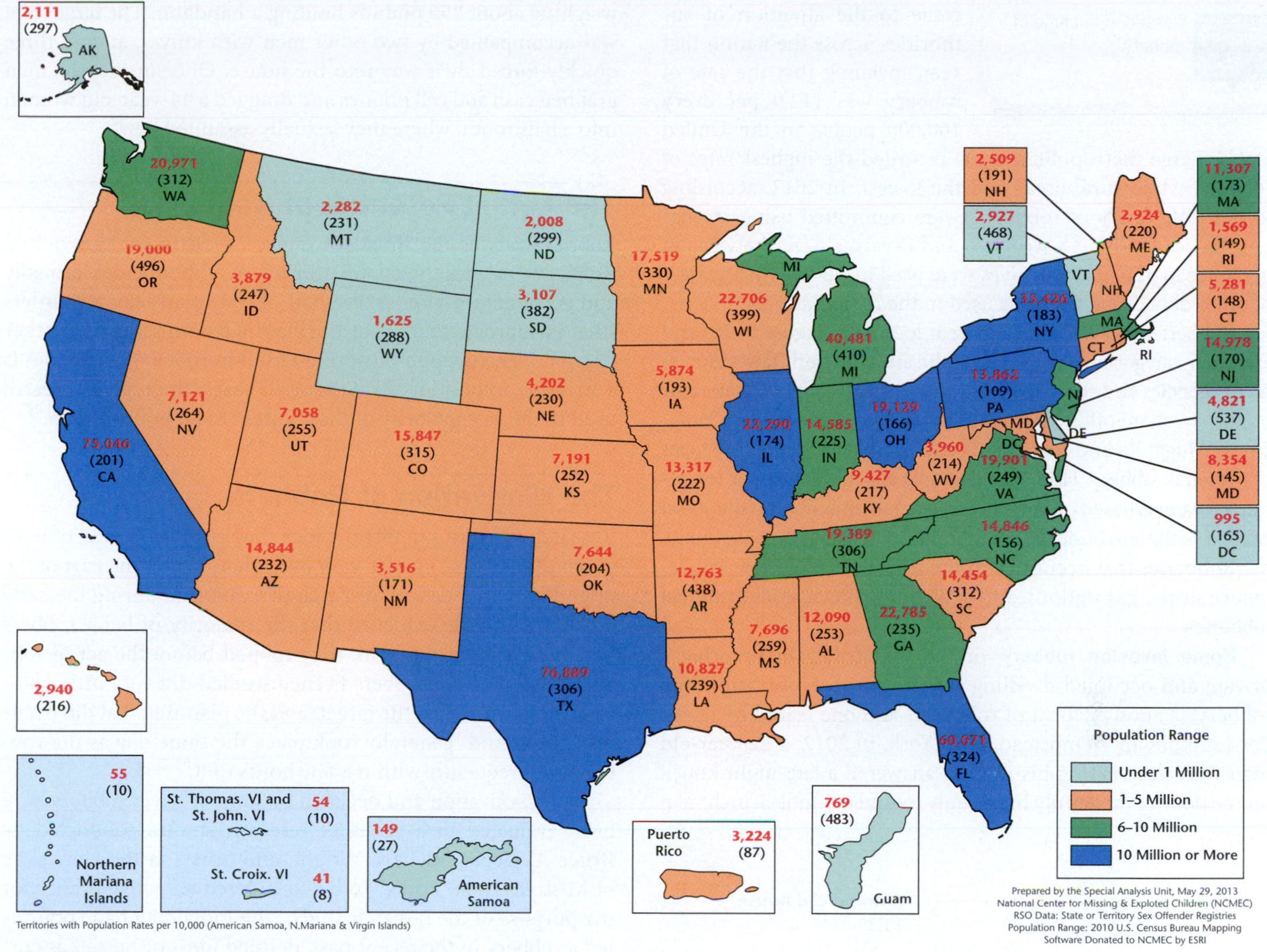

FIGURE 9–9 **Registered Sex Offenders by State.**
Source: National Center for Missing & Exploited Children. Copyright by National Center for Missing & Exploited Children. Used by permission of National Center for Missing & Exploited Children..

Not all adults involved in the sexual abuse of children pursue personal sexual gratification. Some have a profit motive, as is the case in instances of *commercial sexual exploitation of children*, or CSEC. CSEC refers to all offenses in which an adult victimizes a child sexually for profit, including the prostituting of a child and creating or trafficking in child pornography.

Awareness of **child pornography** exploded onto the American scene in the 1990s, as the advent of rapid transmission of high-quality images and video became possible through the growth of the Internet. Child pornography can be defined as a visual representation of any kind that depicts a minor engaging in sexually explicit conduct that is obscene and that lacks serious literary, artistic, political, or scientific value.

The Internet created special problems in enforcement of the laws designed to control pedophiles and child pornographers. Because it is an international medium, the Internet is hard to police, and activities through which information on the Internet is transmitted may be illegal in one jurisdiction and not so in another. Similarly, the relative anonymity of buyers and sellers of child pornography over the Internet provides both a sense of security and impersonality to those involved in such transactions.

According to the United Nations Children's Fund (UNICEF), tens of thousands of children in the United States and tens of millions of children worldwide are involved in CSEC.[93] UNICEF says the number of sexually exploited children worldwide may exceed 100 million, not all of whom are located in "poor" or "developing" countries. Read a comprehensive report on the commercial sexual exploitation of children in the United States, Canada, and Mexico via **Web Extra 9–7**.

Some evidence exists to suggest that child molestation may be related to an offender's restaging of his or her own childhood sexual victimization.

Robbery

Robbery is classified as a violent crime because it involves the threat or use of force. It is, however, a property crime as well in that the express purpose of robbery is to take the property of another.[94] UCR/NIBRS data for 2012 show that 354,520 robberies

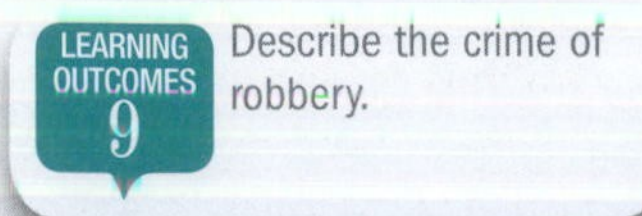

Describe the crime of robbery.

came to the attention of authorities across the nation that year, meaning that the rate of robbery was 112.9 per every 100,000 people in the United States. Large metropolitan areas recorded the highest rates of robbery, while rural areas had the lowest. In 2012, according to the FBI, 42.5% of robberies were committed using strong-arm tactics (without a weapon) and firearms were the weapon of choice in 41% more. Knives were used in 7.8%, with a variety of other dangerous weapons used in the remainder.

Robberies can occur in different locations (Figure 9–10) and are often categorized according to location by both law enforcement agencies and social science researchers. Robberies that occur on the street are often referred to as **highway robberies**, or "muggings." Muggings and robberies that happen in residences are types of personal robbery. Homes and people appear as more or less attractive targets based on their perceived vulnerability and the social context of the surrounding neighborhood in which they are found.

Robberies that occur in commercial settings, such as convenience stores, gas stations, and banks, are known as **institutional robberies**.[95]

Home invasion robbery, or the act of illegally entering a private and occupied dwelling for the purpose of committing robbery, is another form of robbery—and one feared by many. For example, in Hempstead, New York, in 2012, a 22-year-old man who was visiting his mother answered a late-night knock on the door of the family home only to find a 6-foot-3-inch man weighing about 250 pounds holding a handgun. The large man was accompanied by two other men with knives, and all three quickly forced their way into the house. Once inside, the men grabbed cash and cell phones and dragged a 44-year-old woman into a bathroom, where they sexually assaulted her.[96]

Commercial house 13.3%
Gas or service station 2.4%
Convenience store 5.1%
Residence 16.9%
Bank 1.9%
Miscellaneous 16.9%
Street/highway 43.5%

FIGURE 9–10 **Robbery Locations.**
Source: Federal Bureau of Investigation, *Crime in the United States, 2012* (Washington, DC: FBI, 2013).

The Lethal Potential of Robbery

Robbery carries the threat of injury or death for the victim. Robbery provides the context for 6% of all homicides annually and accounts for almost one-half (42%) of all felony murders (that is, murders that occur during the commission of another felony).[97] The weapon most often used in robbery homicides is a firearm, accounting for 42% of all cases; the type of firearm used in the vast majority of these cases (85%) is a handgun.[98]

The Motivation of Robbers

Research tends to support the idea that most robberies, of both people and places, involve very little planning on the part of the offender. Floyd Feeney's research in California during the early 1970s found little evidence that the majority of bank robbers had even been in the bank they robbed before the act of robbery.[99] Most of the robbers Feeney studied did very little planning, no matter what the target, and the planning that did occur was minor and "generally took place the same day as the robbery and frequently within a few hours of it."[100]

The motivation and decision making of street robbers have been evaluated in a series of research studies conducted by Bruce A. Jacobs, Richard Wright, and others at the University of Missouri at St. Louis. To be considered an active robber for the purpose of the research study, "the individual had committed a robbery in the recent past, defined him- or herself as currently active, and was regarded as active by other offenders."[101] Researchers found that the decision to offend, like other decisions, occurs as part of ongoing social action that is "mediated by prevailing situations and subcultural conditions."[102] "Fast cash" is the direct need that robbery satisfied, but this need can be properly understood only against the backdrop of street culture. Jacobs and Wright hypothesized that street culture was the intervening force that connected background factors (such as low self-esteem, deviant peer relations, and weak social bonds) to the motivation to offend. They found that the majority of robbers gave little thought to planning robberies until they found themselves needing money. For less than half of the robbers, the financial need was for basic necessities; mostly, it was connected to a fairly hedonistic lifestyle. The daily activity of most street robbers was characterized as a "quest for excitement and sensory stimulation" with a "general lack of social stability" in terms of residence or ties to conventional activities or institutions.[103]

Jacobs and Wright conclude that the economic motivation behind robbery should not be interpreted as "genuine financial hardship," but as a constant ongoing crisis situation experienced as a result of the logic of the street context of robbers' daily lives.[104] For the individuals whom Jacobs and Wright interviewed, "being a street robber is a way of behaving, a way of thinking, an approach to life."[105]

Robbery is perhaps the most gender-differentiated serious crime in the United States.

The Gendered Nature of Robbery

According to researcher Jody Miller, "[w]ith the exception of forcible rape, robbery is perhaps the most gender differentiated serious crime in the United States."[106] Women represent robbery offenders in only 11% of all incidents.[107] Miller's research goal was to assess the extent to which gender organizes robbery offending. To accomplish this, she analyzed a subset of the interviews with active robbers from the research data used by Jacobs and Wright. The sample that Miller used consisted of 37 robbers, 14 of whom were women and 23 of whom were men. Miller found that economic incentives were the primary motivation among both men and women. There were, however, significant differences in the way in which men and women carried out street robberies. Men exhibited a fairly uniform pattern. Their robberies were characterized by "using physical violence and/or a gun placed on or at close proximity to the victim in a confrontational manner."[108] The presence of a gun was almost a constant in robberies conducted by men. While perceiving women to be easier targets, male robbers tended to rob men rather than women because of the perception that men carried more money. The majority of the males targeted as victims were those involved in "street life."

Female robbers, on the other hand, did not exhibit one clear style; instead, they tended to fall into one of three patterns. The robbery of other women in a "physically confrontational manner" was the most prevalent way in which female robbers worked, but also present were the strategies of using their sexuality to attract male victims and acting as accomplices to male robbers in offenses against other men.[109] Except when robbing men, female robbers, as a general rule, did not use guns. Miller concludes that rather than reflecting different motivations, the different strategies for robbery selected by men and women "reflect practical choices made in the context of a gender-stratified environment—one in which, on the whole, men are perceived as strong and women are perceived as weak."[110] Although similar cultural and structural forces can drive the offending of men and women in the same way, gender continues to exert an influence on shaping the nature of these interactions in robbery incidents. Up-to-date robbery information from the Bureau of Justice Statistics can be seen at **Web Extra 9–8**.

Aggravated Assault

On Christmas Eve, 2011, Jacquetta Simmons, 26, a Batavia, New York, resident was arrested after she punched a Walmart female greeter in the face and knocked her down, resulting in fractures to her facial bones.[111] The greeter had asked Simmons to see receipts for items she was carrying before she hit the greeter and ran out of the store. Employees and customers gave chase and held Simmons until police arrived. A state police spokesperson later told reporters that Simmons, who was charged with two counts of assault, had store receipts for everything in her possession.

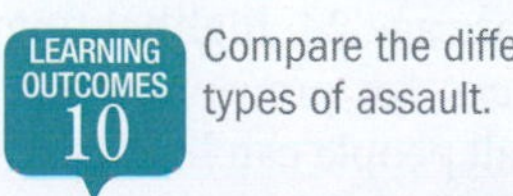

LEARNING OUTCOMES 10 Compare the different types of assault.

There are two types of assault: simple and aggravated. **Aggravated assault**, which the FBI defines as "the unlawful attack by one person upon another wherein the offender uses a weapon or displays it in a threatening manner, or the victim suffers obvious or severe bodily injury,"[112] is the more serious type of assault and the one that concerns us here. According to the FBI, 760,739 aggravated assaults were reported to police agencies across the nation in 2012, producing an aggravated assault rate of 242.3 for every 100,000 people in the country.

The profile of a typical offender in aggravated assault mirrors that of homicide, with disproportionate involvement of males, African Americans, 15- to 34-year-olds, those of lower-socioeconomic status, those with prior arrest records, and offenders demonstrating little evidence of offense specialization.[113] Also consistent with most homicides, aggravated assaults are "spontaneous, triggered by a trivial altercation or argument that quickly escalates in the heat of passion."[114]

Based on statistics from the National Crime Victimization Survey (NCVS), which tallies simple as well as aggravated assault, the majority of assaults reported by victims to NCVS interviewers are simple rather than aggravated assault. According to the NCVS, the overall decline in the nation's crime rate between 1993 and 2012 was mostly due to decreases in the rate of simple assault.

Aggravated assaults are distinguished according to those involving injury and those not involving injury. The victims and offenders in aggravated assault are, for the most part, equally likely to be strangers or nonstrangers to each other. When you look at the gender of the victim, a pattern emerges. A slight majority of male victims are assaulted by a stranger, whereas slightly more than one-third (39%) of female victims are assaulted by a stranger in aggravated assaults. Simple assaults, by contrast, are more likely to involve nonstrangers (58%). Almost one-half (47%) of male victims are assaulted by nonstrangers, whereas 71% of female victims are assaulted by nonstrangers in these cases. Whether it is an aggravated or simple assault, the largest category of nonstranger offenders of female victims is represented by friends and acquaintances followed by intimate partners. Weapons are present in less than one-fourth (23%) of all assaults, and when a weapon is present, it is most likely to be something other than a gun or a knife.[115]

Stranger Assault

The possibility of stranger violence elicits a great deal of fear and concern among most members of the population. But based on research using victimization data in both the United States and Great Britain, "the probability of suffering a serious personal crime by strangers is very low,"[116] with this likelihood varying by demographic characteristics such as gender, age, ethnicity, marital status, and lifestyle. For example, individuals who have an active social life away from home and in the evening are far more likely to be victimized by strangers, but this effect depends very much on the community context in which the individuals engage in their leisure pursuits.

Assault within Families

The majority of assaults involve victims and offenders who are known to each other, quite often in a familial or intimate relationship. Criminology as a discipline began to give more attention to violent behavior within the family just as society began viewing the wall of privacy that has long surrounded the family with a bit more scrutiny. The family as a social institution is intensely private, and the discussion of physical, emotional, and sexual violence among family members invades this privacy. These types of abuse also represent extremely sensitive parts of a person's experience, which individuals may be reluctant to discuss. Two of the most common reasons for not reporting crimes to the police are that it was a "private matter" and that there might be reprisal from the offender. Current research shows that such rationales supporting nonreporting continue to characterize incidents involving violence among family members.[117]

Initial research on violence within the family came from official records and small clinical studies that consistently revealed that women were more likely than men to become victims. Based on an examination of emergency room victims in the late 1970s, Evan Stark and colleagues found that approximately 25% of all women who had been injured had been the victim of a spousal attack.[118]

In the years since survey research was first used to estimate violence against family members, other surveys have emerged to assess this phenomenon and existing data sources have been improved to better measure family violence. NIBRS data reveal that while assault is the most frequently occurring violent crime both among the general population and within the family, the percentage is even higher within the family.[119]

Compared with aggravated assaults generally, firearms are less likely to be used within the family; instead, fists, hands, and knives are more common. A slight majority of aggravated assault offenses involve some type of injury both in the general population (57.5%) and within the family (60.8%). Women are more likely to be the victims of both aggravated assaults and simple assaults within the family than in the general population (60% versus 41% and 72% versus 60%, respectively).[120]

Intimate Partner Violence

Intimate partner violence (IPV), a special area of study in criminology, includes sexual violence, physical abuse, and stalking. According to the 2010 National Intimate Partner and Sexual Violence Survey, which was conducted by the National Center for Injury Prevention and Control (part of the Centers for Disease Control and Prevention), rates of sexual violence, stalking, and IPV are alarmingly high for adult Americans. The survey found that IPV alone affects more than 12 million people each year and that women are disproportionately impacted. Female victims experience far higher rates of severe IPV, rape, and stalking and suffer from long-term chronic disease and other health impacts as a result of that violence—such as symptoms of post-traumatic stress disorder (PTSD).

The majority of assaults involve victims and offenders who are known to each other.

Intimate partner assault is one of several terms used to characterize assaultive behavior that takes place between individuals involved in an intimate relationship. Several researchers have noted that terms such as *spouse assault* are inappropriate because they give the misleading impression that male and female spouses are equally likely to be victims.[121] The overwhelming majority of victims of marital violence within heterosexual relationships are women. This empirical reality does not deny that men can be the victims of violence at the hands of their wives; it merely acknowledges that based on official records, self-reports, hospital emergency room records, and small clinical samples, it is women who emerge as victims.

Assault between intimate partners that results in a breakup of the relationship is referred to as **separation assault**.[122] Separation assault illustrates what feminists such as Liz Kelly mean when they say "the use of explicit force/violence is in fact a response to the failure of, or resistance to, other forms of control."[123] A woman who attempts to leave a violent relationship might be seen as violating the right of her husband to control her, and even if she does manage to leave, many times the husband will follow her and attempt to take her back. Physical assaults often involve other tactics of abuse, such as emotional abuse and attacks or threats against children. This is especially salient in that most women who have reported abuse by intimate partners also had dependent children.[124]

Generally speaking, results from the National Intimate Partner and Sexual Violence Survey reveal that female victims experience multiple forms of IPV, whereas male victims most often experience only physical violence. The survey found that nearly 1 in 10 women in the United States (9.4%) has been raped by an intimate partner in her lifetime and that an estimated 16.9% of women and 8.0% of men have experienced sexual violence other than rape by an intimate partner at some point in their lifetime. According to the survey, more than 1 in 3 women experienced multiple forms of rape, stalking, or physical violence in 2010, and 92.1% of male victims experienced physical violence alone and 6.3% experienced physical violence and stalking (Figure 9–11). The NISVS also shows that most rape and IPV are first experienced before age 24, highlighting the importance, according to researchers, "of preventing this violence before it occurs to ensure that all people can live life to their fullest potential."[125]

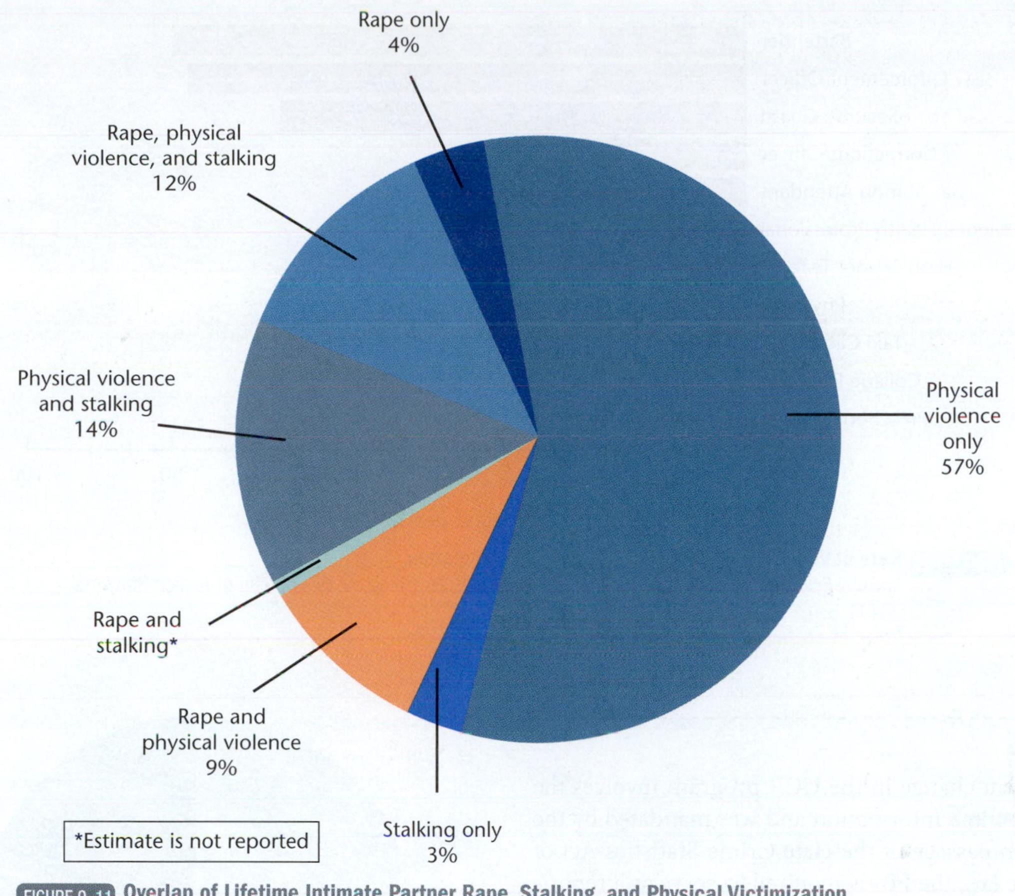

FIGURE 9–11 **Overlap of Lifetime Intimate Partner Rape, Stalking, and Physical Victimization.**
Source: Centers for Disease Control and Prevention, National Center for Injury Prevention and Control, *The National Intimate Partner and Sexual Violence Survey: Factsheet 2010* (Atlanta, GA: Centers for Disease Control and Prevention, National Center for Injury Prevention and Control), p. 2.

Other Forms of Interpersonal Violence

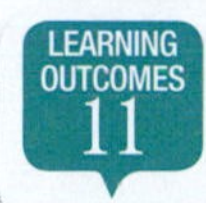

Describe other violent crimes, including hate crimes, workplace violence, and stalking.

This chapter concludes with an overview of three special forms of interpersonal violence: (1) workplace violence, (2) hate crimes, and (3) stalking.

Workplace Violence

Workplace violence (murder, rape, robbery, and assault committed against persons who are at work or on duty) is a significant problem in America today. The FBI says that "workplace violence is now recognized as a specific category of violent crime that calls for distinct responses from employers, law enforcement, and the community." In a given year, approximately 570,000 nonfatal violent crimes (rape/sexual assault, robbery, and aggravated and simple assault) occurred against persons aged 16 or older while they were at work or on duty, based on findings from the NCVS.[126] Assaults, both simple and aggravated, account for the largest number of workplace violence incidents, affecting approximately 11.7 out of every 1,000 persons in the workforce annually. Another 520 or so work-related homicides occur annually.[127] About 70% of workplace homicides are committed by robbers and other assailants and about 21% are committed by work associates.[128] Workplace violence accounts for approximately 18% of all violent crime that occurs in the United States. As might be expected, police officers experience workplace violence at rates higher than people employed in almost any other occupation, whereas college and university professors are among those least likely to be victimized (Figure 9–12) Learn more about occupational and workplace violence at **Web Extra 9–9**.

All workplace violence falls into four broad categories, as follows:

Type 1. Violent acts by criminals who have no other connection with the workplace, but enter to commit robbery, acts of terrorism, or another crime

Type 2. Violence directed at employees by customers, clients, patients, students, inmates, or any others for whom an organization provides services

Type 3. Violence against coworkers, supervisors, or managers by a present or former employee

Type 4. Violence committed in the workplace by someone who doesn't work there, but has a personal relationship with an employee, such as an abusive spouse or domestic partner

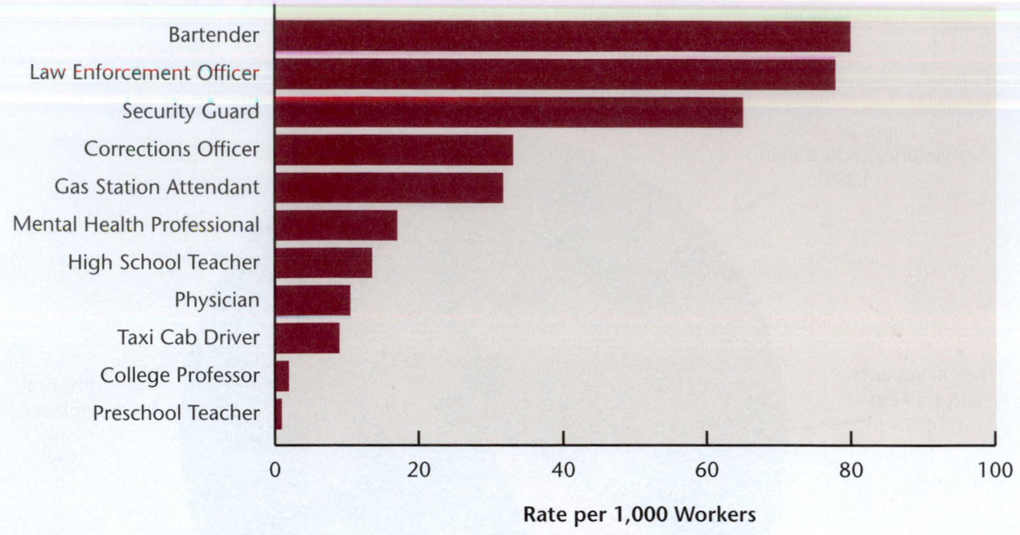

FIGURE 9–12 **Rate of Violent Workplace Victimization by Occupation.**
Source: Erika Harrell, *Workplace Violence, 1993–2009* (Washington, DC: Bureau of Justice Statistics, 2011), p. 4.

Hate Crimes

An important recent change in the UCR program involves the collection of **hate crime** information and was mandated by the U.S. Congress with passage of the Hate Crime Statistics Act of 1990.[129] Under the law, the FBI is required to serve as a repository for data collected on crimes motivated by religious, ethnic, racial, or sexual orientation prejudice. The Violent Crime Control and Law Enforcement Act of 1994[130] mandated the addition to the hate crimes category of crimes motivated by biases against people with disabilities, and the UCR program began reporting such crimes in 1997.

According to the BJS, hate crimes, also called "bias crimes," are crimes characterized by "manifest evidence of prejudice based on race, religion, sexual orientation, or ethnicity, including where appropriate the crimes of murder, non-negligent manslaughter, forcible rape, aggravated assault, simple assault, intimidation, arson, and destruction, damage, or vandalism of property."[131] Figure 9–13 shows the motivational bases of the 5,790 hate-crime incidents that were reported in 2012. Hate-crime resources of the National Criminal Justice Reference Service are available at **Web Extra 9–10**.

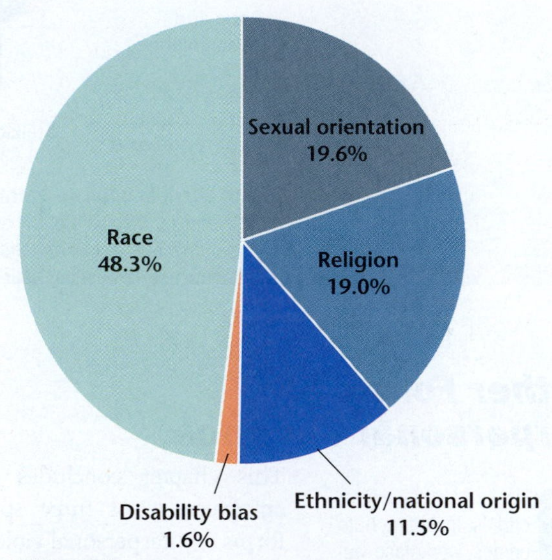

FIGURE 9–13 **Motivation of Hate-Crime Offenders, 2012.**
Source: Based on data from FBI, *Hate Crime Statistics: Incidents and Offenses, 2012*, http://www.fbi.gov/about-us/cjis/ucr/hate-crime/2012/topic-pages/incidents-and-offenses/incidentsandoffenses_final (accessed October 7, 2014).

Stalking

Although **stalking** behavior is not new, the labeling of such behavior as criminal is relatively recent. Stalking can be defined as a course of conduct directed at a specific person that involves visual or physical proximity, nonconsensual verbal communication, or implied threats that would cause a reasonable person fear. All states and the federal government have antistalking laws. Rather than being an offense that occurs once, stalking is a repeated pattern of behavior that causes victims to fear for their personal safety.

Statutory definitions of *stalking* encompass a number of diverse but interrelated behaviors, such as making phone calls, following the victim, sending letters, making threats in some manner, vandalizing property, and watching the victim. Rather than viewing these behaviors in isolation from one another, antistalking laws take into account the totality of the circumstances, so that seemingly benign behaviors are seen in light of how they are connected to other behaviors. This acknowledges that while sending unwanted letters might be seen as innocuous behavior, when this activity is combined with following the victim and standing outside his or her place of work or residence, the behavior takes on a more threatening tone and may be the precursor for more serious offenses such as assault, rape, and murder.[132]

The only national-level data on the nature and extent of stalking come from the National Violence Against Women Survey (NVAWS). For behavior to satisfy the definition of *stalking* used in the NVAWS, the respondents had to have reported victimization on more than one occasion and to have reported that they were "very frightened or feared bodily harm."[133]

Employing these criteria, the survey asked individuals to report relevant experiences both over their lifetime and during the past 12 months. Approximately 8% of women and 2% of men reported being stalked at some point in their life. Using the survey data to generate estimates for the general population, this means that about 1 in every 12 women (8.2 million) and 1 in every 45 men (2 million) are stalked at some point in their life. An overwhelming majority (90%) of individuals surveyed reported being stalked by only one individual.[134] When a lower threshold of reported fear is used to measure stalking, the estimates are even higher: 12% of women and 4% of men reported being stalked at some point, and 6% of women and 1.5% of men reported being stalked annually.[135]

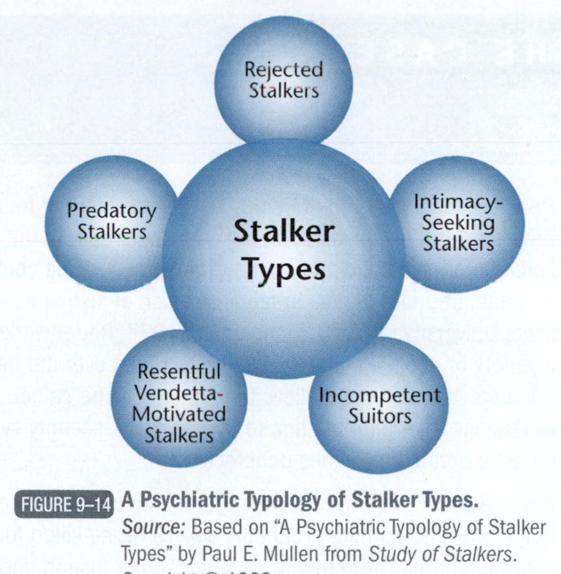

FIGURE 9–14 **A Psychiatric Typology of Stalker Types.**
Source: Based on "A Psychiatric Typology of Stalker Types" by Paul E. Mullen from *Study of Stalkers*. Copyright © 1999.

Types of Stalkers

A psychiatric study of 145 Canadian stalkers who had been referred to a forensic psychiatry center for treatment found that most were men (79%) and that many were unemployed (39%).[136] Perhaps not surprisingly, most (52%) had never had an intimate relationship. Five types of stalkers were identified (Figure 9–14):

- **Rejected stalkers** who pursue their victims to reverse, correct, or avenge a felt rejection (for example, divorce, separation, or termination)
- **Intimacy-seeking stalkers** who want to establish an intimate, loving relationship with their victims and may see the victim as a soul mate with whom they are fated to have a relationship with
- **Incompetent suitors** who have a romantic or sexual interest in their victims despite having poor social or courting skills
- **Resentful vendetta-motivated stalkers** who act out of a sense of wrong or a grievance against their victims and whose intent is generally to frighten and distress the victim
- **Predatory stalkers** who spy on their victims in preparation for attacks, which are usually sexual in nature

Delusional disorders were found to be common among the stalkers treated, and 30% were determined to suffer consistently from delusions about those they stalked. Stalking behavior among those studied lasted anywhere from 4 weeks to 20 years, with an average of 12 months. Rejected and intimacy-seeking stalkers tended to persist the longest in stalking behavior. Sixty-three percent of the stalkers made threats toward their victims, and 36% were assaultive. The researchers concluded that "stalkers have a range of motivations, from reasserting power over a partner who rejected them to the quest for a loving relationship."[137]

Cyberstalking

Another type of stalking, **cyberstalking**, has received attention as efforts progress to better understand the consequences of our increased reliance on electronic communication and the Internet.[138] Although no standard definition of cyberstalking exists, this term refers to the use of technology, such as email and the Internet, to harass individuals. Learn more about stalking by visiting the National Center for Victims of Crime's Stalking Resource Center at **Web Extra 9–11**.

THE CASE

Dennis Rader (The BTK Killer)

Travis Heying/Associated Press

Dennis Rader was born March 9, 1945, the eldest of four brothers. After high school, he did a four-year stint in the U.S. Air Force before returning to Park City, Kansas, where he completed an undergraduate degree in administration of justice at Wichita State University in 1979. Beginning in 1974, Rader worked in a variety of positions at ADT Security Services over the next 14 years. Investigators believe that knowledge he gained in this experience later enabled him to bypass home security systems so as to break into homes undetected.[i]

It was also in 1974 that Rader's murderous criminal career began. On the morning of January 15, 1974, he killed four members of the Otero family, including father Joseph, mother Julie, 11-year-old Josephine, and 9-year-old Joseph II. Each victim was subjected to various acts of torture before ultimately being killed. The two males died from asphyxiation after Rader tied them up at gunpoint and placed plastic bags over their heads. The females were strangled, with Rader later reporting that the mother woke up after he thought she was dead and had to be strangled again. In court testimony many years later, he attributed the killings to sexual needs, and he apparently molested at least one of the females. The four bodies were discovered when 15-year-old Charlie Otero returned from school later that afternoon.[ii]

The Otero murders were the start of a long series of murders. Kathryn Bright, 20, was stabbed to death just three months later, on April 4, 1974. Amazingly, her 19-year-old brother, Kevin, survived the attack by Rader despite being shot twice in the head.

Almost three years elapsed before the BTK struck again on March 17, 1977, by strangling 26-year-old Shirley Vian. Uncharacteristically, the BTK locked the three young Vian children in the closet, permitting them to survive. Just nine months later, on December 8, 1977, police found Nancy Jo Fox, 25, dead in her bedroom, strangled with a nylon stocking. BTK's final three killings occurred on April 27, 1985 (Marine Hedge), September 16, 1986 (Vicki Wegerle), and January 18, 1991 (Dolores Davis); all were strangled.[iii]

A strange component of the BTK murders was the way the killer periodically wrote taunting letters to the local police and newspapers. His goal seemed to be to receive some kind of credit for the murders. In some writings, he expressed his indignation that other suspects were being accused of crimes he had committed or that the story of his murderous activities was not receiving adequate press coverage. "How many do I have to kill before I get my name in the paper or some national attention?" he complained in the letter in which he also coined his BTK nickname.[iv]

The frequency of the BTK letters decreased by the end of the 1980s, as he apparently became dormant. In 1991, Rader became a Park City Compliance Officer,[v] where he developed a reputation as a by-the-book "bureaucratic bully."[vi]

In March 2004, new BTK letters began surfacing. Over the course of the next year, a total of 11 communications were received. One, which had been mailed to police on a computer floppy disk, was forensically identified as having been created on Rader's church computer and had electronic residue that included the name *Dennis*. That disk led directly to Rader's arrest on February 25, 2005. At his arraignment on May 3, Rader stood mute and a trial date of June 27 was set.

Rader subsequently surprised everyone when, on June 27, he confessed in open court to the murders of ten people. In response to direct questioning from the judge, Rader recounted in chillingly graphic and dispassionate detail exactly how he had killed each of his victims.

Author's Note: Graphic testimony from Dennis Rader's 2007 trial is available at http://www.kansas.com/2005/06/28/16541/raders-testimony.html.

Notes

[i]"Neighbors Paint Mixed Picture of BTK Suspect," MSNBC, February 27, 2005, http://www.msnbc.msn.com/id/7036219 (accessed June 16, 2007).

[ii]Marilyn Bardsley, Rachael Bell, and David Lohr, "BTK–Birth of a Serial Killer," CourtTV Crime Library, http://www.crimelibrary.com/serial_killers/unsolved/btk/index_1.html (accessed June 16, 2007).

[iii]Ibid.

[iv]"Neighbors Paint Mixed Picture of BTK Suspect," MSNBC.

[v]"Report: Daughter of BTK Suspect Alerted Police," Cable News Network, April 19, 2005.

[vi]Bardsley et al., "BTK–Birth of a Serial Killer."

The case of Dennis Rader raises a number of interesting questions. Among them are the following:

1. **Does Rader fit the profile of serial killers described in this chapter? Why or why not?**
2. **Why did Rader kill? What other motivations might serial killers have?**
3. **How was Rader able to hide his crimes for so long?**
4. **What can Rader's behavior help us understand about serial killers?**

CHAPTER 9 Crimes against Persons—*What We Fear*

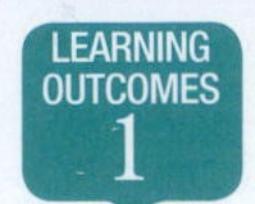

Describe the major national crime-data-gathering programs and explain the differences between them.

Today's official U.S. crime statistics come from the Bureau of Justice Statistics (BJS), which conducts the annual National Crime Victimization Survey (NCVS), and from the Federal Bureau of Investigation (FBI), which publishes yearly data under its summary-based Uniform Crime Reporting (UCR) program and its more detailed National Incident Based Reporting System (NIBRS). Both the UCR and NIBRS compile data on reported or discovered crimes, although the latter provides a more complete picture of crimes reported and committed. NCVS data are gathered through an annual national household survey.

1. What are the main differences between the National Crime Victimization Survey (NCVS) and the Uniform Crime Reports (UCR)? Which do you think is more accurate?
2. How does the National Incident Based Reporting System (NIBRS) enhance UCR data?

National Crime Victimization Survey (NCVS) An annual survey of selected American households conducted by the Bureau of Justice Statistics to determine the extent of criminal victimization—especially unreported victimization—in the United States.

Uniform Crime Reporting (UCR) program A Federal Bureau of Investigation data-gathering initiative that provides an annual tally of statistics consisting primarily of information on crimes reported to the police and on arrests.

National Incident Based Reporting System (NIBRS) An enhanced statistical reporting system to collect data on each incident and arrest within 22 crime categories.

LEARNING OUTCOMES 2

Summarize various types and patterns of murder.

Homicide is the willful killing of one human being by another, whereas murder is an unlawful homicide. Some homicides, such as those committed in defense of oneself or one's family, may be justifiable and therefore legal. Criminal homicide refers to causing the death of another person without legal justification or excuse. Jurisdictions generally distinguish among various types of murder, including first-degree murder, second-degree murder, negligent homicide, and felony murder.

1. What different kinds of murder were discussed in this chapter?
2. What is felony murder? How does it differ from other types of murder?

murder The willful (nonnegligent) and unlawful killing of one human being by another.

criminal homicide The causing of the death of another person without legal justification or excuse.

first-degree murder Criminal homicide that is planned or that involves premeditation.

second-degree murder Criminal homicide that is unplanned and is often described as "a crime of passion."

negligent homicide The act of causing the death of another person by recklessness or gross negligence.

felony murder A special class of criminal homicide in which an offender may be charged with first-degree murder when that person's criminal activity results in another person's death.

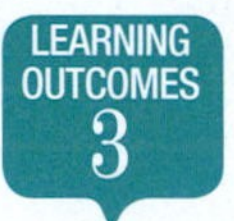

Provide a closer look at the crime of murder.

A closer look at homicide statistics tells us about the nature of the relationship between the victim and the offender, the types of weapons used, and the most likely time and location of occurrence.

1. What key issues must be considered in explaining patterns of homicide?
2. What is a sibling offense? How is a sibling offense related to the crime of homicide?

primary homicide A murder involving a family member, friend, or acquaintance.

expressive homicide A criminal offense that results from acts of interpersonal hostility, such as jealousy, revenge, romantic triangles, and quarrels.

nonprimary homicide A murder that involves a victim and an offender who have no prior relationship and that usually occurs during the course of another crime, such as robbery.

instrumental crimes Goal-directed offenses that involve some degree of planning by the offender and little or no precipitation by the victim.

sibling offense An offense or incident that culminates in homicide. The offense or incident may be a crime, such as robbery, or an incident that meets a less stringent criminal definition, such as a lover's quarrel involving assault or battery.

victim precipitation Contributions made by the victim to the criminal event, especially those that led to its initiation.

Key Name

Robert Nash Parker A criminologist who conducted the first systematic research focused on differentiating homicide according to the victim–offender relationship.

LEARNING OUTCOMES 4

Define *serial murder* and list the different types of serial killers.

Serial murder is criminal homicide that "involves the killing of several victims in three or more separate events." Typologies of serial killers are organized around different, but generally related, themes. Some criminologists identify four different types of serial killers: visionary serial killers, comfort serial killers, hedonistic serial killers, and power seekers.

1. What is serial murder? What are the different types of serial killers?

serial murder Criminal homicide that "involves the killing of several victims in three or more separate events."

visionary serial killers Serial killers who hear voices and have visions that are the basis for a compulsion to murder.

comfort serial killers Serial killers who are motivated by financial or material gain.

hedonistic serial killers Serial killers who murder because they find it enjoyable and derive psychological pleasure from killing.

power seekers Serial killers who operate from some position of authority over others.

Key Names

James Alan Fox and ***Jack Levin*** Criminologists who believe that the vast majority of serial killers are not legally insane or medically psychotic.

LEARNING OUTCOMES 5

Explain how mass murder differs from serial murder and list the different types of mass murderers.

Mass murder involves the killing of a number of victims at the same location and within a compressed time frame. Mass murderers may be of the revenge, love, profit, or terror type.

1. What is mass murder? What different types of mass murderers were discussed in this chapter?
2. How does mass murder differ from serial murder?

mass murder The illegal killing of four or more victims at one location within one event.

LEARNING OUTCOMES 6

Show how definitions of rape differ and describe the various perspectives that have been offered to explain the crime of rape.

Some of the definitions of rape that this chapter considers are the common law definition, the revised FBI definition, and the definition of forcible rape. Earlier definitions allowed only for the rape of a female and incorporated the term *carnal knowledge* to describe the type of act that constituted rape. Contemporary definitions tend to be gender-neutral and count a variety of specific acts of sexual violence under the category of rape.

1. What is the common law definition of rape? Why is it is not gender-neutral?
2. What is the difference between the crimes of rape and forcible rape?

rape The penetration, no matter how slight, of the vagina or anus with any body part or object, or oral penetration by a sex organ of another person, without the consent of the victim.

forcible rape The carnal knowledge of a person forcibly and against their will.

common law definition of rape The carnal knowledge of a woman, not one's wife, by force or against her will.

rape shield laws Statutes intended to protect rape victims by ensuring that defendants do not introduce irrelevant facts about the victim's sexual past into evidence.

Key Names

Nicholas Groth A criminologist who found that over half of rapists reported that they committed the crime to exert power and control over women.

Robert R. Hazelwood and ***Ann Burgess*** Developers of a four-part typology of rapists based on the motivation of the offender, and revolving around the themes of power, anger, and sadism.

Diane Scully A researcher who interviewed rapists, concluding that rape was not a reflection of pathology but rather a reflection of a continuum of normality in which it is important to understand "how sexual violence is made possible in a society [and] what men who rape gain from their sexually violent behavior."

LEARNING OUTCOMES 7

Summarize the various types and patterns of rape and violence against women.

Acquaintance rape is the most common scenario for rapes. Among adults, acquaintance rape usually occurs within the context of a dating relationship and is sometimes referred to as *date rape*. Spousal rape is another type of sexual assault that may involve beatings and other violence. Rape in prison or in other institutions is an additional type of rape that this chapter discusses.

1. What is acquaintance rape? How common is it? What are the most common social contexts in which it is likely to occur?
2. What key issues are to be considered in explaining as well as preventing the crime of rape?

acquaintance rape Rape characterized by a prior social, although not necessarily intimate or familial, relationship between the victim and the perpetrator.

spousal rape The rape of one spouse by the other. The term usually refers to the rape of a woman by her husband.

Key Name

Diana E. H. Russell A researcher who found that rather than being one-dimensional, rape within marriage has several forms that reflect the various nuances of motivations on the part of others.

LEARNING OUTCOMES 8

Describe the types and patterns of child physical and sexual abuse.

Child abuse varies in terms of the age and gender of the child, the kind of abuse (physical, sexual, or a combination of both), whether it is accompanied by verbal abuse or other forms of co-abuse, and who commits it (a parent, caregiver, teacher, or stranger).

1. What is child pornography? How does it differ from child sexual abuse?

child sexual abuse (CSA) Encompasses a variety of criminal and civil offenses in which an adult engages in sexual activity with a minor, exploits a minor for purposes of sexual gratification, or exploits a minor sexually for purposes of profit.

child pornography A visual representation of any kind that depicts a minor engaging in sexually explicit conduct that is obscene and that lacks serious literary, artistic, political, or scientific value.

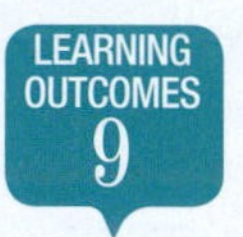

Describe the crime of robbery.

Robbery is classified as a violent crime because it involves the threat or use of force. It is, however, also a property crime in that the express purpose of robbery is to take the property of another. Robberies can also be classified in terms of where they occur, leading to a three-part distinction to include highway robberies, institutional robberies, and home invasion robberies.

1. What are the different types of robbery?
2. Which form of robbery is most common?

robbery The taking of or attempting to take anything of value under confrontational circumstances from the control, custody, or care of another person by force or threat of force or violence and/or by putting the victim in fear of immediate harm.

highway robberies Robberies that occur on the highway or street or in a public place (and are often referred to as "muggings").

institutional robberies Robberies of commercial establishments, such as convenience stores, gas stations, and banks.

home invasion robbery The act of illegally entering a private and occupied dwelling for the purpose of committing robbery.

Compare the different types of assault.

This chapter discusses four types of assault: aggravated assault, simple assault, intimate partner assault, and stranger assault. The first two are distinguished by their severity, and the last two are distinguished by the nature of the relationship between the offender and the victim.

1. What's the difference between simple and aggravated assault?
2. What is an intimate partner? What is intimate partner assault?

aggravated assault The unlawful attack by one person upon another wherein the offender uses a weapon or displays it in a threatening manner, or the victim suffers obvious or severe bodily injury."

intimate partner violence (IPV) A special area of study in criminology that includes sexual violence, physical abuse, and stalking committed by a current or former partner or spouse of the victim.

intimate partner assault A gender-neutral term used to characterize assaultive behavior that takes place between individuals involved in an intimate relationship.

separation assault Violence inflicted by partners on significant others who attempt to leave an intimate relationship.

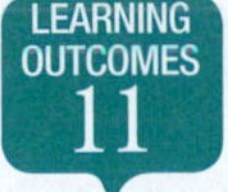

Describe other violent crimes, including hate crimes, workplace violence, and stalking.

This chapter concludes with an overview of three special forms of interpersonal violence: workplace violence, hate crimes, and stalking.

1. Define workplace violence. What do we know about the offense?
2. What is hate crime? What kinds of hate crimes are most common?
3. What is cyberstalking? How does it differ from the traditional crime of stalking?

workplace violence The crimes of murder, rape, robbery, and assault committed against people who are at work or on duty.

hate crime A criminal offense in which the motive is hatred, bias, or prejudice based on the actual or perceived race, color, religion, national origin, ethnicity, gender, or sexual orientation of another individual or group of individuals. Also called *bias crime*.

stalking A course of conduct directed at a specific person that involves repeated visual or physical proximity; nonconsensual communication; verbal, written, or implied threats; or a combination thereof that would cause a reasonable person fear.

cyberstalking The use of technology, such as email and the Internet, to harass individuals.

"... the professional thief rejoices in the welfare of the public. He would like to see society enjoy continuous prosperity, for then his own touches will naturally be greater."

—*Chic Conwell in Edwin Sutherland's* The Professional Thief

10 Crimes Against Property—It's What We Lose

1. **Summarize the nature and pattern of property crime.**
2. **Describe the crime of burglary and various forms of burglary.**
3. **Describe the crime of larceny-theft and the various kinds of theft.**
4. **Describe identity theft and some of the techniques used by identity thieves.**
5. **Describe the crime of motor vehicle theft.**
6. **Summarize the characteristics of arson.**
7. **Distinguish between persistent and professional thieves.**
8. **Expound upon the three basic categories of burglars and detail the process of target selection in burglary.**
9. **Characterize burglars and their motivation.**
10. **Describe the role and various types of fences and criminal receivers.**

Paolese/Fotolia

THEFT ON THE JOB

In 2012 Pedro Antonio Marcuello Guzman, 46, and Maria Martha Elisa Ornelas Lazo, 50, were arrested and charged with possession of stolen goods when they tried to sell a painting created in 1925 by the French Impressionist Matisse.[1] The painting, titled *Odalisque a la culotte rouge,* depicts a bare-chested woman sitting cross-legged on the floor wearing a pair of scarlet trousers. It is estimated to be worth over $3 million, and had been stolen from the Caracas Museum of Contemporary Art in Venezuela a decade earlier. Guzman and Lazo, who admitted knowing that the painting was stolen, had offered to sell it for $740,000 to undercover agents from the Federal Bureau of Investigation (FBI) posing as art collectors.

Art theft can be a lucrative business. In May 2010, a lone thief stole five paintings from the Paris Museum of Modern Art, including works by Picasso and Matisse.[2] Estimates put the value of the art stolen at hundreds of millions of dollars. Two years prior to the Paris incident, armed robbers stole four paintings from a private museum in Zurich, Switzerland, with an estimated value of $163 million. The art included works by van Gogh and Monet, some of which were recovered. Similarly, in 2007, three paintings by Pablo Picasso were stolen in two separate incidents—one in Brazil and the other in Paris, France. The latter involved a nighttime burglary at the home of one of Picaso's granddaughters. Art thefts are relatively common, and occur with great regularity.

The largest art theft in U.S. history took place at the Isabella Stewart Gardner Museum in Boston in 1990, when thieves made off with several paintings worth more than $300 million. In that case, two people disguised as Boston police officers entered the museum, incapacitated security guards, and made off with the paintings as well as surveillance tapes.[3] Learn more about art theft at **Web Extra 10–1**.

SuperStock/Glow Images

Henri Matisse's painting, "Pastoral" (1905), stolen from the National Museum of Modern Art in Paris in 2010. The painting remains unrecovered. Do you think that most art thieves know the value of the art that they steal?

DISCUSS **Few people realize that art theft can be big business. What other forms of theft can you think of that have a high-profit potential, but are out of the ordinary?**

Types of Property Crime

LEARNING OUTCOMES 1 Summarize the extent and patterning of property crime.

Both the Uniform Crime Reporting (UCR) Program and the National Crime Victimization Survey (NCVS) report data on property crimes. According to the FBI, the major **property crimes** are burglary, larceny, motor vehicle theft, and arson. Definitions used by the FBI for statistical data-gathering purposes are shown in Figure 10–1.

Burglary

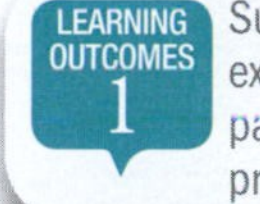

LEARNING OUTCOMES 2 Describe the crime of burglary and various forms of burglary.

Burglary is a common crime. The FBI defines **burglary** as the unlawful entry into a structure for the purpose of felony commission, generally a theft. The structure may be a business, a residence, or some other type of building. Force is not a necessary ingredient of burglary, and various types of burglaries can be identified (see Figure 10–2).[4] Based on a recent examination of victimization data, 72% of households within the United States are burglarized at least once.[5] In contrast to lifetime risk, however, the risk of burglary occurring within any given year is much lower. Even so, burglary is feared because the offense invades the sanctity of the home and threatens the existence of businesses.

In 2012, according to the FBI, there were an estimated 2,103,787 burglaries throughout the country. In that year, burglary accounted for 23.4% of the total number of property crimes committed. In 2012, burglary offenses cost victims an estimated $4.7 billion in lost property, and the average dollar

Force is not a necessary ingredient of burglary.

PROPERTY CRIMES	
Burglary	The unlawful entry of a structure to commit a felony or theft. The use of force to gain entry is not required to classify an offense as a burglary. Burglary is categorized into three subclassifications: forcible entry, unlawful entry where no force is used, and attempted forcible entry.
Larceny-Theft	The unlawful taking, carrying, leading, or riding away of property from the possession or constructive possession of another. It includes crimes such as shoplifting, pocket picking, purse snatching, thefts from motor vehicles, thefts of motor vehicle parts and accessories, and bicycle thefts in which no use of force, violence, or fraud occurs. Motor vehicle theft is also excluded from this category.
Motor Vehicle Theft	The theft or attempted theft of a motor vehicle. This offense includes the stealing of automobiles, trucks, buses, motorcycles, motor scooters, snowmobiles and so forth. The taking of a motor vehicle for temporary use by persons having lawful access is excluded from this definition.
Arson	Any willful or malicious burning or attempt to burn, with or without intent to defraud, a dwelling house, public building, motor vehicle or aircraft, or personal property of another. Only fires determined through investigation to be willfully or maliciously set are classified as arson.

FIGURE 10–1 **Property Crimes and Their Definitions.**
Source: Federal Bureau of Investigation, Uniform Crime Reporting Program.

loss per burglary offense was $2,230. Burglary of residential properties accounted for 74.5% of all burglary offenses, and 36% of residential burglaries occurred during the daytime, while 56.4% of nonresidential burglaries occurred during nighttime hours. As Chapter 1 pointed out, only about 15% of burglaries were cleared by arrest or other means in 2012.

In contrast to reports from the UCR and National Incident-Based Reporting System (NIBRS), NCVS statistics on burglary paint quite a different picture. The NCVS reported 3,764,540 household burglaries and attempted burglaries in 2012—nearly 90% more than UCR/NIBRS estimates.[6] Rates of burglary were generally higher for African American households than for white households, regardless of family income levels, although wealthy African American families had far lower burglary rates than did low-income white families.

According to UCR/NIBRS data for 2012, most burglaries involve forcible entry, followed in prevalence by unlawful entry and then by attempted forcible entry. Most residential burglaries are likely to occur during the day.[7] Most residential burglars commit their offenses at a time when residents are unlikely to be home. This is an important factor in their choice of target.

The consequences of both residential and commercial burglary can be profound for the victim. Residential burglaries, by definition, do not involve direct confrontation between

Attempted forcible entry	Force is used in an attempt to gain entry to a residence.
Attempted unlawful entry	No force is involved in an attempt to gain entry. An example is jiggling a door knob to see if the door is unlocked. The NCVS does not collect information about attempted unlawful entry.
Completed forcible entry	Force is used to successfully gain entry to a residence. Examples include breaking a window or slashing a screen.
Completed unlawful entry	No force is used but the residence is entered by someone having no legal right to be on the premises. Examples include entering through an unlocked door or an open window.
Completed burglary	Includes completed forcible entries and completed unlawful entries. Completed burglaries do not necessarily involve stolen or damaged property.

FIGURE 10–2 **Types of Burglary.**
Source: Jennifer Hardison Walters, et al., "Household Burglary, 1994–2011" (Washington, DC: Bureau of Justice Statistics, 2013).

the victims and the perpetrators, although the invasion of one's home produces a level of fear and apprehension beyond the dollar loss of the property taken. In cases of commercial burglary, because the targets are likely to be smaller, less stable businesses, the loss from burglaries can seriously affect the business's viability.[8]

The Social Ecology of Burglary

Burglary rates are higher in large metropolitan areas and in particular regions of the country, such as the South. Most research on variations in property crime at the aggregate level has examined how economics influences rates of crime. Lifestyle theory[9] and routine activities theory[10] have had a significant impact on explanations of how the nature and level of property crime offending have changed in response to alterations in the routine activities and structures of daily living. As Figure 10–3 shows, for a property crime to occur, three ingredients are necessary: (1) someone who wants something (a *motivated offender*) coming into direct contact with (2) someone who has that thing (a *suitable target*) and (3) the lack of anything or anyone to inhibit the crime (a *capable guardian*).

Advances in technology have made electronic devices lighter, smaller, and more portable. Hence, they've become more suitable targets because they are easier to steal.[11] Consequently, some of the observed changes in crime rates since the 1970s, when downsizing of electronics began in earnest, are not solely related to an increased supply of motivated offenders, but to changes in the patterns of routine activities. The basic contention of both lifestyle theory and routine activities theory is that what people do, where they do it, how often they do it, and with whom they do it all influence the risk of criminal victimization. The idea is to explore not why people commit crimes, but rather "how the structure of social life makes it easy or difficult for people to carry out these inclinations," which are taken as a given.[12] The structure of everyday life in one's city, neighborhood, home, workplace, and so forth, not only constrains the opportunity for individuals to act on inclinations to commit crimes, but also limits the ability of people to avoid victimization.

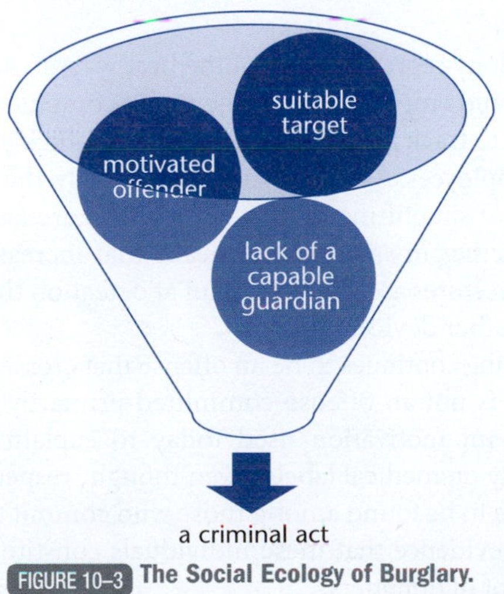

FIGURE 10–3 **The Social Ecology of Burglary.**

The structure of everyday life in one's city, neighborhood, home, workplace, and so forth, not only constrains the opportunity for individuals to act on inclinations to commit crimes, but also limits the ability of people to avoid victimization.

Residential Burglary

In a study of residential burglary, Lawrence E. Cohen and David Cantor set out to resolve often contradictory findings of previous research on the relationship between the impact of income and race on burglary victimization.[13] Cohen and Cantor found that, independent of race, the highest-income households and the lowest-income households in areas both within and outside the central city had the highest victimization risk. Their findings appear to show that both high-income and low-income households are targeted—one because it is thought to have items of special value and the other because it provides ease of access.

A 2013 Bureau of Justice Statistics special report on burglary showed that although household burglaries deceased by 56% between 1994 and 2011, completed burglaries involving the theft of an electronic device or household appliance increased from 28% to 34% of all burglaries over the same period. Similarly, the average dollar value of items and cash stolen increased by 54%—from $389 to $600 per year.[14]

The Costs of Burglary

According to the NCVS, well over three-fourths (86%) of all household burglaries involve some type of economic loss. Approximately 20% of household burglaries involve losses exceeding $1,000, with 21% involving loss amounts between $250 and $1,000, 24% involving loss amounts between $50 and $249, and slightly more than 14% involving losses under $50.[15] Remaining categories, not described here, total another 21%. Twenty-nine percent of items stolen from homes are personal in nature, with the largest category being jewelry or clothing. Household furnishings represent 11% of all stolen items, and tools and cash represent the items most likely to be stolen in about 12% (6% each) of incidents. Another type of crime cost can be gauged by looking at whether victims lose time from work as a result of their victimization. Among all victims of household burglaries, approximately 7% lose some time from work. Of this group, one-third lose less than one day and slightly over one-half lose anywhere from one to five days, with the remaining 7% losing six days or more.[16]

Another cost can be found in stability of residence. Using NCVS data to test the relationship between criminal victimization and a household's decision to move, research by criminologist **Laura Dugan** reveals that property crimes such as burglary have a greater effect on the decision to move than do violent crimes.[17]

Think About It…

This chapter says that for a property crime to occur, three ingredients are necessary: (1) a *motivated offender*, (2) a suitable target, and (3) the lack of a *capable guardian*. Using the example of a purse lying in an unlocked car, describe how each of these ingredients would apply.

Trombax/Fotolia

Larceny-Theft

Larceny-theft is defined by the UCR Program as "the unlawful taking, carrying, leading, or riding away of property from the possession, or constructive possession, of another."[18] Just about anything can be stolen. In 2013, for example, Kaven Kamooneh of suburban Atlanta was arrested by a Chamblee Police Department officer after he plugged his Nissan Leaf (an electric car) into an external outlet at the Chamblee Middle School while he watched his son play tennis. Although Kamooneh protested, saying that he had used only a few cents worth of electricity, a spokesperson for the police department told reporters for a local TV station that "A theft is a theft. He broke the law. He stole something that wasn't his."[19]

LEARNING OUTCOMES 3 Describe the crime of larceny-theft and the various kinds of theft.

The FBI reports that during 2012, there were an estimated 6.2 million larceny-thefts nationwide and larceny-thefts accounted for an estimated 68.5% of all property crimes. The rate of larceny-theft is 1,959 per every 100,000 people living in the United States. On average, larceny-theft offenses cost victims an estimated $6.1 billion in lost property annually.

Larceny is the most frequently occurring property offense according to official data compiled by the FBI and data from the NCVS. Within the offenses subsumed under the category of larceny in UCR/NIBRS data, the largest category is theft from motor vehicles, followed by shoplifting and theft from buildings (Figure 10–4).[20] Offenses such as pocket picking and purse snatching constitute a small percentage of all larcenies, less than 1% each. Just as rates of different offenses within the category of larceny differ, so, too, do estimated losses to victims.

As a form of theft, larceny (as opposed to burglary) does not involve the use of force or other means of illegal entry. For this reason, among others, larceny is a crime "less frightening than burglary because to a large, perhaps even to a preponderant extent, it is a crime of opportunity, a matter of making off with whatever happens to be lying around loose: Christmas presents in an unlocked car, merchandise on a store counter, a bicycle in a front yard."[21]

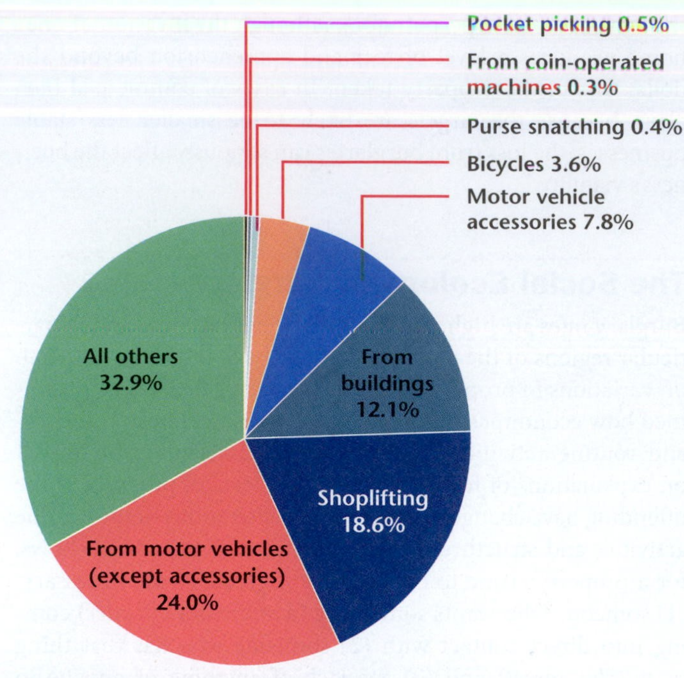

FIGURE 10–4 **Larceny-Theft Distribution, 2012.**
Source: Federal Bureau of Investigation, *Crime in the United States, 2012*.

Shoplifting and Employee Theft

Thefts cost U.S. retailers a staggering $33.6 billion in an average year.[22] Some retail theft is shoplifting, but other theft is committed by store employees. "The theft of merchandise by employees can range from the simple act of walking out the door with stolen goods to complex schemes requiring the manipulation of documents and/or involving several employees."[23] Most of the employees engaging in theft of either cash or merchandise are short-term workers. They are typically found in retail establishments with higher-than-average sales and a significant degree of turnover in management. Many retailers perceive the issue of internal theft to be more serious than the economic loss caused by customer shoplifting.

Nonetheless, retailers must consider that efforts to combat shoplifting might impact sales. This concern was reflected by a marketing director who commented, "You don't want to hinder sales by intimidating the shopper. We used to think just about stopping shoplifting. We didn't think enough about selling more merchandise."[24]

Technology represents one of the best ways to address both shoplifting and employee theft. The use of computerized inventory counts to track merchandise is useful in quickly identifying thefts by employees. As will be discussed shortly, the widespread prevalence of shoplifting among youths who are fast and often operate together in small gangs means that increased security personnel in stores are less successful at detection than are electronic and other devices.

Shoplifting continues to be an offense that crosses class lines, although it is not an offense committed primarily by women. The dominant motivation used today to explain shoplifting does not rely on medical labels. Even though "respectable" people continue to be found among those who commit this offense, there is no evidence that these individuals constitute a significant segment of offenders.

Who Shoplifts?

On August 4, 2010, Caroline Giuliani, the 20-year-old daughter of former New York City Mayor Rudolph Giuliani, was arrested and placed in handcuffs after she stuffed makeup worth about $100 into her jacket pockets at a Sephora store in New York's Upper East Side.[25] The younger Giuliani, a Harvard University student, was caught on store security cameras and charged with larceny. Many people viewed the arrest as ironic because her father, a former presidential candidate, became famous as a strong law-and-order mayor. One month later, in a plea deal arranged in Manhattan Criminal Court, Giuliani was ordered to serve one day of community service working for the city's Sanitation Department.[26]

Giuliani is not the first well-known person to be charged with shoplifting. In another case, on December 6, 2002, actress Winona Ryder was sentenced to three years of probation and required to perform 480 hours of community service for shoplifting more than $5,500 in merchandise from a Beverly Hills, California, Saks Fifth Avenue store a year earlier.

Neither the Ryder nor the Giuliani case, however, is that of a typical shoplifter. In self-reports of offending, official arrest data, and store records, juveniles are overrepresented as shoplifters. Although variation exists in the frequency of offending among adolescents, most offending patterns are fairly sporadic and are characterized by a greater prevalence among younger adolescents. The sporadic nature of shoplifting among adolescents is typical across all social classes even though the most serious and chronic forms are found among the economically disadvantaged. Although females represent the majority of offenders in some shoplifting data sources, this finding has been seriously challenged in research since the 1970s.[27]

Research by **Lloyd W. Klemke**, which used self-report techniques to assess juvenile shoplifting, revealed that almost two-thirds of the sample had shoplifted at some point in their lifetime.[28] Although previous research by **Mary Owen Cameron**, using department store records, had revealed that females were more likely than males to be apprehended for shoplifting,[29] Klemke found the reverse to be true. The difference in these findings may be attributed to the fact that Klemke's research included only adolescents, whereas Cameron's research also included adults.

Youths from lower-income households are more likely to shoplift than are their higher-income counterparts. However, this relationship is a moderate one at best, and the fact remains that shoplifting is reported by a solid majority of youths in several self-report studies. The relationship between social class and likelihood of shoplifting is stronger among adults.

Think About It...

This chapter provides examples of shoplifters who had the money to buy what they stole and were clearly not economically motivated. What causes such people to steal?

Steve Lovegrove/Shutterstock

Among Klemke's other findings was a "maturing out" pattern, whereby "shoplifting activity peaked in the under ten age category" and decreased considerably as the youths entered adolescence.[30] These findings are contrary to other research that supports escalation during late adolescence. Learn more about the crime of shoplifting and shoplifting prevention from the National Association for Shoplifting Prevention at **Web Extra 10-2**.

Flash Mobs and Larceny

Over the past few years, a new term has entered the popular lexicon—flash mobs. Flash mobs are purposeful crowds of people brought together on a moment's notice through the use of social media websites such as Twitter and Facebook. Sometimes the gatherings are peaceful and fun—as was the case in 2011 when a McDonald's restaurant in Chicago asked people to dress in beach attire and to converge on its location.[31] Other flash mobs, however, can have more insidious purposes and even involve organized criminal activity. In April 2011, for example, scores of teenagers organized through Tweets descended on a high-end men's clothing retailer in Washington, D.C., and stole about $20,000 worth of merchandise. Frantic employees tried to grab the apparel back as it was taken from shelves, but the crowd was too large.

Loss-prevention specialists refer to larcenies committed by flash mobs as multiple-offender crimes, and statistics show that 10% of retail establishments report being victimized by multiple offenders who formed flash mobs during a recent 12-month period.[32] In 2012, in recognition of the problem, the National Retail Federation issued a report outlining steps that stores could take to combat criminal flash mobs.[33] Those steps include documenting the larceny, especially through the use of video recordings and store security cameras, and quickly reporting the events to law enforcement agencies. Some states have even considered criminalizing flash mobs in an effort to prevent the kinds of crimes to which they can lead.

Identity Theft

Identify theft—the misuse of another individual's personal information to commit fraud[34]— is a relatively new form of larceny that appears to be growing rapidly. Identity theft involves obtaining credit, merchandise, or services by fraudulent personal representation. Usually, individuals learn that they have become identity theft victims only after being denied credit or employment or when a debt collector seeks payment for a debt the victim did not incur. The most threatening aspects of identity theft are its potential relationship to international terrorism. Even where terrorism is not involved, identity theft can be used broadly by transnational crime rings.

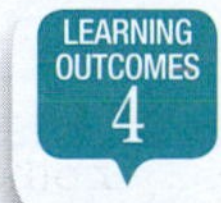

Describe identity theft and some of the techniques used by identity thieves.

The misuse of stolen personal information can be classified into two broad categories. *Existing account fraud* occurs when thieves obtain account information involving credit, brokerage, banking, or utility accounts that are already open. Existing account fraud is typically less costly, but more prevalent. A stolen credit card may lead to thousands of dollars in fraudulent charges, for example, but the card generally will not provide a thief with enough information to establish a false identity. Moreover, most credit card companies do not hold consumers liable for fraudulent charges, and federal law caps liability of victims of credit card theft at $50.

The second and more serious category is *new account fraud*. In new account fraud, identity thieves use personal information such as Social Security numbers, birth dates, and home addresses to open new accounts in the victim's name, make charges indiscriminately, and then disappear. Although this type of identity theft is less likely to occur, it imposes much greater costs and hardships on victims. In addition, identity thieves sometimes use stolen personal information to obtain government, medical, or other benefits to which the criminal is not legally entitled.

In addition to the losses that result when identity thieves fraudulently open accounts or misuse existing accounts, monetary costs of identity theft include indirect costs to businesses for fraud prevention and mitigation of the harm once it has occurred (for example, for mailing notices to consumers and upgrading systems). Similarly, individual victims often suffer indirect financial costs, including the costs incurred in dealing with civil litigation initiated by creditors and in overcoming the many obstacles they face in obtaining or retaining credit. Victims of nonfinancial identity theft, for example, including health-related or criminal record fraud, face other types of harm and frustration.

Consumers' fears of becoming identity theft victims can also harm the digital economy. In a recent online survey conducted by the Business Software Alliance and Harris Interactive, nearly 30% of adults interviewed said that security fears caused them to shop online less or not at all.[35] Identity theft became a federal crime in 1998 with the passage of the **Identity Theft and Assumption Deterrence Act**.[36] The law makes it a crime whenever anyone "knowingly transfers or uses, without lawful authority, a means of identification of another person with the intent to commit, or to aid or abet, any unlawful activity that constitutes a violation of federal law, or that constitutes a felony under any applicable state or local law."

The 2004 **Identity Theft Penalty Enhancement Act**[37] added two years to federal prison sentences for criminals convicted of using stolen credit card numbers and other personal data to commit crimes. It also prescribed prison sentences for those who use identity theft to commit other crimes, including terrorism, and it increased penalties for defendants who exceed or abuse the authority of their position in unlawfully obtaining or misusing means of personal identification.

The Incidence of Identity Theft

Recently, the Bureau of Justice Statistics (BJS) provided information on the incidence of identity theft derived from the National Crime Victimization Survey (NCVS).[38] For statistical-reporting purposes, the BJS defines *identity theft* to include the following three behaviors: (1) the unauthorized use or attempted use of existing credit cards, (2) the unauthorized use or attempted use of other existing accounts such as checking accounts, and (3) the misuse of personal information to obtain new accounts or loans or to commit other crimes.

BJS surveyors found that approximately 7% of all U.S. residents age 16 or older, or about 16.6 million people, had been the victim of identity theft during 2012[39] (Figure 10–5). About 1.7 million people reported being victimized by the theft of an existing account other than a credit card account, such as the use or attempted use of a cell phone account, bank account, or debit/check card account without permission.

The BJS survey also revealed that about one in six victimized households had to pay higher interest rates as the result of identity theft and that one in nine households was denied phone or utility service as a consequence of being victimized.[40] About 7% of victimized households were turned down for insurance or had to pay higher rates, 5% became the subject of a civil suit or judgment, 4% became the subject of a criminal investigation, and about 20% reported other kinds of problems.

Think About It...

Identity theft is a serious and growing problem. How do identity thieves work? What steps can you take to prevent the theft of your identity?

blas/Fotolia

Identity Thieves: Who They Are

Unlike some groups of criminals, identity thieves cannot be readily classified.[41] According to the survey of identity theft by the Federal Trade Commission (FTC), about 14% of victims claim to know the perpetrator, who may be a family member, a friend, or an in-home employee. Identity thieves can act alone or as part of a criminal enterprise. Each poses unique threats to the public.

Identity thieves often have no prior criminal background and sometimes have preexisting relationships with the victims. They have been known to prey on people they know, including coworkers, senior citizens for whom they may be serving as caretakers, and even family members. Some identity thieves use minimal sophistication, such as stealing mail from homeowners' mailboxes or trash containing financial documents. In some jurisdictions, identity theft by illegal immigrants has resulted in passport, employment, and Social Security fraud. Occasionally, loosely knit groups of individuals with no significant criminal records work together to obtain personal information and even to create false or fraudulent documents.[42]

Law enforcement agencies also have seen increased involvement of foreign organized criminal groups in computer- or Internet-related identity theft schemes. In Asia and Eastern Europe, for example, organized groups are increasingly sophisticated both in the techniques they use and in the complexity of their tools. According to law enforcement agencies, such groups also are demonstrating increasing levels of sophistication and specialization in their online crime, even selling goods and services—such as software templates for making counterfeit identification cards and payment card magnetic strip encoders—that make the stolen data even more valuable to those who have it.

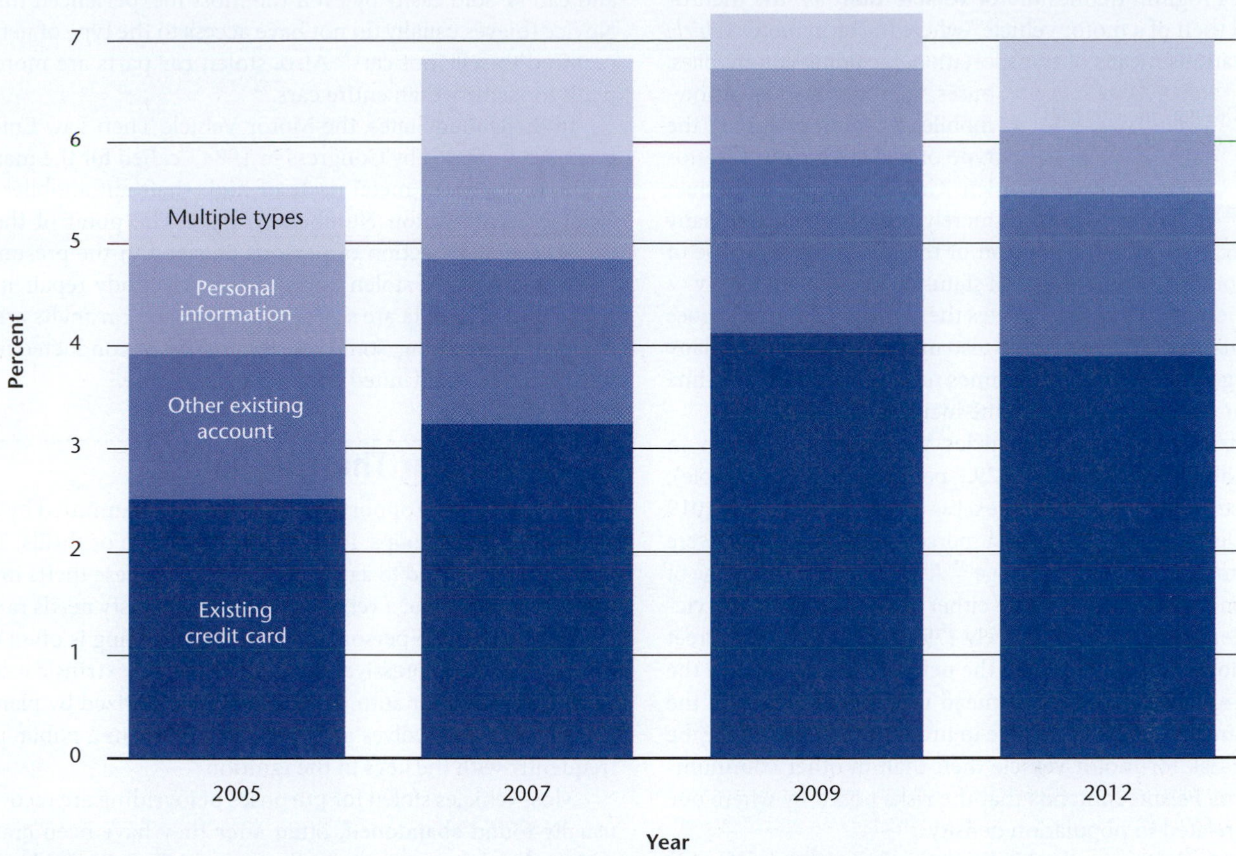

FIGURE 10–5 **Percent of Households That Experienced Identity Theft, by Type of Theft, 2005–2012.**
Source: Lynn Langton, *Identity Theft Reported by Households, 2005–2010* (Washington, DC: Bureau of Justice Statistics, 2011), p. 1; and Erika Harrell and Lynn Langton, *Victims of Identity Theft, 2012* (Washington, DC: Bureau of Justice Statistics, 2013).

WHO'S TO BLAME—The Individual or Society

Body Parts for Sale

On March 20, 2014, Dr. Paul Sutter, a Palm Beach, Florida, plastic surgeon, was arrested and charged with a federal crime after he allegedly purchased facial bones that he knew had been illegally removed from a cadaver, and implanted them into a wealthy female patient undergoing elective facial reconstructive surgery following a car accident. The doctor and a mortician, who sold him the bones, were both charged with violating the National Organ Transplant Act of 1984, which expressly prohibits interstate trafficking in human tissue for profit.

In an interview the doctor gave after posting bail, Sutter told reporters, "I understand that there's a law against what I did. But it's not my fault that the materials I need to work with are frequently so hard to acquire. There needs to be a better system in place for the distribution of bones and other tissues that are so desperately needed by patients like the woman whose face I reconstructed in this case."

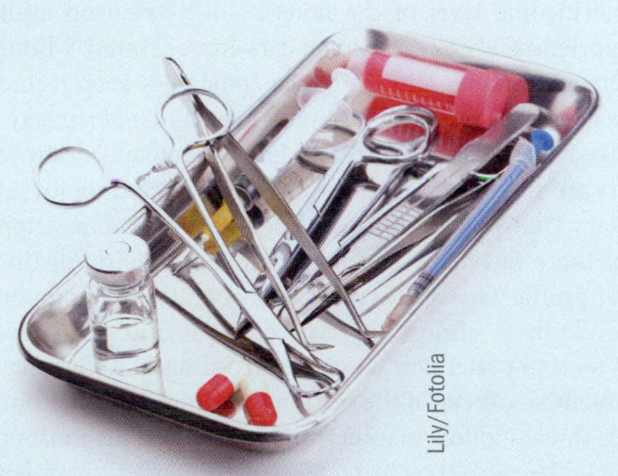

Think About It

1. Why did Sutter violate the law? What do you think was his primary motivation for what he did?
2. Do you think it would have mattered to Sutter's patient had she known that the bones used in her surgery had been acquired illegally?
3. Can body parts be considered items of property, like a person's other possessions? If so, should he or she have the right to sell them—perhaps to the highest bidder?

Note: Who's to Blame boxes provide fictionalized critical thinking opportunities, and are not actual cases.

Motor Vehicle Theft

The UCR Program defines **motor vehicle theft** as "the theft or attempted theft of a motor vehicle," where the term *motor vehicle* refers to various means of transportation, including automobiles, buses, motorcycles, and snowmobiles.[43] Automobiles are the type of vehicle most often stolen. Cars represent more than merely a possession; for many Americans, they are an extension of their identity. The type of car a person drives reflects social status and personal identity.

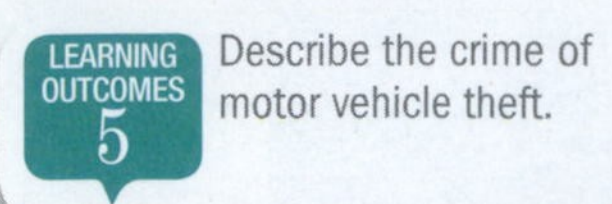

Describe the crime of motor vehicle theft.

The theft of a car, then, violates the victim in a way that goes beyond financial loss. Auto theft also makes it difficult for many people to get to work and sometimes requires them to take time away from work to take care of the incident.[44]

Approximately 721,000 vehicles were reported stolen in 2012 (for an auto theft rate of 229.7 per every 100,000 people), with an estimated total value in excess of $4.3 billion (or $6,019 per vehicle stolen). The largest percentage of vehicles were stolen from a parking lot or garage.[45] A significant percentage of motor vehicle thefts takes place either at or quite near the victim's residence, with approximately 17% taking place on a street near the home.[46] Depending on the neighborhood in which the victim resides, *near home* can mean different things, and the same distance from the residence in urban communities may be more of a risk for motor vehicle theft than in other communities. Marcus Felson contends that the risks posed by where one parks are related to population density.

Based on data from the NCVS, on average, 81% of all motor vehicle thefts, both attempted and completed, are reported to the police. As is seen with other offenses, the reporting percentage is higher (79%) for completed motor vehicle thefts than for attempted incidents (54%).[47] Although the rate of motor vehicle victimization is the same for the lowest-income households (under $7,500 per year) as for the highest-income households ($75,000 or more per year), the rate of reporting increases with the income level of the household.[48] Based on available data, approximately 62% of stolen cars are recovered.[49] Both law enforcement agencies and insurance companies keep records of recovered vehicles, but each uses its own definition of *recovery*, and some "recovered" cars may actually have been totally destroyed.

Cars are stolen for a variety of reasons, including joyriding, temporary transportation needs, use in a crime, and stripping. Each of these rationales is representative of a fairly distinctive offender profile. Given the wide variety of rationales supporting automobile theft, almost any type of car is a target. However, thieves tend to prefer certain cars. According to Robert Bryant, chief executive officer of the National Insurance Crime Bureau, "Vehicle thieves follow market trends and target the most popular vehicles because they provide the best market for stolen vehicle parts and illegal export to other countries."[50]

Theft of Car Parts

Approximately one-third of stolen vehicles that are scored as "recovered" are completely stripped at chop shops, and another third are stripped of easy-to-sell accessories like radios, air bags, and seats.[51] The theft of car parts is variously motivated. Some car parts are worth a significant sum on the illegal market and can be sold easily by even the most inexperienced thieves. Novice thieves usually do not have access to the type of network required to sell "hot cars." Also, stolen car parts are more difficult to identify than entire cars.[52]

In the United States, the Motor Vehicle Theft Law Enforcement Act,[53] passed by Congress in 1984, "called for the marking of the major sheet metal parts of high-theft automobiles with Vehicle Identification Numbers (VINs). The point of the law was to enable detection of persons engaged in the presumably widespread sale of stolen parts to the auto body repair industry."[54] Although data are scarce on how many car thefts are carried out for stripping, some research has been conducted in this regard both in the United States and elsewhere.

Joyriders: Car Theft for Fun

Some car thefts are opportunistic in nature, committed by teenagers, usually in groups, for the purpose of fun or thrills. These offenses are referred to as **joyriding**. Because these thefts involve the temporary use of a vehicle primarily to satisfy needs ranging from excitement to personal autonomy, joyriding is often characterized as an "expressive act with little or no extrinsic value."[55] This motivation for auto theft is not characterized by planning and quite often involves an unlocked car left in a public place, frequently with the keys in the ignition.[56]

Most vehicles stolen for purposes of joyriding are recovered, usually found abandoned, often after they have been crashed. Although adolescents may select a vehicle for joyriding that belongs to strangers, they are more likely to select the car of a known owner.[57]

Research offers no definite answer as to whether there is a distinctive social-class profile of the joyriding offender. Some research indicates that higher social class can be associated with greater involvement in auto theft because of greater access to cars and an earlier association of cars as status symbols. On the other hand, the "disadvantaged-group hypothesis" contends that youths from lower socioeconomic classes are more likely to be involved in car thefts because conventional means of acquiring status symbols such as cars are blocked, and they are left with only the avenue of illegitimate acquisition.[58] Although some support has been found for each of these perspectives, other research has failed to find a link between social class and involvement in auto theft among adolescents.[59]

Although they represent the most costly and most serious form of auto theft, professional thefts are not as common as thefts for other uses, such as joyriding. Like joyriders, professional auto thieves operate in groups, but their groups are characterized by a great deal more planning and calculation in target selection. The cars targeted by professional thieves are luxury cars that may be driven across national borders or shipped overseas. Professional thefts have the lowest recovery rates. Still, professionals are only a small part of the vehicle theft problem. For anyone concerned about preventing motor vehicle theft, the Bureau of Justice Assistance provides a fact sheet on the Watch Your Car Program available via **Web Extra 10–3**.

Arson

The FBI defines **arson** as "any willful or malicious burning or attempt to burn, with or without intent to defraud, a dwelling house, public building, motor vehicle or aircraft, personal property of another, etc."[60] It is only after a fire has been investigated and officially classified as arson by the proper investigative authorities that the FBI records the incident as an arson. Fires that are suspicious or of unknown origin are not included in the FBI's arson statistics.[61]

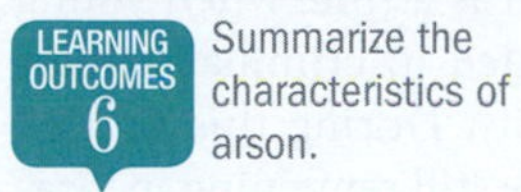

Summarize the characteristics of arson.

In 2012, the FBI received reports of 52,766 arsons the occurred throughout the country. Arsons involving structures (for example, residential, storage, and public) accounted for 46.8% of the total number of arson offenses. Mobile property was involved in 23.1% of arsons, and other types of property, such as crops, timber, and fences, accounted for 30.1% of reported arsons. The average dollar loss due to arson was $12,796 per offense, whereas arsons of industrial/manufacturing structures resulted in the highest average dollar losses (an average of $42,133 per arson). In 2012, arson offenses decreased slightly when compared with arson data reported in 2011. Nationally, the clearance rate for arson was only 20.6% in 2012. Of all arson arrests, 37% involve juveniles—a higher percentage than for any other major crime. In addition, 76% of arson arrestees are white and 83% are male.

Several diverse motives may underlie arson, from profit to thrill seeking. On August 1, 2003, for example, a 206-unit San Diego condominium complex burned down while under construction. A 12-foot banner found at the scene declared, "If you build it, we will burn it." The banner was signed with the letters *ELF*, which stand for the Earth Liberation Front. Less than a month later, ELF arsonists attacked a number of car dealerships in Los Angeles, targeting those that sold gas-guzzling SUVs such as Hummers. In a more recent attack, the letters "ELF" were found spray-painted in red letters at the site of an arson fire in which explosive devices were used to set fire to four empty multimillion-dollar homes in Echo Lake, Washington, in 2008.[62] Ironically, the houses were part of a luxury homes showcase whose theme was "green and sustainable building."

The ELF, described as an ecoterrorist group by law enforcement officials, may have begun in California as the Environmental Life Force in 1977. The present-day ELF targets what it deems to be threats to the environment—including residential and commercial construction in environmentally sensitive areas, certain types of animal research facilities, and sometimes Starbucks restaurants.

Fire Setters

Whatever the motive, the vast majority of those involved in arson are juveniles. According to UCR/NIBRS data, juveniles represent the offenders in arson incidents at a much higher rate than is found in any other index offense; 37% of all arsons that are cleared are found to have involved a juvenile offender. Juveniles are a bit more likely to be involved in arsons in cities than in suburbs or rural areas.[63] According to Jay K. Bradish, editor of *Firehouse* magazine, "Arson is the third-leading cause of residential fires and the second-leading cause of residential fire deaths nationwide. Arson is the leading cause of deaths and injuries and accounts for the highest dollar loss in commercial fires."[64] In both residential and commercial arson, juveniles are involved more often than adults.

Three general groups of juvenile fire setters can be identified.[65] The first consists of children younger than seven who generally start fires by accident or out of curiosity. The second group is children between the ages of 8 and 12 who may start fires out of curiosity, but "a greater proportion of their fire setting represents underlying psychosocial conflicts."[66] The final group, youths between the ages of 13 and 18, has had a history of fire setting, usually undetected. It is believed that many of the fires started by juveniles go undetected by law enforcement officials because they are started on school property, perhaps even accidentally, and are discovered early by janitors or other school staff who do not report the incidents. In response to a growing awareness of the problem created by juvenile fire setters, several agencies and organizations, including the U.S. Fire Administration, have developed model programs to mobilize community agencies across the nation to deal more effectively with juvenile fire setters. Learn more about arson through the National Fire Data Center at **Web Extra 10–4**.

Persistent and Professional Thieves

Although legal distinctions separate the offenses of larceny and burglary, both are basically property crimes of theft, and those who commit such offenses are thieves. Many thieves are persistent, but this does not make them professionals. Willie Sutton, a famous bank robber, saw himself as a professional and defined a professional thief quite simply as "a man who wakes up every morning thinking about committing a crime, the same way another man gets up and goes to his job."[67] In a classic study of the professional thief, Edwin H. Sutherland defines this offender as one who "makes a regular business of stealing," plans carefully, possesses "technical skills and methods which are different from those of other professional criminals," and moves from locale to locale in offending pursuits.[68] The criminologist **Neil Shover** defines **professional criminals** as those "who commit crime with some degree of skill, earn reasonably well from their crimes, and despite stealing over long periods of time, spend rather little time incarcerated."[69] This is certainly not the profile of most offenders, who continue to commit crimes but never exhibit signs of a professional approach to crime. Rather than being viewed as professional, they are best understood as persistent.

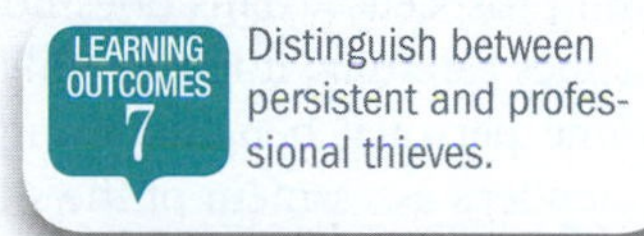

Distinguish between persistent and professional thieves.

Persistent thieves continue in "common-law property crimes despite their, at best, ordinary level of success."[70] Rather than specializing, the vast majority of persistent thieves alternate between a variety of crimes such as burglary, robbery, car theft, and confidence games. Even though they exhibit a

Burglars choose burglary over other crimes such as robbery because burglary does not involve direct contact with victims.

generalist approach to offending, persistent thieves may have "crime preferences" that take the form of characteristics such as "whether to avoid or to confront their victim(s)."[71]

Similarly, property offenders rarely have a preference for a particular kind of offense. Significant numbers of property offenders are fully immersed in a street culture and lifestyle characterized by a hedonistic approach to life and a disregard for conventional pursuits. Their everyday lives are usually filled with a wide array of petty crimes, including confidence games, gambling, and minor thefts.[72]

Shover, who has studied burglary and professional thieves, suggests that designations such as "burglar" have little meaning if conceived of in a strict sense of exclusive offending. Many burglary offenders prefer this type of offending to other crimes such as robbery because burglary does not involve direct contact with victims. Still, burglars may engage in other types of offenses, even occasional robbery, when the need for money arises.[73]

Because of the short-term and sporadic nature of their offending, property offenders are also known as **occasional offenders**.[74] The label "occasional" refers not to the frequency of offending, but to the nature and character of offending. John R. Hepburn defines occasional property offenders as those whose crimes "occur on those occasions in which there is an opportunity or situational inducement to commit the crime."[75] This observation, which fits well with rational choice theory, has been confirmed in subsequent research, most recently in the work of Richard T. Wright and Scott H. Decker. Wright and Decker found that the burglars they interviewed are not a "continually motivated group of criminals; the motivation for them to offend is closely tied to their assessment of current circumstances and prospects."[76] This does not mean that offenders plan their crimes carefully; it means only that they are seeking to achieve some personal benefit through criminal activity. Because an offender's assessment of the situation at hand may not even be accurate, some don't succeed in obtaining the benefits they desire. This is because they rarely have all the information they need, they do not devote enough time to planning their actions, they take unnecessary risks, and they make mistakes. This is how we all behave in everyday decision making, and it is what theorists call *limited* or *bounded rationality*.[77] So although some degree of rationality characterizes the criminal activity of most property offenders, it is limited.

The Criminal Careers of Property Offenders

Criminologists have long studied the criminal careers of offenders, both violent offenders and property offenders. The concept of a *career* reflects the same meaning as a traditional career to a limited extent. It implies a rational progression through defined stages, with some type of planning or formalized logic to the progression.

According to Alfred Blumstein and colleagues, a criminal career in property offending consists of three distinct phases.[78] The first phase is the "break-in" period, which characterizes the early years of an offender's career. It is a time when young offenders become increasingly committed to criminal careers and explore various kinds of criminality. During this period, residual career length (the expected time still remaining in a career) increases. The initial phase generally lasts for the first 10 to 12 years of a property offender's career. The second, or "stable" period, which begins around age 30 for those who first embark on criminal careers when they are around 18, is the time of highest commitment. It is the period in an offender's career when he or she identifies most closely with a criminal lifestyle; it is probably also the period when rehabilitation efforts are most likely to fail. The final, or "burnout," phase of a criminal career begins around age 40, says Blumstein. It is characterized by increasing dropout rates and by a lowered commitment to criminal lifestyles.

In a study of violent offending, however, D. S. Elliott and his colleagues examined data from the National Youth Survey and found that the careers of violent offenders were typically quite short—averaging just 1.58 years.[79] Only about 4% of subjects studied by Elliott had a violent criminal career of five years or more. Unlike other researchers, however, Elliott defined career length as the maximum number of consecutive years the individual was classified as a serious violent offender during the study period.

An assumption long attached to criminal careers was the idea that offending becomes more serious and more frequent over time, an assumption strongly challenged by Michael R. Gottfredson and Travis Hirschi.[80] Although the idea of deviance and crime as an orderly process may be appealing for social policy purposes, evidence shows that crime is more a fragmented pursuit than a "career." Some researchers have found that a certain logic to the lifestyle of most offenders does exist, but it is not one that easily complies with "a concept appropriate in a distinctly different culture (lawful society)."[81]

Property Offenders and Rational Choice

Research on property crimes is often scrutinized from the perspective of rational choice theories. One definition of *rationality* is "activities identified by their impersonal, methodical, efficient, and logical components."[82] Although the decision making, motivation, and target selection of property offenders will be explored throughout this chapter, it is crucial to understand now that the rationality of the typical criminal offender is not the same as "the rationality used by the civil engineer."[83] In line with the research of Thomas Bennett and Richard Wright on the rationality surrounding decision making by burglars,[84] Walsh's research concludes that offenders employ a "limited, temporal rationality." Walsh says, "Not all these men are highly intelligent, and few are equipped to calculate Bentham-style, even supposing the information were available. Yet it is very common for rationality to be used. Of course it is partial and limited rather than total, but at the time, the actor feels he has planned enough and weighed enough data."[85] This is in many ways no different from the limited type of rationality that many conventional individuals employ in their daily activities. Although some offenders, certainly those closer to the end of the continuum marked "professional," will use a higher degree of rationality and still others will at times exhibit behavior that is totally senseless, most expressions of rationality are not as dramatically clear. The extent to which property crimes are rational pursuits for either expressive or instrumental gains is a question that will be addressed throughout this chapter.

Types of Burglars

Although the image of the professional burglar is part of our popular culture, it does not accurately describe most burglars. **Mike Maguire** offers three basic categories of burglars: low-level, middle-range, and high-level (Figure 10–6).[86] *Low-level burglars*, primarily juveniles, often commit their crimes "on the spur of the moment," usually work with others, and are easily deterred from a target by secure locks, alarms, and/or other such security devices. The rewards gained from offending for this group are generally not significant, and many desist from burglary as they get older and as they feel "the pull of conventional relationships and fear of more severe adult sanctions."[87]

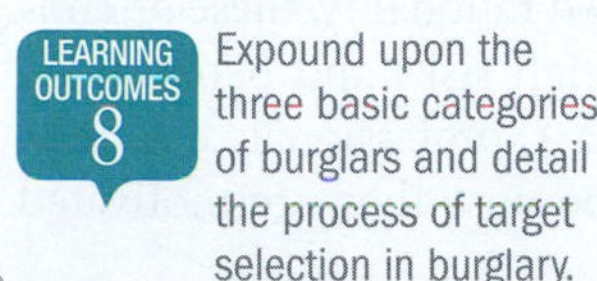

Expound upon the three basic categories of burglars and detail the process of target selection in burglary.

Middle-range burglars are generally a bit older, although they may have begun their offending in burglary as juveniles. These offenders quite often go back and forth between legitimate pursuits and involvement in crime. The use of alcohol and other drugs is more common among middle-range offenders than among the other two groups of burglars. These offenders select targets that take into account both the potential payoff and the risk involved; however, this group is not as easily discouraged by security devices as are the low-level burglars. Although their take from their crimes may be substantial at times, they lack the connections for dealing in stolen goods on a large scale.

High-level burglars are professionals. Burglary is an offense characterized by a large prevalence of co-offending, and high-level burglars work in organized crews and "are connected with reliable sources of information about targets."[88] Members of this group earn a good living from the proceeds of their crimes, which are carefully planned, including target selection, generally with the assistance of outside sources. Professional burglars may be known to the police, but due to their "task-force approach to organization," their activities remain largely concealed from detection.[89] Only high-level burglars would attempt large-scale art thefts. Learn more about the stolen goods market from the Center for Problem-Oriented Policing at **Web Extra 10–5**.

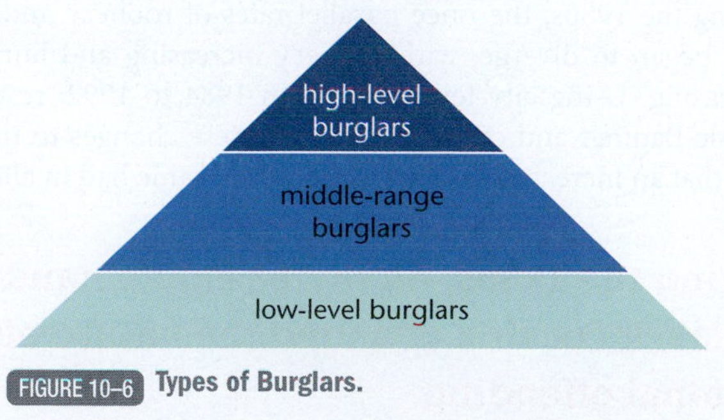

FIGURE 10–6 **Types of Burglars.**

Burglary Locales

Burglars at any level may target both residences and commercial buildings. Police reports detail the time of the burglary; nighttime residential burglary and daytime commercial burglary are considered most serious. Evening hours are the time that burglars are most likely to face homeowners, and daytime hours are the time considered to present the greatest risk of confrontation between offenders and customers or workers.[90] According to NCVS data, however, a larger percentage of residential burglaries take place during the day than during the evening hours.[91]

Burglary is known as a "cold" crime because there is usually very little physical evidence to link the offender to the offense, and by the time the victims realize they have been burglarized and have called the police, the burglar is usually long gone. This is truer of residential than commercial burglaries, as the latter are more likely to involve alarms or other security devices.[92]

Target Selection

Retail establishments are four times as likely to be burglarized as are other types of establishments, such as wholesale or service businesses. Based on a study of commercial burglaries in Philadelphia, economics researchers Simon Hakim and Yochanan Shachmurove offer three reasons for the dominance of retail stores as burglary targets: "The merchandise is exposed so that the burglar knows precisely what his expected loot is, the merchandise is new and enjoys a high resale value to a fence, and burglars do not need to spend intrusion time searching for the loot."[93] Because burglars can "survey the facility while legitimately shopping or browsing through the store," retail establishments, especially those located away from major thoroughfares in places where police response time will be slower, are prime targets.[94]

Burglars may select a target based on information from "tipsters," those who "regularly pass on intelligence about good burglary opportunities for a fee or a cut of the take."[95] Some offenders use tipsters who work in service capacities within households and businesses, whereas others act in collusion with insurance agents or other middle-class people who feed the offender information in exchange for money or for some of the stolen merchandise.

The ethnographic research that Wright and Decker conducted in St. Louis made clear that only very rarely is a burglary target chosen on the "spur of the moment," but the type of observation that went into the selection was often quite fragmented. Even so, fragmented observation may sometimes be all that is required. Given the lackadaisical nature of much household security and the fact that approximately one-fourth of burglaries do not involve any type of forced entry, "the world affords abundant poorly protected opportunities for burglars."[96] This does not mean, however, that burglars are primarily opportunistic. An open door or window is viewed less as an opportunity

Some burglars select targets based on information provided by "tipsters."

to commit burglary and more as a sign that the residence is occupied and hence an undesirable target. More commonly, by chance alone, the offender happens to be in a place to observe the resident of a household departing.

Target selection is also influenced by other key elements. One of the most important is signs of occupancy because most offenders are reluctant to burglarize occupied dwellings. Burglars have reported that they avoid occupied homes because they want to avoid injury to their victims and to themselves. For some offenders, the fear of their own injury was greater than the fear of apprehension. Most residential burglars avoid residences with complex security devices because they generally lack the expertise to bypass the system. Even offenders who engaged targets with alarms would only do so with certain alarms, again because of their lack of expertise. Dogs will deter an offender from a potential target as well. Many offenders will choose a target that is in the same area and within walking distance of their residence because of a lack of access to cars. As one offender in Wright and Decker's research noted, "It's hard as hell getting on a bus carrying a big picture or a vase."[97]

The Motivation of Burglars

Rational choice perspectives have guided a great deal of research on decision making among property offenders. Decision making is thought to be guided by the peculiar logic of the offender's perspective. The way in which offenders work out the logic of their decisions may not make sense objectively, but their decisions have their own internal logic from the standpoint of the offenders' social world.[98]

LEARNING OUTCOMES
9
Characterize burglars and their motivation.

The most prevalent rationale behind the offense of residential burglary is the need for fast cash.[99] However, this need for cash is not necessarily characterized by the demand to satisfy the basic necessities of life or to maintain a conventional lifestyle. Based on ethnographic research conducted in Texas[100] and in St. Louis,[101] active burglars do not, as a whole, have a conventional lifestyle; most of their everyday concerns revolve around maintaining their street status and supporting a lifestyle of self-indulgence and often gratuitous consumption of drugs. Wright and Decker contend that the need to maintain a party lifestyle, to "keep up appearances," and to provide basic necessities for themselves and their families are all key factors that drive offenders' decisions to commit a burglary.[102]

As in the ethnographic research on the lifestyle of armed robbers, Wright and Decker found that the vast majority of the residential burglars they interviewed were committed to an "every night is a Saturday night" lifestyle. Thus, when offenders discussed their offending as a means of survival, it had to be interpreted against the backdrop of this lifestyle, for it was only within this context that an understanding of what they meant by "survival" emerged. The vast majority of offenders were committed to street culture, and almost three-fourths of the money they obtained from burglary went to support their lifestyle—a lifestyle that included illicit drugs, alcohol, and sexual pursuits. Keeping up appearances, another crucial part of street culture resulted in the "need" to buy things that helped them to maintain street status, such as the right clothes and the right car. Although some of the offenders interviewed by Wright and Decker did use the proceeds from their burglaries to pay their bills, the researchers also note that "the bills were badly delinquent because the offenders avoided paying them for as long as possible—even when they had the cash—in favor of buying, most typically, drugs."[103] Burglaries of commercial establishments are generally thought to be associated even more with instrumental ends, usually economic gain, than are residential burglaries. The same is true of professional burglars who invest more planning and strategy into their offenses. Far from operating from a standpoint of limited rationality, these offenders are calculating and carefully weigh risks and benefits. As Shover details in his work on burglars, professionals use quite sophisticated planning techniques because they are motivated to find targets with high payoffs.[104]

Because most of the offenders interviewed by Wright and Decker regarded themselves as hustlers, or "people who were always looking to get over by making some fast cash," they would commit offenses other than burglary if a chance opportunity presented itself.[105] Otherwise, they stayed with the familiar, which was burglary. For many, burglary was not as risky as selling drugs. Robbery was perceived as too risky because it involved direct confrontation with the victim and hence a higher likelihood of being injured. Some offenders stated that they did not own the necessary equipment for robberies—namely, guns. Because guns can be easily translated into cash in the street economy, "offenders who are in need of immediate cash often are tempted to sell their weapon instead of resorting to a difficult or risky crime."[106]

A small number of offenders in Wright and Decker's research in St. Louis indicated that "they did not typically commit burglaries as much for the money as for the psychic rewards."[107] This is consistent with Jack Katz's concept of sneaky thrills. As Katz contends, "If we looked more closely at how [offenders] define material needs, we might get a different image of these 'serious thieves.'"[108] Based on his ethnographic research with property offenders, Kenneth D. Tunnell concluded that "excitement was present but only as a latent benefit—a by-product of the criminal act."[109]

The Burglary–Drug Connection

During the 1980s, the once parallel rates of robbery and burglary began to diverge, with robbery increasing and burglary decreasing. Using city-level data from 1984 to 1992, research by Eric Baumer and colleagues linked these changes to the effects that an increased demand for crack cocaine had in altering

During the 1980s, an increased demand for crack cocaine changed the nature of criminal offending.

structures of offending.[110] As a stimulant, crack use is characterized by short highs that are "followed by an intense desire for more crack."[111] If users are funding their drug habit through criminal pursuits, they need to rely on offenses that complement the demands of their drug of choice. This means that offenses such as robbery, which can net cash quickly and directly and at any time, are better suited to the habits and needs of crack users than is burglary, which is more likely to net stolen goods than cash.

Workers in Stolen Property

As previously discussed, a small number of thieves steal for their own consumption and steal mostly cash. In these cases, there is no need to translate the goods into cash. But in other cases, it is necessary to turn stolen goods into cash. In such cases, "there are many paths that stolen property may take from thieves to eventual customers."[112] Receiving stolen property allows for various levels of profit by individuals and groups with varying skill levels. Some burglars commit their offenses specifically to get something they know someone wants. In this case, the burglar may sell the merchandise directly to a waiting customer.[113] Burglars also may sell to people who are known to them or may take stolen goods to flea markets or auctions. Other paths to disposing of stolen goods include "dabbling middlemen" who buy and sell stolen property "under the cover of a bar, a luncheonette, or an auto service station with the encouragement, if not the active participation, of the proprietor."[114] Some burglars also sell their merchandise to legitimate retailers, representing it as legal goods.

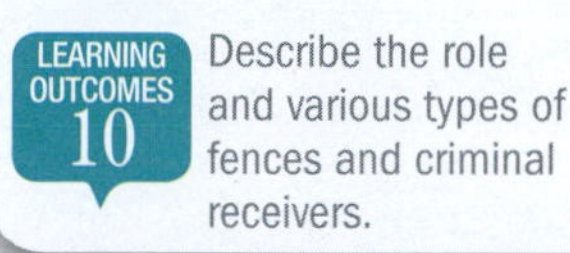

Describe the role and various types of fences and criminal receivers.

The most complicated path from the thief to end users is through a **fence**. The use of a professional fence is the least common method of disposing of stolen goods for the majority of thieves, but it is the most common method used by professional thieves. **Carl Klockars**, a criminologist who studied the lives of thieves, detailed the career of a professional fence named Vincent Swaggi, who had worked as a fence for more than 20 years.[115] Building on Klockars's work, **Darrell Steffensmeier** defines a *fence* as a person who "purchases stolen goods both on a regular basis, and for resale."[116] The most crucial defining characteristics of the professional fence, says Steffensmeier, are that he or she has "direct contact with thieves," "buys and resells stolen goods regularly and persistently," and thus is a "public dealer—recognized as a fence by thieves, the police, and others acquainted with the criminal community."[117]

The Role of Criminal Receivers

In their research on residential burglary, **Paul F. Cromwell** and his colleagues offer a three-part typology of criminal receivers: professional receivers, avocational receivers, and amateur receivers.[118] *Professional receivers* are those who fit the definition provided by Steffensmeier. Use of a professional fence to dispose of stolen goods is uncommon among the majority of residential burglars, who lack "sophisticated underworld connections."[119] Such connections often distinguish "high-level burglars" from the more typical and prevalent residential burglars.[120] Burglars and other thieves who have relationships with fences have a number of advantages in disposing of stolen goods. The professional fence offers a safe and quick means of resale. This is especially the case with burglars who have committed a high-visibility crime, stealing goods that are easily recognizable. Fences are also the best outlet for a large volume of stolen goods, which is one factor that distinguishes professional fences from other types. Some professional fences are "generalists" who deal in a wide variety of stolen goods, and others are "specialists" who deal only in certain types of goods. Goodman, the professional fence described in Steffensmeier's research, started as a specialist but evolved into a generalist as a "function of greater capital and a growing knowledge of varied merchandise."[121]

According to insights provided by Goodman, fences need several conditions to be successful. Because they deal in cash, they must have plenty of cash available. They must understand the trade by knowing acceptable prices and the right time to buy. They must have relationships with those who supply stolen goods and know those who will buy the goods, often with the knowledge that they are stolen. And, finally, they must have a relationship with law enforcement that may involve bribery or barter.

The majority of professional fences are involved in legitimate businesses that serve as cover for their criminal activity. A "partly covered fence," may, for example, operate a secondhand store whose inventory largely matches the stolen goods received. Fences who are "fully covered" do not deal in stolen goods that are outside their inventory in their legitimate business. "Noncovered" fences are those whose "illicit lines of goods are distinct from the legitimate commerce."[122] The more a fence is able to cover illicit activities by incorporating them into legitimate enterprises, the safer the fence is from criminal detection and prosecution.

Fences use many types of businesses as fronts for criminal activity. They generally range from businesses seen by the "community-at-large as strictly clean," such as restaurants, to businesses that "are perceived as clean but somewhat suspect," such as auto parts shops and antique shops, to businesses that are viewed as "quasi-legitimate or marginal," such as pawnshops.[123]

Some residential burglars avoid pawnshops when disposing of stolen goods because owners often demand identification and take photos of people selling to them and because they have "hot sheets" of recently stolen goods. In addition, pawnshops generally do not provide the greatest return on stolen merchandise. Residential burglars who do regularly use pawnshops have probably established a relationship with the owner that enables them "to pawn stolen property 'off camera.' "[124]

A second type of fence is the *avocational receiver*. For this person, the buying of stolen property is a part-time endeavor "secondary to, but usually associated with, their primary business activity."[125] This fairly diverse group can include individuals involved in respectable occupations, such as the lawyers or bail bondsmen who "provide legitimate professional services to property offenders who cannot pay for these services with anything but stolen property."[126] Others involved in illegitimate occupations, such as drug dealers, may also accept stolen goods in lieu of cash. As opposed to the professional fence, the avocational receiver is distinguished by the "frequency of purchase, volume of activity, and level of commitment to the criminal enterprise."[127]

Amateur receivers are those "otherwise honest citizens who buy stolen property on a relatively small scale, primarily, but not exclusively, for personal consumption. Crime is peripheral rather than central to their lives."[128] These individuals are sporadic in their involvement in activities that generate stolen goods. Cromwell and colleagues cite as an example a "public-school teacher who began her part-time fencing when she was approached by a student who offered her a 'really good deal' on certain items."[129] Although these individuals do not engage in receiving stolen property at the same level as professional or avocational fences, "they represent a large market for stolen goods" because they "compensate for lack of volume with their sheer numbers."[130] An interesting YouTube video about the life of a young criminal receiver can be viewed at **Web Extra 10–6**

THE CASE

Colton Harris-Moore (The Barefoot Bandit)

On January 27, 2012, Colton Harris-Moore, 21, was sentenced to six and one-half years in federal prison for dozens of crimes he had committed in three different countries. Harris-Moore, who gained celebrity for his widely publicized attempts to evade arrest, came to be known as the "Barefoot Bandit" because he reportedly committed some of his crimes while barefoot.[i]

Harris-Moore began living a survivalist lifestyle in his home state of Washington at age seven and would break into homes and businesses to steal food, blankets, and other supplies. At 12, he was convicted of possessing stolen property, and he quickly built a record of continued juvenile offenses. Diagnosed with attention deficit disorder and depression, he was ordered to community service or brief stays in a detention facility following each offense. By 2008, then-17-year-old Harris-Moore was stealing ever-more-expensive items and was sentenced to spend three years in a halfway house. He fled soon after arriving at the home.[ii]

His criminal career eventually expanded to include more than 100 larcenies, involving thefts of cars, bicycles, boats, and airplanes. Eventually, Harris-Moore went on the run, leaving a trail of thefts and stolen vehicles from the state of Washington to Indiana. He became a sensation on Facebook when a fan page was created to follow his exploits. On July 4, 2010, he stole a Cessna single-engine airplane from the Bloomington, Indiana, airport and, using skills he had learned from flight simulation software and airplane manuals, flew it to Great Abaco Island in the Bahamas, where he crash-landed in water. After drinking beer in a local bar, Harris-Moore stole a 44-foot power boat from a marina on Great Abaco and used it to travel to nearby Eleuthera Island. Spotted by authorities, he attempted to flee, but officers shot out the engine and captured him.

On December 16, 2011, Harris-Moore was sentenced in Island County, Washington, to more than seven years in prison on charges ranging from identity theft and theft of a firearm to residential burglary. His lawyers had argued that he was abused as a child, suffered from prenatal alcohol exposure, and was raised by a drunken mother. In a statement provided to the judge, Harris-Moore said that his childhood was one he wouldn't wish on his "darkest enemies." Judge Vickie Churchill apparently agreed, saying, "This case is a tragedy in many ways, but it's a triumph of the human spirit in other ways." Describing Harris-Moore's childhood as a "mind numbing absence of hope," she stated that the 20-year-old was genuinely remorseful for his crimes.[iii]

RHB WENN Photos/Newscom

Colton Harris-Moore, the "Barefoot Bandit," under arrest. Harris-Moore committed dozens of crimes in three different countries and became something of a folk hero before his arrest. Why did Harris-Moore turn to crime?

In an email a few days after his sentencing in state court, Harris-Moore wrote to his supporters, saying, "When all the acting and spreading of high propaganda on the part of the state was over and my lawyers argued the true facts, the judge gave me a much-appreciated recognition and validation, calling my story a 'triumph of the human spirit.' She wasn't having none of the weak argument the prosecution tried to peddle, and ended up handing down a sentence that was the lowest possible within the range. . . . Once again, I made it through a situation I shouldn't have."[iv]

Harris-Moore has said that he plans to study in preparation for applying to college to earn a degree in aeronautical engineering. Fox bought the movie rights in a deal that could be worth $1.3 million, and Dustin Lance Black, who won an Academy Award for writing the movie "Milk," about the gay rights activist Harvey Milk, is working on the screenplay.

(*continued*)

THE CASE

Colton Harris-Moore (The Barefoot Bandit) (*Continued*)

Notes

[i]Laura L. Myers, " 'Barefoot Bandit' Gets 6.5 Years of Federal Time," *Chicago Tribune* via Reuters, January 27, 2012, http://www.chicagotribune.com/news/sns-rt-us-barefoot-bandit-sentencingtre80q1tm-20120127,0,4418476.story (accessed March 1, 2012).

[ii]Manual Valdes, " 'Barefoot Bandit' Sentenced to 6 ½ Years," Pantagraph.com via AP, January 31, 2012, http://www.pantagraph.com/news/weird-news/barefoot-bandit-sentenced-to-years/article_e671e808-4c28-11e1-81c6-0019bb2963f4.html (accessed May 2, 2012).

[iii]Charles Montaldo, "'Barefoot Bandit' Gets 6 1/2 Federal Years," About.com/Crime and Punishment, January 28, 2012, http://crime.about.com/b/2012/01/28/barefoot-bandit-gets-7-federal-years.htm (accessed March 2, 2012).

[iv]Gene Johnson, " 'Barefoot Bandit' Emails Ridicule Law Enforcement," Associated Press, January 25, 2012, http://abcnews.go.com/US/wireStory/barefoot-bandit-emails-ridicule-law-enforcement-15432245#.Tyln_mNSRak (accessed May 1, 2012).

The case of the Barefoot Bandit raises a number of interesting questions. Among them are the following:

1. **What led Harris-Moore to embark on a crime spree?**
2. **What role did his mother and father (or his mother's boyfriends) play in contributing to Harris-Moore's criminal lifestyle?**
3. **Would Harris-Moore have turned to crime had he been raised under different circumstances? Explain.**

CHAPTER 10 Crimes Against Property—*It's What We Lose*

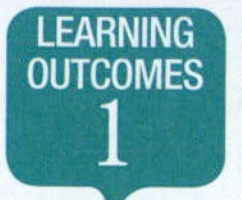

Summarize the nature and pattern of property crime.

Property crimes are distinguished from violent personal crimes because they target things rather than people. According to the FBI, the major property crimes are burglary, larceny, motor vehicle theft, and arson. This chapter presents a wealth of property crime statistics provided by federal sources.

1. What are the major forms of property crime?

property crime According to the FBI's Uniform Crime Reporting Program, a crime category that includes burglary, larceny, motor vehicle theft, and arson.

LEARNING OUTCOMES 2

Describe the crime of burglary and various forms of burglary.

The crime of burglary consists of the unlawful entry into a structure for the purpose of felony commission, generally a theft. The FBI distinguishes between burglaries involving forcible entry, unlawful entry, and attempted forcible entry.

1. How do the motivations of burglars vary? In what ways are they the same?

burglary The unlawful entry into a structure for the purpose of felony commission, generally a theft.

Key Name

Laura Dugan A criminologist who found that property crimes rather than violent crimes can cause a family to move from a neighborhood.

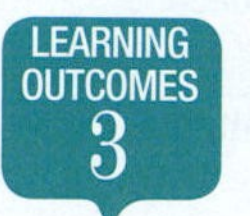

Describe the crime of larceny-theft and the various kinds of theft.

Larceny is the most frequently occurring property offense according to both official data compiled by the FBI and data from the NCVS. Within the offenses subsumed under the category of larceny in UCR/NIBRS data, the largest category is theft from motor vehicles, followed by shoplifting and theft from buildings. Offenses such as pocket picking and purse snatching constitute a small percentage of all larcenies, but employee theft is a more frequent form of larceny.

1. What is larceny-theft? How does it differ from burglary? From robbery?

larceny-theft "The unlawful taking, carrying, leading, or riding away of property from the possession, or constructive possession, of another."

Key Names

Lloyd W. Klemke A criminologist who used self-report research to reveal that almost two-thirds of individuals had shoplifted at some time in their lives.

Mary Owen Cameron A researcher who used department store records to reveal that females are more likely to be apprehended for shoplifting than are males.

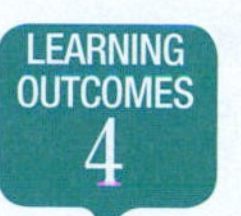

Describe identity theft and some of the techniques used by identity thieves.

Identity theft is a new and special kind of larceny that involves obtaining credit, merchandise, or services by fraudulent personal representation.

1. What is identity theft? How can identities be stolen?
2. Name and describe two important pieces of federal legislation aimed at thwarting identity thieves.

identity theft The unauthorized use of another individual's personal identity to fraudulently obtain money, goods, or services; to avoid the payment of debt; or to avoid criminal prosecution.

Identity Theft and Assumption Deterrence Act The first federal law to make identity theft a crime. The 1998 statute makes it a crime whenever anyone "knowingly transfers or uses, without lawful authority, a means of identification of another person with the intent to commit, or to aid or abet, any unlawful activity that constitutes a violation of federal law, or that constitutes a felony under any applicable state or local law."

Identity Theft Penalty Enhancement Act A 2004 federal law that added two years to federal prison sentences for criminals convicted of using stolen credit card numbers and other personal data to commit crimes.

Describe the crime of motor vehicle theft.

Motor vehicle theft involves "the theft or attempted theft of a motor vehicle," where the term *motor vehicle* includes automobiles, buses, motorcycles, and snowmobiles. It may be committed for a variety of purposes, including joyriding and the sale of motor vehicle parts through the use of chop shops that dismantle stolen cars and resell their parts.

1. What is a motor vehicle for statistical reporting purposes? What kinds of motorized vehicles are excluded?
2. What reasons for motor vehicle theft does this chapter provide?

motor vehicle theft "The theft or attempted theft of a motor vehicle," where the term *motor vehicle* refers to various means of transportation, including automobiles, buses, motorcycles, and snowmobiles.

joyriding An opportunistic car theft, often committed by a teenager seeking fun or thrills.

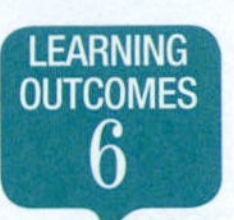

Summarize the characteristics of arson.

Arson refers to an intentionally set fire that maliciously damages property, to include vehicles, structures, and the personal property of another. According to UCR/NIBRS data, juveniles represent the offenders in arson incidents at a much higher rate than is found in any other index offense.

1. What three general groups of juvenile fire setters does this chapter identify? What are the differences between them?

arson Any willful or malicious burning or attempt to burn (with or without intent to defraud) a dwelling, a house, a public building, a motor vehicle, aircraft, or personal property of another.

Distinguish between persistent and professional thieves.

Many thieves are persistent, but this does not make them professionals. A professional thief makes a living from criminal pursuits, is recognized by other offenders as professional, and engages in offending that is planned and calculated.

1. Explain the differences between persistent and professional thieves.

professional criminal A criminal offender who makes a living from criminal pursuits, is recognized by other offenders as professional, and engages in offending that is planned and calculated.

persistent thief A person who continues in property crimes despite no better than an ordinary level of success.

occasional offender A criminal offender whose offending patterns are guided primarily by opportunity.

Key Name

Neil Shover A criminologist who distinguished between persistent and professional thieves.

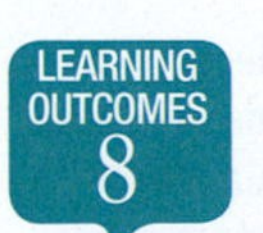

Expound upon the three basic categories of burglars and detail the process of target selection in burglary.

The three basic categories of burglars are low-level, middle-range, and high-level. *Low-level burglars* are primarily juveniles who often commit their crimes on the spur of the moment. Middle-range burglars often go back and forth between legitimate pursuits and involvement in crime, but they select targets that take into account both the potential payoff and the risk involved. *High-level burglars* are professionals who earn a good living from the proceeds of their crimes, which are carefully planned, including target selection.

1. What are the three basic categories of burglars?
2. How do burglars select their targets?

Key Name

Mike Maguire A criminologist who offers three basic categories of burglars: low-level, middle-range, and high-level burglars.

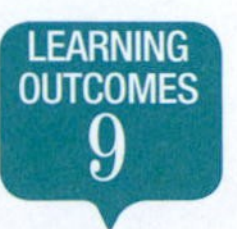

Characterize burglars and their motivation.

The most prevalent rationale behind the offense of residential burglary is the need for fast cash. The vast majority of burglars are committed to street culture, and the money they obtain from burglary goes to support their lifestyle—a lifestyle that includes illicit drugs, alcohol, and sexual pursuits, as well as "keeping up appearances."

1. To what extent are property offenders, especially burglars, rational actors?

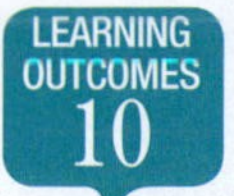

Describe the role and various types of fences and criminal receivers.

There are three kinds of fences, or criminal receivers: professional receivers, avocational receivers, and amateur receivers. The use of a professional fence is the least common method of disposing of stolen goods for the majority of thieves, but it is the most common method used by professional thieves.

1. In what kinds of illegal activities are receivers of stolen property generally involved?
2. How do stolen goods get resold?

fence An individual or a group involved in buying, selling, and distributing stolen items. Also called a *criminal receiver*.

Key Names

Carl Klockars A criminologist who used the case study method to detail the career of a professional fence.

Darrell Steffensmeier A criminologist who studied the life of the professional fence.

Paul F. Cromwell A researcher who offered a three-part typology of criminal receivers: professional receivers, avocational receivers, and amateur receivers.

"More money has been stolen at the point of a pen than at the point of a gun."

—Woody Guthrie

White-Collar and Organized Crime—Crime as a Job

1 Describe the various types of white-collar crime.

2 Define *corporate crime* and explain how a corporation can commit a crime.

3 Describe the causes of white-collar crime.

4 Summarize the efforts to curtail white-collar crime.

5 Outline the history and activities of organized crime.

6 Explain criminal enterprise and identify some of the more important criminal gangs operating in the United States.

7 Explain transnational organized crime.

8 Summarize the efforts, including federal legislation, aimed at curtailing organized crime.

9 Describe what can be done to combat organized crime.

Fotolia

INTRO

FINANCIAL FRAUD INVESTIGATIONS

In 2011, Attorney General Eric Holder announced the results of a nationwide takedown that involved Medicare Fraud Strike Force operations in Houston, Baton Rouge, Brooklyn, Chicago, Dallas, Detroit, Los Angeles, and Miami.[1] As a result of the operation, a total of 91 individuals were arrested and charged with various Medicare-fraud-related offenses, including fraudulent billings of approximately $295 million to the U.S. government. Included among those charged were:

- 45 individuals in Miami—including a doctor and a nurse—who were charged for their participation in various fraud schemes involving a total of $159 million in fraudulent Medicare billings in the areas of home health care, mental health services, occupational and physical therapy, durable medical equipment, and HIV infusion
- 6 people in Los Angeles—including one doctor—who were charged for their roles in schemes to defraud Medicare of more than $10.7 million.
- 3 defendants in Brooklyn—including two doctors—who were charged in a fraud scheme involving more than $3.4 million in false claims for medically unnecessary physical therapy
- 18 people in Detroit—including doctors, nurses, clinic operators, and other health care professionals—who were charged for schemes involving an additional $28 million in false billing

The Medicare Fraud Strike Force, coordinated jointly by the Department of Justice (DOJ) and the Department of Health and Human Services (HHS), is a multiagency team of federal, state, and local investigators who combat Medicare fraud by analyzing Medicare claims and payout data. Learn more about efforts the federal government is making to prevent Medicare fraud at **Web Extra 11–1**.

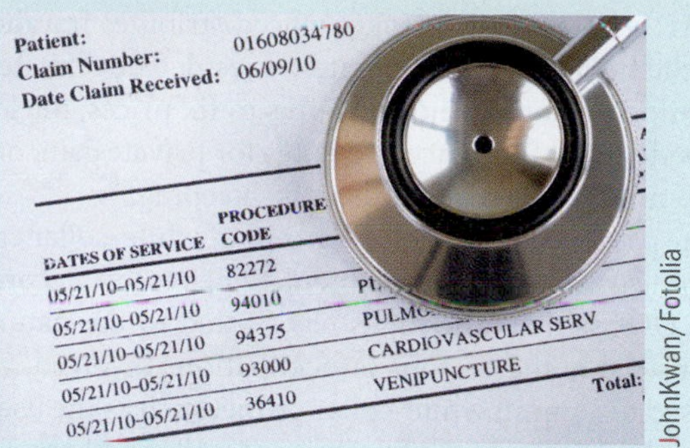

JohnKwan/Fotolia

DISCUSS **Unlike traditional forms of crime, white-collar crime is a relatively new offense made possible by the complex financial transactions characteristic of modern society. Should white-collar criminals, once convicted, be treated like offenders who commit more traditional crimes? Explain.**

White-Collar Crime

In 1939, **Edwin H. Sutherland** defined **white-collar crime** as violations of the criminal law "committed by a person of respectability and high social status in the course of his occupation."[2] Many criminologists do not properly understand crime, Sutherland claimed, because they fail to recognize that the secretive violations of public and corporate trust by those in positions of authority are just as criminal as predatory acts committed by people of lower social standing.

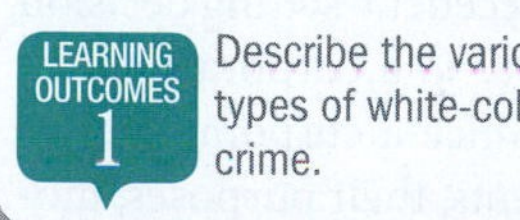
LEARNING OUTCOMES 1 Describe the various types of white-collar crime.

Sutherland also noted that white-collar criminals are far less likely to be investigated, arrested, or prosecuted than are other types of offenders. In Sutherland's day, when they were convicted, white-collar offenders were much less likely to receive active prison terms than were "common criminals." The deference shown to white-collar criminals, said Sutherland, is due primarily to their social standing. Many white-collar criminals have been well respected in their communities, and many have taken part in national affairs.

Given these kinds of sentiments, criminologists felt compelled for years to address the question "Is white-collar crime really crime?" As recently as 1987, writers on the subject were still asking, "Do persons of high standing commit crimes?"[3] Although most criminologists today would answer the question with a resounding *yes*, members of the public were slower to accept the notion that violations of the criminal law by businesspeople share conceptual similarities with street crime. Attitudes, however, have quickly changed during the past few years as headline-making charges have been filed against a number of corporate scam artists and financial managers who duped investors out of billions of dollars.

Definitional Evolution of White-Collar Crime

The chief criterion for a crime to be "white collar" is that "it occurs as a part of, or a deviation from, the violator's occupational role."[4] This focus on the violator, rather than on the offense, in deciding whether to classify a crime as white collar was accepted by the 1967 Presidential Commission on Law Enforcement and

Administration of Justice. In its classic report *The Challenge of Crime in a Free Society*, members of the commission wrote, "The 'white-collar' criminal is the broker who distributes fraudulent securities, the builder who deliberately uses defective material, the corporation executive who conspires to fix prices, the legislator who peddles his influence and votes for private gain, or the banker who misappropriates funds in his keeping."[5]

Over the past few decades, the concept of white-collar crime has undergone considerable refinement.[6] The reason, according to the U.S. DOJ, is that "the focus has shifted to the nature of the crime instead of the persons or occupations involved."[7] The methods used to commit white-collar crime, such as the use of a computer and the Internet, and the special skills and knowledge necessary for attempted law violation have resulted in a contemporary understanding of white-collar crime that emphasizes the type of offense being committed rather than the social standing or occupational role of the person committing it. Some reasons for this shift are changes in the work environment and in the business world itself. Other reasons are pragmatic. In the words of the Justice Department, "The categorization of 'white-collar crime' as crime having a particular modus operandi [committed in a manner that utilizes deception and special knowledge of business practices and committed in a particular kind of economic environment] is of use in coordinating the resources of the appropriate agencies for purposes of investigation and prosecution."[8]

The National White Collar Crime Center (http://www.NW3C.org), for example, operates the Internet Crime Complaint Center (http://www.IC3.gov), referred to as IC3, and reports on white-collar crimes committed via the Internet. Figure 11–1 shows the top-ten Internet crime complaint categories recorded by the IC3 for 2010.

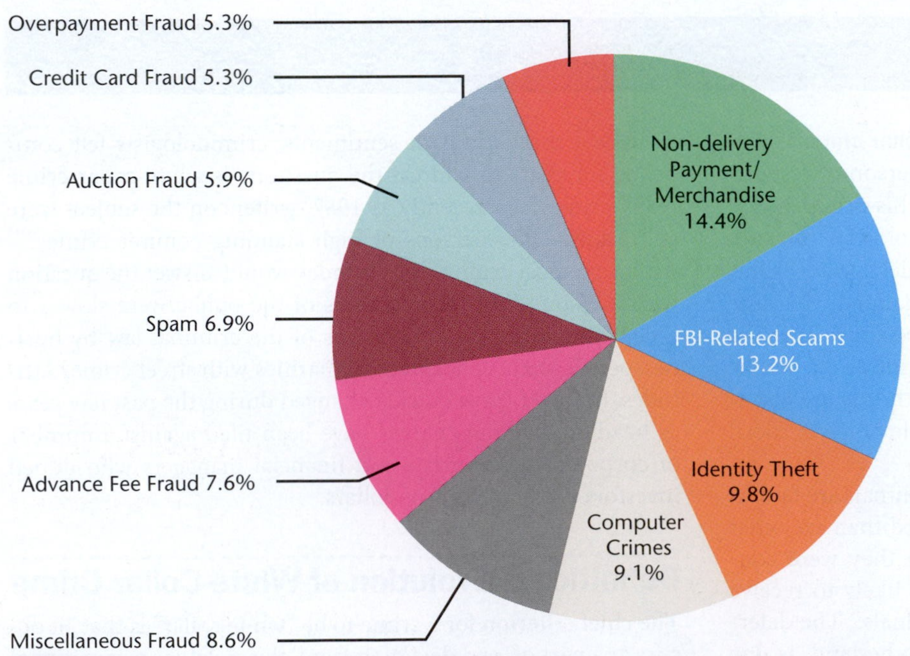

Occupational crime has recently emerged as a kind of new catchall category. **Occupational crime** can be defined as "any act punishable by law that is committed through opportunity created in the course of an occupation which is legal."[9] Occupational crimes include the job-related law violations of both white- and blue-collar workers. According to experts, white-collar crimes result in more than $300 billion in losses to the American economy every year.[10] Other terms associated with occupational and white-collar crime are shown in Table 11–1. Visit the White Collar Crime Professor's Blog at **Web Extra 11–2**. Cornell University Law School's white-collar crime web page is available at **Web Extra 11–3**.

Corporate Crime

Corporate malfeasance, which is essentially another form of white-collar crime, has been dubbed "corporate crime." **Corporate crime** can be defined as "a violation of a criminal statute either by a corporate entity or by its executives, employees, or agents acting on behalf of and for the benefit of the corporation, partnership, or other form of business entity."[11] Corporate crimes come in many forms, ranging from prior knowledge about automobile defects to price fixing and insider securities trading. Culpability, which often results in civil suits against the corporation along with possible criminal prosecutions, is greatest where company officials can be shown to have had advance knowledge about product defects, dangerous conditions, or illegal behavior on the part of employees.

LEARNING OUTCOMES 2 Define *corporate crime* and explain how a corporation can commit a crime.

In 1909, in the case of *New York Central and Hudson River Railroad Co.* v. *United States*,[12] the U.S. Supreme Court reasoned that the criminal acts and intentions of a company's employees can extend to the company itself. The Court said that because corporations could be held liable for civil wrongs involving their employees' bad conduct, it would be appropriate to hold them criminally liable as well. In its precedent-setting decision assigning legal liability to a corporate entity, the justices wrote, "Since a corporation acts by its officers and agents, their purposes, motives, and intent are just as much those of the corporation as are the things done."

In 2002, in an example of how corporations can be held criminally responsible for the acts of their officials, the accounting firm of Arthur Andersen was convicted of obstruction of justice after its employees destroyed documents related to Enron Corporation audits. Arthur Andersen, which had served as Enron's auditor, was forced to relinquish its U.S. licenses and closed its American offices. The company also paid more than $130 million to settle issues

FIGURE 11–1 **Top-Ten Internet Crime Complaint Categories.**
Source: National White Collar Crime Center, *Annual Report, 2010*, p. 10, http://www.ic3.gov/media/annualreport/2010_ic3report.pdf (accessed March 11, 2012). Used with permission.

TABLE 11–1 THE TERMINOLOGY OF WHITE-COLLAR CRIME

Antitrust violation: Any activity that illegally inhibits competition between companies within an industry, such as price fixing and monopolies in restraint of trade. Antitrust violations are infractions of the Sherman Act (15 U.S.C. Sections 1–7) and the Clayton Act (15 U.S.C. Sections 12–27).

Bank fraud (also financial fraud or financial institution fraud): Fraud or embezzlement that occurs within or against financial institutions that are insured or regulated by the U.S. government. Financial institution fraud includes commercial loan fraud, check fraud, counterfeit negotiable instruments, mortgage fraud, and false credit applications.

Bankruptcy fraud: The misleading of creditors through the concealment and misstatement of assets. Bankruptcy fraud also involves illegal pressure on bankruptcy petitioners.

Economic espionage/trade secret theft: The theft or misappropriation of proprietary economic information (that is, trade secrets) from an individual, a business, or an industry.

Embezzlement: The unlawful misappropriation for personal use of money, property, or other thing of value entrusted to the offender's care, custody, or control.

Environmental law violation: Any business activity in violation of federal and state environmental laws, including the discharge of toxic substances into the air, water, or soil, especially when those substances pose a significant threat of harm to people, property, or the environment.

Government fraud: Fraud against the government, especially in connection with federal government contracting and fraud in connection with federal and/or federally funded programs. Such programs include public housing, agricultural programs, defense procurement, and government-funded educational programs. Fraudulent activities involving government contracting include bribery in contracts or procurement, collusion among contractors, false or double billing, false certification of the quality of parts or of test results, and substitution of bogus or otherwise inferior parts.

Health care fraud: Fraudulent billing practices by health care providers, including hospitals, home health care, ambulance services, doctors, chiropractors, psychiatric hospitals, laboratories, pharmacies, and nursing homes that affect health care consumers, insurance providers, and government-funded payment providers such as Medicare and Medicaid. Fraudulent activities include receiving kickbacks, billing for services not rendered, billing for unnecessary equipment, and billing for services performed by a less qualified person.

Insider trading: Equity trading based on confidential information about important events that may affect the price of the issue being traded. Because confidential information confers advantages on those who possess it, federal law prohibits them from using that knowledge to reap profits or to avoid losses in the stock market.

Insurance fraud: Fraudulent activity committed by insurance applicants, policy holders, third-party claimants, or professionals who provide insurance services to claimants. Such fraudulent activities include inflating, or "padding," actual claims and fraudulent inducements to issue policies and/or establish a lower premium rate.

Kickbacks: The return of a certain amount of money from seller to buyer as a result of a collusive agreement.

Mail fraud: The use of the U.S. mail in furtherance of criminal activity.

Money laundering: The process of converting illegally earned assets, originating as cash, to one or more alternative forms to conceal such incriminating factors as illegal origin and true ownership.

Securities fraud: The theft of money resulting from intentional manipulation of the value of equities, including stocks and bonds. Securities fraud also includes theft from securities accounts and wire fraud.

Tax evasion: Fraud committed by filing false tax returns or not filing tax returns at all.

Wire fraud: The use of an electric or electronic communications facility to intentionally transmit a false and/or deceptive message in furtherance of a fraudulent activity.

Sources: Cynthia Barnett, "The Measurement of White-Collar Crime Using Uniform Crime Reporting Data," FBI, Criminal Justice Information Services Division, http://www.fbi.gov/ucr/whitecollarforweb.pdf (accessed June 18, 2009); Clifford Karchmer and Douglas Ruch, "State and Local Money Laundering Control Strategies," *NIJ Research in Brief* (Washington, DC: National Institute of Justice, 1992); and Legal Information Institute, "White-Collar Crime: An Overview," http://www.law.cornell.edu/topics/white_collar.html (accessed July 1, 2011).

relating to questionable accounting practices in its work with another company, Waste Management, in the late 1990s. The company had provided accounting services for WorldCom, Inc., prior to the arrest of that company's chief financial officer and other executives.[13] In 2005, however, the firm was at least partially vindicated when its conviction was overturned by the U.S. Supreme Court, which found that the instructions given to the jury in the 2002 trial had been flawed.[14]

Power Fasterners, Inc., of Brewster, New York, was indicted in 2007 on charges of manslaughter by Massachusetts

Think About It…

The financial debacle that grew out of the energy trading activities of Enron Corporation in the early 2000s and the infamous Gulf oil spill in 2010 are often cited by those who would hold corporations criminally responsible for the acts of their officials. Can a corporation be tried for criminal activity the same way an individual can? Why or why not?

Coco Robicheaux/Alamy

prosecutors after the epoxy products it manufactured failed in Boston's "Big Dig" tunnel in 2006, allowing 20 tons of concrete ceiling panels to collapse onto a car below, killing the passenger.[15] In 2008, the company agreed to pay $16 million to settle a civil lawsuit brought against it in exchange for a promise by prosecutors to drop manslaughter charges.[16]

Finally, in 2012, British Petroleum (BP) pleaded guilty to criminal charges and agreed to pay a $4.5 billion in fines—in addition to the tens of billions of dollars it had already agreed to pay for cleanup and to reimburse victims whose livelihood had been affected by the oil spill from the company's *Deepwater Horizon* oil rig in 2010 in the Gulf of Mexico.[17]

It should be noted, however, that corporate criminal liability is what some have called a unique form of "American exceptionalism," as few other countries hold corporations criminally accountable.[18]

Financial Crime

Most white-collar crimes are financial crimes, meaning illegal activities generally committed for monetary profit by businesses and those who run them. The FBI classifies the following types of activities as financial crimes: corporate fraud, securities and commodities fraud, health care fraud, mortgage fraud, insurance fraud, mass-marketing fraud, and money laundering (Figure 11–2).[19] We will discuss each in the pages that follow.

Corporate Fraud

The term **corporate fraud** refers to accounting schemes, self-dealing by corporate executives, and obstruction of justice as well as insider trading, kickbacks, and misuse of corporate property for personal gain. The majority of these cases pursued at the federal level are built on accounting schemes intended to deceive investors, auditors, and analysts about the financial health of a corporation; in addition to significant financial losses to investors, corporate fraud has the potential to cause damage to both investor confidence and the U.S. economy.

Securities and commodities fraud includes crimes such as stock market manipulation and investment fraud.

Corporate fraud sometimes involves the backdating of executive stock options under which the date of options is set to a time in the past when the price of the stock was lower than on the date the options were actually issued. Backdating stock options inflates the value of the options to the holder at the expense of regular shareholders.

Obstruction of justice occurs when activities are undertaken that are designed to conceal any of the types of criminal conduct noted here, particularly when the obstruction impedes the inquiries of the Securities and Exchange Commission (SEC), other regulatory agencies, and/or law enforcement agencies.

Securities and Commodities Fraud

Securities and commodities fraud includes crimes such as stock market manipulation, high-yield investment fraud (Ponzi schemes, pyramid schemes, and prime bank schemes), advance fee fraud, hedge fund fraud, commodities fraud, foreign exchange fraud, and broker embezzlement.

Stock market manipulation schemes (commonly referred to as "pump and dumps") create artificial buying pressure for a targeted security, generally a low-volume stock in the over-the-counter securities market, that is largely controlled by the fraud perpetrators. This artificially increased trading volume unfairly increases the price of the targeted security (the "pump"), which is rapidly sold off into the inflated market created for the

FIGURE 11–2 **Types of Financial Crime.**
Source: From *Criminology Today: An Integrative Introduction*, 7e by Frank A. Schmalleger. Copyright © 2014 by Pearson Education. Used by permission of Pearson Education.

Ponzi schemes use money collected from new investors to pay off earlier investors.

security by the fraud perpetrators (the "dump"), resulting in illicit gains for the perpetrators and losses for innocent third-party investors.

High-yield investment fraud takes various forms, all of which are characterized by offers of low- or no-risk investments that guarantee unusually high rates of return. **Ponzi schemes** use money collected from new investors, rather than business profits, to pay high rates of return promised to earlier investors, giving them the impression that this is a legitimate money-making enterprise when, in reality, investors' money is the only source of funding. The term *pyramid scheme* refers to money collected from newer victims of the fraud to pay earlier victims to provide a veneer of legitimacy; the victims themselves are induced to recruit more victims through the payment of recruitment commissions. *Prime bank schemes* (another form of high-yield investment fraud) induce victims to invest in financial instruments, allegedly issued by well-known institutions, offering risk-free opportunities for high rates of return. The benefits are supposedly the result of access to a secret worldwide exchange ordinarily open only to the world's largest financial institutions, but such networks don't exist or the perpetrators don't have access to them, and the perpetrators keep the money with which they've been entrusted.

Advance fee fraud encompasses a broad variety of schemes designed to induce victims into remitting up-front payments in exchange for the promise of goods, services, and/or prizes; victims are informed that to participate in this promising investment opportunity, they must first pay various taxes and/or fees—which go directly to the perpetrators. *Hedge fund fraud* uses private investment partnerships that have generally experienced a relative lack of regulatory scrutiny, and the fraud perpetrated by fund managers can involve the overstatement or misappropriation of fund assets overcharges for fund management fees, insider trading, market timing, and late trading.

Commodities fraud typically involves the deceptive or fraudulent sale of commodities investments (for example, gold, silver, oil, copper, and natural gas); false or deceptive sales practices are used to solicit victim funds for commodities transactions that either never occur or are inconsistent with the original sales promises. Commodities market participants may also attempt to illegally manipulate the market for a commodity by fraudulently reporting price information or cornering the market to artificially increase the price of the targeted commodity.

Foreign exchange fraud uses false or deceptive sales practices alleging high rates of return for minimal risk to induce victims to invest in the foreign currency exchange market. The transactions never occur or are executed for the sole purpose of generating excessive trading commission—in breach of the trader's responsibilities to the client. Alternatively, individual currency traders employed by large financial institutions may illegally attempt to manipulate foreign currency exchange prices to generate illicit trading profits for their own enrichment.

Schemes using *broker embezzlement* involve illicit, unauthorized actions by brokers to steal directly from their clients; these may be facilitated by the forging of client documents, the doctoring of account statements, or the unauthorized trading and fund transfers in violation of the broker's legal obligations to the client.

According to the FBI, the losses associated with these types of fraud range from the macroeconomic (erosion of investor confidence in capital markets) to the corporate (reduction in the economic health of corporations/industries due to decreased market capitalization) to the intensely personal (devastation of retirement and investment portfolios).[20] Victims of these kinds of fraud include government entities, corporations, financial institutions, pension funds, and individual investors.

Health Care Fraud

All health care programs are subject to fraud, with Medicare and Medicaid being most victimized. Estimates of fraudulent billings to health care programs (public and private) are said to be between 3% and 10% of all health care expenditures. According to the FBI, health care fraud is not limited to any particular geographic area, targets large health care programs (public and private) as well as beneficiaries, has become more sophisticated and complex over time, and is even being perpetrated by a number of organized crime groups.

The FBI stated that "one of the most significant trends in recent health care fraud cases includes the willingness of medical professionals to risk patient harm in their schemes."[21] These cases involve health care providers who conduct unnecessary surgeries, prescribe dangerous drugs without medical necessity, and engage in abusive or substandard care practices. Other schemes involve fraudulent billing for services not rendered and upcoding of charges for services provided.[22]

Mortgage Fraud

The federal government has reported a spike in the number of corporate fraud cases involving subprime mortgage–lending companies[23] (businesses that lend to borrowers who do not qualify for loans from mainstream loan companies). The subprime market grew from 2% of all home mortgages in 1998 to 20% of mortgages in 2006, but as the housing market declined, subprime lenders were forced to buy back a number of nonperforming loans. Many of these subprime lenders had relied on a continuous increase in real estate values to allow borrowers to refinance or sell their properties before defaulting, but due to the slowdown in the housing market, loan defaults increased.

As subprime lenders suffered financial difficulties due to rising defaults, analyses of company financials by regulators identified instances of false accounting entries and fraudulently inflated assets and revenues. Federal investigations then determined that many now-bankrupt subprime lenders manipulated their reported loan portfolio risks and used various accounting schemes to inflate and falsify their financial reports; in addition, before the value of these subprime lenders' stocks rapidly declined in value, some executives with insider information sold their equity positions and made illegal profits.

Mortgage fraud, which is not confined to the subprime market, involves material misstatements, misrepresentations, and/or omissions relating to the property or potential mortgage relied on by an underwriter or lender to fund, purchase, or insure a loan. As initial mortgage products are repackaged and sold on secondary markets, the process can conceal or distort the original fraud so that it is not reported, leading the FBI to explain that "the true level of mortgage fraud is largely unknown."[24]

Current mortgage fraud, according to the FBI, includes equity skimming, property flipping, and mortgage debt elimination. *Equity skimming* uses corporate shell companies, corporate identity theft, and bankruptcy/foreclosure (or the threat of it) to dupe homeowners and investors. *Property flipping* involves purchasing properties and artificially inflating their value through false appraisals; the overvalued properties are then repurchased several times for a higher price by associates of the "flipper." After three or four sham sales, the properties are foreclosed on by victim lenders. Often flipped properties are ultimately repurchased for 50% to 100% of their original value. *Mortgage debt elimination* uses email or Web-based ads to promote the elimination of mortgage loans, credit card debt, and other debt for an up-front fee to prepare documents to satisfy the debt, but these documents (typically referred to as Declaration of Voidance, Bond for Discharge of Debt, Bill of Exchange, Due Bill, or Redemption Certificate) do not achieve debt-elimination goals; they only gain profit for the scammers.

Insurance Fraud

The U.S. insurance industry consists of thousands of companies and collects nearly $1 trillion in premiums each year, so its size makes it a prime target for criminal activity.[25] The Coalition Against Insurance Fraud (CAIF) estimated that the cost of fraud in the industry is as high as $80 billion each year, a cost passed on to consumers in the form of higher premiums. The National Insurance Crime Bureau (NICB) calculated that insurance fraud raises the yearly cost of premiums by $300 for the average household.

Insurance fraud involving arson is also related to the mortgage crisis. Some distressed homeowners, property flippers, and other real estate investors have resorted to committing arson to avoid real estate foreclosure; the insurance policyholders for these properties receive otherwise-unobtainable proceeds/profits through the filing of false insurance claims.

With the downturn in the American and worldwide economies that started in the first decade of this century, workers' compensation fraud has soared. Workers' compensation insurance accounts for as much as 46% of small-business owners' operating expenses, so small-business owners have an incentive to shop for workers' compensation insurance on a regular basis. This has created an illicit opportunity for entities purporting to provide workers' compensation insurance to enter the marketplace, offer reduced premiums, and misappropriate funds without providing insurance, leaving injured and deceased victims and their families without workers' compensation coverage to pay medical bills.

Flipping involves purchasing properties and inflating their value through false appraisals; overvalued properties are repurchased several times for higher prices by associates of the "flipper."

Mass-Marketing Fraud

Mass-marketing fraud is a general term for any fraud connected with communications media such as telemarketing, mass mailings, and the Internet. Mass-marketing fraud takes a variety of forms that share a common theme: use of false and/or deceptive representations to induce potential victims to make advance-fee-type payments to fraud perpetrators. Although there are no comprehensive statistics on the subject, it is estimated that mass-marketing frauds victimize millions of Americans each year and generate losses in the hundreds of millions of dollars. Following is a brief description of three key concepts and schemes associated with mass-marketing fraud.

1. *Nigerian letter fraud.* Victims of Nigerian letter fraud are contacted regarding substantial sums of money held in foreign accounts that they are told is owed to them, and they are requested to pay various fees to secure the transfer of these monies to the United States; these fees are kept by the perpetrators. Victims also may be asked to act as U.S. agents in securing the release of such funds and are provided with counterfeit instruments to be cashed to pay any required fees, only to discover that they must reimburse their financial institutions for cashing counterfeit instruments.
2. *Foreign lottery/sweepstakes fraud.* Victims are informed that they have won a substantial prize in a foreign lottery or sweepstakes but must remit payment for various taxes/fees to receive their winnings; the taxes/fees are paid to the perpetrators. Victims may be given financial documents, supposedly representing a portion of the winnings, to be cashed to pay the required fees, only to discover that they must reimburse their financial institutions for cashing counterfeit instruments.
3. *Overpayment fraud.* Victims who have advertised some item for sale are contacted by buyers who remit counterfeit instruments in excess of the purchase price for payment; the victims are told to cash the instruments, deduct any expenses, and return or forward the excess funds to an individual identified by the buyer, only to discover that they must reimburse their financial institution for cashing counterfeit instruments.

Money Laundering

Money laundering is the process by which illegal gains are disguised as legal income. A more formal definition is offered by the National Institute of Justice for *money laundering*: "the process of converting illegally earned assets, originating as cash, to one or more alternative forms to conceal such incriminating factors as illegal origin and true ownership."[26] In 2010, Wachovia Corporation (now part of Wells Fargo & Company) agreed

In money laundering, illegal gains are disguised as legal income.

to pay $160 million to settle federal charges that it failed to establish an adequate program to prevent money laundering through its facilities.[27] The plea resulted from transactions involving Wachovia and Mexican money exchanges between 2004 and 2007 that facilitated money transfers between the United States and Mexico; a federal investigation found that drug dealers routinely used them to move funds between the two countries.

Title 18, Section 1956, of the U.S. Criminal Code specifically prohibited what it called the "laundering of monetary instruments" and defined *money laundering* as "[efforts] to conceal or disguise the nature, the location, the source, the ownership, or the control of the proceeds of specified unlawful activity."[28] To assist in the identification of money launderers, a provision of the 1986 federal Money Laundering Control Act required that banks report to the government all currency transactions in excess of $10,000. The Bank Secrecy Act (BSA), formally known as the Currency and Foreign Transactions Reporting Act, required financial institutions to assist government agencies in detecting and preventing activities related to money laundering, to report cash transactions exceeding an aggregate amount of $10,000 daily per account, and to report suspicious financial activity. However, high-end money launderers know these requirements and routinely evade them by dealing in commodities such as gold, using foreign banks, or making a series of smaller deposits and transfers, often involving numerous financial institutions. Reliable official estimates of the amount of money laundered in the United States are hard to establish. However, the Drug Enforcement Administration reported that estimates provided by the International Monetary Fund pegged worldwide money-laundering activities at between 2% and 5% of the world's gross domestic product, or about $600 billion annually.[29]

The problem of money laundering may be getting worse: A 2010 report by the Senate Permanent Subcommittee on Investigations found that billions of dollars are leaving the United States every year to be put into the flow of commerce and returned to this country as laundered capital.[30] The report also identified a number of individuals and organizations suspected of bringing millions of dollars from illegal activities into the country by funneling it through offshore accounts.

Environmental Crimes

A relatively new area of corporate and white-collar criminality, which is defined solely in terms of violations of the criminal law, is that of crimes against the environment.[31] **Environmental crimes** are violations of the criminal law that, although typically committed by businesses or business officials, may also be committed by other individuals or organizational entities and that damage some protected or otherwise significant aspect of the natural environment.

Whaling in violation of international conventions, for example, constitutes a form of environmental crime. So, too, does

Crimes against the environment constitute a relatively new area of corporate and white-collar criminality.

intentional pollution, especially when state or federal law contravenes the practice. Sometimes negligence contributes to environmental criminality, as in the case of the 1,000-foot *Valdez* supertanker owned by Exxon Corporation, which ran aground off the coast of Alaska in 1989, spilling 11 million gallons of crude oil over 1,700 miles of pristine coastline. In September 1994, an Alaskan jury ordered Exxon to pay $5 billion in punitive damages to 14,000 people affected by the 1989 spill and another $287 million in actual damages to commercial fishermen in the region. Exxon also agreed to pay $100 million in criminal fines.

British Petroleum Products North America, Inc. (BPPNA) pleaded guilty in 2007 to one felony count of violating the federal Clean Air Act; it was ordered to pay $50 million in fines and was placed on three years of federal probation. The conviction stemmed from an explosion at the BPPNA Texas City refinery on March 23, 2005, that caused the death of 15 employees. The company admitted that several procedures required under the Clean Air Act for ensuring the integrity of safety equipment either had not been established or were being ignored. The British Petroleum subsidiary BP Exploration Alaska (BPXA) pleaded guilty to one count of violating the federal Clean Water Act as a result of a 2006 oil spill of 267,000 gallons at its facility on Alaska's North Slope.[32] Authorities charged that the spill occurred because company officials had conspired to save money by acting to conceal corrosion in a pipeline used to transfer oil and falsifying financial reports detailing money spent to fix the corrosion. The company agreed to pay a $20 million fine and was placed on three years' probation.[33]

As this book goes to press, British Petroleum is facing dozens of civil and criminal charges stemming from the Gulf oil spill that began on April 20, 2010, when the company's deep-water drilling platform *Deep Water Horizon* suffered an explosion and fire and sank, releasing 206 million gallons of oil into the Gulf of Mexico from a wellhead 5,000 feet below the surface.[34] So far, the company has agreed to pay out $37 billion in oil spill expenses.[35]

The devastating fires set in oil fields throughout Kuwait by retreating Iraqi Army troops during the Gulf War in 1991 provide an example of arson that resulted in global pollution while negatively affecting fossil fuel reserves throughout much of the Middle East. These intentional fires, although properly classified as environmental criminality, also serve as an example of ecological terrorism because they were set for the purpose of political intimidation.

Terrorism and White-Collar Crime

Terrorist activity frequently involves some form of white-collar crime because terrorists need money for daily living expenses and for weapons, travel, and communications.

Involvement in white-collar crime allows terrorist groups to maintain a significantly lower profile.

Terrorist groups also frequently send a portion of the money acquired from illegal activities back to their home country or pass it along to those higher up in the chain of command. Involvement in white-collar crime allows terrorist groups to maintain a significantly lower profile than if they raised funds through other crimes such as bank robberies and illegal drug sales.

John Kane and April Wall, in a report prepared for the White Collar Crime Center, pointed out that "curtailing terrorist activity may be achieved through the combined efforts of nations, through legislation that criminalizes the financing of terrorism, modifications to regulations that govern non-profit or charity-based corporations, international cooperation, and a willingness of the international banking community to adhere to reporting rules designed to detect money laundering and suspicious activity" and that shell companies have been used by terrorist groups to receive and distribute money.[36] The term *shell companies* refers to entities engaged in legitimate activities to establish a good reputation in the business community and provide a veneer of legitimacy; they can launder funds by creating invoices for nonexistent products or services that then appear to be paid by another company to provide a channel for profits from illegal activities (such as insurance fraud and identity theft) so that the money enters the legitimate flow of cash disguised as revenue from legitimate activities. In 2001, for example, an American telecommunications company was indicted on charges of aiding members of al-Qaeda in preparation for the 9/11 terrorist attacks by handling more than $500,000 in monthly money transfers. Table 11–2 provides examples of the kinds of white-collar crimes associated with terrorism in recent years, along with information on federal criminal statutes that these kinds of activities violate.

Causes of White-Collar Crime

When Edwin H. Sutherland first coined the term *white-collar crime*, he wrote, "A hypothesis is needed that will explain both white-collar criminality and lower-class criminality."[37] The answer Sutherland gave to his own challenge was that "white-collar criminality, just as other systematic criminality, is learned."[38] He went on to apply elements of his famous theory of differential association (discussed in Chapter 6) to white-collar crime, saying that "it is learned in direct or indirect association with those who already practice the behavior."[39]

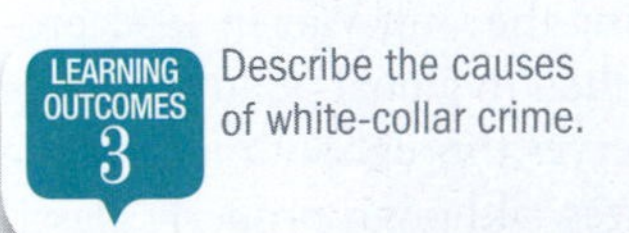

Describe the causes of white-collar crime.

Other authors have since offered similar integrative perspectives. Travis Hirschi and Michael Gottfredson, for example, in an issue of the journal *Criminology* published half a century after Sutherland's initial work, write, "In this paper we outline a general theory of crime capable of organizing the facts about white-collar crime at the same time it is capable of organizing the facts about all forms of crime."[40] Their analysis of white-collar crime focuses squarely on the development of the concept itself. Hirschi and Gottfredson suggest that if we were not aware of the fact that the concept of white-collar crime arose "as a reaction to the idea that crime is concentrated in the lower class, there would be nothing to distinguish it from other" forms of crime.[41] "It may be, then," they write, "that the discovery of white-collar criminals is important only in a context in which their existence is denied by theory or policy."[42] In other words, nothing is unusual about the idea of white-collar crime other than the fact that many people are loath to admit that high-status individuals commit crimes just as people of lower status do.

In fact, say Hirschi and Gottfredson, white-collar criminals are motivated by the same forces that drive other criminals: self-interest, the pursuit of pleasure, and the avoidance of pain. White-collar crimes certainly have special characteristics. They are not as dangerous as other "common" forms of crime, they provide relatively large rewards, the rewards they produce may follow quickly from their commission, sanctions associated with them may be vague or only rarely imposed, and they may require only minimal effort from those with the requisite skills to engage in them.

Hirschi and Gottfredson conclude, however, that criminologists err in assuming that white-collar criminality is common or that it is as common as the forms of criminality found among the lower classes. They reason that the personal characteristics of most white-collar workers are precisely those we would expect to produce conformity in behavior. High educational levels, a commitment to the status quo, personal motivation to succeed, deference to others, attention to conventional appearance, and other inherent aspects of social conformity—all of which tend to characterize those who operate at the white-collar level—are not the kinds of personal characteristics associated with crime commission. "In other words," say Hirschi and Gottfredson, "selection processes inherent to the high end of the occupational structure tend to recruit people with relatively low propensity to crime."[43]

One other reason most criminologists are mistaken about the assumed high rate of white-collar criminality is because "white-collar researchers often take organizations as the unit of analysis" and confuse the crimes committed by organizational entities with those of individuals within those organizations.[44] Similarly, rates of white-collar offending tend to lump together the crimes of corporations with crimes committed by individual representatives of those organizations when making comparisons with the rate of criminal activity among blue-collar and other groups.

Edwin Sutherland said that white-collar criminality is learned, just like other forms of criminal activity.

TABLE 11–2 WHITE-COLLAR CRIMES ASSOCIATED WITH TERRORISM CASES

Type of Offense	Description of Offense	Statute
Identification Document Fraud	Fraud in connection with identification documents	18 USC 1028
	Forgery or false use of passports	18 USC 1543
	Misuse of passports	18 USC 1544
	Fraud and misuse of visas, permits, and other documents	18 USC 1546
	Social Security fraud	42 USC 408
Financial Fraud	Bribery of public officials and witnesses	18 USC 201
	Counterfeited or forged securities of states and private entities	18 USC 513
	False statements on credit application	18 USC 1014
	Bank fraud	18 USC 1344
	Money laundering	18 USC 1956
	Unlicensed money-transmitting business	18 USC 1960
	Racketeering	18 USC 1962
	Transactions structured to evade reporting requirements	31 USC 5324
Mail and Wire Fraud	Mail fraud	18 USC 1341
	Fraud by wire, radio, or television	18 USC 1343
Credit Card Fraud	Fraud in connection with access devices	18 USC 1029
Tax Fraud	Materially false income tax returns	26 USC 7206
	Corrupt endeavors to impede IRS laws	26 USC 7212
Immigration Fraud	Deportable alien	8 USC 1227
	Alien failing to report address change	8 USC 1305
	Alien smuggling	8 USC 1324
	Evasion of immigration laws	8 USC 1325
	False representations as U.S. citizen	18 USC 911
	Illegal alien	18 USC 922
	False statements regarding naturalization, citizenship, or alien registry	18 USC 1015
	Unlawful procurement of citizenship or naturalization	18 USC 1425
Other Related Charges	Aiding and abetting	18 USC 2
	Conspiracy to commit offenses against or defraud the U.S.	18 USC 371
	Materially false statements	18 USC 1001
	Perjury	18 USC 1621
	Provision of material support to terrorists	18 USC 2339
	Conspiracy to give or receive funds, goods, or services for designated terrorist	50 USC 595

Note: Subchapters are not listed.
Source: John Kane and April Wall, *Identifying the Links between White-Collar Crime and Terrorism* (Glen Allen, VA: National White Collar Crime Center, September 2004), p. 13.

A complementary perspective by Australian criminologist **John Braithwaite** says that white-collar criminals are frequently motivated by a disparity between corporate goals and the limited opportunities available to businesspeople through conventional business practices.[45] When pressured to achieve goals that may be unattainable within the existing framework of laws and regulations surrounding their business's area of endeavor, innovative corporate officers may turn to crime to meet organizational demands.[46]

Braithwaite believes that a general theory covering both white-collar and other forms of crime can be developed by focusing on inequality as the central explanatory variable in all criminal activity.[47] Although alienation from legitimate paths to success may lead lower-class offenders to criminal activity in an effort to acquire the material possessions necessary for survival, greed can similarly motivate relatively successful individuals to violate the law to acquire even more power and more wealth.[48] New types of criminal opportunities and new paths to immunity from accountability arise from inequitable concentrations of wealth and power. Inequality thus worsens crimes of poverty motivated by the need to survive as well as crimes of wealth motivated by greed.

Braithwaite also suggests that corporate culture socializes budding executives into clandestine and frequently illegal behavioral modalities, making it easier for them to violate the law when pressures to perform mount. The hostile relationship that frequently exists between businesses and the government agencies that regulate them may further spur corporate officers to evade the law. Braithwaite emphasizes his belief that the potential for shame associated with discovery—whether by enforcement agencies, the public, or internal corporate regulators—can have a powerful deterrent effect on most corporate executives because they are fundamentally conservative individuals who are otherwise seeking success through legitimate means.[49]

Braithwaite also recommends implementation of an "accountability model," which would hold all those responsible for corporate crimes accountable.[50] Rather than merely punishing corporations through fines, personal punishment meted out to corporate lawbreakers, says Braithwaite, should have the potential to substantially reduce white-collar offending.[51]

In sum, Braithwaite contends that an integrated theory of organizational crime would include insights garnered from (1) strain theories, as to the distribution of legitimate and illegitimate opportunities; (2) subcultural theory, as applied to business subcultures; (3) labeling theory, or the way stigmatization can foster criminal subculture formation; and (4) control theory, as to how potential white-collar offenders can be made accountable.[52]

Curtailing White-Collar and Corporate Crime

It is far easier to convict street criminals than white-collar criminals, and it may even be difficult for prosecutors to show that a white-collar crime has occurred. "When someone breaks into a house and takes the TV and VCR," says Harvard University criminal law professor William Stuntz, "it's a matter of proving who did it. With white-collar crime it's usually not even clear what happened."[53]

LEARNING OUTCOMES 4 Summarize the efforts to curtail white-collar crime.

White-collar crimes are often difficult to investigate and prosecute for a number of other reasons. For one thing, white-collar criminals are generally better educated compared to other offenders and are therefore better able to conceal their activities.[54] Similarly, cases against white-collar offenders must often be built on evidence of a continuing series of offenses, not a single crime, such as a bank robbery. Often the evidence involved is only understandable to financial or legal experts and can be difficult to explain to jurors. Finally, business executives, because they often have the financial resources of an entire corporation at their disposal and because they sometimes earn salaries and bonuses in the millions of dollars, are able to hire excellent defense attorneys and can tie up the courts with motions and appeals that might not be as readily available to defendants with fewer resources.

Events such as the 2001 collapse of Enron Corporation left investors around the world leery of American stock markets and forced federal legislators to enact sweeping financial reform. At the same time, the SEC renewed efforts to enforce existing regulations and mandated new rules for investment bankers. By the start of 2001, the atmosphere of distrust that had been created by corporate criminals had become so severe that President George W. Bush believed it was necessary to make significant efforts to help restore investor confidence and to bring order to American financial markets. Consequently, the president created a federal **Corporate Fraud Task Force** within the U.S. DOJ, and on July 30, 2002, he signed the **Sarbanes-Oxley Act** (officially known as the Public Company Accounting Reform and Investor Protection Act), which set stiff penalties for corporate wrongdoers.[55] View the Sarbanes-Oxley Act at **Web Extra 11–4**.

In 2007, the U.S. DOJ announced that activities of the task force had resulted in 1,236 fraud convictions, including those of 214 chief executive officers and 53 chief financial officers, since 2002.[56] In announcing the convictions, then-attorney general Alberto Gonzales noted that "perhaps the most important accomplishment is the criminal conduct that never occurred because of the widespread deterrent effect" of the task force.[57]

In 2009, President Barack Obama replaced President Bush's Corporate Fraud Task Force with an interagency task force targeting financial crimes. Called the **Financial Fraud Enforcement Task Force**, the organization consists of senior-level officials from more than 20 federal departments, agencies, and offices.[58] The new task force, which was given a wider mandate than its predecessor, was charged with combating mortgage fraud, securities fraud, Recovery Act fraud, and discrimination by financial institutions in the making of loans and in other financial activities. The task force also aimed to fully enforce the Fraud Enforcement and Recovery Act of 2009,[59] which targeted the recovery of federal funds spent on fraudulent claims made under the American Recovery and Reinvestment Act of 2009 (also known as the Financial Stimulus Act),[60] fraudulent claims under the Troubled Assets Relief Program (TARP),[61] and financial fraud related to any "other form of Federal assistance."

In his 2012 State of the Union Address to Congress, President Obama announced the creation of two more enforcement initiatives—one of which will be charged with targeting financial crimes; the other, with fighting unfair trade practices. The first, the Residential Mortgage-Backed Securities Working Group, will operate under the previously created Financial Fraud Enforcement Task Force; the second, which will investigate unfair trade practices in countries such as China, will likely be run from the White House under the Deputy National Security Advisor for International Affairs.[62]

The Sarbanes-Oxley Act, referred to earlier, has been called the most far-reaching reform of U.S. business practices since the time of Franklin Delano Roosevelt. The law authorizes funding for investigators and for the development of new technologies at the SEC targeted at uncovering corporate wrongdoing. Under the Sarbanes-Oxley Act, the SEC has the authority to bar dishonest corporate directors and officers from ever again serving in positions of corporate responsibility. Similarly, penalties for obstructing justice and shredding documents are greatly increased, corporate officers who profit illegally can be forced to return their gains to investors, and the maximum federal prison term for common types of corporate fraud has been increased from 5 to 20 years.

The Sarbanes-Oxley Act also requires chief executive officers and chief financial officers to personally vouch for the truth and fairness of their companies' financial disclosures and establishes an independent oversight board to regulate the accounting profession. The board is required to set clear standards to uphold the integrity of public audits and has the authority to investigate abuses and discipline offenders. Similarly, the Sarbanes-Oxley Act prohibits auditing firms from providing consulting services that create conflicts of interest. Finally, under the law, officials in public corporations are barred from buying or selling stock during periods when employees are prevented from making stock transactions in their retirement or 401(k) accounts.

The Sarbanes-Oxley Act was the latest in a long line of federal legislation relating to the conduct of U.S. business that extends back more than 100 years. Some of the earliest such legislation can be found in the federal Sherman Act,[63] which became law in 1890. The Sherman Act was passed to eliminate restraints on trade and competition and specifically to prevent the development of trusts and monopolies in restraint of trade. The Clayton Act,[64] passed in 1914, prohibits mergers and acquisitions in which the effect "may be substantially to lessen competition, or to tend to create a monopoly."

The Securities Act of 1933[65] and the Securities Exchange Act of 1934[66] were enacted by federal legislators reeling from the effects of the Great Depression, which began with the stock market crash of 1929. Often referred to as the "truth in securities" law, the Securities Act of 1933 has two basic objectives: (1) to require that investors receive financial and other significant information concerning securities being offered for public sale and (2) to prohibit deceit, misrepresentations, and other fraud in the sale of securities.

The Securities Exchange Act of 1934 gave birth to the SEC and conferred upon the SEC broad authority over all aspects of the securities industry. This includes the power to register, regulate, and oversee brokerage firms, transfer agents, and clearing agencies as well as the nation's stock exchanges. The act also identified and prohibited certain types of conduct in the markets and provides the SEC with disciplinary powers over regulated entities and people associated with them. Finally, the act empowered the SEC to require periodic reporting of information by companies with publicly traded securities.

Think About It…

The Sarbanes-Oxley Act has been called the most far-reaching reform of U.S. business practices since the time of Franklin Delano Roosevelt. Read the Sarbanes-Oxley Act online at http://www.soxlaw.com. What does the act do to increase fairness in American business practices? What more could it do?

RRS/Fotolia

Certain forms of occupational crime may be easier to address than others. Individual occupational crimes especially may be reduced by concerted enforcement and protective efforts, including enhanced Internal Revenue Service (IRS) auditing programs, theft-deterrent systems, and good internal financial procedures. Consumer information services can help eliminate fraudulent business practices, and increases in both victim awareness and reporting can help target businesses and individuals responsible for various forms of white-collar or occupational crime.

Organized Crime

Organized crime specifically refers to unlawful activities of the members of a highly organized, disciplined association engaged in supplying illegal goods and services, including prostitution, gambling, loan-sharking, narcotics, and labor racketeering. In 1967, the President's Commission on Law Enforcement and Administration of Justice investigated organized crime in the United States and found that—at the time—many organized crime families were of Italian descent. The Commission depicted the structure of a typical Italian American organized crime family as shown in Figure 11–3.

Outline the history and activities of organized crime.

Much of what most Americans traditionally think of today as organized crime—sometimes called the **Mafia** or **La Cosa Nostra**—has roots that predate the establishment of the United States. For hundreds of years, secret societies have flourished in

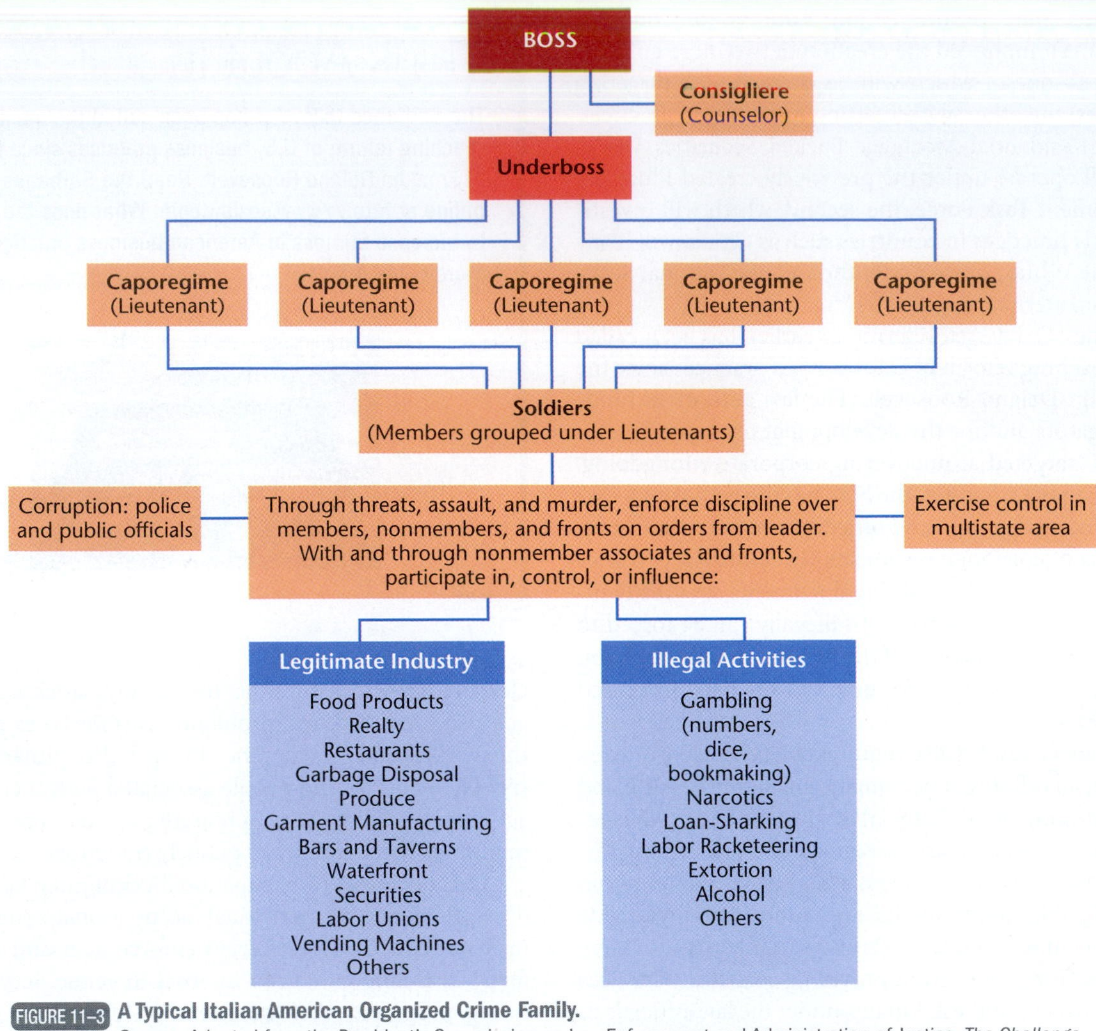

FIGURE 11–3 **A Typical Italian American Organized Crime Family.**
Source: Adapted from the President's Commission on Law Enforcement and Administration of Justice, *The Challenge of Crime in a Free Society* (Washington, DC: U.S. Government Printing Office, 1967), p. 47.

Italy.[67] Italian criminal organizations that came to the United States with the wave of European immigrants during the late nineteenth and early twentieth centuries included the Mafia and the Black Hand. The Black Hand (in Italian, *La Mano Negro*) "specialized in the intimidation of Italian immigrants,"[68] typically extorting protection money and valuables.

The Mafia worked to become a quasi-police organization in the Italian ghetto areas of the burgeoning American cities of the industrial era—often enforcing its own set of laws and codes. Secret societies in Italy were all but expunged during the 1930s and early 1940s under Fascist dictator Benito Mussolini. Surviving Mafia members became vehemently anti-Fascist, sentiments that endeared them to American and allied intelligence services during World War II. Following the war, mafioso leaders resumed their traditional positions of power within Italian society, and links grew between American criminal organizations and those in Italy.

Other organized criminal groups, including Jewish and Irish gangs, flourished in New York City prior to the arrival of large numbers of Italian immigrants in the late 1800s. Ethnic succession has been as much a reality in organized crime as in most other aspects of American life. **Ethnic succession** refers to the continuing process whereby one immigrant or ethnic group succeeds another through assumption of a particular position in society.

Throughout the late nineteenth and early twentieth centuries, for example, Jewish gangsters such as Meyer Lansky, Benjamin "Bugsy" Siegel, "Dutch" Schultz, and Lepke Buchalter ran many of the "rackets" in New York City, only to have Italian immigrants who arrived a few years later take their places.

Around the middle of the twentieth century, organized criminal activity in the United States became the domain of Italian American immigrants and their descendants, especially those of Sicilian descent. Keep in mind that most Sicilians who immigrated to this country did not have ties or experience with Mafia organizations in the old country. Many Sicilian Americans immigrated to the United States to escape Mafia despotism at home, and most became productive members of their adopted society. The few who did involve themselves in organized crime created an organization known variously as the Mafia, the Outfit, the Mob, La Cosa Nostra ("our thing"), the syndicate, or simply the organization. Because *Mafia* is used most often, we will use it to describe Sicilian American organized criminal groups. Learn more about La Cosa Nostra families operating in the United States at **Web Extra 11–5**.

Prohibition and Official Corruption

In many ways, the advent of Prohibition was a godsend for Mafia leaders. Prior to Prohibition, Mafia operations in American cities were concerned mostly with gambling, protection rackets, and loan-sharking. Many mafiosi, however, were well versed in the manufacture of low-cost, high-proof, untaxed alcohol,[69] an expertise they had brought from their native country. In addition, the existing infrastructure of organized crime permitted easy and efficient entry into the running and sale of contraband liquor. The huge profits to be had from bootlegging led to the wholesale bribery of government officials and to the quick corruption of many law enforcement officers throughout the country. Nowhere was corruption more complete than in Chicago, where runners working for organized crime distributed illegal alcohol under police protection[70] and corrupt city government officials received regular payoffs from criminal cartels.

Activities of Organized Crime

The 1976 federal Task Force on Organized Crime identified five types of activity that may qualify as organized crime: racketeering, vice operations, theft/fence rings, gangs, and terrorism. Throughout the past half century, Sicilian American criminal cartels have continued to be involved in (1) the establishment and control of both legalized and illicit forms of gambling, including lotteries, bookmaking, horse race wagering, and bets on athletic contests; (2) loan-sharking, which involves the lending of money at rates far higher than legally prescribed limits; (3) large-scale drug trafficking; (4) the fencing of stolen goods, including securities; (5) infiltration of legitimate businesses, including labor unions and corporations that can be used as quasi-legitimate fronts for money laundering and other activities; and (6) labor union racketeering through which legitimate businesses are intimidated by threats of strikes, walkouts, and sabotage.

Organized crime is involved in many kinds of rackets, including gambling and the illegal copying and distribution of copyrighted software, music, and other forms of recorded media. The provision of elaborately staged recorded pornographic productions, including "snuff movies" (in which a sex "star" is actually killed in front of the camera), and elements of child pornography can also be traced to organized criminal activity.

▶ Other Organized Criminal Groups

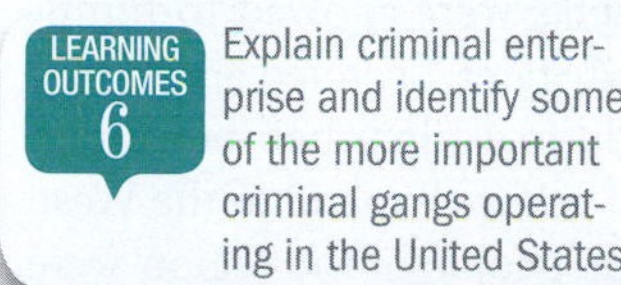

Explain criminal enterprise and identify some of the more important criminal gangs operating in the United States.

In 2013, a masked attacker threw sulfuric acid into the face of 42-year-old Sergei Filin as he walked down a Moscow street. Filin, the artistic director of the world-famous Moscow-based Bolshi Ballet, was seriously injured, and his eyesight has never fully recovered. Only two days earlier, 75-year-old Aslan Usoyan, known as the godfather of Russian organized crime, was killed by two bullets fired by a sniper as he left a restaurant in central Moscow, less than a mile from the Kremlin.

Some Russian news reporters speculated that the attacks may have been related—perhaps even carried out by the government, which some claim collaborates with organized crime to share financial and other resources, and uses criminal organizations to do its dirty work. Usoyan was suspected of controlling much of the trade in illegal arms, drugs, and gambling, and to be involved in the theft of state-owned natural resources. Filin, on the other hand, may have been targeted because the Bolshi, a national treasure in Russia, had recently focused on themes that promoted political discord.[71]

The FBI defines a **criminal enterprise** as "a group of individuals with an identifiable hierarchy, and extensive supporting networks, engaged in significant criminal activity."[72] According to **Howard Abadinsky**, the hallmark of true criminal organizations is that they function independently of any of their members, including their leaders, and have continuity over time as personnel within them change.[73] Abadinsky mentioned the James Gang, which dissolved with the death of its leader, Jesse James. In contrast, says Abadinsky, "When Al Capone was imprisoned fifty years later, the 'Capone Organization' continued, and in its more modern form (the 'Outfit') it continues to operate in Chicago."[74]

The terms *organized crime* and *criminal enterprise* are closely related and are often used interchangeably, but various federal criminal statutes have specifically defined the elements of a criminal enterprise that need to be proven to convict individuals or groups of individuals under those statutes. The federal Continuing Criminal Enterprise statute defines a *criminal enterprise* as any group of six or more people—with one of the six occupying an organizing, supervisory, or management position—that generates substantial income or resources and is engaged in a continuing series of violations of Subchapters I and II of Chapter 13 of Title 21 of the U.S. Code (Chapter 13 is that portion of federal law concerned with drug-abuse prevention and control).[75]

State laws defining criminal enterprise are generally more inclusive than federal statutes. The laws of New York, for example, stated that "the concept of criminal enterprise should not be limited to traditional criminal syndicates or crime families, and may include persons who join together in a criminal enterprise . . . for the purpose of corrupting . . . legitimate enterprises or infiltrating and illicitly influencing industries."[76] New York criminal statutes have defined *criminal enterprise* as "a group of persons sharing a common purpose of engaging in criminal conduct, associated in an ascertainable structure distinct from a pattern of criminal activity, and with a continuity of existence, structure and criminal purpose beyond the scope of individual criminal incidents."[77]

When people think of criminal enterprises, they often picture the Italian and Sicilian mafioso of popular television shows and movies, but the face of organized crime in the United States

The terms *organized crime* and *criminal enterprise* are often used interchangeably.

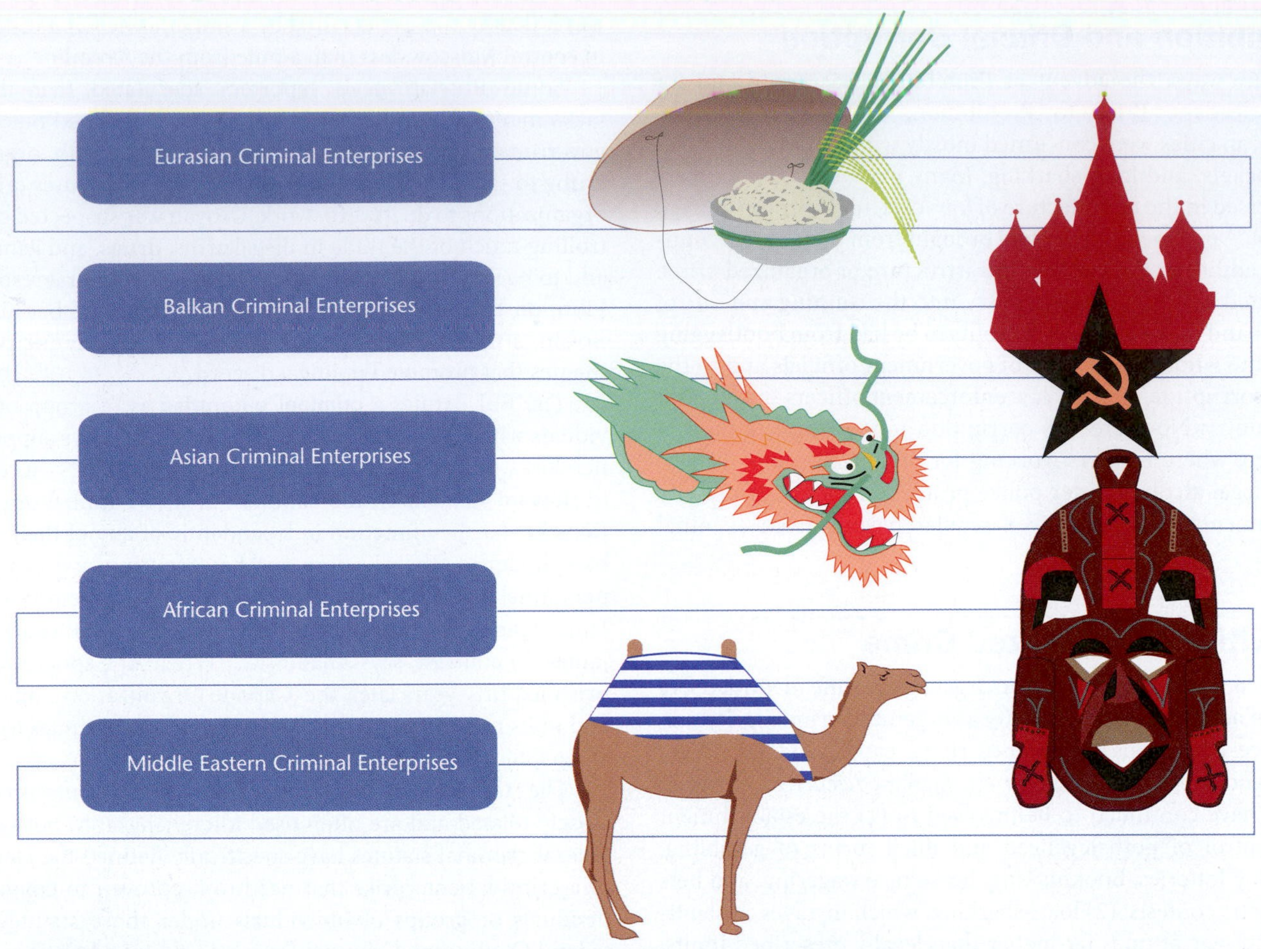

FIGURE 11–4 **International Organized Criminal Groups Whose Activities Impact the United States.**

has changed, and its threat is broader and more complex than ever, with criminal enterprises of different origins. Some especially noteworthy groups include the following:

- Russian mobsters who fled to the United States in the wake of the Soviet Union's collapse
- Groups from African countries such as Nigeria that engage in drug trafficking and financial scams
- Chinese tongs, Japanese *Boryokudan*, and other Asian crime rings
- Enterprises based in Eastern European nations such as Hungary and Romania

Many organized crime groups of different nationalities—including Eurasian, Balkan, Asian, African, and Middle Eastern—currently operate in the United States or are targeting U.S. citizens from afar using the Internet and other technologies; we will describe each of these. (See Figure 11–4)

Eurasian Criminal Enterprises

The term *Eurasian organized crime* refers to organized crime groups comprising criminals born in or with family ties to the former Soviet Union or Central or Eastern Europe.[78] Eurasian organized crime in the United States is rooted in the *Vory V Zakone* (meaning "thieves in law"), career criminals who banded together for support and profit in the Soviet prison system; their leaders operated outside the official Soviet system and were illegally paid to acquire scarce consumer goods and to divert raw materials and finished goods from production lines for the benefit of *Nomenklatura* (the educated elite) and criminals.

With the collapse of the Soviet Union in 1991, members of the *Vory V Zakone* joined with corrupt public officials to acquire control of industries and resources that were being privatized, which gave the criminal syndicate a one-time infusion of wealth and supplied the infrastructure with continuing cash flows and opportunities to launder criminal proceeds. In February 1993, Boris Yeltsin, the first elected president of the Federation of Russian States, said, "Organized crime has become the No. 1 threat to Russia's strategic interests and to national security. . . . Corrupted structures on the highest level have no interest in reform."

Organized crime members first emerged in the West in the 1970s when so-called Soviet *Refuseniks* were allowed to immigrate to Europe, Israel, and the United States. Secreted among the *Refuseniks* were criminals who sought to exploit their newfound freedoms and helped major criminal groups expand to the West; when the Soviet Union collapsed, the people of the region were able to move about freely, with many coming to join their criminal colleagues already in the United States and Western Europe.

Today, Russian organized crime operates in many nations. As one expert puts it: "The Russian Mafia does not just operate

Many organized crime groups of different nationalities currently operate in the United States.

multinationally. It *is* multinational. . . . It makes maximum use of the dual or multiple nationality status many people are entitled to as a result of the breakup of the Soviet Union, and exploits differences in transliteration practices so that names in passports are often spelt differently. There are also well over a million former Soviet citizens living in Israel with citizenship there, free to travel to the EU and North America without visas."[79]

In the United States, Eurasian criminal organizations are heavily involved in health care fraud, auto insurance fraud, securities and investment fraud, money laundering, drug trafficking, extortion, auto theft, and interstate transportation of stolen property as well as human smuggling and prostitution.

Balkan Criminal Enterprises

The term *Balkan organized crime* applies to criminal enterprises originating from or operating in Albania, Bosnia-Herzegovina, Bulgaria, Croatia, Greece, Kosovo, the former Yugoslav Republic of Macedonia, Romania, and Serbia and Montenegro and is an emerging threat in the United States today. The FBI noted that while several of these groups are active in various cities across the country, "they do not yet exhibit the established criminal sophistication of traditional Eurasian or La Cosa Nostra (LCN) organizations."

Organized crime in the rural areas of the Balkans sprang from traditional clan structures, which had large familial ties for protection and mutual assistance. Starting in the fifteenth century, clan relationships operated under the *kanun* (code), which values loyalty and *besa*, or secrecy. Each clan established itself in specific territories and controlled the criminal activities and illicit interests there; the protection of these interests often led to violence between clans.

Years of communist rule led to black market activities in the Balkans, but the impact of those activities was mostly limited to the region. However, when Soviet-style communism collapsed in the late 1980s and early 1990s, Balkan organized crime activities expanded. Within the Balkans, organized crime groups infiltrated newly established democratic institutions, further expanding opportunities for criminal profits. Criminal markets once closed to Balkan groups suddenly opened, which led to the creation of an international criminal network.

Balkan criminal organizations have been active in the United States since the mid-1980s.[80] Initially, they were involved in low-level crimes, such as bank robberies, ATM burglaries, and home invasions. Later, ethnic Albanians affiliated themselves with established Mafia families in New York and acted as low-level participants; as their communities and presence became more established, they expanded their own organizations.

Balkan organized crime is not structured like the traditional Sicilian Mafia. The members brought their clanlike structure to the United States, meaning they are not clearly defined or organized, but instead are grouped around central leaders who maintain ties with the Balkan region while establishing close-knit communities in many cities across the nation. According to the FBI, "Albanian organized crime activities in the United States include gambling, money laundering, drug trafficking, human smuggling, extortion, violent witness intimidation, robbery, attempted murder, and murder" and are said to "have recently expanded into more sophisticated crimes including real estate fraud."[81]

Asian Criminal Enterprises

Asian criminal enterprises have been active in the United States since the early 1900s.[82] The first of these groups evolved from Chinese tongs—social organizations formed by early Chinese American immigrants. A century later, the criminalized tongs continue to thrive and have been joined by similar organizations with ties to East and Southeast Asia. The FBI has stated that "members of the most dominant Asian criminal enterprises affecting the United States have ties—either directly or culturally—to China, Korea, Japan, Thailand, the Philippines, Cambodia, Laos, and Vietnam."[83] Groups from the South Pacific island nations are also emerging as a threat.

Asian organized criminal groups rely on extensive networks of national and international criminal associates that are fluid and mobile, easily adapt to changes, have multilingual abilities, are sophisticated in their criminal operations, and have extensive financial capabilities. Some enterprises have commercialized their criminal activities and can be considered business firms, ranging from small family-run operations to large corporations.

Asian criminal enterprises have prospered due to communications technology, international travel, and the globalization of world economies. The FBI explained that "generous immigration policies have provided many members of Asian criminal enterprises the ability to enter and live on every populated continent in the world today undetected."[84]

Two categories of Asian criminal enterprises have been identified. Traditional criminal enterprises include the Chinese triads (or underground societies) based in Hong Kong, Taiwan, and Macau, as well as the Japanese *Yakuza* or *Boryokudan*; nontraditional criminal enterprises comprise criminally influenced Chinese tongs, triad affiliates, and other ethnic Asian street gangs found in several countries with sizable Asian communities.

Today's Asian criminal enterprises conduct traditional racketeering activities: extortion, murder, kidnapping, illegal gambling, prostitution, and loan-sharking. They also smuggle aliens, traffic in heroin and methamphetamine, commit financial fraud, steal automobiles and computer chips, produce counterfeit computer and clothing products, and launder money.

In this country, Asian criminal enterprises have been identified in more than 50 metropolitan areas but are more prevalent in Boston; Chicago; Honolulu; Las Vegas; Los Angeles; Newark; New Orleans; New York; Philadelphia; Portland; San Francisco; Seattle; and Washington, D.C.

Asian criminal enterprises have prospered due to the globalization of world economies.

African Criminal Enterprises

African criminal enterprises have developed quickly since the 1980s due to advances in communications technology and the globalization of the world's economies.[85] Easier international travel, expanded world trade, and transnational financial transactions have enabled these groups to target international victims and to develop criminal networks within prosperous countries and regions. The political, social, and economic conditions in African countries such as Ghana, Liberia, and Nigeria also have helped some enterprises expand globally.

African criminal enterprises actively operate in several major metropolitan areas in the United States but are most prevalent in Atlanta; Baltimore; Chicago; Dallas; Houston; Milwaukee; Newark; New York; and Washington, D.C. Nigerian criminal enterprises are the most significant group and operate in more than 80 countries around the world. The FBI stated that "they are among the most aggressive and expansionist international criminal groups and are primarily engaged in drug trafficking and financial frauds."[86]

The most profitable activity for Nigerian groups is drug trafficking, primarily the delivery of cocaine from South America into Europe and South Africa and heroin from Southeast and Southwest Asia into Europe and the United States. (Large populations of ethnic Nigerians in India, Pakistan, and Thailand have given them direct access to 90% of the world's heroin production.) Money laundering has also helped establish Nigerian criminal enterprises around the world.

Nigerian groups are famous for their financial frauds, which cost U.S. citizens, businesses, and government offices an estimated $1 billion to $2 billion each year. Their schemes are diverse: "insurance fraud involving auto accidents; health care billing scams; life insurance schemes; bank, check, and credit card fraud; advance-fee schemes known as 4-1-9 letters; and document fraud to develop false identities." The Internet and email have made such crimes even more profitable and prevalent.

Middle Eastern Criminal Enterprises

The FBI has pointed out that "that some Middle Eastern criminal groups have no nexus to terror. Instead, these groups have the same goals as any traditional organized crime ring—to make money through illegal activities."[87] Middle Eastern criminal enterprises originate from Afghanistan, Algeria, Bahrain, Egypt, India, Iran, Iraq, Israel, Jordan, Kuwait, Lebanon, Libya, Morocco, Oman, Pakistan, Qatar, Saudi Arabia, Syria, Tunisia, Turkey, United Arab Emirates, and Yemen.

Middle Eastern criminal groups have been active in the United States since the 1970s, tending to operate in areas with significant Middle Eastern or Southwest Asian populations; according to the FBI, they are most active in Illinois, Ohio, New Jersey, and New York.

The FBI explained that these enterprises engage in "automobile theft, financial fraud, money laundering, interstate transportation of stolen property, smuggling, drug trafficking, document fraud, health care fraud, identity fraud, cigarette smuggling, and the theft and redistribution of infant formula."[88] They rely on extensive networks of international criminal associates and can be highly sophisticated in their criminal operations; internationally, they thrive in Afghanistan, Canada, Iran, Pakistan, Turkey, and the United Arab Emirates.

Think About It...

How does transnational organized crime differ from the more traditional forms of organized crime discussed in this chapter? How does official corruption facilitate the operation of transnational organized criminal groups? How does it contribute to the success of organized crime?

Jose Gil/Fotolia

▶ *Transnational Organized Crime*

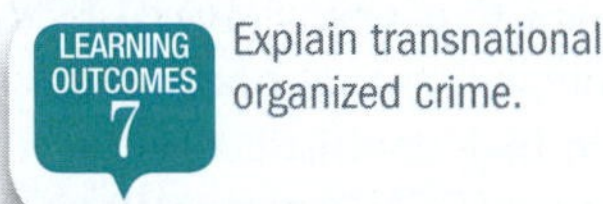
LEARNING OUTCOMES
7
Explain transnational organized crime.

Transnational organized crime, which refers to unlawful activity undertaken and supported by organized criminal groups operating across national boundaries, is emerging as one of the most pressing challenges of the early twenty-first century.[89]

Russian organized crime is of special interest because it has grown quickly following the collapse of the Soviet Union and because it has taken root in the United States and other countries outside the former Soviet sphere of influence.

With the dissolution of Soviet-style controls between 1992 and 1994, the Russian Mafia quickly seized control of the country's banking system through the investment of ill-gotten gains, money laundering, intimidation, fraud, murder, and the outright purchase of financial institutions. Ninety-five Russian bankers were murdered by *Mafiya* operatives between 1995 and 2000, and hundreds of reform-minded business leaders and investigative journalists have been assassinated or kidnapped.[90] In September 2006, Russian Central Bank deputy chairman Andrei Kozlov was fatally shot as he left a soccer stadium in Moscow. Kozlov had been a crusader against money laundering and had suspended or withdrawn the licenses of dozens of banks. After Kozlov's death, President Vladimir Putin created a task force to combat financial crime.

The Analytical Center for Social and Economic Policies, a Russian think tank, estimates that four out of every five Russian businesses pay protection money to the mob.[91] In response to the wave of organized crime that Russia is currently experiencing, more than 25,000 private security firms have sprung up throughout the country. Analysts say, however, that few of these firms are legitimate, with many being fronts for Russian gangsters.[92]

Russian organized criminals differ from their counterparts in the United States because their ranks consist largely of ex-KGB officers, veterans of the 1979–1989 war in Afghanistan, underpaid military officers, and former Communist Party operatives who formed powerful economic alliances with traditional gangsters and black marketers years ago. As some observers note, Russian organized crime seems to be a natural outgrowth of the corrupt practices of officials who operated in the days of strict Soviet control, combined with a huge underground criminal black market that had already developed a complex organizational structure long before the Soviet Union fell apart.[93]

Although Russian organized crime profits from American-style activities such as narcotics, prostitution, racketeering, and illicit gambling, it is also heavily involved in human trafficking, product diversion and counterfeiting of popular Western goods (including software, video, and music duplication), and illicit arms sales and smuggling on a massive scale.

Over the past decade or two, hundreds of thousands of Russian citizens have immigrated to the United States. As U.S. officials have now discovered, many of these people were former black market profiteers and hardcore offenders who had been released by the KGB from the Soviet gulag.[94]

Russian organized criminal groups today operate out of 17 American cities in 14 states. According to one source, "The FBI believes there are 15 separate organized crime groups and 4,000 hard-core Mafia criminals from the former Soviet Union at work in the U.S. They are engaged in money laundering, automobile theft, smuggling, contract murder, loan-sharking, medical insurance fraud, narcotics, and credit card and telecommunications fraud. The theft of electronic serial numbers from cellular phones and the duplication (cloning) of these PIN numbers have grown into a multimillion-dollar industry."[95]

The globalization of crime has necessitated the enhanced coordination of law enforcement efforts in different parts of the world and the expansion of American law enforcement activities beyond national borders. U.S. police agencies routinely send agents to assist law enforcement officers in other countries who are involved in transnational investigations. A four-part YouTube overview of transnational organized crime is available at **Web Extra 11-6**.

Organized Crime and the Law

For many years, American law enforcement agencies had few special weapons in the fight against organized crime. Instead, they prosecuted organized criminal operatives under statutes directed at solitary offenders, using laws such as those against theft, robbery, assault, gambling, prostitution, drug abuse, and murder. Innovative prosecutors at times drew upon other statutory resources in the drive to indict leaders of organized crime. On October 17, 1931, for example, Al Capone was convicted on various charges of income tax evasion after federal investigators were able to show that he had paid no taxes on an income in excess of $1 million. Laws regulating the sale of alcohol and drugs and statutes circumscribing acts of prostitution have also been used against organized criminals, although with varying degrees of success.

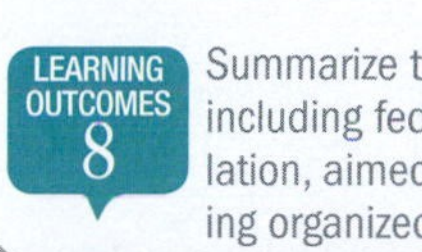

Summarize the efforts, including federal legislation, aimed at curtailing organized crime.

The first federal legislation aimed specifically at curtailing the activities of organized crime was the Hobbs Act, which encompassed a series of statutes that were passed beginning in 1946. In essence, the Hobbs Act made it a violation of federal law to engage in any form of criminal behavior that interferes with interstate commerce. It also criminalized interstate or foreign travel in furtherance of criminal activity and made it a crime to use the highways, telephone, or mail in support of activities such as gambling, drug trafficking, loan-sharking, and other forms of racketeering.

The single most important piece of federal legislation ever passed that specifically targets the activities of organized crime is the **Racketeer Influenced and Corrupt Organizations (RICO) Act**, which was part of the federal Organized Crime Control Act of 1970. The Organized Crime Control Act defines *organized crime* as "the unlawful activities of the members of a highly organized, disciplined association engaged in supplying illegal goods and services, including but not limited to gambling, prostitution, loansharking, narcotics, labor racketeering, and other unlawful activities of members of such organizations."[96] The RICO portion of the act brought under one single piece of legislation the many and diverse activities of American organized crime and made each punishable in a variety of new ways. RICO did not make racketeering itself illegal but, rather, focused on the ill-gotten gains derived from such activity, specifying that it will be unlawful for anyone involved in a pattern of racketeering to derive any income or proceeds from that activity.

Punishments provided for under RICO include **asset forfeiture**, which makes it possible for federal officials to seize the proceeds of those involved in racketeering. In the words of the statute, "Whoever violates any provision of this chapter shall be fined or imprisoned not more than 20 years (or for life if the violation is based on a racketeering activity for which the maximum penalty includes life imprisonment), or both, and shall forfeit to the United States, irrespective of any provision of State law any property derived from any proceeds that the person obtained, directly or indirectly, from racketeering activity or unlawful debt collection."[97] Hence, as a result of RICO, federal agents are empowered to seize the financial and other tangible fruits of organized criminal activity, including businesses, real estate, money, equities, gold and other commodities, vehicles (including airplanes and boats), and just about anything else that can be shown to have been acquired through a pattern of racketeering activity.

Policy Issues: The Control of Organized Crime

In a cogent analysis of organized crime, **Gary W. Potter** tells us that "the question of what we [should] do about organized crime is largely predicated on how we conceptualize [of] organized crime."[98] To understand organized crime and to deal effectively with it, according to Potter, we must study the social context in which it occurs. Such study reveals "that organized

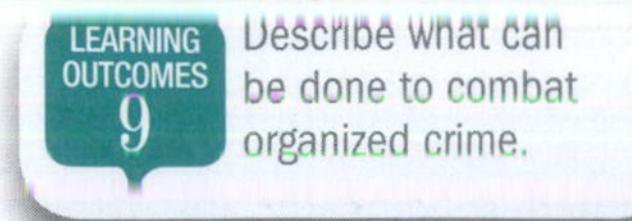

crime is simply an integral part of the social, political, and economic system,"[99] says Potter. Any effective attack on organized crime, therefore, would involve either meeting or eliminating the demands of the consumers of organized crime's products and services. Potter suggests that this can be accomplished by punishing the consumers more effectively and/or by educating them about the perils of their own behavior.

Fighting corruption in politics and among law enforcement personnel and administrators is another track Potter suggests in the battle against organized crime. If organized crime has been successful at least partially because it has been able to corrupt local politicians and enforcement agents, then, Potter asks, why not work to reduce corruption at the local level?

Howard Abadinsky recommends four approaches to the control of organized crime, each involving changes at the policymaking level:[100]

- Increasing the risk of involvement in organized crime by increasing the resources available to law enforcement agencies that are useful in fighting organized crime.
- Increasing law enforcement authority so as to increase the risks of involvement in organized crime. Money-laundering statutes that expand the scope of law enforcement authority, racketeering laws, and forfeiture statutes may be helpful in this regard.[101]
- Reducing the economic lure of involvement in organized crime by making legitimate opportunities more readily available. Educational programs, scholarships, job-training initiatives, and so on, might play a role in such a strategy.
- Decreasing organized criminal opportunity through decriminalization or legalization. This last strategy is perhaps the most controversial. It would decriminalize or legalize many of the activities from which organized crime now draws income, including state-run gambling and the ready and legitimate availability of narcotics.

Strict enforcement of existing laws is another option. This strategy has been used with considerable success by a number of federal and state law enforcement operations that have targeted organized crime. One of the most spectacular mob trials was that of John "Dapper Don" Gotti, who took over control of New York's Gambino crime family after orchestrating the murder of "Big Paul" Castellano in 1985. Over the years, Gotti had been arrested on many occasions and had been prosecuted at least five times for various offenses. His ability to escape conviction earned him the title "Teflon Don." That changed on April 2, 1992, when Gotti was convicted on 13 federal charges, including murder and racketeering, and was sentenced to life in prison without the possibility of parole. Gotti's major mistake was personally participating in several executions, including that of Castellano. After Gotti went to prison, his son, John, Jr., took over control of the family, but in 1999, he pleaded guilty to charges of bribery, extortion, gambling, fraud, tax evasion, and loan-sharking and was sentenced to six and a half years in prison.[102] After being released from prison, John, Jr., was tried on a number of racketeering charges, resulting in three hung juries, and following his last trial, he vowed to leave New York, saying he might move his family to the Midwest or to Florida; his father died of cancer at a federal prison hospital in 2002 at the age of 61.

The senior Gotti's downfall came at the hands of Salvatore "Sammy the Bull" Gravano, a former underboss in the Gambino crime family. Gravano, who admitted to 19 murders, shared family secrets with federal investigators in return for leniency and succor through the federal witness protection program. Gravano spent days on the witness stand testifying against his former boss, and federal prosecutor Zachary Carter later called Gravano "the most significant witness in the history of organized crime."[103]

In 1997, Gravano again assumed center stage when he testified in federal district court in Brooklyn as the star prosecution witness in the murder and racketeering trial of Vincent Gigante, reputed head of the powerful Genovese crime family. Gravano was assailed by defense lawyers for being a notorious liar and for leading "a life of lies," facts he largely admitted in his best-selling book *Underboss*.[104] Although Gravano was sent to Phoenix, Arizona, under the witness protection program, he found it hard to lead a straight life. In 2000, he was arrested on three separate occasions on drug-running and money-laundering charges and was indicted by a New York federal grand jury and charged with financing and running a major Ecstasy drug ring in conjunction with an Israeli organized crime syndicate.[105]

Finally, in 2013, in a sign that traditional American organized crime remains active, Stephen Rakes, a 59-year-old South Boston man who had waited decades for the opportunity to testify against crime boss James "Whitey" Bulger, was found dead prior to being put on the witness stand.[101] Later that same year, Bulger was convicted of racketeering and conspiracy by a Boston jury that found he was involved in 11 murders and numerous other crimes.[106] Bulger had been on the run for 16 years, and had apparently lived quietly in California before his capture.

THE CASE

Bernie Madoff

On July 24, 2009, convicted Ponzi schemer and formerly wealthy investment counselor Bernard (Bernie) Madoff arrived by prison bus at the federal correctional institution in Butner, North Carolina, to begin serving a 150-year sentence.[i] The 71-year-old Madoff had been convicted only days earlier of multiple fraud and securities violations stemming from a scheme in which he exploited thousands of clients who had entrusted him with their money for over 20 years. Among his victims were very wealthy people from places as diverse as New York City and Palm Beach, Florida.[ii]

Some estimates put losses to investors as high as $65 billion dollars—money that seemed to evaporate into thin air and that investigators struggled to recover. By the time Madoff went to prison, only about $1.2 billion had been found and insurance payments of around $500,000 had been made to investors.[iii] Madoff's scheme has been called "the largest investor fraud ever committed by a single person."[iv]

In fact, Madoff may not have invested any of his clients' money, instead paying off redemptions from his fund with money from new clients. The false account statements that Madoff issued to "investors" showed their accounts rapidly growing in value—outpacing the investment results of even the most savvy investment managers. The stock market downturn of 2008, however, led to a record number of redemption requests—and when Madoff was unable to meet them, the game was up.

Everett Collection Inc/Alamy

Disgraced financier Bernard Madoff leaving the federal court in Manhattan after appearing at a bail hearing on January 5, 2009, in New York City. Madoff was convicted of operating a Ponzi scheme that bilked investors out of $65 billion. He is currently serving a 150-year sentence at the medium-security Federal Correctional Institution in Butner, North Carolina. Some people thought that his sentence was too harsh; others felt that it was too lenient. What do you think?

Born Bernard Lawrence Madoff on April 29, 1938, in Queens, New York, Madoff began his adult life as a plumber; he also worked as a lifeguard and a landscaper. He soon went to college, graduating from New York's Hofstra University in 1960 with a degree in political science. A year later, he dropped out of Brooklyn Law School to become a stockbroker, eventually rising through the financial ranks to serve as a chairman of the NASDAQ stock exchange. In 1960, Madoff founded his own firm, Bernard L. Madoff Investment Securities, LLC. He served as chairman of that company until his arrest on December 11, 2008.

Doubts about Madoff preceded his arrest by at least ten years, as his firm had faced a number of investigations by the SEC, some of which had apparently been dropped by the SEC for lack of money. At the time of this writing, only one other person—Madoff's longtime accountant, David Friehling—has been charged in connection with the fraud, although authorities suspect that others must have been involved. Madoff refused to cooperate in the investigation, claiming that he was the only person with knowledge of the scam. Federal prosecutors reached a settlement with Madoff's wife under which she abandoned claims to $85 million in assets that the couple had owned, leaving her with $2.5 million in cash. The couple's sons, Mark and Andrew, both of whom had worked with their father, denied claims of any wrongdoing.

During the sentencing stage of the proceedings against him, Madoff apologized to his victims, saying, "I have left a legacy of shame . . . to my family and my grandchildren. This is something I will live with for the rest of my life. I'm sorry."[v]

(continued)

THE CASE

Bernie Madoff (*Continued*)

Notes

[i]Zachery Kouwe, "Madoff Arrives at Federal Prison in North Carolina," *New York Times*, July 14, 2009, http://www.nytimes.com/2009/07/15/business/15madoff.html (accessed July 21, 2009).

[ii]Michael Moore, "Bernie Madoff," The 2009 TIME 100, http://www.time.com/time/specials/packages/article/0,28804,1894410_1893837_1894189,00.html (accessed July 20, 2009).

[iii]The Ticker, *Washington Post*, July 14, 2009; and Elizabeth Dwoskin, "Bernie Madoff's Accountant Charged, Pleads Not Guilty," *The Village Voice*, July 17, 2009, http://blogs.villagevoice.com/runninscared/archives/2009/07/bernie_madoffs.php (accessed July 21, 2009).

[iv]"Topic: Bernard Madoff," *New York Post* (various dates), http://www.nypost.com/topics/topic.php?t=Bernard_Madoff (accessed August 12, 2009).

[v]"Transcript of Madoff's Sentencing Statement," *New York Post*, June 29, 2009, http://www.nypost.com/seven/06292009/news/regionalnews/partial_transcript_of_madoffs_sentencing_176718.htm (accessed August 12, 2009).

The case of Bernie Madoff raises a number of interesting questions. Among them are the following:

1. **Do you think that Madoff originally set out to build a Ponzi scheme? If not, how might the scheme have evolved?**
2. **Why haven't more people been arrested in the Madoff scandal?**
3. **How would you compare Madoff to other white-collar criminals? What do they have in common?**
4. **Do you think that Madoff is truly sorry for his crimes—or merely for the fact that he got caught? How can we know?**

CHAPTER 11 White-Collar and Organized Crime—*Crime as a Job*

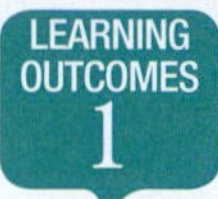

Describe the various types of white-collar crime.

This chapter distinguishes between white-collar, occupational, corporate, and organized crime. White-collar crimes can be further broken down into antitrust violations, bank fraud, bankruptcy fraud, economic espionage, embezzlement, environmental law violations, government fraud, health care fraud, insider trading, insurance fraud, kickbacks, mail fraud, securities fraud, tax evasion, and wire fraud.

1. What is white-collar crime?
2. How does white-collar crime differ from most of the other kinds of criminal offenses discussed in this book?
3. How does white-collar crime differ from occupational crime?

white-collar crime Violations of the criminal law committed by persons of respectability and high social status in the course of their occupation.

occupational crime Any act punishable by law that is committed through opportunity created in the course of an occupation that is legal.

Key Name

Edwin H. Sutherland A criminologist who found that white-collar crime is little understood by some criminologists because they fail to recognize that the secretive violations of public and corporate trust by those in positions of authority are just as criminal as predatory acts committed by people of lower social standing.

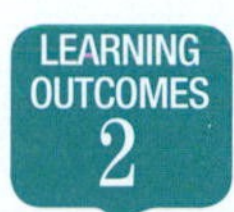

Define *corporate crime* and explain how a corporation can commit a crime.

Corporate crimes, or corporate malfeasance, come in many forms, ranging from prior knowledge about dangerous automobile defects to price fixing and insider securities trading. Businesses may be charged with corporate crimes for the acts of their corporate officers, as can individuals for legal wrongs committed in their corporate capacity.

1. Why is corporate crime considered to be a form of white-collar crime?
2. What legal theory allows for a corporation to be charged under the law with committing a crime?
3. What is a Ponzi scheme? How does it work?
4. What is an environmental crime? How can crimes against the environment be committed?

corporate crime "A violation of a criminal statute either by a corporate entity or by its executives, employees, or agents acting on behalf of and for the benefit of the corporation, partnership, or other form of business entity."

corporate fraud A term that refers to accounting schemes, self-dealing by corporate executives, and obstruction of justice as well as insider trading, kickbacks, and misuse of corporate property for personal gain.

securities and commodities fraud A term that refers to crimes such as stock market manipulation, high-yield investment fraud, advance fee fraud, hedge fund fraud, commodities fraud, foreign exchange fraud, and broker embezzlement.

Ponzi scheme A form of high-yield investment fraud that uses money collected from new investors, rather than profits from the purported underlying business venture, to pay the high rates of return promised to earlier investors.

money laundering The process of converting illegally earned assets, originating as cash, to one or more alternative forms to conceal such incriminating factors as illegal origin and true ownership.

environmental crime A violation of the criminal law that, although typically committed by businesses or by business officials, may also be committed by other people or by organizational entities and that damages some protected or otherwise significant aspect of the natural environment.

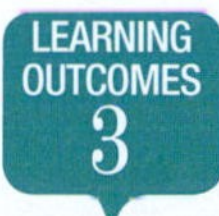

Describe the causes of white-collar crime.

White-collar criminals have many of the same motivations as do other criminals, and criminologists generally agree that white-collar crime, like other crime, is learned. Although white-collar criminals may not be directly dangerous to the health and physical well-being of their victims, they are motivated by the same forces that drive other criminals: self-interest, the pursuit of pleasure, and the avoidance of pain. Other authors have held that white-collar criminals are motivated by a disparity between corporate goals and the limited opportunities available to businesspeople through conventional business practices.

1. What leads people to commit white-collar crime?
2. How similar is Braithwaite's explanation for white-collar crime to Merton's notion of goals and means disparity discussed in Chapter 5?

Key Name

John Braithwaite A criminologist who said that white-collar criminals are frequently motivated by a disparity between corporate goals and the limited opportunities available to businesspeople through conventional business practices.

LEARNING OUTCOMES 4

Summarize the efforts to curtail white-collar crime.

White-collar crimes are often difficult to investigate and prosecute. Nonetheless, the U.S. SEC has recently renewed efforts to enforce existing regulations and has mandated new rules for investment bankers. The now-defunct U.S. DOJ's Corporate Fraud Task Force, the Obama administration's Financial Fraud Enforcement Task Force, and the 2002 Sarbanes-Oxley Act all provided law enforcers with new organizations and tools to fight white-collar crime.

1. Why are white-collar crimes more difficult to investigate and prosecute than more traditional forms of crime?

Corporate Fraud Task Force A U.S. Department of Justice organization created under the administration of George W. Bush to investigate corporate fraud. It has since been superseded by the Obama administration's Financial Fraud Enforcement Task Force.

Sarbanes-Oxley Act A 2002 federal law that set stiff penalties for corporate wrongdoers (officially known as the Public Company Accounting Reform and Investor Protection Act).

Financial Fraud Enforcement Task Force An organization created under the Obama administration in 2009 to combat financial fraud, including false claims made under various federal economic stimulus legislation.

LEARNING OUTCOMES 5

Outline the history and activities of organized crime.

Much of what most Americans traditionally think of today as organized crime—sometimes called the Mafia or La Cosa Nostra—has roots that predate the establishment of the United States and extends to secret societies that have flourished in Italy for hundreds of years. Other organized criminal groups, including Jewish and Irish gangs, flourished in New York City prior to the arrival of large numbers of Italian immigrants in the late 1800s, and ethnic succession has been as much a reality in organized crime as it has in most other aspects of American life. The huge profits to be had from bootlegging under Prohibition in the United States led to the wholesale bribery of government officials and to the quick corruption of many law enforcement officers throughout the country. The activities of organized crime include the establishment and control of both legalized and illicit forms of gambling; loan-sharking; large-scale drug trafficking; the fencing of stolen goods (including securities); the infiltration of legitimate businesses, including labor unions and corporations; labor union racketeering; and other crimes.

1. What linkages, if any, exist between white-collar and organized crime?
2. What is meant by the term *ethnic succession*? How does it apply to organized crime?

organized crime The unlawful activities of the members of a highly organized, disciplined association engaged in supplying illegal goods and services, including gambling, prostitution, loan-sharking, narcotics, and labor racketeering.

Mafia Another name for Sicilian organized crime, or *La Cosa Nostra*.

La Cosa Nostra Literally, "our thing." A criminal organization of Sicilian origin. Also called *the Mafia*, *the Outfit*, *the Mob*, *the syndicate*, or simply *the organization*.

ethnic succession The continuing process whereby one immigrant or ethnic group succeeds another by assuming its position in society.

LEARNING OUTCOMES 6

Explain criminal enterprise and identify some of the more important criminal gangs operating in the United States.

A criminal enterprise is a group of individuals with an identifiable hierarchy, and extensive supporting networks, engaged in significant criminal activity. Some of the most important criminal gangs operating in the United States today are Eurasian criminal enterprises such as the *Vory V Zakone*, Balkan organized criminal groups, Asian criminal enterprises such as the *Yakuza*, African criminal groups, and Middle Eastern criminal enterprises.

1. What is the definition of the term *criminal enterprise*?

criminal enterprise A group of individuals with an identifiable hierarchy, and extensive supporting networks, engaged in significant criminal activity.

Key Name

Howard Abadinsky A criminologist who believed that a hallmark of true criminal organizations is that they function independently of any of their members, including their leaders, and have a continuity over time as personnel within them change.

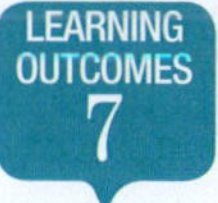

Explain transnational organized crime.

Transnational organized crime refers to unlawful activity undertaken and supported by organized criminal groups operating across national boundaries.

1. How does transnational organized crime differ from traditional forms of organized crime?
2. What special enforcement efforts are required to combat transnational organized crime?

transnational organized crime Unlawful activity undertaken and supported by organized criminal groups operating across national boundaries.

Summarize the efforts, including federal legislation, aimed at curtailing organized crime.

The first federal legislation aimed specifically at curtailing the activities of organized crime was the Hobbs Act, which encompassed a series of statutes that were passed beginning in 1946. The single most important piece of federal legislation ever passed that specifically targets the activities of organized crime, however, is the Racketeer Influenced and Corrupt Organizations (RICO) Act, which was part of the federal Organized Crime Control Act of 1970.

1. How does the RICO statute purport to fight organized crime?
2. What is asset forfeiture? How can it be used in the fight against organized crime?

Racketeer Influenced and Corrupt Organizations (RICO) Act A statute that was part of the federal Organized Crime Control Act of 1970 and is intended to combat criminal conspiracies.

asset forfeiture The authorized seizure of money, negotiable instruments, securities, or other things of value. In federal antidrug laws, "the authorization of judicial representatives to seize all monies, negotiable instruments, securities, or other things of value furnished or intended to be furnished by any person in exchange for a controlled substance, and all proceeds traceable to such an exchange."

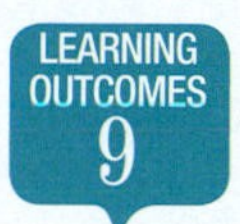

Describe what can be done to combat organized crime.

Organized crime is an integral part of the social, political, and economic systems in our society. As such, any effective attack on organized crime would involve meeting or eliminating the demands of the consumers of organized crime's products and services.

1. What strategies seem to work best to combat the activities of organized crime? Why?

Key Name

Gary W. Potter A criminologist who believed that any effective attack on organized crime would involve either eliminating or meeting the demands of the consumers of organized crime's products and services.

12

"I . . . believe that locking up more and more people who are nonviolent drug offenders, people whose real problem is that they are addicted to drugs, is simply a waste of money and human resources."

—New Mexico Governor Gary E. Johnson

Drug and Sex Crimes—
Recreational Offenses

1 Summarize the early history of drug use in the United States, and describe the extent of contemporary drug abuse.

2 Identify the types of legal and illegal drugs that are commonly abused in the United States today.

3 Describe some of the methods used today to traffic drugs.

4 Explain legislative and social strategies to combat drug abuse.

5 Summarize the drug legalization/decriminalization debate.

6 Summarize prostitution in the United States.

7 Summarize the prostitution legalization/decriminalization debate.

Monkey Business Images/Shutterstock

INTRO

FAKE POT

In late 2013, law enforcement officials in the United States announced that they had closed down a website called Silk Road, pulling the plug on the site's servers and arresting its operator, Ross William Ulbricht.[1] Silk Road brought together buyers and sellers of illegal drugs and other illicit wares. The site used the virtual currency known as Bitcoins to facilitate transactions, leaving no financial trail that authorities could track.

Since Silk Road's demise, other websites with names like Atlantis, Black Market Reloaded, and the Sheep Marketplace have stepped up their operations—selling everything from marijuana to ecstasy and illegal firearms. Customers access the sites with anonymizing software to protect their identities and often have products shipped via private courier.

Eugenio Marongiu/Foto ia

DISCUSS **Why are so many young people drawn to drug use? Why does society believe it is so important to regulate the use of illicit drugs?**

History and Extent of Drug Abuse in the United States

Online drug marketplaces are relatively new inventions, but the rampant and widespread use and abuse of mind- and mood-altering drugs has been around for at least fifty years. In the early years of our country, however, the use of mind-altering drugs was mostly confined to a small group of artists seeking to enhance their creativity. Although it is true that medicinal elixirs of the 1800s and early 1900s contained a variety of potent substances, including cocaine, alcohol, and opium, relatively few Americans were seriously affected at the time by any drug other than alcohol. One significant exception was opium, which was brought to the United States by Chinese immigrants and used in dens in West Coast cities. Opium eventually made its way across the country as a result of increased Asian immigration.

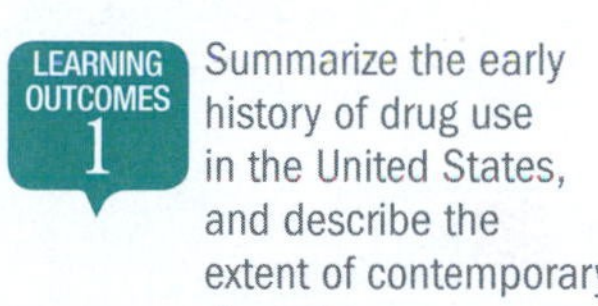
LEARNING OUTCOMES 1 Summarize the early history of drug use in the United States, and describe the extent of contemporary drug abuse.

Psychoactive substances gained widespread acceptance during the hippie movement, a period of newfound freedoms embraced by a large number of American youths during the late 1960s and early 1970s.

According to today's criminal law, a **drug offense** is any violation of the laws prohibiting or regulating the possession, use, distribution, sale, or manufacture of illegal drugs. Because many offenses are not directly threatening to life and property, the law sees them somewhat differently. In a sense, we can think of most drug crimes as *recreational crimes* because many of them are the kinds of offenses in which people tend to get involved when they have too much time on their hands or when they seek relaxation in inappropriate ways. Such crimes share the fact that they are generally disapproved of and, as in the case of drug crimes, may be related to other more serious offenses, including property and violent crimes. Learn more about illicit drugs and related issues from the U.S. Drug Enforcement Administration via **Web Extra 12–1**.

The rampant and widespread use and abuse of mind- and mood-altering drugs is of relatively recent origin.

Extent of Drug Abuse Today

Data on drug abuse in the United States are available through a variety of sources, such as the *Monitoring the Future* (MTF) study, conducted by the University of Michigan's Institute for Social Research; the **National Survey on Drug Use and Health (NSDUH)**, conducted annually by the Substance Abuse and Mental Health Services Administration (SAMHSA); the National Narcotics Intelligence Consumers Committee *NNICC Report*, published in conjunction with the Drug Enforcement Administration (DEA); the National Institute of Justice (NIJ) quarterly Arrestee Drug Abuse Monitoring Program report; the Office of National Drug Control Policy's (ONDCP) *Pulse Check: National Trends in Drug Abuse*, which reports at least once a year on drug-use trends; and annual reports published by SAMHSA's Drug Abuse Warning Network.

According to NSDUH data released in 2013, an estimated 22.5 million Americans ages 12 and older were current users of illicit drugs in 2011, meaning they used an illicit drug at least once during the 30 days prior to being interviewed (Figure 12–1).[2] This estimate represents 8.9% of the population

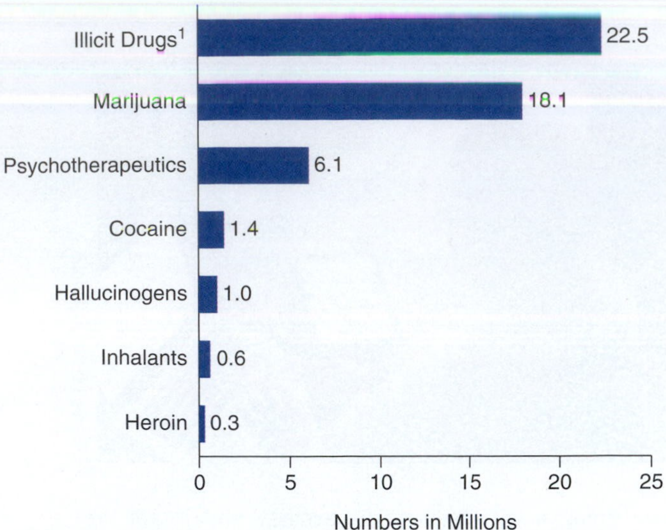

[1]Illicit Drugs include marijuana/hashish, cocaine (including crack), heroin, hallucinogens, inhalants, or prescription-type psychotherapeutics used nonmedically.

FIGURE 12–1 **Past-Month Use of Selected Illicit Drugs among Persons Ages 12 and Older by Type of Drug, 2011.**
Source: Substance Abuse and Mental Health Services Administration, *National Survey on Drug Use and Health, 2011* (Washington, DC: U.S. Government Printing Office, 2012).

aged 12 or older. Illicit drugs include marijuana/hashish, cocaine (including crack), heroin, hallucinogens, inhalants, or prescription-type psychotherapeutics used nonmedically. The report describes the number and percentage of persons aged 12 or older who were current users of specific drugs in 2011 as follows:[3]

- Marijuana was the most commonly used illicit drug, with 18.1 million current users (or 8.7% of the American population aged 12 or older). It was used by 85.0% of current illicit drug users and was the only drug used by 64.3% of them.
- Between 2007 and 2011, the rate of marijuana use increased from 5.8% to 7.0%, and the number of users increased from 14.4 million to 18.1 million.
- 6.1 million persons (2.4% of the population) were nonmedical users of prescription-type psychotherapeutic drugs, including 5.1 million users of pain relievers, 2.2 million users of tranquilizers, 1.1 million users of stimulants, and 374,000 users of sedatives.
- 439,000 (0.1%) were methamphetamine users.
- 1.4 million (0.5%) were current users of cocaine.
- Hallucinogens were used in the past month by almost 1 million persons (0.5%) aged 12 or older, including 695,000 (0.3%) who had used ecstasy.
- The overall rate of current illicit drug use among persons aged 12 or older in 2011 (8.7%) was similar to the rate in 2010, but it was higher than the rates in 2002 through 2008.
- In 2011, the rate of illicit drug use was highest among young adults aged 18 to 25 (21.4%). As Figure 12–2 shows, rates of use generally declined in each successively older age group, with only 6.34% of people ages 55 to 59 and 1.0% of those ages 65 and older reporting current illicit use.

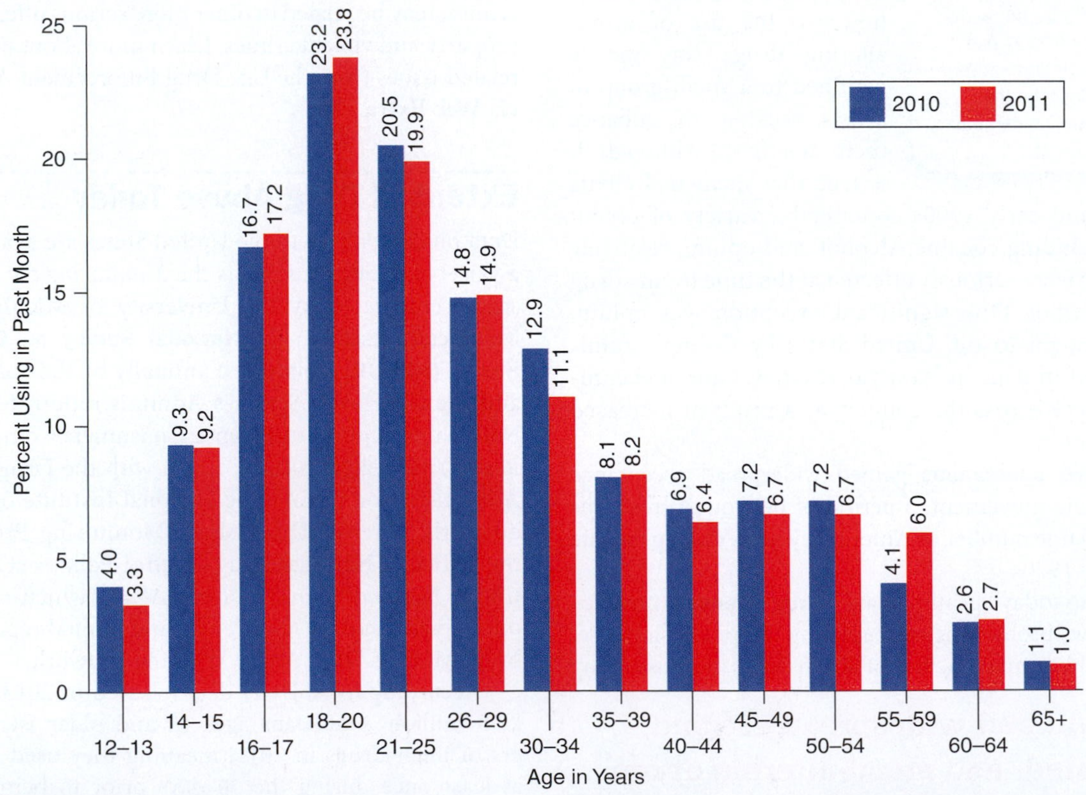

FIGURE 12–2 **Past-Month Illicit Drug Use among Persons Ages 12 and Older by Age, 2010 and 2011.**
Source: Substance Abuse and Mental Health Services Administration, *National Survey on Drug Use and Health, 2011* (Washington, DC: U.S. Government Printing Office, 2012).

Other findings show that:

- Most illicit drug users were employed. Of the 20.2 million current illicit drug users aged 18 or older in 2011, 13.1 million (65.7%) were employed either full or part time.
- Among unemployed adults aged 18 or older in 2011, 17.2% were current illicit drug users, which was higher than the 8.0% of those employed full time and 11.6% of those employed part time.
- In 2011, 9.4 million persons aged 12 or older reported driving under the influence of illicit drugs during the past year. This corresponds to 3.7% of the population aged 12 or older, which was lower than the rate in 2002 (4.7%).

The NSDUH found that rates of illicit drug use for major racial and ethnic groups in 2011 were 8.2% for whites, 8.7% for Hispanics, and 7.2% for blacks. The rates were highest among the American Indian/Alaska Native population (16.8%) and among people reporting multiple races (9.0%); Asians had the lowest rate (3.3%).

The rate of illicit drug use in metropolitan areas was higher than in nonmetropolitan areas: 8.4% in large metropolitan areas, 8.2% in small metropolitan areas, and 6.3% in nonmetropolitan areas. Rural counties had a 4.6% rate of illicit drug use. The NSDUH and the MTF study showed a leveling or declining national trend in illicit drug use, marijuana use, and cigarette use among adolescents since 1997, following a period of significant increases in the early 1990s.

If NSDUH results are accurate, they would seem to indicate that drug abuse is now substantially less of a problem than it was two decades ago. In 1979, the number of current illicit drug users was at its highest level, when estimates of current users reached 25 million; the largest ever annual estimate of marijuana use put routine users at 22.5 million in 1979, and the greatest cocaine use was estimated at 5.3 million in 1985—figures that are considerably greater than those of today. Growth of the American population over time gives the estimated decline even greater weight. Read the latest NSDUH report at **Web Extra 12–2**.

Whereas the use of illicit drugs provides one measure of the drug problem facing our country, the ready availability of such drugs provides another. Data from the National Crime Victimization Survey (NCVS) show that two of three students ages 12 to 19 report ready availability of illegal drugs at their school.[4] Students in public schools report a wider availability of drugs than those in private schools, and students in higher grades (9 through 12) report more drugs available to them than those in the lower grades. Similar rates of availability were reported by white students (69% of whom said drugs were available to them at school), black students (67%), and students living in cities (66%), suburban areas (67%), and rural areas (71%).

In the late twentieth century, drug use among young Americans reached very high levels.

Costs of Drug Abuse

In 2014, The **Office of National Drug Control Policy (ONDCP)** estimated that Americans annually spend around $109 billion to purchase illegal drugs (see Figure 12–3.)[5] The total costs of drug abuse, however, are difficult to measure, but a recent report by the National Drug Intelligence Center (NDIC) placed the total annual cost of illicit drug abuse in the United States at $193 billion.[6] As Figures 12–4, 12–5, and 12–6 show, the NDIC

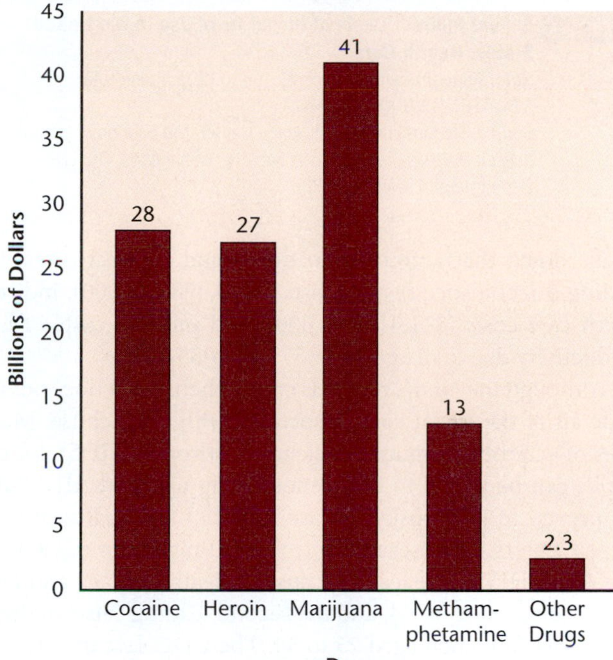

FIGURE 12–3 **Annual Amount Spent on Illegal Drugs in the United States.**
Source: Based on B. Kilmer, S. Everingham, J. Caulkins, G. Midgette, R. Pacula, P. Reuter, R. Burns, B. Han, R. Lundberg, *What America's Users Spend on Illegal Drugs: 2000–2010* (Santa Monica, CA; RAND Corporation, 2014).

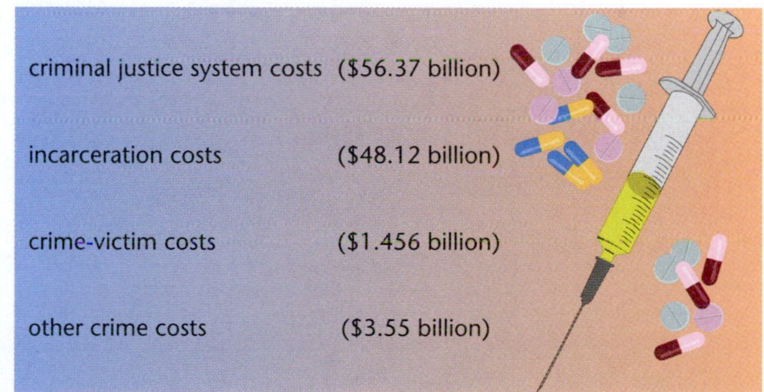

criminal justice system costs ($56.37 billion)
incarceration costs ($48.12 billion)
crime-victim costs ($1.456 billion)
other crime costs ($3.55 billion)

FIGURE 12–4 **Annual Direct Costs of Illegal Drug Use in the United States: Justice System and Victimization.**
Note: Annual criminal justice system amounts due to drug abuse total $109,498,643,000. They include the costs associated with investigation, arrest, adjudication, and parole and probation, plus the costs of incarceration, which are shown separately.
Source: National Drug Intelligence Center, *The Economic Impact of Illicit Drug Use on American Society* (Washington, DC: U.S. Department of Justice, 2011).

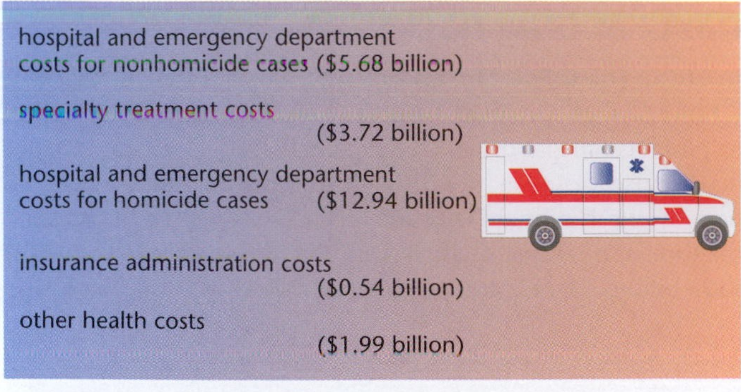

hospital and emergency department
costs for nonhomicide cases ($5.68 billion)
specialty treatment costs
($3.72 billion)
hospital and emergency department
costs for homicide cases ($12.94 billion)
insurance administration costs
($0.54 billion)
other health costs
($1.99 billion)

FIGURE 12–5 **Annual Indirect Costs of Illegal Drug Use in the United States: Health Care.**
Note: Annual health care costs due to drug abuse total $11,416,232,000.
Source: National Drug Intelligence Center, *The Economic Impact of Illicit Drug Use on American Society* (Washington, DC: U.S. Department of Justice, 2011).

breaks down that amount into direct and indirect costs, including direct justice system costs ($109,498,643,000), indirect health care costs ($11,416,232,000), and indirect costs of lost productivity due to drug abuse ($72,182,055,000).

Although the NDIC report is comprehensive, it does not include all of the social costs associated with drug abuse. Many cases of acquired immunodeficiency syndrome (AIDS), for example, can be traced to intravenous drug use, and AIDS/HIV has proved to be a costly disease in social terms. Researchers at the Centers for Disease Control and Prevention (CDC) say that AIDS/HIV is the leading cause of death of black and Hispanic men aged 25 to 44, and the second leading cause of death among black women aged 25 to 44. The CDC says that 47% of HIV infection among minority women is traceable to intravenous drug use, whereas 37% appears to be due to heterosexual intercourse.[7]

Some people, however, have argued that drugs and prostitution, although costly in some ways, also make a significant contribution to economic activity. In 2014, for example, the United Kingdom changed its accounting practices to include contributions made by drugs and prostitution to the national economy.[8] In its first attempt to measure illegal activity other than smuggling, the British Office of National Statistics estimated that the prostitution industry adds about $7.22 billion to the country's Gross Domestic Product, and that the trade in illegal drugs adds an additional $6.0 billion. Together, the two illicit endeavors increase measures of the national economy by 2.3%. For more information on the extent and costs of drug abuse, visit the Office of National Drug Control Policy via **Web Extra 12–3**.

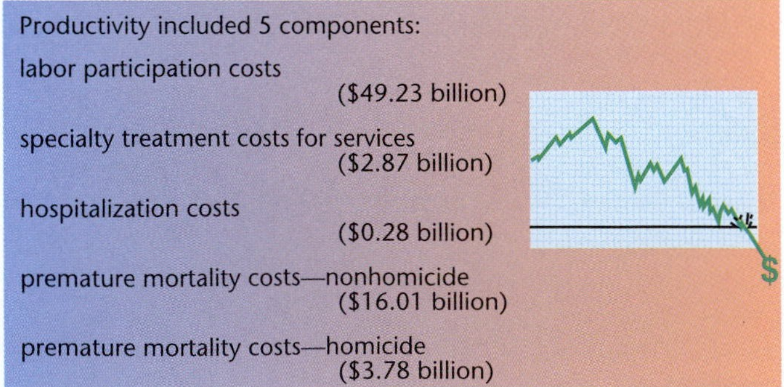

Productivity included 5 components:
labor participation costs
($49.23 billion)
specialty treatment costs for services
($2.87 billion)
hospitalization costs
($0.28 billion)
premature mortality costs—nonhomicide
($16.01 billion)
premature mortality costs—homicide
($3.78 billion)

FIGURE 12–6 **Annual Indirect Costs of Illegal Drug Use in the United States: Lost Productivity.**
Note: Annual costs of lost productivity due to drug abuse total $72,182,055,000.
Source: National Drug Intelligence Center, *The Economic Impact of Illicit Drug Use on American Society* (Washington, DC: U.S. Department of Justice, 2011).

The DEA identifies seven categories of "dangerous drugs": stimulants, depressants, cannabis, narcotics, hallucinogens, anabolic steroids, and inhalants, whereas the 1970 Controlled Substances Act includes five "schedules" of illegal drugs.

Types of Illegal Drugs

Identify the types of legal and illegal drugs that are commonly abused in the United States today.

Controlled substances are grouped into five *schedules* under the 1970 Controlled Substances Act (CSA). Table 12–1 shows those schedules, the criteria for inclusion of a drug under each schedule, a list of drugs in each schedule, and street names for drugs.

Federal law also allows for the control of other **dangerous drugs**, a term used by the DEA to refer to "broad categories or classes of controlled substances other than cocaine, opiates, and cannabis products."[9] The availability of precursor chemicals, such as the popular decongestant pseudoephedrine used in the manufacture of methamphetamine, is also limited under the Combat Methamphetamine Epidemic Act of 2005.

One category of drugs that deserves special mention is inhalants. Nitrous oxide, carbon tetrachloride, amyl nitrite, butyl nitrite, chloroform, Freon, acetate, and toluene, as well as other volatile solvents, are all in the inhalant category. Inhalants are found in fast-drying glues, nail polish remover, room and car deodorizers, lighter fluid, paint thinner, kerosene, cleaning fluids, household sealants, and gasoline. Although some of these substances (for example, ether, nitrous oxide, amyl nitrate, and chloroform) have legitimate medical uses, others are employed only to produce a sense of light-headedness often described in colloquial terms as a "rush." Inhalants are generally sniffed, inhaled, huffed, or snorted. It has been estimated that there are over 1,000 substances that are abused. The use of inhalants "can disturb vision, impair judgment, and reduce muscle and reflex control."[10] The National Inhalant Prevention Coalition can be reached via **Web Extra 12–4**.

TABLE 12–1 CONTROLLED SUBSTANCES UNDER THE FEDERAL CONTROLLED SUBSTANCES ACT

Schedule	Description of Schedule	Drugs in Schedule	Street Names
I	• high potential for abuse • no currently accepted medical use in the United States • lacks accepted safety standards for use under medical supervision	marijuana, heroin, opioids, hallucinogenic substances, peyote, mescaline, gamma-hydroxybutyric acid (GHB), and others	pot, weed, grass, reefer, joint, angel dust, horse
II	• high potential for abuse • currently accepted for medical use • may lead to severe psychological or physical dependence	cocaine, opium, oxycodone, methadone, morphine, Seconal, methamphetamine, and other amphetamines	snow, crack, coke, meth, speed, uppers
III	• potential for abuse less than the drugs or other substances in Schedules I and II • currently accepted for medical use • may lead to moderate or low physical dependence or high psychological dependence	anabolic steroids, ketamine, hydrocodone, and a number of barbiturates and sedatives	downers, goof balls, yellow jackets
IV	• lower potential for abuse relative to the drugs or other substances in Schedule III • currently accepted for medical use • may lead to limited physical dependence or psychological dependence relative to the drugs or other substances in Schedule III	some antidiarrheal drugs; some partial opioid analgesics; some sleeping pills such as Zolpidem; long-acting barbiturates; and benzodiazepines such as Xanax, Librium, and Valium	blues, peaches, bars, zombie pills, no-go-pills, A-minus
V	• low potential for abuse relative to the drugs or other substances in Schedule IV • currently accepted for medical use • may lead to limited physical dependence or psychological dependence relative to the drugs or other substances in Schedule IV	some cough suppressants, anticonvulsants, and selected perscription pain pills	

Drug Trafficking

The term *drug trafficking* has a variety of meanings. On one hand, it refers to the illegal shipment of controlled substances across state and national boundaries. On the other hand, it means the sale of controlled substances. Hence, in colloquial usage, a person who "traffics" in drugs may simply sell them. Technically speaking, **drug trafficking** includes manufacturing, distributing, dispensing, importing, and exporting (or possessing with intent to do the same) a controlled or counterfeit substance.[11] Federal law enforcement agencies, in their effort to reduce trafficking, focus largely on the prevention of smuggling and on the apprehension of smugglers.

Describe some of the methods used today to traffic drugs.

Drugs such as cocaine, heroin, and LSD are especially easy to smuggle because relatively small quantities of these drugs can be adulterated with other substances to provide large amounts of illicit commodities for sale on the street. Figure 12–7 and Figure 12–8 provide maps of major cocaine and heroin trafficking routes (sometimes called "pipelines"), respectively, worldwide. Most cocaine that enters the United States originates in the Western Hemisphere, especially in the South American nations of Colombia, Peru, and Bolivia. Transportation routes into the United States include (1) shipment overland from South America through Central America, (2) direct shipments to U.S. ports while concealed in containers or packed with legitimate products, (3) flights into the United States via commercial airplanes or in private aircraft, and (4) airdrops to vessels waiting offshore for smuggling into the United States.

The DEA follows heroin trafficking through its **heroin signature program (HSP)**, which identifies the geographic source

Drug trafficking involves manufacturing, distributing, dispensing, importing, or exporting a controlled substance.

WHO'S TO BLAME—The Individual or Society

His Brother's Keeper

In March 2012, Nicole Smithfield received a letter from her former boyfriend, Derek Little. The letter came from the state's maximum-security prison where Derek was serving life without possibility of parole for the murder of his older brother, Hamilton. The brothers had grown up together and attended school in the same small town where Nicole lived. Derek began dealing drugs at age 13, bringing in a few dollars selling marijuana to some friends at school. By the time he was 24, Derek was operating one of the largest drug distribution networks in the county and bringing in thousands of dollars a week. He drove an expensive car, had the best clothes and high-tech gadgets, and carried a lot of cash with him wherever he went. People who knew him said that he also carried a 9-shot semiautomatic pistol strapped to his waist.

Hamilton took a different path and joined the army. He went to Afghanistan and then to Iraq for two tours of duty. One night, when he was home on leave, Hamilton stopped by his brother's house and an argument ensued. Hamilton wanted Derek to get out of the drug business and to turn his life around. "It's only a matter of time before you get arrested," Hamilton told his brother. "Do you want to spend the rest of your life in prison?"

"I'm too smart for that," Derek responded. "I've got too many layers (of dealers) protecting me. They'll never get anything on me."

"Yeah—but what about all the lives you're affecting? What about all the kids from our neighborhood who are getting strung out on drugs because of you? You're preying on society," Hamilton said, angry now. "And if you don't quit, I'll make you."

"What do you mean by that?" Derek asked, jumping out of his chair.

"I just think you need to stop, and if I have to, then I'll find a way to make you," Hamilton said, and left, beginning the walk home to his mother's mobile home less than a mile away.

According to evidence presented at his trial, that's when Derek got into his pickup truck and started down the road, accelerating to 80 mph before swerving onto the shoulder and hitting his brother.

Justasc/Shutterstock

Hamilton's body flew 40 feet through the air before hitting the ground and then tumbled another 30 feet through the brush.

Prosecutors tried to present additional evidence showing that Derek was likely responsible for the deaths of three other people who had threatened him during the past two years, or who had said that they would turn him in to authorities—but the judge would not allow the jury to hear those claims. When the trial concluded, Derek was found guilty of killing his brother and sentenced to life in prison without the possibility of parole.

Think About It

1. How is it that two brothers raised in the same environment might choose such different paths? What might explain their choices?
2. How would you explain the attraction that the drug trade seems to have for so many people in this country?
3. If you were able to set crime-control policies for the nation, how would you address the drug problem? Would you consider the decriminalization of any substances? If so, which ones and why?

Note: Who's to Blame boxes provide fictionalized critical thinking opportunities, and are not actual cases.

area of a heroin sample through the laboratory detection of specific chemical characteristics in the sample that are peculiar to that area. The signature program employs special chemical analyses to identify and measure chemical constituents of a sample of seized heroin. Results of the HSP show that 62% of heroin in the United States originates in South America, 17% in Southeast Asia, 16% in Southwest Asia, and 5% in Mexico. According to the DEA, most heroin originating in Southeast Asia is produced in the Golden Triangle area, which encompasses Burma, Laos, and Thailand. Shipments are "controlled by ethnic Chinese criminal groups . . . while U.S.-based ethnic Chinese traffickers with links to these international criminal groups [are] the most prolific importers and distributors of Southeast Asian heroin" within the United States.[12] HSP data were based on examination of over 800 random samples, including some obtained through undercover purchases, domestic seizures, and seizures made at U.S. ports of entry.

Pharmaceutical Diversion and Designer Drugs

The pharmaceutical diversion and subsequent abuse of legitimately manufactured controlled substances are a major source of drug-related addiction or dependence, medical emergencies, and death. **Pharmaceutical diversion** occurs through illegal prescribing by physicians and illegal dispensing by pharmacists. "Doctor shopping," the process of finding a physician who is liberal in prescribing types and amounts of certain drugs, and visits to numerous physicians for the purpose of collecting large quantities of prescribed medicines exacerbate the problem. Depressants, including sedatives, tranquilizers, and antianxiety drugs (especially Xanax and Valium), along with stimulants and anabolic steroids, constitute the types of drugs most often diverted.

A number of drugs, especially those that fall into the "designer" category, are manufactured in drug facilities that are sometimes

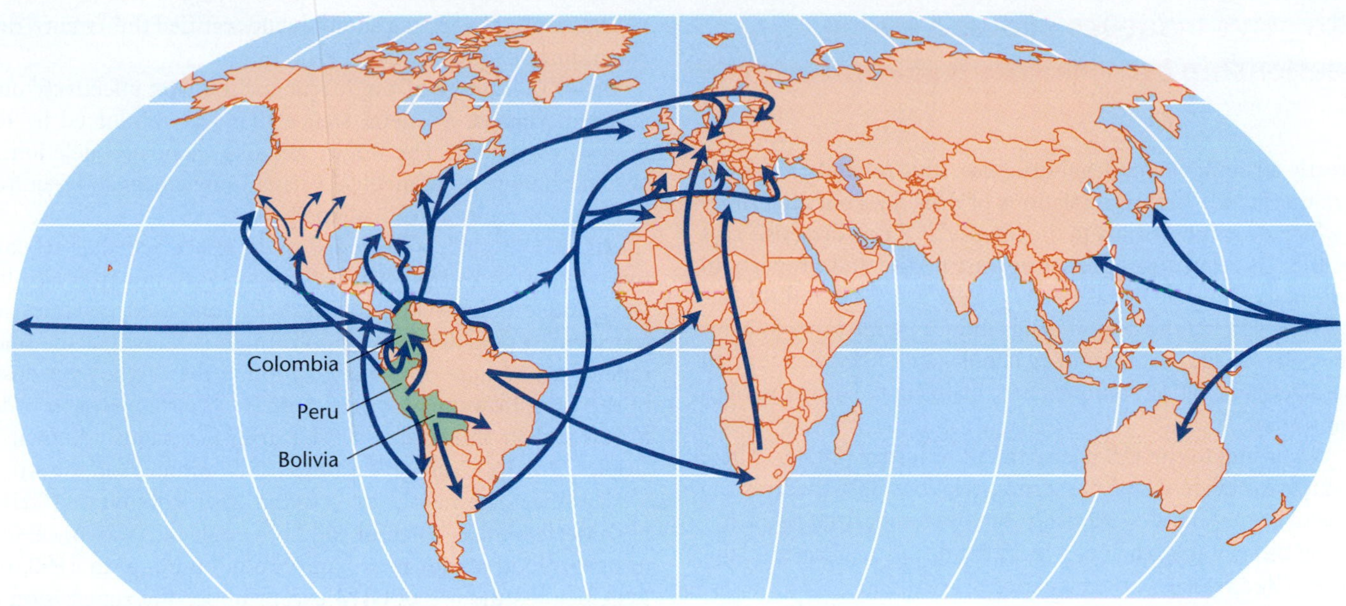

FIGURE 12–7 **Global Cocaine Trafficking: Source Countries and Pipelines.**
Source: Adapted from the Office of National Drug Control Policy, *The National Drug Control Strategy: 2000 Annual Report* (Washington, DC: U.S. Government Printing Office, 2000), p. 78.

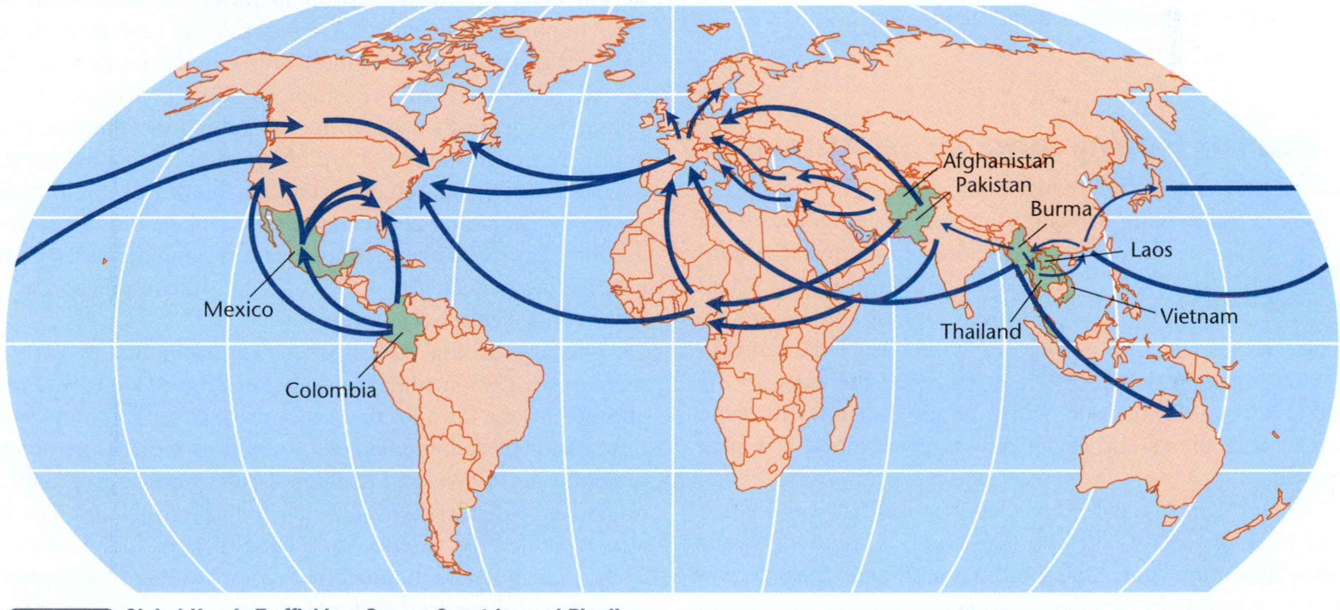

FIGURE 12–8 **Global Heroin Trafficking: Source Countries and Pipelines.**
Source: Adapted from Office of National Drug Control Policy, *The National Drug Control Strategy: 2000 Annual Report* (Washington, DC: U.S. Government Printing Office, 2000), p. 81.

called "basement laboratories" because they are operated by individuals out of their homes. **Designer drugs** are so named because "they are new substances designed by slightly altering the chemical makeup of other illegal or tightly controlled drugs."[13] Designer drugs such as Nexus, a new reputed aphrodisiac, usually fall under the rubric "synthetic narcotic" or "synthetic hallucinogen."

Drugs and Crime

Although the manufacture, sale, transportation, and use of controlled substances are themselves criminal, drugs and crime are also linked in other ways. The addict who is so habituated to the use of illegal drugs that he or she steals to support a "habit," the drug importer who kills a rival dealer, and the offender who commits a criminal act due to the stimulation provided by drugs are examples of how drug abuse may be linked to other forms of criminal activity.

Recognizing these differences, the Bureau of Justice Statistics (BJS) distinguishes between drug-defined and drug-related crimes. **Drug-defined crimes** are "violations of laws prohibiting or regulating the possession, use, or distribution of illegal drugs."[14] The costs of all drug-defined crime, says the BJS, are

Extensive evidence shows a strong relationship between drug use and crime.

directly attributable to illegal drug use. **Drug-related crimes**, on the other hand, "are not violations of drug laws but are crimes in which drugs contribute to the offense."[15] Illegal drug use, says the BJS, "is related to offenses against people and property in three major ways: (1) pharmacologically drugs can induce violent behavior, (2) the cost of drugs induces some users to commit crimes to support their drug habits, [and] (3) violence often characterizes relations among participants in the drug distribution system."[16]

According to the U.S. Department of Justice (DOJ), "There is extensive evidence of the strong relationship between drug use and crime." This relationship can be summarized in the following three points, each of which, the department says, is supported "by a review of the evidence":[17]

- Drug users report greater involvement in crime and are more likely than nonusers to have criminal records.
- People with criminal records are much more likely than others to report being drug users.
- Crimes rise in number as drug use increases.

Social Policy and Drug Abuse

Prior to 1907, any and all drugs could be bought and sold in the United States without restriction. Manufacturers were not required to disclose the contents of their products. Patent medicines of the time were trade secrets. This came to an end with the federal Pure Food and Drug Act of 1906, which required manufacturers to list their ingredients and specifically targeted mood-changing chemicals.

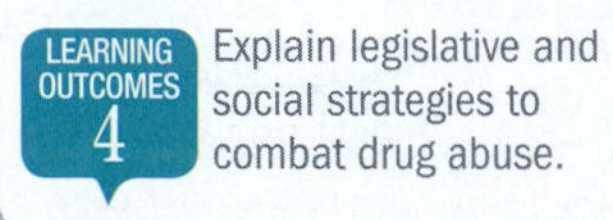

The Harrison Act, passed by Congress in 1914, was the first major piece of federal antidrug legislation. It required anyone dealing in opium, morphine, heroin, cocaine, or their derivatives to register with the federal government and to pay a tax of $1 per year. The act, however, only authorized the registration of physicians, pharmacists, and other medical professionals, effectively outlawing street use of these drugs. However, by 1920, court rulings severely curtailed the use of heroin for medical purposes, claiming that it only caused addiction.

In 1919, the Eighteenth Amendment to the U.S. Constitution, which prohibited the manufacture, sale, and transportation of alcoholic beverages, was ratified. Support for Prohibition began to wane not long after the amendment was enacted. Objections to Prohibition included the claims that it gave the government too much power over people's personal lives, was impossible to enforce, corrupted agents of enforcement, and made many bootleggers wealthy. The coming of the Great Depression, which began in 1929, magnified the effect of lost alcohol tax revenues on the federal government, and in 1933, Congress proposed and the states ratified the Twenty-first Amendment, which repealed Prohibition.

In 1937, passage of the Marijuana Tax Act effectively outlawed marijuana, a federal stance that was reinforced by the Boggs Act of 1951. The Boggs Act also mandated deletion of heroin from the list of medically useful substances and required its complete removal from all medicines.

In 1991, steroids were added to the list of Schedule III controlled substances by congressional action, and in 1996, the Drug-Induced Rape Prevention Act[18] increased penalties for trafficking in the drug Rohypnol, which is known as the "date rape drug" because of its use by "young men [who] put doses of the drug in women's drinks without their consent in order to lower their inhibitions."[19] The drug is variously known as "roples," "roche," "ruffles," "roofies," and "rophies" on the street.

Another date rape drug, gamma hydroxybutyrate (GHB), has effects similar to those of Rohypnol, but was once sold in health food stories to enhance body building. In 1990, the FDA banned the use of GHB except under the supervision of a physician.

Recent Legislation

Recent drug control legislation includes the Comprehensive Methamphetamine Control Act (CMCA) of 1996 and relevant portions of the Violent Crime Control and Law Enforcement Act of 1994. The CMCA, which contains provisions for the seizure of chemicals used in the manufacture of methamphetamine, regulated the use of iodine (used in meth labs); created new reporting requirements for distributors of combination products containing ephedrine, pseudoephedrine (a common decongestant), and phenylpropanolamine; and increased penalties for the manufacture and possession of equipment used to make controlled substances.

The far-reaching Violent Crime Control and Law Enforcement Act of 1994 included a number of drug-related provisions. Specifically, the act allocated other drug-treatment moneys for the creation of state and federal programs to treat drug-addicted prisoners and provided $1 billion for drug court programs for nonviolent offenders with substance abuse problems. The law also expanded the federal death penalty to include large-scale drug trafficking and mandated life imprisonment for criminals convicted of three drug-related felonies.

Drug Control Strategies

Major policy initiatives in the battle against illicit drugs have included antidrug legislation and strict law enforcement, interdiction, international crop control, and prevention (i.e., antidrug education and drug treatment).[20] Much legislative emphasis in recent years has shifted from targeting users to arresting, prosecuting, and incarcerating the distributors of controlled substances. Similar shifts have occurred among employers requiring routine drug testing as a condition of employment and retention.

Interdiction is an international drug control policy designed to stop drugs from entering the country illegally. Another antidrug strategy, crop control, has both international and

Those who favor educational attacks on the problem of drug abuse claim that other techniques have not been effective.

domestic aspects. During 2010, for example, the DEA's Domestic Cannabis Eradication and Suppression Program was responsible for the eradication of 9,866,766 cultivated outdoor marijuana plants and 462,419 indoor marijuana plants in the United States. In addition, the same program was responsible for 9,687 arrests, and agents seized 5,081 weapons and $34,311,819 in assets.[21]

Forfeiture, or asset forfeiture, is another strategy in the battle against illegal drugs. **Forfeiture** is a legal procedure that authorizes judicial representatives to seize "all moneys, negotiable instruments, securities, or other things of value furnished or intended to be furnished by any person in exchange for a controlled substance . . . [and] all proceeds traceable to such an exchange."[22]

Another strategy, antidrug education and drug treatment, has gained significant popularity over the past decade. Those favoring education as a means to attack the problem of drug abuse are quick to claim that other measures have not been effective in reducing the incidence of abuse. Antidrug education programs often reach targeted individuals through schools, corporations, and media campaigns.

The Drug Legalization/ Decriminalization Debate

The war on drugs has been costly. Domestic law enforcement activities (including all federal law enforcement programs within the nation's borders) account for the lion's share of federal antidrug expenditures, whereas demand-reduction programs (that is, educational activities) absorb the smallest part of the antidrug budget. Figure 12–9 depicts federal drug control spending by functional area for fiscal years 2012–2014. When state moneys are added in, the total cost of the war on drugs has been enormous.

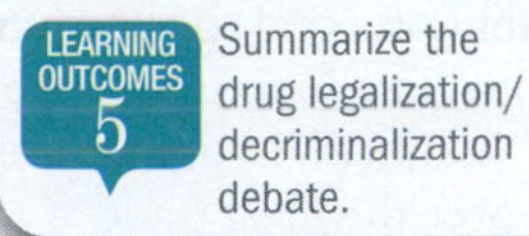

The drug war has been costly in other ways as well. Court resources must be diverted to deal with the enormous influx of drug prosecutions. In some jurisdictions, drug cases account for as much as two-thirds of the criminal case filings. America's major cities have been especially affected.[23] Strict enforcement has combined with a lock-'em-up philosophy to produce astonishingly high rates of imprisonment for drug offenders. The proportion of federal prisoners who are sentenced drug offenders rose from 38% to over 50% today.[24] Part of the increase is due to congressional action that has required high mandatory minimum sentences in drug cases, so that even first-time offenders were sentenced to long prison terms instead of probation. Approximately 70% of all first-time offenders in federal prisons are serving drug sentences. This is also true of 85% of illegal immigrants who are federal prisoners and 66% of female federal prisoners.[25] Explore the history of America's War on Drugs via **Web Extra 12–5.**

Alternative Drug Policies

Decriminalization and legalization have both been suggested drug-control policies at the state and local levels. Both strategies are "based on the assumption that drug abuse will never be eliminated."[26] Whereas **decriminalization** typically reduces criminal penalties associated with the personal possession of a controlled substance, **legalization** eliminates "the laws and associated criminal penalties that prohibit its production, sale,

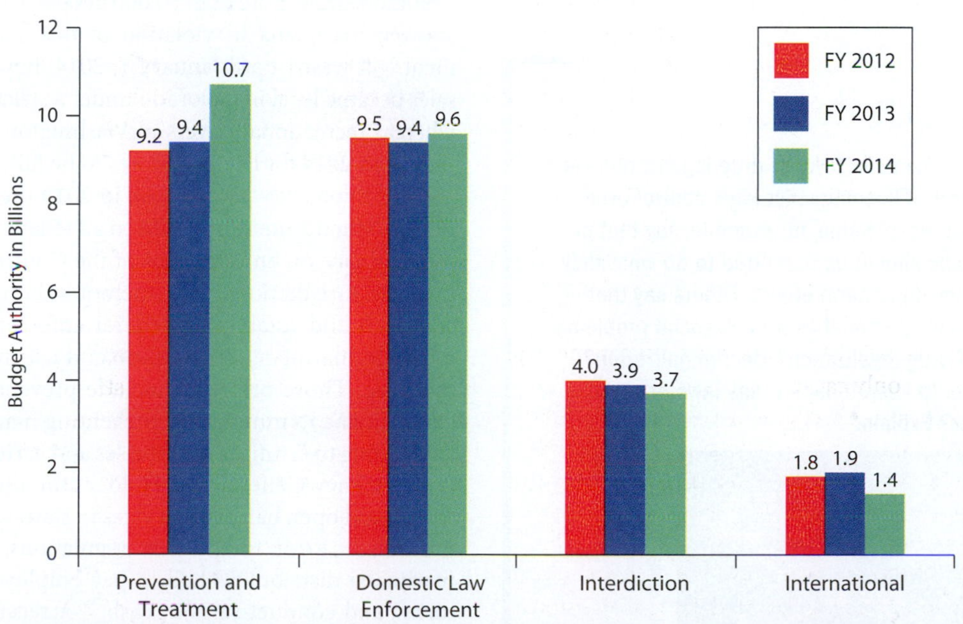

FIGURE 12–9 **Federal Drug Control Spending, Fiscal Years 2012–2014.**
Source: Executive Office of the President of the United States, *National Drug Control Budget: FY 2014 Funding Highlights* (Washington, DC: April 2013), p. 2.

distribution, and possession."[27] Decriminalization enhances personal freedoms in the face of state control, whereas legalization "is aimed," in part, "at reducing the control that criminals have over the drug trade."[28] Other arguments in favor of legalization include the following notions:

- In a free society, people should be permitted to do what they want as long as they don't harm others.
- Keeping drugs illegal means that they will continue to be high-priced commodities. Legalizing them could greatly lower the price and make them taxable—providing the states with much-needed revenue.
- The expense of illicit drugs, kept artificially high by their illegal status, encourages the commission of many drug-related crimes, including prostitution, robbery, and burglary, by users seeking to feed their habits.
- Legalizing drugs would reduce the influence of criminal cartels.
- The illegal status and associated high cost of drugs indirectly victimize others, such as property owners in drug-infested areas and taxpayers who foot the enforcement bill.
- Drug legalization would dramatically reduce the opportunity for official corruption, which is now frequently associated with the illicit drug trade.
- The legalization of drugs would allow for better control over public health issues related to drug use. The spread of AIDS, for example, caused in large part by the use of dirty needles in heroin injection, could be better controlled if sterilized needles were made legally available. Similarly, drug quality and potency could be monitored and ensured.

Think About It...

There are many arguments in favor of drug legalization—and just as many in favor of keeping strict legal control over mind-altering substances. Some, for example, say that in a free society, people should be permitted to do what they want as long as they don't harm others. Others say that drug use causes many personal as well as social problems. Are you in favor of drug legalization? Decriminalization? Or would you prefer to keep today's drugs laws or make them even tougher? Explain.

Griessel/Fotolia

Opponents of drug legalization argue the following:

- Reducing official control over psychoactive substances is immoral, is socially irresponsible, and would result in heightened costs to society from drug abuse.
- Drug legalization would simply increase the types of problems now associated with alcohol abuse, such as lost time from work, drug-induced criminality, the loss of personal self-control, and the severing of important social relationships.
- The fact that laws are not *easily* enforceable is no reason to eliminate them.

In 1996, California and Arizona voters passed resolutions legalizing the medical use of marijuana under certain circumstances. Arizona law requires prescribing physicians to write a scientific opinion explaining why the drug is appropriate for a specific patient, and a second opinion is required before the drug can be legally used. California's law, called the Compassionate Use Act,[29] was further modified by action of the state senate in 2003,[30] limiting the amount of marijuana a patient and his or her primary caregivers may possess.

In 1999, Maine voters passed a referendum permitting some sick people to use small amounts of marijuana, and 26 other states and the District of Columbia have passed various laws and resolutions allowing therapeutic research programs involving the use of marijuana or asking the federal government to lift its ban on medical use of the drug.[31] In May 2001, the U.S. Supreme Court prohibited California marijuana-growing clubs from distributing the drug to those who are ill or in pain.[32] The ruling technically prohibits the use of medical marijuana in virtually all situations.

In 2012, voters in Colorado and Washington State approved ballot initiatives that legalized the possession and use of small amounts of marijuana for recreational use in private; and on April 20–21 of that year the nation's first Cannabis Cup held in Denver, Colorado, drew more than 50,000 people—many of whom openly smoked marijuana in violation of that state's privacy requirement.[33] It wasn't until January 1, 2014, however, that marijuana sales became legal in Colorado under a strict set of requirements, whereas recreational buyers in Washington State needed to wait until mid-2014 for licensed stores to be fully stocked.

In response to state action, in 2013 the U.S. Department of Justice issued a memorandum to all federal prosecutors providing guidance on enforcement of the Controlled Substances Act in those jurisdictions. The memorandum took a "hands-off" approach and established federal enforcement priorities with regard to marijuana distribution and use in states that legalized the drug. Those priorities include preventing the distribution of marijuana to minors and preventing marijuana sales revenue from going to criminal enterprises and cartels.[34] Finally, in 2014, U.S. Attorney General Eric Holder announced new regulations that would open banking services to state-sanctioned marijuana businesses. Prior to the new regulations, most state-licensed marijuana distributors had to pay employees, purchase inventories, and conduct sales in cash.[35] A recent Gallup poll found that 58% of those surveyed favored marijuana legalization.[36] In contrast, only 12% favored legalizing the drug in 1969 when the poll was first conducted.

Prostitution

Recently, officials in Zurich, Switzerland, began experimenting with drive-in "sex boxes" for safer prostitution.[37] Prostitution has been legal in Switzerland since 1942, but many prostitutes had to work in sleazy locations and were sometimes harassed by pimps and customers. The new publicly funded facilities, which are open all night and patrolled by police officers, have emergency call buttons for use by sex-workers who may feel threatened. They are located away from the city center in an effort to shield foreign tourists from what they might regard as an immoral climate.

Prostitution can be defined as the offering of one's self for hire for the purpose of engaging in sexual relations or the act or practice of engaging in sexual activity for money or its equivalent. As the second part of this definition indicates, in heterosexual prostitution involving men as clients (or "johns") and women as sexual "service providers," the man can also be charged with and found guilty of the offense of prostitution. Except for parts of Nevada, prostitution is a criminal act throughout the United States and is generally classified as a misdemeanor.

In the United States, over 92,000 men, women, and juveniles are arrested yearly for the crime of prostitution.[38] The number of juveniles engaging in prostitution is estimated to be between 100,000 and 300,000 annually. While male prostitution is a common practice in many parts of the United States, this chapter will focus on female prostitutes or, as some of the literature describes them, "working girls."

Prostitution: A Changing Business

In 2010, the National Institute of Justice (NIJ) funded the Washington-based Urban Institute to measure the size and structure of the underground commercial sex economy (UCSE) in the United States. The resulting Urban Institute report, which was published in 2014, found that "The UCSE has changed significantly over time—it used to mainly consist of street prostitution, whereas over the last decade, a majority of the business takes place on the Internet."[39] The shift from street prostitution to Internet-based "escort" services not only removed many prostitutes from the streets, but has also changed the structure of prostitution; including how "dates" are arranged, the nature of recruitment efforts (for new girls), solicitation of new customers (or "Johns"), the advertisement of services, fee setting, and other forms of communications between prostitutes, their clients, and their pimps. The Urban Institute report notes that "The Internet has become a powerful tool for employee recruitment," used by many pimps nationwide. It concludes by saying that "The widespread availability and rapid expansion of the Internet has redefined the spatial and social limitations of the sex market by introducing new markets for both recruitment and advertisement."

A Typology of Prostitutes

Using location as the basis for a typology of prostitutes results in the following categories: streetwalkers, bar/hotel prostitutes, club girls (stripclubs); hotel/brothel prostitutes, online escorts ("outcall girls"), and others who don't clearly fit any of these categories (Figure 12–10).

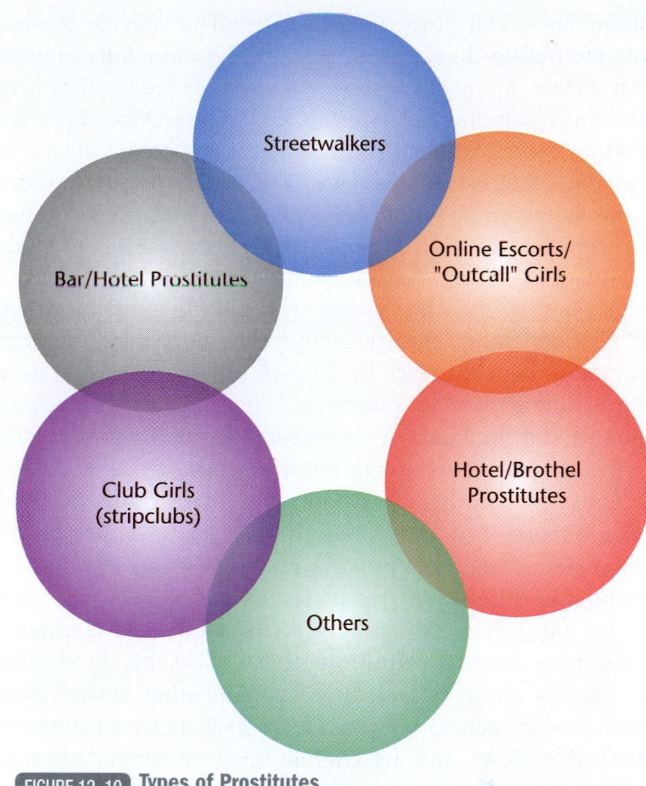

FIGURE 12–10 **Types of Prostitutes.**
Source: From *Criminology Today: An Integrative Introduction*, 7e by Frank A. Schmalleger. Copyright © 2014 by Pearson Education. Used by permission of Pearson Education.

Streetwalkers, whose numbers are dwindling due to the widespread use of the Internet in today's sex trade, are generally seen as the lowest class of prostitute because they solicit customers in public. Their dress is revealing, which advertises their services and entices customers. Streetwalkers service customers in cars, alleyways, hotels, and darkened doorways. Streetwalkers command the lowest prices (often as little as $15 per sex act) and have little bargaining power over condom use and choice of sexual practices. They also face the highest risk of harm from customers and others and the highest risk of arrest.

Bar/hotel prostitutes work in bars and hotels. They may have a standing relationship with hotel professionals, with whom they share their profits. They tend to "work" conventions, sporting events, and business meetings. Services are typically provided in the establishment itself. The prices charged by bar/hotel prostitutes vary considerably according to the prestige of the establishment. The woman's risk of harm and arrest are low to moderate as long as the collaborative relation with the establishment is maintained.

Club girls operate much the same way as bar/hotel prostitutes, except that the settings in which they work are strip clubs (often referred to as "gentlemen's clubs"), and the sex workers do double duty as on-stage performers and prostitutes. A girl's performance on stage often acts as an enticement for customers to "book" her for private performances and sexual intercourse.

Online escorts and outcall all girls work for escort services. Escort services frequently advertise via the Internet, and with flyers; in newspapers; on TV, and even in the yellow pages.

Consequently, call girls are not restricted to specific locales. Most see well-to-do clients who prefer the anonymity of a referral service. Many of the service's customers are regulars who maintain a standing relationship with the service. Fees are sometimes charged to customers' credit cards before the girl is dispatched, and can range upwards of $1,000 per hour. Once on site, however, prostitutes may negotiate with the customer for specific services at additional fees. This arrangement tends to insulate itself from legal action—with prostitutes and their pimps claiming that they simply arranged for companionship. Call girls depend on the agency to screen customers. Prices in this market segment reach the highest levels, and escorts have considerable bargaining power over such things as the use of condoms and the kinds of sexual services provided. Call girls face the lowest risk of harm or arrest.

House or brothel prostitutes ply their trade in legal environments—but are limited to only a few venues in the United States. Legalized prostitution, however, is common in a number of other countries, including Australia (where laws vary by state), New Zealand, the Netherlands, and Germany. In countries where prostitution is legal, it is subject to health and locality controls as well as age and other restrictions. Prostitutes are generally licensed sex workers who pay taxes, belong to unions, and are eligible for government benefits such as unemployment wages and medical services. In the United States, brothel prostitution is an option available to the governments of rural counties in Nevada. Nevada's house prostitutes operate with posted fees and generally earn 40% to 60% of the revenue they generate. State law requires that they be fingerprinted, undergo regular health examinations, and keep financial records for tax purposes. Rhode Island is the only other state in the United States in which the selling of sexual services is not specifically outlawed, although operating a brothel and engaging in solicitation for the purpose of prostitution are illegal.

Feminist Perspectives on Prostitution

Prostitution is a significant issue in today's feminist thought. Some feminist thinkers argue that prostitution exploits and demeans women, while also subjecting them to the dangers of violence and disease.

Others take quite a different approach, saying that selling sex need not be exploitative and might actually be liberating because it fulfills a woman's rights to control her body and her sexuality. They are likely to see prostitution as legitimate and to argue for the legalization of prostitution with added protections for those who choose sex work as a trade. The recent redefinition of prostitution as sex work has been accompanied by the development of a sex worker activism movement, comprising organizations such Call Off Your Old Tired Ethics (COYOTE) in the United States and the Australian Prostitutes Collective in Australia.

Most call girls see well-to-do clients who prefer the anonymity of a referral service.

Think About It...

uperfield/Fotolia

Some feminist thinkers argue that prostitution exploits and demeans women, while also subjecting them to the dangers of violence and disease. Others take quite a different approach, saying that selling sex need not be exploitative and might actually be liberating because it fulfills a woman's rights to control her body and her sexuality. Which point of view comes closest to your own?

The Prostitution Legalization/ Decriminalization Debate

Numerous arguments have been made in favor of legalizing or decriminalizing prostitution. Under outright legalization, women beyond a specified age would be able to offer paid sexual services with few restrictions, as is currently the case in parts of Nevada. Decriminalization, on the other hand, would significantly reduce the criminal penalties associated with prostitution, but it would still regulate the practice and, in an effort to curtail the practice, might require counseling and alternative employment programs for women in that line of work.

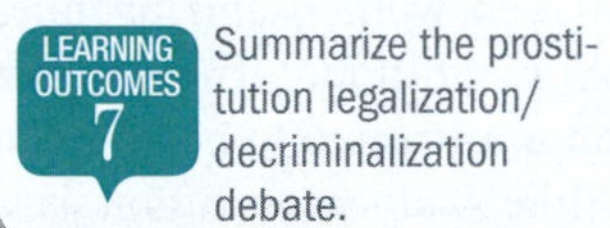

Summarize the prostitution legalization/decriminalization debate.

Those who argue in favor of legalization say that current practices by the justice system tend to force prostitution out of areas where it might naturally be found (that is, certain hotels and massage parlors) and onto the streets and into other parts of the community. Similarly, they say, keeping prostitution illegal means that prostitutes will continue to be viewed as easy targets for pimps, sex offenders, and violent predators. Finally, legalization frees law enforcement resources to be used in the prevention and investigation of more serious types of crime.

Those who argue for keeping prostitution illegal point out that it is regarded as morally and ethically wrong, that it is often not a line of work that is freely chosen, and that it is dangerous for sex workers as well as for their clients because of the disease and violence often associated with it. Read more about the potential legalization of prostitution in a number of jurisdictions at **Web Extra 12–6**.

Legalization of prostitution would free up law enforcement resources to be used in the investigation of more serious types of crime.

THE CASE

Heidi Lynne Fleiss

At the height of her fame, Heidi Fleiss, the so-called Hollywood Madame, told reporters, "Alexander the Great conquered the world at 32. I conquered it at 22."[i] What more could the media have asked for? This case had it all: Hollywood; young, good-looking women selling sex; a mysterious list of rich celebrity clients that kept threatening to crop up; and a young, attractive, articulate, and outspoken advocate of a woman's right to sell her body for sex sensationally touted as the "Madam to the Stars."[ii]

Fleiss's cachet in the sex trade was the stable of exceptionally beautiful young women she kept available for clients willing to pay top dollar. And top dollar it was, with some of the prostitutes making from $1,500 to as much as $1 million per customer. Their services even included travel to Paris, London, and other overseas locations to meet the demands of the rich and desiring.[iii]

But Fleiss did not recruit members for her workforce—they found her. Some were drawn by the potential for high earnings, as Fleiss paid her girls 40% of the profit from each "booking," including tips. For others, the lure was the chance to frolic in the environment of the rich and famous. The lifestyle Fleiss's women enjoyed was beyond the dreams of most and included the opportunity to party with some of the richest and most powerful men in the world. Through mid-1993, Fleiss pocketed several million dollars per year from her role in the enterprise.

Heidi Fleiss's notorious high-priced prostitution ring was the stuff of Hollywood lore, but no more so than her arrest, trial, incarceration, and post-release emergence as an unrepentant sex entrepreneur. Fleiss was initially arrested in June 1993 on state charges that included five counts of pandering and one count of narcotics possession. On July 28, 1994, during her state trial, she was indicted by a federal grand jury on charges of income tax evasion, money laundering, and 14 counts of conspiracy.

In August 1995, Fleiss was convicted in federal court of income tax evasion, money laundering, and eight counts of conspiracy. She also pled guilty in state court to the pandering charges. The combined sentences resulted in her serving three years in prison.

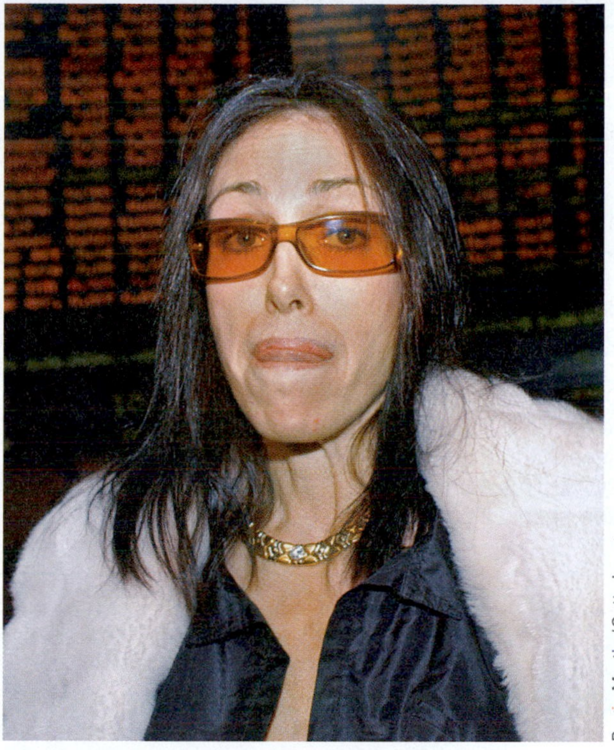

Regis Martin/Getty Images

After her release from prison, Fleiss parlayed her notoriety into a series of successful business ventures, including a men's apparel store in Los Angeles called "Heidi's Wear." A book (*Pandering*), a DVD (*Sex Tips*), a website, and repeated appearances on late-night talk shows kept her in the public eye. Ever the sensationalist, one of Fleiss's recent projects, which she described as a "stud farm,"[iv] involved converting a brothel in southern Nevada into a resort staffed by male prostitutes to service Fleiss's hoped-for female customers.[v]

Notes

[i]"Then & Now: Heidi Fleiss," CNN, June 19, 2005, http://www.cnn.com/2005/US/02/28/cnn25.tan.fleiss (accessed June 1, 2007).

[ii]Rachael Bell, "Heidi Fleiss: The Million Dollar Madam," Court TV Crime Library, http://www.crimelibrary.com/notorious_murders/celebrity/heidi_fleiss/index.html (accessed June 1, 2007).

[iii]Ibid.

[iv]"Fleiss Plans Makeover for Nevada Brothel," *USA Today*, November 16, 2005, http://www.usatoday.com/life/people/2005-11-16-fleiss_x.htm (accessed June 1, 2007).

[v]Steve Friess, "Betting on the Studs," *Newsweek*, December 12, 2005, http://www.msnbc.msn.com/id/10313009/site/newsweek (accessed June 1, 2007).

The case of Heidi Fleiss raises a number of interesting questions. Among them are the following:

1. **In your opinion, was Fleiss a smart businesswoman or a madam committing a series of crimes? Could she have been both? Explain.**
2. **Fleiss parlayed her illegal activities into a sex industry generating large amounts of money. Does that mean that high-level prostitution pays? Explain.**
3. **If prostitution were legal in the United States, what kind of impact would it have?**

CHAPTER 12 Drug and Sex Crimes—*Recreational Offenses*

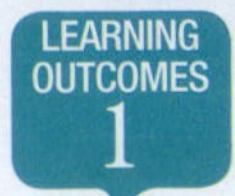

Summarize the early history of drug use in the United States, and describe the extent of contemporary drug abuse

The use of what were to become controlled substances was not regulated until the 1900s in the United States. Prior to that time, drug use was mostly confined to small groups of artists or other people seeking to enhance their creativity. Data on drug abuse in the United States are available through a variety of sources, such as the Monitoring the Future (MTF) study, conducted by the University of Michigan's Institute for Social Research; the National Survey on Drug Use and Health (NSDUH) conducted annually by federal agencies; the Office of National Drug Control Policy's (ONDCP) *Pulse Check: National Trends in Drug Abuse*; and annual reports published by SAMHSA's Drug Abuse Warning Network. According to NSDUH data released in 2013, an estimated 22.6 million Americans ages 12 and older were current users of illicit drugs in 2011. This estimate represents 8.9% of the U.S. population aged 12 or older.

1. How did drug control laws come into being? Why?
2. What types of activities fall under the heading of drug crimes?
3. How much drug abuse is there in the United States?

psychoactive substance A substance that affects the mind, mental processes, or emotions.

drug offense Any violation of the laws prohibiting or regulating the possession, use, distribution, sale, or manufacture of illegal drugs.

National Survey on Drug Use and Health (NSDUH) A national survey of illicit drug use among people 12 years of age and older that is conducted annually by the Substance Abuse and Mental Health Services Administration.

Office of National Drug Control Policy (ONDCP) A national office charged by Congress with establishing policies, priorities, and objectives for the nation's drug control program. The ONDCP is responsible for annually developing and disseminating the *National Drug Control Strategy*.

LEARNING OUTCOMES 2

Identify the types of legal and illegal drugs that are commonly abused in the United States today.

The types of drugs commonly abused in this country include controlled substances, or those that fall into one of five schedules under the 1970 Controlled Substances Act (CSA). Included here are drugs like marijuana, heroin, opioids, hallucinogenic substances, cocaine, oxycodone, methamphetamines, barbiturates, steroids, and certain prescription pain medications. Inhalants, such as gasoline, paint thinner, and household cleaners, along with cigarettes, nicotine, and caffeine, generally fall into the category of legal drugs. Precursor chemicals, or those substances used in the manufacture of illicit drugs, are also controlled under various federal and state laws.

1. What are the five schedules contained within the federal Controlled Substances Act? What kinds of drugs fall under each?

controlled substances Chemical substances or drugs as defined under the 1970 federal Controlled Substances Act.

dangerous drug A term used by the Drug Enforcement Administration to refer to broad categories or classes of controlled substances other than cocaine, opiates, hallucinogens, inhalants, and cannabis products.

Describe some of the methods used today to traffic drugs.

Drug trafficking includes the manufacturing, distributing, dispensing, importing, and exporting of controlled or counterfeit substances. It can also include activities such as smuggling and, technically speaking, even the sale of illegal drugs.

1. What is the relationship between drug trafficking, drug abuse, and other forms of crime?
2. What is pharmaceutical diversion, and who is responsible for such diversion?

drug trafficking The manufacturing, distributing, dispensing, importing, and exporting (or possession with intent to do the same) of a controlled or counterfeit substance.

heroin signature program (HSP) A program of the Drug Enforcement Administration that identifies the geographic source of a heroin sample through the detection of specific chemical characteristics in the sample peculiar to the source area.

pharmaceutical diversion The process by which legitimately manufactured controlled substances are diverted for illicit use.

designer drugs New substances designed by slightly altering the chemical makeup of other illegal or tightly controlled drugs.

drug-defined crime A violation of the laws prohibiting or regulating the possession, use, or distribution of illegal drugs.

drug-related crime A crime in which drugs contribute to the offense (excluding violations of drug laws).

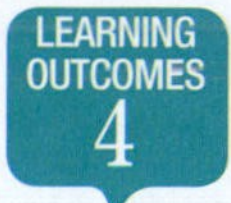

Explain legislative and social strategies to combat drug abuse.

Legislative initiatives to curtail drug use include the Harrison Act, passed by Congress in 1914. It was the first major piece of federal antidrug legislation, and required anyone dealing in opium, morphine, heroin, cocaine, or their derivatives to register with the federal government and to pay a tax. In 1937, passage of the Marijuana Tax Act effectively outlawed marijuana, a federal stance that was reinforced by the Boggs Act of 1951. The centerpiece of federal antidrug legislation, however, is the 1970 Controlled Substances Act, which established a list of five "schedules" or categories of illicit drugs. Other strategies to prevent illegal drug use include interdiction and forfeiture.

1. What are some of the costs of illicit drug use in the United States today?
2. How would you reduce those costs?

interdiction An international drug control policy designed to stop drugs from entering the country illegally.

forfeiture A legal procedure that authorizes judicial representatives to seize "all moneys, negotiable instruments, securities, or other things of value furnished or intended to be furnished by any person in exchange for a controlled substance and all proceeds traceable to such an exchange."

Summarize the drug legalization/ decriminalization debate.

Some people advocate either the legalization or decriminalization of at least some controlled substances. Legalization would involve the elimination of all criminal penalties associated with drug use and/or drug production, sale, and distribution; decriminalization would reduce the seriousness of drug offenses, making them "ticketable" rather than "arrestable." Advocates of drug legalization point out that the war on drugs has been costly, has ruined many lives, and seems to disproportionately involve certain disadvantaged populations. Moreover, such advocates argue, potential tax revenues that would accrue from drug legalization could help balance state and local government budgets. Those opposed to legalization generally support the status quo, and argue that drug use and abuse is the root cause of many social and personal ills.

1. What is the difference between decriminalization and legalization?
2. What do you think of the arguments in favor of drug legalization? Of those against?

decriminalization The redefinition of certain previously criminal behaviors into regulated activities that become "ticketable" rather than "arrestable."

legalization Elimination of the laws and criminal penalties associated with certain behaviors—usually the production, sale, distribution, and possession of a controlled substance.

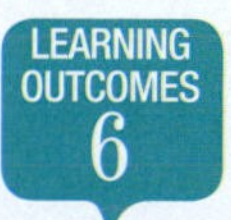

Summarize prostitution in the United States.

In the United States, over 92,000 men, women, and juveniles are arrested yearly for the crime of prostitution. The number of juveniles engaged in prostitution is estimated to be between 100,000 and 300,000 annually. Sexual services are sold in red-light districts, in commercial houses of prostitution, in massage parlors, in nude photography studios, in strip clubs, in erotic dance theaters, and at stag parties. Using location as the basis for a typology of prostitutes results in the following categories: streetwalkers, bar/hotel prostitutes, call girls, hotel/brothel prostitutes, and others who don't clearly fit any of these categories.

1. What is prostitution? What are the various types of prostitutes?
2. How is prostitution like other crimes? How does it differ?

prostitution The offering of one's self for hire for the purpose of engaging in sexual relations or the act or practice of engaging in sexual activity for money or its equivalent.

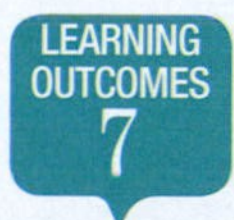

Summarize the prostitution legalization/ decriminalization debate.

Numerous arguments have been made in favor of legalizing or decriminalizing prostitution. Under outright legalization, women beyond a specified age would be able to offer paid sexual services with few restrictions, as is currently the case in parts of Nevada. Decriminalization, on the other hand, would significantly reduce the criminal penalties associated with prostitution, but it would still regulate the practice. Advocates of legalization say that it would allow for the reallocation of law enforcement and justice system resources to more pressing areas, and would provide safer conditions for sex workers. Those against the legalization or decriminalization of prostitution point to the moral issues involved in the practice and claim that it demeans women while threatening family stability.

1. What's the difference between the legalization and decriminalization of prostitution?
2. Would you be in favor of either? Why or why not?

"The world isn't run by weapons anymore, or energy, or money. It's run by ones and zeros—little bits of data—it's all electrons. . . . It's all about information."

—Sneakers (*The Movie*)

Technology and Crime—

It's a Double-Edged Sword

1. Explain cybercrime and describe how it is committed.
2. Describe the extent and forms of cybercrime.
3. Describe the legislation that has been enacted in an effort to curb cybercrime.
4. Describe the typical profile of computer criminals.
5. Explain how technology arms criminals with new methods of crime commission while simultaneously providing criminal justice personnel with the tools to combat crime.
6. Summarize the steps being taken to combat computer crime.
7. Identify freedom-of-speech issues that modern technology has introduced.

Elnur/Fotolia

INTRO PIRACY PAYOFF

On January 20, 2012, New Zealand police broke into the mega-mansion of ex-German national Kim Dotcom.[1] Dotcom, 38, whose given name is Kim Schmitz, created the Internet piracy website Megaupload.com—a site that U.S. officials estimate cost legal copyright holders in this country at least $500 million in lost revenues. Megaupload, which is registered in Hong Kong, was reported to have 150 million registered users and 50 million daily visitors. The site, which accounted for 4% of all daily traffic on the Web,[2] illegally made music, videos, PDFs, and other copyrighted files available to anyone willing to pay a small fee. Those fees, however, along with money spent on advertisements posted to the site, added up, and authorities estimate that Dotcom earned hundreds of millions of dollars from his illegal operations, including $42 million in 2010 alone.

When police arrived at his $30 million mansion, one of the largest private homes in New Zealand, the 6-foot, 7-inch 300-pound Dotcom locked them out using high-tech electronic security devices and fled to a safe room stocked with weapons. More than 100 officers, many with special equipment, were needed to extract him and to place him under arrest.

Epa European Pressphoto Agency b.v./Alamy

DISCUSS **Kim Dotcom parlayed the site Megaupload into a vast money-making enterprise, which U.S. authorities said violated the law. What types of crimes can be facilitated using computers, the Internet, and other forms of modern technology?**

High Technology and Criminal Opportunity

The twenty-first century has been termed the postindustrial information age. Information is vital to the success of any endeavor, and certain forms of information hold nearly incalculable value for those who possess it. Patents on new products, pharmaceutical formulations, corporate strategies, and the financial resources of corporations all represent competitive and corporate trade secrets. Government databases, if infiltrated, can offer terrorists easy paths to destruction and mayhem.

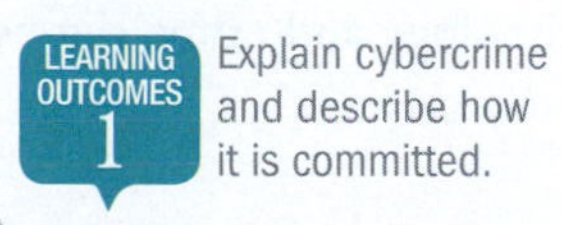
LEARNING OUTCOMES 1 Explain cybercrime and describe how it is committed.

Some criminal perpetrators intend simply to destroy or alter data without otherwise accessing or copying the information. Disgruntled employees, mischievous computer **hackers**, business competitors, and others may have varied degrees of interest in destroying the records or computer capabilities of others.

High-tech criminals seeking illegitimate access to computerized information take a number of routes. One is the path of direct access, wherein office workers or corporate spies, planted as seemingly innocuous employees, use otherwise legitimate work-related entry to a company's computer resources to acquire wanted information.

Another path of illegal access, called *computer trespass*, involves remote access to targeted machines. Anyone equipped with a computer and Internet access has potential access to numerous computer systems. Many such systems have few, if any, effective security procedures in place. Similarly, electromagnetic field (EMF) decoders can scan radio frequency emanations generated by all types of computers. Keystroke activity, internal chip-processed computations, and disk reads, for example, can be detected and interpreted at a distance by such sophisticated devices. Computers secured against such passively invasive practices are rarely found in the commercial marketplace, although the military had adopted them for many applications. Within the last decade, wireless networking has heightened fears of data theft, and cell phone use, handheld devices, and other forms of radio communication offer opportunities for data interception.

The realities of today's digital world have led to a relatively new form of crime, called cybercrime, and to new laws intended to combat it. Simply put, **cybercrime**, or *computer crime*, is any violation of a federal or state computer-crime statute. Many argue that only those crimes that use computer technology as central to their commission may properly be called "cybercrimes." However, a number of other kinds of offenses can also be described as cybercrimes.[3] A typology developed by the Federal Bureau of Investigation (FBI) distinguishes between five types of cybercrimes: (1) internal cybercrimes, such as viruses; (2) Internet and telecommunications crimes, including illegal hacking; (3) support of criminal enterprises, such as databases supporting drug distribution; (4) computer-manipulation crimes, such as embezzlement; and (5) hardware, software, and information theft.[4] Table 13–1 lists these five categories, with additional examples of each.

TABLE 13–1	CATEGORIES OF CYBERCRIME

Internal Cybercrimes (Malware)
Trojan horses
Logic bombs
Trap doors
Viruses
Internet and Telecommunications Crimes
Phone phreaking
Hacking
Denial of service attacks
Illegal websites
Dissemination of illegal material (e.g., child pornography)
Misuse of telecommunications systems
Theft of telecommunications services
Illegal eavesdropping
Illegal Internet-based gambling
Support of Criminal Enterprises
Databases to support drug distribution
Databases to support loan-sharking
Databases to support illegal gambling
Databases to keep records of illegal client transactions
Electronic money laundering
Communications in furtherance of criminal conspiracies
Computer-Manipulation Crimes
Embezzlement
Electronic fund transfer fraud
Other fraud/phishing
Extortion threats/electronic terrorism
Hardware, Software, and Information Theft
Software piracy (warez)
Thefts of computers
Thefts of microprocessor chips
Thefts of trade secrets and proprietary information
Identity theft

When discussing cybercrime, it is important to realize that a huge number of today's financial transactions are computerized. Although most people probably think of money as bills and coins, money today is really just information—information stored in a computer network, possibly located within the physical confines of a bank, but more likely existing as bits and bytes of data on service providers' machines. Typical financial customers give little thought to the fact that very little "real" money is held by their bank, brokerage house, mutual fund, or commodities dealer. Nor do they often consider the threats to their financial well-being by activities such as electronic theft or the sabotage of existing accounts. Unfortunately, however, the threat is very real. Computer criminals equipped with enough information (or able to find the data they need) can quickly and easily locate, steal, and send vast amounts of money anywhere in the world.

Money today is really just information—information stored in a computer network, possibly located within the physical confines of a bank, but more likely existing as bits and bytes of data on service providers' machines.

More recently, in 2012 and 2013, the Obama administration identified the Chinese military as the source of cyber-intrusions into public and private websites throughout the United States, and the 2013 Verizon Data Breach Investigations Report found that "state-affiliated actors tied to China are the biggest mover in 2012. Their efforts to steal IP" addresses, the report said, "comprise about one-fifth of all breaches" covered by the report.[5] At about the same time, U.S. defense officials announced that hackers linked to China's government broke into an American computer system used to send commands to nuclear weapons.[6] In response, the Obama administration began efforts in 2013 to combat the persistent Chinese cyberespionage campaign.[7]

No reliable estimates exist as to the losses suffered in such transactions due to the activities of technologically adept criminal perpetrators. Accurate estimates are lacking largely because sophisticated high-tech thieves are so effective at eluding apprehension. A YouTube video about technology and crime can be viewed at **Web Extra 13–1**.

The Extent of Cybercrime

A recent estimate by the U.S. Secret Service in conjunction with the CERT Cybersecurity Center puts the annual cost of cybercrime in the United States at around \$666 million.[8] The 2011 CSO (Chief Security Officer) Cyber Security Watch Survey, a cooperative effort between the U.S. Secret Service, Deloitte & Touche, Carnegie Mellon's Software Engineering Institute (CERT), and *CSO* magazine, found that a sophisticated cybercrime-fueled underground economy exists in America and that its members continue to develop a sophisticated arsenal of damaging software tools with which most companies cannot keep pace while remaining focused on their core businesses. The website of the CERT Cybersecurity Center can be accessed via **Web Extra 13–2**, and the U.S. government's Computer Emergency Readiness Team can be found at **Web Extra 13–3**.

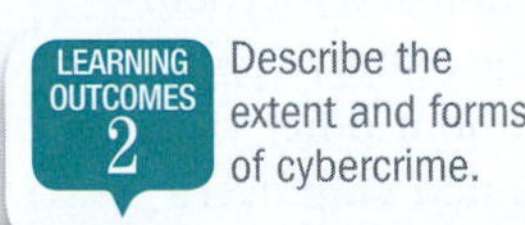

At about the same time, a white paper entitled *Cyber Crime: A Clear and Present Danger* was released by Deloitte & Touche's

WHO'S TO BLAME—The Individual or Society?

Criminal Activity or Mischievous Gaming?

Late last year, Alan Sziran was arrested and charged under federal law with interfering with the operation of computers owned by the federal government. The computers, mostly Apple iMacs, ran Apple's latest operating system, popularly referred to as Mac OS X Mountain Lion, and were located in Veterans Administration (VA) hospitals across the country.

Sziran was especially taken with the long-standing popular impression that Apple's operating system was secure and impenetrable—a myth that computer hackers had long known was untrue, but that Apple corporate officials had done little to dispel. The feeling of those who worked for Apple, Sziran concluded, was that the popular myth could help sell computers. Nonetheless, most hackers continued to focus their efforts on Microsoft's Windows operating system because of its greater popularity, and because it was easier to hack. Since the advent of Windows Vista in 2006, however, and with the introduction of Macintosh computers able to dual-boot both Vista and OS X, and able to run both simultaneously, attention in the hacker community had increasingly turned to identifying backdoors into the Apple operating system.

Soon Sziran was devoting all of his spare time to dispelling Apple's myth of invincibility, and to writing malware—malicious software code—that could successfully invade almost any of Apple's higher-end computers that were connected to the Internet.

After writing a malicious script that he could insert into a tiny QuickTime video, Sziran sent the video as an email attachment to VA hospital computers, making the email look as though it contained administrative data that would be of significance to people in charge of the facilities. Although the email had to be opened and the video file clicked on, and although the person reading the email had to be logged in under an administrative account (most, he found, were), Sziran's plan was very successful, and soon most Apple computers in federally run hospitals across the country were infected. Unfortunately for Sziran, however, federal anticyberterrorism officials had been running a drill responding to a mock cyberterrorism attack when his email made its way onto the Net. Within minutes of its release, Sziran malicious email had been traced to the Internet protocol (IP) address assigned to his home by his Internet service provider (ISP).

Xy/Fotolia

A warrant for his arrest was drawn up, and Sziran was arrested by federal agents who charged him with violating various federal computer-crime laws, including one meant to deter terrorists.

Think About It

1. Do you believe that Sziran saw his activity as criminal? As terrorist activity? If not, how did he perceive it?
2. Was Sziran, as he claimed, doing a service by showing weaknesses in parts of the nation's computer infrastructure?
3. Might there have been other ways for Sziran to make his point? Would those ways have been as effective as the computer mischief in which he engaged? Why or why not?

Note: Who's to Blame boxes provide fictionalized critical thinking opportunities, and are not actual cases.

Center for Security & Privacy Solutions. The paper pointed out the following facts:

- Cybercrime is now serious, widespread, aggressive, growing, and increasingly sophisticated, and it poses major implications for national and economic security.
- Many industries and institutions and public- and private-sector organizations (particularly those within the critical infrastructure) are at significant risk.
- Relatively few organizations have recognized organized cybercriminal networks (instead of hackers) as their greatest potential cybersecurity threat; even fewer are prepared to address this threat.
- Cyberattacks and security breaches are increasing in frequency and sophistication, with discovery usually occurring only after the fact, if at all.
- Current perimeter-intrusion detection, signature-based malware, and antivirus solutions are providing little defense and are rapidly becoming obsolete.
- Effective deterrents to cybercrime are not known, available, or accessible to many practitioners, many of whom underestimate the scope and severity of the problem.
- There is a likely nexus between cybercrime and a variety of other threats, including terrorism, industrial espionage, and foreign intelligence services.[9]

Another industry group, the Computer Security Institute (CSI), surveyed 351 business organizations and found that computer crime cost most companies an average of less than $100,000 in 2010; although two companies lost much more than that—$20 million in one case and more than $25 million in another.[10] **Software piracy**, or the unauthorized and illegal copying of

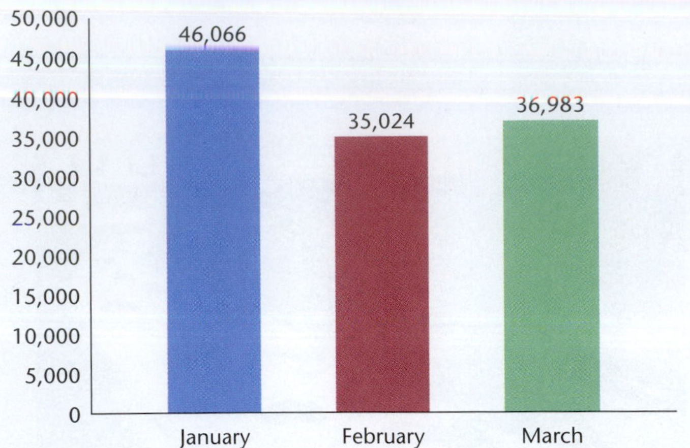

FIGURE 13–1 **Unique Phishing Websites by Month, January–March 2013.** *Source:* The Anti-Phishing Working Group, *Phishing Activity Trends Report, 1st Quarter 2013,* July 23, 2013, p. 4. Copyright by Anti-Phishing Working Group. Used by permission of Anti-Phishing Working Group.

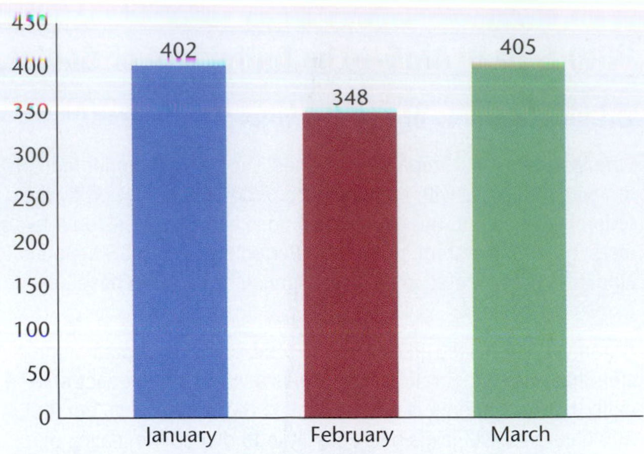

FIGURE 13–2 **Hijacked Brands by Month, January–March, 2013.** *Source:* The Anti-Phishing Working Group, *Phishing Activity Trends Report, 1st Quarter 2013,* July 23, 2013, p. 7. Used by permission of Anti-Phishing Working Group.

software, is rampant. According to the Business Software Alliance, global losses from pirated software (known as *warez* in the computer underground) totaled $59 billion in 2010.[11] The Alliance found that 42% of all personal computer (PC) software installed in 2010 was pirated. The problem is worse in certain countries. In the European country of Georgia, for example, it is estimated that 93% of all software used there has been illegally copied. The Business Software Alliance can be accessed via **Web Extra 13–4**.

Phishing (pronounced "fishing") is a relatively new scam that uses official-looking email to steal valuable information such as credit card numbers, Social Security numbers, user IDs, and passwords from victims. The emails appear to come from a user's bank, credit card company, retail store, or Internet service provider (ISP) and generally inform the recipients that some vital information in their account urgently needs to be updated. Those who respond are provided with an official-looking Web form on which they can enter their private financial information. Once the information is submitted, it enters the phisher's database.

The Anti-Phishing Working Group (APWG), a coalition of banks and ISPs, says that a typical phishing scheme reaches up to 1 million email in-boxes. The watchdog group had identified more than 38,000 different phishing websites that were still in operation as of March 2011.[12] Figure 13–1 shows the number of unique phishing sites the APWG detected during the first part of 2013. Although servers that run those sites can be anywhere in the world, the APGW found that more than 50% of them are located in the United States.

Phishing sites often attempt to hijack brand names, and some phishers are capable of sending emails that are difficult to distinguish from legitimate ones. When that happens and customers respond to those emails in significant numbers, a brand (such as the name of a bank or credit card company) is said to have been hijacked. Figure 13–2 shows the number of hijacked brands by month during the first half of 2013. Some observers have noted that in addition to losses suffered by individuals and institutions, phishing has the potential to threaten the viability of e-commerce and to call into question the safety of all Web-based financial transactions.[13]

Not all cybercrime is committed for financial gain. Some types of computer crime, including the creation and transmission of destructive computer viruses, "worms," spyware, and other malicious forms of programming code (often called *malware*), might better be classified as "criminal mischief." Perhaps not surprisingly, these types of activities are typically associated with young, technologically sophisticated male miscreants seeking a kind of clandestine recognition from their computer-savvy peers. Computer crimes committed by youthful and idealistic offenders may represent a novel form of juvenile delinquency—one aimed at expressing dissatisfaction with the status quo.

Computer viruses have shown signs of becoming effective terrorist-like tools in the hands of young, disaffected "technonerds" intent on attacking or destroying existing social institutions. A **computer virus** is a computer program that is designed to secretly invade computer systems to modify the way in which they operate or to alter the information they store.[14] Other types of destructive programs are logic bombs, worms, and Trojan horse routines. Distinctions among these programs are based on the way in which they infect targeted machines or on the way in which they behave once they have found their way into a computer. Figure 13–3 provides an overview of some of the most damaging computer viruses of all time.

In a recent report on cybersecurity, the U.S. Department of Homeland Security (DHS) provided the following examples of damage caused by malware:[15]

- Symantec Corporation, makers of computer security software, reports that more than 15,000 new types of malware are entering networks worldwide every day.
- *Consumer Reports* estimates that U.S. consumers lost $8.5 billion and replaced 2.1 million computers because of viruses, spyware, and other forms of malware between 2006 and 2008.

Significant government cybersecurity reports (all of which can be accessed at http://www.cyber.st.dhs.gov) are shown in Figure 13–4.

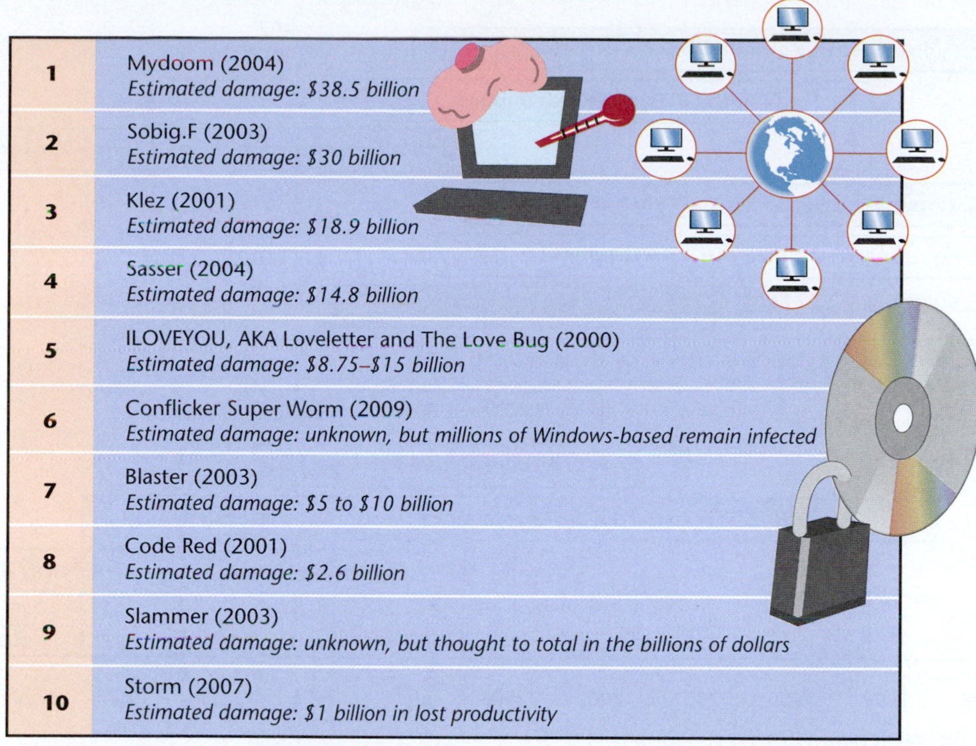

1	Mydoom (2004) *Estimated damage: $38.5 billion*
2	Sobig.F (2003) *Estimated damage: $30 billion*
3	Klez (2001) *Estimated damage: $18.9 billion*
4	Sasser (2004) *Estimated damage: $14.8 billion*
5	ILOVEYOU, AKA Loveletter and The Love Bug (2000) *Estimated damage: $8.75–$15 billion*
6	Conflicker Super Worm (2009) *Estimated damage: unknown, but millions of Windows-based remain infected*
7	Blaster (2003) *Estimated damage: $5 to $10 billion*
8	Code Red (2001) *Estimated damage: $2.6 billion*
9	Slammer (2003) *Estimated damage: unknown, but thought to total in the billions of dollars*
10	Storm (2007) *Estimated damage: $1 billion in lost productivity*

FIGURE 13–3 **The Ten Most Damaging Computer Viruses and Worms of All Time.**
Source: Smithsonian Magazine, "Top Ten Most-Destructive Computer Viruses," http://www.smithsonianmag.com/science-nature/Top-Ten-Most-Destructive-Computer-Viruses.html#ixzz2SNIYZOTz (accessed May 10, 2013); PC Security World, "Most Notorious Computer Virus, Worms of All Time," http://forum.pcsecurityworld.com/showthread.php?tid=233 (accessed February 8, 2013); Buzzle.com, "The Most Damage Causing Computer Viruses Revealed," http://www.buzzle.com/articles/the-most-damage-causing-computer-viruses-revealed.html (accessed October 22, 2013); Christopher Null, "The Worst Computer Viruses of All Time," Yahoo! Tech, http://tech.yahoo.com/blogs/null (accessed October 22, 2011); and George Jones, "The 10 Most Destructive PC Viruses of All Time," Tech Web, July 5, 2006, http://www.techweb.com/tech/160200005 (accessed June 26, 2012).

Cybercrime and the Law

In the early years of computer-based information systems, most U.S. jurisdictions tried to prosecute unauthorized computer access under preexisting property crime statutes, including burglary and larceny laws. Unfortunately, because the actual carrying off of a computer is quite different from copying or altering some of the information it contains, juries were confused by how such laws apply to high-tech crimes and computer criminals were often let free. As a result, all states and the federal government developed computer-crime statutes specifically applicable to invasive activities that illegally access stored information.

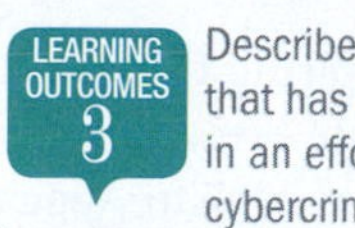

LEARNING OUTCOMES 3 Describe the legislation that has been enacted in an effort to curb cybercrime.

In 1996, President Bill Clinton signed into law the **Communications Decency Act (CDA)**,[16] which sought to protect minors from harmful material on the Internet. A portion of the CDA criminalized the knowing transmission of obscene or indecent messages to any recipient under 18 years of age. Another section prohibited the knowing, sending, or displaying to a person under 18 any message "that, in context, depicts or describes, in terms patently offensive as measured by contemporary community standards, sexual or excretory activities or organs." Shortly after the law was passed, however, the American Civil Liberties Union (ACLU) and a number of other plaintiffs filed suit against the federal government, challenging the constitutionality of the law's two provisions relating to the transmission of obscene materials to minors.

In 1996, a three-judge federal district court entered a preliminary injunction against enforcement of both challenged provisions, ruling that they contravened First Amendment guarantees of free speech. The government then appealed to the U.S. Supreme Court. The Court's 1997 decision ***Reno* v. *ACLU***[17] upheld the lower court's ruling and found that the CDA's "indecent transmission" and "patently offensive display" provisions abridge "the freedom of speech" protected by the First Amendment. Most other federal legislation aimed at keeping online pornography away from the eyes of children has not fared any better when reviewed by the Court. Although the Children's Internet Protection Act (CIPA), which requires public and school libraries receiving certain kinds of federal funding to install pornography filters on their Internet-linked computers, was approved by the justices, most observers acknowledge that the Court has placed the Internet in the same category as newspapers and other print media, where almost no regulation is permitted.

Enacted in 1997, the **No Electronic Theft Act (NETA, or NET Act)** criminalizes the willful infringement of copyrighted works,

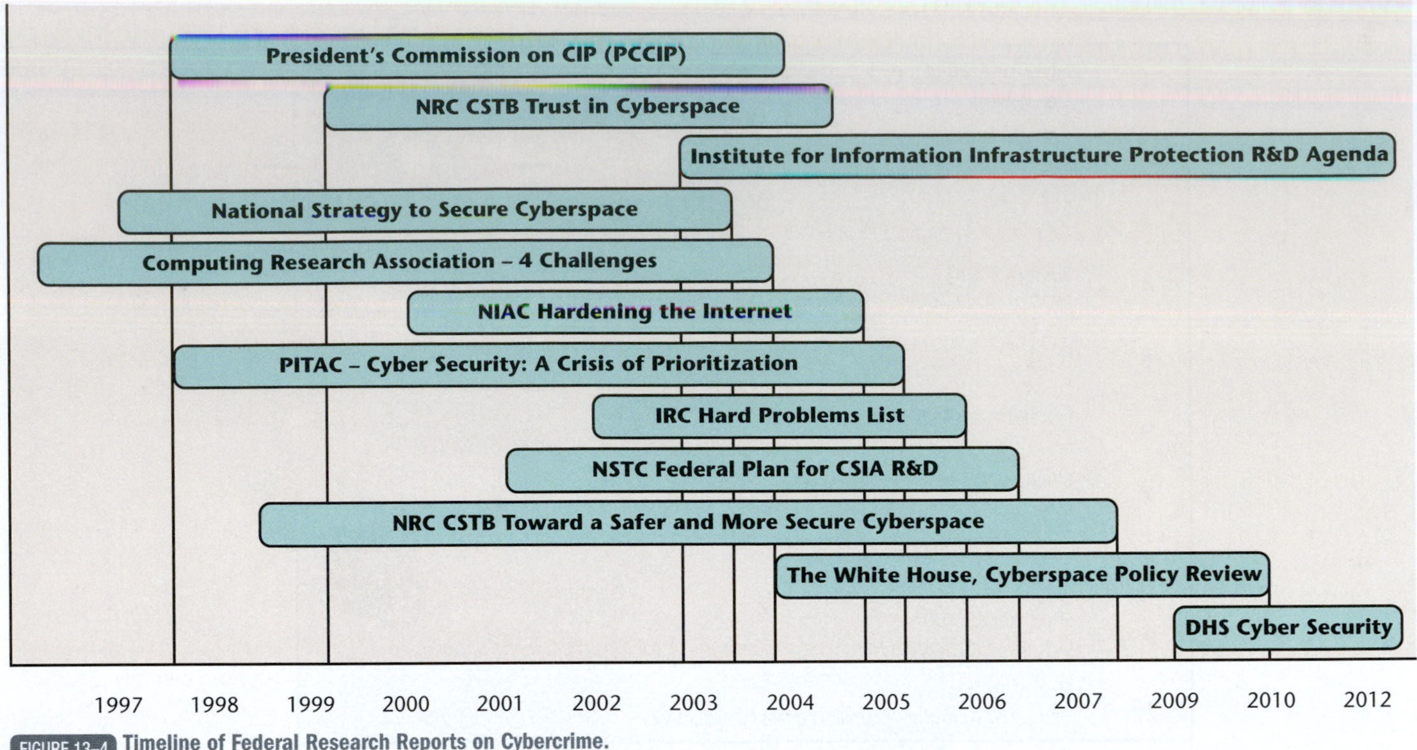

FIGURE 13–4 **Timeline of Federal Research Reports on Cybercrime.**
Source: Adapted from *Criminology Today: An Integrative Introduction*, 7e by Frank A. Schmalleger. Copyright © 2014 by Pearson Education. Used by permission of Pearson Education.

including by electronic means, even when the infringing party derives no direct financial benefit from the infringement (such as when pirated software is freely distributed online). In keeping with requirements of the NETA, the U.S. Sentencing Commission enacted amendments to its guidelines to increase penalties associated with electronic theft. The **Digital Theft Deterrence and Copyright Damages Improvement Act** of 1999 increased the amount of damages that could be awarded in cases of copyright infringement—a crime that is intimately associated with software piracy. The **Cyber Security Enhancement Act (CSEA)** of 2002,[18] which is part of the Homeland Security Act of 2002, directed the U.S. Sentencing Commission to take several factors into account in creating new sentencing guidelines for computer criminals. The law told the commission to consider not only what financial loss was caused by computer crime, but also the what level of planning was involved in the offense, whether the crime was committed for commercial or private advantage, and whether malicious intent existed on the part of the perpetrator. Under the law, computer criminals can face life in prison if they put human lives in jeopardy. Certain future illegitimate activities using computer equipment may not be adequately covered by existing law. On the other hand, some crimes committed with the use of a computer may be more appropriately prosecuted under "traditional" laws. For that reason, some experts distinguish between computer crime, computer-related crime, and computer abuse. **Computer-related crime** is "any illegal act for which knowledge of computer technology is involved for its investigation, perpetration, or prosecution," whereas **computer abuse** is said to be "any incident without color of right associated with computer technology in which a victim suffered or could have suffered loss and/or a perpetrator by intention made or could have made gain."[19]

A Profile of Computer Criminals

In November 2012, a federal grand jury in New Hampshire returned an indictment charging Anil Kheda, 24, of the Netherlands, with conspiring to hack into and disable computer servers belonging to Rampid Interactive, a New Hampshire–based company that publishes and hosts *Outwar*, a multiplayer online role-playing game.[20] Kheda was charged with the federal crimes of conspiring to commit computer intrusion and one count of interstate extortion.

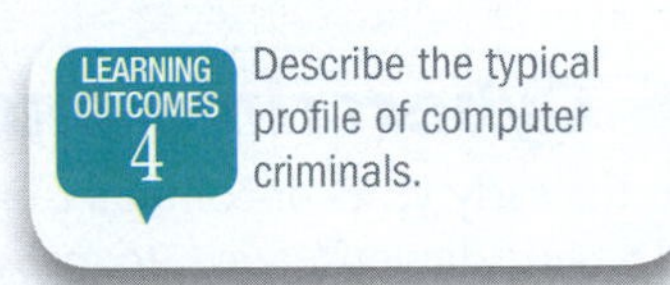

The indictment alleges that from November 2007 to August 2008, Kheda and other members of the conspiracy, all of whom were avid *Outwar* players, accessed Rampid's computer servers without authorization and rendered *Outwar* unplayable for days at a time. According to the indictment, Kheda and his alleged co-conspirators also used their unauthorized access to Rampid's servers to alter user accounts—causing the restoration of suspended player accounts and the accrual of unearned game points—and to obtain a copy of all or portions of the *Outwar* computer source code, which they used to help create a competitor online game, *Outcraft*. The indictment also alleges that Kheda and his alleged co-conspirators sent Rampid interstate email communications threatening to continue to hack into Rampid's computer systems unless Rampid agreed to pay them money.

The indictment says that, as a result of the defendants' hacking activities, Rampid was unable to operate *Outwar* for a total of approximately two weeks over a nine-month period and incurred over $100,000 in lost revenues, wages, hosting costs, and long-term loss of business, as well as the loss of exclusive use of Rampid's proprietary source code, which it had invested approximately $1.5 million in creating.

According to court documents, Kheda earned approximately $10,000 in profits from operating *Outcraft*, which has approximately 10,000 players worldwide. If convicted, Kheda faces a maximum sentence of five years in prison on the conspiracy charge and two years in prison on the interstate threats charge.

The indictment of Anil Kheda illustrates both the potential for high-technology offenders to thwart government efforts at prosecution by operating internationally as well as the transnational nature of hacker subculture. Hackers and hacker identities are a product of **cyberspace**, that etheric realm where computer technology and human psychology meet. Cyberspace exists only within electronic networks and is the place where computers and human beings interact with one another. For many hackers, cyberspace provides the opportunity for impersonal interpersonal contact, technological challenges, and game playing. Fantasy role-playing games are popular among hackers and may engross many "wave riders," who appear to prefer what in technological parlance is called "virtual reality" to the external physical and social worlds that surround them.

Computer security experts have come up with a rough profile of the average hacker.[21] He is a male between the ages of 16 and 25 who lives in the United States. He is a computer user, but not a programmer, who hacks with software written by others. His primary motivation is to gain access to websites and computer networks, not to profit financially.

Unfortunately, not all computer hackers are simply kids trying their hand at beating technological challenges. Many are "high-tech computer operators using computers to engage in unlawful conduct."[22]

The History and Nature of Hacking

Some authors suggest that computer hacking began with the creation of the interstate phone system and direct distance dialing implemented by AT&T in the late 1950s.[23] Early switching devices used audible tones that were easily duplicated by electronics hobbyists, and "blue boxes" capable of emulating such tones quickly entered the illicit marketplace. **Phone phreaks** used special telecommunications access codes and other restricted technical information to avoid paying long-distance charges. Some were able to place calls from pay phones, and others fooled telephone equipment into billing other callers.

A modern form of phone phreaking involves the electronic theft of cellular telephone numbers and access codes. Thieves armed with simple mail-order scanners and low-end computers can "literally grab a caller's phone number and identification number out of the air."[24] Say experts, "Those numbers are [then] used to program computer chips, which are placed inside other cellular phones—or 'clones'—so the long-distance calls appear on the victim's bill."[25] Such high-profile figures as former New York Mayor Rudolph Giuliani and his police commissioner have been among the victims of cellular phone piracy.

Another form of illegal telephone access that has recently become popular is voice-mail hacking. Private voice-mail boxes have become the targets of corporate raiders and young vandals alike. In a recent case, two New York City teenage brothers caused an estimated $2.4 million in lost business by gaining illegal access to the New Hampshire–based International Data Group's voice-mail system. Security experts at the company, who first thought the mailboxes were malfunctioning, were alerted to the intentional disruptions by obscene outgoing messages planted by the brothers that greeted unsuspecting callers.[26]

Because most hackers are adolescent males, it is important to realize that, as one expert on hackers says, "their other favorite risky business is the time-honored adolescent sport of trespassing. They insist on going where they don't belong. . . . The only innovation is in the new form of the forbidden zone and the means of getting in it."[27]

Technology in the Fight Against Crime

Recently, the U.S. Department of Justice's National Law Enforcement and Corrections Technology Center (NLECTC) began testing a high-power compact microwave source designed for vehicle immobilization.[28] The microwave beam emitted by the device can interfere with an automobile's computer circuitry, effectively shutting down a car's engine from up to 35 feet away. As the technology is improved, the device will likely become operable over longer distances, and it may soon become a routine tool in police work.

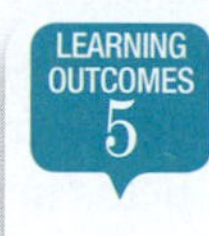

Explain how technology arms criminals with new methods of crime commission while simultaneously providing criminal justice personnel with the tools to combat crime.

Technology is a double-edged sword. On one hand, it arms potential criminals with potent new weapons of crime commission; on the other hand, it provides criminal justice personnel with powerful tools useful in the battle against crime. Law enforcement capabilities commonly leapfrog one another. Consider, for example, the relatively simple case of traffic radar, which has gone through an elaborate technological evolution from early "always-on" units to trigger-operated radar devices to today's sophisticated laser speed-measuring apparatus. On the other hand, radar-jamming devices are now increasingly used by people who are apparently intent on breaking speed limit laws. Not to be outdone, suppliers to law enforcement agencies have created radar-detector detectors, which are used by authorities in states where radar detectors have been outlawed.[29]

DNA Technology

On January 16, 2001, Christopher Ochoa, 34, was released from a Texas prison after serving 13 years for a murder he did not commit.[30] Ochoa had confessed to the rape and murder of 20-year-old Nancy DePriest at a Pizza Hut in Austin in 1988. Although Ochoa later said that he had been coerced by homicide detectives into confessing, no one believed him. A decade after he began serving a life sentence, however, law students at the Wisconsin Innocence Project at the University of Wisconsin–Madison took an interest in his case. They concluded that DNA evidence conclusively proved that someone else had killed DePriest. The students, led by their law professor, took the evidence to State District Judge Bob Perkins, who called the case "a fundamental miscarriage of justice" and ordered Ochoa set free. According to authorities, evidence of DePriest's murder now points to Texas inmate Achim Joseph Marino, who confessed to her murder in 1996 following a religious conversion. The law students involved in the case matched DNA samples taken from mouth swabs of Marino with the DNA found in semen taken from the victim's body. Without the technology known as **DNA profiling**, Ochoa would still be in prison—and DePriest's real killer would be unknown.

DNA evidence is now accepted for courtroom and investigative use in jurisdictions nationwide. Today, a number of states and the federal government (through the FBI laboratory) have established digitized forensic DNA databases. At the federal level, the National DNA Index System (NDIS) enables public forensic laboratories throughout the United States to exchange and compare DNA profiles electronically, thereby linking unsolved serial violent crimes to each other and to known offenders.

Growing numbers of jurisdictions are requiring the gathering of DNA information from arrestees; and in 2013 the U.S. Supreme Court held, in the case of *Maryland* v. *King*, that "When officers make an arrest supported by probable cause . . . and bring the suspect to the station to be detained in custody, taking and analyzing a cheek swab of the arrestee's DNA is, like fingerprinting and photographing, a legitimate police booking procedure that is reasonable under the Fourth Amendment."[31]

Think About It...

Advances in technology have always provided new opportunities for crime. With that thought in mind, examine today's emerging technologies. What cutting-edge technologies can you identify? What new forms of criminal activity do you imagine they will foster?

Phomphan/Shutterstock

Computers as Crime-Fighting Tools

Computers are now used to keep records of every imaginable sort—from point-of-sale contacts to inventory maintenance and production schedules. Computers assist in the design of new technologies and aid in the assignment of resources to problem areas.

Computers also connect people. The Internet contains a large number of law-oriented and law enforcement–oriented newsgroups and provides access to the United Nations and worldwide crime data through its link to the United Nations Criminal Justice Information Network. Other computer services provide access to security information and to software useful in law enforcement administration. Innovative computer technologies facilitate the work of enforcement agents. Among them are automated fingerprint identification systems, or AFISs (often with interstate and even international links); computerized crime-scene simulations and reenactments; expert systems; and online clearinghouses containing data on criminal activity and offenders. AFISs allow investigators to complete in a matter of minutes what would otherwise consume weeks or months of work manually matching a suspect's fingerprints against stored records. AFIS computers are able to compare and eliminate from consideration many thousands of fingerprints per second, sometimes leading to the identification of a suspect in a short time. Once crime-related information or profiles of criminal offenders have been generated, they are typically stored in a database and often made accessible to law enforcement agencies at other sites. Other specialized database programs now track inner-city gang activity and gang membership, contain information on known sexual predators, and describe missing children.

Forensic expert systems deploy machine-based artificial intelligence to draw conclusions and to make recommendations to investigators and others interested in solving problems related to crime and its commission. **Expert systems**, developed by professional "knowledge engineers" who work with "knowledge bases" and computer software called "inference engines," attempt to duplicate the decision-making processes used by skilled investigators in the analysis of evidence and in the recognition of patterns that such evidence might represent. One such system is currently being perfected by the FBI's National Center for the Analysis of Violent Crime (NCAVC). The NCAVC expert system attempts to profile serial killers by matching clues left at a crime scene with individual personality characteristics.

Finally, specialized software programs, such as ImAger, which is produced by Face Software, Inc., and Compu-Sketch, a product of Visatex Corporation, assist police artists in rendering composite images of suspects and missing victims.

Combatting Computer Crime

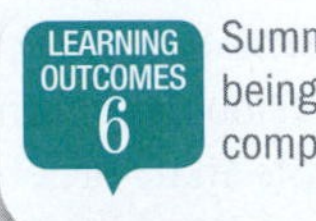

Summarize the steps being taken to combat computer crime.

In 1982, sales of information security software products to private companies and government agencies totaled only \$51 million; by 1997, expenditures exceeded \$425 million; and by 2003, they had grown to \$1.17 billion.[32] Studies conducted by Infonetics Research indicated that worldwide network security appliance and software sales reached more than \$4.5 billion in 2006 and surpassed \$8 billion in 2013.[33] Among the products in use are **data encryption**, key log

Any program intended to secure a company against high-tech crime must be built on a realistic threat analysis.

detectors, and Web servers supporting major security protocols. Data encryption is the process by which information is encoded, making it unreadable to all but its intended recipients.

Software alone, however, is not enough. Any effective program intended to secure a company or business operation against the threat of high-tech crime must be built on a realistic threat analysis. **Threat analysis**, sometimes called "risk analysis," involves a complete and thorough assessment of the potential disasters facing an organization. Some risks, such as floods, tornadoes, hurricanes, and earthquakes, arise from natural events and are often unpredictable. Others, including fire, electrical outages, and disruptions in public services, may be of human origin—but equally difficult to predict. Theft, employee sabotage, and terrorist attacks constitute yet another category of risk. Responses to unpredictable threats can nonetheless be planned, and strategies for dealing with almost any kind of risk can be implemented.

Once specific threats are identified, strategies tailored to dealing with them can be introduced. For example, one powerful tool useful to identify instances of computer crime when they occur is the audit trail. Formally defined, an **audit trail** is "a sequential record of system activities that enables auditors to reconstruct, review, and examine the sequence of states and activities surrounding each event in one or more related transactions from inception to output of final results back to inception."[34] In other words, audit trails, which (once implemented) are recorded in some form of computer memory, trace and record the activities of computer operators and facilitate the apprehension of computer criminals.

Police Investigation of Computer Crime

Many state and local police departments do not have personnel skilled in the investigation of computer crimes. Most officers know little about tracing the activities of computer criminals, and some police investigators find it difficult to understand how a crime can actually have occurred when nothing at the scene appears to be missing or damaged. Horror stories of botched police investigations are plentiful. They include tales of officers standing by while high-tech offenders perform seemingly innocuous activities that destroy evidence, of seized magnetic or optical media allowed to bake in the sun on the dashboards of police vehicles, and of the loss of evidence stored on magnetic media due to exposure to police clipboards and evidence lockers containing magnets.

Police departments also may intentionally avoid computer-crime investigations because they are complex and demanding. The amount of time and money spent on computer-crime investigations, it is often believed, could better be spent elsewhere. In addition, investigators who spend a great deal of time on crimes involving computers tend not to be promoted as readily as their more glamorous counterparts in the homicide and property crime divisions, and personnel who are skilled in computer applications are apt to take jobs with private industries, where pay scales are far higher than in police work. As a consequence of these considerations and others, many police departments and their investigators make cybercrime a low priority.

But the situation has been changing due to federal intervention. In 1992, the FBI formed a National Computer Crime Squad (NCCS)[35] to investigate violations of the federal Computer Fraud and Abuse Act of 1984[36] and other federal computer-crime laws. Prior to the creation of the DHS, the FBI's Washington Field Office housed the agency's Infrastructure Protection and Computer Intrusion Squad (IPCIS). The squad, whose duties have been transferred to the DHS, investigated the illegal interception of signals (especially cable and satellite signal theft) and the infringement of copyright laws related to software. Visit DHS's Office of Infrastructure Protection on the Web via **Web Extra 13–5**.

Automated monitoring of network traffic is an area of considerable interest to law enforcement officials. One network "sniffer" created by the FBI called **DCS-1000** (previously known as "Carnivore") was a diagnostic tool intended to assist in criminal investigations by monitoring and capturing large amounts of Internet traffic. DCS–1000 was to be installed by FBI agents in ISP data centers as necessary to monitor the electronic communications of individuals suspected of federal crimes such as terrorism. The Carnivore/DCS–1000 initiative was later retitled DCS–3000, and its focus was changed to intercepting suspect personal communications delivered via wireless services.[37]

Although goods and materials will always need to be created, transported, and distributed, information is what forms the lifeblood of the new cyberworld. Nations that can effectively manage valuable information and make it accessible to their

Think About It…

The U.S. Constitution guarantees each person freedom of speech and security in his or her "persons, houses, papers, and effects, against unreasonable searches and seizures." The Constitution was written well before the digital age, however, and it is silent on the subject of electronic documents and advanced forms of technology-assisted communications. Given the need to combat high-tech crimes, can significant personal freedoms be retained in an age of digital interconnectedness?

Qoqazian/Fotolia

citizens will receive enhanced productivity and greater wealth as a reward. Moving information safely and securely is also important; today, a large part of that responsibility falls to the Internet. The **Internet**, the world's largest computer network, provides amazing and constantly growing capabilities. Unfortunately, as the Internet has grown, it has been targeted by hackers and computer criminals, some of whom have introduced rogue computer programs into the network's machines.

Policy Issues: Personal Freedoms in the Information Age

The continued development of telecommunications resources has led not only to concerns about security and data integrity, but also to an expanding interest in privacy, free speech, and personal freedoms. Although the **First and Fourth Amendments to the U.S. Constitution** guarantee each person freedom of speech and security in his or her "persons, houses, papers, and effects, against unreasonable searches and seizures," it is understandably silent on the subject of electronic documents and advanced forms of communication facilitated by technologies that did not exist at the time of the Constitutional Convention.

LEARNING OUTCOMES
7
Identify freedom-of-speech issues that modern technology has introduced.

Within the context of contemporary society we are left to ask these questions: What is speech? What are papers? Do electronic communications qualify for protection under the First Amendment, as does the spoken word? In an era when most houses are wired for telephones and many support data links that extend well beyond voice capabilities, it becomes necessary to ask what constitutes one's "speech" or one's "home." Does email qualify as speech? Where does the concept of a home begin and end for purposes of constitutional guarantees? Do activities within the home that can be accessed from without (as when a computer website is run out of a home) fall under the same constitutional guarantees as a private conversation held within the physical confines of a house?

Within the context of contemporary society we are left to ask these questions: What is speech? What are papers? Do electronic communications qualify for protection under the First Amendment?

Complicating matters still further are today's "supersnoop" technologies, which provide investigators with the ability to literally hear through walls (using vibration detectors), listen to conversations over great distances (with parabolic audio receivers), record voices in distant rooms (via laser readings of windowpane vibrations), and even look through walls using forward-looking infrared (FLIR) devices, which can detect temperature differences of as little as two-tenths of a degree.

In 1990, concerned individuals banded together to form the **Electronic Frontier Foundation (EFF)**, a citizens' group funded by private contributions that set for itself the task of actively assisting in refining notions of privacy and legality as they relate to telecommunications and other computer-based media. In the foundation's own words, "The Electronic Frontier Foundation (EFF) was founded in July of 1990 to ensure that the principles embodied in the Constitution and the Bill of Rights are protected as new communications technologies emerge. From the beginning, EFF has worked to shape our nation's communications infrastructure and the policies that govern it in order to maintain and enhance First Amendment, privacy and other democratic values. We believe that our overriding public goal must be the creation of Electronic Democracy."[38]

The EFF, which also supports litigation in the public interest, has been an active supporter of the public advocacy group Computer Professionals for Social Responsibility (CPSR). CPSR maintains a Computing and Civil Liberties Project in keeping with the EFF's purpose. The EFF also supported challenges to the CDA that resulted in the 1997 Supreme Court ruling in *Reno v. ACLU*, which found key provisions of the act unconstitutional. Reach the Electronic Frontier Foundation via **Web Extra 13–6**.

THE CASE

Kevin Mitnick

At the time of his arrest in February 1995, Kevin Mitnick was the most wanted computer criminal in U.S. history. There's little wonder as to why: His crimes included wire fraud, computer fraud, and wire communication interception, and the cost to his victims included millions of dollars in lost licensing fees, marketing delays, lost research and development, and the costs of repairing compromised computer systems.[i]

Cloned cellular telephones, hacker software, "sniffer" devices, and so-called "social engineering" were the tools Mitnick used to conduct the computer-crime spree that launched a lengthy investigation beginning in 1992. The evidence amassed by the FBI during its three-year probe was sufficient to force Mitnick to accept a plea bargain rather than risk more severe penalties by going to trial.[ii] His corporate victims included Motorola, Novell, Fujitsu, Sun Microsystems, and Nokia Mobile Phones, Ltd., among others, and he used University of Southern California computer systems to hide software code and obscure his identity.

An intriguing element of Mitnick's case was the manner in which he was finally caught.[iii] Computer expert Tsutomu Shimomura, infuriated after Mitnick hacked into and stole information from his home computer, employed a dramatic cybersleuthing effort to track down Mitnick, resulting in his arrest by the FBI in a Raleigh, North Carolina, apartment complex. Shimomura and *New York Times* reporter John Markoff subsequently published *Takedown*, an account of Shimomura's experience in chasing down the elusive Mitnick.[iv]

Mitnick became unhappy by what he believed was excessive media hype that led to his being unfairly characterized as "Osama bin Mitnick."[v] His actual transgressions, he contends, were far less serious than those depicted in sensationalistic press reports.

As a result of his 1995 arrest, Mitnick spent more than five years in prison, with more than eight months of it in solitary confinement. Now in his 50s, a significantly matured Mitnick has done a 180-degree turnaround in his approach to computer security. On March 1, 2000, he testified before the U.S. Senate's Governmental Affairs Committee, when he suggested that the millions of dollars corporations spend on firewalls and

Joe Cavaretta/AP Images

Hacker-turned-author Kevin Mitnick posing for a portrait in 2002 in Las Vegas. Barred by the terms of his probation from using computers, ex-convict Mitnick turned to writing about them, baring the tricks of his former trade of hacking in a book titled *The Art of Deception*. Mitnick was granted an exemption to use a computer to write his book. What is he doing today?

secure access devices are negated by the "the weakest link in the security chain: the people who use, administer and operate computer systems."[vi] Mitnick regaled the committee with tales of his use of "social engineering" (what he defines as "using manipulation, influence and deception to get a trusted insider to release information and to perform some sort of action item"[vii]), which enables a hacker to successfully attack the insider's own computer system.

Mitnick now oversees a highly successful computer consulting firm that specializes—not too surprisingly—in advising on computer security issues. Disturbingly, he suggests that it is easier to hack today than it was years ago, citing social engineering as still an extraordinarily effective technique for computer exploit. Mitnick's message is clear: Notwithstanding tremendous advances in both hardware and software security measures, the weak link is still the human element.[viii]

(*continued*)

THE CASE

Kevin Mitnick (*Continued*)

Notes

[i]"Kevin Mitnick Sentenced to Nearly Four Years in Prison," U.S. Department of Justice Press Release, August 9, 1999; and "Computer Hacker Ordered to Pay Restitution to Victim Companies Whose Systems were Compromised," U.S. Attorney's Office, Central District of California, August 9, 1999, http://www.cybercrime.gov/mitnick.htm (accessed June 2, 2007).

[ii]Ibid.

[iii]John Christensen, "The Trials of Kevin Mitnick," CNN, March 18, 1999, http://www.cnn.com/SPECIALS/1999/mitnick.background (accessed June 2, 2007).

[iv]Ibid.

[v]"A Convicted Hacker Debunks Some Myths," CNN, October 13, 2005, http://www.cnn.com/2005/TECH/internet/10/07/kevin.mitnick.cnna (accessed June 2, 2007).

[vi]Elizabeth Wasserman, "Mitnick Schools Feds on Hacking 101," CNN, March 3, 2000, http://archives.cnn.com/2000/TECH/computing/03/03/mitnick.the.prof/mitnick.the.prof.html (accessed June 2, 2007).

[vii]Kevin D. Mitnick, *The Art of Deception: Controlling the Human Element of Security* (Hoboken, NJ: Wiley, 2003).

[viii]"A Convicted Hacker Debunks Some Myths."

The case of Kevin Mitnick raises several interesting questions. Among them are the following:

1. **Had ordinary citizen and computer expert Tsutomu Shimomura not gotten involved in his cybersleuthing effort to track down Mitnick, would Mitnick have been caught? Why or why not?**
2. **Why do you think Mitnick made the decision to testify before Congress?**
3. **How do you feel about the way Mitnick parlayed a career in crime into a successful business?**

CHAPTER 13 Technology and Crime—*It's a Double-Edged Sword*

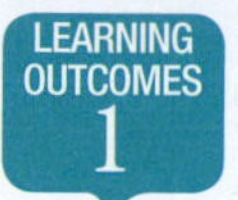

Explain cybercrime and describe how it is committed.

Cybercrime is any violation of a federal or state computer-crime statute. Much of today's crime is committed through the use of technology and consists of efforts to obtain or manipulate data stored on computers or available through the Internet.

1. What is cybercrime? How does it differ from more traditional forms of crime?

hacker A person who uses computers for exploration and exploitation.

cybercrime Any violation of a federal or state computer-crime statute.

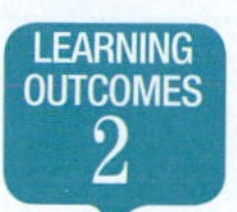

Describe the extent and forms of cybercrime.

A huge number of today's financial transactions are computerized, but the sophistication of cybercriminals makes it difficult to quantify losses due to computer crime. Cybercrimes can take various forms, including thefts from financial institutions, software piracy, phishing, identity theft, and malware authoring.

1. List and describe the forms of cybercrime discussed in this chapter.

software piracy The unauthorized and illegal copying of software.

phishing Pronounced "fishing." An Internet-based scam to steal valuable information such as credit card numbers, Social Security numbers, user IDs, and passwords.

computer virus A set of computer instructions that propagates copies or versions of itself into computer programs or data when it is executed.

Describe the legislation that has been enacted in an effort to curb cybercrime.

In the early years of computer-based information systems, many U.S. jurisdictions tried to prosecute unauthorized computer access under preexisting statutes, including burglary and larceny laws. Since that time, new laws have been developed at both state and federal levels, including the Cyber Security Enhancement Act (CSEA), which is Part of the Homeland Security Act of 2002.

1. List and describe federal laws that have been enacted in an effort to stem the rise of cybercrime.
2. What is a computer-related crime? How does it differ from computer abuse?

Communications Decency Act (CDA) A federal statute signed into law in 1996 that is Title 5 of the federal Telecommunications Act of 1996 (Pub. L. 104-104, 110 Stat. 56). The law sought to protect minors from harmful material on the Internet, and a portion of the CDA criminalized the knowing transmission of obscene or indecent messages to any recipient under 18 years of age.

Reno* v. *ACLU The 1997 U.S. Supreme Court case that found the bulk of the CDA to be unconstitutional, ruling that it contravenes First Amendment free-speech guarantees.

No Electronic Theft Act (NETA, or NET Act) A 1997 federal law that criminalizes the willful infringement of copyrighted works, including by electronic means, even when the infringing party derives no direct financial benefit from the infringement.

Digital Theft Deterrence and Copyright Damages Improvement Act A 1999 federal law that attempted to combat software piracy and other forms of digital theft by amending Section 504(c) of the Copyright Act, thereby increasing the amount of damages that could potentially be awarded in cases of copyright infringement.

Cyber Security Enhancement Act (CSEA) Part of the Homeland Security Act of 2002, this federal law directs the U.S. Sentencing Commission to take several specific factors into account in creating new sentencing guidelines for computer criminals.

computer-related crime Any illegal act for which knowledge of computer technology is involved in its perpetration, investigation, or prosecution.

computer abuse Any unlawful incident associated with computer technology in which a victim suffered or could have suffered loss or in which a perpetrator by intention made or could have made gain.

LEARNING OUTCOMES 4

Describe the typical profile of computer criminals.

The typical computer hacker is a male between the ages of 16 and 25 who lives in the United States; is a computer user, but not a programmer; and is primarily motivated to gain access to websites and computer networks, not to profit financially.

1. Is there a typical kind of cyberoffender? Is so, provide a description.
2. What motivates a computer criminal?

cyberspace The computer-created matrix of virtual possibilities, including online services, wherein human beings interact with one another and with technology itself.

phone phreak A person who uses switched, dialed-access telephone services for exploration and exploitation.

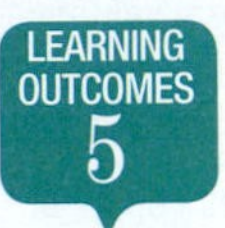

Explain how technology arms criminals with new methods of crime commission while simultaneously providing criminal justice personnel with the tools to combat crime.

Technology is a double-edged sword. On one hand, it arms potential criminals with potent new weapons of crime commission; on the other hand, it provides criminal justice personnel with powerful tools useful in the battle against crime. Technology in law enforcement today involves computer databases of known offenders, expert systems, cellular communications, video surveillance and face recognition technology, electronic eavesdropping, DNA analysis, and less-lethal weapons.

1. What is the difference between high-tech crime and traditional forms of criminal activity?
2. What tools are available to today's law enforcement agencies for use in the fight against technocrimes?

DNA profiling The use of biological residue found at the scene of a crime for genetic comparisons in aiding the identification of criminal suspects.

expert systems Computer hardware and software that attempt to duplicate the decision-making processes used by skilled investigators in the analysis of evidence and in the recognition of patterns that such evidence might represent.

LEARNING OUTCOMES 6

Summarize the steps being taken to combat computer crime.

Moving information safely and securely is vitally important today, and security responsibilities are shared by law enforcement agencies, the public, corporations, businesses, and Internet service providers. Any effective program to combat cybercrime and secure an organization against the threat of high-tech crime must use threat analysis. Once specific threats are identified, strategies tailored to dealing with them can be implemented.

1. What is a threat analysis? What kinds of threats should such an analysis examine?
2. How can the threat of cybercrime victimization be reduced?

data encryption The process by which information is encoded, making it unreadable to all but its intended recipients.

threat analysis A complete and thorough assessment of the kinds of perils facing an organization.

audit trail "A sequential record of system activities that enables auditors to reconstruct, review, and examine the sequence of states and activities surrounding each event in one or more related transactions from inception to output of final results back to inception."

DCS-1000 An FBI-developed network diagnostic tool that is capable of assisting in criminal investigations by monitoring and capturing large amounts of Internet traffic. Previously called "Carnivore."

Internet The world's largest computer network.

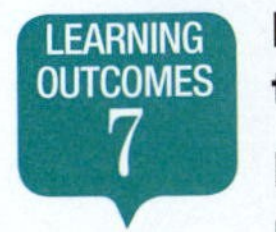

Identify freedom-of-speech issues that modern technology has introduced.

Efforts to control high-tech crime through criminal investigation and prosecution impact issues of individual rights—from free speech to technological privacy in the context of digital interconnectedness. There will need to be an acceptable balance between constitutional guarantees of continued freedom of access to legitimate high-tech activities and effective enforcement initiatives for the massive threat that high-tech crimes represent.

1. What are some of the personal freedoms that are threatened by today's need for enhanced security?

First and Fourth Amendments to the U.S. Constitution The amendments that guarantee each person freedom of speech and security in his or her "persons, houses, papers, and effects, against unreasonable searches and seizures."

Electronic Frontier Foundation (EFF) A nonprofit organization formed in July 1990 to help ensure that the principles embodied in the Constitution and the Bill of Rights are protected as new communications technologies emerge.

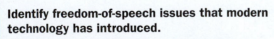

"[I]nternational implications for America's criminal justice system have never been greater. As the country's social, economic, and technological climate continue to undergo major changes, globalization is also producing new challenges for criminal justice practitioners and researchers."

—*Richard Ward,* The Internationalization of Criminal Justice

14 Globalization and Terrorism—Our Small World

1. Define *comparative criminology* and explain what it can tell us about crime worldwide.
2. Explain globalization and show how it is making it more difficult to combat crime around the world.
3. Define *terrorism*, identify its major characteristics, and describe the different kinds of terrorist organizations.
4. Describe the legislative policies that were created after the 9/11 attacks to prevent future incidents of terrorism.

Alain Wacquier/Fotolia

INTRO

TRANSNATIONAL CRIMINAL ENTERPRISE

In January 2012, federal prosecutors indicted ten suspected La Mara Salvatrucha (MS-13) gang members for crimes ranging from conspiracy to commit murder and attempted murder to racketeering and smuggling. Those gang members had nicknames that sounded like cartoon characters, including Doofy, Casper, Sonic, and Lobo.[1]

Federal prosecutors said that the men had committed numerous crimes of violence on the streets of Flushing, a part of Queens, in New York City. Their alleged crimes included extortion rackets in which the men were said to have participated in stabbings, a beating using a baseball bat, and at least one machete attack.

Prosecutors also charged the men with conspiring with other MS-13 gang members around the country and in El Salvador to wire money overseas in an effort to smuggle gang members into the United States. MS-13 is a well-known transnational criminal enterprise whose membership is comprised primarily of immigrants from Central America. It has branches throughout North America, and the Federal Bureau of Investigation (FBI) puts its estimated membership at more than 10,000 in the United States alone.[2]

Ulises Rodriguez/EPA/Newscom

DISCUSS **In the not-too-distant past, crime used to be largely a local phenomenon. Today, however, with the advent of globalization, criminal activity often contains an international component. How can enforcement agencies adjust to these changes? What new laws will be required to cope with them?**

▶ Comparative Criminology

Comparative criminology is the study of crime on a cross-national level. When crime patterns in one country are compared with those in another, theories and policies that have been taken for granted in one place can be reevaluated in the light of world experience. As some noted **comparative criminologists** have observed, "The challenge for comparative criminologists is to develop theories with increased specificity while managing to construct them in such a way that they can be applied across more than one culture or nation-state. This eventually must demand that theories be developed to conceptualize societies as totalities and that theories that manage to provide a world context in which total societies behave be further constructed."[3]

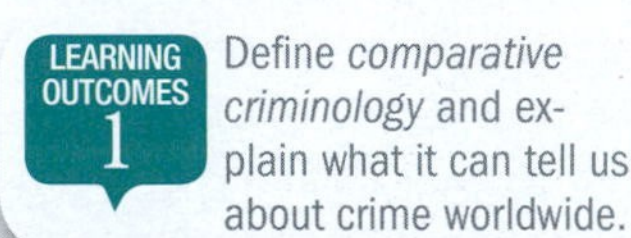

LEARNING OUTCOMES 1 Define *comparative criminology* and explain what it can tell us about crime worldwide.

Ethnocentrism

One important issue facing comparative criminologists is **ethnocentrism**. Ethnocentrism, or culture-centeredness, can interfere with the work of comparative criminologists in a number of ways, including the ways in which crime statistics are gathered, analyzed, and presented.

Only in recent years have American specialists in criminology begun to closely examine crime in other cultures. Not all societies are equally open, and it is not always easy to explore them. In some societies, even the *study* of crime is taboo. As a result, data-gathering strategies taken for granted in Western culture may not be well received elsewhere. One author, for example, has observed that in China, "the seeking of criminal justice information through face-to-face questioning takes on a different meaning than it does generally in the Western world. While we accept this method of inquiry because we prize thinking on our feet and quick answers, it is offensive in China because it shows lack of respect and appreciation for the information given through the preferred means of prepared questions and formal briefings."[4] Most of the information available about Chinese crime rates comes by way of officialdom, and routine Western social science

Think About It…

It is difficult to compare crime statistics and crime rates from one country to another—and the greater the cultural differences between the countries, the greater the difficulty. How do differences in culture lead to differences in crime? In crime reporting?

Giacomo Falcone/Fotolia

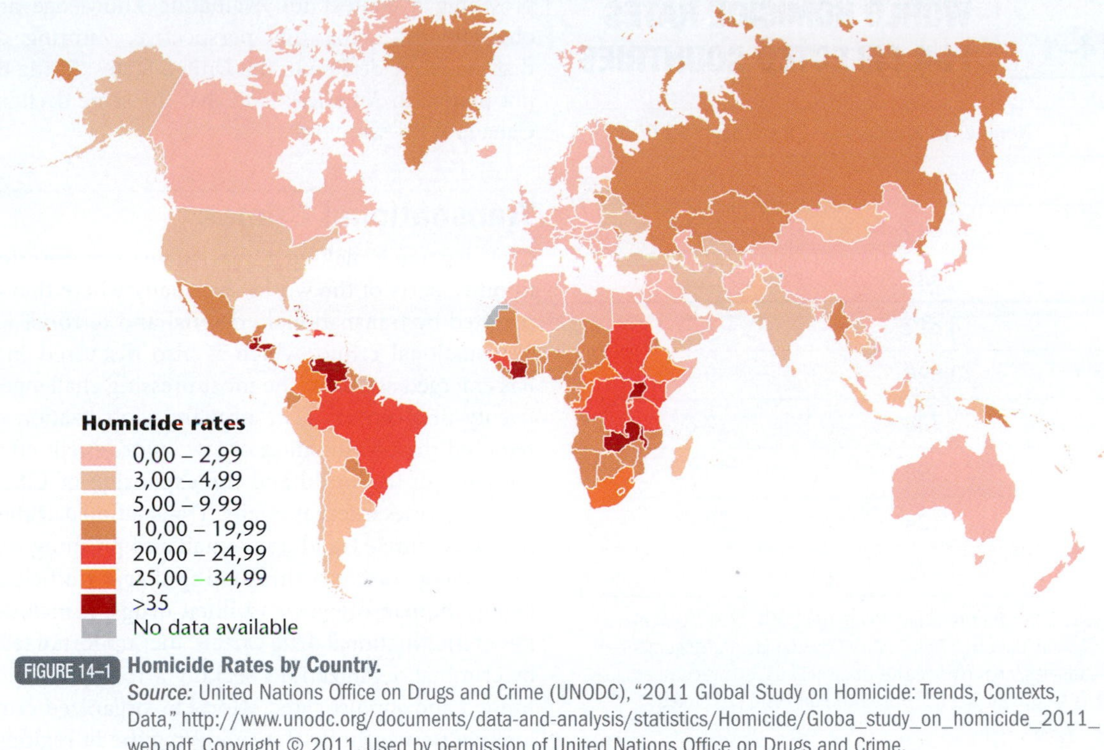

FIGURE 14–1 **Homicide Rates by Country.**
Source: United Nations Office on Drugs and Crime (UNODC), "2011 Global Study on Homicide: Trends, Contexts, Data," http://www.unodc.org/documents/data-and-analysis/statistics/Homicide/Globa_study_on_homicide_2011_web.pdf. Copyright © 2011. Used by permission of United Nations Office on Drugs and Crime.

practices such as door-to-door interviews, participant observation, and random surveys might not produce results in China.

Similar difficulties arise in the comparison of crime rates from one country to another. The crime rates of different nations are difficult to compare because of (1) differences in the way a given crime is defined; (2) diverse crime-reporting practices; and (3) political, social, economic, and other influences on the reporting of statistics to international agencies.[5]

Definitional Issues in Reporting

Definitional differences create what may be the biggest problem. For cross-national comparisons of crime data to be meaningful, they must share conceptual similarities. Unfortunately, that is often not the case. Nations report offenses according to the legal criteria by which arrests are made and under which prosecution can occur. Switzerland, for example, includes bicycle thefts in its reported data on what we call "auto theft." The Netherlands has no crime category for robberies, counting them as thefts. Japan classifies an assault that results in death as an assault or an aggravated assault, not as a homicide. Greek rape statistics include crimes of sodomy, "lewdness," seduction of a child, incest, and prostitution. Communist China reports only robberies and thefts that involve the property of citizens; crimes against state-owned property fall into a separate category.

Crime statistics also reflect social and political contexts. Some nations do not accurately report certain kinds of culturally reprehensible crimes. Communist countries, for example, often do not report crimes such as theft, burglary, and robbery because the very existence of such offenses might appear to create inadequacies in the communist system. Likewise, the social norms in some societies may make it almost impossible for women to report cases of rape or sexual abuse, but in other societies, women are encouraged to come forward.

With all these caveats in mind, it can still be instructive to look at crime rates in other countries and attempt comparisons with U.S. crime rates. A useful tool for international crime rate comparisons is *The Eleventh United Nations Survey on Crime Trends and the Operations of Criminal Justice System*, which covers the years 2007–2008. To some, U.S. violent crime rates seem high compared with violent crime rates of other developed countries, but American crime rates are far from the highest in the world, and United Nations (UN) surveys typically place U.S. crime rates well below world highs. Figure 14–1 shows worldwide homicide rates by country, and Table 14–1 shows homicide rates for selected countries. A 12th UN crime survey is now under way, analyzing comprehensive data from the years 2012–2013.[6] See more international crime statistics at **Web Extra 14–1**, and visit the National Institute of Justice (NIJ) International Center at **Web Extra 14–2**.

▶ Globalization

Globalization can be defined as a process of social homogenization by which the experiences of everyday life, marked by the diffusion of commodities and ideas, can foster a standardization of cultural expressions around the world.[7] The increasing integration of previously isolated events and their impact is an important aspect of globalization, and the idea of globalization encompasses the increasingly

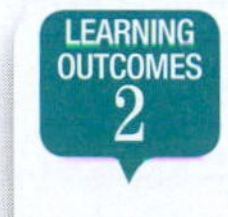

Explain globalization and show how it is making it more difficult to combat crime around the world.

TABLE 14–1 WORLD HOMICIDE RATES FOR SELECTED COUNTRIES

Country	Number of Murders	Rate per 100,000
Denmark	44	0.8
England and Wales	540	1.0
Canada	529	1.5
United States	14,612	4.7
Russia Federation	13,826	9.7
Nicaragua	738	12.6
Mexico	27,199	23.7
Belize	124	39.0
El Salvador	4,371	70.2

Source: United Nations Office on Drugs and Crime (UNODC), "2011 Global Study on Homicide: Trends, Contexts, Data," http://www.unodc.org/documents/data-and-analysis/statistics/crime/Homicide_statistics2013.xls (accessed September 16, 2014). Copyright © 2011. Used by permission of United Nations Office on Drugs and Crime.

Think About It…

What are the positive and negative effects of globalization? How does globalization impact crime in the United States? How does it affect terrorism?

Cristimatei/Fotolia

interconnectedness of people, ideas, and things on a worldwide scale.

Some have used the term *globalization of knowledge* to describe the increase in understanding that results from a sharing of information between cultures. The globalization of knowledge is beginning to play a significant role in both the process of theory formation within criminology and the development of American crime control policies. According to some, globalization will make it increasingly difficult for nation-states to ignore the criminal justice information of other countries. A few years ago, as recipient of the prestigious Vollmer Award in Criminology, Franklin E. Zimring, of the University of California, Berkeley, addressed the American Society of Criminology, complaining about the fact that American criminology had been self-obsessed and "particularly inattentive to the value and necessity of transnational comparisons."[8] Zimring sees comparative efforts as providing a context for evaluating knowledge and reviewing observations. Using this perspective, Zimring demonstrated that the crime decline in the United States during the 1990s was not unique to America—and that the same decline occurred in Canada at the same time.

The term *globalization of knowledge* describes the increase in understanding that results from a sharing of information between cultures.

Transnational Crimes

Globalization is making it impossible to ignore criminal activity in other parts of the world, especially where that crime is perpetrated by transnational criminal and terrorist organizations. Transnational crime, which is also discussed in Chapter 10, has emerged as one of the most pressing challenges of the early twenty-first century. The growing globalization of crime has required the coordination of law enforcement efforts in different parts of the world and the expansion of U.S. law enforcement activities internationally. Transnational crime ranges from relatively simple fraudulent email and phishing schemes to the more dangerous and threatening illegal trafficking in human beings, human organs, and illicit drugs. It includes the activities of multinational drug cartels, the support of terrorist groups by criminal organizations seeking armed protection, and well-funded and sophisticated efforts by organized criminal groups looking to overthrow the ruling regime in regions with others sympathetic to their operations.

Human Smuggling and Trafficking

According to the United Nations,[9] trafficking in persons and human smuggling are some of the fastest-growing areas of international criminal activity today. There are important distinctions between the two. The U.S. State Department defines **human smuggling** as "the facilitation, transportation, attempted transportation or illegal entry of a person(s) across an international border, in violation of one or more country's laws, either clandestinely or through deception, such as the use of fraudulent documents."[10] In other words, human smuggling refers to illegal immigration in which an agent is involved for payment to help a person cross a border clandestinely.[11] Human smuggling may be conducted to obtain financial or other benefits for the smuggler, although sometimes people smuggle others to reunite their families. Human smuggling generally occurs with the consent of the people being smuggled, who often pay for the services. Once in the country they've paid to enter, they usually are no longer be in contact with the smuggler. The State Department notes that the vast majority of people who are assisted in illegally entering the United States annually are smuggled rather than trafficked.

Although smuggling might not involve active coercion, it can be deadly. In January 2007, for example, truck driver Tyrone Williams, 36, a Jamaican citizen living in Schenectady, New York, was sentenced to life in prison for causing the deaths of 19 illegal immigrants in the nation's deadliest known human smuggling attempt.[12]

The Intelligence Reform and Terrorism Prevention Act of 2004[13] established the Human Smuggling and Trafficking Center (HSTC) within the Department of Homeland Security (DHS). The U.S. Immigration and Customs Enforcement (ICE), the largest investigative agency within the DHS, has primary

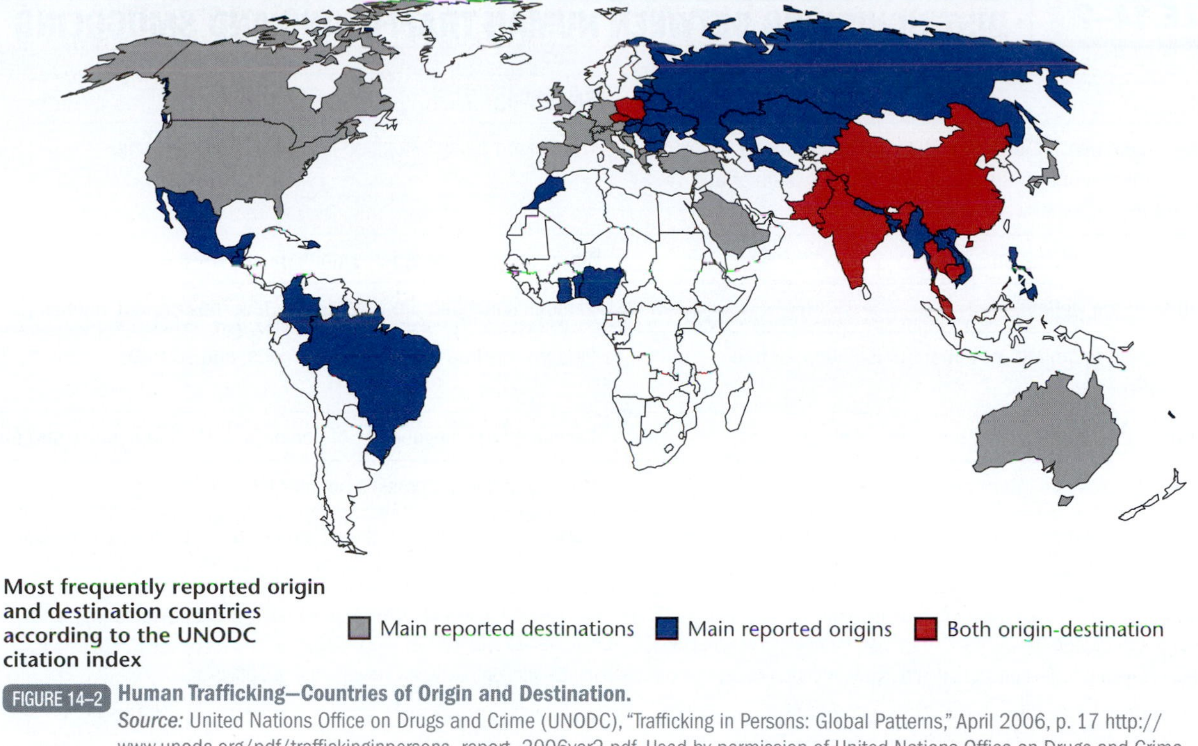

FIGURE 14–2 **Human Trafficking—Countries of Origin and Destination.**
Source: United Nations Office on Drugs and Crime (UNODC), "Trafficking in Persons: Global Patterns," April 2006, p. 17 http://www.unodc.org/pdf/traffickinginpersons_report_2006ver2.pdf. Used by permission of United Nations Office on Drugs and Crime.

responsibility for enforcing laws related to human smuggling and trafficking. As a result, ICE plays a leading role in the fight against human smuggling and trafficking.

In contrast to smuggling, **trafficking in persons (TIP)** can be compared to a modern-day form of slavery. Trafficking involves the exploitation of unwilling people through force, coercion, threat, or deception and includes human rights abuses such as debt bondage, deprivation of liberty, or lack of control over freedom and labor. Trafficking is often undertaken for purposes of sexual exploitation or labor exploitation. The Global Fast Fund, a nonprofit international charity that tracks TIP incidents, says that "the primary countries of destination for victims of trafficking are the United States, Italy, Japan, Canada, Australia, and other 'advanced nations.'"[14] A map from Global Fast is shown in Figure 14–2, showing both countries of origin and destination for victims of trafficking. Figure 14–3 shows where victims of trafficking into the United States end up.

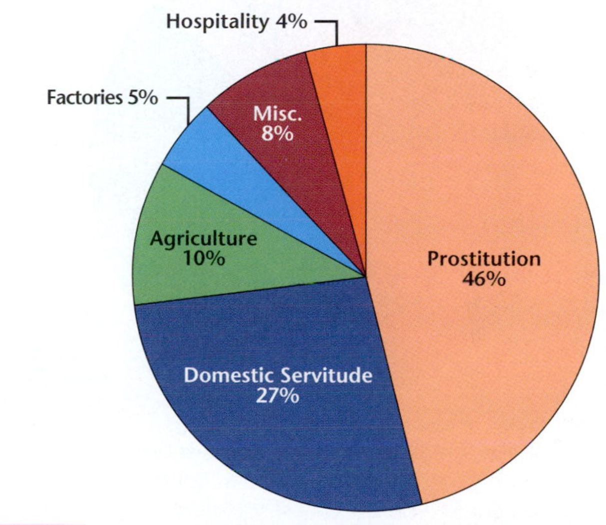

FIGURE 14–3 **Human Trafficking into the United States—Endpoint Sectors.**
Source: Based on Free the Slaves and the Human Rights Center, University of California, Berkeley, "Hidden Slaves: Forced Labor in the United States," September, 2004, p. 1, https://www.freetheslaves.net/Document.Doc?id=17. Copyright © 2004. Used by permission of Human Rights Center.

A recent report by the United Nations Office on Drugs and Crime says that "The term trafficking in persons can be misleading [because] it places emphasis on the transaction aspects of a crime that is more accurately described as enslavement. Exploitation of people, day after day. For years on end."[15]

Practically speaking, it is sometimes difficult to distinguish between a smuggling case and a trafficking case because trafficking often includes an element of smuggling (that is, the illegal crossing of a national border). Some trafficking victims may believe they are being smuggled when they are really being trafficked, but are unaware of their eventual fate. This happens, for example, when women trafficked for sexual exploitation may have thought they were agreeing to work in legitimate industries for decent wages—part of which they may have agreed to pay to the trafficker who smuggled them. They didn't know that upon arrival, the traffickers would keep them in bondage, subject them to physical force or sexual violence, force them to work in the sex trade, and take most or all of their income. Table 14–2 draws some important distinctions between human trafficking and smuggling.

Human Trafficking—The Numbers

U.S. government officials estimate that 800,000 to 900,000 victims are trafficked globally each year and that 17,500 to 18,500

TABLE 14–2 DISTINGUISHING BETWEEN HUMAN TRAFFICKING AND SMUGGLING

Trafficking	Smuggling
Must contain an element of force, fraud, or coercion (actual, perceived, or implied), unless the victim is under 18 years of age and is involved in commercial sex acts.	The person being smuggled is generally cooperating.
Forced labor and/or exploitation.	No forced labor or other exploitation.
Persons trafficked are victims.	Persons smuggled are violating the law. They are not victims.
Enslaved, subjected to limited movement or isolation, or had documents confiscated.	Persons are free to leave, change jobs, and so forth.
Need not involve the actual movement of the victim.	Facilitates the illegal entry of person(s) from one country into another.
No requirement to cross an international border.	Smuggling always crosses an international border.
Person must be involved in labor/services or commercial sex acts (that is, must be "working").	Person must only be in the country or attempting entry illegally.

Source: Adapted from U.S. Department of State, Bureau for International Narcotics and Law Enforcement Affairs, Human Smuggling and Trafficking Center, *Distinctions between Human Smuggling and Human Trafficking* (Washington, DC: Author, January 1, 2005).

Note: This table is meant to be conceptual and is not intended to provide precise legal distinctions between smuggling and trafficking.

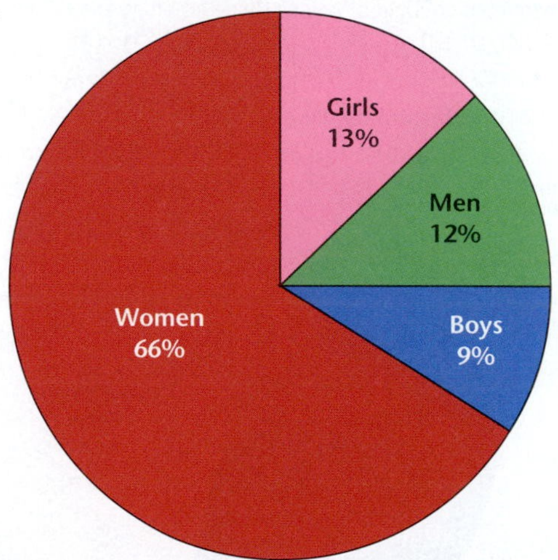

FIGURE 14–4 **Profile of Worldwide Trafficking Victims.**
Source: United Nations Office on Drugs and Crime (UNDOC), *Global Report on Trafficking in Persons* (New York: United Nations, 2009), p. 11. Copyright © 2009. Used by permission of United Nations Office on Drugs and Crime.

are trafficked into the United States. Women and children comprise the largest group of victims, and they are often physically and emotionally abused (see Figure 14–4). Although TIP is often an international crime that involves the crossing of borders, it is important to note that TIP victims can be trafficked within their own country and community. Traffickers can move victims between locations within the same country and often sell them to other trafficking organizations.

A few years ago, the Department of Justice funded the creation of the Human Trafficking Reporting System (HTRS) to report on human trafficking within the United States. The most recent HTRS report provides data on human trafficking incidents that were investigated between January 2008 and June 2010. Those data are shown in Table 14–3.

Globally, the International Labor Organization (ILO), the UN agency charged with addressing labor standards, employment, and social protection issues, estimates that 12.3 million people are in forced labor, bonded labor, forced child labor, and sexual servitude throughout the world today.[16] Other estimates range as high as 27 million.

Federal Immigration and Trafficking Legislation

The United States had open national borders until the 1880s, when limited federal controls on immigration began. One of the nation's first immigration laws was the Chinese Exclusion Act, which became law in 1882 and was enforced for ten years; it was enacted in response to large numbers of Chinese male laborers who had immigrated to the western United States in the mid-1800s looking for work and who often took jobs on railroads and in the mining industry.

A more comprehensive piece of federal immigration legislation was the 1924 Immigration Act limiting the number of immigrants who could be admitted from any one country to 2% of the number of people from that country who were already living here (calculated using the Census of 1890). The law also barred immigration from specific parts of the Asia-Pacific Triangle, including Cambodia, China, Japan, Korea, Laos, the Philippines, and Thailand. The Immigration and Nationality Act (INA) of 1952, establishing the Immigration and Naturalization Service (INS) while continuing numerical ethnic quotas, provided criminal penalties

The United States had open national borders until the 1880s, when limited federal controls on immigration began.

TABLE 14–3 NUMBER OF ALLEGED HUMAN TRAFFICKING INCIDENTS IN THE UNITED STATES, JANUARY 2008 TO JUNE 2010

	Total Incidents	
Type of Human Trafficking Incident	**Number**	**Percent**
All incidents*	2,515	100.0%
Sex trafficking	2,065	82.1%
Adult prostitution	1,218	48.4
Child sex trafficking	1,016	40.4
Sexualized labor	142	5.6
Other sex trafficking	61	2.4
Labor trafficking	350	13.9%
Commercial industry labor	132	5.2
Unregulated industry labor	230	9.1
Other	26	1.0
Other suspected trafficking	65	2.6%
Unknown	172	6.8%

Source: Duren Banks and Tracey Kyckelhahn, *Characteristics of Suspected Human Trafficking Incidents, 2008–2010* (Washington, DC: Bureau of Justice Statistics, 2011), p. 3.
*One trafficking incident may involve many victims.

for anyone bringing or attempting to bring unauthorized aliens into the United States;[17] years later, the INA amendments of 1965 abolished quotas based on ethnicity.[18] The Homeland Security Act of 2002 (HSA) dissolved the INS and transferred most of its functions to three branches of the DHS: Citizenship and Immigration Services (CIS), Customs and Border Protection (CBP), and ICE.

Recognizing that human smuggling and TIP were serious social issues, Congress passed the Trafficking Victims Protection Act of 2000 (TVPA), which addressed the significant problem of TIP for the purposes of having people commit commercial sex acts (termed *sex trafficking*) and of subjecting them to involuntary servitude, peonage, or debt bondage and increased the protections afforded victims of trafficking.[19] The TVPA specified severe forms of trafficking: "a.) sex trafficking in which a commercial sex act is induced by force, fraud, or coercion, or in which the person induced to perform such an act has not attained 18 years of age; or b.) the recruitment, harboring, transportation, provision, or obtaining of a person for labor or services, through the use of force, fraud, or coercion for the purpose of subjection to involuntary servitude, peonage, debt bondage, or slavery."[20]

Under the TVPA, human trafficking does not require the crossing of an international border or even the transportation of victims from one locale to another because victims of certain forms of trafficking are not just illegal aliens, but also U.S. citizens, legal residents, or visitors. Victims do not have to be women or children; they may also be adult males.

The Trafficking Victims Protection Reauthorization Act (TVPRA) of 2003 added a new initiative to the original law to collect foreign data on trafficking investigations, prosecutions, convictions, and sentences. Its 2006 data showed that reporting jurisdictions prosecuted 5,808 people for trafficking-related offenses and secured 3,160 convictions, the lowest number of reported foreign prosecutions since reporting began in 2003.[21] TVPA was again reauthorized in 2005, 2008, and 2013. The most recent reauthorization improves the original legislation by, among other things, authorizing the TIP to negotiate child protection compacts with designated focus countries to increase resources to eradicate child trafficking.

Section 7202 of the Intelligence Reform and Terrorism Prevention Act of 2004 established the HSTC within the U.S. State Department, and the secretary of state, the secretary of the DHS, the attorney general, and members of the National Intelligence Community oversee it. The center was created to achieve greater integration and overall effectiveness in the U.S. government's enforcement of issues related to human smuggling, TIP, and criminal support of clandestine terrorist travel. Learn more about human trafficking in the United States from the U.S. Department of State's Office to Monitor and Combat Trafficking in Persons at http://www.state.gov/j/tip, and from Northeastern University's Human Trafficking Data Collection and Reporting Project at http://www.northeastern.edu/humantrafficking.

Terrorism

The U.S. Department of State defines **terrorism** as "premeditated, politically motivated violence perpetrated against noncombatant targets by subnational groups or clandestine agents, usually intended to influence an audience."[22] Europol says that "[t]errorism is not an ideology or movement, but a tactic or a method for attaining political goals."[23] Paul Pillar, former deputy chief of the Counterterrorist Center of the Central Intelligence Agency (CIA), has identified four key features of terrorism that distinguish it from other forms of violence.[24] Those features are shown in Table 14–4.

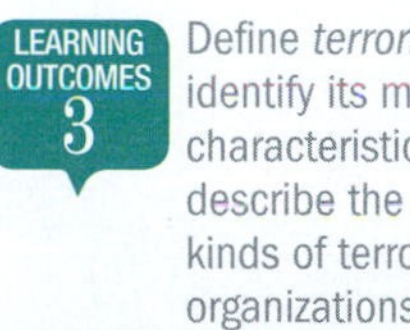

Define *terrorism*, identify its major characteristics, and describe the different kinds of terrorist organizations.

Terrorist acts are criminal because they violate the criminal law, because they involve criminal activity, and because they produce criminal results. The primary distinction between violent criminal acts and acts of terrorism, however, has to do with the political motivation or social ideology of the offender.[25]

TABLE 14–4 CHARACTERISTICS OF TERRORISM

Terrorism Usually Is	Terrorism Usually Is Not
Premeditated or planned	Impulsive or an act of rage
Politically motivated (that is, intended to change the existing political order)	Perpetrated for criminal gain (that is, illicit personal or financial benefit)
Aimed at civilians	Aimed at military targets or combat-ready troops
Carried out by subnational groups	Perpetrated by the army of a country

Terrorist organizations vary in their goals and can be categorized as follows:

1. **Nationalist terrorists** seek to change the entire political, social, and economic system to an extreme right, or ultraconservative, model.
2. **Religious terrorists** use violence to bring about social and cultural changes that are in keeping with their religious views.
3. **State-sponsored terrorists** are deliberately employed by radical nations as foreign policy tools.
4. **Left-wing terrorists** seek to replace economies based on free enterprise with socialist or communist economic systems.
5. **Right-wing terrorists** are motivated by fascist ideals and work toward the dissolution of democratic governments.
6. **Anarchist terrorists** are revolutionary, anticapitalist, and antiauthoritarian. Although these groups are often motivated by domestic politics, they also are usually part of wider international campaigns and may fight against free trade agreements, what they see as ecologically damaging practices, and so forth.

Figure 14–5 lists examples of contemporary terrorist groups according to the categories listed here.

The United States is faced today with two major types of terrorism: domestic and international. **Domestic terrorism** is unlawful force or violence by a group or an individual who is based and operates entirely within the United States and its territories without foreign direction and whose acts are directed at elements of the U.S. government or population.[26] **International terrorism** is unlawful force or violence by a group or an individual who has a connection to a foreign power or whose activities transcend national boundaries against persons or property to intimidate or coerce a government, the civilian population, or any segment thereof, in furtherance of political or social objectives.[27] International terrorism is sometimes incorrectly called *foreign terrorism*, a term that, strictly speaking, refers only to acts of terrorism that occur outside the United States.

Terrorist acts are criminal because they violate the criminal law, because they involve criminal activity, and because they produce criminal results.

FIGURE 14–5 **Types of Terrorist Groups.**
Source: From *Criminology Today: An Integrative Introduction*, 7e by Frank A. Schmalleger. Copyright © 2014 by Pearson Education. Used by permission of Pearson Education.

WHO'S TO BLAME—The Individual or Society

The Making of a Suicide Bomber

Khaled Al-Rasheed was born in New York City to Egyptian parents and repeatedly visited the Middle East with his father. His last trip was in 2010 when Khaled spent part of the summer with his grandparents near the world-famous Aswan dam. Although his American passport didn't show it, Khaled, a Muslim, had traveled extensively throughout the Arab world while he was growing up, sometimes in the company of his father, and sometimes with his grandfather.

He had seen firsthand the damage done by the American invasion of Iraq, much of which hadn't been repaired by the time he first visited the region. He had also experienced the resentment festering among the huge non-Arab populations in Saudi Arabia and Kuwait, where oil money paid for the extravagant lifestyles of the royal families but didn't find its way into the hands of the working class.

Mariusz Blach/Fotolia

By the time he was 15, he had befriended a group of radical young Islamists living in Jordan, who blamed the problems in the Middle East on the Great Satan–their name for America. "Americans are stealing our region's wealth," he was told, "and polluting the holy land with their vice and nonbelief."

Returning to the United States in the fall of 2010, Khaled had become radicalized and was ready to strike a blow in what he saw as a worldwide holy war against nonbelievers. As a U.S. citizen, he could travel easily in and out of the country, and on one of his trips he was able to smuggle in the equipment necessary to manufacture a new kind of explosive–one that could be packed into condoms and swallowed like the heroin and cocaine that often crossed the country's southern borders. Equipped with a small blasting-cap whose thin wire ran up the esophagus and into his mouth, the last charge to be swallowed could be set off by simply biting down on a tiny switch clenched between Khaled's molars. The device, which used very little metal, was virtually undetectable.

One day, Khaled swallowed six explosive-filled condoms, passed through security, and boarded a plane at New York's John F. Kennedy airport. Once the plane, bound for Los Angeles, was airborne, Khaled bit down on the detonator. To his surprise, nothing happened. An hour into the flight, however, one of the swallowed condoms ruptured, and Khaled became violently ill as its contents entered his digestive system. Removed from the plane when it landed in Los Angeles, he was taken to a hospital where the explosives were discovered. An operation saved his life, and he recovered in the medical wing of the Los Angeles County Men's Central Jail.

Think About It

1. What does it mean to say, as this scenario does, that "Khaled had become radicalized"? Might the term be applied to other kinds of offenders? If so, which ones?
2. How could someone like Khaled, born in America, be so taken with a foreign ideology?
3. If you were in charge of policymaking for America's "war on terror," what would you want to see happen to Khaled?
4. If you were a judge in charge of sentencing Khaled for his attempted terrorist attack, what kind of sentence would you give him? Is there any chance that he might be rehabilitated? What does "rehabilitation" mean in this context?

Note: Who's to Blame boxes provide fictionalized critical thinking opportunities, and are not actual cases.

Domestic Terrorism

Twenty years ago, the 1995 terrorist bombing of the Alfred P. Murrah Federal Building in downtown Oklahoma City, Oklahoma, which killed 168 people and wounded hundreds more, showed just how vulnerable the United States is to domestic terrorist attacks. The nine-story building was devastated by a homemade bomb. The fertilizer and diesel fuel device used in the attack was left in a parked rental truck beside the building, and the blast left a crater 30 feet wide and 8 feet deep and spread debris over a ten-block area.

In June 1997, a federal jury found 29-year-old Timothy McVeigh guilty of 11 counts ranging from conspiracy to first-degree murder in the bombing. Jurors concluded that McVeigh had conspired with Terry Nichols, a friend he had met while both were in the U.S. Army, and with unknown others to use a truck bomb to destroy the Murrah building.

Today, a number of groups in the United States fall under the heading of domestic terrorism. One of the largest and fastest growing is the Sovereign Citizens movement, a group of loosely affiliated individuals who argue that they are not subject to local, state, or federal laws. Many do not recognize the authority of the justice system, including the courts and police. Recently, the DHS and the National Counterterrorism Center (NCTC) listed the Sovereign Citizens movement as a major threat, placing it alongside white supremacists and homegrown Islamic terrorists.[28] The FBI classifies the organization as an "extremist antigovernment group." According to Mark Potok, a senior fellow at the Southern Poverty Law Center, more that 100,000 Americans "have aligned themselves" with the Sovereign Citizens movement.[29]

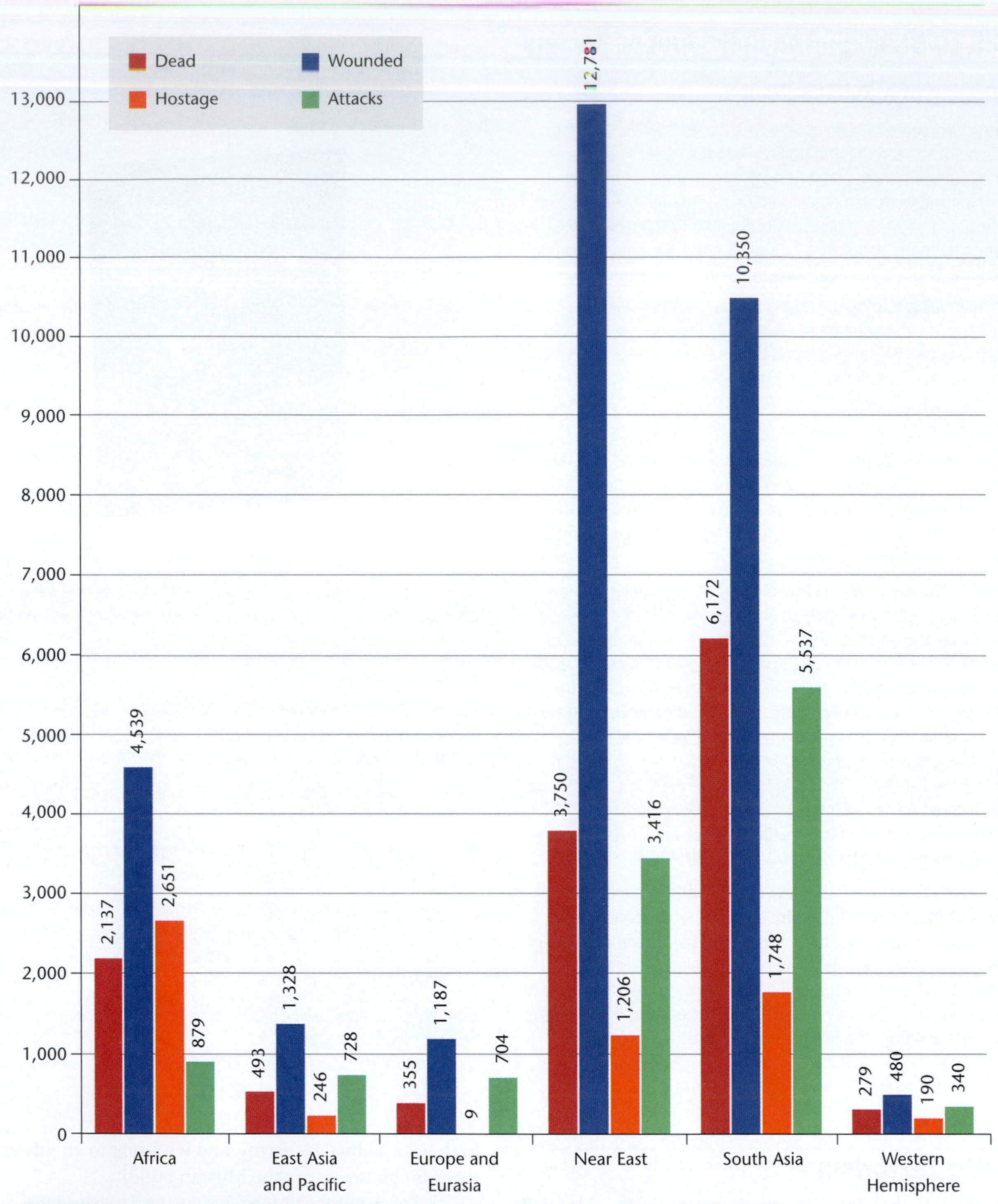

FIGURE 14–6 **Terrorist Attacks and Victims by Region of the World, 2010.**
Source: National Counterterrorism Center (NCC), *2010 Report on Terrorism* (Washington, DC: NCC, April 2011), p. 11, http://www.nctc.gov/witsbanner/docs/2010_report_on_terrorism.pdf.

International Terrorism

According to the NCTC, 11,500 terrorist attacks against noncombatants occurred in 72 countries during 2010, resulting in over 50,000 deaths, injuries, and kidnappings.[30] In that year, the largest number of terrorist attacks took place in the Middle East and South Asia. These two regions were the locations for 75% of the world's terrorist attacks as well as the majority of terrorism-related deaths in 2010. (See Figure 14–6.) The NCTC reports the following for 2010:[31]

- The Near East and South Asia in 2010 suffered a combined total of 8,960 attacks that caused 9,960 deaths.
- Attacks in Afghanistan and Iraq rose in 2010. Almost a quarter of worldwide attacks occurred in Iraq, a slight increase from 2009, although deaths fell for the fourth consecutive year.

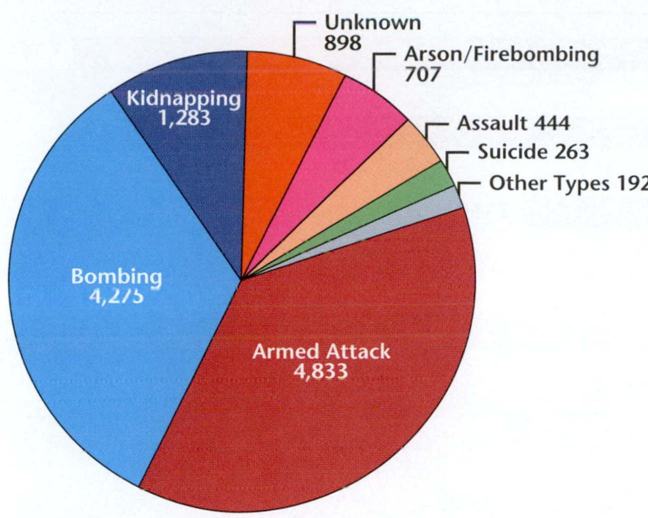

FIGURE 14–7 **Worldwide Terrorism Attacks by Method, 2010.**
Source: National Counterterrorism Center, *2010 Report on Terrorism* (Washington, DC: NCC, April 2011), p. 13, http://www.nctc.gov/witsbanner/docs/2010_report_on_terrorism.pdf.

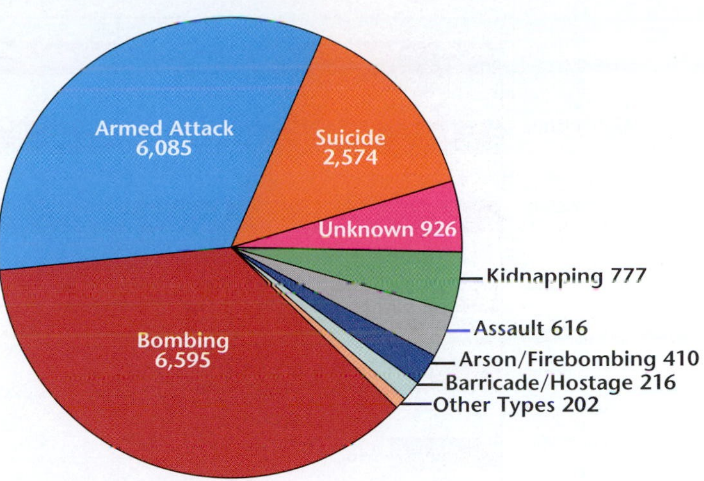

FIGURE 14–8 **Worldwide Deaths from Terrorist Attacks by Method of Attack, 2010.**
Source: National Counterterrorism Center, *2010 Report on Terrorism* (Washington, DC: NCC, April 2011), p. 14, http://www.nctc.gov/witsbanner/docs/2010_report_on_terrorism.pdf.

- The number of deaths in Africa fell by more than 30%, from 3,239 in 2009 to 2,131 in 2010, although attacks rose slightly, from 853 in 2009 to 878 in 2010.
- The number of Lord's Resistance Army attacks in the Democratic Republic of Congo declined sharply, but in June, Algeria saw its first suicide vehicle-borne improvised explosive device (VBIED) since September 2008.
- The number of attacks and deaths in Europe and Eurasia declined slightly in 2010, with the vast majority again occurring in Russia. Attacks fell from 737 in 2009 to 706 in 2010, and deaths fell from 367 in 2009 to 355 in 2010.
- The fewest incidents in 2010 were reported in the Western Hemisphere, where both attacks and deaths declined by roughly 25%. In the Western Hemisphere, attacks fell from 444 in 2009 to 340 in 2010 and deaths fell from 377 in 2009 to 279 in 2010.

Most attacks in 2010 were perpetrated by terrorist organizations using conventional methods of terrorism, such as armed attacks, bombings, and kidnappings. (See Figures 14–7 and 14–8.) Terrorists continued the practice of coordinated attacks that included secondary attacks on first responders at attack sites, and they continued to reconfigure weapons and other materials to create improvised explosive devices.

As has been the case since 2005, substantial numbers of victims of terrorist attacks in 2010 were Muslim. In fact, well over 50% of victims worldwide were Muslims, and most of those were victims of attacks in Iraq, Pakistan, and Afghanistan. Total deaths by country are shown in Figure 14–9.

The War on Terrorism

The most infamous attack of international terrorism in the United States took place on September 11, 2001, when members of Osama Bin Laden's al-Qaeda Islamic terrorist organization attacked New York City's World Trade Center and the Pentagon. The attacks left more than 3,000 people dead[32] and resulted in billions of dollars' worth of property damage. The United States declared a worldwide war on international terrorism.

Describe the legislative policies that were created after the 9/11 attacks to prevent future incidents of terrorism.

During the first years of President George W. Bush's presidency, terrorist attacks and corporate scandals demanded the attention of federal legislators and the Oval Office. Three important legislative initiatives resulted: the USA PATRIOT Act,[33] the Sarbanes-Oxley Act, and the Homeland Security Act. In establishing the new DHS, the act restructured the executive branch of the federal government. A few years later, in 2003, the National Security Council released the *National Strategy for Combating Terrorism*, which has since been revised. The revised strategy, published in 2006, sets the following goals:[34]

- Advance effective democracies as the long-term antidote to the ideology of terrorism
- Prevent attacks by terrorist networks
- Deny weapons of mass destruction to rogue states and terrorist allies who seek to use them
- Deny terrorists the support and sanctuary of rogue states
- Deny terrorists control of any nation they would use as a base and launching pad for terror
- Lay the foundations and build the institutions and structures we need to carry the fight forward against terror and help ensure our ultimate success

The terrorist attacks of September 11, 2001, left more than 3,000 people dead and resulted in billions of dollars' worth of property damage.

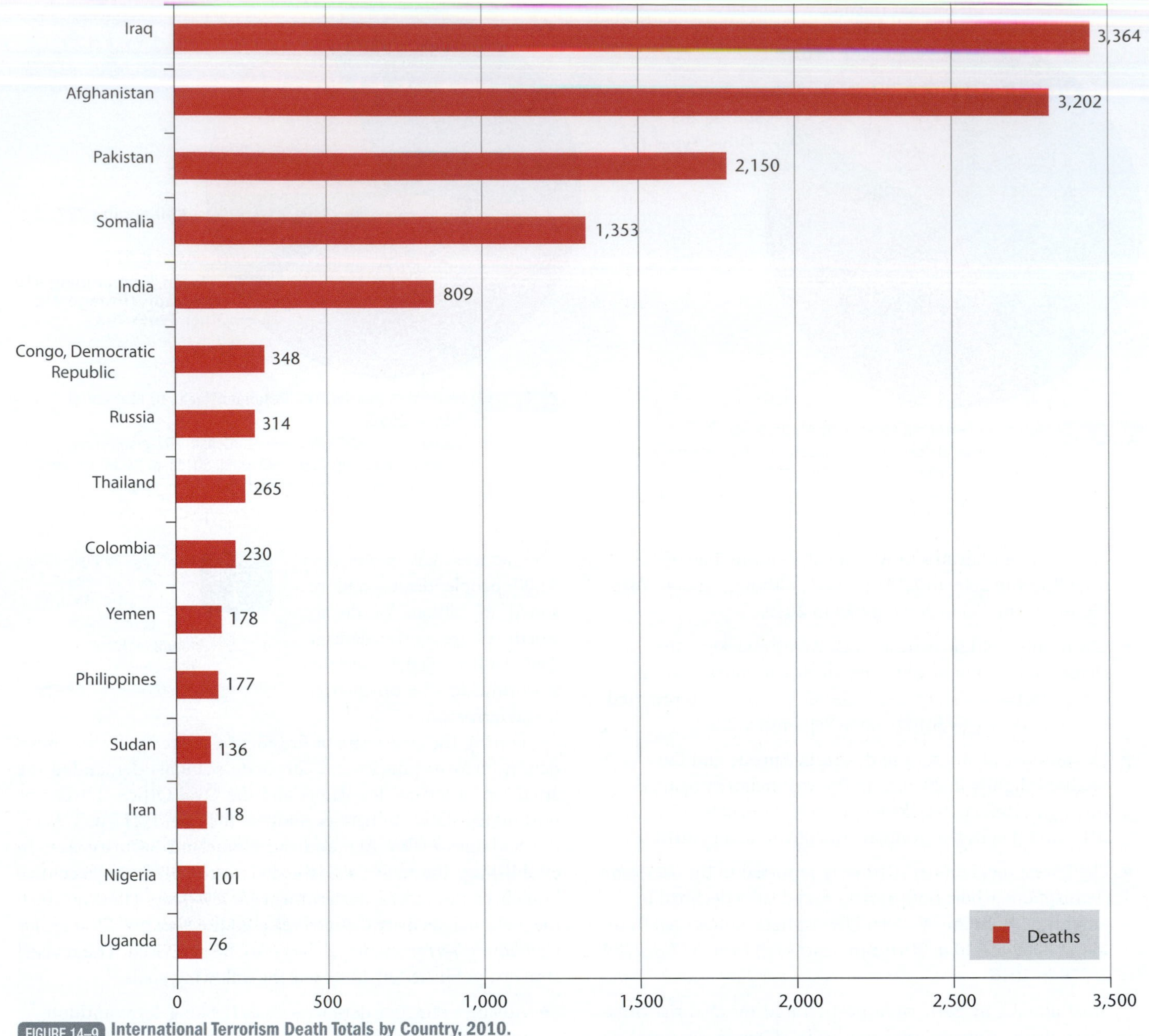

FIGURE 14–9 **International Terrorism Death Totals by Country, 2010.**
Source: National Counterterrorism Center, *2010 Report on Terrorism* (Washington, DC: NCC, April 2011), p. 17, http://www.nctc.gov/witsbanner/docs/2010_report_on_terrorism.pdf.

The USA PATRIOT Act

The **USA PATRIOT Act**, which stands for Uniting and Strengthening America by Providing Appropriate Tools Required to Intercept and Obstruct Terrorism, was designed primarily to fight terrorism, but it contains provisions that apply to other forms of criminal activity as well. The act permits longer jail terms for certain suspects arrested without a warrant, broadens searches conducted without notice, and enhances the power of prosecutors. The law also increases the ability of federal authorities to tap phones (including wireless devices), share intelligence information, track Internet usage, crack down on money laundering, and protect the country's borders.

The USA PATRIOT Act led some to question whether the government threatened powers at the expense of individual rights and civil liberties. Prior to passage, the legislation had been questioned by the American Civil Liberties Union (ACLU), which feared the act would substantially reduce the constitutional rights of individuals facing justice system processing. After the bill became law, the ACLU pledged to work with the president and law enforcement agencies across the country "to ensure that civil liberties in America are not eroded."[35]

The Department of Homeland Security (DHS)

The Homeland Security Act of 2002, enacted to protect America against terrorism, established the federal **Department of Homeland Security (DHS)**, which is also charged with protecting

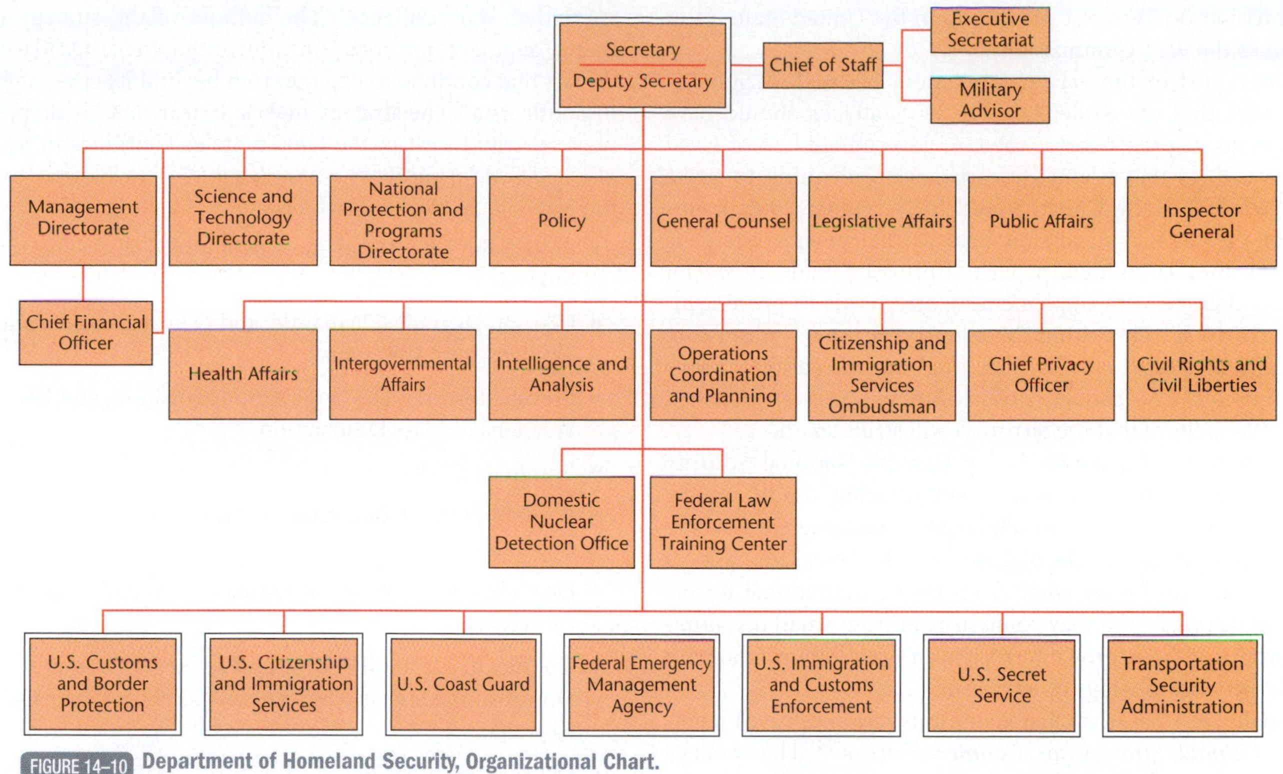

FIGURE 14–10 **Department of Homeland Security, Organizational Chart.**
Source: From *Criminology Today: An Integrative Introduction,* 7e by Frank A. Schmalleger. Copyright © 2014 by Pearson Education. Used by permission of Pearson Education.

the nation's critical **infrastructure** against a terrorist attack.[36] The director is a member of the president's cabinet.

Experts have said that the creation of DHS is the most significant transformation of the U.S. government since 1947, when President Harry S. Truman merged the various branches of the armed forces into the Department of Defense in an effort to better coordinate the nation's defense against military threats.[37] DHS coordinates the activities of 22 disparate domestic agencies, the largest of which are (1) U.S. Customs and Border Protection (CBP), (2) U.S. Citizenship and Immigration Services (CIS), (3) the U.S. Coast Guard (USCG), (4) the Federal Emergency Management Agency (FEMA), (5) U.S. Immigration and Customs Enforcement (ICE), (6) the U.S. Secret Service (USSS), and (7) the Transportation Security Administration (TSA).

The Bureau of Immigration and Customs Enforcement (ICE), also known as U.S. Immigration and Customs Enforcement, is the largest investigative arm of the Department of Homeland Security. ICE is responsible for identifying and eliminating vulnerabilities in the nation's border, economic, transportation, and infrastructure security. The Bureau of Customs and Border Protection (CBP) is the unified border control agency of the United States, and has as its mission the protection of our country's borders and the American people. The Bureau of Citizenship and Immigration Services (CIS), also known as U.S. Citizenship and Immigration Services, or USCIS, dedicates its energies to providing efficient immigration services and easing the transition to American citizenship. Figure 14–10 shows the organizational chart for the DHS. You can reach DHS on the Web via **Web Extra 14–3.**

Think About It…

The USA PATRIOT Act was passed in response to the attacks of September 11, 2001, on the World Trade Center and other sites. Not everyone is happy with the new police powers that some people say the act created. Others argue that the only way to secure freedom is to curtail it during times of national crisis. Is this true? Why or why not?

Beth Dixson/Alamy

Terrorism Commissions and Reports

Numerous important antiterrorism reports and studies have been released during the last ten or more years by various groups, including the Advisory Panel to Assess Domestic Response Capabilities for Terrorism Involving Weapons of Mass Destruction (also known as the Gilmore Commission), the National Commission on Terrorism, the U.S. Commission on National Security in the Twenty-First Century, the New York–based Council on Foreign Relations (CFR), and the National

Commission on Terrorist Attacks upon the United States (also known as the 9/11 Commission).

The report of the 9/11 Commission, released on July 22, 2004, said that the September 11, 2001, attacks should have come as no surprise because the U.S. government had received clear warnings that Islamic terrorists were planning to strike at targets within the United States. In December 2005, members of the 9/11 Commission held a final news conference in which they lambasted the lack of progress made by federal officials charged with implementing safeguards to prevent future terrorist attacks within the country. Former Commission Chair Thomas Kean called it "shocking" that the nation remains so vulnerable. "We shouldn't need another wake-up call," said Kean. "We believe that the terrorists will strike again."

In 2010, the Bipartisan Policy Center's National Security Preparedness Group released a wide-ranging report on the evolving nature of terrorism. The report, *Assessing the Terrorist Threat*, made clear that the biggest threat to American national security may no longer come from large international terrorist organizations—but may come instead from small *decentralized* groups of homegrown terrorists, or even loners, who have bought into the ideology of terrorism.

Finally, in 2011, the Obama administration released its official *National Strategy for Counterterrorism*.[38] The strategy maintained a focus on deterring Islamic-inspired terrorism and promised to pressure "al-Qa'ida's core while emphasizing the need to build foreign partnerships and capacity . . . to strengthen our resilience." The authors of the strategy noted that it "augments our focus on confronting the al-Qa'ida-linked threats that continue to emerge from beyond its core safehaven in South Asia." The strategy makes it clear that "[t]he preeminent security threat to the United States continues to be from *al-Qa'ida and its affiliate and adherents*." The avowed goals of the *National Strategy* are as follows:

- Protect the American People, Homeland, and American Interests.
- Disrupt, Degrade, Dismantle, and Defeat al-Qa'ida and Its Affiliates and Adherents.
- Prevent Terrorist Development, Acquisition, and Use of Weapons of Mass Destruction.
- Eliminate Safehavens.
- Build Enduring Counterterrorism Partnerships and Capabilities.
- Degrade Links between al-Qa'ida and its Affiliates and Adherents.
- Counter al-Qa'ida Ideology and Its Resonance and Diminish the Specific Drivers of Violence that al-Qa'ida Exploits.
- Deprive Terrorists of their Enabling Means.

The *National Strategy for Counterterrorism* is available in its entirety at **Web Extra 14–4**. Visit the NCTC at **Web Extra 14–5**.

THE CASE

The Tsarnaev Brothers

In early 2014, attorneys with the U.S. Department of Justice announced that they would ask a federal trial jury to recommend the death penalty for surviving Boston Marathon bombing suspect Dzhokhar Tsarnaev.[i] A year earlier, Tsarnaev, 19, had been shot by police and arrested, while his brother, Tamerlan, 26, was killed during a massive manhunt launched by authorities who used public video recordings of the crime scene that showed the brothers placing the explosive devices. The blasts, which came from home-made pressure-cooker bombs, killed three people near the marathon's finish line and injured more than 260 others—many of them seriously. During the Tsarnaevs' flight to avoid capture, they hijacked a Mercedes, killed an M.I.T. police officer, threw bombs at pursuing police cars, and engaged in a shootout with Boston law enforcement officers. After Tamerlan was killed, the manhunt ended when Dzhokhar was found hiding in a dry-docked boat in the backyard of a Watertown, Massachusetts, home.[ii]

Shortly after the arrest of Dzhokhar, relatives of the brothers were located by media representatives and interviewed. "You put a shame on our entire family . . . and you put a shame on the entire Chechen ethnicity," said Ruslan Tsarni, the brothers' uncle.[iii]

Investigators soon learned that the Tsarnaevs had emigrated in 2002 from the former Russian Republic of Chechnya, apparently fleeing from the brutal war that had engulfed the country after the fall of the Soviet Union. The family of six had come to America in 2002, settling in Cambridge, Massachusetts. With few financial resources at their disposal, they rented a crowded third-floor apartment in an aging home in an old neighborhood. The mother, Zubeidat, and father, Anzor, claimed to have been well educated in Chechnya and to have held prestigious jobs before emigrating. A *Boston Globe* exposé, however, later disclosed that both parents had few professional skills.

Although the Tsarnaevs had hoped to participate in the "American dream," they found themselves living in near poverty when their desire for steady work, college educations for their sons, and a successful career in boxing for Tamerlan didn't materialize. One of the Tsarnaev daughters became pregnant, marrying only a short time before her baby was born, thus sabotaging her parents' plans for an arranged marriage. Dzhokhar's college career fell apart after he became a popular marijuana dealer on the campus of the University of Massachusetts at Dartmouth. He apparently made a good deal of money selling drugs, causing him to lose academic focus. Friends said that he often carried a handgun to protect his "stash" of drugs and the large sums of money that he carried on his person.

FBI Photo/Alamy

Dzhokhar Tsarnaev, the surviving Boston Marathon bomber. Was Dzhokhar merely following his brother in an attempt to terrorize the American public?

Cambridge Police/Splash News/Newscom

Tamerlan Tsarnaev, killed in a shootout with Boston police officers following the bombing of the Boston Marathon. What led him to attack the marathon?

By the time of the bombings, the two Tsarnaevs daughters, both of whom had divorced after brief marriages, returned home with their infant children, crowding the family's 800-square-foot residence even further. Under the familial strain, Zubeidat and Anzor divorced, and Anzor moved to Dagestan in the Northern Caucasuses. Before his father left, however, Tamerlan told friends that he was hearing voices inside of his head directing him to do things. One doctor suggested that he was suffering from schizophrenia, and that constant marijuana smoking, combined with head injuries received from years of boxing, had caused him to become delusional.

Tamerlan's mother, Zubeidat, could not accept the idea that her son might be mentally ill, and attempted to immerse him in religion, hoping that it would relieve the mental strain he was suffering. As economic problems mounted, the family began to

(*continued*)

THE CASE

The Tsarnaev Brothers (*Continued*)

disintegrate and Tamerlan turned to radical Islam with mounting fervor. Friends later said that Tamerlan, unable to find steady work, and with his boxing career in tatters, spent much of his time on the Internet, reading radical Islamist literature. He soon began attending a local mosque, but was thrown out after interrupting services by shouting his disagreement with the imam's sermons.

Shortly before the bombings, Tamerlan visited Dagestan, where his father lived. Once there, he fell in with members of a radical Muslim group known as the Union of the Just. The group strongly condemned U.S. intervention in Muslim countries. Reports say that Tamerlan spent much of his time in Dagestan studying the Koran and praying with other members of the Union. The Russian Federal Security Service (FSB) later told American intelligence officers that Tamerlan met with members of the Muslim insurgency fighting for independence from the Russian Republic. Although FSB reports were sent to U.S. authorities in 2011 and 2012, FBI officers who investigated them didn't find them alarming enough to interrogate Tamerlan after he returned to the United States. Friends who knew him said that Tamerlan had come home a changed man, and railed against American intervention in the Middle East. Shortly after his return, he opened a YouTube account using the name of muazseyfullah, which can be translated as "The Sword of God."

As Tamerlan grew more and more obsessed with radical Islam, the family's disintegration continued. The oldest Tsarnaev sister, Bella, was arrested in New Jersey and charged with marijuana distribution; and Zubeidat was attempting to evade arrest on an outstanding warrant for a shoplifting charge. Dzhokhar, now failing out of college, and with more than $20,000 of unpaid debts, came back to a troubled household. Making matters worse, the building's landlord forced the Tsarnaevs to leave their Cambridge residence after raising the rent to a level they could not afford. As one source put it, "It was a time of great family upheaval."

After the bombings, it was discovered that the Tsarnaev brothers had read an online al-Qaeda English publication entitled "Make a Bomb in the Kitchen of Your Mom." The article explained how to make pressure-cooker bombs, and how to fill them with shrapnel in order to make them more destructive.

A *Boston Globe* investigative reporter who studied the Tsarnaev family history concluded that "the motivation for the Tsarnaev brothers' violent acts is more likely rooted in the turbulent collapse of their family and their escalating personal and collective failures than, as federal investigators have suggested, on the other side of the globe."[iv]

Notes

[i] Katharine Q. Seelye, "U.S. Weighs Pursuit of Death Penalty for Suspect in Boston Bombings," *The New York Times*, January 24, 2014, http://www.nytimes.com/2014/01/24/us/us-weighs-pursuit-of-death-penalty-in-boston-bombing.html?_r=0 (accessed June 5, 2014).

[ii] Chelsea J. Carter, "Official: Boston Bombing Suspect 'Sedated,'" CNN, April 20, 2013, http://www.cnn.com/2013/04/20/us/boston-attack/index.html (accessed July 5, 2014).

[iii] Alan Cullison, "A Family Terror: The Tsarnaevs and the Boston Bombing," *The Wall Street Journal*, December 13, 2013, http://online.wsj.com/news/articles/SB10001424052702304477704579254482254699674 (accessed May 30, 2014).

[iv] Sally Jacobs, David Filipov, and Patricia Wen, "The Fall of the House of Tsarnaev," *The Boston Globe*, December 2013, http://www.bostonglobe.com/Page/Boston/2011-2020/WebGraphics/Metro/BostonGlobe.com/2013/12/15tsarnaev/tsarnaev.html (accessed January 26, 2014).

The case of the Tsarnaev brothers raises a number of interesting questions. Among them are the following:

1. **Why did the Tsarnaev brothers attack spectators and participants at the 2013 Boston Marathon? What were they hoping to accomplish with those attacks?**
2. **What might policymakers and law enforcement officials have done to prevent the attacks?**

CHAPTER 14 Globalization and Terrorism—*Our Small World*

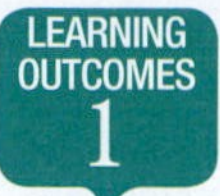

Define *comparative criminology* and explain what it can tell us about crime worldwide.

Comparative criminology is the study of crime on a cross-national level. Many of today's criminologists strive to develop theories that can be successfully applied across more than one culture or nation-state. Globalization will enhance the field of criminology through the sharing of ideas about crime causation and prevention and the interchange of effective crime-control practices between regions and countries.

1. What is ethnocentrism? What is comparative criminology? How are the two related?
2. What are the advantages of a comparative perspective in criminology? Are there any disadvantages? If so, what are they?

comparative criminology The cross-national study of crime.

comparative criminologist A criminologist involved in the cross-national study of crime.

ethnocentrism The phenomenon of "culture-centeredness" by which one uses one's own culture as a benchmark against which to judge all other patterns of behavior.

LEARNING OUTCOMES 2

Explain globalization and show how it is making it more difficult to combat crime around the world.

Globalization refers to the increasing interconnectedness of people, ideas, and things on a worldwide scale. Globalization is making it impossible to ignore criminal activity in other parts of the world, especially where that crime is perpetrated by transnational criminal and terrorist organizations.

1. What is globalization?
2. How does globalization impact criminal activity in today's world?
3. What are the differences between human smuggling and human trafficking?

globalization A process of social homogenization by which the experiences of everyday life, marked by the diffusion of commodities and ideas, fosters a standardization of cultural expressions around the world.

human smuggling Illegal immigration in which an agent is involved for payment to help a person cross a border clandestinely.

trafficking in persons (TIP) The exploitation of unwilling or unwitting people through force, coercion, threat, or deception.

LEARNING OUTCOMES 3

Define *terrorism*, identify its major characteristics, and describe the different kinds of terrorist organizations.

Terrorism is the use of criminal acts of violence as a tactic for attaining political goals. It is characteristically premeditated or planned, is politically motivated, targets civilians, and is carried out by subnational groups. This chapter distinguished between domestic and international terrorism and identified four different types of terrorist organizations: (1) nationalist terrorists, (2) religious terrorists, (3) state-sponsored terrorists, (4) left-wing terrorists, (5) right-wing terrorists, and (6) anarchist terrorists.

1. How is terrorism defined? Why is terrorism a criminal act?
2. What are the two main types of terrorism discussed in this chapter? What are the differences between them?
3. What are the four different types of terrorist organizations identified in this chapter?

terrorism "Premeditated, politically motivated violence perpetrated against noncombatant targets by subnational groups or clandestine agents, usually intended to influence an audience."

domestic terrorism The unlawful use of force or violence by a group or an individual who is based and operates entirely within the United States and its territories without foreign direction and whose acts are directed at elements of the U.S. government or population.

international terrorism The unlawful use of force or violence by a group or an individual who has a connection to a foreign power or whose activities transcend national boundaries against people or property to intimidate or coerce a government, the civilian population, or any segment thereof in furtherance of political or social objectives.

LEARNING OUTCOMES 4

Describe the legislative policies that were created after the 9/11 attacks to prevent future incidents of terrorism.

The United States declared a worldwide war on international terrorism following the attacks of September 1, 2001, that destroyed the World Trade Center in New York City and resulted in other loss of life at the Pentagon and elsewhere. Congress passed and the president signed the USA PATRIOT Act of 2001 and the Homeland Security Act of 2002. The latter created the Department of Homeland Security.

1. What led to passage of the USA PATRIOT Act of 2001? What did the law do?
2. What was the purpose of the Homeland Security Act of 2002? What new federal agency did it create?

USA PATRIOT Act A post-9/11 federal law designed to fight terrorism. The name of the statute is an acronym for Uniting and Strengthening America by Providing Appropriate Tools Required to Intercept and Obstruct Terrorism.

Department of Homeland Security (DHS) A federal agency established by the Homeland Security Act of 2002 that is responsible for protecting America against acts of terrorism.

infrastructure The basic facilities, services, and installations needed for the functioning of a community or society, such as transportation and communications systems, water and power lines, and public institutions, including schools, post offices, and prisons.

Glossary

acquaintance rape Rape characterized by a prior social, though not necessarily intimate or familial, relationship between the victim and the perpetrator.

adolescence-limited offenders Juvenile offenders who abandon delinquency upon reaching maturity.

aggravated assault The unlawful attack by one person upon another wherein the offender uses a weapon or displays it in a threatening manner, or the victim suffers obvious or severe bodily injury.

allele Variation of a gene.

alloplastic adaptation A form of adjustment that results from change in the environment surrounding an individual.

altruism Selfless, helping behavior.

androcentric A single-sex perspective, as in the case of criminologists who study only the criminality of males.

anomie A social condition in which norms are uncertain or lacking.

antisocial personality An individual who is unsocialized and whose behavior pattern brings him or her into repeated conflict with society.

antisocial personality disorder (ASPD) A psychological condition exhibited by individuals who are basically unsocialized and whose behavior pattern brings them repeatedly into conflict with society.

arson Any willful or malicious burning or attempt to burn (with or without intent to defraud) a dwelling, house, public building, motor vehicle, aircraft, or personal property of another.

asset forfeiture The authorized seizure of money, negotiable instruments, securities, or other things of value. In federal antidrug laws, "the authorization of judicial representatives to seize all monies, negotiable instruments, securities, or other things of value furnished or intended to be furnished by any person in exchange for a controlled substance, and all proceeds traceable to such an exchange."

atavism A term used by Cesare Lombroso to suggest that criminals are physiological throwbacks to early stages of human evolution.

attachment theory A social-psychological perspective on delinquent and criminal behavior holding that the successful development of secure attachment between a child and his or her primary caregiver provides the basic foundation for all future psychological development.

audit trail A sequential record of computer system activities that enables auditors to reconstruct, review, and examine the sequence of states and activities surrounding each event in one or more related transactions from inception to output of final results back to inception.

autoplastic adaptation A form of adjustment that results from changes with an individual.

Balanced and Restorative Justice Model (BARJ) A model of restorative justice in which the community, victim, and offender should all receive balanced attention.

behavior theory A psychological perspective positing that behavior that is rewarded will increase in frequency and behavior that is punished will decrease in frequency.

behavioral genetics The study of genetics and environmental contributions to individual variations in human behavior.

behaviorism A psychological perspective that stresses observable behavior and disregards unobservable events that occur in the mind.

biological theories Perspectives maintaining that the basic determinants of human behavior, including criminality, are constitutionally or physiologically based and often inherited.

biosocial criminology A theoretical perspective that sees the interaction between biology and the physical and social environments as key to understanding human behavior, including criminality.

born criminal An individual who is born with a genetic predilection toward criminality.

bourgeoisie The class of people who own the means of production.

broken windows theory A perspective on crime causation that holds that physical deterioration in an area leads to increased concerns for personal safety among area residents and to higher crime rates in that area.

Buck* v. *Bell A Supreme Court case that upheld the practice of sterilization as a way to rid society of those with criminal tendencies.

burglary The unlawful entry into a structure for the purpose of felony commission, generally a theft.

Cambridge Study in Delinquent Development A longitudinal (life-course) study of crime and delinquency tracking a cohort of 411 boys in London.

capable guardian One who effectively discourages crime.

capital punishment The legal imposition of a sentence of death upon a convicted offender.

Chicago Area Project A program focusing on urban ecology and originating at the University of Chicago during the 1930s, which attempted to reduce delinquency, crime, and social disorganization in transitional neighborhoods.

Chicago School of criminology An ecological approach to explaining crime that examined how social disorganization contributes to social pathology.

child pornography A visual representation of any kind that depicts a minor engaging in sexually explicit conduct and is obscene, and which lacks serious literary, artistic, political, or scientific value.

child sexual abuse (CSA) Encompasses a variety of criminal and civil offenses in which an adult engages in sexual activity with a minor, exploits a minor for purposes of sexual gratification, or exploits a minor sexually for purposes of profit.

chromosomes Bundles of genes.

Classical School A criminological perspective developed in the late 1700s and early 1800s. It had its roots in the Enlightenment and held that men and women are rational beings and that crime is the result of the exercise of free will and personal choices based on calculations of perceived costs and benefits.

clearance rate The proportion of reported or discovered crimes within a given offense category that are solved.

cognitive information-processing theory (CIP) A psychological perspective that involves the study of human perceptions, information processing, and decision making.

cohort analysis A social scientific technique that studies over time a population with common characteristics. Cohort analysis usually begins at birth and traces the development of cohort members until they reach a certain age.

comfort serial killers Serial killers who are motivated by financial or material gain.

common law definition of rape The carnal knowledge of a woman, not one's wife, by force or against her will.

Communications Decency Act (CDA) A federal statute signed into law in 1996, the CDA is Title 5 of the federal Telecommunications Act of 1996 (Public Law 104–104, 110 Stat. 56). The law sought to protect minors from harmful material on the Internet, and a portion of the CDA criminalized the knowing transmission of obscene or indecent messages to any recipient under 18 years of age.

comparative criminologist A criminologist involved in the cross-national study of crime.

comparative criminology Refers to the cross-national study of crime.

Comprehensive Strategy for Serious, Violent, and Chronic Juvenile Offenders program A program that works to strengthen families and core institutions in their efforts to reduce risk factors for juvenile offenders and develop their full potential.

computer abuse Any unlawful incident associated with computer technology in which a victim suffered or could have suffered loss, or in which a perpetrator by intention made or could have made gain.

computer virus A set of computer instructions that propagates copies or versions of itself into computer programs or data when it is executed.

computer-related crime Any illegal act for which knowledge of computer technology is involved in its perpetration, investigation, or prosecution.

conditioning A psychological principle that holds that the frequency of any behavior can be increased or decreased through reward, punishment, or association with other stimuli.

conduct norms Shared expectations of a social group relative to personal conduct.

conflict theory A perspective that applies the principles and concepts developed by Karl Marx to the study of crime, and holds that the causes of crime are rooted in social conditions that empower the wealthy and the politically well-organized but disenfranchise those who are less fortunate. Also sometimes referred to as *Marxist criminology*.

consensus perspective A viewpoint that holds that laws should be enacted to criminalize given forms of behavior when members of society agree that such laws are necessary.

constitutional theories Biological theories that explain criminality by reference to offenders' body types, inheritance, genetics, or external observable physical characteristics.

constitutive criminology The assertion that individuals shape their world while also being shaped by it.

containment The stabilizing force that, if effective, blocks pushes and pulls from leading an individual toward crime.

containment theory A form of control theory that suggests that a series of both internal and external factors contributes to law-abiding behavior.

control ratio The amount of control to which a person is subject versus the amount of control that person exerts over others.

controlled substances Chemical substances or drugs as defined under the 1970 federal Controlled Substances Act.

convict criminology A radical paradigm consisting of writings on criminology by convicted felons and ex-inmates who have acquired academic credentials or who are associated with credentialed others; also called *alternative criminology*.

corporate crime A violation of a criminal statute either by a corporate entity or by its executives, employees, or agents acting on behalf of and for the benefit of the corporation, partnership, or other form of business entity.

corporate fraud A term that refers to accounting schemes, self-dealing by corporate executives, and obstruction of justice as well as insider trading, kickbacks, and misuse of corporate property for personal gain.

Corporate Fraud Task Force A U.S. Department of Justice organization created under the administration of George W. Bush to investigate corporate fraud. It has since been superseded by the Obama administration's Financial Fraud Enforcement Task Force.

correctional psychology The branch of forensic psychology concerned with the diagnosis and classification of offenders, the treatment of correctional populations, and the rehabilitation of inmates and other law violators.

crime Human conduct that violates the criminal laws of a state, the federal government, or a local jurisdiction that has the power to make and enforce the laws.

criminal anthropology The scientific study of the relationship between human physical characteristics and criminality.

criminal career The longitudinal sequence of events committed by an individual offender.

criminal homicide The causing of the death of another person without legal justification or excuse.

criminal justice The scientific study of crime, criminal law, the criminal justice system, police, courts, and correctional systems.

criminal psychology The application of the science and profession of psychology to questions and issues relating to law and the legal system; also called *forensic psychology*.

criminalist A specialist in the collection and examination of the physical evidence of crime.

criminalize To make an act illegal.

criminaloids A term used by Cesare Lombroso to describe occasional criminals who were pulled into criminality by environmental influences.

criminologist A person trained in the field of criminology who studies crime, criminals, and criminal behavior.

criminology The scientific study of crime and criminal behavior, including their manifestations, causes, legal aspects, and control.

criminology of place A perspective that emphasizes the importance of geographic location and architectural features as they are associated with the prevalence of criminal victimization.

cultural transmission Through a process of social communication, the transmission of delinquency through successive generations of people living in the same area.

culture A collection of values, ideas, beliefs, and traits that characterize a human group—usually one defined by geographic boundaries, such as a nation.

culture conflict theory A sociological perspective on crime that suggests that the root cause of criminality can be found in a clash of values between variously socialized groups over what is acceptable or proper behavior.

Cyber Security Enhancement Act (CSEA) Part of the Homeland Security Act of 2002, this federal law directs the U.S. Sentencing Commission to take several specific factors into account in creating new sentencing guidelines for computer criminals.

cybercrime Any violation of a federal or state computer-crime statute.

cyberspace The computer-created matrix of virtual possibilities, including online services, wherein human beings interact with one another and with technology itself.

cyberstalking The use of electronic communication, such as email and the Internet, to harass individuals.

cycloid A term developed by Ernst Kretschmer to describe a particular relationship between body build and personality type. The cycloid personality, which was associated with a heavyset, soft type of body, was said to vacillate between normal and abnormality.

dangerous drug A term used by the Drug Enforcement Administration to refer to broad categories or classes of controlled substances other than cocaine, opiates, hallucinogens, inhalants, and cannabis products.

dangerousness The degree of criminal threat that an offender represents.

dark figure of crime The large number of unreported crimes that never make it into official crime statistics.

data encryption The process by which information is encoded, making it unreadable to all but its intended recipients.

DCS–1000 An FBI-developed network diagnostic tool that is capable of assisting in criminal investigations by monitoring and capturing large amounts of Internet traffic. Previously called "Carnivore."

deconstructionist theories A postmodern perspective that challenges existing criminological theories in order to debunk them and that works toward replacing traditional ideas with concepts seen as more appropriate to the postmodern era.

decriminalization The redefinition of certain previously criminal behaviors into regulated activities that become "ticketable" rather than "arrestable."

defensible space The range of mechanisms that combine to bring an environment under the control of its residents.

delinquency Violations of the criminal law and other misbehavior committed by young people.

Department of Homeland Security (DHS) A federal agency established by the Homeland Security Act of 2002 whose responsibility it is to protect America against acts of terrorism.

designer drugs New substances designed by slightly altering the chemical makeup of other illegal or tightly controlled drugs.

desistance The cessation of criminal activity or the termination of a period of involvement in offending behavior (that is, abandoning a criminal career).

determinate sentencing A model of criminal punishment in which an offender is given a fixed term of imprisonment that may be reduced by good behavior or other considerations.

deterrence A goal of criminal sentencing that seeks to inhibit criminal behavior through the fear of punishment.

deviant behavior Human activity that violates social norms.

differential association An explanation for crime and deviance that holds that people pursue criminal or deviant behavior to the extent that they identify themselves with real or imaginary people from whose perspective their criminal or deviant behavior seems acceptable.

Digital Theft Deterrence and Copyright Damages Improvement Act A 1999 federal law that attempted to combat software piracy and other forms of digital theft by amending Section 504(c) of the Copyright Act, thereby increasing the amount of damages that could potentially be awarded in cases of copyright infringement.

diplastic A mixed group of offenders described by constitutional theorist Ernst Kretschmer as highly emotional and often unable to control themselves. They were thought to commit mostly sexual offenses and other crimes of passion.

disengagement The process of devaluing aggression by those who may still engage in it.

distributive justice The rightful, equitable, and just distribution of rewards within a society.

dizygotic (DZ) twins A twin who develops from a separate ovum and who carries the genetic material shared by siblings.

DNA profiling The use of biological residue found at the scene of a crime for genetic comparisons in aiding the identification of criminal suspects.

domestic terrorism The unlawful use of force or violence by a group or an individual who is based and operates entirely within the United States and its territories without foreign direction and whose acts are directed at elements of the U.S. government or population.

drug-defined crime A violation of the laws prohibiting or regulating the possession, use, or distribution of illegal drugs.

drug offense Any violation of the laws prohibiting or regulating the possession, use, distribution, sale, or manufacture of illegal drugs.

drug-related crime A crime in which drugs contribute to the offense (excluding violations of drug laws).

drug trafficking The manufacturing, distributing, dispensing, importing, and exporting (or possession with intent to do the same) of a controlled or counterfeit substance.

ecological theory A type of sociological approach that emphasizes demographics (the characteristics of population groups) and geographics (the mapped location of such groups relative to one another) and that sees the social disorganization that characterizes delinquency areas as a major cause of criminality and victimization.

ectomorph A body type originally described as thin and fragile, with long, slender, poorly muscled extremities and delicate bones.

ego The reality-testing part of the personality. Also called the *reality principle*. More formally, the personality component that is conscious, most immediately controls behavior, and is most in touch with external reality.

electroencephalogram (EEG) The electrical measurement of brainwave activity.

Electronic Frontier Foundation (EFF) A nonprofit organization formed in July of 1990 to help ensure that the principles embodied in the Constitution and the Bill of Rights are protected as new communications technologies emerge.

endomorph A body type originally described as soft and round or overweight.

environmental crime A violation of the criminal law that, although typically committed by businesses or by business officials, may also be committed by other people or by organizational entities and that damages some protected or otherwise significant aspect of the natural environment.

environmental criminology An emerging perspective that emphasizes the importance of geographic location and architectural features as they are associated with the prevalence of criminal victimization.

epigenetics The study of the chemical reactions that occur within a genome, and that switch parts of the genome on or off at strategic times and locations.

ethnic succession The continuing process whereby one immigrant or ethnic group succeeds another by assuming its position in society.

ethnocentrism The phenomenon of "culture-centeredness" by which one uses one's own culture as a benchmark against which to judge all other patterns of behavior.

eugenic criminology A perspective holding that the root causes of criminality are passed from generation to generation in the form of "bad genes."

eugenics The study and implementation of hereditary improvement by genetic control (i.e., selective breeding to "improve" the human race).

evidence-based criminology A form of contemporary criminology that makes use of rigorous social scientific techniques, especially randomized controlled experiments, and the systematic review of research results; also called knowledge-based criminology.

evolutionary ecology A theory that blends elements of previous perspectives—building upon social ecology while emphasizing developmental pathways.

evolutionary perspective A theoretical approach that (1) seeks to explain behavior with reference to human evolutionary history, and (2) recognizes the influence that genes have over human traits.

expert systems Computer hardware and software that attempt to duplicate the decision-making processes used by skilled investigators in the analysis of evidence and in the recognition of patterns that such evidence might represent.

expressive homicide A criminal offense that results from acts of interpersonal hostility, such as jealousy, revenge, romantic triangles, and quarrels.

Farrington's Delinquent Development Theory A theory in which persistence describes continuity in crime and desistance refers to cessation of criminal activity or to a termination in a period of involvement in offending behavior.

felony murder A special class of criminal homicide in which an offender may be charged with first-degree murder when that person's criminal activity results in another person's death.

feminist criminology A corrective model of social analysis intended to redirect the thinking of mainstream criminologists to include gender awareness.

fence An individual or a group involved in the buying, selling, and distribution of stolen calls. Also called a *criminal receiver*.

Financial Fraud Enforcement Task Force An organization created under the Obama administration in 2009 to combat financial fraud, including false claims made under various federal economic stimulus legislation.

First and Fourth Amendments to the U.S. Constitution The amendments that guarantee each person freedom of speech and security in his or her "persons, houses, papers, and effects, against unreasonable searches and seizures."

first-degree murder Criminal homicide that is planned or involves premeditation.

Five Factor Model A psychological perspective that builds on the Big Five core traits of personality.

focal concerns The key values of any culture, especially the key values of a delinquent subculture.

forcible rape The carnal knowledge of a person forcibly and against their will.

forensic psychiatry A branch of psychiatry having to do with the study of crime and criminality.

forensic psychology The application of the science and profession of psychology to questions and issues relating to law and the legal system; also called *criminal psychology*.

forfeiture A legal procedure that authorizes judicial representatives to seize all moneys, negotiable instruments, securities, or other things of value furnished or intended to be furnished by any person in exchange for a controlled substance and all proceeds traceable to such an exchange.

frontal brain hypothesis A perspective that references physical changes in certain parts of the brain to explain criminality.

GBMI (Guilty But Mentally Ill) A GBMI verdict means that a person can be held responsible for a specific criminal act, even though a degree of mental incompetence may be present.

gender gap The observed differences between male and female rates of criminal offending in a given society, such as the United States.

gender ratio problem The need for an explanation of the fact that the number of crimes committed by men routinely far exceeds the number of crimes committed by women in almost all categories.

gene A molecular unit of DNA that carries coded instructions for making everything the body needs.

gene expression The process by which the coded information that is stored within a gene is used to create a biological product, usually a protein. Also, the manifestation of a trait in an individual carrying the gene or genes that determine that trait.

gene pool The total genetic information of all the individuals in a breeding population.

general deterrence A goal of criminal sentencing that seeks to prevent others from committing crimes similar to the one for which a particular offender is being sentenced.

general strain theory (GST) A perspective that suggests that lawbreaking behavior is a coping mechanism that enables those who engage in it to deal with the socioemotional problems generated by negative social relations.

general theory A theory that attempts to explain most forms of criminal conduct through a single, overarching approach.

general theory of crime A theory that attempts to explain all (or at least most) forms of criminal conduct through a single, overarching approach, and which holds that low self-control accounts for all crime at all times.

genetic determinism The belief that genes are the major determining factor in human behavior.

globalization A process of social homogenization by which the experiences of everyday life, marked by the diffusion of commodities and ideas, fosters a standardization of cultural expressions around the world.

hacker A person who uses computers for exploration and exploitation.

hate crime A criminal offense in which the motive is hatred, bias, or prejudice based on the actual or perceived race, color, religion, national origin, ethnicity, gender, or sexual orientation of another individual or group of individuals. Also called *bias crime*.

hedonistic calculus The belief, first proposed by Jeremy Bentham, that behavior holds value to any individual undertaking it according to the amount of pleasure or pain that it can be expected to produce for that person.

hedonistic serial killers Serial killers who murder because they find it enjoyable and derive psychological pleasure from killing.

heritability The proportion of variation in a trait within a group of people that can be attributed to variations in their genes rather than to their environment.

heroin signature program (HSP) A program of the Drug Enforcement Administration that identifies the geographic source of a heroin sample through the detection of specific chemical characteristics in the sample peculiar to the source area.

highway robberies Robberies that occur on the highway or street or in a public place (and that are often referred to as a "mugging").

home invasion robbery The act of illegally entering a private and occupied dwelling for the purpose of committing robbery.

hormone A chemical substance produced by the body that regulates and controls the activity of certain cells or organs.

human agency The idea that Individuals construct their own life course through the choices they make and the actions they take within the opportunities and constraints of history and social circumstances.

human development The relationship between the maturing individual and his or her changing environment, as well as the social processes that the relationship entails.

human ecology The interrelationship between human beings and the physical and cultural environments in which they live.

human smuggling Illegal immigration in which an agent is involved for payment to help a person cross a border clandestinely.

hypoglycemia A medical condition characterized by low blood sugar.

id The aspect of the personality from which drives, wishes, urges, and desires emanate. More formally, the division of the psyche associated with instinctual impulses and demands for immediate satisfaction of primitive needs.

Identity Theft and Assumption Deterrence Act The first federal law to make identity theft a crime. The 1998 statute makes it a crime whenever anyone "knowingly transfers or uses, without lawful authority, a means of identification of another person with the intent to commit, or to aid or abet, any unlawful activity that constitutes a violation of federal law, or that constitutes a felony under any applicable state or local law."

Identity Theft Penalty Enhancement Act A 2004 federal law that added two years to federal prison sentences for criminals convicted of using stolen credit card numbers and other personal data to commit crimes.

identity theft The unauthorized use of another individual's personal identity to fraudulently obtain money, goods, or services; to avoid the payment of debt; or to avoid criminal prosecution.

illegitimate opportunity structure Subcultural pathways to success of which the wider society disapproves.

incapacitation The use of imprisonment or other means to reduce the likelihood that an offender will be capable of committing future offenses.

infrastructure The basic facilities, services, and installations needed for the functioning of a community or society, such as transportation and communications systems, water and power lines, and public institutions, including schools, post offices, and prisons.

insanity A type of defense allowed in criminal courts.

institutional robberies Robberies of commercial establishments, such as convenience stores, gas stations, and banks.

instrumental crimes Criminal offenses that involve some degree of premeditation by the offender and are unlikely to be precipitated by the victim.

integrated theory An explanatory perspective that merges concepts drawn from different sources.

interactional theory A theoretical approach to exploring crime and delinquency that blends social control and social learning perspectives.

interdiction An international drug control policy designed to stop drugs from entering the country illegally.

international terrorism The unlawful use of force or violence by a group or an individual who has a connection to a foreign power, or whose activities transcend national boundaries, against people or property to intimidate or coerce a government, the civilian population, or any segment thereof in furtherance of political or social objectives.

Internet The world's largest computer network.

intimate partner assault A gender-neutral term used to characterize assaultive behavior that takes place between individuals involved in an intimate relationship.

intimate partner violence (IPV) A special area of study in criminology that includes sexual violence, physical abuse, and stalking committed by a current or former partner or spouse of the victim.

irresistible-impulse test A standard for judging legal insanity that holds that a defendant is not guilty of a criminal offense if the person, by virtue of his or her mental state or psychological condition, was not able to resist committing the crime.

Italian School of Criminology A perspective on criminology developed in the late 1800s holding that criminals can be identified by physical features and are throwbacks to earlier stages of human evolution. The Italian School was largely based on studies of criminal anthropology.

joyriding An opportunistic car theft, often committed by a teenager seeking fun or thrills.

Juke family A well-known "criminal family" studied by Richard Dugdale.

just deserts model The notion that criminal offenders deserve the punishment they receive at the hands of the law and that punishments should be appropriate to the type and severity of crime committed.

justice model A contemporary model of imprisonment in which the principle of just deserts forms the underlying social philosophy.

Juvenile Mentoring Program (JUMP) A program that places at-risk youth in a one-on-one relationship with favorable adult role models.

Kallikak family A well-known "criminal family" studied by Henry H. Goddard.

La Cosa Nostra Literally, "our thing." A criminal organization of Sicilian origin. Also called *the Mafia, the Outfit, the Mob, the syndicate,* or simply *the organization*.

larceny-theft "The unlawful taking, carrying, leading, or riding away of property from the possession, or constructive possession, of another."

learning theory A perspective that places primary emphasis upon the role of communication and socialization in the acquisition of learned patterns of criminal behavior and the values that support that behavior.

legalization Elimination of the laws and criminal penalties associated with certain behaviors—usually the production, sale, distribution, and possession of a controlled substance.

legitimate opportunities Opportunities generally available to individuals born into middle-class culture; participants in lower-class subcultures are often denied access to them.

liberal feminism A perspective that holds that the concerns of women can be incorporated within existing social institutions through conventional means and without the need to drastically restructure society.

life course Pathways through the life span involving a sequence of culturally defined, age-graded roles and social transitions enacted over time.

life-course criminology A developmental perspective that draws attention to the fact that criminal behavior tends to follow a distinct pattern across the life cycle.

life course–persistent offenders Offenders who, as a result of neuropsychological deficits combined with poverty and family dysfunction, display patterns of misbehavior throughout life.

lifestyle theory life course–persistent offenders Offenders who, as a result of neuropsychological deficits combined with poverty and family dysfunction, display patterns of misbehavior throughout life.

low self-esteem A reduced sense of self-worth, to include lowered self-assurance and lowered self-respect. Low self-esteem is linked to delinquency.

M'Naughten rule A standard for judging legal insanity that requires that offenders did not know what they were doing, or if they did, that they did not know it was wrong.

Mafia Another name for Sicilian organized crime, or *La Cosa Nostra*.

Marxist criminology A perspective on crime and crime causation based on the writings of Karl Marx.

Marxist feminism A perspective that sees capitalism as the root cause of women's oppression because it perpetuates economic inequality, dependence, and political powerlessness, ultimately leading to unhealthy social relations between men and women.

masculinity hypothesis The belief that criminal women exhibit masculine features and mannerisms.

mass murder The illegal killing of four or more victims at one location within one event.

mesomorph A body type described as athletic and muscular.

modeling A form of learning in which individuals imitate actions or performances by observing other people in order to add those actions to their own behavioral repertoire.

modeling theory A psychological perspective that contends that people learn how to behave by modeling themselves after others whom they have the opportunity to observe.

money laundering Refers to the process of converting illegally earned assets, originating as cash, to one or more alternative forms to conceal such incriminating factors as illegal origin and true ownership.

Monitoring the Future A national self-report survey on drug use that has been conducted since 1975.

monozygotic (MZ) twins Twins who develop from the same egg and have virtually the same genetic material.

Montreal Prevention Treatment Program A program designed to address early childhood risk factors for gang involvement by targeting boys in kindergarten who exhibit disruptive behavior.

moral development theory A perspective on crime causation holding that individuals become criminal when they have not successfully completed their intellectual development from child- to adulthood.

moral enterprise The efforts made by an interest group to have its sense of moral or ethical propriety enacted into law.

moral entrepreneurs Individuals or groups engaged in the process of moral enterprise.

motor vehicle theft "The theft or attempted theft of a motor vehicle," where the term *motor vehicle* refers to various means of transportation, including automobiles, buses, motorcycles, and snowmobiles.

murder The willful (nonneligent) and unlawful killing of one human being by another.

National Crime Victimization Survey (NCVS) An annual survey of selected American households conducted by the Bureau of Justice Statistics to determine the extent of criminal victimization—especially unreported victimization—in the United States.

National Incident-Based Reporting System (NIBRS) An enhanced statistical reporting system to collect data on each incident and arrest within 22 crime categories.

National Survey on Drug Use and Health (NSDUH) A national survey of illicit drug use among people 12 years of age and older that is conducted annually by the Substance Abuse and Mental Health Services Administration.

National Youth Survey (NYS) A longitudinal panel study of a national sample of 1,725 individuals that measured self-reports of delinquency and other types of behavior.

negative affective states Adverse emotions that derive from the experience of strain, such as anger, fear, depression, and disappointment.

negligent homicide The act of causing the death of another person by recklessness or gross negligence.

neoclassical criminology Focuses on the importance of character, the dynamics of character development, and the rational choices that people make as they are faced with opportunities for crime.

neurocriminology A perspective that examines the neurological links between the organism, social factors, and criminal behavior.

neurophysiology A field of research that examines the relationship between neurotransmitters and behavior.

neuroplasticity The ability of the brain to alter its structure and function in response to experience.

neurosis A functional disorder of the mind or of the emotions involving anxiety, phobia, or other abnormal behavior.

neurotransmitters Chemical substances that facilitate the flow of electrical impulses from one neuron to the next across nerve synapses.

No Electronic Theft Act (NETA) A 1997 federal law that criminalizes the willful infringement of copyrighted works, including by electronic means, even when the infringing party derives no direct financial benefit from the infringement.

nonprimary homicide A murder that involves a victim and an offender who have no prior relationship and that usually occurs during the course of another crime, such as robbery.

nothing-works doctrine The belief popularized by Robert Martinson in the 1970s that correctional treatment programs have little success in rehabilitating offenders.

occasional offender A criminal offender whose offending patterns are guided primarily by opportunity.

occupational crime Any act punishable by law that is committed through opportunity created in the course of an occupation that is legal.

Office of National Drug Control Policy (ONDCP) A national office charged by Congress with establishing policies, priorities, and objectives for the nation's drug-control program. ONDCP is responsible for annually developing and disseminating the *National Drug Control Strategy*.

operant behavior Behavior that affects the environment in such a way as to produce responses or further behavioral clues.

organized crime The unlawful activities of the members of a highly organized, disciplined association engaged in supplying illegal goods and services, including gambling, prostitution, loan-sharking, narcotics, and labor racketeering.

Panopticon A prison designed by Jeremy Bentham that was to be a circular building with cells along the circumference, each clearly visible from a central location staffed by guards.

paradigm An example, a model, or a theory.

paranoid schizophrenic A schizophrenic individual who suffers from delusions and hallucinations.

Part I offenses The crimes of murder, rape, robbery, aggravated assault, burglary, larceny, and motor vehicle theft, as defined under the FBI's Uniform Crime Reporting Program. Also called *major crimes*.

participatory justice A relatively informal type of criminal justice case processing that makes use of local community resources rather than requiring traditional forms of official intervention.

patriarchy The tradition of male dominance.

peace model An approach to crime control that focuses on effective ways for developing a shared consensus on critical issues that could seriously affect the quality of life.

peacemaking criminology Holds that crime control agencies and the citizens they serve should work together to alleviate social problems and human suffering and thus reduce crime.

persistence Continuity in crime, or continual involvement in offending.

persistent thief A person who continues in property crimes despite no better than an ordinary level of success.

personality The characteristic patterns of thoughts, feelings, and behaviors that make a person unique, and that tend to remain stable over time. Personality influences an individual's thoughts, behavior, and emotions.

pharmaceutical diversion The process by which legitimately manufactured controlled substances are diverted for illicit use.

phishing Pronounced "fishing." An Internet-based scam to steal valuable information such as credit card numbers, Social Security numbers, user IDs, and passwords.

phone phreak A person who uses switched, dialed-access telephone services for exploration and exploitation.

phrenology The study of the shape of the head to determine anatomical correlates of human behavior.

pluralist perspective A viewpoint that recognizes the importance of diversity in our society and says that behaviors are typically criminalized through a political process.

Ponzi scheme A form of high-yield investment fraud that uses money collected from new investors, rather than profits from the purported underlying business venture, to pay the high rates of return promised to earlier investors.

positivism A scientific approach to the study of crime and its causation. Early positivism was built upon evolutionary principles and saw criminals as throwbacks to earlier evolutionary epochs.

Positivist School An approach that stresses the application of scientific techniques to the study of crime and criminals.

postmodern criminology A brand of criminology that developed following World War II and builds on the tenets inherent in postmodern social thought.

power seekers Serial killers who operate from some position of authority over others.

power-control theory A perspective that holds that the distribution of crime and delinquency within society is to some degree founded upon the consequences that power relationships within the wider society hold for domestic settings and for the everyday relationships among men, women, and children within the context of family life.

prenatal substance exposure Fetal exposure to maternal drug and alcohol use. Prenatal substance exposure can significantly increase a child's risk for developmental and neurological disorders.

Preparing for the Drug-Free Years (PDFY) A program designed to increase effective parenting for children in grades 4 through 8 in an effort to reduce drug abuse and behavioral problems.

primary deviance Initial deviance often undertaken to deal with transient problems in living.

primary homicide A murder involving a family member, friend, or acquaintance.

professional criminal A criminal offender who makes a living from criminal pursuits, is recognized by other offenders as professional, and engages in offending that is planned and calculated.

Project on Human Development in Chicago Neighborhoods (PHDCN) A longitudinal analysis of how individuals, families, institutions, and communities evolve together.

proletariat The working class.

property crime According to the FBI's Uniform Crime Reporting Program, a crime category that includes burglary, larceny, motor vehicle theft, and arson.

prosocial bonds Bonds between the individual and the social group that strengthen the likelihood of conformity. Prosocial bonds are characterized by attachment to conventional social institutions, values, and beliefs.

prostitution The offering of one's self for hire for the purpose of engaging in sexual relations, or the act or practice of engaging in sexual activity for money or its equivalent.

psychiatric criminology A theory that is derived from the medical sciences (including neurology) and that, like other psychological theories, focuses on the individual as the unit of analysis. Psychiatric theories form the basis of psychiatric criminology.

psychoactive substance A substance that affects the mind, mental processes, or emotions.

psychoanalysis The theory of human psychology founded by Sigmund Freud on the concepts of the unconscious, resistance, repression, sexuality, and the Oedipus complex.

psychoanalytic theory A perspective developed by psychiatrist Sigmund Freud in the early 1900s that explains the structure of personality and behavior in terms of both conscious and unconscious components and the conflicts between them.

psychobiotics The study of the psychological and behavioral effects that bacteria (primarily those found in the human gut) can have on the mind, feelings, emotions, and behavior.

psychological profiling The attempt to categorize, understand, and predict the behavior of certain types of offenders based on behavioral clues they provide; also called criminal profiling and behavioral profiling.

psychopath An individual who has a personality disorder, especially one manifested in aggressively antisocial behavior, and who is lacking in empathy; also called *sociopath*.

psychopathy A personality disorder characterized by antisocial behavior and lack of affect.

psychosis A form of mental illness in which sufferers are said to be out of touch with reality.

psychotherapy A form of psychiatric treatment based on psychoanalytical principles and techniques.

public order offense An act that is willfully committed and that disturbs the public peace or tranquility.

punishment An undesirable behavioral consequence likely to decrease the frequency of occurrence of that behavior.

Racketeer Influenced and Corrupt Organizations (RICO) Act A statute that was part of the federal Organized Crime Control Act of 1970 and that is intended to combat criminal conspiracies.

radical-critical criminology A conflict perspective that sees crime as engendered by the unequal distribution of wealth, power, and other resources that its adherents believe is especially characteristic of capitalist societies.

radical feminism A perspective that holds that any significant change in the social status of women can be accomplished only through substantial changes in social institutions such as the family, law, and medicine.

rape The penetration, no matter how slight, of the vagina or anus with any body part or object, or oral penetration by a sex organ of another person, without the consent of the victim.

rape shield laws Statutes intended to protect rape victims by ensuring that defendants do not introduce irrelevant facts about the victim's sexual past into evidence.

rational choice theory A perspective holding that criminality is the result of conscious choice and that predicts that individuals choose to commit crime when the benefits outweigh the costs of disobeying the law.

reaction formation The process by which a person openly rejects that which he or she wants or aspires to but cannot obtain or achieve.

recidivism The repetition of criminal behavior.

relative deprivation A sense of social or economic inequality experienced by those who are unable, for whatever reason, to achieve legitimate success within the surrounding society.

Reno* v. *ACLU The 1997 U.S. Supreme Court case that found the bulk of the CDA to be unconstitutional, ruling that it contravenes First Amendment free-speech guarantees.

repression The psychological process through which a person rejects his or her own desires and impulses toward pleasurable instincts by excluding them from consciousness, thereby removing them from awareness and rendering them unconscious.

restorative justice A postmodern perspective that stresses remedies and restoration rather than prison, punishment, and victim neglect.

reward A desirable behavioral consequence likely to increase the frequency of occurrence of that behavior.

robbery The taking of or attempting to take anything of value under confrontational circumstances from the control, custody, or care of another person by force or threat of force or violence and/or by putting the victim in fear of immediate harm.

routine activities theory (RAT) A brand of rational choice theory suggesting that lifestyles contribute significantly to both the volume and the type of crime found in any society.

Sarbanes-Oxley Act A 2002 federal law that set stiff penalties for corporate wrongdoers (officially known as the Public Company Accounting Reform and Investor Protection Act).

schizoid A person characterized by schizoid personality disorder. Such disordered personalities appear to be aloof, withdrawn, unresponsive, humorless, dull, and solitary to an abnormal degree.

schizophrenia A serious mental illness that distorts the way a person thinks, feels, and behaves. A primary feature of schizophrenia is the inability to distinguish between real and imagined experiences and the inability to think logically.

scripts Generalized knowledge about specific types of situations that is stored in the mind.

second-degree murder Criminal homicide that is unplanned and that is often described as "a crime of passion."

secondary deviance Deviant behavior that results from official labeling and from association with others who have been so labeled.

securities and commodities fraud A term that refers to crimes such as stock market manipulation, high-yield investment fraud, advance fee fraud, hedge fund fraud, commodities fraud, foreign exchange fraud, and broker embezzlement.

seductions of crime The idea that crime is often pleasurable for those committing it and pleasure of one sort or another is the major motivation behind crime.

selective incapacitation An imprisonment policy based on the notion of career criminality; that is, on the long-term confinement of career criminals.

self-control A person's ability to alter his or her own states and responses.

self-report surveys A survey in which anonymous respondents, without fear of disclosure or arrest, are asked to report confidentially any violations of the criminal law they have committed.

semiotics The theory that everything we know, say, do, think, and feel is mediated through signs. Semiotic criminology identifies how language systems communicate uniquely encoded values.

separation assault Violence inflicted by partners on significant others who attempt to leave an intimate relationship.

serial murder Criminal homicide that involves "the killing of several victims in three or more separate events."

serotonin A neurotransmitter that is commonly found in the pineal gland, the digestive tract, the central nervous system, and in blood platelets.

sexual selection A form of natural selection that influences an individual's ability to attain or choose a mate.

sibling offense An offense or incident that culminates in homicide. The offense or incident may be a crime, such as robbery or an incident that meets a less stringent criminal definition, such as a lover's quarrel involving assault or battery.

situational action theory (SAT) A perspective that suggests that an individual's ability to exercise self-control is an outcome of the interaction between his or her personal traits and the situation in which he or she takes part.

situational choice theory A brand of rational choice theory that views criminal behavior "as a function of choices and decisions made within a context of situational constraints and opportunities."

situational crime prevention An approach that looks to develop greater understanding of crime and more effective crime prevention strategies through concern with the physical, organizational, and social environments that make crime possible.

social bond The link created through individuals and the society of which they are a part.

social capital The degree of positive relationships with others and with social institutions that individuals build up over the course of their lives.

social class Distinctions made between individuals on the basis of important defining social characteristics.

social cognition theory A perspective stating that people learn how to act by observing others.

social control theories A perspective that predicts that when social constraints on antisocial behavior are weakened or absent, delinquent behavior emerges.

social development perspective An integrated view of human development that examines multiple levels of maturity simultaneously, including the psychological, biological, familial, interpersonal, cultural, societal, and ecological levels.

social development theories An integrated view of human development that examines multiple levels of maturation simultaneously, including the psychological, biological, familial, interpersonal, cultural, societal, and ecological levels.

social disorganization A condition said to exist when a group is faced with social change, uneven development of culture, maladaptiveness, disharmony, conflict, and lack of consensus.

social disorganization theory A perspective on crime and deviance that highlights the role that the breakdown of social institutions, such as the family, the economy, education, and religion, play in crime causation.

social ecology (also called *ecological school of criminology*) An approach to criminological theorizing that attempts to link the structure and organization of a human community to interactions with its localized environment.

social life The ongoing and (typically) structured interaction that occurs between persons in a society, including socialization and social behavior in general.

social pathology A concept that compares society to a physical organism and that sees criminality as an illness or disease.

social policy A government initiative, person, or plan intended to address problems in society.

social process The interaction between and among social institutions, individuals, and groups.

social process theories Theories that suggest that criminal behavior is learned in interaction with others and that socialization and learning processes occur as the result of group membership and relationships.

social relativity The notion that social events are interpreted differently according to the cultural experiences and personal interests of the initiator, the observer, or recipient of that behavior.

social structure The stable pattern of social relationships that exists within a society.

social structure theories Theories that explain crime by reference to some aspect of the social fabric. These theories emphasize relationships among social institutions and describe the types of behavior that tend to characterize groups of people rather than individuals.

socialist feminism A perspective that examines social roles and the gender-based division of labor within the family, seeing both as a significant source of women's subordination within society.

sociobiology A theoretical perspective developed by Edward O. Wilson that includes "the systematic study of the biological basis of all social behavior." It is a branch of evolutionary biology and particularly of modern population biology.

sociological theories A group of perspectives that focus on the nature of the power relationships that exist between social groups and on the influences that various social phenomena bring to bear on the types of behaviors that tend to characterize groups of people.

sociopath An individual who has a personality disorder, especially one manifested in aggressively antisocial behavior, and who is lacking in empathy; also called *psychopath*.

software piracy The unauthorized and illegal copying of software.

somatotyping Classifying according to body types.

specific deterrence A goal of criminal sentencing that seeks to prevent a particular offender from engaging in repeat criminality.

spousal rape The rape of one spouse by the other. The term usually refers to the rape of a woman by her husband.

stalking A course of conduct directed at a specific person that involves repeated visual or physical proximity; nonconsensual communication; verbal, written, or implied threats; or a combination thereof that would cause a reasonable person fear.

statute A formal written enactment of a legislative body.

stimulus-response See *behavior theory*.

strain theory A sociological approach that posits a disjuncture between socially and subculturally sanctioned means and goals as the cause of criminal behavior.

subcultural theory A sociological perspective that emphasizes the contribution made by variously socialized cultural groups to the phenomenon of crime.

subculture A collection of values and preferences that is communicated to subcultural participants through a process called socialization.

sublimation The psychological process whereby one aspect of consciousness comes to be symbolically substituted for another.

superego The moral aspect of personality, much like the conscience. More formally, the division of the psyche that develops by the incorporation of the perceived moral standards of the community, is mainly unconscious, and includes the conscience.

supermale A male individual displaying the XYY chromosome structure.

tagging A term that explains what happens to offenders following arrest, conviction, and sentencing.

target hardening The reduction in criminal opportunity for a particular location, generally through the use of physical barriers, architectural design, and enhanced security measures.

techniques of neutralization Culturally available justifications that can provide criminal offenders with the means to disavow responsibility for their behavior.

terrorism Premeditated, politically motivated violence perpetrated against noncombatant targets by subnational groups or clandestine agents, usually intended to influence an audience.

testosterone The primary male sex hormone. It is produced in the testes, and its function is to control secondary sex characteristics and sexual drive.

theoretical criminology The type of criminology that is usually studied in colleges and universities, describes crime and its occurrence, and offers explanations for criminal behavior.

threat analysis A complete and thorough assessment of the kinds of perils facing an organization.

trafficking in persons (TIP) The exploitation of unwilling or unwitting people through force, coercion, threat, or deception.

trait A notable feature or quality of a biological entity. Traits may be classified as physical, behavioral, or psychological. Traits are passed on from generation to generation.

traits (psychological) Stable personality patterns that tend to endure throughout the life course and across social and cultural contexts.

translational criminology A form of contemporary criminology that seeks to translate research findings in the field into practical and workable policy initiatives.

transnational organized crime Unlawful activity undertaken and supported by organized criminal groups operating across national boundaries.

tribalism The attitudes and behavior that result from strong feelings of identification with one's own social group.

truth in sentencing A close correspondence between the sentence imposed upon those sent to prison and the time actually served prior to prison release.

turning points Crucial life experiences that can change behavior.

unicausal Of or having one cause. Theories posing one source for all that they attempt to explain.

Uniform Crime Reporting (UCR) Program An FBI statistical reporting program that provides an annual summation of the incidence and rate of reported crimes throughout the United States.

USA PATRIOT Act A post-9/11 federal law designed to fight terrorism. The name of the statute is an acronym that stands for Uniting and Strengthening America by Providing Appropriate Tools Required to Intercept and Obstruct Terrorism.

victim precipitation Contributions made by the victim to the criminal event, especially those that led to its initiation.

visionary serial killers Serial killers who hear voices and have visions that are the basis for a compulsion to murder.

white-collar crime Violations of the criminal law committed by persons of respectability and high social status in the course of their occupation.

workplace violence The crimes of murder, rape, robbery, and assault committed against persons who are at work or on duty.

References

Chapter 1, What Is Criminology?—*Understanding Crime and Criminals*

1 Karl Menninger, *The Crime of Punishment* (New York: Viking, 1968).

2 "'NCIS, S.H.I.E.L.D.' and 'Sleepy Hollow' all Earn Noms in the 2014 PCA's," The Examiner, http://www.examiner.com/article/ncis-s-h-i-e-l-d-and-sleepy-hollow-all-earn-noms-the-2014-pca-s (accessed May 12, 2014).

3 "NCIS Audience Ratings," NCIS Fan Site, http://www.ncisfanwiki.com/page/NCIS+Audience+Ratings (accessed May 26, 2014).

4 CTV Global Media, "CSI: Miami," http://www.ctv.ca/servlet/ArticleNews/show/CTVShows/1064338847511_59746366 (accessed March 10, 2007).

5 Sara Bibel, "'CSI: Crime Scene Investigation' Is the Most-Watched Show in the World," TV by the Numbers, June 14, 2012, http://tvbythenumbers.zap2it.com/2012/06/14/csi-crime-scene-investigation-is-the-most-watched-show-in-the-world-2/138212/ (accessed July 26, 2012).

6 From the standpoint of the law, the proper word is *conduct* rather than *behavior* because the term *conduct* implies intentional and willful activity, whereas *behavior* refers to any human activity—even that which occurs while a person is unconscious, as well as that which is unintended.

7 Edwin Sutherland, *Principles of Criminology*, 4th ed. (New York: Lippincott, 1947).

8 Hector Florin, "A Saggy-Pants Furor in Riviera Beach," *Time*, October 1, 2008, http://www.time.com/time/world/article/0,8599,1846205,00.html (accessed July 26, 2012).

9 Neal J. Riley, "S.F. Barely Passes Public-Nudity Ban," *San Francisco Chronicle*, November 21, 2012, http://www.chron.com/bayarea/article/S-F-barely-passes-public-nudity-ban-4055606.php#photo-3732744 (accessed February 1, 2013).

10 American Gaming Association, FAQ, http://www.americangaming.org/industry-resources/faq (accessed July 26, 2012).

11 Alberto Sisto, "Italian Scientists Convicted over Earthquake Warning," Reuters, October 22, 2012, http://articles.chicagotribune.com/2012-10-22/business/sns-rt-us-italy-earthquake-courtbre89l13v-20121022_1_magnitude-earthquake-enzo-boschi-scientists (accessed January 3, 2014).

12 See The Wineman at http://www.thewineman.com/strangelaw.htm (accessed March 11, 2007).

13 Ibid.

14 *The American Heritage Dictionary of the English Language*, 3rd ed. (Boston: Houghton Mifflin, 1996).

15 Ibid.

16 Piers Beirne, *Inventing Criminology* (Albany: State University of New York Press, 1993).

17 See also Paul Topinard, *Anthropology* (London: Chapman and Hall, 1894).

18 Edwin H. Sutherland, *Criminology* (Philadelphia: Lippincott, 1924), p. 11.

19 Edwin H. Sutherland and Donald R. Cressey, *Criminology*, 9th ed. (Philadelphia: Lippincott, 1974), p. 3.

20 There are, however, those who deny that criminology deserves the name "discipline." See, for example, Don C. Gibbons, *Talking about Crime and Criminals: Problems and Issues in Theory Development in Criminology* (Upper Saddle River, NJ: Prentice Hall, 1994), p. 3.

21 Charles F. Wellford, "Controlling Crime and Achieving Justice: The American Society of Criminology 1996 Presidential Address," *Criminology*, Vol. 35, No. 1 (1997), p. 1.

22 Gibbons, *Talking about Crime and Criminals*, p. 4.

23 Sutherland, *Principles of Criminology*.

24 Don M. Gottfredson, "Criminological Theories: The Truth as Told by Mark Twain," in William S. Laufer and Freda Adler, eds., *Advances in Criminological Theory*, Vol. 1 (New Brunswick, NJ: Transaction, 1989), p. 1.

25 Gregg Barak, *Integrating Criminologies* (Boston: Allyn & Bacon, 1998), p. 5.

26 Gibbons, *Talking about Crime and Criminals*.

27 For a good overview of this issue, see Wesley G. Skogan, ed., *Reactions to Crime and Violence: The Annals of the American Academy of Political and Social Science* (Thousand Oaks, CA: Sage, 1995).

28 For a good discussion of the social construction of crime, see Leslie T. Wilkins, "On Crime and Its Social Construction: Observations on the Social Construction of Crime," *Social Pathology*, Vol. 1, No. 1 (January 1995), pp. 1–11.

29 For a parallel approach, see Terance D. Miethe and Robert F. Meier, *Crime and Its Social Context: Toward an Integrated Theory of Offenders, Victims, and Situations* (Albany: State University of New York Press, 1995).

30 See, for example, Miethe and Meier, *Crime and Its Social Context*.

31 For a good discussion of the historical development of criminology, see Leon Radzinowicz, *In Search of Criminology* (Cambridge: Harvard University Press, 1962).

32 As quoted in W. Wayt Gibbs, "Trends in Behavioral Science: Seeking the Criminal Element," *Scientific American*, Vol. 272, No. 3 (March 1995), pp. 100–107.

33 Wellford, "Controlling Crime and Achieving Justice," p. 4. Not all studies support such a policy, however. See, for example, P. R. Marchant, "A Demonstration That the Claim That Brighter Lighting Reduces Crime Is Unfounded," *British Journal of Criminology*, Vol. 44, No. 3 (2004), p. 441.

34 NCJRS may be reached at 800-851-3420 or on the Web at http://www.ncjrs.gov.

35 Jennifer L. Truman, Lynn Langton, and Michael Planty, *Criminal Victimization, 2012* (Washington, DC: Bureau of Justice Statistics, 2013), from which much of the data in this section come.

36 For further information, see Ronet Bachman and Bruce Taylor, "The Measurement of Family Violence and Rape by the Redesigned National Crime Victimization Survey," *Justice Quarterly*, Vol. 11, No. 3 (September 1994); Bureau of Justice Statistics, "National Crime Victimization Survey Redesign," *BJS Fact Sheet*, October 19, 1994; and BJS, "Questions and Answers about the Redesign," October 30, 1994.

37 FBI, *Uniform Crime Reports*, 2012, http://www.fbi.gov/about-us/cjis/ucr/crime-in-the-u.s/2012/crime-in-the-u.s.-2012/violent-crime/murder (accessed March 12, 2014).

38 See FBI, "About the UCR Program," http://www.fbi.gov/ucr/05cius/about/about_ucr.html (accessed July 10, 2012).

39 Bureau of Justice Statistics, *Dictionary of Criminal Justice Data Terminology*, 2nd ed. (Washington, DC: U.S. Department of Justice, 1981), p. 39.

40 See Association of State UCR Programs, "NIBRS News," http://www.asucrp.org/news/index.html (accessed March 30, 2007).

41 The President's Commission on Law Enforcement and Administration of Justice, *The Challenge of Crime in a Free Society* (Washington, DC: U.S. Government Printing Office, 1967). The President's Commission relied on *Uniform Crime Reports* data, and the other crime statistics reported in this section come from the UCR Program for various years.

42 Frank E. Hagan, *Research Methods in Criminal Justice and Criminology,* 5th ed. (Boston: Allyn & Bacon, 2000).

43 John J. DiIulio, Jr., "The Question of Black Crime," *Public Interest* (Fall 1994), pp. 3–12.

44 The coining of the term *dark figure of crime* is sometimes attributed to Michael Gottfredson. See Michael Gottfredson, "Substantive Contributions of Victimization Surveys," in Michael Tonry and Norval Morris, eds., *Crime and Justice: An Annual Review of Research*, Vol. 7 (Chicago: University of Chicago Press, 1986).

45 Carl Bialik, "Statistics Shed Little Light on Rape Rates," *Wall Street Journal*, August 30, 2013, http://online.wsj.com/news/articles/SB30001424127887324324404579043623106927570 (accessed May 14, 2014).

46 Ibid.

47 Terence P. Thornberry and Marvin D. Krohn, "The Self-Report Method for Measuring Delinquency and Crime," *Criminal Justice 2000* (Washington, DC: National Institute of Justice, 2000), p. 34.

48 See, for example, Delbert S. Elliott, David Huizinga, and Suzanne S. Ageton, *Explaining Delinquency and Drug Use* (Newbury Park, CA: Sage, 1985).

49 National Institute on Drug Abuse, *Monitoring the Future: National Results on Adolescent Drug Use—Overview of Key Findings, 2006* (Rockville, MD: U.S. Department of Health and Human Services, 2007).

50 American Society of Criminology, "The ASC Announces a New Division: The Division of Experimental Criminology," https://www.asc41.com/DECannouncement.html (accessed April 7, 2010).

51 David Weisburd, "Editor's Introduction," *Journal of Experimental Criminology*, Vol. 1 (2005), p. 3.

52 National Institute of Justice, "What Is Translational Criminology?" *NIJ Journal*, No. 268 (November 3, 2011), http://www.nij.gov/nij/journals/268/criminology.htm (accessed October 23, 2014).

53 Editorial, "In Denial about On-Screen Violence," *New Scientist* (April 21, 2007), p. 5, http://www.newscientist.com/channel/opinion/mg19426003.600-editorial-in-denial-about-onscreen-violence.html (accessed August 1, 2007).

54 Ibid.

55 Congressional Public Health Summit, *Joint Statement on the Impact of Entertainment Violence on Children*, July 26, 2000.

56 Federal Trade Commission, *Marketing Violent Entertainment to Children* (Washington, DC: U.S. Government Printing Office, 2000).

57 Sue Pleming, "U.S. Report Says Hollywood Aims Violence at Kids," Reuters wire service, September 11, 2000.

58 Editorial, "In Denial about On-Screen Violence."

59 National Institute of Justice, "What Is Translational Criminology?"

Chapter 2, Classical and Neoclassical Criminology—*Choice and Consequences*

1 "About Listverse," http://listverse.com/about-listverse/ (accessed February 10, 2014).

2 "Top 10 Tips to Commit the Perfect Crime," http://listverse.com/2007/08/16/top-10-tips-to-commit-the-perfect-crime/ (accessed February 10, 2014).

3 Ibid.

4 The quotations attributed to Beccaria in this section are from Beccaria, *Essay on Crimes and Punishments*, second American edition; translated by Edward D. Ingraham (Philadelphia: Philip H. Nicklin, 1819).

5 The quotations attributed to Bentham in this section are from Bentham, *An Introduction to the Principles of Morals and Legislation* (Oxford: Clarendon Press, 1907). First edition published 1789.

6 R. Martinson, "What Works: Questions and Answers about Prison Reform," *Public Interest*, No. 35 (1974), pp. 22–54.

7 James Q. Wilson, *Thinking about Crime* (New York: Vintage, 1975).

8 See Conrad P. Rutkowski, "Fogel's 'Justice Model': Stop Trying to Reform. Punish, but Treat All Alike," *Illinois Issues*, February 1976.

9 *Ewing* v. *California*, 583 U.S. 11 (2003); *Lockyer* v. *Andrade*, 583 U.S. 63 (2003).

10 Under California law, a person who commits petty theft can be charged with a felony if he or she has prior felony convictions. The charge is known as "petty theft with prior convictions." Andrade's actual sentence was two 25-year prison terms to be served consecutively.

11 Felton M. Earls and Albert J. Reiss, *Breaking the Cycle: Predicting and Preventing Crime* (Washington, DC: National Institute of Justice, 1994), p. 49.

12 L. E. Cohen and Marcus Felson, "Social Change and Crime Rate Trends: A Routine Activity Approach," *American Sociological Review*, Vol. 44, No. 4 (August 1979), pp. 588–608.

13 Ibid., p. 595.

14 For a test of routine activities theory as an explanation for victimization in the workplace, see John D. Wooldredge, Francis T. Cullen, and Edward J. Latessa, "Victimization in the Workplace: A Test of Routine Activities Theory," *Justice Quarterly*, Vol. 9, No. 2 (June 1992), pp. 325–335.

15 Michael Hindelang, Michael Gottfredson, and James Garofalo, *Victims of Personal Crime: An Empirical Foundation for a Theory of Personal Victimization* (Cambridge, MA: Ballinger, 1978).

16 Marcus Felson, *Crime and Everyday Life: Insight and Implications for Society* (Thousand Oaks, CA: Pine Forge Press, 1994).

17 Gary LaFree and Christopher Birkbeck, "The Neglected Situation: A Cross-National Study of the Situational Characteristics of Crime," *Criminology*, Vol. 29, No. 1 (February 1991), p. 75.

18 Ronald V. Clarke and Derek B. Cornish, eds., *Crime Control in Britain: A Review of Police and Research* (Albany: State University of New York Press, 1985), p. 8.

19 Ronald V. Clarke, "Situational Crime Prevention—Everybody's Business," paper presented at the 1995 Australian Crime Prevention Council conference.

20 See Derek B. Cornish and Ronald V. Clarke, "Understanding Crime Displacement: An Application of Rational Choice Theory," *Criminology*, Vol. 25, No. 4 (November 1987), p. 933.

21 Clarke and Cornish, *Crime Control in Britain*, p. 48.

22 Werner Einstadter and Stuart Henry, *Criminological Theory: An Analysis of Its Underlying Assumptions* (Fort Worth, TX: Harcourt Brace, 1995), p. 70.

23 Center for Problem-Oriented Policing, "Twenty Five Techniques of Situational Prevention," http://www.popcenter.org/25techniques/ (accessed July 15, 2014).

24 Daniel J. Curran and Claire M. Renzetti, *Theories of Crime* (Boston: Allyn & Bacon, 1994), p. 18.

25 Jack Katz, *Seductions of Crime: Moral and Sensual Attractions in Doing Evil* (New York: Basic Books, 1988), p. 8.

26 Ibid., p. 8.

27 Ibid., p. 3.

28 Ibid., p. 76.

29 Ibid., p. 71.

30 Bill McCarthy, "Not Just 'for the Thrill of It': An Instrumentalist Elaboration of Katz's Explanation of Sneaky Thrill Property Crimes," *Criminology*, Vol. 33, No. 4 (1995), pp. 519–538.

31 The quotations attributed to Weisburd in this section are from David Weisburd, "Reorienting Crime Prevention Research and Policy: From the Causes of Criminality to the Context of Crime," *NIJ Research Report* (Washington, DC: National Institute of Justice, June 1997).

32 See P. Brantingham and P. Brantingham, "Situational Crime Prevention in Practice," *Canadian Journal of Criminology* (January 1990), pp. 17–40; and R. V. Clarke, "Situational Crime Prevention: Achievements and Challenges," in M. Tonry and D. Farrington, eds., *Building a Safer Society: Strategic Approaches to Crime Prevention, Crime and Justice: A Review of Research*, Vol. 19 (Chicago: University of Chicago Press, 1995).

33 Weisburd, "Reorienting Crime Prevention Research and Policy."

34 See, for example, J. E. Eck and D. Weisburd, eds., *Crime and Place: Crime Prevention Studies*, Vol. 4 (Monsey, NY: Willow Tree Press, 1995).

35 See L. Sherman, "Hot Spots of Crime and Criminal Careers of Places," in J. E. Eck and D. Weisburd, eds., *Crime and Place: Crime Prevention Studies*, Vol. 4 (Monsey, NY: Willow Tree Press, 1995); and L. Sherman, P. R. Gartin, and M. E. Buerger, "Hot Spots of Predatory Crime: Routine Activities and the Criminology of Place," *Criminology*, Vol. 27, No. 1 (1989), pp. 27–56.

36 Tracey L. Snell, *Capital Punishment, 2012* (Washington, DC: Bureau of Justice Statistics, 2014), p. 14.

37 See, for example, W. C. Bailey, "Deterrence and the Death Penalty for Murders in Utah: A Time Series Analysis," *Journal of Contemporary Law*, Vol. 5, No. 1 (1978), pp. 1–20; and William Bailey, "An Analysis of the Deterrent Effects of the Death Penalty for Murder in California," *Southern California Law Review*, Vol. 52, No. 3 (1979), pp. 743–764.

38 See, for example, B. E. Forst, "The Deterrent Effect of Capital Punishment: A Cross-State Analysis of the 1960s," *Minnesota Law Review*, Vol. 61 (1977), pp. 743–764.

39 Scott H. Decker and Carol W. Kohfeld, "Capital Punishment and Executions in the Lone Star State: A Deterrence Study," *Criminal Justice Research Bulletin* (Criminal Justice Center, Sam Houston State University), Vol. 3, No. 12 (1988).

40 Tomislav V. Kovandzic, Lynne M. Vieraitis, and Denise Paquette Boots, "Does the Death Penalty Save Lives? New Evidence from State Panel Data, 1977 to 2006," *Crime and Public Policy*, Vol. 8, No. 4 (2009), p. 803.

41 Committee on Law and Justice, *Deterrence and the Death Penalty* (Washington, DC: National Academy of Sciences, 2012).

42 Snell, *Capital Punishment, 2012*.

43 From the Death Penalty Information Center's site, http://www.deathpenaltyinfo.org (accessed December 15, 2013).

44 As some of the evidence presented before the Supreme Court in *Furman* v. *Georgia*, 408 U.S. 238 (1972), suggested.

45 *McCleskey* v. *Kemp*, 481 U.S. 279 (1987).

46 Edward Connors, Thomas Lundregan, Neal Miller, and Tom McEwen, *Convicted by Juries, Exonerated by Science: Case Studies in the Use of DNA Evidence to Establish Innocence after Trial* (Washington, DC: National Institute of Justice, 1996).

47 U.S. Department of Justice, *The Federal Death Penalty System: A Statistical Survey (1988–2000)* (Washington, DC: U.S. Department of Justice, 2000).

48 James S. Liebman, Jeffrey Fagan, and Valerie West, "A Broken System: Error Rates in Capital Cases, 1973–1995," Columbia Law School, 2000, http://www.law.columbia.edu/instructionalservices/liebman (accessed September 10, 2013).

49 Death Penalty Information Center, "Innocence Cases: 2004–Present," http://www.deathpenaltyinfo.org/innocence-cases-2004-present (accessed July 3, 2014). *Released* in this context means exonerated or determined to be innocent. The definition of *innocence* used by the Death Penalty Information Center in placing defendants on the list is that they had been convicted and sentenced to death and that subsequently (a) their convictions were overturned and they were acquitted at a retrial or all charges were dropped or (b) they were given an absolute pardon by the governor of the relevant state based on new evidence of innocence.

50 Jeffrey L. Kirchmeier, "Another Place beyond Here: The Death Penalty Moratorium Movement in the United States," *University of Colorado Law Review*, Vol. 70, No. 1 (2002), pp. 1–116.

51 Governor's Press Office, State of Maryland, "Governor Glendening Issues a Stay of Execution in the Case of Wesley Eugene Baker," May 9, 2002, http://www.gov.state.md.us/gov/press/2002/may/html/baker.html (accessed January 30, 2005).

52 Jeremy W. Peters, "Death Penalty Repealed in New Jersey," *New York Times*, December 17, 2007, http://www.nytimes.com/2007/12/17/nyregion/17cnd-jersey.html (accessed March 3, 2012).

53 "Massachusetts Panel Offers Limited Death Penalty Plan," *Criminal Justice Newsletter*, May 17, 2004, p. 1.

54 "South Dakota Lawmakers Reject Bill to Repeal Death Penalty," *Rapid City Journal*, February 21, 2014, http://rapidcityjournal.com/news/local/south-dakota-lawmakers-reject-bill-to-repeal-death-penalty/article_778fd0c0-57d7-57d0-84d1-a3a12bb91113.html, (accessed April 27, 2014).

55 Title IV of the Justice for All Act of 2004.

56 Public Law 108-405.

57 The act also provides funding for the DNA Sexual Assault Justice Act (Title III of the Justice for All Act of 2004), and the Rape Kits and DNA Evidence Backlog Elimination Act of 2000 (42 U.S.C. 14135), authorizing more than $500 million for programs to improve the capacity of crime labs to conduct DNA analysis, reduce non-DNA backlogs, train evidence examiners, support sexual assault forensic examiner programs, and promote the use of DNA to identify missing persons.

58 In those states that accept federal monies under the legislation.

59 E. Ann Carson and Daniela Golinelli, *Prisoners in 2012—Advance Counts* (Washington, DC: Bureau of Justice Statistics, 2013).

60 Marvin Wolfgang, Thorsten Sellin, and Robert Figlio, *Delinquency in a Birth Cohort* (Chicago: University of Chicago Press, 1972).

61 Walter Moore, "An Alternative Take on the State of Los Angeles," *Press-Telegram*, April 26, 2012, http://www.presstelegram.com/opinions/ci_20461647/oped-an-alternate-take-state-los-angeles (accessed May 20, 2012).

62 Ibid.

63 Laura J. Moriarty and James E. Williams, "Examining the Relationship between Routine Activities Theory and Social Disorganization: An Analysis of Property Crime Victimization," *American Journal of Criminal Justice*, Vol. 21, No. 1 (1996), pp. 43–59.

64 Ibid., p. 43.

65 Ibid., p. 46.

66 M. Lyn Exum, "The Application and Robustness of the Rational Choice Perspective in the Study of Angry Intentions to Aggress," *Criminology*, Vol. 40, No. 4 (2002), p. 933, citing Allen E. Liska and Stephen F. Messner, *Perspectives on Crime and Deviance*, 3rd ed. (Upper Saddle River, NJ: Prentice Hall, 1999).

67 Dolf Zillman, *Hostility and Aggression* (Hillsdale, NJ: Lawrence Erlbaum, 1979), p. 279.

68 Kenneth D. Tunnell, "Choosing Crime: Close Your Eyes and Take Your Chances," *Justice Quarterly*, Vol. 7 (1990), pp. 673–690.

69 See R. Barr and K. Pease, "Crime Placement, Displacement and Deflection," in M. Tonry and N. Morris, eds., *Crime and Justice: A Review of Research*, Vol. 12 (Chicago: University of Chicago Press, 1990).

70 For a good summation of studies on displacement, see R. Hesseling, "Displacement: A Review of the Empirical Literature," in R. V. Clarke, ed., *Crime Prevention Studies*, Vol. 3 (Monsey, NY: Willow Tree Press, 1994).

71 For a good summation of target hardening, see Ronald V. Clarke, *Situational Crime Prevention* (New York: Harrow and Heston, 1992).

Chapter 3, Early Biological Perspectives on Criminal Behavior—*It's What We Are*

1 Cited in Patricia Cohen, "Genetic Basis for Crime: A New Look," *New York Times*, June 19, 2011.

2 Megan Visscher, "How Food Can Cut Crime," *Ode Magazine*, February 9, 2010, http://www.care2.com/greenliving/how-food-can-cut-crime.html?page=4 (accessed March 11, 2014).

3 C. B. Gesch, S. M. Hammond, S. E. Hampson, A. Eves, and M. J. Crowder, "Influence of Supplementary Vitamins, Minerals and Essential Fatty Acids on the Antisocial Behavior of Young Adult Prisoners: Randomized, Placebo-Controlled Trial," *British Journal of Psychiatry*, Vol. 181 (July 2002), pp. 22–28.

4 Visscher, "How Food Can Cut Crime."

5 C. Ray Jeffery, "Biological Perspectives," *Journal of Criminal Justice Education*, Vol. 4, No. 2 (fall 1993), pp. 292–293.

6 Anthony Walsh and Craig Hemmens, eds., *Introduction to Criminology: A Text/Reader*, 2nd ed. (Thousand Oaks, CA: Sage, 2011), p. 272.

7 Auguste Comte, *A System of Positive Polity*, trans. John Henry Bridges (New York: Franklin, 1875; originally published in four volumes, 1851–1854).

8 See K. L. Henwood and N. F. Pidgeon, "Qualitative Research and Psychological Theorising," *British Journal of Psychology*, Vol. 83 (1992), pp. 97–111.

9 Cesare Lombroso, "Introduction," in Gina Lombroso-Ferrero, ed., *Criminal Man According to the Classification of Cesare Lombroso* (1911; reprint, Montclair, NJ: Patterson Smith, 1972), p. xv.

10 Ibid., p. xiv.

11 Charles Goring, *The English Convict: A Statistical Study* (London: His Majesty's Stationery Office, 1913; reprint, Montclair, NJ: Patterson Smith, 1972), p. 15.

12 Ibid.

13 William H. Sheldon, *Varieties of Delinquent Youth* (New York: Harper & Brothers, 1949).

14 See Joseph D. McInerney, "Genes and Behavior: A Complex Relationship," *Judicature*, Vol. 83, No. 3 (November–December 1999).

15 Sir Francis Galton, *Inquiry into Human Faculty and Its Development*, 2nd ed. (London: J. M. Dent and Sons, 1907).

16 Richard Louis Dugdale, *The Jukes: A Study in Crime, Pauperism, Disease, and Heredity*, 3rd ed. (New York: G. P. Putnam's Sons, 1895).

17 Arthur H. Estabrook, *The Jukes in 1915* (Washington, DC: Carnegie Institute of Washington, 1916).

18 Henry Herbert Goddard, *The Kallikak Family: A Study in the Heredity of Feeblemindedness* (New York: Macmillan, 1912).

19 See Nicole Hahn Rafter, *Creating Born Criminals* (Urbana: University of Illinois Press, 1997).

20 See Nicole Hahn Rafter, ed., *White Trash: The Eugenics Family Studies, 1877–1919* (Boston: Northeastern University Press, 1988).

21 *Buck* v. *Bell*, 274 U.S. 200, 207 (1927).

22 P. A. Jacobs, M. Brunton, and M. Melville, "Aggressive Behavior, Mental Subnormality, and the XYY Male," *Nature*, Vol. 208 (1965), p. 1351.

23 Webster's defines *karyotype* as "a photomicrograph of metaphase chromosomes in a standard array" (*Webster's II New College Dictionary* [Chicago, IL: Houghton Mifflin Harcourt, 2005], p. 618).

24 Anthony Walsh, *Biology and Criminology: The Biosocial Synthesis* (New York: Routledge, 2009), p. 268.

25 See David A. Jones, *History of Criminology: A Philosophical Perspective* (Westport, CT: Greenwood Press, 1986), p. 124.

26 T. Sarbin and J. Miller, "Demonism Revisited: The XYY Chromosomal Anomaly," *Issues in Criminology*, Vol. 5 (1970), p. 199.

27 Karl O. Christiansen, "A Preliminary Study of Criminality among Twins," in Sarnoff Mednick and Karl Christiansen, eds., *Biosocial Bases of Criminal Behavior* (New York: Gardner Press, 1977).

28 The Minnesota Twin Family Study, http://www.psych.umn.edu/psylabs/mtfs (accessed August 10, 2013).

29 T. J. Bouchard et al., "Sources of Human Psychological Differences: The Minnesota Study of Twins Reared Apart," *Science*, Vol. 250, No. 4978 (1990), pp. 223–228.

30 Peter McGuffin and Anita Thapar, "Genetic Basis of Bad Behaviour in Adolescents," *Lancet*, Vol. 350 (August 9, 1997), pp. 411–412.

31 Louise Arseneault et al., "Strong Genetic Effects on Cross-Situational Antisocial Behaviour among 5-Year-Old Children According to Mothers, Teachers, Examiner-Observers, and Twins' Self-Reports," *Journal of Child Psychology and Psychiatry*, Vol. 44, No. 6 (September 2003), pp. 832–848.

32 Ibid.

33 Taken from "Hope for the 'Hopeless,'" *Crime Times*, Vol. 10, No. 2 (2004), p. 2.

Chapter 4, Biosocial and Other Contemporary Perspectives—*Interaction is Key*

1 Personal Quote by Nicole Rafter. Used by permission of Nicole Rafter.

2 Marc Lallianilla, "Genetics May Provide Clues to Newton Shooting," Livescience, http://www.livescience.com/25853-newtown-shooter-dna.html December 28, 2012 (accessed January 2, 2014).

3 James Watson and Francis Crick, "Molecular Structure of Nucleic Acids: A Structure for Deoxyribose Nucleic Acid," *Nature*, Vol. 171 (April 1953), p. 737.

4 Mary Kugler, "What Are Genes, DNA and Chromosomes?" About.com, http://rarediseases.about.com/od/geneticdisorders/a/genesbasics.htm (accessed December 6, 2012).

5 Ibid.

6 McKusick-Nathans Institute of Genetic Medicine, "The 1,000 Genomes Project," The Johns Hopkins University, 2010, http://www.hopkinsmedicine.org/geneticmedicine/news/NewsletterStories/2010_12/2010_12_1000_genomes.html (accessed January 3, 2013).

7 Much of the information and some of the wording in this section come from the National Human Genome Research Institute's Web page, http://www.nhgri.nih.gov/HGP (accessed November 16, 2007).

8 Clive Cookson, "Science: Contours of the Mind," *Financial Times*, February 22, 2013, http://www.ft.com/intl/cms/s/0/06568de8-7cc2-11e2-afb6-00144feabdc0.html#axzz2LmTokbXz (accessed March 3, 2013).

9 "Obama's Brain Activity Map Could Be the Future of Neuroscience Research," *Huffington Post*, February 23, 2013, http://www.huffingtonpost.com/2013/02/23/obamas-brain-activity-map_n_2747159.html (accessed February 25, 2013).

10 "Obama's Brain Activity Map," *Huffington Post.*

11 Geoffrey Cowley and Carol Hallin, "The Genetics of Bad Behavior: A Study Links Violence to Heredity," *Newsweek*, November 1, 1993, p. 57.

12 H. G. Brunner, M. Nelen, X. O. Breakefield, H. H. Ropers, and B. A. van Oost, "Abnormal Behavior Associated with a Point Mutation in the Structural Gene for Monoamine Oxidase A," *Science*, Vol. 262, No. 5133 (October 22, 1993), pp. 578–580.

13 Quoted in Tim Friend, "Violence Linked to Gene Defect: Pleasure Deficit May Be the Spark," *USA Today*, May 9, 1996. See the original research at Kenneth Blum et al., "Reward Deficiency Syndrome," *American Scientist*, Vol. 84 (March/April 1996), pp. 132–145, http://www.sigmaxi.org/amsci/Articles/96Articles/Blum-full.html (accessed January 5, 2005).

14 See, for example, M. Rutter, H. Giller, and A. Hagell, *Antisocial Behavior by Young People* (Cambridge: Cambridge University Press, 1998).

15 Avshalom Caspi et al., "Role of Genotype in the Cycle of Violence in Maltreated Children," *Science*, Vol. 298, No. 2 (August 2002), p. 851.

16 For more information on the Dunedin Multidisciplinary Health and Development Study, see T. E. Moffitt et al., *Sex Differences in Antisocial Behavior: Conduct Disorder, Delinquency and Violence in the Dunedin Longitudinal Study* (Cambridge: Cambridge University Press, 2001). Visit the Dunedin Multidisciplinary Health and Development Research Unit on the Web at http://healthsci.otago.ac.nz/dsm/dmhdru.

17 Ibid.

18 Nilsson Oreland et al., "Monoamine Oxidases: Activities, Genotypes and the Shaping of Behaviour," *Journal of Neural Transmission*, April 12, 2007; and Rickard L. Sjöberg et al., "Adolescent Girls and Criminal Activity: Role of MAOA-LPR Genotype and Psychosocial Factor," *American Journal of Medical Genetics Part B: Neuropsychiatric Genetics*, Vol. 144B, No. 2 (October 2006), pp. 159–164.

19 Kevin M. Beaver, Matt DeLisi, Michael G. Vaughn, and John Paul Wright, "The Intersection of Genes and Neuropsychological Deficits in the Prediction of Adolescent Delinquency and Low Self-Control," *International Journal of Offender Therapy and Comparative Criminology*, Vol. 20, No. 10, (2008) p. 17.

20 National Geographic Television, "Inside the Warrior Gene," http://natgeotv.com/ca/inside-the-warrior-gene/about (accessed January 2, 2014).

21 A. E. Baum et al., "A Genome-Wide Association Study Implicates Diacylglycerol Kinase Eta (DGKH) and Several Other Genes in the Etiology of Bipolar Disorder," *Molecular Psychiatry*, advance online publication, http://doi:10.1038/sj.mp.4002012 (accessed May 8, 2007).

22 National Institute on Drug Abuse, "Genetics of Addiction: A Research Update from the National Institute on Drug Abuse," http://www.drugabuse.gov/tib/genetics.html (accessed May 1, 2010).

23 Nathalie M. G. Fontaine, Eamon J. P. McCory, et al., "Predictors and Outcomes of Joint Trajectories of Callous–Unemotional Traits and Conduct Problems in Childhood," *Journal of Abnormal Psychology*, Vol. 123, No. 3 (August 2011), pp. 740–741.

24 Twins Early Development Study, "TEDS," http://www.teds.ac.uk/about.html (accessed January 27, 2012).

25 Eric Lacourse, Michel Boivin, Mara Brendgen, Amélie Petitclerc, Alain Girard, Frank Vitaro, Stéphane Paquin, Isabelle Ouellet-Morin, Ginette Dionne, and Richard E. Tremblay, "A Longitudinal Twin Study of Physical Aggression during Early Childhood: Evidence for a Developmentally Dynamic Genome," *Psychological Medicine*, January 21, 2014.

26 Anthony Walsh, "Behavior Genetics and Anomic/Strain Theory," in Anthony Walsh and Craig Hemmens, eds., *Introduction to Criminology: A Text/Reader* (Thousand Oaks, CA: Sage, 2010), p. 284.

27 The University of Utah, Genetic Science Learning Center, "Epigenetics," http://learn.genetics.utah.edu/content/epigenetics (accessed February 2, 2014).

28 Joseph D. McInerney, "Genes and Behavior: A Complex Relationship," *Judicature*, Vol. 83, No. 3 (November/December 1999).

29 See "The Genome Changes Everything: A Talk with Matt Ridley," http://www.edge.org/3rd_culture/ridley03/ridley_print.html (accessed February 10, 2007).

30 Matt Ridley, "What Makes You Who You Are?" *Time*, June 2, 2003, pp. 55–63.

31 Kevin M. Beaver and Anthony Walsh, "Biosocial Criminology," in Kevin M. Beaver and Anthony Walsh, eds., *The Ashgate Research Companion to Biosocial Theories of Crime* (Burlington, VT: Ashgate Publishing, 2011), p. 7.

32 See Adrian Raine et al., "Prefrontal Glucose Deficits in Murderers Lacking Psychosocial Deprivation," *Neuropsychiatry, Neuropsychology, and Behavioral Neurology*, Vol. 11, No. 1 (1998), pp. 1–7; and Adrian Raine et al., "Selective Reductions in Prefrontal Glucose Metabolism in Murderers," *Biological Psychiatry*, Vol. 36 (September 1, 1994), pp. 319–332.

33 "PET Study: Looking inside the Minds of Murderers," *Crime Times*, Vol. 1, No. 1–2 (1995), http://www.crime-times.org/95a/w95ap1.htm (accessed November 15, 2006).

34 Ibid.

35 Raine et al., "Selective Reductions in Prefrontal Glucose Metabolism in Murderers."

36 Adrian Raine, Monte Buchsbaum, and Lori LaCasse, "Brain Abnormalities in Murderers Indicated by Positron Emission Tomography," in Kevin M. Beaver and Anthony Walsh, eds., *Biosocial Theories of Crime* (Burlington, VT: Ashgate, 2010), pp. 465–478.

37 Adrian Raine, J. Reid Meloy, Susan Bihrle, Jackie Stoddard, Lori LaCasse, and Monte S. Buchsbaum, "Reduced Prefrontal and Increased Subcortical Brain Functioning Assessed Using Positron Emission Tomography in Predatory and Affective Murderers," in Kevin M. Beaver and Anthony Walsh, eds., *Biosocial Theories of Crime* (Burlington, VT: Ashgate, 2010), pp. 479–492.

38 "Researchers Explore the Brain for Clues to the Causes of Anti-Social Behavior," AAAS 2011 Annual Meeting News, February 25, 2011, http://news.aaas.org/2011_annual_meeting/0225nature-nurture-in-antisocial-behavior.shtml (accessed January 27, 2011).

39 "Kids' Brains May Hold Clues to Future Criminals," CNN Health, February 21, 2011, http://thechart.blogs.cnn.com/2011/02/21/kids-brains-may-hold-clues-to-future-criminals (accessed January 27, 2012).

40 James H. Fallon, "Neuroanatomical Background to Understanding the Brain of the Young Psychopath," *Ohio State Journal of Criminal Law*, Vol. 3 (2006), pp. 340–367.

41 Daniel Strueber, Monika Lueck, and Gerhard Roth, "The Violent Brain," *Scientific American*, November 29, 2006, http://www.scientificamerican.com/article.cfm?id=the-violent-brain (accessed October 23, 2014).

42 "Brain's Mirror Cells Help Actions Speak Louder," *New Scientist*, February 2014, p. 11.

43 Ibid.

44 See, for example, A. R. Mawson and K. J. Jacobs, "Corn Consumption, Tryptophan, and Cross National Homicide Rates," *Journal of Orthomolecular Psychiatry*, Vol. 7 (1978), pp. 227–230; and A. Hoffer, "The Relation of Crime to Nutrition," *Humanist in Canada*, Vol. 8 (1975), p. 8.

45 "Flu in Pregnancy Changes Fetal Brain," *New Scientist*, January 30, 2010, p. 15.

46 Douglas S. Massey, "Segregation and Stratification: A Biosocial Perspective," in Kevin M. Beaver and Anthony Walsh, eds., *Biosocial Theories of Crime* (Burlington, VT: Ashgate, 2010), p. 62.

47 "Violence Makes a Kid's Brain Like That of a Soldier," *New Scientist*, December 10, 2011, p. 12.

48 Christian Jarrett, "Predicting Reoffending?" *The Psychologist*, April 23, 2013.

49 See Proceedings of the National Academy of Sciences of the United States of America, "Biological Embedding of Early Social Adversity: From Fruit Flies to Kindergartners—the Sackler Colloquium," October 16, 2012, http://www.pnas.org/content/109/suppl.2 (accessed February 2, 2013).

50 Marla B. Sokolowski, W. Thomas Boyce, and Bruce S. McEwen, "Scarred for Life?" *New Scientist*, January 26, 2013, p. 28.

51 D. Hill and W. Sargent, "A Case of Matricide," *Lancet*, Vol. 244 (1943), pp. 526–527.

52 William Dufty, *Sugar Blues* (Pandor, PA: Chilton, 1975).

53 See Court TV's Crime Library, "Twinkies as a Defense," http://www.crimelibrary.com/criminal_mind/psychology/insanity/7.html (accessed August 8, 2007).

54 See, for example, C. Hawley and R. E. Buckley, "Food Dyes and Hyperkinetic Children," *Academy Therapy*, Vol. 10 (1974), pp. 27–32; and Alexander Schauss, *Diet, Crime and Delinquency* (Berkeley, CA: Parker House, 1980).

55 "Special Report: Measuring Your Life with Coffee Spoons," *Tufts University Diet and Nutrition Letter*, Vol. 2, No. 2 (April 1984), pp. 3–6.

56 See, for example, "Special Report: Does What You Eat Affect Your Mood and Actions?" *Tufts University Diet and Nutrition Letter*, Vol. 2, No. 12 (February 1985), pp. 4–6.

57 See *Tufts University Diet and Nutrition Newsletter*, Vol. 2, No. 11 (January 1985), p. 2; and "Special Report: Why Sugar Continues to Concern Nutritionists," *Tufts University Diet and Nutrition Letter*, Vol. 3, No. 3 (May 1985), pp. 3–6.

58 "School Study: Supplementation Decreases Delinquent Behaviors, Raises IQ," *Crime Times*, Vol. 6, No. 2 (2000), p. 3, http://www.crimetimes.org/00b/w00bp3htm (accessed March 10, 2012).

59 S. J. Schoenthaler and D. Bier, "The Effect of Vitamin-Mineral Supplementation on Juvenile Delinquency among American Schoolchildren: A Randomized, Double-Blind Placebo-Controlled Trial," *Journal of Alternative Complementary Medicine*, Vol. 6, No. 1 (February 2000), pp. 31–35.

60 C. Iribarren et al., "Dietary Intake of Omega-3, Omega-6 Fatty Acids and Fish: Relationship with Hostility in Young Adults—the CARDIA Study," *European Journal of Clinical Nutrition*, Vol. 50, No. 1 (January 2004), pp. 24–31.

61 David Benton, "The Impact of Diet on Anti-Social, Violent and Criminal Behaviour," *Neuroscience and Biobehavioral Reviews*, Vol. 31 (2007), pp. 752–774.

62 Roger D. Masters, Brian Hone, and Anil Doshi, "Environmental Pollution, Neurotoxicity, and Criminal Violence," in J. Rose, ed., *Environmental Toxicology* (London and New York: Gordon and Breach, 1997).

63 Peter Montague, "Toxics and Violent Crime," *Rachel's Environment and Health Weekly*, No. 551 (June 19, 1997).

64 Rick Nevin, "Understanding International Crime Trends: The Legacy of Preschool Lead Exposure," *Environmental Research*, Vol. 104 (February 2007), pp. 315–336.

65 Jim Haner, "Studies Suggest Link between Lead, Violence," *Baltimore Sun*, May 9, 2000, http://www.baltimoresun.com/news/maryland/bal-te.lead09may09,0,584142.story (accessed June 15, 2011).

66 See, for example, Rick Nevin, "How Lead Exposure Relates to Temporal Changes in IQ, Violent Crime, and Unwed Pregnancy," *Environmental Research*, Vol. 83, No. 1 (May 2000), pp. 1–22.

67 Quoted in Alison Motluck, "Pollution May Lead to a Life of Crime," *New Scientist*, Vol. 154, No. 2084 (May 31, 1997), p. 4.

68 L. Goldschmidt, N. L. Day, and G. A. Richardson, "Effects of Prenatal Marijuana Exposure on Child Behavior Problems at Age 10," *Neurotoxicology and Teratology*, Vol. 22, No. 3 (May/June 2000), pp. 325–336.

69 David Fergusson, Lianne Woodward, and L. John Horwood, "Maternal Smoking during Pregnancy and Psychiatric Adjustment in Late Adolescence," *Archives of General Psychiatry*, Vol. 55 (August 1998), pp. 721–727.

70 Jacob F. Orlebeke, Dirk L. Knol, and Frank C. Verhulst, "Increase in Child Behavior Problems Resulting from Maternal Smoking during Pregnancy," *Archives of Environmental Health*, Vol. 52, No. 4 (July/August 1997), pp. 317–321.

71 Travis C. Pratt, Jean Marie McGloin, and Noelle E. Fearn, "Maternal Cigarette Smoking during Pregnancy and Criminal/Deviant Behavior: A Meta-Analysis," *International Journal of Offender Therapy and Comparative Criminology*, Vol. 50, No. 6 (2006), pp. 672–690.

72 Tresa M. Roebuck, Sarah N. Mattson, and Edward P. Riley, "Behavioral and Psychosocial Profiles of Alcohol-Exposed Children," *Alcoholism: Clinical and Experimental Research*, Vol. 23, No. 6 (June 1999), pp. 1070–1076.

73 John Cryan and Timothy Dinan, "A Light on Psychobiotics," *New Scientist*, January 25, 2014, pp. 28–29.

74 Ibid.

75 Ibid., p. 29.

76 Jill Portnoy, Adrian Raine, Frances R. Chen, Dustin Pardini, Rolf Loeber, and J. Richard Jennings, "Heart Rate and Antisocial Behavior: The Mediating Role of Impulsive Sensation Seeking," *Criminology*, doi: 10.1111/1745-9125.12038 (accessed May 9, 2014).

77 See, for example, John G. V. Davies and Rodney Maliphant, "Autonomic Responses of Male Adolescents Exhibiting Refractory Behaviour in School," *Journal of Child Psychology and Psychiatry*, Vol. 12 (1971), pp. 115–127.

78 Adrian Raine, Annis Lai-Chu Fung, Jill Portnoy, Olivia Choy, and Victoria L. Spring, "Low Heart Rate as a Risk Factor for Child and Adolescent Proactive Aggressive and Impulsive Pyschopathic Behavior," *Aggressive Behavior* (2014), doi: 10.1002/ab.21523.

79 Adrian Raine, "The Role of Prefrontal Deficits, Low Autonomic Arousal, and Early Health Factors in the Development of Antisocial and Aggressive Behavior in Children," *Journal of Child Psychology and Psychiatry*, Vol. 43 (2002), pp. 417–434.

80 See, for example, D. H. Fishbein, "The Psychobiology of Female Aggression," *Criminal Justice and Behavior*, Vol. 19 (1992), pp. 99–126.

81 T. I. Paus et al., "Sexual Dimorphism in the Adolescent Brain: Role of Testosterone and Androgen Receptor in Global and Local White Matter," *Hormones and Behavior*, Vol. 57 (2010), pp. 63–75.

82 See, for example, R. T. Rada, D. R. Laws, and R. Kellner, "Plasma Testosterone Levels in the Rapist," *Psychosomatic Medicine*, Vol. 38 (1976), pp. 257–268.

83 "The Insanity of Steroid Abuse," *Newsweek*, May 23, 1988, p. 75.

84 Dan Olweus et al., "Testosterone, Aggression, Physical and Personality Dimensions in Normal Adolescent Males," *Psychosomatic Medicine*, Vol. 42 (1980), pp. 253–269.

85 Richard Udry, "Biosocial Models of Adolescent Problem Behaviors," *Social Biology*, Vol. 37 (1990), pp. 1–10.

86 Alan Booth and D. Wayne Osgood, "The Influence of Testosterone on Deviance in Adulthood: Assessing and Explaining the Relationship," *Criminology*, Vol. 31, No. 1 (1993), p. 93.

87 Richard Udry, Luther Talbert, and Naomi Morris, "Biosocial Foundations for Adolescent Female Sexuality," *Demography*, Vol. 23 (1986), pp. 217–227.

88 James M. Dabbs, Jr., and Marian F. Hargrove, "Age, Testosterone, and Behavior among Female Prison Inmates," *Psychosomatic Medicine*, Vol. 59 (1997), pp. 447–480.

89 *Regina* v. *English*, unreported, Norwich Crown Court, November 10, 1981.

90 Paul C. Bernhardt, "Influences of Serotonin and Testosterone in Aggression and Dominance: Convergence with Social Psychology," *Current Directions in Psychological Science*, Vol. 6, No. 2 (April 1997), pp. 44–48.

91 Anastasia Toufexis, Hannah Bloch, and Dick Thompson, "Seeking the Roots of Violence: A Search for Biological Clues to Crime is Igniting a Brutal Political Controversy." *Time*, April 19, 1993.

92 Terrie E. Moffitt et al., "Whole Blood Serotonin Relates to Violence in an Epidemiological Study," *Biological Psychiatry*, Vol. 43, No. 6 (March 15, 1998), pp. 446–457.

93 Ibid.

94 H. Soderstrom et al., "New Evidence for an Association between the CSF HVA:5-HIAA Ratio and Psychopathic Traits," *Journal of Neurology, Neurosurgery and Psychiatry*, Vol. 74 (2003), pp. 918–921.

95 Angela D. Crews, "Biological Theory," in J. Mitchell Miller, ed., *21st Century Criminology: A Reference Handbook* (Thousand Oaks, CA: Sage, 2009), p. 196.

96 See E. G. Stalenheim, L. von Knorring, and L. Wide, "Serum Levels of Thyroid Hormones as Biological Markers in a Swedish Forensic Psychiatric Population," *Biological Psychiatry*, Vol. 43, No. 10 (May 15, 1998), pp. 755–761; and P. O. Alm et al., "Criminality and Psychopathy as Related to Thyroid Activity in Former Juvenile Delinquents," *Acta Psychiatrica Scandinavica*, Vol. 94, No. 2 (August 1996), pp. 112–117.

97 Paul J. Zak, "The Trust Molecule," WSJ.com, April 27, 2012, http://professional.wsj.com/article/SB10001424052702304811304577365782995320366.html?mod=WSJPRO_hps_MIDDLESecondNews#printMode (accessed August 2, 2012).

98 Leah E. Daigle, "Biochemical Theories of Criminal Behavior," in Richard A. Wright and J. Mitchell Miler, eds., *Encyclopedia of Criminology*, Vol. 1 (London: Routledge, 2005), p. 103.

99 James Q. Wilson and Richard J. Herrnstein, *Crime and Human Nature* (New York: Simon & Schuster, 1985).

100 Quoted in Karen J. Winkler, "Criminals Are Born as Well as Made, Authors of Controversial Book Assert," *Chronicle of Higher Education*, January 16, 1986, p. 5.

101 Wilson and Herrnstein, *Crime and Human Nature*.

102 Winkler, "Criminals Are Born as Well as Made," p. 8.

103 Anthony Walsh, *Biosocial Criminology: Introduction and Integration* (Cincinnati: Anderson, 2002), p. vii.

104 Anthony Walsh, "Biological Theories of Criminal Behavior," in Richard A. Wright and J. Mitchell Miller, eds., *Encyclopedia of Criminology*, Vol. 1 (New York: Routledge, 2005), p. 106.

105 Ibid.

106 Ibid.

107 Diana Fishbein, *Biobehavioral Perspectives in Criminology* (Belmont, CA: Wadsworth, 2001), pp. 2–3.

108 Jeffery, "Biological Perspectives," *Journal of Criminal Justice Education*, Vol. 4, No. 2 (Fall 1993), p. 300.

109 Leanne Fiftal Alarid et al., "Women's Roles in Serious Offenses: A Study of Adult Felons," *Justice Quarterly*, Vol. 13, No. 3 (September 1996), pp. 432–454.

110 Kevin Beaver, "Foreword," in Anthony Walsh, *Feminist Criminology through a Biosocial Lens* (Durham, NC: Carolina Academic Press, 2011), p. 11.

111 Federal Bureau of Investigation, *Crime in the United States, 2012* (Washington, DC: U.S. Department of Justice, 2013).

112 T. Bernard, J. Snipes, and A. Gerould, *Vold's Theoretical Criminology* (New York: Oxford University Press, 2010), cited in Anthony Walsh, *Feminist Criminology through a Biosocial Lens* (Durham, NC: Carolina Academic Press, 2011), p. xi.

113 Anthony Walsh, *Feminist Criminology through a Biosocial Lens* (Durham, NC: Carolina Academic Press, 2011), p. 22.

114 Ibid.

115 Laura Klappenbach, "Sexual Selection," About.com, http://animals.about.com/od/s/g/sexualselection.htm (accessed January 10, 2012).

116 I. Silverman, J. Choi, and M. Peters, "The Hunter-Gatherer Theory of Sex Differences in Spatial Abilities: Data from 40 Countries," *Archives of Sexual Behavior*, Vol. 36 (2007), pp. 261–268.

117 A. Walsh and L. Ellis, *Criminology: An Interdisciplinary Approach* (Thousand Oaks, CA: Sage, 2007).

118 Aurelio José Figueredo, Paul Robert Gladden, and Zachary Hohman, *The Evolutionary Psychology of Criminal Behaviour*. In S. C. Roberts, ed., *Applied Evolutionary Psychology* (Oxford University Press, 2011).

119 Walsh, *Feminist Criminology*, p. 125.

120 Kevin M. Beaver, John Paul Wright, and Anthony Walsh, "A Gene-Based Evolutionary Explanation for the Association between Criminal Involvement and Number of Sex Partners," in Kevin M. Beaver and Anthony Walsh, eds., *Biosocial Theories of Crime* (Burlington, VT: Ashgate, 2010), p. 351.

121 Anthony Walsh and Craig Hemmens, *Introduction to Criminology: A Text/Reader*, 2nd ed. (Thousand Oaks, CA: Sage, 2011), p. 269.

122 Jerome H. Barkow, Leda Cosmides, and John Tooby, eds., *The Adapted Mind: Evolutionary Psychology and the Generation of Culture* (New York: Oxford University Press, 1992).

123 Lee Ellis and Anthony Walsh, "Gene-Based Evolutionary Theories in Criminology," *Criminology*, Vol. 35, No. 2 (1997), pp. 229–230.

124 Terrie E. Moffitt, "The New Look of Behavioral Genetics in Developmental Psychopathology: Gene-Environment Interplay in Antisocial Behaviors," in Kevin M. Beaver and Anthony Walsh, eds., *Biosocial Theories of Crime* (Burlington, VT: Ashgate, 2010), p. 185.

125 Elizabeth Englander, *Understanding Violence*, 3rd ed. (Mahwah, NJ: Lawrence Erlbaum Associates, 2007).

126 Lee Ellis, "Theory Explaining the Biological Correlates of Criminality," *European Journal of Criminology*, Vol. 2, No. 3 (2005), pp. 287–314.

127 Julian Roberts and T. Gabor, "Lombrosian Wine in a New Bottle: Research on Crime and Race," *Canadian Journal of Criminology*, Vol. 32 (1990), pp. 291–313.

Chapter 5, Psychological and Psychiatric Foundations of Criminal Behavior—*It's How We Think*

1 "Giffords, Other Survivors to Observe 1-Year Mark of Shooting Rampage in Tucson," Associated Press, December 29, 2011, http://www.washingtonpost.com/national/giffords-other-survivors-to-observe-1-year-mark-of-shooting-rampage-in-tucson/2011/12/29/gIQAOgNsOP_story.html?hpid=z4 (accessed May 1, 2012).

2 "Jared Loughner Enters Guilty Plea after Being Found Competent to Stand Trial," *The Guardian*, http://www.guardian.co.uk/world/2012/aug/07/jaredloughner-pleads-guilty-arizona (accessed May 5, 2011).

3 Paul Farhi, "Publications Grapple with Jared Loughner Mug Shot," *Washington Post*, January 11, 2011, http://www.washingtonpost.com/wp-dyn/content/article/2011/01/11/AR2011011106921.html (accessed July 17, 2014).

4 American Board of Forensic Psychology, http://www.abfp.com/brochure.html (accessed November 22, 2007).

5 See the American Academy of Psychiatry and the Law, http://www.aapl.org (accessed August 2, 2012).

6 Laurence Steinberg, "The Juvenile Psychopath: Fads, Fictions, and Facts," *National Institute of Justice Perspectives on Crime and Justice: 2001 Lecture Series*, Vol. V (Washington, DC: NIJ, 2002), pp. 35–64.

7 Ibid.

8 Nicole Hahn Rafter, "Psychopathy and the Evolution of Criminological Knowledge," *Theoretical Criminology*, Vol. 1, No. 2 (May 1997), p. 236.

9 As noted by Rafter, "Psychopathy and the Evolution of Criminological Knowledge." See Richard von Krafft-Ebing, *Psychopathia Sexualis* (1886; reprint, New York: Stein and Day, 1965); and Richard von Krafft-Ebing, *Textbook of Insanity* (Germany, 1879; reprint, Philadelphia: F. A. Davis, 1904).

10 Bernard H. Glueck, *Studies in Forensic Psychiatry* (Boston: Little, Brown, 1916).

11 William Healy, *The Individual Delinquent* (Boston: Little, Brown, 1915).

12 Early writings about the psychopathic personality focused almost exclusively on men, and most psychiatrists appeared to believe that very few women (if any) possessed such traits.

13 Hervey M. Cleckley, *The Mask of Sanity*, 4th ed. (St. Louis, MO: C. V. Mosby, 1964).

14 "Charles Manson," Research This Stuff, http://www.researchthisstuff.com/Charles_Manson_001.htm (accessed July 3, 2009).

15 Quoted in Joseph P. Newman and Chad A. Brinkley, "Psychopathy: Rediscovering Cleckley's Construct," *Psychopathology Research*, Vol. 9, No. 1 (March 1998).

16 Gwynn Nettler, *Killing One Another* (Cincinnati: Anderson, 1982), p. 179.

17 Ralph Serin, "Can Criminal Psychopaths Be Identified?" Correctional Service of Canada, October 22, 1999, http://www.csc-scc.gc.ca/text/pblct/forum/e012/e0121.shtml (accessed December 20, 2006).

18 David T. Lykken, *The Antisocial Personalities* (Hillsdale, NJ: Lawrence Erlbaum, 1995).

19 Robert D. Hare, "Checklist for the Assessment of Psychopathy in Criminal Populations," in M. H. Ben-Aron, S. J. Hucker, and C. D. Webster, eds., *Clinical Criminology* (Toronto: University of Toronto, Clarke Institute of Psychiatry, 1985), pp. 157–167. Hare developed this checklist on Cleckley's characteristics commonly found in psychopaths.

20 See Steinberg, "The Juvenile Psychopath," from which some of the wording in this paragraph is adapted.

21 Ivan Semeniuk, "How We Tell Right from Wrong: An Interview with Marc Hauser," *New Scientist*, March 3, 2007, p. 44.

22 Michael Caldwell et al., "Treatment Response of Adolescent Offenders with Psychopathy Features: A 2-Year Follow-Up," *Criminal Justice and Behavior*, Vol. 33, No. 5 (2006), pp. 571–576.

23 American Psychiatric Association, *Diagnostic and Statistical Manual of Mental Disorders*, 2nd ed. (Washington, DC: American Psychiatric Association, 1968).

24 Ibid., p. 43.

25 R. D. Hare, *Psychopathy: Theory and Research* (New York: John Wiley and Sons, 1970).

26 L. N. Robins, *Deviant Children Grow Up* (Baltimore: Williams and Wilkins, 1966).

27 S. B. Guze, *Criminality and Psychiatric Disorders* (New York: Oxford University Press, 1976).

28 Hans J. Eysenck, *Crime and Personality* (Boston: Houghton Mifflin, 1964).

29 Intelligence may also be seen as an ability. See, for example, Colin G. DeYoung, "Intelligence and Personality," in R. J. Sternberg and S. B. Kaufman, eds., *The Cambridge Handbook of Intelligence* (New York: Cambridge University Press, 2011), pp. 711–737.

30 Some early personality theorists considered intelligence to be part of personality. See, for example, R. B. Cattell, *Personality* (New York: McGraw-Hill, 1950); and J. P. Guilford, *Personality* (New York: McGraw-Hill, 1959).

31 Guilford, *Personality*, p. 92.

32 Hans J. Eysenck, "Personality and Criminality: A Dispositional Analysis," in William S. Laufer and Freda Adler, eds., *Advances in Criminology Theory*, Vol. 1 (New Brunswick, NJ: Transaction, 1989), p. 90.

33 Eysenck, *Crime and Personality*, pp. 35–36.

34 DeYoung, "Intelligence and Personality."

35 Jean Piaget, *The Moral Judgment of the Child* (New York: The Free Press, 1965 [originally published 1932]). See also J. Piaget, *The Child's Construction of Reality* (London: Routledge and Kegan Paul, 1955).

36 Cited in Holly K. Craig and Tanya M. Gallagher, "The Structural Characteristics of Monologues in the Speech of Normal Children: Syntactic Nonconversational Aspects," *Journal of Speech, Language, and Hearing Research*, Vol. 22 (March 1979), pp. 46–62.

37 Lawrence Kohlberg, *Stages in the Development of Moral Thought and Action* (New York: Holt, Rinehart and Winston, 1969).

38 Sergio Herzog, "Moral Judgment, Crime Seriousness, and the Relations between Them: An Exploratory Study," *Crime and Delinquency*, December 27, 2012.

39 K. Dodge, "A Social Information Processing Model of Social Competence in Children," *Minnesota Symposium in Child Psychology*, Vol. 8 (1986), pp. 77–125.

40 J. Lochman, "Self and Peer Perceptions of Attributional Biases of Aggressive and Non-aggressive Boys in Dyadic Interactions," *Journal of Consulting and Clinical Psychology*, Vol. 55 (1987), pp. 404–410.

41 Calvin Langton and W. Marshall, "Contagion in Rapists: Theoretical Patterns by Typological Breakdown," *Aggression and Violent Behaviour*, Vol. 6 (2001), pp. 499–518.

42 R. C. Schank and R. P. Abelson, *Scripts, Plans, Goals and Understanding, an Inquiry into Human Knowledge Structures* (Hillsdale, NJ: Lawrence Erlbaum, 1977).

43 Helen Gavin and David Hockey, "Criminal Careers and Cognitive Scripts: An Investigation into Criminal Versatility," *The Qualitative Report*, Vol. 15, No. 2 (March 2010), pp. 389–410.

44 Ibid.

45 Samuel Yochelson and Stanton E. Samenow, *The Criminal Personality*, Vols. I, II, and III (New York, Aronson, 1976 and 1977).

46 Ibid.

47 Stanton E. Samenow, *Inside the Criminal Mind*, 2nd ed. (New York: Crown Publishers, 2004), p. xxi.

48 Ibid, p. 212.

49 August Aichorn, *Wayward Youth* (New York: Viking Press, 1935).

50 Marti Olsen Laney, *The Hidden Gifts of the Introverted Child* (New York: Workman Publishing, 2006).

51 Mark Solms, "Freud Returns," *Scientific American*, Vol. 290, No. 5 (May 2004), pp. 82–90.

52 Eric R. Kandel, "Biology and the Future of Psychoanalysis: A New Intellectual Framework for Psychiatry Revisited," *American Journal of Psychiatry*, Vol. 156 (April 1999), pp. 505–524.

53 Nettler, *Killing One Another*, p. 159.

54 Ibid., p. 155.

55 Runa Munkner, Soeren Haastrup, Torben Joergensen, and Peter Kramp, "The Temporal Relationship between Schizophrenia and Crime," *Social Psychiatry and Psychiatric Epidemiology*, Vol. 38, No. 7 (July 2003), pp. 347–353.

56 Elizabeth Walsh, Alec Buchanan, and Thomas Fahy, "Violence and Schizophrenia: Examining the Evidence," *The British Journal of Psychiatry*, Vol. 180 (2002), pp. 490–495.

57 Seena Fazel, Niklas Långström, Anders Hjern, Martin Grann, and Paul Lichtenstein, "Schizophrenia, Substance Abuse, and Violent Crime," *Journal of the American Medical Association*, Vol. 301, No. 19 (2009), pp. 2016–2023.

58 Michael Ollove, "New Psychosis Center Aims to Prevent Violence," *Stateline* (a publication of the Pew Charitable Trusts), http://www.pewstates.org/projects/stateline/headlines/new-psychosis-center-aims-to-prevent-violence-85899510671 (accessed June 2, 2014).

59 J. Dollard et al., *Frustration and Aggression* (New Haven, CT: Yale University Press, 1939).

60 Andrew F. Henry and James F. Short, Jr., *Suicide and Homicide: Economic, Sociological, and Psychological Aspects of Aggression* (Glencoe, IL: Free Press, 1954).

61 Stewart Palmer, *A Study of Murder* (New York: Crowell, 1960).

62 Seymour L. Halleck, *Psychiatry and the Dilemmas of Crime: A Study of Causes, Punishment and Treatment* (Berkeley: University of California Press, 1971).

63 Ibid., p. 78.

64 Ibid., p. 80.

65 Ibid.

66 Ibid.

67 Arnold S. Linsky, Ronet Bachman, and Murray A. Straus, *Stress, Culture, and Aggression* (New Haven, CT: Yale University Press, 1995).

68 Ibid., p. 7.

69 D. A. Andrews and J. Bonta, *The Psychology of Criminal Conduct*, 2nd ed. (Cincinnati, OH: Anderson Publishing Co., 1998).

70 D. A. Andrews and James Bonta, "Rehabilitating Criminal Justice Policy and Practice," *Psychology, Public Policy, and Law*, Vol. 16, No. 1 (2010), pp. 39–55.

71 Adapted from Tony Ward and Claire Stewart, "Criminogenic Needs and Human Needs: A Theoretical Model," *Psychology, Crime and Law*, Vol. 9, No. 2 (2003), pp. 125–143.

72 Andrews and Bonta, "Rehabilitating Criminal Justice Policy and Practice," p. 46.

73 See Mary D. Salter Ainsworth, "John Bowlby, 1907–1990," *American Psychologist*, Vol. 47 (1992), p. 668.

74 John Bowlby, "The Nature of the Child's Tie to Its Mother," *International Journal of Psycho-Analysis*, Vol. 39 (1958), pp. 350–373.

75 See John Bowlby, *Maternal Care and Mental Health*, World Health Organization Monograph (1951); and John Bowlby, *A Secure Base* (New York: Basic Books, 1988).

76 Bowlby, *A Secure Base*, p. 11.

77 David P. Farrington and Donald J. West, "Effects of Marriage, Separation, and Children on Offending by Adult Males," *Current Perspectives on Aging and the Life Cycle*, Vol. 4 (1995), pp. 249–281.

78 Stephen A. Cernkovich and Peggy C. Giordano, "Family Relationships and Delinquency," *Criminology*, Vol. 25 (1987), pp. 295–313.

79 Gabriel Tarde, *The Laws of Imitation*, trans. E. C. Parsons (1890; reprint, Gloucester, MA: Peter Smith, 1962).

80 Albert Bandura, "The Social Learning Perspective: Mechanisms of Aggression," in Hans Toch, ed., *Psychology of Crime and Criminal Justice* (Prospect Heights, IL: Waveland, 1979), p. 198.

81 Albert Bandura, *Social Learning Theory* (Englewood Cliffs, NJ: Prentice Hall, 1977).

82 Ibid., p. 199.

83 M. M. Lefkowitz et al., "Television Violence and Child Aggression: A Follow-up Study," in G. A. Comstock and E. A. Rubinstein, eds., *Television and Social Behavior*, Vol. 3 (Washington, DC: U.S. Government Printing Office, 1972), pp. 35–135.

84 John C. Norcross, Gerald P. Koocher, and Ariele Garofalo, "Discredited Psychological Treatments and Tests: A Delphi Poll," *Professional Psychology: Research and Practice*, Vol. 37, No. 5 (2006), pp. 515–522.

85 North Carolina Department of Public Safety, Cognitive Behavioral Interventions (CBI): Standard Operating Procedures (December 2001).

86 Friedrich Losel, "Treatment and Management of Psychopaths," *NATO ASI Series*, Vol. 88 (1998), pp. 303–354.

87 Paul C. Vitz, "The Use and Abuse of Freud," a review of *Freudian Fraud: The Malignant Effect of Freud's Theory on American Thought and Culture* by E. Fuller Torrey, Leadership U., 1993, p. 52.

88 J. Bonta, M. Law, and R. K. Hanson, "The Prediction of Criminal and Violent Recidivism among Mentally Disordered Offenders: A Meta-analysis," *Psychological Bulletin*, Vol. 123 (1998), pp. 123–142.

89 Mark Solms, "Freud Returns," *Scientific American*, Vol. 290, No. 5 (May 2004), pp. 82–90.

90 Cathy Spatz Widom and Hans Toch, "The Contribution of Psychology to Criminal Justice Education," *Journal of Criminal Justice Education*, Vol. 4, No. 2 (Fall 1993), p. 253.

91 Interview by Amy Goldman, February 27, 1998, http://www.serialkillers.net/interviews/jdouglas2bak.html (accessed December 20, 2000).

92 See John Douglas and Alan Burgess, "Criminal Profiling: A Viable Investigative Tool against Violent Crime," *FBI Law Enforcement Bulletin,* December 1986.

93 Robert R. Hazelwood and John E. Douglas, "The Lust Murderer," *FBI Law Enforcement Bulletin*, April 1980.

94 Ibid.

95 Ibid.

96 Lea Winerman, "Criminal Profiling: The Reality behind the Myth," *Monitor on Psychology*, July/August 2004, http://www.apa.org/monitor/julaug04/criminal.aspx (accessed May 4, 2013).

97 University of Liverpool, School of Psychology, "Centre for Investigative Psychology," http://www.liv.ac.uk/psychology/centres/centre-for-investigative-psychology/about (accessed May 2, 2013).

98 Scott O. Lilienfeld, Steven Jay Lynn, John Ruscio, and Barry L. Beyerstein, *50 Great Myths of Popular Psychology* (Malden, MA: Wiley-Blackwell, 2010), p. 215.

99 B. Snook, J. Eastwood, P. Gendreau, C. Goggin, and R. M. Cullen, "Taking Stock of Criminal Profiling: A Narrative Review and Meta-analysis," *Criminal Justice and Behavior*, Vol. 34 (2007), pp. 437–453.

Chapter 6, Social Structure—*It's How We Live*

1 See Anthony Walsh, *Biosocial Criminology: Introduction and Integration* (Cincinnati: Anderson, 2002).

2 Emile Durkheim, *The Division of Labor in Society*, trans. George Simpson (1893; reprint, New York: Free Press, 1947).

3 Ferdinand Toennies, *Community and Society*, trans. Charles P. Loomis (1887; reprint, East Lansing: Michigan State University Press, 1957).

4 Georg Simmel, "The Metropolis and Mental Life," in Donald N. Levine, ed., *On Individuality and Social Forms* (Chicago: University of Chicago Press, 1903).

5 Durkheim, *The Division of Labor in Society*, p. 80.

6 Robert Park and Ernest Burgess, *The City* (Chicago: University of Chicago Press, 1925).

7 "Human Ecology," *Encyclopaedia Britannica* online, http://britannica.com (accessed March 7, 2007).

8 For an excellent contemporary review of measuring the extent of social disorganization, see Barbara D. Warner and Glenn L. Pierce, "Reexamining Social Disorganization Theory Using Calls to the Police as a Measure of Crime," *Criminology*, Vol. 31, No. 4 (November 1993), pp. 493–513.

9 Edwin M. Lemert, *Social Pathology* (New York: McGraw-Hill, 1951), p. 3.

10 Ibid., p. 7.

11 Clifford R. Shaw et al., *Delinquency Areas* (Chicago: University of Chicago Press, 1929).

12 David Matza, *Becoming Deviant* (Upper Saddle River, NJ: Prentice Hall, 1969).

13 Lawrence W. Sherman, Patrick R. Gartin, and Michael E. Buerger, "Hot Spots of Predatory Crime: Routine Activities and the Criminology of Place," *Criminology*, Vol. 27, No. 1 (1989), pp. 27–55.

14 See, for example, David Weisburd et al., *Putting Crime in Its Place: Units of Analysis in Geographic Criminology* (New York: Springer Science+Business Media, 2009); John E. Eck and David Weisburd, eds., *Crime and Place* (Monsey, NY: Criminal Justice Press, 1995); and Anthony A. Braga, "The Effects of Hot Spots Policing on Crime," *Annals of the American Academy of Political and Social Science*, Vol. 578 (2001), pp. 104–125.

15 National Research Council, Committee to Review Research on Police Policy and Practices, *Fairness and Effectiveness in Policing: The Evidence*, edited by Wesley Skogan and Kathleen Frydl (Washington, DC: The National Academies Press, 2004), p. 35.

16 Rodney Stark, "Deviant Places: A Theory of the Ecology of Crime," *Criminology*, Vol. 25, No. 4 (1987), p. 893.

17 Ibid., pp. 895–899.

18 James Q. Wilson and George Kelling, "Broken Windows," *Atlantic Monthly*, March 1982, pp. 1–11.

19 David Thacher, "Order Maintenance Reconsidered: Moving beyond Strong Causal Reasoning," *Journal of Criminal Law and Criminology*, Vol. 94, No. 2 (2004), pp. 381–414.

20 Oscar Newman, *Architectural Design for Crime Prevention* (Washington, DC: U.S. Department of Justice, 1973). See also Oscar Newman, *Creating Defensible Space* (Washington, DC: Office of Housing and Urban Development, 1996).

21 Oscar Newman, *Defensible Space: Crime Prevention through Urban Design* (New York: Macmillan, 1972), p. 3. See also Ralph B. Taylor and Adele V. Harrell, *Physical Environment and Crime* (Washington, DC: National Institute of Justice, May 1996).

22 Sherman, Gartin, and Buerger, "Hot Spots of Predatory Crime," p. 31.

23 See, for example, David Weisburd, Laura A. Wyckoff, Justin Ready, John E. Eck, Joshua C. Hinkle, and Frank Gajewski, "Does Crime Just Move around the Corner? A Controlled Study of Spatial Displacement and Diffusion of Crime Control Benefits," *Criminology*, Vol. 44 (2006), pp. 549–592.

24 Robert J. Bursik, "Social Disorganization and Theories of Crime and Delinquency: Problems and Prospects," *Criminology*, Vol. 26, No. 4 (1988), p. 519.

25 Stephen J. Pfohl, *Images of Deviance and Social Control* (New York: McGraw-Hill, 1985), p. 167.

26 Thomas M. Arvanites and Robert H. Defina, "Business Cycles and Street Crime," *Criminology*, Vol. 44, No. 1 (2006), p. 141.

27 Emile Durkheim, *Suicide: A Study in Sociology* (New York: Free Press, 1897).

28 "Social Structure and Anomie," *American Sociological Review*, Vol. 3 (October 1938), pp. 672–682; and Robert K. Merton, *Social Theory and Social Structure*, rev. ed. (New York: Free Press, 1957).

29 J. Blau and P. Blau, "The Cost of Inequality: Metropolitan Structure and Violent Crime," *American Sociological Review*, Vol. 147 (1982), pp. 114–129.

30 Robert Agnew, "Foundation for a General Strain Theory of Crime and Delinquency," *Criminology*, Vol. 30, No. 1 (February 1992), pp. 47–87.

31 Ibid., p. 60.

32 Agnew, "Foundation for a General Strain Theory of Crime and Delinquency."

33 Ibid., p. 48.

34 Travis Hirschi, review of Delbert S. Elliott, David Huizinga, and Suzanne S. Ageton, *Explaining Delinquency and Drug Use*, in *Criminology*, Vol. 25, No. 1 (February 1987), p. 195.

35 John Hagan, "Defiance and Despair: Subcultural and Structural Linkages between Delinquency and Despair in Life Course," *Social Forces*, Vol. 76, No. 1 (September 1997), p. 119.

36 Ibid.

37 Thorsten Sellin, *Culture Conflict and Crime* (New York: Social Science Research Council, 1938).

38 The quotations attributed to Miller in this section are from Walter Miller, "Lower Class Culture as a Generating Milieu of Gang Delinquency," *Journal of Social Issues*, Vol. 14, No. 3 (1958), pp. 5–19.

39 Gresham Sykes and David Matza, "Techniques of Neutralization: A Theory of Delinquency," *American Sociological Review*, Vol. 22 (December 1957), pp. 664–670.

40 Franco Ferracuti and Marvin Wolfgang, *The Subculture of Violence: Toward an Integrated Theory of Criminology* (London: Tavistock, 1967).

41 Richard A. Cloward and Lloyd E. Ohlin, *Delinquency and Opportunity: A Theory of Delinquent Gangs* (Glencoe, IL: Free Press, 1960).

42 Ibid., p. 3.

43 Ibid., pp. 12–13.

44 Albert Cohen, *Delinquent Boys: The Culture of the Gang* (New York: Free Press, 1955).

45 Donald J. Shoemaker, *Theories of Delinquency: An Examination of Explanations of Delinquent Behavior* (New York: Oxford University Press, 1984), p. 102, citing Cohen.

46 Cohen, *Delinquent Boys*, p. 76.

47 Elijah Anderson, *The Code of the Street: Decency, Violence, and the Moral Life of the Inner City* (New York: W. W. Norton, 1990).

48 National Gang Center, *National Youth Gang Survey Analysis*, http://www.nationalgangcenter.gov/survey-analysis (accessed May 8, 2014).

49 Carl Rogers, "Children in Gangs," *Criminal Justice, 1993–94* (Guilford, CT: Dushkin, 1993), pp. 197–199.

50 "Youths Match Power, Fear, Guns," *Fayetteville (NC) Observer-Times*, September 6, 1993, p. 2A.

51 Ibid.

52 Gwynn Nettler, *Killing One Another* (Cincinnati: Anderson, 1982), p. 67.

53 Margaret Anderson, "Review Essay: Rape Theories, Myths, and Social Change," *Contemporary Crises*, Vol. 5 (1983), p. 237.

54 Steven Schlossman et al., *Delinquency Prevention in South Chicago: A Fifty-Year Assessment of the Chicago Area Project* (Santa Monica, CA: Rand, 1984).

55 J. Robert Lilly, Francis T. Cullen, and Richard A. Ball, *Criminological Theory: Context and Consequences* (Newbury Park, CA: Sage, 1989), p. 80.

56 Lamar T. Empey, *American Delinquency: Its Meaning and Construction* (Homewood, IL: Dorsey, 1982), p. 243.

57 See James DeFronzo, "Welfare and Burglary," *Crime and Delinquency*, Vol. 42 (1996), pp. 223–230.

58 Because overall rates of crime rose throughout much of the 1970s and 1980s, the effectiveness of such programs remains very much in doubt.

59 Public Law 104–193 (August 22, 1996).

60 Sec. 103 of the Welfare Reform Act of 1996.

Chapter 7, Social Process and Social Development—*It's What We Learn*

1 Chris Jansing, "Natalee Holloway Suspect Joran van der Sloot Admits Killing Woman in Peru," MSNBC TV, January 12, 2012, http://www.msnbc.msn.com/id/45954171/ns/world_news-americas/#.Tw-fJiO5dhE (accessed March 12, 2013).

2 Frank Bajak, "Peru Court Sentences Van der Sloot to 28 Years," Associated Press, January 13, 2012, http://www.google.com/hostednews/ap/article/ALeqM5jajjHkBVW2klSZb2fTAdyV1sRsOA?docId=b61a4dfc829e429a942854d33b86cde5 (accessed March 12, 2012).

3 Edwin Sutherland, *Principles of Criminology*, 3rd ed. (New York: Lippincott, 1939).

4 Charles R. Tittle, "Theoretical Developments in Criminology," in National Institute of Justice, *Criminal Justice 2000*, Vol. 1, *The Nature of Crime: Continuity and Change* (Washington, DC: National Institute of Justice, 2000), p. 65.

5 For a good overview of social control approaches, see George S. Bridges and Martha Myers, eds., *Inequality, Crime, and Social Control* (Boulder, CO: Westview Press, 1994).

6 Walter C. Reckless, *The Crime Problem*, 4th ed. (New York: Appleton-Century-Crofts, 1967), p. 470.

7 Ibid.

8 Ibid., p. 475.

9 Howard B. Kaplan, "Self-Derogation and Violence," paper presented at the first meeting of the International Society for Research on Aggression, Toronto, August 1974. See also Howard B. Kaplan and A. D. Pokorny, "Self-Derogation as an Antecedent of Suicidal Responses," paper presented at the Eighth International Congress on Suicide Prevention and Crisis Intervention, Jerusalem, October 19–22, 1975.

10 Howard B. Kaplan, *Deviant Behavior in Defense of Self* (New York: Academic Press, 1980).

11 M. Rosenberg, C. Schooler, and C. Schoenbach, "Self-Esteem and Adolescent Problems: Modeling Reciprocal Effects," *American Sociological Review*, Vol. 54 (1989), pp. 1004–1018.

12 L. E. Wells, "Self-Enhancement through Delinquency: A Conditional Test of Self-Derogation Theory," *Journal of Research in Crime and Delinquency*, Vol. 26, No. 3 (1989), pp. 226–252.

13 Travis Hirschi, *Causes of Delinquency* (Berkeley: University of California Press, 1969).

14 Ibid.

15 Ibid.

16 Ibid.

17 Ibid.

18 Ibid.

19 Ibid.

20 Ibid.

21 Michael Gottfredson and Travis Hirschi, *A General Theory of Crime* (Stanford, CA: Stanford University Press, 1990).

22 See also Michael R. Gottfredson and Travis Hirschi, "Criminality and Low Self-Control," in John E. Conklin, ed., *New Perspectives in Criminology* (Boston: Allyn & Bacon, 1996).

23 Gottfredson and Hirschi, *A General Theory of Crime.*

24 Ibid.

25 J. Mitchell Miller, ed., *Encyclopedia of Criminology*, Vol. 3 (New York: Routledge, 2005), pp. 1480–1482.

26 Charles R. Tittle, *Control Balance: Toward a General Theory of Deviance* (Boulder, CO: Westview Press, 1995).

27 For an excellent summation of control-balance theory, see Alex R. Piquero and Matthew Hickman, "An Empirical Test of Tittle's Control Balance Theory," *Criminology*, Vol. 37, No. 2 (1999), pp. 319–341.

28 Tittle, *Control Balance*, p. 181.

29 Piquero and Hickman, "An Empirical Test of Tittle's Control Balance Theory," p. 327.

30 Tittle, *Control Balance*, p. 95. For a good critique of control-balance theory, see Joachim J. Savelsberg, "Human Nature and Social Control in Complex Society: A Critique of Charles Tittle's Control Balance," *Theoretical Criminology*, Vol. 3, No. 3 (August 1999), pp. 331–338.

31 Margaret Colgate Love, "What's in a Name? A Lot, When the Name Is 'Felon,'" *The Crime Report*, March 13, 2012, http://www.thecrimereport.org/viewpoints/2012-03-whats-in-a-name-a-lot-when-the-name-is-felon (accessed August 3, 2014).

32 Frank Tannenbaum, *Crime and the Community* (New York: Atheneum Press, 1938), pp. 17–18.

33 Howard Becker, *Outsiders: Studies in the Sociology of Deviance* (New York: Free Press, 1963), p. 1.

34 Ibid., p. 9.

35 NORML, "About NORML," http://norml.org/about (accessed February 23, 2014).

36 Randy Martin, Robert J. Mutchnick, and W. Timothy Austin, *Criminological Thought: Pioneers Past and Present* (New York: Macmillan, 1990), p. 368.

37 P.L. 93–415; 42 U.S.C. § 5667e.

38 See Kevin Haggerty et al., *Preparing for the Drug Free Years* (Washington, DC: Office of Juvenile Justice and Delinquency Prevention, 1999), http://www.ncjrs.gov/html/jjbulletin/9907/theo.html (accessed March 11, 2005).

39 Ibid., at http://www.ncjrs.gov/html/jjbulletin/9907/theo.html (accessed March 11, 2005).

40 Haggerty et al., *Preparing for the Drug Free Years.*

41 Material in this paragraph is adapted from Finn-Aage Esbensen, "Preventing Adolescent Gang Involvement," *OJJDP Juvenile Justice Bulletin* (Washington, DC: Office of Juvenile Justice and Delinquency Prevention, September 2000).

42 See R. E. Tremblay et al., "From Childhood Physical Aggression to Adolescent Maladjustment: The Montreal Prevention Experiment," in R. D. Peters and R. J. McMahon, eds., *Preventing Childhood Disorders, Substance Abuse, and Delinquency* (Thousand Oaks, CA: Sage, 1996), pp. 268–298.

43 For some influential writings of the period, see K. F. Riegel, "Toward a Dialectical Theory of Development," *Human Development*, Vol. 18 (1975), pp. 50–64; and U. Bronfenbrenner, *The Ecology of Human Development* (Cambridge: Harvard University Press, 1979).

44 Elaine Eggleston Doherty, "Self-Control, Social Bonds, and Desistance," *Criminology*, Vol. 44, No. 4 (November, 2006), pp. 807–808.

45 A. Blumstein et al., eds., *Criminal Careers and Career Criminals* (Washington, DC: National Academy Press, 1986).

46 See Alfred Blumstein et al., "Introduction: Studying Criminal Careers," in A. Blumstein et al., eds., *Criminal Careers and Career Criminals* (Washington, DC: National Academy Press), p. 12.

47 Blumstein et al., *Criminal Careers and Career Criminals*, pp. 12–30.

48 Robert J. Sampson and John H. Laub, *Crime in the Making: Pathways and Turning Points through the Life Course* (Cambridge, MA: Harvard University Press, 1993).

49 G. H. Elder, Jr., "Perspectives on the Life-Course," in G. H. Elder, Jr., ed., *Life-Course Dynamics* (Ithaca, NY: Cornell University Press, 1985).

50 Philip W. Harris, Wayne N. Welsh, and Frank Butler, "A Century of Juvenile Justice," *Criminal Justice 2000*, Vol. 1 (Washington, DC: National Institute of Justice, 2000).

51 G. H. Elder, Jr., ed., *Life-Course Dynamics* (Ithaca, NY: Cornell University Press, 1985).

52 Robert J. Sampson and John H. Laub, "Understanding Variability in Lives through Time: Contributions of Life-Course Criminology," in Alex Piquero and Paul Mazerolle, eds., *Life-Course Criminology: Contemporary and Classic Readings* (Belmont, CA: Wadsworth, 2001), p. 243.

53 Marc LeBlanc and Rolf Loeber, "Developmental Criminology Updated," in Michael Tonry, ed., *Crime and Justice: A Review of Research*, Vol. 23 (Chicago: University of Chicago Press, 1998).

54 Adapted from Harris, Welsh, and Butler, "A Century of Juvenile Justice," p. 379.

55 Glen H. Elder, Jr., "Time, Human Agency, and Social Change: Perspectives on the Life Course," *Social Psychology Quarterly*, Vol. 57, No. 1 (1994), pp. 4–15.

56 Glen H. Elder, Jr., "The Life Course as Developmental Theory," *Child Development*, Vol. 69, No. 1 (1998), pp. 1–12, from which some of the wording in this section is taken.

57 See, for example, the collected papers of Sheldon Glueck, 1916–1972, which are part of the David L. Bazelon collection at Harvard University Law School (Cambridge, MA). Results of the Gluecks' work were reported in S. Glueck and E. Glueck, *Unraveling Juvenile Delinquency* (New York: The Commonwealth Fund, 1950).

58 Sheldon Glueck and Eleanor Glueck, *Delinquents and Nondelinquents in Perspective* (Cambridge, MA: Harvard University Press, 1968).

59 David S. Kirk, "Residential Change as a Turning Point in the Life Course of Crime: Desistance or Temporary Cessation?" *Criminology*, Vol. 50, No. 2 (2012), p. 1.

60 John H. Laub and Robert J. Sampson, "Urban Poverty and the Family Context of Delinquency: A New Look at Structure and Process in a Classic Study," *Child Development*, Vol. 65 (1994), pp. 523–540. See also John H. Laub and Robert J. Sampson, "Turning Points in the Life Course: Why Change Matters to the Study of Crime," *Criminology*, Vol. 31, No. 3 (1993), pp. 301–325; and Robert J. Sampson and John H. Laub, "Crime and Deviance in the Life Course," *Annual Review of Sociology*, Vol. 18 (1992), pp. 63–84.

61 See John H. Laub and Leana C. Allen, "Life Course Criminology and Community Corrections," *Perspectives*, Vol. 24, No. 2 (Spring 2000), pp. 20–29.

62 Sampson and Laub, "Crime and Deviance in the Life Course," pp. 63–84.

63 John H. Laub, "The Life Course of Criminology in the United States: The American Society of Criminology 2003 Presidential Address," *Criminology*, Vol. 42, No. 1 (2004), pp. 1–26.

64 Laub and Sampson, "Turning Points in the Life Course."

65 Ibid.

66 See Laub and Allen, "Life Course Criminology and Community Corrections," pp. 20–29.

67 Sampson and Laub, *Crime in the Making.*

68 Moffitt, "Adolescence-Limited and Life-Course-Persistent Antisocial Behavior," pp. 674–701.

69 Adapted from Tittle, "Theoretical Developments in Criminology."

70 Moffitt, "Adolescence-Limited and Life-Course-Persistent Antisocial Behavior."

71 Family and Youth Services Bureau, *Understanding Youth Development: Promoting Positive Pathways of Growth* (Washington, DC: U.S. Department of Health and Human Services, 2000).

72 Sheldon Glueck and Eleanor Glueck, *Later Criminal Careers* (New York: The Commonwealth Fund, 1937), p. 105.

73 Walter R. Grove, "The Effect of Age and Gender on Deviant Behavior: A Biopsychosocial Perspective," in Alice S. Rossi, ed., *Gender and the Life Course* (New York: Aldine, 1985).

74 Ibid., p. 128.

75 David P. Farrington, "The Twelfth Jack Tizard Memorial Lecture: The Development of Offending and Antisocial Behavior from Childhood—Key Findings

from the Cambridge Study in Delinquent Development," *Journal of Child Psychology and Psychiatry*, Vol. 360 (1995), pp. 929–964.

76 David P. Farrington, "Explaining and Preventing Crime: The Globalization of Knowledge: The American Society of Criminology 1999 Presidential Address," *Criminology*, Vol. 38, No. 1 (February 2000), pp. 1–24.

77 Rolf Loeber and Marc LeBlanc, "Toward a Developmental Criminology," in M. Tonry and N. Morris, eds., *Crime and Justice: A Review of Research*, Vol. 12 (Chicago: University of Chicago Press, 1990).

78 Piquero and Mazerolle, *Life-Course Criminology*, p. xv.

79 Marvin Wolfgang, Robert Figlio, and Thorsten Sellin, *Delinquency in a Birth Cohort* (Chicago: University of Chicago Press, 1972).

80 Marvin Wolfgang, Terence Thornberry, and Robert Figlio, *From Boy to Man, from Delinquency to Crime* (Chicago: University of Chicago Press, 1987).

81 Marvin Wolfgang, "Delinquency in China: Study of a Birth Cohort," *National Institute of Justice Research Preview* (Washington, DC: 1996).

82 Lawrence E. Cohen and Richard Machalek, "A General Theory of Expropriative Crime: An Evolutionary Ecological Approach," *American Journal of Sociology*, Vol. 94, No. 3 (1988), pp. 465–501; and Lawrence E. Cohen and Richard Machalek, "The Normalcy of Crime: From Durkheim to Evolutionary Ecology," *Rationality and Society*, Vol. 6 (1994), pp. 286–308.

83 Bryan Vila, "Human Nature and Crime Control: Improving the Feasibility of Nurturant Strategies," *Politics and the Life Sciences*, Vol. 16, No. 1 (March 1997), pp. 3–21.

84 Ibid.

85 Steven P. Lab, "Analyzing Change in Crime and Delinquency Rates: The Case for Cohort Analysis," *Criminal Justice Research Bulletin*, Vol. 3, No. 10 (Huntsville, TX: Sam Houston State University, 1988), p. 2.

86 Terence Thornberry, "Toward an Interactional Theory of Delinquency," *Criminology*, Vol. 25 (1987), pp. 863–891.

87 See Terence P. Thornberry, Alan J. Lizotte, Marvin D. Krohn, Margaret Farnworth, and Sung Joon Jang, "Delinquent Peers, Beliefs, and Delinquent Behavior: A Longitudinal Test of Interactional Theory," *Criminology*, Vol. 32, No. 1 (1994), pp. 47–53.

88 Terence P. Thornberry, Alan J. Lizotte, Marvin D. Krohn, Margaret Farnworth, and Sung Joon Jang, "Testing Interactional Theory: An Examination of Reciprocal Causal Relationships among Family, School and Delinquency," *Journal of Criminal Law and Criminology*, Vol. 82 (1991), pp. 3–35.

89 Carolyn Smith and Terence P. Thornberry, "The Relationship between Childhood Maltreatment and Adolescent Involvement in Delinquency," *Criminology*, Vol. 33, No. 4 (1995), pp. 451–477.

90 Barbara Tatem Kelley et al., *Developmental Pathways in Boys' Disruptive and Delinquent Behavior* (Washington, DC: Office of Juvenile Justice and Delinquency Prevention, December 1997).

91 R. Loeber and D. F. Hay, "Developmental Approaches to Aggression and Conduct Problems," in M. Rutter and D. F. Hay, eds., *Development through Life: A Handbook for Clinicians* (Oxford, England: Blackwell Scientific, 1994).

92 Ibid.

93 The Causes and Correlates of Delinquency study is being conducted by Terence P. Thornberry of the Rochester Youth Development Study at the State University of New York at Albany, New York, Rolf Loeber of the Pittsburgh Youth Study at the University of Pittsburgh, and David Huizinga of the Denver Youth Survey at the University of Colorado.

94 Adapted from Katharine Browning et al., "Causes and Correlates of Delinquency Program," *OJJDP Fact Sheet* (Washington, DC: U.S. Department of Justice, April 1999).

95 Compiled from Katharine Browning and Rolf Loeber, "Highlights of Findings from the Pittsburgh Youth Study," *OJJDP Fact Sheet* (Washington, DC: U.S. Department of Justice, February 1999); Katharine Browning, Terence P. Thornberry, and Pamela K. Porter, "Highlights of Findings from the Rochester Youth Development Study," *OJJDP Fact Sheet* (Washington, DC: U.S. Department of Justice, April 1999); and Katharine Browning and David Huizinga, "Highlights of Findings from the Denver Youth Survey," *OJJDP Fact Sheet* (Washington, DC: U.S. Department of Justice, April 1999).

96 Browning and Huizinga, "Highlights of Findings from the Denver Youth Survey."

97 Kelley et al., *Developmental Pathways in Boys' Disruptive and Delinquent Behavior.*

98 Ibid., p. 14.

99 See Felton J. Earls and Albert J. Reiss, *Breaking the Cycle: Predicting and Preventing Crime* (Washington, DC: National Institute of Justice, 1994), http://www.ncjrs.gov/txtfiles/break.txt (accessed March 12, 2006).

100 Ibid.

101 Ibid.

102 Adapted from the MacArthur Foundation, "The Project on Human Development in Chicago Neighborhoods," http://www.macfound.org/research/hcd/hcd_5.htm (accessed January 5, 2006).

103 Project on Human Development in Chicago Neighborhoods press release, "Study of Chicago Finds Neighborhood Efficacy Explains Reductions in Violence," no date, http://phdcn.harvard.edu/press/index.htm (accessed January 5, 2006).

104 Vila, "Human Nature and Crime Control," p. 10.

105 Robert W. Sweet, Jr., "Preserving Families to Prevent Delinquency," *Office of Juvenile Justice and Delinquency Prevention Model Programs, 1990* (Washington, DC: U.S. Department of Justice, April 1992).

106 Ibid.

Chapter 8, Social Conflict—*It's How We Relate*

1 "Occupy Wall Street: About," http://occupywallst.org/about (accessed May 3, 2014).

2 Excerpt from We Are The 99 Percent. Copyright by wearethe99percent.us. Used by permission of wearethe99percent.

3 Burke R. Hopkins, *An Introduction to Criminological Theory*, 2nd ed. (Cullompton, England: Willan Publishing, 2006), p. 173.

4 Vance Packard, *The Status Seekers* (London: Harmondsworth, 1961).

5 Willem Bonger, *Criminality and Economic Conditions* (Bloomington: Indiana University Press, 1969). Originally published in Amsterdam as *Criminalite et Conditions Economiques* (1905); translated into English in 1916.

6 Georg Simmel, *Conflict and the Web of Group Affiliations* (New York: Free Press, 1964). Originally published in 1908.

7 George B. Void, *Theoretical Criminology* (New York: Oxford University Press, 1958).

8 Ibid., p. 205.

9 Ibid., p. 206.

10 Ibid., pp. 208–209.

11 Ibid., p. 309.

12 Ralf Dahrendorf, *Class and Class Conflict in Industrial Society* (Stanford, CA: Stanford University Press, 1959).

13 Ralf Dahrendorf, "Out of Utopia: Toward a Reorientation of Sociological Analysis," *American Journal of Sociology*, Vol. 64 (1958), pp. 115–127.

14 Austin Turk, *Criminality and Legal Order* (Chicago: Rand McNally, 1969), p. vii.

15 lbid.

16 William J. Chambliss, "Toward a Political Economy of Crime," in C. Reasons and R. Rich, eds., *The Sociology of Law* (Toronto: Butterworth, 1978), p. 193.

17 William Chambliss and Robert T. Seidman, *Law, Order, and Power* (Reading, MA: Addison-Wesley, 1971), p. 33.

18 Adapted from ibid., pp. 473–474.

19 William J. Chambliss, *Crime and the Legal Process* (New York: McGraw-Hill, 1969), p. 88.

20 Chambliss, "Toward a Political Economy of Crime."

21 Ibid.

22 Ibid., p. 152.

23 Ibid.

24 Richard Quinney, *Critique of the Legal Order: Crime Control in Capitalist Society* (Boston: Little, Brown, 1974), p. 16; and Richard Quinney, *Bearing Witness to Crime and Social Justice* (Albany, NY: SUNY Press, 2000), p. 107.

25 Quinney, *Bearing Witness to Crime and Social Justice*, p. 110.

26 Richard Quinney, *Class, State, and Crime: On the Theory and Practice of Criminal Justice* (New York: David McKay, 1977), p. 58.

27 Ibid.

28 Ibid., p. 61.

29 William V. Pelfrey, *The Evolution of Criminology* (Cincinnati: Anderson, 1980), p. 86.

30 For a good overview of critiques of radical criminology, see J. F. Galliher, "Life and Death of Liberal Criminology," *Contemporary Crisis*, Vol. 2, No. 3 (July 1978), pp. 245–263.

31 Jackson Toby, "The New Criminology Is the Old Sentimentality," *Criminology*, Vol. 16 (1979), pp. 516–526.

32 Carl Klockars, "The Contemporary Crisis of Marxist Criminology," *Criminology*, Vol. 16 (1979), pp. 477–515.

33 Ibid.

34 Hermann Mannheim, *Comparative Criminology* (Boston: Houghton Mifflin, 1965), p. 445.

35 Ibid., p. 65.

36 Quinney, *Bearing Witness to Crime and Social Justice*, p. 110.

37 The quotations attributed to Currie in this section are from Elliott Currie, "Market, Crime, and Community," *Theoretical Criminology*, Vol. 1, No. 2 (May 1997), pp. 147–172.

38 For examples of how this might be accomplished, see F. H. Knopp, "Community Solutions to Sexual Violence: Feminist/Abolitionist Perspectives," in Harold E. Pepinsky and Richard Quinney, eds., *Criminology as Peacemaking* (Bloomington: Indiana University Press), pp. 181–193; and S. Caringella-MacDonald and D. Humphries, "Sexual Assault, Women, and the Community: Organizing to Prevent Sexual Violence," in Pepinsky and Quinney, eds., *Criminology as Peacemaking*, pp. 98–113.

39 Richard Quinney, "Life of Crime: Criminology and Public Policy as Peacemaking," *Journal of Crime and Justice*, Vol. 16, No. 2 (1993), pp. 3–9.

40 See, for example, Harold E. Pepinsky, "This Can't Be Peace: A Pessimist Looks at Punishment," in W. B. Groves and G. Newman, eds., *Punishment and Privilege* (Albany, NY: Harrow and Heston, 1986); Harold E. Pepinsky, "Violence as Unresponsiveness: Toward a New Conception of Crime," *Justice Quarterly*, Vol. 5 (1988), pp. 539–563; and Pepinsky and Quinney, eds., *Criminology as Peacemaking*.

41 See, for example, Richard Quinney, "Crime, Suffering, Service: Toward a Criminology of Peacemaking," *Quest*, Vol. 1 (1988), pp. 66–75; Richard Quinney, "The Theory and Practice of Peacemaking in the Development of Radical Criminology," *Critical Criminologist*, Vol. 1, No. 5 (1989), p. 5; and Richard Quinney and John Wildeman, *The Problem of Crime: A Peace and Social Justice Perspective*, 3rd ed. (Mayfield, CA: Mountain View Press, 1991). Originally published as *The Problem of Crime: A Critical Introduction to Criminology* (New York: Bantam, 1977).

42 Hal Pepinsky, "Peacemaking," in Stuart Henry and Mark M. Lanier, eds., *The Essential Criminology Reader* (Cambridge, MA: Westview Press, 2006), p. 278.

43 All of these themes are addressed, for example, in Pepinsky and Quinney, eds., *Criminology as Peacemaking*.

44 Quinney and Wildeman, *The Problem of Crime*, pp. vii–viii.

45 Quinney, "Life of Crime," abstract.

46 Bo Lozoff and Michael Braswell, *Inner Corrections: Finding Peace and Peace Making* (Cincinnati: Anderson, 1989).

47 Clemens Bartollas and Michael Braswell, "Correctional Treatment, Peacemaking, and the New Age Movement," *Journal of Crime and Justice*, Vol. 16, No. 2 (1993), pp. 43–58.

48 Ram Dass and Paul Gorman, *How Can I Help? Stories and Reflections on Service* (New York: Alfred A. Knopf, 1985), p. 165, as cited in Quinney and Wildeman, *The Problem of Crime*, p. 116.

49 Bo Lozoff and Michael Braswell, *Inner Corrections: Finding Peace and Peace Making* (Cincinnati: Anderson, 1989), p. vii.

50 E. M. Schur, *Labeling Women Deviant: Gender, Stigma, and Social Control* (Philadelphia: Temple University Press, 1984), p. 10.

51 Walter S. DeKeseredy, *Contemporary Critical Criminology* (New York: Routledge, 2011), p. 29.

52 K. Daly and M. Chesney-Lind, "Feminism and Criminology," *Justice Quarterly*, Vol. 5 (1988), p. 502.

53 James W. Messerschmidt, *Capitalism, Patriarchy and Crime: Toward a Socialist Feminist Criminology* (Totowa, NJ: Rowman and Littlefield, 1986).

54 Don C. Gibbons, *Talking about Crime and Criminals*, p. 165, citing Loraine Gelsthorpe and Alison Morris, "Feminism and Criminology in Britain," *British Journal of Criminology* (Spring 1988), pp. 93–110.

55 Sally S. Simpson, "Feminist Theory, Crime and Justice," *Criminology*, Vol. 27, No. 4 (1989), p. 605.

56 Carol Pateman, "Feminist Critiques of the Public/Private Dichotomy," in Anne Phillips, ed., *Feminism and Equality* (Oxford, England: Blackwell, 1987).

57 F. P. Williams III and M. D. McShane, *Criminological Theory* (Upper Saddle River, NJ: Prentice Hall, 1994), p. 238.

58 Freda Adler, *Sisters in Crime: The Rise of the New Female Criminal* (New York: McGraw-Hill, 1975).

59 Rita J. Simon, *Women and Crime* (Lexington, MA: Lexington Books, 1975).

60 Carol Smart, *Women, Crime and Criminology: A Feminist Critique* (London: Routledge, 1977).

61 Kathleen Daly and Meda Chesney-Lind, "Feminism and Criminology," *Justice Quarterly*, Vol. 5, No. 4 (December 1988), pp. 497–538.

62 Ibid.

63 Ibid., p. 514.

64 For an intriguing analysis of how existing laws tend to criminalize women and their reproductive activities, see Roslyn Muraskin, ed., *Women and Justice: It's a Crime*, 5e. (Upper Saddle River, NJ: Prentice Hall, 2012).

65 Ngaire Naffine, *Feminism and Criminology* (Philadelphia: Temple University Press, 1996).

66 John Hagan, *Structural Criminology* (New Brunswick, NJ: Rutgers University Press, 1989), p. 130.

67 Ibid., p. 13.

68 Ibid.

69 For an excellent overview of feminist theory in criminology and a comprehensive review of research regarding female offenders, see Joanne Belknap, *The Invisible Woman: Gender, Crime and Justice* (Belmont, CA: Wadsworth, 1996).

70 Ronald L. Akers, *Criminological Theories: Introduction and Evaluation* (Los Angeles: Roxbury, 1994), p. 39.

71 Such studies are still ongoing and continue to add to the descriptive literature of feminist criminology. See, for example, Deborah R. Baskin and Ira Sommers, "Female Initiation into Violent Street Crime," *Justice Quarterly*, Vol. 10, No. 4 (December 1993), pp. 559–583; Scott Decker et al., "A Woman's Place Is in the Home: Females and Residential Burglary," *Justice Quarterly*, Vol. 10, No. 1 (March 1993), pp. 143–162; and Jill L. Rosenbaum, "The Female Delinquent: Another Look at the Role of the Family," in Roslyn Muraskin and Ted Alleman, eds., *It's a Crime: Woman and Justice* (Upper Saddle River, NJ: Prentice Hall, 1993), pp. 399–420.

72 For additional insight into the notion of deconstruction as it applies to feminist thought within criminology, see Carol Smart, *Feminism and the Power of Law* (New York: Routledge, 1989).

73 Karen Heimer, "Changes in the Gender Gap in Crime and Women's Economic Marginalization," in *The Nature of Crime: Continuity and Change, Criminal Justice 2000*, Vol. 1 (Washington, DC: National Institute of Justice, 2000), p. 428.

74 Citing Allison Morris, *Women, Crime and Criminal Justice* (New York: Blackwell, 1987).

75 Stephen C. Richards, "Introducing the New School of Convict Criminology," *Social Justice*, Vol. 28, No. 1 (2001), p. 177.

76 Stephen C. Richards and Jeffrey Ian Ross, "Convict Criminology," in Richard A. Wright and J. Mitchell Miller, eds., *Encyclopedia of Criminology*, Vol. 1 (New York: Routledge, 2005), pp. 232–236.

77 Ibid., p. 233.

78 John Irwin, *The Felon* (Upper Saddle River, NJ: Prentice Hall, 1970).

79 K. C. Carceral et al., *Behind a Convict's Eyes: Doing Time in a Modern Prison* (New York: Wadsworth, 2003).

80 K. C. Carceral and Thomas J. Bernard, *Prison, Inc.: A Convict Exposes Life inside a Private Prison* (New York: New York University Press, 2006).

81 Stephen C. Richards and Jeffrey Ian Ross, "Convict Criminology," in Richard A. Wright and J. Mitchell Miller, eds., *Encyclopedia of Criminology*, Vol. 1 (New York: Routledge, 2005), pp. 232–236; and Matthew B. Robinson, *Justice Blind: Ideals and Realities of American Criminal Justice*, 2nd ed. (Upper Saddle River, NJ: Prentice Hall, 2005).

82 Richards and Ross, p. 235.

83 Gregg Barak, "Introduction: Criminological Theory in the 'Postmodernist' Era," in Barak, ed., *Varieties of Criminology* (Santa Barbara, CA: Praeger, 1993), pp. 1–11.

84 Stuart Henry and Dragan Milovanovic, "Postmodernism and Constitutive Theories of Criminal Behavior," in Richard A. Wright and J. Mitchell Miller, eds., *Encyclopedia of Criminology*, Vol. 2 (New York: Routledge, 2005), pp. 1245–1249.

85 Joycelyn M. Pollock, *Criminal Women* (Cincinnati: Anderson, 1999), p. 146.

86 Walter S. DeKeseredy, *Contemporary Critical Criminology* (New York: Routledge, 2011), p. 48.

87 For an excellent and detailed discussion of many of these approaches, see Dragan Milovanovic, *Postmodern Criminology* (Hamden, CT: Garland, 1997).

88 See, for example, Stuart Henry and Dragan Milovanovic, *Constitutive Criminology: Beyond Postmodernism* (London: Sage, 1995); and Milovanovic, *Postmodern Criminology*.

89 Milovanovic, *Postmodern Criminology*.

90 Dragan Milovanovic, *Primer in the Sociology of Law*, 2nd ed. (New York: Harrow and Heston, 1994).

91 Ibid.

92 Henry and Milovanovic, *Constitutive Criminology*, p. 118.

93 Werner Einstadter and Stuart Henry, *Criminological Theory: An Analysis of Its Underlying Assumptions* (Fort Worth, TX: Harcourt Brace, 1995), p. 291.

94 Ian Taylor, Paul Walton, and Jock Young, *The New Criminology: For a Social Theory of Deviance* (London: Routledge, 1973); and Ian Taylor, Paul Walton, and Jock Young, *Critical Criminology* (London: Routledge, 1975).

95 Ian Taylor, "Crime and Social Criticism," *Social Justice*, Vol. 26, No. 2 (1999), p. 150.

96 Ibid.

97 Ibid.

98 Bruce A. Arrigo, "Postmodern Theory and Criminology," in Stuart Henry and Mark M. Lanier, eds., *The Essential Criminology Reader* (Boulder, CO: Westview, 2006), p. 225.

99 Raymond J. Michalowski, *Order, Law, and Crime: An Introduction to Criminology* (New York: Random House, 1985), p. 410.

100 Ibid., p. 128.

101 Walter S. DeKeseredy, *Contemporary Critical Criminology* (New York: Routledge, 2011)), pp. 89–93.

102 U.S. Department of Education, National Center for Education Statistics, National Assessment of Education Progress, http://nces.ed.gov/nationsreportcard (accessed February 15, 2012).

103 Paul Ashton, "The Education of D.C.: How Washington D.C.'s Investments in Education Can Help Increase Public Safety," Justice Policy Institute, February 15, 2012, http://www.justicepolicy.org/research/3535?utm_source=Education+of+D.C.-2%2F14%2F12&utm_campaign=DC+Education+Brief&utm_medium=email (accessed February 15, 2014).

104 For a good overview of such programs, see Thomas E. Carbonneau, *Alternative Dispute Resolution: Melting the Lances and Dismounting the Steeds* (Chicago: University of Illinois Press, 1989).

105 Fay Honey Knopp, "Community Solutions to Sexual Violence: Feminist-Abolitionist Perspectives," in Pepinsky and Quinney, eds., *Criminology as Peacemaking*, p. 183.

106 Ibid.

107 Daniel Van Ness and Karen Heetderks Strong, *Restoring Justice* (Cincinnati: Anderson, 1997), p. 31.

108 Office of Juvenile Justice and Delinquency Prevention, *Balanced and Restorative Justice: Program Summary* (Washington, DC: OJJDP, no date), p. 2, from which some of the wording in this section is adapted.

109 Milwaukee County District Attorney's Office, "Community Conferencing Program," no date.

110 Ibid.

Chapter 9, Crimes against Persons—*What We Fear*

1 "Police Union Warns Visitors about 'War-Like' Detroit," *Police Magazine*, October 8, 2012, http://www.policemag.com/channel/patrol/news/2012/10/08/police-union-warns-visitors-about-war-like-detroit.aspx (accessed May 3, 2013).

2 FBI, *Crime in the United States, 2012* (Washington, DC: U.S. Department of Justice, 2013).

3. Access NCJRS on the Web at http://www.ncjrs.gov.

4. This and other UCR statistics in this chapter are taken from FBI, *Crime in the United States, 2012.*

5 Marvin Wolfgang and Franco Ferracuti, *The Subculture of Violence: Towards an Integrated Theory in Criminology* (1967; reprint, Beverly Hills, CA: Sage, 1982).

6 Marc Reidel and Margaret A. Zahn, *The Nature and Patterns of American Homicide* (Washington, DC: U.S. Government Printing Office, 1985). See also Margaret A. Zahn and P. C. Sagi, "Stranger Homicide in Nine American Cities," *Journal of Criminal Law and Criminology*, Vol. 78, No. 2 (1987), pp. 377–397.

7 Kirk R. Williams and Robert L. Flewelling, "The Social Production of Criminal Homicide: A Comparative Study of Disaggregated Rates in American Cities," *American Sociological Review*, Vol. 53, No. 3 (1988), pp. 421–431.

8 Lynne A. Curtis, *American Violence and Public Policy* (New Haven, CT: Yale University Press, 1985); and Lynne A. Curtis, *Violence, Race and Culture* (Lexington, MA: Lexington Books, 1975).

9 Claude S. Fisher, "Toward a Subcultural Theory of Urbanism," *American Journal of Sociology*, Vol. 80 (1975), p. 1335.

10 Steven Messner, "Poverty, Inequality and Urban Homicide Rate," *Criminology*, Vol. 20 (1982), pp. 103–114; and Steven Messner, "Regional and Racial Effects on the Urban Homicide Rate," *American Journal of Sociology*, Vol. 88 (1983), pp. 997–1007.

11 Robert Sampson, "Neighborhood Family Structure and the Risk of Personal Victimization," in James Byrne and Robert J. Sampson, eds., *The Social Ecology of Crime* (New York: Springer-Verlag, 1985), and Robert J. Sampson, "Structural Sources in Variation in Race-Age Specific Rates of Offending across Major U.S. Cities," *Criminology*, Vol. 23, No. 4 (1985), pp. 647–673.

12 Marvin E. Wolfgang, *Patterns in Criminal Homicide* (New York: Wiley, 1958).

13 Ibid.

14 Robert Nash Parker and Dwayne M. Smith, "Deterrence, Poverty and Type of Homicide" *American Journal of Sociology*, Vol. 85 (1979), pp. 614–624; and M. Dwayne Smith and Robert Nash Parker, "Types of Homicide and Variation in Regional Rates," *Social Forces*, Vol. 59 (1980), pp. 136–147.

15 The distinction between expressive and instrumental crimes has been incorporated into much research on different crimes. This approach originated in the work of Richard Block and Franklin Zimring, "Homicide in Chicago, 1965–1970," *Journal of Research in Crime and Delinquency*, Vol. 10 (1973), pp. 1–12.

16 Terance D. Miethe and Kriss A. Drass, "Exploring the Social Context of Instrumental and Expressive Homicides: An Application of Qualitative Comparative Analysis," *Journal of Quantitative Criminology*, Vol. 15, No. 1 (1999), p. 3.

17 Carolyn Rebecca Block and Richard Block, "Beginning with Wolfgang: An Agenda for Homicide Research," *Journal of Crime and Justice*, Vol. 24, No. 2 (1991), p. 42.

18 Ibid., p. 54.

19 Wolfgang, *Patterns in Criminal Homicide*, p. 2.

20 Ibid., p. 9.

21 Ibid.

22 Philip J. Cook and Mark H. Moore, "Guns, Gun Control, and Homicide," in M. Dwayne Smith and Margaret A. Zahn, eds., *Studying and Preventing Homicide: Issues and Challenges* (Thousand Oaks, CA: Sage, 1999), p. 252.

23 Ibid., p. 254.

24 Ibid., p. 266.

25 Bureau of Justice Statistics, *Report to the Nation on Crime and Justice*, 2nd ed. (Washington, DC: U.S. Government Printing Office, 1988), p. 4. According to the FBI, the term "serial killings" means "a series of three or more killings, not less than one of which was committed within the United States, having common characteristics such as to suggest the reasonable possibility that the crimes were committed by the same actor or actors." See http://www.fbi.gov/stats-services/publications/serial-murder/serial-murder-1.

26 James Alan Fox and Jack Levin, "Serial Murder: Myths and Realities," in Smith and Zahn, eds., *Studying and Preventing Homicide: Issues and Challenges* (Thousand Oaks, CA: Sage, 1999), p. 84.

27 Ibid.

28 Ibid.

29 Ronald Holmes and J. DeBurger, "Profiles in Terror: The Serial Murderer," *Federal Probation*, Vol. 49, No. 3 (1985), pp. 29–34.

30 Fox and Levin, "Serial Murder."

31 Stephen T. Holmes, Eric Hickey, and Ronald M. Holmes, "Female Serial Murderesses: Constructing Different Typologies," *Journal of Contemporary Criminal Justice*, Vol. 7, No. 4 (1991), pp. 245–256.

32 Ibid.

33 Ibid.

34 Michael D. Kelleher and C. L. Kelleher, *Murder Most Rare: The Female Serial Killer* (Westport, CT: Praeger, 1998).

35 Ibid., p. 11.

36 Ibid., p. 7.

37 Thomas O'Reilly-Fleming, "The Evolution of Multiple Murder in Historical Perspective," in Thomas O'Reilly-Fleming, ed., *Serial and Mass Murder: Theory, Research, and Policy* (Toronto: Canadian Scholars' Press, 1996).

38 Richard Winton, Rosanna Xia, Rong-Gong Lin II, "Isla Vista Shooting: Read Eliot Rodger's Elaborate Attack Plan," *Los Angeles Times*, http://www.latimes.com/local/lanow/la-me-ln-isla-vista-document-20140524-story.html, May 25, 2014 (accessed May 26, 2014).

39 Solomon Banda, "James Holmes, Alleged Aurora Shooter, Shows No Emotion to Court Discussion of Victims' Charity," *Huffington Post*, August 16, 2012, http://www.huffingtonpost.com/2012/08/17/james-holmes-court-appearance-victims_n_1795932.html (accessed August 17, 2014).

40 Joe Taschler, "Security Experts Prepare Steps to Deal with 'Active Shooters,'" *Journal Sentinel*, August 13, 2012, http://www.jsonline.com/business/security-experts-prepare-steps-to-deal-with-active-shooters-9t6d08i-166029386.html (accessed August 17, 2013).

41 Jack Levin and James Alan Fox, "A Psycho-social Analysis of Mass Murder," in O'Reilly-Fleming, ed., *Serial and Mass Murder*, p. 65.

42 Ibid., p. 66.

43 Ibid., p. 69.

44 Per Nyberg and Laura Smith-Spark, "Anger in Norway over Claim Anders Breivik Has Applied to University," CNN, http://www.cnn.com/2013/07/31/world/europe/norway-breivik-university (accessed August 5, 2013).

45 Susan Candioti, Greg Botelho, and Tom Watkins, "Newtown Shooting Details Revealed in Newly Released Documents," CNN, March 29, 2013, http://www.cnn.com/2013/03/28/us/connecticut-shooting-documents (accessed August 5, 2013).

46 Ibid., p. 69.

47 James Alan Fox and Jack Levin, *Overkill: Mass Murder and Serial Killing Exposed* (New York: Dell, 1996), p. 149.

48 U.S. Department of Justice, Office of Public Affairs, news release, "Attorney General Eric Holder Announces Revisions to the Uniform Crime Report's Definition of Rape," January 6, 2012, http://www.justice.gov/opa/pr/2012/January/12-ag-018.html (accessed March 12, 2012).

49 Email communication with the Criminal Justice Information Services Division of the FBI, January 6, 2012.

50 Centers for Disease Control, National Center for Injury Prevention and Control, *National Intimate Partner and Sexual Violence Survey Factsheet*, November 2011.

51 Susan Brownmiller, *Against Our Will: Men, Women, and Rape* (New York: Simon & Schuster, 1975).

52 Dianne Herman, "The Rape Culture," in Jo Freeman, ed., *Women: A Feminist Perspective* (Palo Alto, CA: Mayfield, 1984).

53 Diana Scully and Joseph Marolla, "Riding the Bull at Gilley's: Convicted Rapists Describe the Rewards of Rape," *Social Problems*, Vol. 32, No. 2 (1985), p. 252.

54 Nicholas Groth, *Men Who Rape: The Psychology of the Offender* (New York: Plenum, 1979).

55 Nicholas Groth, "Rape and Sexual Offenses," in Neil Alan Weiner, Margaret A. Zahn, and Rita J. Sagi, eds., *Violence: Patterns, Causes, Public Policy* (New York: Harcourt Brace Jovanovich, 1990), p. 76.

56 Groth, *Men Who Rape.*

57 Robert T. Sigler, Ida M. Johnson, and Etta F. Morgan, "Forced Sexual Intercourse: Contemporary Views," in Roslyn Muraskin, ed., *It's a Crime: Women and Justice* (Upper Saddle River, NJ: Prentice Hall, 2000), p. 352.

58 Randy Thornhill and Craig T. Palmer, *A Natural History of Rape* (Cambridge, MA: MIT Press, 2000), p. 53.

59 Martin Daly and Margo Wilson, *Homicide* (New York: Aldine De Gruyter, 1988), p. 140.

60 Thornhill and Palmer, *A Natural History of Rape*, p. 199.See also Katharine K. Baker, "What Rape Is and What It Ought Not to Be," *Jurimetrics*, Vol. 30, No. 3 (1999), p. 233.

61 A. Nicholas Groth and H. Jean Birnbaum, *Men Who Rape: The Psychology of the Offender* (New York: Plenum Press, 1979).

62 R. R. Hazelwood and A. N. Burgess, eds., *Practical Aspects of Rape Investigation: A Multidisciplinary Approach* (New York: CRC Press, 1995).

63 Dennis J. Stevens, *Inside the Mind of a Serial Rapist* (San Francisco: Austin and Winfield, 1999), p. 39.

64 Diana Scully, *Understanding Sexual Violence: A Study of Convicted Rapists* (New York: Routledge, 1990).

65 Ibid., p. 59.

66 Ibid.

67 Ibid.

68 Gary LaFree, *Rape and Criminal Justice: The Social Construction of Sexual Assault* (Belmont, CA: Wadsworth, 1989). See also Jeanne C. Marsh, Alison Geist, and Nathan Caplan, *Rape and the Limits of Law Reform* (Boston: Auburn, 1982).

69 Harriet R. Galvin, "Shielding Rape Victims in the State and Federal Courts: A Proposal for the Second Decade," *Minnesota Law Review*, Vol. 70 (1986), pp. 763–916.

70 Cassia Spohn and Julie Horney, *Rape Law Reform: A Grassroots Revolution and Its Impact* (New York: Plenum, 1992).

71 Ibid.

72 See Frances P. Bernat, "Rape Law Reform," in James F. Hodgson and Debra S. Kelley, eds., *Sexual Violence: Policies, Practices, and Challenges in the United States and Canada* (New Brunswick, CT: Praeger, 2001).

73 Pub. L. 102–325, section 486(c).

74 Carol Bohmer and Andrea Parrot, *Sexual Assault on Campus: The Problem and the Solution* (New York: Lexington Books, 1993), pp. 15–16.

75 Patricia Yancey Martin and Robert A. Hummer, "Fraternities and Rape on Campus," *Gender and Society*, Vol. 3, No. 4 (1989), p. 462.

76 Pub. L. 108–79.

77 Bureau of Justice Statistics, *PREA Data Collection Activities, 2013* (Washington, DC: U.S. Department of Justice, June 2013).

78 Ibid.

79 Lee H. Bowker, *Prisoner Subcultures* (Lanham, MA: Lexington Books, 1977), p. 42.

80 Ibid., p. 1.

81 Hans Toch, *Living in Prison: The Ecology of Survival* (New York: Free Press, 1977), p. 151.

82 Robert A. Prentky, Raymond A. Knight, and Austin F. S. Lee, *Child Sexual Molestation: Research Issues* (Washington, DC: National Institute of Justice, 1997), p. 1.

83 G. G. Abel, J. V. Becker, M. S. Mittelman, J. Cunningham-Rathner, J. L. Rouleau, and W. D. Murphy, "Self-Reported Sex Crimes of Nonincarcerated Paraphiliacs," *Journal of Interpersonal Violence*, Vol. 2 (1987), pp. 3–25.

84 Child Molestation Research & Prevention Institute, "Some Facts," http://www.childmolestationprevention.org (accessed June 5, 2013).

85 Abel et al., "Self-Reported Sex Crimes of Nonincarcerated Paraphilics."

86 B. M. Maletzky, "Factors Associated with Success and Failure in the Behavioral and Cognitive Treatment of Sexual Offenders," *Annals of Sex Research*, Vol. 6 (1993), pp. 241–258.

87 Robert A. Prentky, Raymond A. Knight, and Austin F. S. Lee, *Child Sexual Molestation: Research Issues* (Washington, DC: National Institute of Justice, 1997), from which much of the information and some of the wording in this section is taken.

88 A. Nicholas Groth, W. F. Hobson, and T. S. Gary, "The Child Molester: Clinical Observations," *Journal of Social Work and Child Sexual Abuse,* Vol. 1, No. 2 (1982), pp. 129–144.

89 Prentky et al., *Child Sexual Molestation: Research Issues.*

90 Ibid., p. 3.

91 R. A. Prentky and R. A. Knight, "Age of Onset of Sexual Assault: Criminal and Life History Correlates," in G. C. N. Hall, R. Hirschman, J. R. Graham, and M. S. Zaragoza, eds., *Sexual Aggression: Issues in Etiology, Assessment, and Treatment,* (Washington, DC: Taylor & Francis, 1993), pp. 43–62.

92 Prentky et al., *Child Sexual Molestation: Research Issues.*

93 Charlotte Bunch, "The Intolerable Status Quo: Violence against Women and Children," in UNICEF, *The Progress of Nations* (1997).

94 Note that while purse snatching and pocket picking involve the express goal of taking someone's property, they are classified as property crimes because they do not involve the same type of direct contact with the victim as does robbery.

95 Miethe and McCorkle, *Crime Profiles,* p. 87.

96 "Stunning Home Invasion Robbery Shocks Hempstead," CBS New York, January 9, 2012, http://newyork.cbslocal.com/2012/01/09/stunning-home-invasion-robbery-shocks-hempstead/ (accessed May 6, 2012)

97 FBI, *Crime in the United States, 2006.* (Washington, DC: U.S. Department of Justice, 2007).

98 Ibid.

99 Floyd Feeney, "Robbers as Decision Makers," in Derek B. Cornish and Ronald V. Clarke, eds., *The Reasoning Criminal* (New York: Springer-Verlag, 1986).

100 Ibid., p. 59.

101 Bruce A. Jacobs and Richard Wright, "Stick-Up, Street Culture, and Offender Motivation," *Criminology*, Vol. 37, No. 1 (1999), p. 150.

102 Ibid.

103 Ibid., p. 155.

104 Ibid.

105 Ibid., pp. 167–168.

106 Jody Miller, "Up It Up: Gender and the Accomplishment of Street Robbery," *Criminology*, Vol. 36, No. 1 (1998), p. 43.

107 FBI, *Crime in the United States*, 2006.

108 Miller, "Up It Up," p. 47.

109 Ibid., p. 51.

110 Ibid., p. 61.

111 Bennett Loudon, "Woman Accused of Punching Walmart Greeter," December 26, 2011, *Rochester Democrat and Chronicle*, http://www.democratandchronicle.com/article/20111226/NEWS01/112260313/Jacquetta-Simmons-accused-hitting-elderly-Walmart-worker.

112 Bureau of Justice Statistics, *Criminal Victimization 2006* (Washington, DC: U.S. Department of Justice, Office of Justice Programs, 2007), p. 172.

113 Miethe and McCorkle, *Crime Profiles*, p. 25.

114 Ibid., p. 27.

115 Callie Marie Rennison, *Criminal Victimization, 1999: Changes 1998–1999 with Trends 1993–1999* (Washington, DC: U.S. Department of Justice, Office of Justice Programs, 2000).

116 Robert J. Sampson, "Personal Violence by Strangers: An Extension and Test of Predatory Victimization," *Journal of Criminal Law and Criminology*, Vol. 78, No. 2 (1987), p. 342.

117 Michael Hindelang, *Criminal Victimization in Eight American Cities* (Cambridge, MA: Ballinger, 1976).

118 Evan Stark, A. Flitcraft, and W. Frazier, "Medicine and Patriarchal Violence: The Social Construction of a Private Event," *International Journal of Health Service*, Vol. 9, No. 3 (1979), pp. 461–493.

119 FBI, *Crime in the United States, 2006.*

120 Ibid.

121 For representative examples of this, see R. E. Dobash et al., "The Myth of Sexual Symmetry in Marital Violence," *Social Problems*, Vol. 39, No. 1 (1992), pp. 71–91; and R. E. Dobash and R. Dobash, *Women, Violence, and Social Change* (New York: Routledge, 1992).

122 Martha R. Mahoney, "Legal Issues of Battered Women: Redefining the Issue of Separation," *Michigan Law Review*, Vol. 90, No. 1 (1991), p. 6.

123 Liz Kelly, *Surviving Sexual Violence* (Minneapolis: University of Minnesota Press, 1988), p. 23.

124 Neil Websdale, *Rural Woman Battering and the Justice System: An Ethnography* (Thousand Oaks, CA: Sage, 1998), p. 208.

125 Centers for Disease Control and Prevention, National Center for Injury Prevention and Control, *The National Intimate Partner and Sexual Violence Survey: Factsheet 2010*, p. 2.

126 Erika Harrell, *Workplace Violence, 1993–2009* (Washington, DC: Bureau of Justice Statistics, 2011).

127 Ibid., p. 1

128 Ibid., p. 1

129 28 U.S.C.A. § 534.

130 Pub. L. 103–322.

131 Bureau of Justice Assistance, *Addressing Hate Crimes: Six Initiatives That Are Enhancing the Efforts of Criminal Justice Practitioners* (Washington, DC: U.S. Department of Justice, 2000).

132 Violence against Women Grants Office, *Stalking and Domestic Violence: The Third Annual Report to Congress under the Violence against Women Act* (Washington, DC: Violence against Women Grants Office, 1998).

133 Ibid.

134 Ibid.

135 Ibid.

136 Paul E. Mullen et al., "Assessing and Managing the Risks in the Stalking Situation," *Journal of the American Academy of Psychiatry and Law*, Vol. 34 (2006), pp. 439–450; and Paul E. Mullen et al., "Study of Stalkers," *American Journal of Psychiatry*, Vol. 156 (August 1999), pp. 1244–1249.

137 Paul E. Mullen et al., "Study of Stalkers."

138 T. Gregorie, *Cyberstalking: Dangers on the Information Highway* (Arlington, VA: National Center for Victims of Crime, 2000).

Chapter 10, Crimes Against Property—*It's What We Lose*

1 "Stolen Matisse Recovered in US," BBC, http://www.bbc.co.uk/news/entertainment-arts-18898804 (accessed March 5, 2013).

2 "Some of the Biggest Art Thefts in Recent Times," Associated Press, May 20, 2010, http://www.boston.com/news/world/europe/articles/2010/05/20/some_of_the_biggest_art_thefts_in_recent_times/ (accessed May 3, 2013).

3 William Spain, "Art Crime of the Century Still Frustrates: Empty Frames Still Hang in Boston Museum," APB News, June 16, 2000, http://apbnews.com/newscenter/breakingnews/2000/06/16/artcrime_gardner0161_01.html (accessed December 1, 2000).

4 Federal Bureau of Investigation, *Crime in the United States, 2011* (Washington, DC: U.S. Government Printing Office, 2012).

5 Herbert Koppel, *Lifetime Likelihood of Victimization* (Washington, DC: Bureau of Justice Statistics, 1987).

6 This is true even though the NCVS does not record burglaries of businesses or commercial properties.

7 Federal Bureau of Investigation, *Crime in the United States, 2012* (Washington, DC: U.S. Government Printing Office, 2013).

8 Neil Shover, "Burglary," in Michael Tonry, ed., *Crime and Justice: A Review of Research* (Chicago: University of Chicago Press, 1991).

9 For representative examples of this perspective, see Michael J. Hindelang, *Criminal Victimization in Eight American Cities* (Cambridge, MA: Ballinger, 1978); and Michael J. Hindelang, Michael R. Gottfredson, and James Garolfalo, *Victims of Personal Crime: An Empirical Foundation for a Theory of Personal Victimization* (Cambridge, MA: Ballinger, 1978).

10 For representative discussions of this perspective, see Lawrence E. Cohen and Marcus Felson, "Social Change and Crime Rate Trends: A Routine Activity Approach," *American Sociological Review*, Vol. 44 (1979), pp. 588–607; and Marcus Felson and Lawrence E. Cohen, "Human Ecology and Crime: A Routine Activity Approach," *Human Ecology*, Vol. 8 (1980), pp. 398–405.

11 Felson and Cohen, "Human Ecology and Crime."

12 Marcus Felson, "Linking Criminal Choices, Routine Activities, Informal Control, and Criminal Outcomes," in Derek B. Cornish and Ronald V. Clarke, eds., *The Reasoning Criminal: Rational Choice Perspectives on Offending* (New York: Springer-Verlag, 1986).

13 Lawrence E. Cohen and David Cantor, "Residential Burglary in the United States: Life-Style and Demographic Factors Associated with the Probability of Victimization," *Journal of Research in Crime and Delinquency*, Vol. 18, No. 1 (1981), pp. 113–127.

14 Jennifer Hardison Walters, et al., *Household Burglary, 1994–2011* (Washington, DC: Bureau of Justice Statistics, 2013).

15 Bureau of Justice Statistics, *Criminal Victimization, 1999*, Tables 81 and 83 (Washington, DC: Bureau of Justice Statistics, 2000).

16 Ibid., Tables 87 and 89.

17 Laura Dugan, "The Effect of Criminal Victimization on a Household's Moving Decision," *Criminology*, Vol. 37, No. 4 (1999), pp. 903–930.

18 Ramona R. Rantala and Thomas J. Edwards, *Effects of NIBRS on Crime Statistics* (Washington, DC: Office of Justice Programs, 2000), p. 12.

19 James Gerken, "Kaveh Hamooneh Arrested for Charging Electric Car at Chamblee, Georgia Middle School," *The Huffington Post*, December 4, 2013 (accessed January 23, 2014).

20 Federal Bureau of Investigation, *Crime in the United States, 2012.*

21 President's Commission on Law Enforcement and Administration of Justice, *The Challenge of Crime in a Free Society* (New York: Avon, 1968), p. 64.

22 Richard C. Hollinger and Lynn Langton, *2003 National Retail Security Survey: Final Report* (Tallahassee, FL: University of Florida, 2004).

23 Thomas Gabor, *Everybody Does It! Crime by the Public* (Toronto: University of Toronto Press), p. 80.

24 Dick Silverman, "Crime and Punishment," *Footwear News*, November 1999, http://www.allbusiness.com/crime-law/criminal-offenses-property/9030609-1.html (accessed July 28, 2009).

25 Sheila Marikar, "Caroline Giuliani, Daughter of Ex-NYC Mayor, Arrested for Shoplifting," ABC News, August 4, 2010, http://abcnews.go.com/Entertainment/TheLaw/caroline-giuliani-daughter-rudy-giuliani-arrested-shoplifting/story?id=11326577#.Ty7OkV2WZyo (accessed March 3, 2012).

26 "Caroline Giuliani Makes Deal in Shoplifting Case," Associated Press, August 31, 2010, http://abclocal.go.com/wabc/story?section=news/local&id=7641361 (accessed March 3, 2012).

27 Lloyd W. Klemke, *The Sociology of Shoplifting* (Westport, CT: Praeger, 1992).

28 Lloyd W. Klemke, "Exploring Juvenile Shoplifting," *Sociology and Social Research*, Vol. 67, No. 1 (1982), pp. 59–75.

29 Mary Owen Cameron, *The Booster and the Snitch: Department Store Shoplifting* (New York: Free Press of Glencoe, 1964).

30 Klemke, "Exploring Juvenile Shoplifting," p. 71.

31 Eric Tucker and Thomas Watkins, "For Flash Mobsters, Crowd Size a Tempting Cover," Associated Press, August 9, 2011 (accessed February 21, 2012).

32 Joe Larocca, "NRF Issues Guidelines for Retailers in Handling 'Criminal Flash Mobs,'" National Retail Federation, Retail's Big Blog, http://blog.nrf.com/2011/08/02/nrf-issues-guidelines-for-retailers-in-handling-criminal-flash-mobs/ (accessed February 21, 2012).

33 National Retail Federation, "Multiple Offender Crimes: Preparing for and Understanding the Impact of Their Tactics," http://www.nrf.com/modules.php?name=Documents&op=viewlive&sp_id=6788 (accessed February 21, 2012).

34 The President's Identity Theft Task Force, *Combating Identity Theft: A Strategic Plan* (Washington, DC: U.S. Department of Justice, 2007), from which much of the information comes and from which some of the wording is taken or adapted.

35 See Business Software Alliance, "Consumer Confidence in Online Shopping Buoyed by Security Software Protection, BSA Survey Suggests," January 12, 2006, http://www.bsacybersafety.com/news/2005-Online-Shopping-Confidence.cfm.

36 U.S. Code, Title 18, Section 1028.

37 H.R. 1731 (2004).

38 Lynn Langton, *Identity Theft Reported by Households, 2005–2010* (Washington, DC: Bureau of Justice Statistics, 2011).

39 Erika Harrell and Lynn Langton, *Victims of Identity Theft, 2012* (Washington, DC: Bureau of Justice Statistics, 2013).

40 Information in this paragraph comes from Katrina Baum, *Identity Theft, 2005* (Washington, DC: Bureau of Justice Statistics, 2007).

41 The information and some of the wording in this section is taken from The President's Identity Theft Task Force, *Combating Identity Theft: A Strategic Plan*.

42 See U.S. Attorney's Office, Southern District of Florida, press release, July 19, 2006, http://www.usdoj.gov/usao/fls/PressReleases/060719-01.html.

43 Federal Bureau of Investigation, *Crime in the United States, 2012*.

44 Bureau of Justice Statistics, *Criminal Victimization, 1999*, Tables 87 and 89.

45 Ibid.; and http://www.fbi.gov/about-us/cjis/ucr/crime-in-the-u.s/2012/crime-in-the-u.s.-2012/property-crime/motor-vehicle-theft.

46 Ibid.

47 Jennifer Truman, Lynn Langton, and Michael Planty, *Criminal Victimization, 2012* (Washington, DC: Bureau of Justice Statistics, 2013).

48 Ibid.

49 Caroline Wolf Harlow, *Motor Vehicle Theft* (Washington, DC: Bureau of Justice Statistics, 1988).

50 Ibid.

51 Kevin Blake, "What You Should Know about Car Theft," *Consumer's Research*, October 1995, cited in Terance D. Miethe and Richard McCorkle, *Crime Profiles: The Anatomy of Dangerous Persons, Places, and Situations* (Los Angeles: Roxbury, 1998), p. 156.

52 Miethe and McCorkle, *Crime Profiles*.

53 Pub. L. 98–547, 98 Stat. 2754 (1984).

54 Patricia M. Harris and Ronald V. Clarke, "Car Chopping, Parts Marking and the Motor Vehicle Theft Law Enforcement Act of 1984," *Sociology and Social Research*, Vol. 75 (1991).

55 Miethe and McCorkle, *Crime Profiles*, p. 156.

56 Michael Gottfredson and Travis Hirschi, *A General Theory of Crime* (Stanford, CA: Stanford University Press, 1990), p. 35.

57 Miethe and McCorkle, *Crime Profiles*; and Ronald V. Clarke and Patricia M. Harris, "Auto Theft and Its Prevention," in Tonry, ed., *Crime and Justice*.

58 Miethe and McCorkle, *Crime Profiles*.

59 For research reporting on effect of social class, see Charles H. McCaghy, Peggy C. Giordano, and Trudy Knicely Henson, "Auto Theft: Offender and Offense Characteristics," *Criminology*, Vol. 15 (1977), pp. 367–385.

60 Federal Bureau of Investigation, *Crime in the United States, 2006* (Washington, DC: U.S. Government Printing Office, 2007).

61 Ibid.

62 Peyton Whitely, "Suspicious Fires Destroy 3 Street of Dreams Homes, Damage 1, in Snohomish County," *Seattle Times*, March 3, 2008, http://seattletimes.com/html/localnews/2004256586_webdreamsfire03m.html (accessed August 5, 2013).

63 Federal Bureau of Investigation, *Crime in the United States, 2004* (Washington, DC: U.S. Government Printing Office, 2005).

64 Ken Brownlee, "Ignoring Juvenile Arson Is Like Playing with Fire," *Claims*, Vol. 48, No. 3 (March 2000), p. 106.

65 Eileen M. Garry, *Juvenile Firesetting and Arson*, Office of Juvenile Justice and Delinquency Prevention Fact Sheet 51 (Washington, DC: Office of Juvenile Justice and Delinquency Prevention, 1997).

66 Ibid., p. 1.

67 Cited in Gabor, *Everybody Does It!*, p. 11.

68 Edwin H. Sutherland, *The Professional Thief* (Chicago: University of Chicago Press, 1937), p. 3.

69 Neil Shover, *Great Pretenders: Pursuits and Careers of Persistent Thieves* (Boulder, CO: Westview Press, 1996), p. xiii.

70 Ibid., pp. xii–xiii.

71 Ibid., p. 63.

72 Mark S. Fleisher, *Beggars and Thieves: Lives of Urban Street Criminals* (Madison: University of Wisconsin Press, 1995), p. 29.

73 See Shover, *Great Pretenders;* and Shover, "Burglary."

74 John R. Hepburn, "Occasional Property Crime," in Robert F. Meier, ed., *Major Forms of Crime* (Beverly Hills, CA: Sage, 1984).

75 Ibid., p. 76.

76 Richard T. Wright and Scott H. Decker, *Burglars on the Job: Streetlife and Residential Break-Ins* (Boston: Northeastern University Press, 1994), p. 35.

77 See Center for Problem-Oriented Policing, "Crime Analysis for Problem Solvers in 60 Small Steps," from which the wording for this definition is taken, http://www.popcenter.org/learning/60steps/index.cfm?stepNum=10 (accessed May 31, 2007).

78 A. Blumstein, J. Cohen, J. A. Roth, and C. A. Visher, eds., *Criminal Careers and "Career Criminals,"* 2 vols. (Washington, DC: National Academy Press, 1986).

79 D. S. Elliott, "Serious Violent Offenders: Onset, Developmental Course, and Termination: 1993 Presidential Address," *Criminology*, Vol. 32, No. 1 (1994), pp. 1–22. See also D. S. Elliott, D. Huizinga, and B. Morse, "Self-Reported Violent Offending: A Descriptive Analysis of Juvenile Violent Offenders and Their Offending Careers," *Journal of Interpersonal Violence*, Vol. 1, No. 4 (1987), pp. 472–514.

80 Michael R. Gottfredson and Travis Hirschi, "Science, Public Policy, and the Career Paradigm," *Criminology*, Vol. 26 (1988), pp. 37–55.

81 Fleisher, *Beggars and Thieves*, p. 11.

82 Dermot Walsh, "Victim Selection Procedures among Economic Criminals: The Rational Choice Perspective," in Cornish and Clarke, eds., *The Reasoning Criminal*, p. 40.

83 Ibid., p. 50.

84 Thomas Bennett and Richard Wright, *Burglars on Burglary* (Aldershot, Hants, England: Gower, 1984).

85 Walsh, "Victim Selection Procedures among Economic Criminals," p. 50.

86 Mike Maguire, *Burglary in a Dwelling* (London: Heinemann, 1982), cited in Shover, "Burglary," p. 89.

87 Shover, "Burglary," p. 90.

88 Ibid., p. 91.

89 Ibid.

90 Miethe and McCorkle, *Crime Profiles*.

91 Truman et al., *Criminal Victimization, 2012*, Table 59.

92 Ibid., Table 64.

93 Simon Hakim and Yochanan Shachmurove, "Spatial and Temporal Patterns of Commercial Burglaries: The Evidence Examined," *American Journal of Economics and Sociology*, Vol. 55, No. 4 (1996), p. 445.

94 Ibid., p. 452.

95 Ibid., p. 73.

96 Shover, "Burglary," p. 83.

97 Ibid., p. 86.

98 Kenneth D. Tunnell, *Choosing Crime: The Criminal Calculus of Property Offenders* (Chicago: Nelson-Hall, 1992), p. 5.

99 See Paul F. Cromwell, James N. Olson, and D'Aunn Wester Avary, *Breaking and Entering: An Ethnographic Analysis of Burglary* (Newbury Park, CA: Sage, 1991); and Wright and Decker, *Burglars on the Job*.

100 Cromwell, Olson, and Avary, *Breaking and Entering*.

101 Wright and Decker, *Burglars on the Job*.

102 Ibid., p. 38.

103 Ibid., pp. 45–46.

104 See Shover, *Great Pretenders*.

105 Ibid., p. 52.

106 Ibid., p. 56.

107 Ibid.

108 Jack Katz, *Seductions of Crime: Moral and Sensual Attractions in Doing Evil* (New York: Basic Books, 1988), p. 79.

109 Tunnell, *Choosing Crime*, p. 41.

110 Eric Baumer et al., "The Influence of Crack Cocaine on Robbery, Burglary, and Homicide Rates: A Cross-City, Longitudinal Analysis," *Journal of Research in Crime and Delinquency*, Vol. 35, No. 3 (1998), pp. 316–340.

111 Ibid., p. 317.

112 Ibid., p. 9.

113 Ibid. See also Wright and Decker, *Burglars on the Job*.

114 Darrell J. Steffensmeier, *The Fence: In the Shadow of Two Worlds* (Savage, MD: Rowman and Littlefield, 1986), p. 9.

115 Carl B. Klockers, *The Professional Fence* (New York: Free Press, 1974).

116 Ibid., p. 13.
117 Ibid.
118 Cromwell, Olson, and Avary, *Breaking and Entering*.
119 Wright and Decker, *Burglars on the Job*, p. 167.
120 Shover, "Burglary," p. 103.
121 Steffensmeier, *The Fence*, p. 25.
122 Ibid., p. 23.
123 Ibid., p. 21.
124 Wright and Decker, *Burglars on the Job*, pp. 175–176.
125 Cromwell, Olson, and Avary, *Breaking and Entering*, p. 74.
126 Ibid., p. 75.
127 Ibid., p. 76.
128 Cromwell, Olson, and Avary, *Breaking and Entering*, p. 76.
129 Ibid., p. 77.
130 Ibid.

Chapter 11, White-Collar and Organized Crime—*Crime as a Job*

1 Details for this story come from Federal Bureau of Investigation, "Health Care Fraud Takedown," press release, September 7, 2011, http://www.fbi.gov/news/stories/2011/september/fraud_090711/fraud_090711 (accessed March 15, 2012).
2 Edwin H. Sutherland, "White-Collar Criminality," *American Sociological Review*, Vol. 5, No. 1 (February 1940), pp. 2–10.
3 Travis Hirschi and Michael Gottfredson, "Causes of White-Collar Crime," *Criminology*, Vol. 25, No. 4 (1987), p. 952.
4 Donald J. Newman, "White-Collar Crime: An Overview and Analysis," *Law and Contemporary Problems*, Vol. 23, No. 4 (Autumn 1958).
5 President's Commission on Law Enforcement and Administration of Justice, *The Challenge of Crime in a Free Society* (Washington, DC: U.S. Government Printing Office, 1967), p. 47.
6 For excellent reviews of the evolution of the concept of white-collar crime, see K. Schlegel and D. Weisburd, "White-Collar Crime: The Parallax View," in Kip Schlegel and David Weisburd, eds., *White-Collar Crime Reconsidered* (Boston: Northeastern University Press, 1992), pp. 3–27; and K. Schlegel and D. Weisburd, "Returning to the Mainstream: Reflections on Past and Future White-Collar Crime Study," in Schlegel and Weisburd, eds., *White-Collar Crime Reconsidered*, pp. 352–365.
7 Task Force on Organized Crime, *Organized Crime* (Washington, DC: U.S. Government Printing Office, 1976).
8 Ibid.
9 Gary S. Green, *Occupational Crime* (Chicago: Nelson-Hall, 1990), p. 12.
10 J. Kane and A. D. Wall, *2005 National Public Survey on White-Collar Crime* (Fairmont, VA: National White-Collar Crime Center, 2006).
11 Michael L. Benson, Francis T. Cullen, and William J. Maakestad, *Local Prosecutors and Corporate Crime* (Washington, DC: National Institute of Justice, 1993).
12 *New York Central and Hudson River Railroad Co.* v. *United States*, 212 U.S. 481 (1909).
13 Jonathan D. Glater and Kurt Eichenwald, "Audit Lapse at WorldCom Puzzles Some," *New York Times*, June 28, 2002, p. 1C.
14 *Arthur Andersen LLP* v. *United States*, 544 U.S. 696 (2005).
15 "Epoxy Company Indicted for Manslaughter in Big Dig Death," *Tollroads News*, August 8, 2007, http://www.tollroadsnews.com/node/3063 (accessed April 10, 2010).
16 "Epoxy Company to Pay Millions in Big Dig Collapse," WBZ-TV, December 17, 2008, http://wbztv.com/bigdig/big.dig.agreement.2.889425.html (accessed April 9, 2010).
17 Charles Kennedy, "BP Pleads Guilty to Criminal Charges in Deepwater Horizon Case," Oil Price, November 15, 2012, http://oilprice.com/Latest-Energy-News/World-News/BPPleads-Guilty-to-Criminal-Charges-in-Deep-water-Horizon-Case.html (accessed August 29, 2013).
18 Brandon L. Garrett, "Globalized Corporate Prosecutions," *Virginia Law Review*, Vol. 97 (December 2011), p. 1775.
19 Federal Bureau of Investigation, *Financial Crimes Report to the Public, Fiscal Year 2007*, http://www.fbi.gov/publications/financial/fcs_report2007/financial_crime_2007.htm#financial (accessed May 10, 2012), from which much of the material in this section is derived.
20 Ibid.
21 Ibid.
22 Ibid.
23 Ibid.
24 Ibid.
25 Ibid.
26 Clifford Karchmer and Douglas Ruch, "State and Local Money Laundering Control Strategies," *NIJ Research in Brief* (Washington, DC: National Institute of Justice, 1992), p. 1.
27 "Wachovia to Pay $160M Settlement," *Business Journal*, March 18, 2010, http://www.bizjournals.com/triad/stories/2010/03/15/daily30.html (accessed May 2, 2010).
28 U.S. Code, Title 18, Section 1956.
29 U.S. Drug Enforcement Administration, "Money Laundering," http://www.usdoj.gov/dea/programs/money.htm (accessed June 18, 2007).
30 See, Bernie Becker, "U.S. Report Details Money Laundering," *New York Times*, February 4, 2010, http://dealbook.blogs.nytimes.com/2010/02/04/us-report-details-money-laundering (accessed August 24, 2010).
31 Of course, environmental damage inflicted by corporations can result in civil liability as well as violate criminal statutes.
32 "Alaska Hit by 'Massive' Oil Spill," BBC News, March 11, 2006, http://news.bbc.co.uk/2/hi/americas/4795866.stm (accessed May 2, 2010).
33 "BP Fined $60 Million for Alaska Oil Spill, Texas Air Toxics," Environment News Service, November 1, 2007, http://www.ens-newswire.com/ens/nov2007/2007-11-01-095.asp (accessed May 2, 2010).
34 "BP Could Pay U.S. $25 Billion for Gulf Oil Spill: Analyst," Google News, January 19, 2012, http://www.google.com/hostednews/afp/article/ALeqM5if9Va_XAcDMrIPE7x6ppzdy8YMSw?docId=CNG.cb899fe5256d3216e8a921771e991d78.301 (accessed May 10, 2012).
35 Paul Danziger, "Deepwater Horizon," http://www.deepwaterhorizon.co/history-of-the-deepwater-horizon-settlement/ (accessed January 30, 2014).
36 John Kane and April Wall, "Identifying the Links between White-Collar Crime and Terrorism," National White Collar Crime Center, September 2004.
37 Edwin H. Sutherland, "White-Collar Criminality."
38 Ibid.
39 Ibid.
40 Hirschi and Gottfredson, "Causes of White-Collar Crime," p. 949.
41 Ibid., p. 951.
42 Ibid., p. 956.
43 Ibid., p. 960.
44 Ibid.
45 Braithwaite began many of his studies of white-collar crime with investigations into the criminal activities of pharmaceutical company executives. See, for example, John Braithwaite, *Corporate Crime in the Pharmaceutical Industry* (London: Routledge and Kegan Paul, 1984).
46 For a test of this thesis, see Anne Jenkins and John Braithwaite, "Profits, Pressure and Corporate Lawbreaking," *Crime, Law, and Social Change*, Vol. 20, No. 3 (1993), pp. 221–232.
47 John Braithwaite, "Poverty, Power, White-Collar Crime and the Paradoxes of Criminological Theory," *Australian and New Zealand Journal of Criminology*, Vol. 24, No. 1 (1991), pp. 40–48.
48 Toni Makkai and John Braithwaite, "Criminological Theories and Regulatory Compliance," *Criminology*, Vol. 29, No. 2 (1991), pp. 191–217.
49 John Braithwaite and Gilbert Geis, "On Theory and Action for Corporate Crime Control," *Crime and Delinquency*, Vol. 28, No. 2 (1982), pp. 292–314. See also Brent Fisse and John Braithwaite, *The Impact of Publicity on Corporate Offenders* (Albany: State University of New York Press, 1983).
50 Brent Fisse and John Braithwaite, "Accountability and the Control of Corporate Crime: Making the Buck Stop," in Mark Findlay and Russell Hogg, eds., *Understanding Crime and Criminal Justice* (North Ryde, Australia: Law, 1988), pp. 93–127.
51 Brent Fisse and John Braithwaite, *Corporations, Crime and Accountability* (New York: Cambridge University Press, 1994).
52 John Braithwaite, "Criminological Theory and Organizational Crime," *Justice Quarterly*, Vol. 6, No. 3 (1989), pp. 333–358.
53 Joan Biskupic, "Why It's Tough to Indict CEOs," *USA Today*, July 24, 2002, p. 1A.
54 Ibid.
55 See "Executive Order Establishment of the Corporate Fraud Task Force," July 9, 2002, http://www.whitehouse.gov/news/releases/2002/07/20020709-2.html (accessed January 2, 2005).
56 John R. Wilke, *The Wall Street Journal Online*, July 17, 2007, http://online.wsj.com/article/SB118469845609569168.html (accessed September 1, 2007).

57 Ibid.

58 Joe Palazzolo, "DOJ Unveils Financial Crime Task Force," *Main Justice*, November 17, 2009 (accessed May 8, 2012).

59 Pub. L. 111–21.

60 Pub. L. 111–5.

61 Pub. L. 110–343.

62 "Financial Crimes, Trade Enforcement Targeted in State of the Union," *The Blog of Legal Times*, January 25, 2012, http://legaltimes.typepad.com/blt/2012/01/financial-crimestrade-enforcement-targeted-in-state-of-the-union-.html (accessed January 25, 2012).

63 15 U.S.C. Section 1.

64 15 U.S.C. Sections 12–27.

65 15 U.S.C. Section 77.

66 15 U.S.C. Section 78.

67 Much of the information in this section comes from Julian Symons, *A Pictorial History of Crime* (New York: Bonanza, 1966).

68 Ibid.

69 Howard Abadinsky, *Organized Crime*, 9th ed. (New York: Wadsworth, 2010), p. 132.

70 John Kilber, *Capone: The Life and World of Al Capone* (Greenwich, CT: Fawcett, 1971).

71 Leonid Bershidsky, "The Russian Mafia Is Dead. Or Is It?" *Bloomberg*, January 18, 2013, http://www.bloomberg.com/news/2013-01-18/the-russian-mafia-is-dead-or-is-it-.html (accessed February 23, 2013).

72 William R. Schroeder, "Money Laundering," *FBI Law Enforcement Bulletin*, May 2001, p. 1.

73 Abadinsky, *Organized Crime*.

74 Ibid., p. 5.

75 U.S. Code, Title 21, Section 848(c)(2).

76 New York Penal Law, Section 460.00.

77 New York Penal Law, Section 460.10(3).

78 Much of the information and the quotes in this section come from Federal Bureau of Investigation, "Organized Crime: Eurasian Organized Crime," http://www.fbi.gov/hq/cid/orgcrime/eocindex.htm (accessed May 20, 2010).

79 Euan Grant, "The Russian Mafia and Organized Crime: How Can This Global Force Be Tamed?" Open Democracy, October 12, 2012, http://www.opendemocracy.net/od-russia/euan-grant/russian-mafia-and-organised-crime-how-can-this-global-force-be-tamed (accessed February 22, 2013).

80 Ibid.

81 Ibid.

82 Much of the information and the quotes in this section come from Federal Bureau of Investigation, "Organized Crime: Asian Criminal Enterprises," http://www.fbi.gov/hq/cid/orgcrime/asiancrim.htm (accessed May 20, 2014).

83 Ibid.

84 Ibid.

85 Much of the information and the quotes in this section come from Federal Bureau of Investigation, "Organized Crime: African Criminal Enterprise," http://www.fbi.gov/hq/cid/orgcrime/africancrim.htm (accessed May 20, 2014).

86 Ibid.

87 Much of the information and the quotes in this section come from Federal Bureau of Investigation, "Organized Crime: Middle Eastern Criminal Enterprises," http://www.fbi.gov/hq/cid/orgcrime/middle_eastern.htm (accessed May 20, 2014).

88 Ibid.

89 John T. Picarelli, "Responding to Transnational Organized Crime: Supporting Research, Improving Practice," *NIJ Journal*, No. 268 (October 2011), pp. 4–9.

90 Gary T. Dempsey, "Is Russia Controlled by Organized Crime?" *USA Today* magazine, May 1999.

91 Richard Lindberg and Vesna Markovic, *Organized Crime Outlook in the New Russia: Russia Is Paying the Price of a Market Economy in Blood*, Search International, http://www.searchinternational.com/Articles/crime/russiacrime.htm (accessed January 24, 2012).

92 Ibid.

93 Dempsey, "Is Russia Controlled by Organized Crime?"

94 Lindberg and Markovic, *Organized Crime Outlook in the New Russia*.

95 Ibid.

96 The Organized Crime Control Act of 1970, Pub. L. 91–452, 84 Stat. 922 (October 15, 1970).

97 United States Code, Title 18, Chapter 96, Section 1961.

98 Gary W. Potter, *Criminal Organizations: Vice, Racketeering, and Politics in an American City* (Prospect Heights, IL: Waveland, 1994), p. 183.

99 Ibid.

100 Abadinsky, *Organized Crime*, p. 507.

101 Ibid., p. 508.

102 "'Junior' Gotti Gets Nearly 6 1/2 Years," Associated Press, September 3, 1999.

103 "5-Year Prison Term for Mafia Turncoat," *USA Today*, September 27, 1994, p. 3A.

104 Peter Maas, *Underboss: Sammy the Bull Gravano's Story of Life in the Mafia* (New York: HarperCollins, 1997). According to Ronald Kuby, an attorney suing Gravano to reclaim book royalties under New York's Son of Sam law, to avoid provisions of the law, a roundabout method had been used to pay Gravano. Kuby claimed that documents would show that author Peter Maas, Gravano, HarperCollins, and International Creative Management (the agent for the book) had conspired to hide payments made to Gravano. To learn more about the case, visit http://www.crimelibrary.com/gangsters2/gravano/24.htm.

105 "'Sammy the Bull' Faces More Drug Charges," Associated Press, December 21, 2000.

106 Alexandra Pournaras and Tracy Connor, "Whitey Bulger Convicted of Racketeering, Conspiracy," NBC News, http://usnews.nbcnews.com/_news/2013/08/12/19989231-whitey-bulgerconvicted-of-racketeering-conspiracy?lite (accessed August 29, 2013).

Chapter 12, Drug and Sex Crimes—*Recreational Offenses*

1 Christopher Matthews, "Online Drug Markets Are Alive and Thriving," *Time*, October 4, 2013, http://business.time.com/2013/10/04/online-drug-markets-are-alive-and-thriving/ (accessed June 3, 2014).

2 Data in this section are derived from Substance Abuse and Mental Health Services Administration, *2011 National Survey on Drug Use and Health* (Rockville, MD: SAMHSA, 2013).

3 Numbers total more than 100% because of rounding.

4 Bureau of Justice Statistics, *Drug and Crime Facts, 1993* (Washington, DC: U.S. Department of Justice, August 1994).

5 B. Kilmer, S. Everingham, J. Caulkins, G. Midgette, R. Pacula, P. Reuter, R. Burns, B. Han, R. Lundberg, *What America's Users Spend on Illegal Drugs: 2000-2010* (Santa Monica, CA; RAND Corporation, 2014).

6 National Drug Intelligence Center, *The Economic Impact of Illicit Drug Use on American Society* (Washington, DC: U.S. Department of Justice, 2011).

7 Centers for Disease Control and Prevention, "Drug-Associated HIV Transmission Continues in the United States," http://www.cdc.gov/hiv/resources/factsheets/idu.htm (accessed March 12, 2014).

8 Sarah O'Connor, "Drugs and Prostitution Add 10bn to UK Economy," *The Financial Times*, May 29, 2014, http://www.ft.com/intl/cms/s/2/65704ba0-e730-11e3-88be-00144feabdc0.html, (accessed June 2, 2014).

9 National Narcotics Intelligence Consumers Committee, *The NNICC Report, 1996: The Supply of Illicit Drugs to the United States* (Arlington, VA: Drug Enforcement Administration, 1997), p. 69.

10 Michael D. Lyman and Gary W. Potter, *Drugs in Society: Causes, Concepts and Control* (Cincinnati: Anderson, 1991), p. 45.

11 As defined by federal law and precedent.

12 Ibid., p. 35.

13 Ibid., p. 79.

14 Bureau of Justice Statistics, *Drugs, Crime and the Justice System* (Washington, DC: U.S. Government Printing Office, 1992), p. 2.

15 Ibid.

16 Ibid., p. 126.

17 Ibid., p. 2.

18 Pub. L. 104–305.

19 "'Rophies' Reported Spreading Quickly throughout the South," *Drug Enforcement Report*, June 23, 1995, pp. 1–5.

20 For an excellent overview of policy initiatives in the area of drug control, see Doris Layton MacKenzie and Craig D. Uchida, *Drugs and Crime: Evaluating Public Policy Initiatives* (Thousand Oaks, CA: Sage, 1994).

21 Drug Enforcement Administration, *2010 Domestic Cannabis Eradication/Suppression Program Statistical Report*, http://www.justice.gov/dea/programs/marijuana_seizure_results.pdf (accessed March 5, 2012).

22 21 U.S.C. Section 881(a)(6).

23 J. Michael McWilliams, "Setting the Record Straight: Facts about Litigation Costs and Delay," *Business Economics*, Vol. 27, No. 4 (October 1992), p. 19.

24 Paige M. Harrison and Allen J. Beck, *Prisoners in 2005* (Washington, DC: U.S. Bureau of Justice Statistics, November 2006); and Bureau of Prisons, "Offenses," http://www.bop.gov/about/statistics/statistics_inmate_offenses.jsp (accessed May 2, 2014).

25 "Who Is in Federal Prison?" *Washington Post*, October 3, 1994.

26 Lyman and Potter, *Drugs in Society*, p. 316.

27 James Inciardi, *The War on Drugs II* (New York: McGraw-Hill, 1992), p. 239.

28 Lyman and Potter, *Drugs in Society*, p. 316.

29 Proposition 215, passed by California voters on November 5, 1996.

30 California Senate Bill 420.

31 *Newsweek*, February 3, 1997, pp. 20–23.

32 *United States* v. *Oakland Cannabis Buyers, Cooperative*, 532 U.S. 483 (2001).

33 Kristen Wyatt, "Legal Weed Draws Tourists to Colorado, Washington, for 4/20 Marijuana Holiday," *Huffington Post*, April 15, 2013, http://www.huffingtonpost.com/2013/04/15/legal-pot-draws-tourists-_0_n_3084301.html (accessed May 30, 2013).

34 U.S. Dept. of Justice, Memorandum for all United States Attorneys, "Guidance Regarding Marijuana Enforcement," August 29, 2013.

35 David Ingram, "Eric Holder Just Announced a Major Shift on U.S. Marijuana Policy," *Huffington Post*, January 23, 2014, http://www.huffingtonpost.com/2014/01/23/marijuana-bank_n_4656145.html?utm_hp_ref=tw (accessed June 4, 2014).

36 Tim Gaynor, "For First Time, Most Americans Favor Legalizing Marijuana: Poll," Reuters, October 22, 2013, http://www.reuters.com/article/2013/10/22/us-usa-marijuana-poll-idUSBRE99L1J420131022 (accessed June 4, 2014).

37 "Swiss Try Drive-in 'Sex Boxes' for Safer Prostitution," *USA Today*, August 26, 2013, http://www.usatoday.com/story/news/world/2013/08/26/switzerland-prostitution-sex-boxes/2700877/ (accessed January 23, 2014).

38 Federal Bureau of Investigation, *Crime in the United States, 2006* (Washington, DC: U.S. Government Printing Office, 2007).

39 Meredith Dank, Bilal Khan, P. Mitchell Downey, Cybele Kotonias, Deborah Mayer, Colleen Owens, Laura Pacifici, and Lilly Yu, *Estimating the Size and Structure of the Underground Commercial Sex Economy in Eight Major US Cities* (Washington, DC: The Urban Institute, 2014).

Chapter 13, Technology and Crime—*It's a Double-Edged Sword*

1 Details for this story come from Mantik Kusjanto, "Kim Dotcom: Police Cut Way into Mansion to Arrest Megaupload Founder," *Huffington Post*, via Reuters, January 21, 2012, http://www.huffingtonpost.com/2012/01/21/kim-dotcom-megaupload-arrest_n_1220491.html (accessed January 21, 2012).

2 Patrik Jonsson, "If Feds Can Bust Megaupload, Why Bother with Anti-piracy Bills?" *Christian Science Monitor*, January 21, 2012, http://www.csmonitor.com/USA/2012/0121/If-feds-can-bust-Megaupload-why-bother-with-anti-piracy-bills (accessed January 21, 2012).

3 Catherine H. Conly and J. Thomas McEwen, "Computer Crime," *NIJ Reports*, January/February 1990, p. 3.

4 Ibid.

5 Verizon, "2013 Data Breach Investigations Report," http://www.verizonenterprise.com/DBIR/2013/ (accessed May 21, 2013).

6 Bill Gertz, "White House Hack Attack," September 30, 2012, http://freebeacon.com/white-house-hack-attack (accessed May 21, 2013).

7 "US Mulls Actions against China Cyberattacks," Associated Press, January 31, 2013, http://www.foxnews.com/tech/2013/01/31/us-mulls-action-against-china-cyberattacks/ (accessed May 31, 2013).

8 David McGuire, "Study: Online Crime Costs Rising," *Washington Post*, May 24, 2004, http://www.washingtonpost.com/wp-dyn/articles/A53042-2004May24.html (accessed July 30, 2005).

9 Adapted from Deloitte & Touche, Center for Security & Privacy Solutions, *Cyber Crime: A Clear and Present Danger* (Deloitte & Touche, 2010), http://www.deloitte.com/assets/Dcom-UnitedStates/Local%20Assets/Documents/AERS/us_aers_Deloitte%20Cyber%20Crime%20POV%20Jan252010.pdf (accessed March 12, 2012), pp. 5 and 7.

10 Computer Security Institute, "2010/2011 Computer Crime and Security Survey," http://scadahacker.com/library/Documents/Insider_Threats/CSI%20-%202010-2011%20Computer%20Crime%20and%20Security%20Survey.pdf.

11 Business Software Alliance, "2010 Global Piracy Study," http://portal.bsa.org/globalpiracy2010/downloads/study_pdf/2010_BSA_Piracy_Study-Standard.pdf, May 2011 (accessed July 27, 2012).

12 The Anti-Phishing Working Group, "Phishing Activity Trends Report: 1st Half 2011," http://www.antiphishing.org/reports/apwg_trends_report_h1_2011.pdf (accessed July 27, 2012).

13 Gregg Keizer, "Gartner: Phishing Attacks Threaten E-Commerce," Security Pipeline.com, http://www.securitypipeline.com/news/20000036 (accessed July 30, 2007).

14 This and most other definitions related to computer crime in this chapter are taken from Donn B. Parker, *Computer Crime: Criminal Justice Resource Manual* (Washington, DC: National Institute of Justice, 1989).

15 Kevin Thompson, *Cyber Security* (Washington, DC: U.S. Department of Homeland Security, Command, Control and Interoperability Division, June 24, 2009), p. 6.

16 Pub. L. 104–104, 110 Stat. 56.

17 *Reno* v. *ACLU*, 521 U.S. 844 (1997).

18 Enacted as Section 225 of the Homeland Security Act of 2002, H.R. 5710.

19 Parker, *Computer Crime.*

20 Federal Bureau of Investigation, "Gamer Charged with Hacking into and Disabling New Hampshire Gaming Company's Computer Servers," November 15, 2012, press release, http://www.fbi.gov/boston/press-releases/2012/gamer-charged-with-hacking-into-and-disabling-new-hampshire-gaming-companys-computer-servers (accessed May 3, 2014), from which much of the wording of this story is taken.

21 John Markoff, "Cyberpunks," *New York Times Upfront*, Vol. 132, No. 15 (March 27, 2000), pp. 10–14.

22 Ibid.

23 J. Bloombecker, "A Security Manager's Guide to Hacking," *DATAPRO Reports on Information Security*, Report IS35–450–101, 1986.

24 Paul Keegan, "High Tech Pirates Collecting Phone Calls," *USA Today*, September 23, 1994, p. 4A.

25 Ibid.

26 Marc Robins, "Case of the Ticked-Off Teens," *Infosecurity News*, July/August 1993, p. 48.

27 John Perry Barlow, "Crime and Puzzlement: In Advance of the Law on the Electronic Frontier," *Whole Earth Review* (Fall 1990), p. 44.

28 Eureka Aerospace, "High-Power Compact Microwave Source for Vehicle Immobilization: Final Report," U.S. Department of Justice, National Institute of Justice, April 20, 2006.

29 For insight into how security techniques often lag behind the abilities of criminal perpetrators in the high-technology arena, see James A. Fagin, "Computer Crime: A Technology Gap," *International Journal of Comparative and Applied Criminal Justice*, Vol. 15, Nos. 1 and 2 (Spring/Fall 1991), pp. 285–297.

30 "DNA Frees Man Sentenced to Life," Associated Press, January 16, 2001, http://www.msnbc.com/news/517172.asp (accessed January 17, 2005).

31 *Maryland* v. *King*, U.S. Supreme Court, No. 12-207 (decided June 3, 2013).

32 Japan Electronics Industry Association, *Industry Monitor: High-Tech Sector*, "Security Software Demand to Show Strong Growth—Week Ended June 27, 2004," http://www.irstreet.com/top/im/im20040627.pdf (accessed July 30, 2006).

33 "Global Revenue Made by Security Appliance Vendors from 1st Quarter 2011 to 1st Quarter 2013," *Statista*, June, 2013, http://www.statista.com/statistics/235342/global-security-appliance-revenue-of-leading-security-appliance-vendors/ (accessed August 27, 2013).

34 Parker, *Computer Crime*, p. xiii.

35 The FBI's contemporary cyberinvestigations Web page is available at http://www.fbi.gov/cyberinvest/cyberhome.htm.

36 As modified in 1986, 1988, and later years.

37 The Liberty Coalition, "Carnivore/DCS–1000," http://www.libertycoalition.net/backgrounders/carnivore-dcs-1000 (accessed June 17, 2007).

38 "Original EFF Statement of Purpose," from the EFF website, http://eff.org/abouteff.html (accessed April 20, 2001). For the EFF's most recent statement of purpose, see http://www.eff.org/about (accessed June 2, 2014).

Chapter 14, Globalization and Terrorism—*Our Small World*

1 Mosi Secret, "Doofy? Casper? Scarface Would Cringe," *New York Times*, January 5, 2012, http://www.nytimes.com/2012/01/06/nyregion/ten-suspected-members-of-feared-gang-indicted.html?_r=1&ref=organizedcrime& gwh=097BB65522B2DEA0AA410CF6BBBB4578 (accessed January 15, 2012).

2 Kevin Johnson, "MS-13 Gang Growing Extremely Dangerous, FBI Says," *USA Today*, January 5, 2006, http://www.usatoday.com/news/nation/2006-01-05-gang-grows_x.htm (accessed January 25, 2012).

3 Gregory J. Howard, Graeme Newman, and William Alex Pridemore, "Theory, Method, and Data in Comparative Criminology," in David Duffee, ed., *Criminal Justice 2000: Volume IV—Measurement and Analysis of Criminal Justice* (Washington, DC: NIJ, 2000), p. 189.

4 Robert Lilly, "Forks and Chopsticks: Understanding Criminal Justice in the PRC," *Criminal Justice International* (March/April 1986), p. 15.

5 See United Nations Office on Drugs and Crime, "Compiling and Comparing International Crime Statistics," http://www.unodc.org/en/crime_cicp_surveys_3.html (accessed June 5, 2007).

6 United Nations Office on Drugs and Crime, "The 2013 United Nations Survey of Crime Trends and Operations of Criminal Justice Systems," http://www.unodc.org/unodc/en/dataand-analysis/statistics/crime/cts-data-collection.html (accessed April 25, 2014).

7 Adapted from "Globalization," *Encyclopedia Britannica, 2007*, Encyclopedia Britannica Premium Service, http://www.britannica.com/eb/article?eu5369857 (accessed July 23, 2007).

8 Franklin Zimring, "The Necessity and Value of Transnational Comparative Study: Some Preaching from a Recent Convert," *Criminology and Public Policy*, Vol. 5, No. 4 (2006), pp. 615–622.

9 Human Smuggling and Trafficking Center, *Distinctions between Human Smuggling and Human Trafficking* (Washington, DC: January, 2005).

10 Ibid., p. 2.

11 Raimo Väyrynen, "Illegal Immigration, Human Trafficking, and Organized Crime," United Nations University/World Institute for Development Economics Research, Discussion Paper No. 2003/72 (October, 2003), p. 16.

12 Details for this story come from "Immigrant Smuggler Faulted in 19 Deaths Sentenced to Life in Prison," Associated Press, January 18, 2007, http://www.usatoday.com/news/nation/2007-01-18-smuggler_x.htm.

13 Pub. L. 108–458, December 17, 2004.

14 Global Fast, "Impact Areas: Freedom," http://www.globalfast.org/gfx/end_slavery.php (accessed August 1, 2009).

15 United Nations Office on Drugs and Crime, *Global Report on Trafficking in Persons* (New York: United Nations, 2009), p. 6.

16 International Labor Organization, "Fact Sheet: Trafficking of Children, a Worst Form of Child Labour," http://www.ilo.org/public/english/region/asro/bangkok/child/trafficking/downloads/fact_sheet_november_01_tdm.pdf (accessed August 1, 2009).

17 U.S. Code, Title 8, Section 1324.

18 Pub. L. 89–236.

19 Trafficking Victims Protection Act of 2000, Division A of Pub. L. 106–386, Section 108, as amended.

20 *Global Report on Trafficking in Persons*, p. 7.

21 Ibid.

22 U.S. Department of State, *Patterns of Global Terrorism, 2001* (Washington, DC: U.S. Government Printing Office, 2002), http://www.state.gov/s/ct/rls/pgtrpt/2001/ (accessed January 2, 2003). Note: Until 2004, the U.S. Department of State made *Patterns of Global Terrorism* available to the public annually. As of 2004, however, the report became unavailable after its methodology was challenged by the Bush administration.

23 European Union, *Terrorism Situation and Trend Report* (Europol, 2007), p. 9.

24 Paul R. Pillar, *Terrorism and U.S. Foreign Policy* (Washington, DC: The Brookings Institution, 2001).

25 See Michael J. Lynch and W. Byron Groves, *A Primer in Radical Criminology* (Monsey, NY: Willow Tree Press, 1990), p. 39; and Michael J. Lynch et al., *The New Primer in Radical Criminology: Critical Perspectives on Crime, Power & Identity* (Monsey, NY: Willow Tree Press, 2000).

26 Adapted from "FBI Policy and Guidelines: Counterterrorism," http://www.fbi.gov/contact/fo/jackson/cntrterr.htm (accessed March 4, 2008).

27 Adapted from "FBI Policy and Guidelines: Counterterrorism."

28 Brian Bennett, "'Sovereign Citizen' Movement Now on FBI's Radar," *Los Angeles Times*, February 23, 2012, http://www.latimes.com/news/nationworld/nation/la-na-terror-cop-killers-20120224,0,5474022.story (accessed February 25, 2012).

29 Ibid.

30 National Counterterrorism Center, *2010 Report on Terrorism* (Washington, DC: NCC, April 2011), http://www.nctc.gov/witsbanner/docs/2010_report_on_terrorism.pdf (accessed March 5, 2012).

31 Ibid., pp. 5–10.

32 The New York City Office of Emergency Management said that 2,795 people died in the attacks on the World Trade Center. Another 184 people died in the attack on the Pentagon (including those aboard the crashed airliner), and 44 people died aboard hijacked United Airlines Flight 93, which crashed in a Pennsylvania field.

33 Pub. L. 107–56.

34 National Security Council, *National Strategy for Combating Terrorism* (Washington, DC, NSC, 2006), p. 1.

35 Stefanie Olsen. "PATRIOT Act Draws Privacy Concerns," CNET News.com, October 26, 2001, http://news.cnet.com/news/0-1005-200-7671240.htm?tag=rltdnws (accessed November 3, 2002).

36 Public Law 107–296.

37 U.S. Department of Homeland Security, "DHS Organization: Building a Secure Homeland," http://www.dhs.gov/dhspublic/theme_home1.jsp (accessed August 2, 2014).

38 *National Strategy for Counterterrorism* (Washington, DC: The White House, June 2011).

Name Index

Note: The letter n indicates information in a reference note on the listed page.

D

E

F

G

H

I

J

K

L

P

Q

R

S

Subject Index

E

F

G

H

I

J

K

L

M

N

R

S

T

U

V

W

X

Y